AESTHETIC THEORY

Theodor W. Adorno

Gretel Adorno and Rolf Tiedemann, Editors

Newly translated, edited, and with a translator's introduction by
Robert Hullot-Kentor

continuum

Continuum International Publishing Group

The Tower Building	80 Maiden Lane
11 York Road	Suite 704
London SE1 7NX	New York NY 10038

www.continuumbooks.com

Originally published as Asthetische Theorie, © 1970 Suhrkamp Verlag, Frankfurt am Main
This translation published 1997 by The Athlone Press Ltd

This edition published 2004 by Continuum
Reprinted 2007, 2008, 2009, 2010

British Library Cataloguing-in-Publication Data
A catalogue record for this book is available from The British Library

ISBN: 978-0-8264-7691-3

Typeset by Interactive Sciences Ltd, Gloucester
Printed and bound in Great Britain

Contents

CONTENTS

Translator's Acknowlegments

It is not recorded that Job was working on a translation, but I wouldn't doubt it. Whatever could interfere in this project interfered: illness, earthquake, and unemployment took turns with lesser scourges. The translation stretched years beyond the year planned. That it did not finally get left on a doorstep or slid behind a bookshelf I owe in part to friends, to Steve Babson, Jery Zaslove, Marty Jay, Bill Donoghue, Milton Cantor, and most of all to my wife, Odile Hullot-Kentor. And every reader of this book is indebted to Juliane Brand, who painstakingly checked the translation against the original, word by word, suggested innumerable improvements, ánd, as its copy editor as well, helped bring the translation to an altogether new level. Her expertise, generosity, and calm goodwill made her a wonderful and indispensable ally. I also want to thank Shierry Nicholsen, Mike Richardson, and Don Shumaker for their various contributions.

Translator's Introduction

Every translation must fit one world inside another, but not every work to be translated has been shaped by emphatic opposition to the world into which it must be fitted. This is, however, the case with *Aesthetic Theory*, which Theodor Adorno was able to write only by leaving the United States, where he had lived for a decade during the war years, became a citizen, and often thought he might need to remain. Any review of the many American phrases that Adorno scornfully quotes throughout *Aesthetic Theory*—the "tired businessman," the "pin-up," the "what do I get out of it?"—will confirm that not least of all the book was written in refusal of a country that it depicts as a completely commercial order. Even so unproblematically scannable a phrase as "Only what is useless can stand in for the stunted use value" draws on the transformation of distinctly European experiences of aristocracy. In the United States, such an idea, if it gets as far as cognition, falls askance of the inheritances of a puritanical mind that has always suspected that art does not properly work for a living and might encourage others to do the same. And just opening to any page, without bothering to read a word, one sees that the book is visibly antagonistic. No one from the land of edutainment would compose these starkly unbeckoning sheer sides of type, uninterrupted by chapter titles or typographic markers, that have severed and jettisoned every approach and patched over most every apparent handhold.

The book's stylistic peculiarities derive, as a whole, from what makes *Aesthetic Theory* inimical to an American context: that it is oriented not to its readers but to the thing-in-itself. This is not, as will be immediately suspected, motivated by indifference to its readers. On the contrary, the book makes itself remote from its consumption out of interest in, and by its power of, self-immersion. *Aesthetic Theory* is an attempt to overcome the generally recognized failing of aesthetics—its externality to its object—that Barnett Newman once did the world the favor of putting in a nutshell when he famously quipped, speaking of himself as a painter, that "aesthetics is for me like what ornithology must be like for the birds."[1] Artworks are after all unique, not least in that, when they are experienced, they are experienced from within. It is possible to vanish into a novel or a painting and be half-surprised, looking away for a moment, that the world was ever there at all. Anyone turning to aesthetics would expect that, to call itself aesthetics, it would be allied with what is exceptional in the experience of its object. But what is discovered instead is a discipline that throughout its history has worked at the conceptual undergirding of standards of beauty, the sublime, taste, art's dignity, and so on, while failing to achieve the standard of the experience of what it purports to treat. The suspicion is irrepressible that either aesthetics is the work of the willfully deaf, blind, and insensate or that art is under a spell that prohibits its inner comprehension, as if here one is permitted entry as nowhere else only on the condition that one leave empty-handed and never be able to say what the difference is between it and just having been distracted.

Adorno's *Aesthetic Theory* means to breach this externality of aesthetics to art. It is hardly the first effort to do so. But when aesthetics has become dissatisfied with itself and tried to escape its externality it has almost always taken the form of pretending to be art in a pictorial, effusive voice, or it has offered to act as maître d' to a specialized domain of pleasure. Either effort, however, only camouflages the presupposition that intellect must renounce knowing art from within. *Aesthetic Theory*, by contrast, is oriented to an early aphorism that Adorno wrote about music that was seminal to his thinking about art as a whole: "We don't understand music, it understands us."[2] The aesthetics required by this perception would be remote to all art appreciation; its sight lines would run opposite those angled by the intensifying need for art that makes people mill around art museums in constantly greater numbers: it would be art's own understanding; the presentation of its truth content.

Conjuring this genie out of the bottle would seem to require the sacrifice of subjectivity to what is beyond itself. If the thing-in-itself is to speak, subjectivity's own voice must only interfere. This thesis could perhaps look for confirmation in *Dialectic of Enlightenment* in which Adorno and Hork-heimer show that fascism did not simply coax cornered reason into delirium but was itself a potential implicit in reason's own compulsion toward all-encompassing domination. Yet the authors never sought to subvert subjectivity or to countermand enlightenment, the course of subjectivity's development as reason. If enlightenment had come to a dead end in fascism, its abrogation would make terror permanent. Rather, Adorno and Horkheimer took the side of enlightenment and tried to discern the logic of its failure. What they showed was that it missed its aim of human emancipation from natural necessity and the second nature of social constraint because the domination of nature unwittingly requires the sacrifice of subjectivity. The recognition that *in maxima potentia minima licentia* is millennia old. But *Dialectic of Enlightenment* took this thought in a strictly modern direction: if the self is progressively limited and deprived through the domination of its object, if humanity is subordinated to necessity by the struggle against it, then the emancipation of the subject depends on its capacity to emancipate its object, and this requires all possible subjective spontaneity.

Adorno's thesis that subjectivity could only be transcended by way of subjectivity, and not by its limitation, is one way of formulating his seminal insight: that identity is the power of nonidentity. The philosophical means for giving shape to what is more than subjectivity would be, paradoxically, those of conceptual cognition that, since Kant's Copernican turn, specifi-cally limited knowledge to the world constituted by subjectivity this side of the thing-in-itself. As Adorno wrote in the introduction to *Negative Dialectics*, he considered it the task of his thought "to use the strength of the subject to break through the fraud of constitutive subjectivity."[3] The power of identity—manifest in Kant's transcendentalism as concepts that con-stitutively define the likeness of the world with the subject—would go beyond constitutive subjectivity if concepts could be developed in such a way as to present what is more than conceptual in them. That concepts are more than their definitional content is implicit in the idea of a dialectic of enlightenment: for if enlightenment regresses to the natural necessity that it attempts to dominate, then concepts, which ostensibly serve to identify the world with its knower, are actually artifacts most deeply shaped by what enlightenment never mastered. Identity must be more than identity in that it draws back into itself what it purports to overcome. The concealed content of enlightenment, the content of concepts, would be that nature that subjectivity sought to dominate in its own rise to power.

This defines Adorno's approach in *Aesthetic Theory* to the possibility of breaching the externality of aesthetics to art: an aesthetics that wants to know art from within—to present what art itself understands—would consist of what a contemporary nominalist intelligence, always verging on irrationalism, dismisses as the oppressive, overstuffed furnishings of an age credulous of absolutes: natural beauty, art beauty, truth, semblance, and so on, the fundamental concepts of aesthetics.

Although these concepts emerged in the effort to master their material, they are more than that. Freed from the compulsion of domination they would potentially reveal their participation in what they sought to dominate and the impress of that through which they developed. Aesthetic concepts would become the memory of nature sedimented in art, which for Adorno takes shape in *Aesthetic Theory* as the unconscious, mimetically written history of human suffering against which enlightenment elsewhere seals itself off. Only this content could possibly bring reason's struggle for domination to its senses and direct its power to what would actually fulfill it. Thus Adorno organized *Aesthetic Theory* as a paratactical presentation of aesthetic concepts that, by eschewing subordinating structures, breaks them away from their systematic philosophical intention so that the self-relinquishment that is implicit in identity could be critically explicated as what is nonintentional in them: the primacy of the object.

Throughout his years in the United States, Adorno on many occasions met with the rejection of his work by publishers who saw his writings simply as disorganized. It was obvious to Adorno that what he was pursuing required his return to Germany if only because in the 1950s publishing was still less commercially unified than in the United States and permitted writers greater control over their work than here.[4] One event did, however, finally prompt him to leave. When the editorial board at the Psychoanalytic Society of San Francisco finished with his essay "Psychoanalysis Revised," he found that "the entire text was disfigured beyond recognition, the basic intention could not be discerned."[5] As Adorno recounted, the head editor explained that the standards to which the essay had been adjusted, which made it look like every other essay in the journal, were those of the profession: "I would only be standing in my own way"—Adorno was told—"if I passed up its advantages. I passed them up nevertheless."[6] Adorno moved back to Europe.

Adorno's sense that staying here would have impossibly burdened his work was confirmed long after the fact by the first English translation of *Aesthetic Theory* in 1984.[7] The publisher, partially against the will of the translator, discarded the book's form as a superstitiously imposed impediment that would only stymie the book's consumption.[8] Diametrically opposed to the course the book took in its various drafts in Adorno's own hands, a process that led in the final version to the rejection of the division of the book into chapters, the 1984 translation arrived on bookstore shelves divided into numbered chapters with main headings and subheadings inserted in the text. Paragraph indentations were distributed arbitrarily throughout, completing the image of a monodirectional sequence of topic sentences that could be followed stepwise from chapter 1 through chapter 12. This subordinated the text's paratactical order to a semblance of progressive argumentation that offered to present the book's content conveniently. This device provided a steady external grip on the book while causing it to collapse internally. For in lieu of any argumentative structure in the text itself, because it contains no homogeneous substance that can be followed from start to finish, the flaring clarity of paragraph indentations only produced a contrast by which the simulated paragraphs appeared murky in their refusal to parse into stages of thesis and evidence. And whereas the paratactical text demands that every sentence undertake to be the topic sentence and that the book be composed of long, complex phrases, each of which seems under the obligation to present the book as a whole, the 1984 translation carved up sentences in the image of declarative vehicles of content. The original paratactical text is concentrically arranged around a mute middle point through which every word seeks to be refracted and that it must express. The text cannot refer forward or backward without disturbing this nexus through which the parts become binding on each other. The linear argumentative structure imposed on the text by the translation thus dismissed the text's middle point as a detour and severed its nexus. Compulsory unification serves only to fragment: the imposed structure set whole passages adrift whose suddenly evident isolation required further apparatus to span them. Therefore, transitional phrases were interpolated such as: "as we saw" or "as we said" or "let us remember." The narrative persona that was projected into the text at these points and elsewhere was credible insofar as it seemed to substantiate an argumentative model of knowledge and its transmission. But this further contributed to muffling a text that, by its own standards, succeeds only insofar as what is particular in it begins to speak for itself. The rejection of the work's form as a superstition was carried over to the treatment of the original's many Greek, Latin, and French concepts and phrases. They were rendered literally, in English, and without any marking, as if their content was clear enough once they had been freed from their alphabetical inconvenience. Thus, for instance, *chorismos*—the contrary of *methexis*—was translated as "separatism," obfuscating the articulation of the problem of the participation of idea and object from Plato to Benjamin that is, so to speak, the topic of *Aesthetic Theory* and the whole of Adorno's writings. The many American phrases, which have such abrupt expressive power in the original, were likewise seamlessly absorbed into the scenery. Almost ingeniously the language of the 1984 text pulls away from the movement of thought that can still be sensed gesturing underneath, giving the book a disembodied quality, as if it were dubbed rather than translated. Subordinated to the principle of exchange by its coerced identity with the subject's form of consumption, *Aesthetische Theorie* in translation became a model of what it protests against: the primacy of the constitutive subject. The irony is, of course, that by narrowing the distance of the book from its readers, ostensibly for their own good, but fundamentally to sell it to them, the work was put beyond them.[9]

This volume is an entirely new translation of *Aesthetische Theorie*. The spatial organization of the text is identical to the original. The major sections of the English text are divided only where the original divides. The sentence structure and phrasing of the original were maintained wherever possible, given the tremendous differences of English syntax from the original. All words foreign to the original, including English words, occur here in italic. This translation, however, took its lead not so much from the aim to copy the appearance of the original, but rather from Adorno's description of the hearing implicit to Mahler's music: an "amplitude of a hearing encompassing the far distance, to which the most remote analogies and consequences are virtually present."[10] In *Aesthetic Theory* this amplitude occurs, however, not in the mimetic response of musical passages to each other but in the medium of concepts as their subterranean, dynamic relations.

The coherence of these subterranean relations depends on the text's paratactical form and survives only by a density of insight, not by external structure. This defines the text's—and its translation's—particular vulnerability: the slightest slackening of intensity threatens to dissolve the text into a miscellany. Nothing supports the text except the intensity with which it draws on and pushes against itself. With few exceptions paratactical works are therefore short, fragmentary, and compacted by the crisis of their own abbreviation. Paratactical texts are intensive, almost to the denial of their quality of extension; and the more extensive the paratactical work actually is—and *Aesthetic Theory* is almost unparalleled in this—the greater the potential for its unraveling at each and every point. The text therefore requires a rhetoric that will heighten concentration and density and absorb the dozens of ways in which it is constantly exposed. Every reader will note the work's recurrence to abrupt, staccato, sometimes delphically abbreviated expression that heightens the push–pull of the text. Because it rejects certitude as a standard of truth in favor of exactness of insight, it necessarily tends toward the apodictic. Adorno is also able to produce concentration out of nowhere by beginning sentences with long-haul subordinate clauses that engage with a "That . . . " that grips cognition like the ratchet on a rollercoaster with a demand for cooperative antigravitational struggle to the top of the first slope so momentum can be discovered shooting down the main clause into any number of concluding subordinate sweeps. A paratactical text is inimical to exposition, and Adorno uses the most condensed gestures to invoke rather than propound relevant philosophical arguments: a single "sickness unto death" does the work of all of Kierkegaard, "positive negation" all of Hegel and any phrasing that even subliminally hints at "in the age of" is expected to conjure the entire argument of Benjamin's "Artwork in the Age of Mechanical Reproduction," to which the book is, as a whole, a response. Out of the same demand for density, Adorno refers wherever possible to artists and artworks in the familiar: *Recherche* is more than enough for Proust's title, the *Marriage* could not be anything but that of Figaro, and George is plenty for Stefan George.

Wherever parallel linguistic resources were available these and Adorno's many other techniques of condensation and heightening have been used to maintain the density of this translation. In the case of some titles and authors, however, especially of German authors and works that have become progressively unknown in the aftermath of World War II, they are too improbably remote even to pretend they could not be recognized and had to be provided with first names and full titles. And there is another technique of condensed reference, used constantly by Adorno, that could not be incorporated at all because it is uniquely a potential of the original vis-à-vis English. As is well know, German is able to refer by pronouns with specificity across any distance of text, long or short, and juggle many nouns with referential consistency. Adorno employs this linguistic resource to an extreme in order to avoid the repetition of nouns in a text that is allergic to even the few millimeters of slack such repetition would feed in. In some passages the weave of pronouns becomes so remote and tenuous that it seems it could only be followed by someone who would comprehend their referents anamnestically, as if known from eternity. They demand a level of concentration that inhabits the text completely. Since English has no comparable pronominal structure, this internal weave of reference could not possibly be matched in translation. It has, therefore, throughout been necessary to choose between potential glibness and precision of reference. Without exception the latter was preferred, however ungainly the result. This is the recognition of an aporia of translation and its result is not entirely a betrayal of Adorno's text. For however difficult his writing may be, it is never vague or simply evocative.

This translation has not supposed that it is simply a failed replica of the perfections of the original. The original has plenty of problems of its own that it imposes on the translation. Some of these problems are reciprocal with the capacities of the original. On one hand, for instance, this paratactical text provides unmatched freedom: Since the text does not labor under schematic requirements it can and must take a decisively new breath for every line; those insights that authors of traditional forms know to be some of the best of what they have thought but must constantly reject as structurally inapposite are what at every point motivate a paratactical text. But, on the other hand, this paratactical style is, by that same measure, unable—as mentioned—to refer backward or forward: Adorno never writes, "as mentioned." Every transition must be a transition in the object itself if it is not to unhinge the text. Thus the text is deprived of a major technique for building on what has been, or of explicitly organizing itself toward what will be, developed elsewhere; and it cannot take the sting out of repetition by acknowledging it. Instead, Adorno is constantly compelled to start anew saying what has already been said. The text produces a need for repetition that is its innermost antagonist. Thus Adorno throughout repeatedly restates major motifs: that the artwork is a monad, that it is a social microcosm, that society is most intensely active in an artwork where it is most remote from society. If Adorno is a master of thematic variation and able to use the dynamic energy of these repeated motifs not just to justify what is waiting to be said, but as a catapult for new insights, all the same, anyone who actually studies the book will rankle at a repetitiveness that really is as inevitable as it comes to seem. The text is single-mindedly concerned with escaping jargon and developing what is potentially new in concepts that have become rigidified and obsolete, but the obligatory repetitiveness of its formulations courts jargon and makes the central motifs of the work vulnerable to facile trivialization by anyone who cares to do so. The paratactical capacity that prompts the text's protean insights engenders repetition that becomes disorienting: all those markers that measure out space and time longitudinally in traditional forms are discarded and there is a constantly looming sense of being caught in a vortex, as if there is no knowing whether one has been through a particular passage before, or if perhaps one has never left the spot. The virtual presence of the whole of the text at any one point is impeded by the form in which it is maintained.

This level of repetitiveness is damaging to the original and it takes its toll on the translation. More regrettable, however, because it does not derive from any capacity of the text, is the repetition that originates in the fact that it is an opus posthumous. Adorno completed *Aesthetic Theory,* but he did not finish it: every section that he intended to write for the book was written; the main body of the text was for the most part complete and composed at the highest level that Adorno achieved in any of his work. Yet Adorno did not live to carry out the final, crucial revision of the text. In this revision he would have rewritten a sig-nificant number of passages, inserted a group of passages that had accumulated in various ways external to the main text in the decade during which the book was written, and he would have written a new introduction to the book that would have replaced a draft with which he was dissatisfied.[11] After Adorno's death, this editing work could only partially be fulfilled by his longtime student and friend, Rolf Tiedemann, and by Adorno's widow, Gretel Adorno. They deciphered Adorno's handwriting in the main text, collected the fragments into the *Paral-ipomena* that in this edition comes after the main text, and appended the "Draft Introduction" and an excursus entitled "Theories on the Origin of Art." At the end of this volume they have provided an afterword in which they describe in detail the state of the text at Adorno's death and how they constructed the present volume. As they point out, they could not rewrite passages even when the needed improvements were self-evident. And the intense philological pressures in a country whose Protestantism invented the discipline and where there are, for instance, left-wing and right-wing editions of Hölderlin, prohibited the exclusion of even obviously contradictory formulations. What weighs most on this text, weighs on it literally: there is much more here than is needed, by about one-fifth. In his final revision Adorno would have been able to discard a great deal. The repetitive discussions of classicism and genius, for instance, which now seem strewn around, could have been grouped and condensed. And had Adorno had the chance to definitvely position three extensive sections that were still external to the text at the time of his death, he would have been able to exclude duplicate passages that permit their integration at several different points. The editors combined and inserted these extensive sections in plausible ways, but there is no doubt that this has resulted in several overlong main parts that disturb the organization of the book. For instance—as Tiedemann and Gretel Adorno point out—various aspects of "Situation" are needed in the book's development from "Art, Society, Aesthetics" to "On the Categories of the Ugly, the Beautiful, and Technique." But the sheer girth of "Situation" combines so much material that it diffusely interferes with the tightly wrought organization of the first five main parts. It is, furthermore, questionable whether the excursus, "Theories on the Origin of Art," could have been included in the final version. Although it is obviously germane to the problems Adorno treats throughout *Aesthetic Theory*, it is a research essay and in majority stylistically at odds with the rest of the text; and it doesn't make sense to have an "excursus" in a text that is all paratactical divagation anyway. As a guess, however, it is easy to imagine how parts of the excursus could have been used in the new introduction that Adorno wanted to write.

Nothing is to be done about these layers of repetitiveness in the text. They burden the book at every point. But it is worth knowing that however overlong the book is, there is nothing to skim. There is, for instance, much in the *Paralipomena* that is not to be found anywhere else in the text. And if Adorno found the "Draft Introduction" inadequate, it may take some years of research to figure out why. It is in any case probably the best place to begin reading *Aesthetic Theory*. The paratactical organization of the book does not mean that it can be read equally well in any direction. It is not argumentative; it does not seek to convince; but it does present a logic of insight that has a distinct forward direction that develops concentrically, and, as indicated, this is best perceived by initially reading "Situation" separate from the first five main parts.

The less finished main parts, such as "Situation," were often more difficult to translate than the more finished parts, though this was only a slight difference of degree. No reader will imagine the linguistic mayhem out of which this translation is built. And the ditches, craters, and rubble over which each English sentence passes are more than crushed syntax. The historical breach on the other side of which German now stands makes even this translator involuntarily prefer to say the "original" rather than the German, and made it necessary to say, page by page, that it is, or was, a Jewish language, too. This translation is allied with Adorno's return to Germany in that his need to return there to be able to write works such as *Aesthetic Theory* was inseparable from an impulse to pick up the severed threads of what was not fascist in Germany's past and the value of which, however alloyed, he never doubted. His enormous importance in the postwar decades was that he succeeded in helping to reestablish Germany's own relation to that past, not in the search of the primal or in alliance with any antihumanism, but—as in *Aesthetic Theory*—in defense of a modernism that would not betray the hopes of the past.[12]

This is not to say that Adorno returned to Germany to fit in and help restore the nation to what it once was. What he wrote was completely unpalatable to the former-Nazi faculty, still in its prime, that controlled Frankfurt University after the war. They rejected writings such as *Minima Moralia* as unscholarly and the whole of Adorno's work as essayistic and fragmentary and saw to it that he was not offered a professorship. Only under coercion did they grudgingly bestow on him what became known as a *Wiedergutmachungsstuhl*, a faculty position made not because he merited it as a philosopher, but in reparation to a Jew who had been deprived by the war of his property, his teaching post.[13] Barely two decades after his return, leftist students who had idolized him and embraced his works rioted in his seminars because he refused to lead them to the barricades. Adorno's freedom to teach was forcibly rescinded, as it had been in the thirties. In the summer recess following the student demonstrations of 1969, he died of a heart attack while trying to finish this book.

After Adorno's death, interest in his writings soon dissipated, and today, when he is studied in Germany, he is regarded mainly as a historical curiosity and more likely to be diminished than admired. For over a decade, the most thorough, widely read, and esteemed history of his work—Rolf Wiggershaus's *The Frankfurt School*—dismisses him as a bitter, hyperemotional complainer, monotonously prejudiced in his views, irresponsibly protean in his thought, and unable to formulate testable hypotheses.[14] Wiggerhaus's book, in that it embodies a generation's rejection of Adorno echoed in dozens of similar works, points up the fact that *Aesthetic Theory* is currently as obliquely remote to Germany as it is to the United States. And this remoteness is requisite to any plausible value it may have. For as Adorno wrote in constantly varied formulations, only what does not fit in can be true. He would not have been interested in seeing this book "received" here. Like all those works whose strands Adorno returned to Germany to pick up, when *Aesthetic Theory* is seen for what it is, it stands outside and looks in. Although the book does in many ways appear obsolete to us—today no one would try a dialectical reversal, now nothing seems precisely the opposite of anything else, and that shift of quantity into quality such as when water cooling become ice is no longer an inspiring mystery—this perspective that condescends from the vantage of being up-to-date as to the odd cut of an old coat or dress reveals its delusiveness when instead it is wondered how we look to it. For even though students once complained that Adorno had no interest in praxis but was preoccupied only with art, from the book's perspective it will be noticed that the word has completely disappeared from contemporary language, whereas for this book on art, "Praxis would be the ensemble of means for minimizing material necessity, and as such it would be identical with pleasure, happiness, and that autonomy in which these means are sublimated." Much of what catches the eye as obsolete in *Aesthetic Theory* is what would be new if it were not blocked; here what is perceived as old hat masks the disappointment of what can no longer be hoped for. *Aesthetic Theory* wants to be what is German that is not German, and if it finds real resonance here, it will be with what is American that is not American, none of which could be put on a list of national character traits.

What is hard about translation is not—as those who have never tried it imagine—finding the right word. The right word is always there, it just can't be used: inevitably it starts with the same letter as the three words on either side of it and, in a translation, pulling four oranges says fake, not jackpot. Line by line, the wrong word is always, unbearably, coming to the rescue. The sureness with which translation taps fate puts the I-Ching to shame: the word needed at any one point has somehow always just been used in the previous clause to cover for some other right word that would not fit. If translation were just pinning the tail on the donkey it would be easy, but the donkey is running and the translator is riding another beast, going in some other direction: each language, and each and every word, has its own momentary vector. So, for instance, even when the original wants to dictate the right word—e.g., *Programm*—directly into English, with only a slight shift of spelling, it turns out that the English equivalent now instinctually summons up computers—not the self-understood political sense of the original—with barely containable textual implications. Since the right word was always waiting, and had to be left waiting, this translation is made of whatever else was handy: a carrot for the nose, lightbulbs for eyes, some feathers for the mustache. Propped on a bench in the distance with its back to the sunset, perhaps it even looks alive. But it is not to be leaned against and neither will it bear all that much scrutiny. In German this book is almost too interesting to read; for those many passages in English where this is no longer the case, where it was just not possible to find any better way to do it, for the many sentences that were each finally accepted as not really but sort of what it means, I can only say, it was not for lack of trying.

Notes

1 Barnett Newman, in *Painters Painting: The New York Art Scene, 1940–1970*, directed by Emile de Antonio.
2 Adorno, *Beethoven*, ed. Rolf Tiedemann (Frankfurt, 1993), p. 15.
3 Adorno, *Negative Dialectics*, trans. E. B. Ashton (New York, 1973), p. xx (translation amended).
4 Adorno, "Auf die Frage: Was ist deutsch," in *Gesammelte Schriften* 10.2 (Frankfurt, 1977), p. 693.
5 Ibid., p. 698.
6 Ibid.
7 *Aesthetic Theory*, trans. C. Lenhardt (New York, 1984).
8 C. Lenhardt, "Response to Hullot-Kentor," *Telos*, no. 65 (Fall 1985): 153.
9 See Hullot-Kentor, "Aesthetic Theory: The Translation," *Telos*, no. 65 (Fall 1985): 147–152.
10 Adorno, *Mahler: A Musical Physiognomy*, trans. Edmund Jephcott (Chicago, 1992), p. 84.
11 See the Afterword to this translation.
12 See Jürgen Habermas, "A Letter to Christa Wolf," from *The Normalcy of a Berlin Republic*, trans. Michael Roloff (forthcoming).
13 Conversation with Rolf Tiedemann, October 15, 1995.
14 Rolf Wiggershaus, *The Frankfurt School: Its History, Theories, and Political Significance*, trans. Michael Robertson (Cambridge, Mass.: 1994); see, e.g., pp. 245, 246, 254, 458, and 510.

There are three levels of notes: Adorno's own, some of which were added by the German editors in accord with the author's sparse style of annotation; those few additional comments contributed by the German editors, which are marked as such and are in square brackets; and those explanatory notes specific to this translation, also in square brackets and identified by trans. *Citations are given exclusively in English except when German or French poetry is quoted in the text, in which case the original is provided in the note. In the several instances in which no English citation is given for translations of poetry in the main text, the translations are my own.*

Aesthetic Theory

1
Art, Society, Aesthetics

It is self-evident that nothing concerning art is self-evident anymore, not its inner life, not its relation to the world, not even its right to exist. The forfeiture of what could be done spontaneously or unproblematically has not been compensated for by the open infinitude of new possibilities that reflection confronts. In many regards, expansion appears as contraction. The sea of the formerly inconceivable, on which around 1910 revolutionary art movements set out, did not bestow the promised happiness of adventure. Instead, the process that was unleashed consumed the categories in the name of that for which it was undertaken. More was constantly pulled into the vortex of the newly taboo; everywhere artists rejoiced less over the newly won realm of freedom than that they immediately sought once again after ostensible yet scarcely adequate order. For absolute freedom in art, always limited to a particular, comes into contradiction with the perennial unfreedom of the whole. In it the place of art became uncertain. The autonomy it achieved, after having freed itself from cultic function and its images, was nourished by the idea of humanity. As society became ever less a human one, this autonomy was shattered. Drawn from the ideal of humanity, art's constituent elements withered by art's own law of movement. Yet art's autonomy remains irrevocable. All efforts to restore art by giving it a social function—of which art is itself uncertain and by which it expresses its own uncertainty—are doomed. Indeed, art's autonomy shows signs of blindness. Blindness was ever an aspect of art; in the age of art's emancipation, however, this blindness has begun to predominate in spite of, if not because of, art's lost naïveté, which, as Hegel already perceived, art cannot undo. This binds art to a naïveté of a second order: the uncertainty over what purpose it serves. It is uncertain whether art is still possible; whether, with its complete emancipation, it did not sever its own preconditions. This question is kindled by art's own past. Artworks detach themselves from the empirical world and bring forth another world, one opposed to the empirical world as if this other world too were an autonomous entity. Thus, however tragic they appear, artworks tend a priori toward affirmation. The clichés of art's reconciling glow enfolding the world are repugnant not only because they parody the emphatic concept of art with its bourgeois version and class it among those Sunday institutions that provide solace. These clichés rub against the wound that art itself bears. As a result of its inevitable withdrawal from theology, from the unqualified claim to the truth of salvation, a secularization without which art would never have developed, art is condemned to provide the world as it exists with a consolation that—shorn of any hope of a world beyond—strengthens the spell of that from which the autonomy of art wants to free itself. The principle of autonomy is itself suspect of giving consolation: By undertaking to posit totality out of itself, whole and self-encompassing, this image is transferred to the world in which art exists and that engenders it. By virtue of its rejection of the empirical world—a rejection that inheres in art's concept and thus is no mere *escape*, but a law immanent to it—art sanctions the primacy of reality. In a work dedicated to the praise of art, Helmut Kuhn warranted that art's each and every work is a paean.[1] His thesis would be true, were it meant critically. In the face of the abnormity into which reality is developing, art's inescapable affirmative essence has become insufferable. Art must turn against itself, in opposition to its own concept, and thus become uncertain of itself right into its innermost fiber. Yet art is not to be dismissed simply by its abstract negation. By attacking what seemed to be its foundation throughout the whole of its tradition, art has been qualitatively transformed; it itself becomes qualitatively other. It can do this because through the ages by means of its form, art has turned against the status quo and what merely exists just as much as it has come to its aid by giving form to its elements. Art can no more be reduced to the general formula of consolation than to its opposite.

The concept of art is located in a historically changing constellation of elements; it refuses definition. Its essence cannot be deduced from its origin as if the first work were a foundation on which everything that followed were constructed and would collapse if shaken. The belief that the first artworks are the highest and purest is warmed-over romanticism;

with no less justification it could be claimed that the earliest artistic works are dull and impure in that they are not yet separated from magic, historical documentation, and such pragmatic aims as communicating over great distances by means of calls or horn sounds; the classical conception of art gladly made use of such arguments. In bluntly historical terms, the facts blur.[2] The effort to subsume the historical genesis of art ontologically under an ultimate motif would necessarily flounder in such disparate material that the theory would emerge empty-handed except for the obviously relevant insight that the arts will not fit into any gapless concept of art.[3] In those studies devoted to the aesthetic αρχαι, positivistic sampling of material and such speculation as is otherwise disdained by the sciences flourish wildly alongside each other; Bachofen is the best example of this. If, nevertheless, one wanted in the usual philosophical fashion categorically to distinguish the so-called question of origin—as that of art's essence—from the question of art's historical origin, that would amount only to turning the concept of origin arbitrarily against the usual sense of the word. The definition of art is at every point indicated by what art once was, but it is legitimated only by what art became with regard to what it wants to, and perhaps can, become. Although art's difference from the merely empirical is to be maintained, this difference is transformed in itself qualitatively; much that was not art—cultic works, for instance—has over the course of history metamorphosed into art; and much that was once art is that no longer. Posed from on high, the question whether something such as film is or is no longer art leads nowhere. Because art is what it has become, its concept refers to what it does not contain. The tension between what motivates art and art's past circumscribes the so-called questions of aesthetic constitution. Art can be understood only by its laws of movement, not according to any set of invariants. It is defined by its relation to what it is not. The specifically artistic in art must be derived concretely from its other; that alone would fulfill the demands of a materialistic-dialectical aesthetics. Art acquires its specificity by separating itself from what it developed out of; its law of movement is its law of form. It exists only in relation to its other; it is the process that transpires with its other. Nietzsche's late insight, honed in opposition to traditional philosophy, that even what has become can be true, is axiomatic for a reoriented aesthetic. The traditional view, which he demolished, is to be turned on its head: Truth exists exclusively as that which has become. What appears in the artwork as its own lawfulness is the late product of an inner-technical evolution as well as art's position within progressive secularization; yet

3

doubtless artworks became artworks only by negating their origin. They are not to be called to account for the disgrace of their ancient dependency on magic, their servitude to kings and amusement, as if this were art's original sin, for art retroactively annihilated that from which it emerged. Dinner music is not inescapable for liberated music, nor was dinner music honest service from which autonomous art outrageously withdrew. The former's miserable mechanical clattering is on no account improved because the overwhelming part of what now passes for art drowns out the echo of that clatter.

The Hegelian vision of the possible death of art accords with the fact that art is a product of history. That Hegel considered art transitory while all the same chalking it up to absolute spirit stands in harmony with the double character of his system, yet it prompts a thought that would never have occurred to him: that the substance of art, according to him its absoluteness, is not identical with art's life and death. Rather, art's substance could be its transitoriness. It is thinkable, and not merely an abstract possibility, that great music—a late development—was possible only during a limited phase of humanity. The revolt of art, teleologically posited in its "attitude to objectivity"[4] toward the historical world, has become a revolt against art; it is futile to prophesy whether art will survive it. What reactionary cultural pessimism once vociferated against cannot be suppressed by the critique of culture: that, as Hegel ruminated a hundred and fifty years ago, art may have entered the age of its demise.[5] Just as Rimbaud's stunning dictum[6] one hundred years ago divined definitively the history of new art, his later silence, his stepping into line as an employee, anticipated art's decline. It is outside the purview of aesthetics today whether it is to become art's necrology; yet it must not play at delivering graveside sermons, certifying the end, savoring the past, and abdicating in favor of one sort of barbarism that is no better than the culture that has earned barbarism as recompense for its own monstrosity. Whether art is abolished, perishes, or despairingly hangs on, it is not mandated that the content [*Gehalt*][7] of past art perish. It could survive art in a society that had freed itself of the barbarism of its culture. Not just aesthetic forms but innumerable themes have already become extinct, adultery being one of them. Although adultery filled Victorian and early-twentieth-century novels, it is scarcely possible to empathize directly with this literature now, given the dissolution of the high-bourgeois nuclear family and the loosening of monogamy; distorted and impoverished, this literature lives on only in illustrated magazines. At the same time, however, what is authentic in

Madame Bovary and was once embedded in its thematic content has long since outstripped this content and its deterioration. Obviously this is not grounds for historicophilosophical optimism over the invincibility of spirit. It is equally possible for the thematic material in its own demise to take with it that which is more than merely thematic. Art and artworks are perishable, not simply because by their heteronomy they are dependent, but because right into the smallest detail of their autonomy, which sanctions the socially determined splitting off of spirit by the division of labor, they are not only art but something foreign and opposed to it. Admixed with art's own concept is the ferment of its own abolition.

There is no aesthetic refraction without something being refracted; no imagination without something imagined. This holds true particularly in the case of art's immanent purposiveness.[8] In its relation to empirical reality art sublimates the latter's governing principle of *sese conservare* as the ideal of the self-identity of its works; as Schoenberg said, one paints a painting, not what it represents. Inherently every artwork desires identity with itself, an identity that in empirical reality is violently forced on all objects as identity with the subject and thus travestied. Aesthetic identity seeks to aid the nonidentical, which in reality is repressed by reality's compulsion to identity. Only by virtue of separation from empirical reality, which sanctions art to model the relation of the whole and the part according to the work's own need, does the artwork achieve a heightened order of existence. Artworks are afterimages of empirical life insofar as they help the latter to what is denied them outside their own sphere and thereby free it from that to which they are condemned by reified external experience. Although the demarcation line between art and the empirical must not be effaced, and least of all by the glorification of the artist, artworks nevertheless have a life sui generis. This life is not just their external fate. Important artworks constantly divulge new layers; they age, grow cold, and die. It is a tautology to point out that as humanly manufactured artifacts they do not live as do people. But the emphasis on the artifactual element in art concerns less the fact that it is manufactured than its own inner constitution, regardless of how it came to be. Artworks are alive in that they speak in a fashion that is denied to natural objects and the subjects who make them. They speak by virtue of the communication of everything particular in them. Thus they come into contrast with the arbitrariness of what simply exists. Yet it is precisely as artifacts, as products of social labor, that they also communicate with the empirical experience that they reject and from which they draw their content [*Inhalt*]. Art

5

negates the categorial determinations stamped on the empirical world and yet harbors what is empirically existing in its own substance. If art opposes the empirical through the element of form—and the mediation of form and content is not to be grasped without their differentiation—the mediation is to be sought in the recognition of aesthetic form as sedimented content. What are taken to be the purest forms (e.g., traditional musical forms) can be traced back even in the smallest idiomatic detail to content such as dance. In many instances ornaments in the visual arts were once primarily cultic symbols. Tracing aesthetic forms back to contents, such as the Warburg Institute undertook to do by following the afterlife of classical antiquity, deserves to be more broadly undertaken. The communication of artworks with what is external to them, with the world from which they blissfully or unhappily seal themselves off, occurs through noncommunication; precisely thereby they prove themselves refracted. It is easy to imagine that art's autonomous realm has nothing in common with the external world other than borrowed elements that have entered into a fully changed context. Nevertheless, there is no contesting the cliché of which cultural history is so fond, that the development of artistic processes, usually classed under the heading of style, corresponds to social development. Even the most sublime artwork takes up a determinate attitude to empirical reality by stepping outside of the constraining spell it casts, not once and for all, but rather ever and again, concretely, unconsciously polemical toward this spell at each historical moment. That artworks as windowless monads "represent" what they themselves are not can scarcely be understood except in that their own dynamic, their immanent historicity as a dialectic of nature and its domination, not only is of the same essence as the dialectic external to them but resembles it without imitating it. The aesthetic force of production is the same as that of productive labor and has the same teleology; and what may be called aesthetic relations of production—all that in which the productive force is embedded and in which it is active—are sedimentations or imprintings of social relations of production. Art's double character as both autonomous and *fait social* is incessantly reproduced on the level of its autonomy. It is by virtue of this relation to the empirical that artworks recuperate, neutralized, what once was literally and directly experienced in life and what was expelled by spirit. Artworks participate in enlightenment because they do not lie: They do not feign the literalness of what speaks out of them. They are real as answers to the puzzle externally posed to them. Their own tension is binding in relation to the tension external to them.

The basic levels of experience that motivate art are related to those of the objective world from which they recoil. The unsolved antagonisms of reality return in artworks as immanent problems of form. This, not the insertion of objective elements, defines the relation of art to society. The complex of tensions in artworks crystallizes undisturbed in these problems of form and through emancipation from the external world's factual facade converges with the real essence. Art, χωρίς from the empirically existing, takes up a position to it in accord with Hegel's argument against Kant: The moment a limit is posited, it is overstepped and that against which the limit was established is absorbed. Only this, not moralizing, is the critique of the principle of *l'art pour l'art*, which by abstract negation posits the χωρισμός of art as absolute. The freedom of artworks, in which their self-consciousness glories and without which these works would not exist, is the ruse of art's own reason. Each and every one of their elements binds them to that over which, for their happiness, they must soar and back into which at every moment they threaten once again to tumble. In their relation to empirical reality, artworks recall the theologumenon that in the redeemed world everything would be as it is and yet wholly other. There is no mistaking the analogy with the tendency of the profane to secularize the realm of the sacred to the point that only as secularized does the latter endure; the realm of the sacred is objectified, effectively staked off, because its own element of untruth at once awaits secularization and through conjuration wards off the secular. Accordingly, the pure concept of art could not define the fixed circumference of a sphere that has been secured once and for all; rather, its closure is achieved only in an intermittent and fragile balance that is more than just comparable to the psychological balance between ego and id. The act of repulsion must be constantly renewed. Every artwork is an instant; every successful work is a cessation, a suspended moment of the process, as which it reveals itself to the unwavering eye. If artworks are answers to their own questions, they themselves thereby truly become questions. The tendency to perceive art either in extra-aesthetic or preaesthetic fashion, which to this day is undiminished by an obviously failed education, is not only a barbaric residue or a danger of regressive consciousness. Something in art calls for this response. Art perceived strictly aesthetically is art aesthetically misperceived. Only when art's other is sensed as a primary layer in the experience of art does it become possible to sublimate this layer, to dissolve the thematic bonds, without the autonomy of the artwork becoming a matter of indifference. Art is autonomous and it is not; without what is heterogeneous to it, its autonomy eludes it. The great epics, which have survived even their own oblivion, were in their own age intermingled with historical and geographical reportage; Valéry the artist took note of how much of their material had yet to be recast by the formal requirements of the Homeric, pagan-Germanic, and Christian epics, without this reducing their rank vis-à-vis drossless works. Likewise tragedy, which may have been the origin of the idea of aesthetic autonomy, was an afterimage of cultic acts that were intended to have real effects. The history of art as that of its progressive autonomy never succeeded in extirpating this element, and not just because the bonds were too strong. At the height of its form, in the nineteenth century, the realistic novel had something of what the theory of so-called socialist realism rationally plotted for its debasement: reportage, the anticipation of what social science would later ascertain. The fanatic linguistic perfection of *Madame Bovary* is probably a symptom of precisely this contrary element; the unity of both, of reportage and linguistic perfectionism, accounts for the book's unfaded actuality. In artworks, the criterion of success is twofold: whether they succeed in integrating thematic strata and details into their immanent law of form and in this integration at the same time maintain what resists it and the fissures that occur in the process of integration. Integration as such does not assure quality; in the history of art, integration and quality have often diverged. For no single select category, not even the aesthetically central concept of the law of form, names the essence of art and suffices to judge its products. Essential to art are defining characteristics that contradict its fixed art-philosophical concept. Hegel's content-aesthetics [*Inhaltsästhetik*] recognized that element of otherness immanent to art and thus superseded formal aesthetics, which apparently operates with a so much purer concept of art and of course liberated historical developments such as non-representational painting that are blocked by Hegel's and Kierkegaard's content-aesthetics. At the same time, however, Hegel's idealist dialectic, which conceives form as content, regresses to a crude, preaesthetic level. It confuses the representational or discursive treatment of thematic material with the otherness that is constitutive of art. Hegel transgresses against his own dialectical conception of aesthetics, with consequences he did not foresee; he in effect helped transform art into an ideology of domination. Conversely, what is unreal and nonexistent in art is not independent of reality. It is not arbitrarily posited, not invented, as is commonly thought; rather, it is structured by proportions between what exists, proportions that are themselves defined by what exists, its deficiency, distress, and contradictoriness as well as its potentialities; even in these proportions real contexts resonate. Art is related to its other as is a magnet to a field of iron filings. Not only art's elements, but their constellation as well, that which is specifically aesthetic and to which its spirit is usually chalked up, refer back to its other. The identity of the artwork with existing reality is also that of the work's gravitational force, which gathers around itself its *membra disjecta*, traces of the existing. The artwork is related to the world by the principle that contrasts it with the world, and that is the same principle by which spirit organized the world. The synthesis achieved by means of the artwork is not simply forced on its elements; rather, it recapitulates that in which these elements communicate with one another; thus the synthesis is itself a product of otherness. Indeed, synthesis has its foundation in the spirit-distant material dimension of works, in that in which synthesis is active. This unites the aesthetic element of form with noncoercion. By its difference from empirical reality the artwork necessarily constitutes itself in relation to what it is not, and to what makes it an artwork in the first place. The insistence on the nonintentional in art—which is apparent in art's sympathy with its lower manifestations beginning at a specific historical point with Wedekind's derision of the "art-artist," with Apollinaire, and indeed with the beginnings of cubism—points up art's unconscious self-consciousness in its participation in what is contrary to it; this self-consciousness motivated art's culture-critical turn that cast off the illusion of its purely spiritual being.

Art is the social antithesis of society, not directly deducible from it. The constitution of art's sphere corresponds to the constitution of an inward space of men as the space of their representation: A priori the constitution of this space participates in sublimation. It is therefore plausible to conceive of developing the definition of art out of a theory of psychic life. Skepticism toward anthropological theories of human invariants recommends psychoanalytic theory. But this theory is more productive psychologically than aesthetically. For psychoanalysis considers artworks to be essentially unconscious projections of those who have produced them, and, preoccupied with the hermeneutics of thematic material, it forgets the categories of form and, so to speak, transfers the pedantry of sensitive doctors to the most inappropriate objects, such as Leonardo da Vinci or Baudelaire. The narrow-mindedness, in spite of all the emphasis on sex, is revealed by the fact that as a result of these studies, which are often offshoots of the biographical fad, artists whose work gave uncensored shape to the negativity of life are dimissed as neurotics. Laforgue's book[9] actually in all seriousness accuses Baudelaire of having suffered from a mother complex. The question is never once broached whether a psychically sound Baudelaire would have been able to write *The Flowers of Evil*, not to mention whether the poems turned out worse because of the neurosis. Psychological normalcy is outrageously established as the criterion even, as in Baudelaire, where aesthetic quality is bluntly predicated on the absence of *mens sana*. According to the tone of psychoanalytic monographs, art should deal affirmatively with the negativity of experience. The negative element is held to be nothing more than the mark of that process of repression that obviously goes into the artwork. For psychoanalysis, artworks are daydreams; it confuses them with documents and displaces them into the mind of a dreamer, while on the other hand, as compensation for the exclusion of the extramental sphere, it reduces art-works to crude thematic material, falling strangely short of Freud's own theory of the "dreamwork." As with all positivists, the fictional element in artworks is vastly overestimated by the presumed analogy with the dream. In the process of production, what is projected is only one element in the artist's relation to the art-work and hardly the definitive one; idiom and material have their own importance, as does, above all, the product itself; this rarely if ever occurs to the analysts. The psychoanalytic thesis, for instance, that music is a defense against the threat of paranoia, does indeed for the most part hold true clinically, yet it says nothing about the quality and content of a particular composition. The psychoanalytic theory of art is superior to idealist aesthetics in that it brings to light what is internal to art and not itself artistic. It helps free art from the spell of absolute spirit. Whereas vulgar idealism, rancorously opposed to knowledge of the artwork and especially knowledge of its entwinement with instinct, would like to quarantine art in a putatively higher sphere, psychoanalysis works in the opposite direction, in the spirit of enlightenment. Where it deciphers the social character that speaks from a work and in which on many occasions the character of its author is manifest, psychoanalysis furnishes the concrete mediating links between the structure of artworks and the social structure. But psychoanalysis too casts a spell related to idealism, that of an absolutely subjective sign system denoting subjective instinctual impulses. It unlocks phenomena, but falls short of the phenomenon of art. Psychoanalysis treats artworks as nothing but facts, yet it neglects their own objectivity, their inner consistency, their level of form, their critical impulse, their relation to nonpsychical reality, and, finally, their idea of truth. When a painter, obeying the pact of total frankness between analyst and patient, mocked the bad Viennese engravings that defaced his walls, she was informed by the analyst that this was nothing but aggression on her part. Artworks are incomparably less a copy and possession of the artist than a doctor who knows the artist exclusively from the couch can imagine. Only dilettantes reduce everything in art to the unconscious, repeating clichés. In artistic production, unconscious forces are one sort of impulse, material among many others. They enter the work mediated by the law of form; if this were not the case, the actual subject portrayed by a work would be nothing but a copy. Artworks are not *Thematic Apperception Tests* of their makers. Part of the responsibility for this philistinism is the devotion of psychoanalysis to the reality principle: Whatever refuses to obey this principle is always merely "escape"; adaptation to reality becomes the *summum bonum.* Yet reality provides too many legitimate reasons for fleeing it for the impulse to be met by the indignation of an ideology sworn to harmony: on psychological grounds alone, art is more legitimate than psychology acknowledges. True, imagination is escape, but not exclusively so: What transcends the reality principle toward something superior is always also part of what is beneath it; to point a taunting finger at it is malicious. The image of the artist, as one of the tolerated, integrated as a neurotic in a society sworn to the division of labor, is distorted. Among artists of the highest rank, such as Beethoven or Rembrandt, the sharpest sense of reality was joined with estrangement from reality; this, truly, would be a worthwhile object for the psychology of art. It would need to decipher the artwork not just as being like the artist but as being unlike as well, as labor on a reality resisting the artist. If art has psychoanalytic roots, then they are the roots of fantasy in the fantasy of omnipotence. This fantasy includes the wish to bring about a better world. This frees the total dialectic, whereas the view of art as a merely subjective language of the unconscious does not even touch it.

Kant's aesthetics is the antithesis of Freud's theory of art as wish fulfillment. Disinterested liking is the first element of the judgment of taste in the "Analytic of the Beautiful."[10] There interest is termed "the liking that we combine with the representation of the existence of an object."[11] It is not clear, however, if what is meant by the "representation of the existence of an object" is its content, the thematic material in the sense of the object treated in the work, or the artwork itself; the pretty nude model or the sweet resonance of a musical tone can be kitsch or it can be an integral element of artistic quality. The accent on "representation" is a consequence of Kant's subjectivistic approach, which in accord with the rationalistic tradition, notably that of Moses Mendelssohn, tacitly seeks aesthetic quality in the effect the artwork has on the observer. What is revolutionary in the *Critique of Judgment* is that without leaving the circle of the older effect-aesthetics Kant at the same time restricted it through immanent criticism; this is in keeping with the whole of his subjectivism, which plays a significant part in his objective effort to save objectivity through the analysis of subjective elements. Disinterestedness sets itself at a distance from the immediate effect that liking seeks to conserve, and this initiates the fragmentation of the supremacy of liking. For, once shorn of what Kant calls interest, satisfaction becomes so indeterminate that it no longer serves to define beauty. The doctrine of disinterested satisfaction is impoverished vis-à-vis the aesthetic; it reduces the phenomenon either to formal beauty, which when isolated is highly dubious, or to the so-called sublime natural object. The sublimation of the work to absolute form neglects the spirit of the work in the interest of which sublimation was undertaken in the first place. This is honestly and involuntarily attested by Kant's strained footnote,[12] in which he asserts that a judgment of an object of liking may indeed be disinterested, yet interesting; that is, it may produce interest even when it is not based on it. Kant divides aesthetic feeling—and thus, in accord with the whole of his model, art itself—from the power of desire, to which the "representation of the existence of an object" refers; the liking of such a representation "always has reference to the power of desire."[13] Kant was the first to achieve the insight, never since forgotten, that aesthetic comportment is free from immediate desire; he snatched art away from that avaricious philistinism that always wants to touch it and taste it. Nevertheless, the Kantian motif is not altogether alien to psycho-analytic art theory: Even for Freud artworks are not immediate wish fulfillments but transform unsatisfied libido into a socially productive achievement, whereby the social value of art is simply assumed, with uncritical respect for art's public reputation. Although Kant emphasizes the difference between art and the power of desire—and thereby between art and empirical reality—much more energetically than does Freud, he does not simply idealize art: The separation of the aesthetic sphere from the empirical constitutes art. Yet Kant transcendentally arrested this constitution, which is a historical process, and simplistically equated it with the essence of the artistic, unconcerned that the subjective, instinctual components of art return metamorphosed even in art's maturest form, which negates them. The dynamic character of the artistic is much more fully grasped by Freud's theory of sublimation. But for this Freud clearly had to pay no smaller a price than did Kant. If in the latter's case, in spite of his preference for sensual intuition, the spiritual essence of the artwork originates in the distinction between aesthetic and practical, appetitive behavior, Freud's adaptation of the aesthetic to the theory of the instincts seems to seal itself off from art's spiritual essence; for Freud, artworks are indeed, even though sublimated, little more than plenipotentiaries of sensual impulses, which they at best make unrecognizable through a sort of dreamwork. The confrontation of these two heterogeneous thinkers —Kant not only rejected philosophical psychologism but in his old age increasingly rejected all psychology—is nevertheless permitted by a commonality that outweighs the apparently absolute difference between the Kantian construction of the transcendental subject, on the one hand, and the Freudian recourse to the empirically psychological on the other: Both are in principle subjectively oriented by the power of desire, whether it is interpreted negatively or positively. For both, the artwork exists only in relation to its observer or maker. By a mechanism to which his moral philosophy is subordinate, even Kant is compelled to consider the existing individual, the ontic element, more than is compatible with the idea of the transcendental subject. There is no liking without a living person who would enjoy it. Though it is never made explicit, the *Critique of Judgment* is as a whole devoted to the analysis of *constituta*. Thus what was planned as a bridge between theoretical and practical pure reason is vis-à-vis both an ὄλλο γένος. Indeed, the taboo on art—and so far as art is defined it obeys a taboo, for definitions are rational taboos—forbids that one take an animalistic stance toward the object, that is, that one dominate it by physically devouring it. But the power of the taboo corresponds to the power that it prohibits. There is no art that does not contain in itself as an element, negated, what it repulses. If it is more than mere indifference, the Kantian "without interest" must be shadowed by the wildest interest, and there is much to be said for the idea that the dignity of artworks depends on the intensity of the interest from which they are wrested. Kant denies this in favor of a concept of freedom that castigates as heteronomous whatever is not born exclusively of the subject. His theory of art is distorted by the insufficiency of the doctrine of practical reason. The idea of something beautiful, which possesses or has acquired some degree of autonomy in the face of the sovereign I, would, given the tenor of his philosophy, be disparaged as wandering off into intelligible realms. But along with that from which art antithetically originated, art is shorn of all content, and in its place he posits something as formal as aesthetic satisfaction. For Kant, aesthetics becomes paradoxically a castrated hedonism, desire without desire. An equal injustice is done both to artistic experience, in which liking is by no means the whole of it but plays a subordinate role, and to sensual interest, the suppressed and unsatisfied needs that resonate in their aesthetic negation and make artworks more than empty patterns. Aesthetic disinterestedness has broadened interest beyond particularity. The interest in the aesthetic totality wanted to be, objectively, an interest in a correct organization of the whole. It aims not at the fulfillment of the particular but rather at unbound possibility, though that would be no possibility at all without the presupposition of the fulfillment of the particular. Correlative to the weakness of Kant's aesthetics, Freud's is much more idealistic than it suspects. When artworks are translated purely into psychical immanence, they are deprived of their antithetic stance to the not-I, which remains unchallenged by the thorniness of artworks. They are exhausted in the psychical performance of gaining mastery over instinctual renunciation and, ultimately, in the achievement of conformity. The psychologism of aesthetic interpretation easily agrees with the philistine view of the artwork as harmoniously quieting antagonisms, a dream image of a better life, unconcerned with the misery from which this image is wrested. The conformist psychoanalytic endorsement of the prevailing view of the artwork as a well-meaning cultural commodity corresponds to an aesthetic hedonism that banishes art's negativity to the instinctual conflicts of its genesis and suppresses any negativity in the finished work. If successful sublimation and integration are made the end-all and be-all of the artwork, it loses the force by which it exceeds the given, which it renounces by its mere existence. The moment, however, the artwork comports itself by retaining the negativity of reality and taking a position to it, the concept of disinterestedness is also modified. Contrary to the Kantian and Freudian interpretation of art, artworks imply in themselves a relation between interest and its renunciation. Even the contemplative attitude to artworks, wrested from objects of action, is felt as the announcement of an immediate praxis and—to this extent itself practical—as a refusal to play along. Only artworks that are to be sensed as a form of comportment have a raison d'être. Art is not only the plenipotentiary of a better praxis than that which has to date predominated, but is equally the critique of praxis as the rule of brutal self-preservation at the heart of the status quo and in its service. It gives the lie to production for production's sake and opts for a form of praxis beyond the spell of labor. Art's *promesse du bonheur* means not only that hitherto praxis has blocked happiness but that happiness is beyond praxis. The measure of the chasm separating praxis from happiness is taken by the force of negativity in the artwork. Certainly Kafka does not awaken the power of desire. Yet the real fear triggered by prose works like *Metamorphosis* or *The Penal Colony*, that shock of revulsion and disgust that shakes the physis, has, as defense, more to do with desire than with the old disinterestedness canceled by Kafka and what followed him. As a response, disinterestedness would be crudely inadequate to his writings. Ultimately disinterestedness debases art to what Hegel mocked, a pleasant or useful plaything of Horace's *Ars Poetica*. It is from this that the aesthetics of the idealist age, contemporaneously with art itself, freed itself. Only once it is done with tasteful savoring does artistic experience become autonomous. The route to aesthetic autonomy proceeds by way of disinterestedness; the emancipation of art from cuisine or pornography is irrevocable. Yet art does not come to rest in disinterestedness. For disinterestedness immanently reproduces—and transforms—interest. In the false world all ηδονη is false. For the sake of happiness, happiness is renounced. It is thus that desire survives in art.

Pleasure masquerades beyond recognition in the Kantian disinterestedness. What popular consciousness and a complaisant aesthetics regard as the taking pleasure in art, modeled on real enjoyment, probably does not exist. The empirical subject has only a limited and modified part in artistic experience *tel quel*, and this part may well be diminished the higher the work's rank. Whoever concretely enjoys artworks is a philistine; he is convicted by expressions like "a feast for the ears." Yet if the last traces of pleasure were extirpated, the question of what artworks are for would be an embarrassment. Actually, the more they are understood, the less they are enjoyed. Formerly, even the traditional attitude to the artwork, if it was to be absolutely relevant to the work, was that of admiration that the works exist as they do in themselves and not for the sake of the observer. What opened up to, and overpowered, the beholder was their truth, which as in works of Kafka's type outweighs every other element. They were not a higher order of amusement. The relation to art was not that of its physical devouring; on the contrary, the beholder disappeared into the material; this is even more so in modern works that shoot toward the viewer as on occasion a locomotive does in a film. Ask a musician if the music is a pleasure, the reply is likely to be—as in the American joke of the grimacing cellist under Toscanini—"*I just hate music.*" For him who has a genuine relation to art, in which he himself vanishes, art is not an object;

deprivation of art would be unbearable for him, yet he does not consider individual works sources of joy. Incontestably, no one would devote himself to art without—as the bourgeois put it—getting something out of it; yet this is not true in the sense that a balance sheet could be drawn up: "heard the Ninth Symphony tonight, enjoyed myself so and so much" even though such feeble-mindedness has by now established itself as common sense. The bourgeois want art voluptuous and life ascetic; the reverse would be better. Reified consciousness provides an ersatz for the sensual immediacy of which it deprives people in a sphere that is not its abode. While the artwork's sensual appeal seemingly brings it close to the consumer, it is alienated from him by being a commodity that he possesses and the loss of which he must constantly fear. The false relation to art is akin to anxiety over possession. The fetishistic idea of the artwork as property that can be possessed and destroyed by reflection has its exact correlative in the idea of exploitable property within the psychological economy of the self. If according to its own concept art has become what it is, this is no less the case with its classification as a source of pleasure; indeed, as components of ritual praxis the magical and animistic predecessors of art were not autonomous; yet precisely because they were sacred they were not objects of enjoyment. The spiritualization of art incited the rancor of the excluded and spawned consumer art as a genre, while conversely antipathy toward consumer art compelled artists to ever more reckless spiritualization. No naked Greek sculpture was a *pin-up*. The affinity of the modern for the distant past and the exotic is explicable on the same grounds: Artists were drawn by the abstraction from natural objects as desirable; incidentally, in the construction of "symbolic art" Hegel did not overlook the unsensuous element of the archaic. The element of pleasure in art, a protest against the universally mediated commodity character, is in its own fashion mediable: Whoever disappears into the artwork thereby gains dispensation from the impoverishment of a life that is always too little. This pleasure may mount to an ecstasy for which the meager concept of enjoyment is hardly adequate, other than to produce disgust for enjoying anything. It is striking, incidentally, that an aesthetic that constantly insists on subjective feeling as the basis of all beauty never seriously analyzed this feeling. Almost without exception its descriptions were banausic, perhaps because from the beginning the subjective approach made it impossible to recognize that something compelling can be grasped of aesthetic experience only on the basis of a relation to the aesthetic object, not by recurring to the fun of the art lover.

The concept of artistic enjoyment was a bad compromise between the social and the socially critical essence of the artwork. If art is useless for the business of self-preservation—bourgeois society never quite forgives that—it should at least demonstrate a sort of use-value modeled on sensual pleasure. This distorts art as well as the physical fulfillment that art's aesthetic representatives do not dispense. That a person who is incapable of sensual differentiation—who cannot distinguish a beautiful from a flat sound, a brilliant from a dull color—is hardly capable of artistic experience, is hypostatized. Aesthetic experience does indeed benefit from an intensified sensual differentiation as a medium of giving form, yet the pleasure in this is always indirect. The importance of the sensual in art has varied; after an age of asceticism pleasure becomes an organ of liberation and vivaciousness, as it did in the Renaissance and then again in the anti-Victorian impulse of impressionism; at other moments creatural sadness has borne witness to a metaphysical content by erotic excitement permeating the forms. Yet however powerful, historically, the force of pleasure to return may be, whenever it appears in art literally, undefracted, it has an infantile quality. Only in memory and longing, not as a copy or as an immediate effect, is pleasure absorbed by art. Ultimately, aversion to the crudely sensual alienates even those periods in which pleasure and form could still communicate in a more direct fashion; this not least of all may have motivated the rejection of impressionism.

Underlying the element of truth in aesthetic hedonism is the fact that in art the means and the ends are not identical. In their dialectic, the former constantly asserts a certain, and indeed mediated, independence. Through the element of sensuous satisfaction the work's sine qua non, its appearance, is constituted. As Alban Berg said, it is a prosaic matter to make sure that the work shows no nails sticking out and that the glue does not stink; and in many of Mozart's compositions the delicacy of expression evokes the sweetness of the human voice. In important artworks the sensous illuminated by its art shines forth as spiritual just as the abstract detail, however indifferent to appearance it may be, gains sensuous luster from the spirit of the work. Sometimes by virtue of their differentiated formal language, artworks that are developed and articulated in themselves play over, secondarily, into the sensuously pleasing. Even in its equivalents in the visual arts, dissonance, the seal of everything modern, gives access to the alluringly sensuous by transfiguring it into its antithesis, pain: an aesthetic archetype of ambivalence. The source of the immense importance of all dissonance for new art since Baudelaire and *Tristan*—veritably an invariant of the modern—is that the immanent play of forces in the artwork converges with external reality: Its power over the subject intensifies in parallel with the increasing autonomy of the work. Dissonance elicits from within the work that which vulgar sociology calls its social alienation. In the meantime, of course, artworks have set a taboo even on spiritually mediated suavity as being too similar to its vulgar form. This development may well lead to a sharpening of the taboo on the sensual, although it is sometimes hard to distinguish to what extent this taboo is grounded in the law of form and to what extent simply in the failure of craft; a question, incidentally, that like many of its ilk becomes a fruitless topic of aesthetic debate. The taboo on the sensual ultimately encroaches on the opposite of pleasure because, even as the remotest echo, pleasure is sensed in its specific negation. For this aesthetic sensorium dissonance bears all too closely on its contrary, reconciliation; it rebuffs the semblance of the human as an ideology of the inhuman and prefers to join forces with reified consciousness. Dissonance congeals into an indifferent material; indeed, it becomes a new form of immediacy, without any memory trace of what it developed out of, and therefore gutted and anonymous. For a society in which art no longer has a place and which is pathological in all its reactions to it, art fragments on one hand into a reified, hardened cultural possession and on the other into a source of pleasure that the customer pockets and that for the most part has little to do with the object itself. Subjective pleasure in the artwork would approximate a state of release from the empirical as from the totality of heteronomous. Schopenhauer may have been the first to realize this. The happiness gained from artworks is that of having suddenly escaped, not a morsel of that from which art escaped; it is accidental and less essential to art than the happiness in its knowledge; the concept of aesthetic pleasure as constitutive of art is to be superseded. If in keeping with Hegel's insight all feeling related to an aesthetic object has an accidental aspect, usually that of psychological projection, then what the work demands from its beholder is knowledge, and indeed, knowledge that does justice to it: The work wants its truth and untruth to be grasped. Aesthetic hedonism is to be confronted with the passage from Kant's doctrine of the sublime, which he timidly excluded from art: Happiness in artworks would be the feeling they instill of standing firm. This holds true for the aesthetic sphere as a whole more than for any particular work.

Notes

1 Helmut Kuhn, *Schriften zur Aesthetik* (Munich, 1966), pp. 236ff.

2 [See "Excursus: Theories on the Origin of Art."]

3 See Adorno, "Die Kunst und die Künste," in *Ohne Leitbild, Gesammelte Schriften*, vol. 10.1 (Frankfurt, 1977), p. 432ff.

4 ["Stellung zur Objektivität": The phrase is from Georg Wilhelm Friedrich Hegel's *Science of Logic*, trans. William Wallace (Oxford, 1975), pp. 47–112, in which three "attitudes of thought to objectivity" are elucidated.—trans.]

5 [Although the direct reference is to Hegel, the phraseology at the same time quotes the title of Walter Benjamin's essay "Das Kunstwerk im Zeitalter seiner technischen Reproduzierbarkeit" ("The Work of Art in the Age of Its Mechanical Reproduction"), a title on which Adorno works repeated variations, often in ways that cannot be matched with adequate compactness in translation. —trans.]

6 ["Il faut être absolument moderne."—trans.]

7 [For the English "content" German has both "Inhalt" and "Gehalt," which, in aesthetic contexts, serve to distinguish the idea of thematic content or subject matter from that of content in the sense of import, essence, or substance of a work. This distinction, however, is not terminologically fixed in German or in Adorno's writings. One concept may well be used in place of the other. In some sections of *Aesthetic Theory* it is relatively easy to recognize which concept is at stake, as for instance in the lengthy development of the relation of form and content, where content is obviously "Inhalt." In these passages, the German is given when the concept is first introduced. At other points in the text, however, differentiation becomes more difficult. Where it has been necessary to emphasize the distinction between the terms, the much less frequently used term "Inhalt" accompanies the English concept. At points,

19

however, where there is an ongoing, explicit, contrasting discussion of the two concepts, or where confusion seemed likely, the German concepts accompany the single English concept. At one point it has been necessary to translate "Gehalt" as "substance"; in all other instances "substance" is the translation of "Substanz." There are, furthermore, various circumstances in which other German concepts than those just mentioned are also best translated as "content."—trans.]

8 ["Zweckmäßigkeit": For Kantian terms I generally follow Werner S. Pluhar's translation of *Critique of Judgment* (Indianapolis, 1987).—trans.]

9 [René Laforgue, *The Defeat of Baudelaire* (Folcroft, 1977).—trans.]

10 See Immanuel Kant, *Critique of Judgment*, section 2, pp. 45ff.

11 Ibid., p. 45.

12 Ibid., p. 46.

13 Ibid., p. 45.

2
Situation

Along with the categories, the materials too have lost their a priori self-evidence, and this is apparent in the case of poetic language. The disintegration of the materials is the triumph of their being-for-other. Hofmannsthal's *The Lord Chandos Letter*[1] became famous as the first striking evidence of this. Neo-romantic poetry as a whole can be considered as an effort to oppose this disintegration and to win back for language and other materials a degree of substantiality. The aversion felt toward *Jugendstil*, however, is a response to the failure of this effort. Retrospectively, in Kafka's words, it appears as a lighthearted journey going nowhere. In the opening poem to a cycle from the "Seventh Ring," an invocation of a forest, George needed only to juxtapose *Gold* and *Karneol* [carnelian] to be able to hope that, in keeping with his principle of stylization, the choice of words would glimmer poetically.[2] Six decades later the word choice can be recognized as a decorative arrangement, no longer superior to the crude accumulation of all possible precious materials in Wilde's *Dorian Gray*, where the interiors of a chic aestheticism resemble smart antique shops and auction halls and thus the commercial world Wilde ostensibly disdained. Analogously, Schoenberg remarked that Chopin was fortunate: He needed only to compose in F-sharp major, a still unexploited key, for his music to be beautiful. This, however, requires the historicophilosophical caveat that the materials of early musical romanticism, such as Chopin's rare tonalities, did indeed radiate the force of the untrodden, whereas these same materials were by 1900 already debased to the condition of being "select." The fate suffered by this generation's works, their juxtapositions and keys, inexorably befell the traditional concept of the poetic as something categorically higher and sacred. Poetry retreated into what abandons itself unreservedly to the process of disillusionment. It is this that constitutes the irresistibility of Beckett's work.

Art responds to the loss of its self-evidence not simply by concrete transformations of its procedures and comportments but by trying to pull itself free from its own concept as from a shackle: the fact that it is art. This is most strikingly confirmed by what were once the lower arts and entertainment, which are today administered, integrated, and qualitatively reshaped by the culture industry. For this lower sphere never obeyed the concept of pure art, which itself developed late. This sphere, a testimony of culture's failure that is constantly intruded upon this culture, made it will itself to failure—just what all humor, blessedly concordant in both its traditional and contemporary forms, accomplishes. Those who have been duped by the culture industry and are eager for its commodities were never familiar with art: They are therefore able to perceive art's inadequacy to the present life process of society—though not society's own untruth—more unobstructedly than do those who still remember what an artwork once was. They push for the deaestheticization[3] of art.[4] Its unmistakable symptom is the passion to touch everything, to allow no work to be what it is, to dress it up, to narrow its distance from its viewer. The humiliating difference between art and the life people lead, and in which they do not want to be bothered because they could not bear it otherwise, must be made to disappear: This is the subjective basis for classifying art among the consumer goods under the control of *vested interests*. If despite all this, art does not become simply consumable, then at least the relation to it can be modeled on the relation to actual commodity goods. This is made easier because in the age of overproduction the commodity's use value has become questionable and yields to the secondary gratification of prestige, of being in step, and, finally, of the commodity character itself: a parody of aesthetic semblance. Nothing remains of the autonomy of art—that artworks should be considered better than they consider themselves to be arouses indignation in culture customers—other than the fetish character of the commodity, regression to the archaic fetishism in the origin of art: To this extent the contemporary attitude to art is regressive. What is consumed is the abstract being-for-other of the cultural commodities, though without their actually being for others; by serving the customers, they themselves are betrayed. The old affinity of the beholder and the beheld is turned on its head. Insofar as the now typical attitude makes the artwork something merely factual, even art's mimetic element, itself incompatible with whatever is purely a thing, is bartered off as a commodity. The consumer arbitrarily projects his impulses—mimetic remnants—on whatever is presented to him. Prior to total administration, the subject who viewed, heard, or read a work was to lose himself, forget himself, extinguish himself in the artwork. The identification carried out by the subject was ideally not that of making the artwork like himself, but rather that of making himself like the artwork. This identification constituted aesthetic sublimation; Hegel named this comportment freedom to the object. He thus paid homage to the subject that becomes subject in spiritual experience through self-relinquishment, the opposite of the philistine demand that the artwork give him something. As a tabula rasa of subjective projections, however, the artwork is shorn of its qualitative dimension. The poles of the artwork's deaestheticization are that it is made as much a thing among things as a psychological vehicle of the spectator. What the reified artworks are no longer able to say is replaced by the beholder with the standardized echo of himself, to which he hearkens. This mechanism is set in motion and exploited by the culture industry. It contrives to make that appear near and familiar to its audience that has been estranged from them and brought close again only by having been heteronomously manipulated. Even the social argumentation against the culture-industry, however, has its ideological component. Autonomous art was not completely free of the culture industry's authoritarian ignominy. The artwork's autonomy is, indeed, not a priori but the sedimentation of a historical process that constitutes its concept. In the most authentic works the authority that cultic objects were once meant to exercise over the *gentes* became the immanent law of form. The idea of freedom, akin to aesthetic autonomy, was shaped by domination, which it universalized. This holds true as well for artworks. The more they freed themselves from external goals, the more completely they determined themselves as their own masters. Because, however, artworks always turn one side toward society, the domination they internalized also radiated externally. Once conscious of this nexus, it is impossible to insist on a critique of the culture industry that draws the line at art. Yet whoever, rightly, senses unfreedom in all art is tempted to capitulate, to resign in the face of the gathering forces of administration, with the dismissive assertion that "nothing ever changes," whereas instead, in the semblance of what is other, its possibility also unfolds. That in the midst of the imageless world the need for art intensifies—as it does also among the masses, who were first confronted with art through mechanical means of reproduction—tends to arouse doubts rather than, given the externality of this need for art, enabling art's continued existence to be defended. The complementary character of this need, an afterimage of magic as consolation for disenchantment, degrades art to an example of *mundus vult decipi* and deforms it. Also belonging to the ontology of false consciousness are those characteristics in which the bourgeoisie, which liberated at the same time that it bridled spirit, self-maliciously accepts and enjoys of spirit only what it cannot completely believe of it. To the extent that art corresponds to manifest social need it is primarily a profit-driven industry that carries on for as long as it pays, and by its smooth functioning it obscures the fact that it is already dead. There are flourishing genres and sub-genres of art, traditional opera for one, that are totally eviscerated without this being in the slightest apparent in official culture; in the difficulties however of just approximating its own standard of perfection, opera's spiritual insufficiency presents insurmountable practical problems; its actual demise is imminent. Trust in the needs of those who with heightened productive powers were to raise the whole to a higher form no longer makes sense, now that these needs have been integrated by a false society and transformed into false ones. Those needs do, just as was prognosticated, find satisfaction, but this satisfaction is itself false and robs humans of their human rights.

Today it would be fitting to approach art, in Kantian fashion, as a given; whoever pleads its cause manufactures ideologies and makes art one of them. If thought is in any way to gain a relation to art it must be on the basis that something in reality, something back of the veil spun by the interplay of institutions and false needs, objectively demands art, and that it demands an art that speaks for what the veil hides. Though discursive knowledge is adequate to reality, and even to its irrationalities, which originate in its laws of motion, something in reality rebuffs rational knowledge. Suffering remains foreign to knowledge; though knowledge can subordinate it conceptually and provide means for its amelioration, knowledge can scarcely express it through its own means of experience without itself becoming irrational. Suffering conceptualized remains mute and inconsequential, as is obvious in post-Hitler Germany. In an age of incomprehensible horror, Hegel's principle, which Brecht adopted as his motto, that truth is concrete, can perhaps suffice only for art. Hegel's thesis that art is consciousness of plight has been confirmed beyond anything he could have envisioned. Thus his thesis was transformed into a protest against his own verdict on art, a cultural pessimism that throws into relief his scarcely secularized theological optimism, his expectation of an actual realization of freedom. The darkening of the world makes the irrationality of art rational: radically darkened art. What the enemies of modern art, with a better instinct than its anxious apologists, call its negativity is the epitome of what established culture has repressed and that toward which art is drawn. In its pleasure in the repressed, art at the same time takes into itself the disaster, the principle of repression, rather than merely protesting hopelessly against it. That art enunciates the disaster by identifying with it anticipates its enervation; this, not any photograph of the disaster or false happiness, defines the attitude of authentic contemporary art to a radically darkened objectivity; the sweetness of any other gives itself the lie.

Fantastic art in romanticism, as well as its traces in mannerism and the baroque, presents something nonexistent as existing. The fictions are modifications of empirical reality. The effect they produce is the presentation of the nonempirical as if it were empirical. This effect is facilitated because the fictions originate in the empirical. New art is so burdened by the weight of the empirical that its pleasure in fiction lapses. Even less does it want to reproduce the facade. By avoiding contamination from what simply is, art expresses it all the more inexorably. Already Kafka's power is that of a negative feel for reality; what those who misunderstand him take to be fantastic in his work is *"Comment c'est"* By its ἐποχή from the empirical world, new art ceases to be fantastic. Only literary historians would class Kafka and Meyrink[5] together, and it takes an art historian to class Klee and Kubin together. Admittedly, in its greatest works, such as parts of Poe's *Pym*, Kürnberger's *Der Amerika-Müde*,[6] and Wedekind's *Mine-Haha*, fantastic art plays over into what modernity achieved in its freedom from normal referentiality. All the same, nothing is more damaging to theoretical knowledge of modern art than its reduction to what it has in common with older periods. What is specific to it slips through the methodological net of "nothing new under the sun"; it is reduced to the undialectical, gapless continuum of tranquil development that it in fact explodes. There is no denying the fatality that cultural phenomena cannot be interpreted without some translation of the new into the old, yet this implies an element of betrayal. Second reflection would have the responsibility of correcting this. In the relation of modern artworks to older ones that are similar, it is their differences that should be elicited. Immersion in the historical dimension should reveal what previously remained unsolved; in no other way can a relation between the present and the past be established. In comparison, the aim of the current history of ideas is virtually to demonstrate that the new does not exist. Yet since the mid-nineteenth century and the rise of high capitalism, the category of the new has been central, though admittedly in conjunction with the question whether anything new had ever existed. Since that moment no artwork has succeeded that rebuffed the ever fluctuating concept of the modern. Works that thought they would save themselves from the problematic attributed to the modern only accelerated their demise. Even a composer as immune to the charge of modernism as Anton Bruckner, would not have attained his most important achievements had he not worked with the most advanced material of his period, Wagner's harmony, which he then of course paradoxically transformed. His symphonies pose the question how the old is after all still possible, which is to say as something new; the question testifies to the irresistibility of the modern, whereas the "after all" is already something false, which the conservatives of the time could deride as something incoherent. That the category of the new cannot be brushed off as art-alien sensationalism is apparent in its irresistibility. When, prior to World War I, the conservative yet eminently sensitive English music critic Ernest Newman heard Schoenberg's Pieces for Orchestra, op. 16, he warned that one should not underestimate this man Schoenberg: With him it was all or nothing. Newman's hatred thus registered the destructive element of the new with a surer instinct than that of the apologists of the new. Even the old Saint-Saëns sensed something of this when, rejecting the effect of Debussy's music, he insisted that surely there must be alternatives to it. Whatever shuns or evades those transformations in the material that important innovations entail thereby shows itself to be impoverished and ineffectual. Newman must have noticed that the sounds liberated by Schoenberg's Pieces for Orchestra could no longer be dreamed away and henceforward bore consequences that would ultimately displace the traditional language of composition altogether. This process continues throughout the arts; after a play by Beckett one need only see a work by a moderate lesser contemporary to realize how much the new is a nonjudging judgment. Even the ultrareactionary Rudolf Borchadt confirmed that an artist must dispose over the achieved standard of his period. The new is necessarily abstract: It is no more known than the most terrible secret of Poe's pit. Yet something decisive, with regard to its content, is encapsuled in the abstractness of the new. Toward the end of his life Victor Hugo touched on it in his comment that Rimbaud bestowed a *frisson nouveau* on poetry. The shudder is a reaction to the cryptically shut, which is a function of that element of indeterminacy. At the same time, however, the shudder is a mimetic comportment reacting mimetically to abstractness. Only in the new does mimesis unite with rationality without regression: *Ratio* itself becomes mimetic in the shudder of the new and it does so with incomparable power in Edgar Allan Poe, truly a beacon for Baudelaire and all modernity. The new is a blind spot, as empty as the purely indexical gesture "look here." Like every historicophilosophical category, tradition is not to be understood as if, in an eternal relay race, the art of one generation, one style, one maestro, were passed on to the succeeding one. Sociologically and economically, since Max Weber and Sombart, the distinction is made between traditional and nontraditional periods; tradition itself, as a medium of historical movement, depends essentially on economic and social structures and is qualitatively transformed along with them. The attitude of contemporary art toward tradition, usually reviled as a loss of tradition, is predicated on the inner transformation of the category of tradition itself. In an essentially nontraditional society, aesthetic tradition a priori is dubious. The authority of the new is that of the historically inevitable. To this extent it implies objective criticism of the individual, the vehicle of the new: In the new the knot is tied aesthetically between individual and society. The experience of the modern says more even though its concept, however qualitative it may be, labors under its own abstractness. Its concept is privative; since its origins it is more the negation of what no longer holds than a positive slogan. It does not, however, negate previous artistic practices, as styles have done throughout the ages, but rather tradition itself; to this extent it simply ratifies the bourgeois principle in art. The abstractness of the new is bound up with the commodity character of art. This is why the modern when it was first theoretically articulated—in Baudelaire—bore an ominous aspect. The new is akin to death. What adopts a satanic bearing in Baudelaire is the negative self-reflection of identification with the real negativity of the social situation. Weltschmerz defects to the enemy, the world. Something of this remains admixed as ferment in everything modern. For direct protest that did not surrender to its opponent would in art be reactionary: This is why in Baudelaire the imago of nature is strictly taboo. To this day the modern has capitulated whenever it disavowed this taboo; this is the source of the harangues about decadence and of the racket that obstinately accompanies the modern. *Nouveauté* is aesthetically the result of historical development, the trademark of consumer goods appropriated by art by means of which artworks distinguish themselves from the ever-same inventory in obedience to the need for the exploitation of capital, which, if it does not expand, if it does not—in its own language—offer something new, is eclipsed. The new is the aesthetic seal of expanded reproduction, with its promise of undiminished plentitude. Baudelaire's poetry was the first to codify that, in the midst of the fully developed commodity society, art can ignore this tendency only at the price of its own powerlessness. Only by immersing its autonomy in society's *imagerie* can art surmount the heteronomous market. Art is modern art through mimesis of the hardened and alienated; only thereby, and not by the refusal of a mute reality, does art become eloquent; this is why art no longer tolerates the innocuous. Baudelaire neither railed against nor portrayed reification; he protested against it in the experience of its archetypes, and the medium of this experience is the poetic form. This raises him supremely above late romantic sentimentality. The power of his work is that it syncopates the overwhelming objectivity of the commodity character—which wipes out any human trace—with the objectivity of the work in itself, anterior to the living subject: The absolute artwork converges with the absolute commodity. The modern pays tribute to this in the vestige of the abstract in its concept. If in monopoly capitalism it is primarily exchange value, not use value, that is consumed,[7] in the modern artwork it is its abstractness, that irritating indeterminateness of what it is and to what purpose it is, that becomes a cipher of what the work is. This abstractness has nothing in common with the formal character of older aesthetic norms such as Kant's. On the contrary, it is a provocation, it challenges the illusion that life goes on, and at the same time it is a means for that aesthetic distancing that traditional fantasy no longer achieves. From the outset, aesthetic abstraction, which in Baudelaire was a still rudimentary and allegorical reaction to a world that had become abstract, was foremost a prohibition on graven images. This prohibition falls on what provincials[8] ultimately hoped to salvage under the name "message":[9] appearance as meaningful; after the catastrophe of meaning, appearance becomes abstract. From Rimbaud to contemporary avant-garde art, the obstinacy of this prohibition is unflagging. It has changed no more than has the fundamental structure of society. The modern is abstract by virtue of its relation to what is past; irreconcilable with magic, it is unable to bespeak what has yet to be, and yet must seek it, protesting against the ignominy of the ever-same: This is why Baudelaire's crypto-grams equate the new with the unknown, with the hidden telos, as well as with what is monstrous by virtue of its incommensurability with the ever-same and thus with the *goût du néant*. The arguments against the aesthetic *cupiditas rerum novarum,* which so plausibly call as evidence the content-lessness of the category, are at heart pharisaical. The new is not a subjective category, rather it is a compulsion of the object itself, which cannot in any other way come to itself and resist heteronomy. The force of the old presses toward the new, without which the old cannot be fulfilled. Yet the moment this is invoked, artistic practice and its manifestations become suspect; the old that it claims to safeguard usually disavows the specificity of the work; aesthetic reflection, however, is not indifferent to the entwinement of the old and new. The old has refuge only at the vanguard of the new: in the gaps, not in continuity. Schoenberg's simple motto—If you do not seek, you will not find—is a watchword of the new; whatever fails to honor it in the context of the artwork becomes a deficiency; not least among the aesthetic abilities is the capacity, in the process of the work's production, to sound for residual constraints; through the new, critique—the refusal—becomes an objective element of art itself. Even the camp followers of the new, whom everyone disdains, are more forceful than those who boldly insist on the tried and true. If in accord with its model, the fetish character of the commodity, the new becomes a fetish, this is to be criticized in the work itself, not externally simply because it became a fetish; usually the problem is a discrepancy between new means and old ends. If a possibility for innovation is exhausted, if innovation is mechanically pursued in a direction that has already been tried, the direction of innovation must be changed and sought in another dimension. The abstractly new can stagnate and fall back into the ever-same. Fetishiza-tion expresses the paradox of all art that is no longer self-evident to itself: the paradox that something made exists for its own sake; precisely this paradox is the vital nerve of new art. By exigency, the new must be something willed; as what is other, however, it could not be what was willed. Velleity binds the new to the ever-same, and this establishes the inner communication of the modern and myth. The new wants non-identity, yet intention reduces it to identity; modern art constantly works at the Münchhausean trick of carrying out the identification of the non-identical.

Scars of damage and disruption are the modern's seal of authenticity; by their means, art desperately negates the closed confines of the ever-same; explosion is one of its invariants. Antitraditional energy becomes a voracious vortex. To this extent, the modern is myth turned against itself; the timelessness of myth becomes the catastrophic instant that destroys temporal continuity; Benjamin's concept of the dialectical image contains this element. Even when modern art maintains traditional achievements in the form of technical resources, these are transcended by the shock that lets nothing inherited go unchallenged. Given that the category of the new was the result of a historical process that began by destroying a specific tradition and then destroyed tradition as such, modern art cannot be an aberration susceptible to correction by returning to foundations that no longer do or should exist; this is, paradoxically, the foundation of the modern and normative for it. Even in aesthetics, invariants are not to be denied; surgically extracted and displayed, however, they are insignificant. Music can serve as a model. It would be senseless to contest that it is a temporal art or that, however little it coincides with the temporality of real experience, it too is irreversible. If, however, one wanted to pass beyond vague generalities, such as that music has the task of articulating the relation of its "content" [*Inhalt*], its intratemporal elements, to time, one falls immediately into pedantry or subreption. For the relation of music to formal musical time is determined exclusively in the relation between the concrete musical event and time. Certainly it was long held that music must organize the intratemporal succession of events meaningfully: Each event should ensue from the previous one in a fashion that no more permits reversal than does time itself. However, the necessity of this temporal sequence was never literal; it participated in art's semblance character. Today music rebels against conventional temporal order; in any case, the treatment of musical time allows for widely diverging solutions. As questionable as it is that music can ever wrest itself from the invariant of time, it is just as certain that once this invariant is an object of reflection it becomes an element of composition and no longer an apriori.——The violence of the new, for which the name "experimental" was adopted, is not to be attributed to subjective convictions or the psychological character of the artist. When impulse can no longer find preestablished security in forms or content, productive artists are objectively compelled to experiment. This concept of experiment has, however, transformed itself in a fashion that is exemplary for the categories of the modern. Originally it meant simply that the will, conscious of itself, tested unknown or unsanctioned technical procedures. Fundamental to this idea of experimentation was the latently traditionalistic belief that it would automatically become clear whether the results were a match for what had already been established and could thus legitimate themselves. This conception of artistic experimentation became accepted as obvious at the same time that it became problematic in its trust in continuity. The gesture of experimentation, the name for artistic comportments that are obligatorily new, has endured but now, in keeping with the transition of aesthetic interest from the communicating subject to the coherence of the object, it means something qualitatively different: that the artistic subject employs methods whose objective results cannot be foreseen. Even this turn is not absolutely new. The concept of construction, which is fundamental to modern art, always implied the primacy of constructive methods over subjective imagination. Construction necessitates solutions that the imagining ear or eye does not immediately encompass or know in full detail. Not only is the unforeseen an effect, it also has an objective dimension, which was transformed into a new quality. The subject, conscious of the loss of power that it has suffered as a result of the technology unleashed by himself, raised this powerlessness to the level of a program and did so perhaps in response to an unconscious impulse to tame the threatening heteronomy by integrating it into subjectivity's own undertaking as an element of the process of production. What helped make this possible is the fact that imagination, the course taken by the object through the subject, does not, as Stockhausen pointed out, have a fixed focus but can adjust to degrees of acuity. What is hazily imagined can be imagined in its vagueness. This is a veritable balancing act for the experimental comportment. Whether this dates back to Mallarmé and was formulated by Valéry as the subject proving its aesthetic power by remaining in self-control even while abandoning itself to heteronomy, or if by this balancing act the subject ratifies its self-abdication, is yet to be decided. In any case, it is clear that insofar as experimental procedures, in the most recent sense, are in spite of everything undertaken subjectively, the belief is chimerical that through them art will divest itself of its subjectivity and become the illusionless thing in itself which to date art has only feigned.

The painfulness of experimentation finds response in the animosity toward the so-called isms: programmatic, self-conscious, and often collective art movements. This rancor is shared by the likes of Hitler, who loved to rail against "these im-and expressionists," and by writers who out of a politically avant-garde zealousness are wary of the idea of an aesthetic avant-garde. Picasso expressly confirmed this with regard to pre-World War I cubism. Within an ism the quality of individual artists can be clearly distinguished, although initially those who most explicitly draw attention to the peculiar characteristics of the school tend to be overrated in comparison with those who, like Pissarro among the impressionists,

31

cannot be reduced so conclusively to the program. Certainly a faint contradiction is inherent in the linguistic use of ism insofar as in emphasizing conviction and intention it seems to expel the element of involuntariness from art; yet this criticism is formalistic with regard to movements maligned as isms, just as expressionism and surrealism specifically made involuntary production their willful program. Further, the concept of the avant-garde, reserved for many decades for whatever movement declared itself the most advanced, now has some of the comic quality of aged youth. The difficulties in which isms are entangled express the problematics of an art emancipated from its self-evidence. The very consciousness to which all questions of what is genuinely binding in art must be submitted has at the same time demolished all standards of aesthetic bindingness: This is the source of the shadow of mere velleity that hangs over the hated isms. The fact that no important art practice has ever existed without conscious will merely comes to self-consciousness in the much beleaguered isms. This compels artworks to become organized in themselves and requires as well an external organization for the artworks to the extent that they want to survive in a monopolistically fully organized society. Whatever may be true in the comparison of art with an organism must be mediated by way of the subject and his reason. The truth of this comparison has long since been taken into the service of an irrationalistic ideology of a rationalized society; this is why the isms that deny that truth are truer. The isms by no means shackled the individual productive forces but rather heightened them, and they did so in part through mutual collaboration.

One aspect of isms has only recently become relevant. The truth content of many artistic movements does not necessarily culminate in great artworks; Benjamin demonstrated this in his study of German baroque drama.[10] Presumably the same holds true for German expressionism and French surrealism; not by accident the latter challenged the concept of art itself, a defiance that has ever since remained admixed with all authentic new art. Since art all the same remained art, the essence of the provocation may be sought in the preponderance of art over the artwork. This preponderance is embodied in the isms. What in terms of the work seems failed or no more than a citation, also testifies to impulses that can scarcely be objectivated in the particular work any longer; impulses of an art that transcends itself; its idea awaits rescue. It is worth noting that the uneasiness with isms seldom includes their historical equivalent, the schools. Isms are, so to speak, the secularization of these schools in an age that destroyed them as traditionalistic. Isms are scandalous because they do not fit into the schema of absolute individuation but remain as an island of a tradition that was shattered by the principle of individuation. The disdained should at the very least be completely alone, as surety for its powerlessness, its historical inefficacy, and its early, traceless demise. The schools entered into opposition to the modern in a way that was expressed eccentrically in the measures taken by the academies against students suspected of sympathy for modern directions. Isms are potentially schools that replace traditional and institutional authority with an objective authority. Solidarity with them is better than to disavow them, even if this were on the basis of the antithesis of the modern and modernism. The critique of what is *up to date*, yet without structural legitimation, is not without its justification: The functionless, for instance, that imitates function is regressive. Still, the separation of modernism as the opinions and convictions of the hangers-on of the authentically modern is invalid because without the subjective opinions that are stimulated by the new, no objectively modern art would crystallize. In truth the distinction is demagogical: Whoever complains about modernism means the modern, just as hangers-on are always attacked in order to strike at the protagonists whom one fears to challenge and whose prestige inspires deference among conformists. The standard of honesty by which the modernists are pharisaically measured implies acquiescence with being who one is, no more nor less, and a refusal to change, a fundamental *habitus* of the aesthetic reactionary. Its false nature is dissolved by the reflection that has now become the essence of artistic education. The critique of modernism in favor of the putatively truly modern functions as a pretext for judging the moderate—whose thinking fronts for the dross of a trivial intellectualism—as being better than the radical; actually it is the other way around. What lagged behind also fails to master the older means that it employs. History rules even those works that disavow it.

In sharp contrast to traditional art, new art accents the once hidden element of being something made, something produced. The portion of it that is θέσει grew to such an extent that all efforts to secret away the process of production in the work could not but fail. The previous generation had already limited the pure immanence of artworks, which at the same time they drove to its extreme: by employing the author as commentator, by the use of irony, and by the quantity of detail artfully protected from the intervention of art. From this arose the pleasure of substituting for the artworks the process of their own production. Today every work is virtually what Joyce declared *Finnegans Wake* to be before he published the whole: *work in progress*. But a work that in its own terms, in its own texture and complexion, is only possible as emergent and developing, cannot without lying at the same time lay claim to being complete and "finished." Art is unable to extricate itself from this aporia by an act of will. Decades ago Adolf Loos wrote that ornaments cannot be invented;[11] the point he was making has a broader range than he signaled. In art the more that must be made, sought, invented, the more uncertain it becomes if it can be made or invented. Art that is radically and explicitly something made must ultimately confront its own feasibility. What provokes protest in works of the past is precisely what was arranged and calculated, what did not—as one would have said in the years around 1800—in turn become nature. Progress in art as the process of making and doubts about just that run in counterpoint to each other; in fact, such progress has been accompanied by a tendency toward absolute involuntariness, from the automatic writing of fifty years ago to today's tachism and aleatoric music; the observation is correct that the technically integral, completely made artwork converges with the absolutely accidental work; the work that is ostensibly not the result of making is of course all the more fabricated.

The truth of the new, as the truth of what is not already used up, is situated in the intentionless. This sets truth in opposition to reflection, which is the motor of the new, and raises reflection to a second order, to second reflection. It is the opposite of its usual philosophical concept, as it is used, for instance, in Schiller's doctrine of sentimental poetry, where reflection means burdening artworks down with intentions. Second reflection lays hold of the technical procedures, the language of the artwork in the broadest sense, but it aims at blindness. "The absurd," however inadequate as a slogan, testifies to this. Beckett's refusal to interpret his works, combined with the most extreme consciousness of techniques and of the implications of the theatrical and linguistic material, is not merely a subjective aversion: As reflection increases in scope and power, content itself becomes ever more opaque. Certainly this does not mean that interpretation can be dispensed with as if there were nothing to interpret; to remain content with that is the confused claim that all the talk about the absurd gave rise to. Any artwork that supposes it is in possession of its content is plainly naïve in its rationalism; this may define the historically foreseeable limit of Brecht's work. Unexpectedly confirming Hegel's thesis of the transformation of mediation into immediacy, second reflection restores naïveté in the relation of content to first reflection. What is today called a "message" is no more to be squeezed out of Shakespeare's great dramas than out of Beckett's works. But the increasing opacity is itself a function of transformed content. As the negation of the absolute idea, content can no longer be identified with reason as it is postulated by idealism; content has become the critique of the omnipotence of reason, and it can therefore no longer be reasonable according to the norms set by discursive thought. The darkness of the absurd is the old darkness of the new. This darkness must be interpreted, not replaced by the clarity of meaning.

The category of the new produced a conflict. Not unlike the seventeenth-century *querelle des anciens et des modernes*, this is a conflict between the new and duration. Artworks were always meant to endure; it is related to their concept, that of objectivation. Through duration art protests against death; the paradoxically transient eternity of artworks is the allegory of an eternity bare of semblance. Art is the semblance of what is beyond death's reach. To say that no art endures is as abstract a dictum as that of the transience of all things earthly; it would gain content only metaphysically, in relation to the idea of resurrection. It is not only reactionary rancor that provokes horror over the fact that the longing for the new represses duration. The effort to create enduring masterpieces has been undermined. What has terminated tradition can hardly count on one in which it would be given a place. There is all the less reason to call on tradition, in that retroactively countless works once endowed with the qualities of endurance—qualities the concept of classicism strove to encompass—no longer open their eyes: The enduring perished and drew the category of duration into its vortex. The concept of the archaic defines not so much a phase of art history as the condition of works that have gone dead. Artworks have no power over whether they endure; it is least of all guaranteed when the putatively time-bound is eliminated in favor of the timeless. For that can only take place at the cost of the work's relation to those contexts in which permanence is exclusively constituted. It was out of Cervantes' ephemeral intention to parody the medieval romances that *Don Quixote* originated. The concept of duration has an implicitly Egyptian, archaic quality of mythical helplessness; the thought of duration seems to have been remote during productive periods. Probably it becomes an acute concern only when duration becomes problematic and artworks, sensing their latent powerlessness, cling to it. Confusion occurs between what a detestable nationalist exhortation once called the "permanent value of artworks"—everything dead, formal, and neutralized in them—and the hidden seed of their survival. Ever since the praise Horace bestowed on himself for a monument "more durable than bronze," the category of the lasting resonates with an apologetic quality that is foreign to artworks not erected by grace of an Augustan exercise of mercy for the sake of an idea of authenticity that bears more than the trace of the authoritarian. "Beauty itself must die!":[12] This is more true than Schiller imagined. It holds not only for those who are beautiful, not simply for works that are destroyed or forgotten or that have sunk back into the hieroglyphic, but for everything composed of beauty and of what according to its traditional idea was meant to be unchangeable, the constituents of form. In this regard, the category of tragedy should be considered. It seems to be the aesthetic imprint of evil and death and as enduring as they are. Nevertheless it is no longer possible. All that by which aesthetic pedants once zealously distinguished the tragic from the mournful—the affirmation of death, the idea that the infinite glimmers through the demise of the finite, the meaning of suffering—all this now returns to pass judgment on tragedy. Wholly negative artworks now parody the tragic. Rather than being tragic, all art is mournful, especially those works that appear cheerful and harmonious. What lives on in the concept of aesthetic duration, as in much else, is *prima philosophia*, which takes refuge in isolated and absolutized derivatives after having been compelled to abdicate as totality. Obviously the duration to which artworks aspire is modeled on fixed, inheritable possession; the spiritual should, like material, become property, an outrage ineluctably committed by spirit against itself. As soon as artworks make a fetish of their hope of duration, they begin to suffer from their sickness unto death: The veneer of inalienability that they draw over themselves at the same time suffocates them. Many artworks of the highest caliber effectively seek to lose themselves in time so as not to become its prey, entering thus into insoluble antimony with the necessity for objectivation. Ernst Schoen once praised the unsurpassable noblesse of fireworks as the only art that aspires not to duration but only to glow for an instant and fade away. It is ultimately in terms of this idea that the temporal arts of drama and music are to be interpreted, the counterpart of a reification without which they would not exist and yet that degrades them. In the face of the means of mechanical reproduction, these considerations appear obsolete, yet the discontent with these means may nevertheless also be a discontent with the emerging omnipotence of the permanence of art that runs parallel with the collapse of duration. If art were to free itself from the once perceived illusion of duration, were to internalize its own transience in sympathy with the ephemeral life, it would approximate an idea of truth conceived not as something abstractly enduring but in consciousness of its temporal essence. If all art is the secularization of transcendence, it participates in the dialectic of enlightenment. Art has confronted this dialectic with the aesthetic conception of antiart; indeed, without this element art is no longer thinkable. This implies nothing less than that art must go beyond its own concept in order to remain faithful to that concept. The idea of its abolition does it homage by honoring its claim to truth. Nevertheless, the survival of undermined art is not only an expression of *cultural lag*, that ever sluggish revolution of the superstructure. The source of art's power of resistance is that a realized materialism would at the same time be the abolition of materialism, the abolition of the domination of material interests. In its powerlessness, art anticipates a spirit that would only then step forth. To this corresponds an objective need, the neediness of the world, which is contrary to the subjective and now no more than ideological individual need for art. Art can find its continuation nowhere else than in this objective need.

In art what once took care of itself became a specific undertaking, and as a result integration increasingly binds the centrifugal counterforces. Like a whirlpool, integration absorbs the manifold that once defined art. What is left is an abstract unity shorn of the antithetical element by virtue of which art becomes a unity in the first place. The more successful the integration, the more it becomes an empty spinning of gears; teleologically it tends toward infantile tinkering. The power of the aesthetic subject to integrate whatever it takes hold of is at the same time its weakness. It capitulates to a unity that is alienated by virtue of its abstractness and resignedly casts its lot with blind necessity. If the whole of modern art can be understood as the perpetual intervention of the subject, one that is at no point disposed to allow the unreflected governance of the traditional play of forces within the artwork, the permanent interventions of the ego are matched by a tendency of the ego to abdicate out of weakness. True to the age-old mechanical principle of the bourgeois spirit, this abdication takes the form of the reification of subjective achievements, effectively locating them exterior to the subject and mistaking the abdication of the subject for a guarantee of ironclad objectivity. Technique, the extended arm of the subject, also always leads away from that subject. The shadow of art's autarchic radicalism is its harmlessness: Absolute color compositions verge on wallpaper patterns. Now that American hotels are decorated with abstract paintings *à la manière de* . . . and aesthetic radicalism has shown itself to be socially affordable, radicalism itself must pay the price that it is no longer radical. Among the dangers faced by new art, the worst is the absence of danger. The more art expels the preestablished, the more it is thrown back on what purports to get by, as it were, without borrowing from what has become distant and foreign: Art is thrown back on the dimensionless point of pure subjectivity, strictly on its particular and thus abstract subjectivity. This tendency was passionately anticipated by the radical wing of expressionism up to and including dada. The absence of social resonance, however, was not alone to blame for the collapse of expressionism: It was not possible to persevere within the bounds of a dimensionless point; the contraction of the accessible, the totality of the refusal, terminates in complete impoverishment: the scream or the destitute, powerless gesture, literally the syllables "da-da." This became an amusement for all concerned, the dadaists as well as the conformists they challenged, because it confessed the impossibility of artistic objectivation that is postulated by each and every artistic manifestation, whether intentionally or not; what after all is left to do but scream. The dadaists consistently tried to abrogate this postulate; the program of their surrealist successors rejected art, yet without being able to shake itself free of it. Their truth was that it would be better not to have art than to have a false one. But they fell to the mercy of the semblance of an absolute subjectivity existing purely for-itself and objectively mediated, yet without the ability to go beyond the position of being-for-itself. Surrealism expresses the foreignness of the alienated only by seeking recourse in itself. Mimesis ties art to individual human experience, which is now exclusively that of being-for-itself. That there is no persevering at this subjective point is by no means only because the artwork forfeits that otherness in which the aesthetic subject is exclusively able to objectivate itself. Clearly the concept of duration—as ineluctable as it is problematic—cannot be unified with the idea that the subjective point is also a temporal one. Not only did the expressionists make concessions as they became older and had to earn a living; not only did dadaists convert to Catholicism or enroll in the Communist Party: Artists with the integrity of Picasso and Schoenberg went beyond the subjective point. Their difficulties in this could be sensed and feared right from their first efforts to achieve a so-called new order. Since then these difficulties developed into the difficulties of art as such. To date, all requisite progress beyond the subjective point has been bought at the price of regression through assimilation to the past and by the arbitrariness of a self-posited order. In recent years it has been fashionable to accuse Samuel Beckett of simply repeating his basic idea; he exposed himself to this accusation in a provocative fashion. In this his consciousness was correct that the need for progress is inextricable from its impossibility. The gesture of walking in place at the end of *Godot*, which is the fundamental motif of the whole of his work, reacts precisely to this situation. Without exception his response is violent. His work is the extrapolation of a negative καιρός. The fulfilled moment reverses into perpetual repetition that converges with desolation. His narratives, which he sardonically calls novels, no more offer objective descriptions of social reality than—as the widespread misunderstanding supposes—they present the reduction of life to basic human relationships, that minimum of existence that subsists *in extremis*. These novels do, however, touch on fundamental layers of experience *hic et nunc*, which are brought together into a paradoxical dynamic at a standstill. The narratives are marked as much by an objectively motivated loss of the object as by its correlative, the impoverishment of the subject. Beckett draws the lesson from montage and documentation, from all the attempts to free oneself from the illusion of a subjectivity that bestows meaning. Even where reality finds entry into the narrative, precisely at those points at which reality threatens to suppress what the literary subject once performed, it is evident that there is something uncanny about this reality. Its disproportion to the powerless subject, which makes it incommensurable with experience, renders reality unreal with a vengeance. The surplus of reality amounts to its collapse; by striking the subject dead, reality itself becomes deathly; this transition is the artfulness of all antiart, and in Beckett it is pushed to the point of the manifest annihilation of reality. The more total society becomes, the more completely it contracts to a unanimous system, and all the more do the artworks in which this experience is sedimented become the other of this society. If one applies the concept of abstraction in the vaguest possible sense, it signals the retreat from a world of which nothing remains except its *caput mortuum*. New art is as abstract as social relations have in truth become. In like manner, the concepts of the realistic and the symbolic are put out of service. Because the spell of external reality over its subjects and their reactions has become absolute, the artwork can only oppose this spell by assimilating itself to it. At ground zero, however, where Beckett's plays unfold like forces in infinitesimal physics, a second world of images springs forth, both sad and rich, the concentrate of historical experiences that otherwise, in their immediacy, fail to articulate the essential: the evisceration of subject and reality. This shabby, damaged world of images is the negative imprint of the administered world. To this extent Beckett is realistic. Even in what passes *vaguement* under the name of abstract art, something survives of the tradition it effaced; presumably it corresponds to what one already perceives in traditional painting insofar as one sees images and not copies of something. Art carries out the eclipse of concretion, an eclipse to which expression is refused by a reality in which the concrete continues to exist only as a mask of the abstract and the determinate particular is nothing more than an exemplar of the universal that serves as its camouflage and is fundamentally identical with the ubiquity of monopoly. This critique of pseudoconcreteness directs its barbs retrospectively at the whole of art as it has come down to the present. The tangents of the empirical world need only be slightly extended to see that they converge in the insight that the concrete serves for nothing better than that something, by being in some way distinct, can be identified, possessed, and sold. The marrow of experience has been sucked out; there is none, not even that apparently set at a remove from commerce, that has not been gnawed away. At the heart of the economy is a process of concentration and centralization that has the power to absorb what is scattered. It leaves traces of independent existences only for professional statistics and permeates the most subtle spiritual innervations often without its being possible to perceive the mediations. The mendacious personalization of politics and the blather about "man in the age of inhumanity" are appropriate to the objective pseudoindividualization; but this becomes an unbearable burden for art because there is no art without individuation. In other words, the contemporary situation of art is hostile to what the jargon of authenticity calls the "message." The question so insistently posed by East German dramaturgy, "What does he mean?" just barely suffices to frighten hectored authors but would be absurd if applied to any one of Brecht's plays, whose program actually was to set thought processes in motion, not to communicate maxims; otherwise the idea of dialectical theater would have been meaningless from the start. Brecht's efforts to destroy subjective nuances and halftones with a blunt objectivity, and to do this conceptually as well, are artistic means; in the best of his work they become a principle of stylization, not a *fabula docet*. It is hard to determine just what the author of *Galileo* or *The Good Woman of Setzuan* himself meant, let alone broach the question of the objectivity of these works, which does not coincide with the subjective intention. The allergy to nuanced expression, Brecht's preference for a linguistic quality that may have been the result of his misunderstanding of positivist protocol sentences, is itself a form of expression that is eloquent only as determinate negation of that expression. Just as art cannot be, and never was, a language of pure feeling, nor a language of the affirmation of the soul, neither is it for art to pursue the results of ordinary knowledge, as for instance in the form of social documentaries that are to function as down payments on empirical research yet to be done. The space between discursive barbarism and poetic euphemism that remains to artworks is scarcely larger than the point of indifference into which Beckett burrowed.

The relation to the new is modeled on a child at the piano searching for a chord never previously heard. This chord, however, was always there; the possible combinations are limited and actually everything that can be played on it is implicitly given in the keyboard. The new is the longing for the new, not the new itself: That is what everything new suffers from. What takes itself to be utopia remains the negation of what exists and is obedient to it. At the center of contemporary antinomies is that art must be and wants to be utopia, and the more utopia is blocked by the real functional order, the more this is true; yet at the same time art may not be utopia in order not to betray it by providing semblance and consolation. If the utopia of art were fulfilled, it would be art's temporal end. Hegel was the first to realize that the end of art is implicit in its concept. That his prophecy was not fulfilled is based, paradoxically, on his historical optimism. He betrayed utopia by construing the existing as if it were the utopia of the absolute idea. Hegel's theory that the world spirit has sublated art as a form is contradicted by another theory of art to be found in his work, which subordinates art to an antagonistic existence that prevails against all affirmative philosophy. This is compelling in architecture: If out of disgust with functional forms and their inherent conformism it wanted to give free reign to fantasy, it would fall immediately into kitsch. Art is no more able than theory to concretize utopia, not even negatively. A cryptogram of the new is the image of collapse; only by virtue of the absolute negativity of collapse does art enunciate the unspeakable: utopia. In this image of collapse all the stigmata of the repulsive and loathsome in modern art gather. Through the irreconcilable renunciation of the semblance of reconciliation, art holds fast to the promise of reconciliation in the midst of the unreconciled: This is the true consciousness of an age in which the real possibility of utopia—that given the level of productive forces the earth could here and now be paradise—converges with the possibility of total catastrophe. In the image of catastrophe, an image that is not a copy of the event but the cipher of its potential, the magical trace of art's most distant pre-history reappears under the total spell, as if art wanted to prevent the catastrophe by conjuring up its image. The taboo set on the historical telos is the single legitimation of that whereby the new compromises itself politically and practically: its claim to being an end in itself.

The shaft that art directs at society is itself social; it is counterpressure to the force exerted by the *body social*; like inner-aesthetic progress, which is progress in productive and, above all, technical forces, this counterpressure is bound up with progress of extra-aesthetic productive forces. There are historical moments in which forces of production emancipated in art represent a real emancipation that is impeded by the relations of production. Artworks organized by the subject are capable *tant bien que mal* of what a society not organized by a subject does not allow; city planning necessarily lags far behind the planning of a major, purposeless, artwork. The antagonism in the concept of technique as something determined inner-aesthetically and as something developed externally to artworks, should not be conceived as absolute. It originated historically and can pass. In electronics it is already possible to produce artistically by manipulating means that originated extra-aesthetically. There is an obvious qualitative leap between the hand that draws an animal on the wall of a cave and the camera that makes it possible for the same image to appear simultaneously at innumerable places. But the objectivation of the cave drawing vis-à-vis what is unmediatedly seen already contains the potential of the technical procedure that effects the separation of what is seen from the subjective act of seeing. Each work, insofar as it is intended for many, is already its own reproduction. That in his dichotomization of the auratic and the techno-logical artwork, Benjamin suppressed this element common to both in favor of their difference, would be the dialectical critique of his theory. Certainly the concept of the modern is to be placed chronologically long before the idea of the modern as a historicophilosophical category; the modern, however, in the latter sense is not a chronological concept but the Rimbaudian postulate of an art of the most advanced consciousness, an art in which the most progressive and differentiated technical procedures are saturated with the most progressive and differentiated experiences. But these experiences, being social, are critical. Modern works in this sense must show themselves to be the equal of high industrialism, not simply make it a topic. Their own comportment and formal language must react spontaneously to the objective situation; the idea of a spontaneous reaction that is a norm defines a perennial paradox of art. Because there is nothing that can avoid the experience of the situation, nothing counts that purports to have escaped it. In many authentic modern works industrial thematic material is strictly avoided out of mistrust of machine art as a pseudomorphism. But in that this material is negated by heightened construction and the reduction of the material tolerated, the industrial returns with a vengeance, as in the work of Paul Klee. This aspect of the modern has changed as little as has the fact of industrialization for the life process of human beings; for the time being, this grants the aesthetic concept of the modern its peculiar invariance. The recognition of this invariance, however, admits no less breadth to the historical dynamic than does the industrial mode of production itself, which during the last hundred years has been transformed from the nineteenth-century factory to mass production and automation. The substantive element of artistic modernism draws its power from the fact that the most advanced procedures of material production and organization are not limited to the sphere in which they originate. In a manner scarcely analyzed yet by sociology, they radiate out into areas of life far removed from them, deep into the zones of subjective experience, which does not notice this and guards the sanctity of its reserves. Art is modern when, by its mode of experience and as the expression of the crisis of experience, it absorbs what industrialization has developed under the given relations of production. This involves a negative canon, a set of prohibitions against what the modern has disavowed in experience and technique; and such determinate negation is virtually the canon of what is to be done. That this modernity is more than a vague Zeitgeist or being cleverly *up to date* depends on the liberation of the forces of production. Modern art is equally determined socially by the conflict with the conditions of production and inner-aesthetically by the exclusion of exhausted and obsolete procedures. Modernity tends rather to oppose the ruling Zeitgeist, and today it must do so; to confirmed culture consumers, radical modern art seems marked by an old-fashioned seriousness and for that reason, among others, crazy. The historical essence of all art is nowhere expressed so emphatically as in the qualitative irresistibility of modern art; that the idea of inventions in material production comes to mind is not an accidental association. By an inherent tendency, important artworks annihilate everything of their own time that does not achieve their standard. Rancor is therefore one of the reasons why so many of the cultured oppose radical modern art: The murderous historical force of the modern is equated with the disintegration of all that to which the proprietors of culture despairingly cling. Modern art is questionable not when it goes too far—as the cliché runs—but when it does not go far enough, which is the point at which works falter out of a lack of internal consistency. Only works that expose themselves to every risk have the chance of living on, not those that out of fear of the ephemeral cast their lot with the past. Those renaissances of temperate modernism, promoted by a restorative consciousness and its interested parties, fizzle even in the eyes and ears of a public that is hardly avant-garde.

In emphatic opposition to the illusion of the organic nature of art, the material concept of the modern implies conscious control over its means. Even here material production and artistic production converge. The necessity of going to the extreme is the necessity for this particular rationality in relation to the material, and not the result of a pseudoscientific competition with the rationalization of the demystified world. This necessity categorically distinguishes the materially modern from traditionalism. Aesthetic rationality demands that all artistic means reach the utmost determinacy in themselves and according to their own function so as to be able to perform what traditional means can no longer fulfill. The extreme is demanded by artistic technology; it is not just the yearning of a rebellious attitude. The idea of a moderate modernism is self-contradictory because it restrains aesthetic rationality. That every element in a work absolutely accomplish what it is supposed to accomplish coincides directly with the modern as desideratum: The moderate work evades this requirement because it receives its means from an available or fictitious tradition to which it attributes a power it no longer possesses. If moderate modernists pride themselves on their honesty, which supposedly protects them from getting carried away with every fad, this is dishonest given the ways in which moderation makes things easier for them. The purported immediacy of their artistic comportment is thoroughly mediated. The socially most advanced level of the productive forces, one of which is consciousness, is the level of the problem posed at the interior of the aesthetic monad. In their own figuration, artworks indicate the solution to this problem, which they are unable to provide on their own without intervention; this alone is legitimate tradition in art. Each and every important work of art leaves traces behind in its material and technique, and following them defines the modern as what needs to be done, which is contrary to having a nose for what is in the air. Critique makes this definition concrete. The traces to be found in the material and the technical procedures, from which every qualitatively new work takes its lead, are scars: They are the loci at which the preceding works misfired. By laboring on them, the new work turns against those that left these traces behind; this, not shifts in subjective feelings for life or in established styles, is the actual object of what historicism treated as the generational problem in art. The *agon* of Greek tragedy still gave evidence of this; only the pantheon of neutralized culture concealed it. The truth content of artworks is fused with their critical content. That is why works are also critics of one another. This, not the historical continuity of their dependencies, binds artworks to one another; "each artwork is the mortal enemy of the other";[13] the unity of the history of art is the dialectical figure of determinate negation. Only in this way does art serve its idea of reconciliation. A meager and impure idea of this dialectical unity is given by the way in which artists of a single genre perceive themselves to be working in a subterranean collective that is virtually independent of their individual products.

In empirical reality the negation of the negative is hardly ever affirmation, yet in the aesthetic sphere this dialectical maxim bears some truth: The power of immanent negation is not shackled in subjective artistic production as it is externally. Artists with extreme sensitivity of taste, such as Stravinsky and Brecht, brushed taste against the grain on the basis of taste; dialectic lay hold of taste and drove it beyond itself, and this certainly is also its truth. By virtue of aesthetic elements under the facade, realistic artworks in the nineteenth century on occasion proved to be more substantial than those works that paid obeisance to the ideal of art's purity; Baudelaire extolled Manet and took Flaubert's side. In terms of *peinture pure*, Manet towered incomparably over Puvis de Chavannes; comparing them is almost comical. The mistake of aestheticism was aesthetic: It confused its own guiding concept with the work accomplished. Idiosyncrasies of artists are sedimented in the canon of prohibitions, but they in turn become objectively binding so that in art the particular is literally the universal. For the idiosyncratic comportment, which is at first unconscious and hardly theoretically transparent to itself, is the sedimentation of a collective form of reaction. Kitsch is an idiosyncratic concept that is as binding as it is elusive to definition. That reflection is a requisite of art today means that it must become conscious of its idiosyncrasies and articulate them. As a consequence, art threatens to become allergic to itself; the quintessence of the determinate negation that art exercises is its own negation. Through correspondences with the past, what resurfaces becomes something qualitatively other. The deformation of figures and human faces in modern sculpture and paintings are reminiscent *prima vista* of archaic works in which the cultic replication of people was either not intended or impossible to achieve with the techniques available. But it makes a world of difference whether art, having once achieved the power of replication, negates it, as the word deformation implies, or if this power has yet to be gained; for aesthetics the difference is greater than the similarity. It is hard to imagine that art, having once experienced the heteronomy of portrayal, would again forget it and return to what it determinately and intentionally negated. Yet, admittedly, even prohibitions that originated historically are not to be hypostatized; otherwise they call up that favorite sleight of hand of modernists of Cocteau's variety that consists of suddenly conjuring up what has been temporarily prohibited and presenting it as if it were altogether fresh, and of relishing the violation of the modern taboo as itself something modern; in this fashion modernity has frequently been shunted into reaction. It is problems that return, not preproblematic categories and solutions. The older Schoenberg is reliably reported to have said that for the moment there was no discussing harmony. Clearly this was not a prophecy that some day one would again be able to compose with triads, which he by the expansion of the material had relegated to exhausted special circumstances. The question, however, remains open whether the dimension of simultaneity in music as a whole was not degraded to a mere result, an irrelevance, something virtually accidental; music lost one of its dimensions, that of the eloquent simultaneous combination of sound, and this was not the least of the reasons why the immeasurably enriched material was impoverished. Triads and other chords from the treasury of tonality are not to be restituted; it is conceivable, however, that if qualitative counterforces someday stir in opposition to the total quantification of music, the vertical dimension could once again become "a matter of discussion" in such a fashion as to allow the ear to listen for harmonies that had regained their specific value. An analogous prediction could be made for counterpoint, which was similarly scuttled by blind integration. Of course the possibility of reactionary misuse cannot be disregarded; rediscovered harmony, however it is constituted, would accommodate itself to harmonic tendencies; one need only imagine how easily the equally well-founded longing for the reconstruction of monodic lines could be transformed into the false resurrection of what the enemies of new music miss so painfully as melody. The prohibitions are both gentle and strict. The thesis that homeostasis is only binding as the result of a play of forces and not as slack well-proportionedness, implies the weighty prohibition of those aesthetic phenomena that in *The Spirit of Utopia* Bloch called carpet motifs, a prohibition whose powers are expanding retrospectively, as if it were an invariant. Even though it is avoided and negated, however, the need for homeostasis persists. Rather than resolving antagonisms, art at times expresses overwhelming tensions negatively through extreme distance from them. Aesthetic norms, however great their historical importance may be, lag behind the concrete life of artworks; yet all the same these norms participate in the latter's magnetic fields. Nothing, however, is served by affixing a temporal index externally to these norms; the dialectic of artworks takes place between these norms—more precisely, between the most advanced norms—and the works' specific form.

The need to take risks is actualized in the idea of the experimental, which—in opposition to the image of the artist's unconscious organic labor—simultaneously transfers from science to art the conscious control over materials. Currently official culture grants special funds to what it mistrustfully, half hoping for failure, calls artistic experimentation, thus neutralizing it. Actually, art is now scarcely possible unless it does experiment. The disproportion between established culture and the level of productive forces has become blatant: What is internally consistent appears to society at large as a bogus promissory note on the future, and art, socially dispossessed, is in no way sure that it has any binding force of its own. For the most part, experimentation takes shape as the testing of possibilities, usually of types and species; it therefore tends to degrade the concrete work to a mere example: This is one of the reasons for the aging of new art. Certainly aesthetic means and ends cannot be separated, yet almost by its concept experimentation is primarily concerned with means and content to leave the world waiting in vain for the ends. What is more, during the last several decades the concept of the experiment has itself become equivocal. If even as late as 1930 experimentation referred to efforts filtered through critical consciousness in opposition to the continuation of unreflected aesthetic practices, in the meantime the concept has acquired the stipulation that a work should have contents that are not foreseeable in the process of production, that, subjectively, the artist should be surprised by the work that results. In this transformation of the concept of experimentation, art becomes conscious of something that was always present in it and was pointed out by Mallarmé. The artist's imagination scarcely ever completely encompassed what it brought forth. The combinatorial arts, *ars nova*, for instance, and later that of the Netherland School, infiltrated the music of the late Middle Ages with effects that probably surpassed the composers' subjective imagination. A combinatorial art that required of the artist—as alienated artist—the mediation of subjective imagination, was essential to the development of artistic techniques. This magnified the risk that aesthetic products would deteriorate because of inadequate or feeble imagination. The risk is that of aesthetic regression. Artistic spirit raises itself above what merely exists at the point where the imagination does not capitulate to the mere existence of materials and techniques. Since the emancipation of the subject, the mediation of the work through it is not to be renounced without its reversion to the status of a thing. Music theoreticians of the sixteenth century already recognized this. On the other hand, only stubbornness could deny the productive function of many "surprise" elements in much modern art, in *action painting* and aleatoric art, that did not result from being passed through the imagination. The solution to this contradiction is that all imagination has an arena of indeterminateness that is not, however, in rigid opposition to it. As long as Richard Strauss still wrote somewhat complex works, the virtuoso himself may have been unable to imagine each sound, each color, and each sounding combination precisely; it is well known that even composers with the best ears are usually astonished when they actually hear their orchestral works performed. This indeterminateness, however—including the indeterminateness that results from the inability of the ear, as Stockhausen has noted, to distinguish, much less imagine, each tone of a tone cluster—is built into determinateness as an element of it rather than that it encompasses the whole. In the jargon of musicians: You have to know exactly *if* something sounds, and only to a certain extent *how* it sounds. This leaves room for surprises, those that are desired as well as those that require correction; what made its precocious appearance as *l'imprévu* in Berlioz is a surprise not only for the listener but objectively as well; and yet the ear can anticipate it. In the experiment, the ego-alien must be respected as well as subjectively mastered: Only as something mastered does it bear witness to what has been liberated. The real source of the risk taken by all artworks, however, is not located in their level of contingency but rather in the fact that each one must follow the whippoorwill of objectivity immanent to it, without any guarantee that the productive forces—the spirit of the artist and his procedures—will be equal to that objectivity. If such a guarantee did exist it would block the possibility of the new, which itself contributes to the objectivity and coherence of the work. What can, without stirring up the musty odors of idealism, justly be called *serious* in art is the pathos of an objectivity that confronts the individual with what is more and other than he is in his historically imperative insufficiency. The risk taken by artworks participates in their seriousness; it is the image of death in their own sphere. This seriousness is relativized, however, in that aesthetic autonomy remains external to suffering, of which the work is an image and from which the work draws its seriousness. The artwork is not only the echo of suffering, it diminishes it; form, the organon of its seriousness, is at the same time the organon of the neutralization of suffering. Art thereby falls into an unsolvable aporia. The demand for complete responsibility on the part of artworks increases the burden of their guilt; therefore this demand is to be set in counterpoint with the antithetical demand for irresponsibility. The latter is reminiscent of the element of play, without which there is no more possibility of art than of theory. As play, art seeks to absolve itself of the guilt of its semblance. Art is in any case irresponsible as delusion, as *spleen*, and without it there is no art whatsoever. The art of absolute responsibility terminates in sterility, whose breath can be felt on almost all consistently developed artworks; absolute irresponsibility degrades art to *fun*; a synthesis of responsibility and irresponsibility is precluded by the concept itself. Any relation to what was once thought of as the dignity of art—what Hölderlin called that "noble, grave genius"[14]—has become ambivalent. True, in the face of the culture industry art maintains that dignity; it enrobes two measures of a Beethoven quartet snatched up from between the murky stream of hit tunes while tuning the radio dial. By contrast, modern art that laid claim to dignity would be pitilessly ideological. To act dignified it would have to put on airs, strike a pose, claim to be other than what it can be. It is precisely its seriousness that compels modern art to lay aside pretensions long since hopelessly compromised by the Wagnerian art religion. A solemn tone would condemn artworks to ridiculousness, just as would the gestures of grandeur and might. Certainly, without the subjective form-giving power art is not thinkable, yet this capacity has nothing to do with an artwork's achieving expressive strength through its form. Even subjectively this strength is heavily compromised, for art partakes of weakness no less than of strength. In the artwork the unconditional surrender of dignity can become an organon of its strength. Consider the strength it took for the rich and brilliant bourgeois heir, Verlaine, to let himself go, to sink so drastically in the world, to turn himself into the passively tumbling instrument of his poetry. To accuse him, as did Stefan Zweig, of having been a weakling, is not only petty but obtuse with regard to the variety of productive artistic comportments: Without his weakness Verlaine would no more have been able to write his most beautiful works than to write those miserable verses he later marketed as *raté*.

To survive reality at its most extreme and grim, artworks that do not want to sell themselves as consolation must equate themselves with that reality. Radical art today is synonymous with dark art; its primary color is black. Much contemporary production is irrelevant because it takes no note of this and childishly delights in color. The ideal of blackness with regard to content is one of the deepest impulses of abstraction. It may well be that the current trifling with sound and color effects is a reaction to the impoverishment entailed by the ideal of black; perhaps art will one day be able to abolish this axiom without self-betrayal, which is what Brecht may have sensed when he wrote: "What times are these, when / to speak of trees is almost a crime / because it passes in silence over such infamy!"[15] Art indicts superfluous poverty by voluntarily undergoing its own; but it indicts asceticism as well and cannot establish it as its own norm. Along with the impoverishment of means entailed by the ideal of blackness—if not by every sort of aesthetic *Sachlichkeit*—what is written, painted, and composed is also impoverished; the most advanced arts push this impoverishment to the brink of silence. That the world, which, as Baudelaire wrote,[16] has lost its fragrance and since then its color, could have them restored by art strikes only the artless as possible. This further convulses the possibility of art, though without bringing it down. Incidentally, an early romantic artist, Schubert, who was later so widely exploited by the insistently happy, already felt compelled to ask if there were such a thing as happy music. The injustice committed by all cheerful art, especially by entertainment, is probably an injustice to the dead; to accumulated, speechless pain. Still, black art bears features that would, if they were definitive, set their seal on historical despair; to the extent that change is always still possible they too may be ephemeral. The radically darkened art—established by the surrealists as black humor—which the aesthetic hedonism that survived the catastrophes defamed for the perversity of expecting that the dark should give something like pleasure, is in essence nothing but the postulate that art and a true consciousness of it can today find happiness only in the capacity of standing firm. This happiness illuminates the artwork's sensuous appearance from within. Just as in internally consistent artworks spirit is communicated even to the most recalcitrant phenomenon, effectively rescuing it sensuously, ever since Baudelaire the dark has also offered sensuous enticement as the antithesis of the fraudulent sensuality of culture's facade. There is more joy in dissonance than in consonance: This metes out justice, eye for eye, to hedonism. The caustic discordant moment, dynamically honed, is differentiated in itself as well as from the affirmative and becomes alluring; and this allure, scarcely less than revulsion for the imbecility of positive thinking draws modern art into a no-man's-land that is the plenipotentiary of a livable world. Schoenberg's *Pierrot lunaire*, that crystalline unity of imaginary essence and a totality of dissonance, was the first to achieve this aspect of the modern. Negation may reverse into pleasure, not into affirmation.

Authentic art of the past that for the time being must remain veiled is not thereby sentenced. Great works wait. While their metaphysical meaning dissolves, something of their truth content, however little it can be pinned down, does not; it is that whereby they remain eloquent. A liberated humanity would be able to inherit its historical legacy free of guilt. What was once true in an artwork and then disclaimed by history is only able to disclose itself again when the conditions have changed on whose account that truth was invalidated: Aesthetic truth content and history are that deeply meshed. A reconciled reality and the restituted truth of the past could converge. What can still be experienced in the art of the past and is still attainable by interpretation is a directive toward this state. Nothing guarantees that it will ever be followed. Tradition is to be not abstractly negated but criticized without naïveté according to the current situation: Thus the present constitutes the past. Nothing is to be accepted unexamined just because it is available and was once held valuable; nor is anything to be dismissed because it belongs to the past; time alone provides no criterion. An incalculable store of what is past proves immanently to be inadequate, though in its own time and for the consciousness of its own period this may not have been the case. It is the course of time that unmasks these deficiencies, yet they are objective in quality and not a matter of shifting taste.——Only the most advanced art of any period has any chance against the decay wrought by time. In the afterlife of works, however, qualitative differences become apparent that in no way coincide with the level of modernity achieved in their own periods. In the secret *bellum omnium contra omnes* that fills the history of art, the older modern may be victorious over the newer modern. This is not to say that someday what is *par ordre du jour* old-fashioned could prove superior and more enduring than the more advanced. Hopes for renaissances of Pfitzner and Sibelius, Carossa or Hans Thoma, say more about those who cherish the hope than about the enduring value of the works of such souls. But works can be actualized through historical development, through *correspondance* with later developments: Names such as Gesualdo de Venosa, El Greco, Turner, Büchner are all famous examples, not accidentally rediscovered after the break with continuous tradition. Even works that did not reach the technical standard of their periods, such as Mahler's early symphonies, communicate with later developments and indeed precisely by means of what separated them from their own time. Mahler's music is progressive just by its clumsy and at the same time objective refusal of the neo-romantic intoxication with sound, but this refusal was in its own time scandalous, modern perhaps in the same way as were the simplifications of van Gogh and the fauves vis-à-vis impressionism.

However true it is that art is no replica of the subject and that Hegel was right in his criticism of the popular idea that the artist must be more than his work—for not infrequently he is less, the empty husk of what he objectivated in the work—it holds equally true that no artwork can succeed except to the degree that the subject gives it shape from out of himself. It is not for the subject, as the organon of art, to overleap the process of divisive individuation that is imposed on him and not a matter of opinion or accidental consciousness. This situation therefore compels art—as something spiritual—to undergo subjective mediation in its objective constitution. The share of subjectivity in the artwork is itself a piece of objectivity. Certainly the mimetic element that is indispensable to art is, as regards its substance, universal, but it cannot be reached other than by way of the inextinguishably idiosyncratic particular subject. Although art in its innermost essence is a comportment, it cannot be isolated from expression, and there is no expression without a subject. The transition to the discursively recognized universal by which the politically reflecting particular subject hopes to escape atomization and powerlessness is in the aesthetic sphere a desertion to heteronomy. If the artist's work is to reach beyond his own contingency, then he must in return pay the price that he, in contrast to the discursively thinking person, cannot transcend himself and the objectively established boundaries. Even if one day the atomistic structure of society itself were changed, art would not have to sacrifice its social idea—in essence whether a particular is even possible—to the socially universal: As long as the particular and the universal diverge there is no freedom. Rather, freedom would secure for the subject the right that today manifests itself exclusively in the idiosyncratic compulsions that artists must obey. Whoever resists the overwhelming collective force in order to insist on the passage of art through the subject, need on no account at the same time think underneath the veil of subjectivism. Aesthetic autonomy encompasses what is collectively most advanced, what has escaped the spell. By virtue of its mimetic preindividual elements, every idiosyncrasy lives from collective forces of which it is unconscious. The critical reflection of the subject, however isolated that subject, stands watch that these forces do not provoke regression. Social reflection on aesthetics habitually neglects the concept of productive force. Yet deeply embedded in the technological processes this force is the subject, the subject congealed as technology. Productions that avoid it, that effectively want to make themselves technically autonomous, are obliged to correct themselves by way of the subject.

The rebellion of art against its false—intentional—spiritualization, Wedekind's for example in his program of a corporeal art, is itself a rebellion of spirit that, though it is not perpetually negative, does indeed negate itself.[17] Indeed, in the contemporary social situation spirit is present only by virtue of the *principium individuationis*. Collective labor is conceivable in art; the extinguishing of its immanent subjectivity is not. Any change in this would depend on the total social consciousness having reached a level where it no longer conflicts with the most progressive consciousness, which today is exclusively that of the individual. In spite of the most subtle modifications, bourgeois idealist philosophy has been unable epistemologically to break through solipsism. For normal bourgeois consciousness the epistemology modeled on it was of no consequence. For this consciousness art appears necessary and directly "intersubjective." This relation of epistemology and art should be reversed. The former has the ability through critical self-reflection to destroy the spell of solipsism, whereas the subjective point of reference in art remains that which solipsism has merely feigned in reality. Art is the historicophilosophical truth of a solipsism that is untrue in-itself. In art there is no possible willful overcoming of the situation that philosophy has unjustly hypostatized. Aesthetic semblance is what solipsism extra-aesthetically confuses with truth. By participating in this confusion, Lukács's attack on radical modern art totally misses the point. He contaminates art with real or alleged solipsistic currents in philosophy. What appears identical, however, can now and again be fundamentally opposite.——A critical element of the mimetic taboo is directed against a tepid warmth that is increasingly supposed to pass for expression. Expressive impulses produce a type of contact in which conformism rejoices. This is the mentality that has absorbed Berg's *Wozzeck* and reactionarily played it off against the Schoenberg School, which not a single measure of the opera disavows. The paradox of the situation is concentrated in Schoenberg's preface to Webern's Six Bagatelles for String Quartet, a work at the extreme limit of expressivity: Schoenberg praises it because, in his own words, it spurns animal warmth. All the same, the warmth has by now also been attributed to those works that rejected it for the sake of authentic expression. Valid art today is polarized into, on the one hand, an unassuaged and inconsolable expressivity that rejects every last trace of conciliation and becomes autonomous construction; and, on the other, the expressionlessness of construction that expresses the dawning powerlessness of expression.——The discussion of the taboo that weighs on subject and expression touches on a dialectic of maturity. Its Kantian postulate, that of emancipation from the spell of the infantile, holds not only for reason but equally for art. The history of modern art is that of a straining toward maturity as the organized and heightened aversion toward the childish in art, which becomes childish in the first place by the measure of a pragmatically narrow rationality. No less, however, does art rebel against precisely this form of rationality, which, in the relation of means and ends, forgets the ends and fetishizes the means as an end in itself. This irrationality in the principle of reason is unmasked by the avowedly rational irrationality of art, evident in its technical procedures. Art brings to light what is infantile in the ideal of being grown up. Immaturity via maturity is the prototype of play.

In modern art, *métier* is fundamentally different from traditional artisanal methods. Its concept indicates the *totum* of capacities through which the artist does justice to the conception of the work and precisely thereby severs the umbilical cord of tradition. All the same, the artist's *métier* never originates wholly out of a single work. No artist approaches his work with nothing but the eyes, ears, or linguistic capacity for just it. The realization of a specific work always presupposes qualities gained beyond the spell of the work's specification; only dilettantes confuse originality with tabula rasa. Although it appears to be merely subjective, the *totum* of forces invested in the work is the potential presence of the collective according to the level of the available productive forces: Windowless, it contains the monad. This is most strikingly evident in the critical corrections made by artists. In every improvement to which he is compelled, often enough in conflict with what he considers his primary impulse, the artist works as social agent, indifferent to society's own consciousness. He embodies the social forces of production without necessarily being bound by the censorship dictated by the relations of production, which he continually criticizes by following the rigors of his *métier*. In the many particular situations with which the work confronts its author there are always many available solutions, but the multiplicity of solutions is finite and surveyable as a whole. *Métier* sets boundaries against the bad infinity in works. It makes concrete what, in the language of Hegel's *Logic*, might be called the abstract possibility of artworks. Therefore every authentic artist is obsessed with technical procedures; the fetishism of means also has a legitimate aspect.

Art is not to be reduced to the unquestionable polarity of the mimetic and the constructive, as if this were an invariant formula, for otherwise works of high quality would be obliged to strike a balance between the two principles. But what was fruitful in modern art was what gravitated toward one of the extremes, not what sought to mediate between them; those works that strove after both, in search of synthesis, were rewarded with a dubious consensus. The dialectic of these elements is similar to dialectical logic, in that each pole realizes itself only in the other, and not in some middle ground. Construction is not the corrective of expression, nor does it serve as its guarantor by fulfilling the need for objectivation; rather, construction must conform to the mimetic impulses without planning, as it were; in this lies the superiority of Schoenberg's *Erwartung* over a great many compositions that made that work into a principle that had for its part been one of construction; what survives of expressionism as something objective are those works that abstained from constructive organization. Similarly, construction cannot, as a form empty of human content, wait to be filled with expression. Rather, construction gains expression through coldness. Picasso's cubist works and their later transformations are, by virtue of asceticism against expression, far more expressive than those works that were inspired by cubism but feared to lose expression and became supplicant. This may lead the way beyond the debate over functionalism. The critique of *Sachlichkeit* as a form of reified consciousness must not smuggle in a laxness that would imagine that the reduction of the requirement of construction would result in the restoration of an allegedly free fantasy and thus of the element of expression. Functionalism today, prototypically in architecture, would need to push construction so far that it would win expression through the rejection of traditional and semitraditional forms. Great architecture gains its suprafunctional language when it works directly from its purposes, effectively announcing them mimetically as the work's content. H. B. Scharoun's Philharmonic Hall in Berlin is beautiful because, in order to create the ideal spatial conditions for orchestral music, it assimilates itself to these conditions rather than borrowing from them. By expressing its purpose through the building, it transcends mere purposiveness though, incidentally, this transition is never guaranteed to purposive forms. *Neue Sachlichkeit*'s condemnation of expression and all mimesis as ornamental and superfluous, as arbitrary subjective garnishing, holds true only for construction provided with a veneer of expression, not for works of absolute expression. Absolute expression would be objective, the object itself. The phenomenon of aura, which Benjamin described at once nostalgically and critically, has become bad wherever it is instituted and simulated; wherever works that in their production and reproduction oppose the *hic et nunc* are, like the commercial film, provided with the semblance of this immediacy. To be sure, this also damages the individually produced work when, seeking to preserve aura, it concocts uniqueness and thus springs to the aid of an ideology that regales itself with the well-individuated, as if in the administered world such still existed. On the other hand, conceived nondialectically the theory of aura lends itself to misuse. It becomes a slogan of the deaestheticization of art that is under way in the age of the technical reproducibility of the artwork. Aura is not only—as Benjamin claimed—the here and now of the artwork, it is whatever goes beyond its factual givenness, its content; one cannot abolish it and still want art. Even demystified artworks are more than what is literally the case.[18] The "exhibition value" that, according to Benjamin, supplants "cult value" is an *imago* of the exchange process. Art that devotes itself to its exhibition value is ruled by the exchange process in just the same way as the categories of socialist realism accommodate themselves to the status quo of the culture industry. The refusal by artworks to compromise becomes a critique even of the idea of their inner coherence, their drossless perfection and integration. Inner coherence shatters on what is superior to it, the truth of the content, which no longer finds satisfaction in expression—for expression recompenses helpless individuality with a deceptive importance—or in construction, for coherence is more than a mere analogy of the administered world. The utmost integration is utmost semblance and this causes the former's reversal: Ever since Beethoven's last works those artists who pushed integration to an extreme have mobilized disintegration. The truth content of art, whose organon was integration, turns against art and in this turn art has its emphatic moments. Artists discover the compulsion toward disintegration in their own works, in the surplus of organization and regimen; it moves them to set aside the magic wand as does Shakespeare's Prospero, who is the poet's own voice. However, the truth of such disintegration is achieved by way of nothing less than the triumph and guilt of integration. The category of the fragmentary—which has its locus here—is not to be confused with the category of contingent particularity: The fragment is that part of the totality of the work that opposes totality.

Notes

1 [Hugo von Hofmannsthal, *The Lord Chandos Letter* (Marlboro, 1986).—trans.]
2 See Stefan George, "Darkness of Dream" ["Foliage and fruit of carnelian and gold"], in *The Works of Stefan George*, trans. Marx and Merwitz (Chapel Hill, 1974), p. 270.
3 ["Entkunstung": Literally, the destruction of art's quality as art.—trans.]
4 See Adorno, "Cultural Criticism and Society," in *Prisms*, trans. Samuel Weber and Shierry Weber (Cambridge, 1981), pp. 17ff.
5 [Gustav Meyrink (1868–1932), the Austrian novelist of eerie and grotesque novels, most famously *The Golem*.—trans.]
6 [Ferdinand Kürnberger (1821–1879), the Austrian dramatist and novelist.—trans.]
7 See Adorno, *Dissonanzen. Musik in der verwalteten Welt*, 4th ed. (Göttingen, 1969), pp. 19ff.
8 [A reference especially to Martin Heidegger.—trans.]
9 ["Aussage": See Adorno, *The Jargon of Authenticity*, trans. Knut Tarnowsky and Frederic Will (Evanston, 1976), p. 14.—trans.]
10 Walter Benjamin, *The Origin of German Tragic Drama*, trans. John Osborne (London, 1977).
11 See Adolf Loos, *Sämtliche Schriften*, ed. F. Glück, vol. 1 (Vienna and Munich, 1962), pp. 278, 393, and *passim*.
12 Friedrich Schiller, "Nenia," in *Poetical Works*, trans. Percy E. Pinkerton (Boston, 1902), p. 253.
13 [Adorno is quoting from his own *Ohne Leitbild, Gesammelte Schriften*, vol. 10. 1 (Frankfurt, 1977).—trans.]
14 Friedrich Hölderlin, "German Song," in *Friedrich Hölderlin: Poems and Fragments*, trans. Michael Hamburger (Cambridge, 1966), p. 505.

15 Bertolt Brecht, "An die Nachgeborenen," in *Gesammelte Werke*, vol. 9 (Frankfurt, 1967), p. 723. ["Was sind das für Zeiten, wo / Ein Gespräch über Bäume fast ein Verbrechen ist / Weil es ein Schweigen über so viele Untaten einschließt"; "To Posterity," in *German Poetry, 1910–1975*, trans. and ed. Michael Hamburger (New York, 1976). p. 168.—trans.]

16 See Charles Baudelaire, "The Taste for nothingness," from *Flowers of Evil*, trans. S. McGowan (Oxford, 1993), p. 153: "The Spring, once wonderful, has lost its scent!" p. 72.

17 [A reference to the Mephistopheles of Johann Wolfgang von Goethe's *Faust*, described there as "The spirit that negates itself."—trans.]

18 [A critical reference to Ludwig Wittgenstein's maxim in the *Tractatus Logico-Philosophicus* that "Die Welt ist alles was der Fall ist" (The world is all that is the case). Throughout *Aesthetic Theory* and many of his other writings Adorno similarly recasts Wittgenstein's expression.—trans.]

3

On the categories of the ugly, the beautiful and technique

To say that art is not identical with the concept of beauty, but requires for its realization the concept of the ugly as its negation, is a platitude. Yet this does not amount to the annulment of the category of the ugly as a canon of prohibitions. This canon no longer forbids offenses against universal rules, but it debars violations of the work's immanent consistency. The universality of this canon is nothing other than the primacy of the particular: There should no longer be anything that is not specific. The prohibition of the ugly has become an interdiction of whatever is not formed *hic et nunc*, of the incompletely formed, the raw. Dissonance is the technical term for the reception through art of what aesthetics as well as naïveté calls ugly. Whatever it may be, the ugly must constitute, or be able to constitute, an element of art; a work by the Hegelian Karl Rosenkranz bears the title *The Aesthetics of the Ugly.*[1] Archaic art and then traditional art, especially since the fauns and sileni of Hellenism, abound in the portrayal of subjects that were considered ugly. In modern art the weight of this element increased to such a degree that a new quality emerged. According to traditional aesthetics, the ugly is that element that opposes the work's ruling law of form; it is integrated by that formal law and thereby confirms it, along with the power of subjective freedom in the artwork vis-à-vis the subject matter. This subject matter would indeed become beautiful in a higher sense through its function in the pictorial composition, for instance, or by its participation in the production of a dynamic equilibrium; for, according to a Hegelian topos, beauty is the result not of a simple equilibrium per se, but rather of the tension that results. Harmony that, as a mere result, denies the tensions that have entered into it, becomes something disturbing, false, and effectively dissonant. The harmonistic view of the ugly was voided in modern art, and something qualitatively new emerged. The anatomical horror in Rimbaud and Benn, the physically revolting and repellent in Beckett, the scatological traits of many contemporary dramas, have nothing in common with the rustic uncouthness of seventeenth-century Dutch paintings. Anal pleasure, and the pride of art at facilely being able to integrate it, abdicate; powerlessly the law of form capitulates to ugliness. That is how completely dynamic the category of the ugly is, and necessarily its counterimage, the category of the beautiful, is no less so. Both mock definitional fixation such as is imagined by that aesthetic whose norms are, however indirectly, oriented by these categories. The statement that a devastated industrial landscape or a face deformed by a painting is just plain ugly may answer spontaneously to the phenomenon but lacks the self-evidence it assumes. The impression of the ugliness of technology and industrial landscapes cannot be adequately explained in formal terms, and aesthetically well-integrated functional forms, in Adolf Loos's sense, would probably leave the impression of ugliness unchanged. The impression of ugliness stems from the principle of violence and destruction. The aims posited are unreconciled with what nature, however mediated it may be, wants to say on its own. In technique, violence toward nature is not reflected through artistic portrayal, but it is immediately apparent. It could be transformed only by a reorientation of technical forces of production that would direct these forces not only according to desired aims but equally according to the nature that is to be technically formed. After the abolition of scarcity, the liberation of the forces of production could extend into other dimensions than exclusively that of the quantitative growth of production. There are intimations of this when functional buildings are adapted to the forms and contours of the landscape, as well as when building materials have originated from and been integrated into the surrounding landscape, as for instance with châteaux and castles. What is called a "cultural landscape" [*Kulturlandschaft*] is a beautiful model of this possibility. A rationality that embraced these motifs would be able to help heal the wounds that rationality inflicted. Even as bourgeois consciousness naïvely condemns the ugliness of a torn-up industrial landscape, a relation is established that reveals a glimpse of the domination of nature, where nature shows humans its facade of having yet to be mastered. This bourgeois indignation therefore is part of the ideology of domination. Ugliness would vanish if the relation of man to nature renounced its repressive character, which perpetuates—rather than being perpetuated by—the repression of man. The potential for this in a world laid waste by technique resides in a pacified technique, not in planned enclaves. There is nothing putatively ugly that would not be able through a transformation of its position in the work, freed from the culinary, to discard its ugliness. What appears ugly is in the first place what is historically older, what art rejected on its path toward autonomy, and what is therefore mediated in itself. The concept of the ugly may well have originated in the separation of art from its archaic phase: It marks the permanent return of the archaic, intertwined with the dialectic of enlightenment in which art participates. Archaic ugliness, the cannibalistically threatening cult masks and grimaces, was the substantive imitation of fear, which it disseminated around itself in expiation. As mythical fear diminished with the awakening of subjectivity, the traits of this fear fell subject to the taboo whose organon they were; they first became ugly vis-à-vis the idea of reconciliation, which comes into the world with the subject and his nascent freedom. But the old images of terror persist in history, which has yet to redeem the promise of freedom, and in which the subject—as the agent of unfreedom—perpetuates the mythical spell, against which he rebels and to which he is subordinate. Nietzsche's dictum that all good things were once dreadful things, like Schellings's insight into the terror of the beginning, may well have had their origins in the experience of art. The overthrown and recurrent content [*Inhalt*] is sublimated in imagination and form. Beauty is not the platonically pure beginning but rather something that originated in the renunciation of what was once feared, which only as a result of this renunciation—retrospectively, so to speak, according to its own telos—became the ugly. Beauty is the spell over the spell, which devolves upon it. The ambiguousness of the ugly results from the fact that the subject subsumes under the abstract and formal category of ugliness everything condemned by art: polymorphous sexuality as well as the violently mutilated and lethal. The perpetually recurring becomes that antithetical other without which art, according to its own concept, would not exist; appropriated through negation, this other—the antithesis to beauty, whose antithesis beauty was—gnaws away correctively on the affirmativeness of spiritualizing art. In the history of art, the dialectic of the ugly has drawn the category of the beautiful into itself as well; kitsch is, in this regard, the beautiful as the ugly, taboo in the name of that very beauty that it once was and that it now contradicts in the absence of its own opposite. That, however, only formal definition may be given to the concept of the ugly, as well as to its positive correlate, is internally related to art's immanent process of enlightenment. For the more art is dominated throughout by subjectivity and must show itself to be irreconcilable with everything preestablished, the more that subjective reason—the formal principle itself—becomes the canon of aesthetics.[2] This formal principle, obedient to subjective lawfulness regardless of what is other to it, and unshaken by its other, continues to give pleasure: In it subjectivity, unconscious of itself, enjoys the feeling of power. The aesthetic of pleasure, once free of crude materiality, coincides with mathematical relations in the artistic object, the most famous in the plastic arts being the golden mean, which has its musical correlative in the overtone relations of musical consonance. The appropriate caption for all aesthetics of pleasure is the paradoxical title of Max Frisch's play about Don Juan: *The Love of Geometry*. The formalism inherent in the concept of the ugly and the beautiful, as is acknowledged by Kant's aesthetics, a formalism against which artistic form is not immune, is the price art has to pay for raising itself above the domination of natural powers only in order to perpetuate them as domination over nature and human beings. Formalistic classicism commits an affront: Precisely the beauty that its concept glorifies is sullied by the manipulative, "composed" violence of its exemplary works. All that is imposed and added secretly gives the lie to the harmony that domination undertakes to produce: Bindingness that is decreed remains arbitrary. Although the formal character of the ugly and the beautiful cannot be retroactively annulled by any content aesthetics, its own content [*Inhalt*] can be determined. Precisely this is what gives it the weight that prevents the correction of the immanent abstractness of the beautiful by a clumsy surplus of material. Reconciliation as an act of violence, aesthetic formalism, and unreconciled life forms a triad.

The latent content [*Inhalt*] of the formal distinction between the ugly and the beautiful has its social aspect. The motive for the admission of the ugly was antifeudal: The peasants became a fit subject for art. Later, in Rimbaud, whose poems about mutilated corpses pursued this dimension even more relentlessly than did Baudelaire's "Martyr," the woman says, during the storming of the Tuileries: "I am scum,"[3] that is: fourth estate, or lumpenproletariat. The repressed who sides with the revolution is, according to the standards of the beautiful life in an ugly society, uncouth and distorted by resentment, and he bears all the stigmas of degradation under the burden of unfree—moreover, manual—labor. Among the human rights of those who foot the bill for culture is one that is polemically

63

directed against the affirmative, ideological totality: That the stigmas of degradation be dedicated to Mnemosyne in the form of an image. Art must take up the cause of what is proscribed as ugly, though no longer in order to integrate or mitigate it or to reconcile it with its own existence through humor that is more offensive than anything repulsive. Rather, in the ugly, art must denounce the world that creates and reproduces the ugly in its own image, even if in this too the possibility persists that sympathy with the degraded will reverse into concurrence with degradation. In the penchant of modern art for the nauseating and physically revolting—in objecting to which the apologists of the status quo can think of nothing more substantial than that the world is ugly enough as it is and art therefore should be responsible for idle beauty—the critical material motif shows through: In its autonomous forms art decries domination, even that which has been sublimated as a spiritual principle and stands witness for what domination represses and disavows. Even as semblance this materialistic motif's form remains what it had been external to that form: critical. Powerful aesthetic *valeurs* are liberated by social ugliness, as in the previously unimaginable blackness of the first part of *Hannele's Ascension*.[4] The process is comparable to the introduction of negative magnitudes: They retain their negativity in the continuum of the work. The status quo, by contrast, can only deal with this same material by swallowing hard at graphics of starving working-class children and other extreme images as documents of that beneficent heart that beats even in the face of the worst, thereby promising that it is not the worst. Art struggles against this kind of collusion by excluding through its language of form that remainder of affirmation maintained by social realism: This is the social element in radical formalism. The infiltration of the aesthetic by the moral—as for example Kant sought external to artworks in the sublime—is defamed by cultural apologists as degenerate. Art has struggled hard over the course of its development to establish its boundaries and so rarely fully respected them when defined as those of amusement, that any indication of the frailty of these boundaries, anything hybrid, provokes the strongest rejection. The aesthetic condemnation of the ugly is dependent on the inclination, verified by social psychology, to equate, justly, the ugly with the expression of suffering and, by projecting it, to despise it. Hitler's empire put this theorem to the test, as it put the whole of bourgeois ideology to the test: The more torture went on in the basement, the more insistently they made sure that the roof rested on columns. Doctrines of aesthetic invariance have the tendency to raise the reproach of degeneracy.

Yet the counterconcept of degeneracy is precisely that nature that doctrines of aesthetic invariance defame as degenerate. Art need not defend itself against the rebuke that it is degenerate; art meets this rebuke by refusing to affirm the miserable course of the world as the iron law of nature. However, because art has the power to harbor its own opposite without slackening its longing, indeed because it changes its longing into this power, the element of the ugly is bound up with art's spiritualization; George clear-sightedly recognized this in his preface to his translation of *Flowers of Evil*. This is alluded to by the subtitle "Spleen and Ideal": Back of the word spleen is the obsession with what resists being formed, with the transformation of what is hostile to art into art's own agent, which thus extends art's concept beyond that of the ideal. The ugly serves this purpose in art. But ugliness and cruelty are not merely the subject matter of art. As Nietzsche knew, art's own gesture is cruel. In aesthetic forms, cruelty becomes imagination: Something is excised from the living, from the body of language, from tones, from visual experience. The purer the form and the higher the autonomy of the works, the more cruel they are. Appeals for more humane art, for conformity to those who are its virtual public, regularly dilute the quality and weaken the law of form. What art in the broadest sense works with, it oppresses: This is the ritual of the domination of nature that lives on in play. It is the original sin of art as well as its permanent protest against morality, which revenges cruelty with cruelty. Yet those artworks succeed that rescue over into form something of the amorphous to which they ineluctably do violence. This alone is the reconciling aspect of form. The violence done to the material imitates the violence that issued from the material and that endures in its resistance to form. The subjective domination of the act of forming is not imposed on irrelevant materials but is read out of them; the cruelty of forming is mimesis of myth, with which it struggles. Greek genius expressed this idea, allegorizing it unconsciously: An early Doric relief from Selinunte, at the archaeological museum in Palermo, portrays Pegasus as having sprung from the blood of Medusa. If in modern artworks cruelty raises its head undisguised, it confirms the truth that in the face of the overwhelming force of reality art can no longer rely on its a priori ability to transform the dreadful into form. Cruelty is an element of art's critical reflection on itself; art despairs over the claim to power that it fulfills in being reconciled. Cruelty steps forward unadorned from the artworks as soon as their own spell is broken. The mythical terror of beauty extends into artworks as their irresistibility, a trait once attributed to Aphrodite Peithon. Just as during the Olympian stage the amorphous power of myth was concentrated in a single deity who subordinated the all and the many and retained its destructiveness, great artworks, as destructive works, have also retained the power to destroy in the authority of their success. Their radiance is dark; the beautiful permeates negativity, which appears to have mastered it. As if they feared that immortality would draw out their life blood, even the most seemingly neutral objects that art has sought to eternalize as beautiful radiate—entirely out of their materials—hardness, unassimilability, indeed ugliness. The formal category of resistance, requisite of an artwork if it is not to sink to that level of empty play dismissed by Hegel, introduces the cruelty of method even into artworks of happy periods such as that of impressionism. Likewise, the *sujets* around which the movement developed its greatest works are rarely those of a strictly peaceful nature but have scattered throughout fragments of civilization that the *peinture* blissfully seeks to incorporate.

If one originated in the other, it is beauty that originated in the ugly, and not the reverse. However, putting the concept of beauty on the Index—as many psychologies have done with the concept of the soul and many sociologies with that of society—would amount to resignation on the part of aesthetics. The definition of aesthetics as the theory of the beautiful is so unfruitful because the formal character of the concept of beauty is inadequate to the full content [*Inhalt*] of the aesthetic. If aesthetics were nothing but a systematic catalogue of whatever is called beautiful, it would give no idea of the life that transpires in the concept of beauty. In terms of the intention of aesthetic reflection, the concept of beauty is but one element. The idea of beauty draws attention to something essential to art without, however, articulating it directly. If artifacts were not in various ways judged to be beautiful the interest in them would be incomprehensible and blind, and no one—neither artist nor beholder—would have reason to make that exodus from the sphere of practical aims, those of self-preservation and pleasure, that art requires by virtue of its constitution. Hegel arrests the aesthetic dialectic by his static definition of the beautiful as the sensual appearance of the idea. The beautiful is no more to be defined than its concept can be dispensed with, a strict antinomy. If it dispensed with categories, aesthetics would be no more than a hermetic historico-relativistic description of what beauty has signified in various societies and styles; any distillation of common characteristics would be no better than a parody and would be confounded by any new example. The fatal universality of the concept of beauty is, however, not contingent. The transition to the primacy of form codified by the category of the beautiful inherently tends toward that formalism—the convergence of the aesthetic object with the most universal subjective determinations—from which the concept of beauty suffers. Nothing would be achieved by setting up a material essence over and against formal beauty: The principle, as something that became what it is, must be grasped in terms of its dynamic, and to this extent substantively. The image of beauty as that of a single and differentiated something originates with the emancipation from the fear of the overpowering wholeness and undifferentiatedness of nature. The shudder in the face of this is rescued by beauty into itself by making itself impervious to the immediately existent; beauty establishes a sphere of untouchability; works become beautiful by the force of their opposition to what simply exists. Of that on which it was active the aesthetically forming spirit allowed entry only to what resembled it, what it understood, or what it hoped to make like itself. This was a process of formalization; therefore beauty is, in terms of its historical tendency, formal. The reduction that beauty imposes on the terrifying, over and out of which beauty raises itself and which it banishes from itself as from a sacred temple, has—in the face of the terrifying—something powerless about it. For the terrifying digs in on the perimeter like the enemy in front of the walls of the beleaguered city and starves it out. If beauty is not to fail its own telos, it must work against its enemy even if this struggle is contrary to its own tendency. The history of the Hellenic spirit discerned by Nietzsche is unforgettable because it followed through and presented the historical process between myth and genius. The archaic giants reclining in one of the temples of Agrigento are no more rudiments than are the demons of Attic drama. Form requires them if it is not to capitulate to myth, which persists in it so long as form merely rejects it. In all subsequent art of any import this counterelement to beauty is maintained and transformed. This occurred already in Euripedes' dramas, where the horror of mythical violence redounds to the unblemished divinities, the Olympian consorts of beauty, who are in turn decried as demons; afterward Epicurean philosophy wanted to free consciousness from this horror of the gods. Since, however, the images of a terrifying nature have from the outset mollified those gods mimetically, the archaic grimaces, monsters, and minotaurs already assume a human likeness. Orderly reason already governs these mixed creatures; natural history did not allow their kind to survive. They are frightening because they warn of the fragility of human identity, but they are not chaotic because threat and order are intertwined in them. In the repetitive rhythms of primitive music the menacing aspect originates in the principle of order itself. In this principle the antithesis to the archaic is implicit as the play of forces of the beautiful single whole; the qualitative leap of art is a smallest transition.[5] By virtue of this dialectic the image of the beautiful is metamorphosed into the movement of enlightenment as a whole. The law of the formalization of beauty was a moment of balance that was progressively destroyed by its relation to its contrary, which the identity of the beautiful hopelessly tries to hold at bay. Terror itself peers out of the eyes of beauty as the coercion that emanates from form; the concept of the blinding glare of beauty articulates this experience. The irresistibility of the beautiful, a sublimation of sexuality that extends into the highest artworks, is exerted by their purity, their distance from materiality and any concern with effect. This irresistibility becomes content [*Inhalt*]. With all the ambivalence of triumph, what subjugates expression—the formal character of beauty—is transformed into expression, in which what is menacing in the domination of nature is wed with a longing for the vanquished, a longing stirred by domination. But it is the expression of suffering under subjugation and subjugation's vanishing point, death. The affinity of all beauty with death has its nexus in the idea of pure form that art imposes on the diversity of the living and that is extinguished in it. In serene beauty its recalcitrant other would be completely pacified, and such aesthetic reconciliation is fatal for the extra-aesthetic. That is the melancholy of art. It achieves an unreal reconciliation at the price of real reconciliation. All that art can do is grieve for the sacrifice it makes, which, in its powerlessness, art itself is. Beauty not only speaks like a messenger of death—as does Wagner's Valkyrie to Siegmund —but in its own process it assimilates itself to death. The course toward the artwork's integration, identical with the development of its autonomy, is the death of the particular elements in the whole. What compels the artwork to go beyond itself, beyond its own particularity, seeks its own demise, the quintessence of which is the totality of the work. If the idea of artworks is eternal life, they can attain this only by annihilating everything living within their domain: This too inheres in their expression. It is the expression of the demise of the whole, just as the whole speaks of the demise of expression. In the impulse of every particular element of an artwork toward integration, the disintegrative impulse of nature secretly manifests itself. The more integrated artworks are, the more what constitutes them disintegrates in them. To this extent their success is their decomposition and that lends them their fathomlessness. Decomposition at the same time releases the immanent counterforce of art, its centrifugal force.——Ever less is the beautiful achieved in a particular, purified form; beauty is shifted to the dynamic totality of the work and thus, through heightened emancipation from the particularity, advances formalization at the same time that it melds particularity with the diffuse. By virtue of the fact that the reciprocal relations operative in art in the image actually break through the cycle of guilt and atonement in which art participates, that reciprocity reveals something of a condition beyond myth. The reciprocity transposes the cycle of guilt into the image, which reflects it and thereby transcends it. Loyalty to the image of beauty results in an idiosyncratic reaction against it. This loyalty demands tension and ultimately turns against its resolution. The loss of tension, an insignificance of the relation of parts to the whole, is the strongest objection to be made against much contemporary art. Yet the abstract demand for tension would itself be mediocre and artificial: The concept of tension applies to what is always under tension, namely form and its other, which is represented in the work by the particularities. Once however the beautiful, as homeostasis of tension, is transferred to the totality, beauty is drawn into the vortex. For totality, the coherence of the parts in a unity, requires or presupposes in some regard the substantiality of the elements and indeed to a degree greater than in older art, in which tension remained much more latent beneath established idioms. Because totality ultimately engorges tension and makes itself fit for ideology, homeostasis itself is annulled: This is the crisis of the beautiful and of art, and here the efforts of the last twenty years may converge. But even here the idea of the beautiful prevails, which must exclude everything heterogeneous to it, the conventionally established, all traces of reification. Indeed, it is for the sake of the beautiful that there is no longer beauty: because it is no longer beautiful. What can only appear negatively mocks a resolution that it recognizes as false and which therefore debases the idea of the beautiful. Beauty's aversion to the overly smooth, the pat mathematical solution, which has compromised art with the lie throughout its history, becomes an aversion to any resultant, without which art can be conceived no more than it can be without the tensions out of which it emerges. The prospect of the rejection of art for the sake of art is foreseeable. It is intimated by those artworks that fall silent or disappear. Even socially they are correct consciousness: Rather no art than socialist realism.

Art is a refuge for mimetic comportment. In art the subject exposes itself, at various levels of autonomy, to its other, separated from it and yet not altogether separated. Art's disavowal of magical practices—its antecedents—implies participation in rationality. That art, something mimetic, is possible in the midst of rationality, and that it employs its means, is a response to the faulty irrationality of the rational world as an overadministered world. For the aim of all rationality—the quintessence of the means for dominating nature—would have to be something other than means, hence something not rational. Capitalist society hides and disavows precisely this irrationality, and in contrast to this, art represents truth in a double sense: It maintains the image of its aim, which has been obscured by rationality, and it convicts the status quo of its irrationality and absurdity. The relinquishment of the delusion of the unmediated intervention of spirit, which intermittently and insatiably recurs in the history of humanity, establishes a prohibition against recollection's employing art to turn unmediatedly toward nature. Only separation can countermand separation. This at once strengthens and exculpates the rational element in art because it resists real domination, even though, as ideology, this element is ever and again bound up with domination. To speak of "the magic of art" is trite because art is allergic to any relapses into magic. Art is a stage in the process of what Max Weber called the disenchantment of the world, and it is entwined with rationalization; this is the source of all of art's means and methods of production; technique that disparages its ideology inheres in this ideology as much as it threatens it because art's magical heritage stubbornly persisted throughout art's transformations. Yet art mobilizes technique in an opposite direction than does domination. The sentimentality and debility of almost the whole tradition of aesthetic thought is that it has suppressed the dialectic of rationality and mimesis immanent to art. This persists in the astonishment over the technical work of art as if it had fallen from heaven: The two points of view are actually complementary. Nevertheless, the cliché about the magic of art has something true about it. The survival of mimesis, the nonconceptual affinity of the subjectively produced with its unposited other, defines art as a form of knowledge and to that extent as "rational." For that to which the mimetic comportment responds is the telos of knowledge, which art simultaneously blocks with its own categories. Art completes knowledge with what is excluded from knowledge and thereby once again impairs its character as knowledge, its univocity. Art threatens to be pulled apart because magic, which art secularizes, actually refuses this process, while in the midst of secularization the essence of magic sinks to the level of a mythological vestige, to superstition. What today emerges as the crisis of art, as its new quality, is as old as art's concept. How an artwork deals with this antinomy determines its possibility and quality. Art cannot fulfill its concept. This strikes each and every one of its works, even the highest, with an ineluctable imperfectness that repudiates the idea of perfection toward which artworks must aspire. Unreflected, perfectly logical enlightenment would have to discard art just as the prosaic pragmatist in fact does. The aporia of art, pulled between regression to literal magic or surrender of the mimetic impulse to thinglike rationality, dictates its law of motion; the aporia cannot be eliminated. The depth of the process, which every artwork is, is excavated by the unreconcilability of these elements; it must be imported into the idea of art as an image of reconciliation. Only because no artwork can succeed emphatically are its forces set free; only as a result of this does art catch a glimpse of reconciliation. Art is rationality that criticizes rationality without withdrawing from it; art is not something prerational or irrational, which would peremptorily condemn it as untruth in the face of the entanglement of all human activity in the social totality. Rational and irrational theories of art are therefore equally faulty. If enlightenment principles are bluntly applied to art, the result is that philistine prosaism that made it easy for the Weimar classicists and their romantic contemporaries to drown in ridicule the meager sentiment of bourgeois revolutionary spirit in Germany; a philistinism that was admittedly surpassed one hundred and fifty years later by that of a narrow bourgeois religion of art. That form of rationalism that argues powerlessly against artworks, by applying extra-aesthetic logical and causal criteria to art, has not died off; it is provoked by the ideological misuse of art. If someone writing a realist novel after it had become outmoded objected about one of Eichendorff's verses that clouds cannot be equated with dreams but that at best dreams might perhaps be equated with clouds, the verse itself, "Clouds pass by like heavy dreams,"[6] would in its own sphere, where nature is transformed into a premonitory metaphor of inner life, be immune to such homegrown correctness. Whoever denies the expressive power of this verse—a prototype of sentimental poetry in the best sense—blunders and trips in the twilight of the work instead of entering it and responsively working out the *valeurs* of the words and their constellations. Rationality in the artwork is the unity-founding, organizing element, not unrelated to the rationality that governs externally, but it does not reflect its categorizing order. What empirical rationality takes to be the irrational characteristics of artworks is not a symptom of an irrational mind, not even a symptom of an irrational opinion among its viewers;

opinion generally produces opinionated artworks that are, in a certain sense, rationalistic. Rather, the lyric poet's *désinvolture*, his dispensation from the strictures of logic—which enter his sphere only as shadows —grants him the possibility of following the immanent lawfulness of his works. Artworks do not repress; through expression they help to make present to consciousness the diffuse and elusive without, as psychoanalysis insists, "rationalization."——To accuse irrational art of irrationalism for playing a trick on the praxis-oriented rules of reason is in its own way no less ideological than the irrationality of official faith in art; it serves the needs of apparatchiks of every persuasion. Movements such as expressionism and surrealism, whose irrationality alienated, were an attack on violence, authority, and obscurantism. That various tributaries of German expressionism and French surrealism too converged in Fascism—for which spirit was merely the means to an end, which is why Fascism devoured everything—is insignificant with regard to the objective idea of those movements, and it has been deliberately blown out of proportion by Zhdanov and his followers for political purposes. It is one thing to manifest the irrationality of the psyche or the political order artistically, giving it form and thereby in a certain sense making it rational, but it is something else again to preach irrationality, as it has almost always been done under the auspices of a rationalism of aesthetic means, in crude, mathematically commensurable superficial connections. Benjamin's theory of the artwork in the age of its technical reproduction may have failed to do full justice to this. The simple antithesis between the auratic and the mass-reproduced work, which for the sake of simplicity neglected the dialectic of the two types, became the booty of a view of art that takes photography as its model and is no less barbaric than the view of the artist as creator. It is of interest that initially, in his "Small History of Photography," Benjamin in no way pronounced this antithesis as undialectically as he did five years later in his essay on reproduction.[7] Whereas the later work adopted the definition of aura word for word from the earlier one, the early study praises the aura of early photographs, which they lost only with the critique of their commercial exploitation by Atget. This may come much closer to the actual situation than does the simplification that made the essay on reproduction so popular. What slips through the wide mesh of this theory, which tends toward copyrealism, is the element opposed to cultic contexts that motivated Benjamin to introduce the concept of aura in the first place, that is, that which moves into the distance and is critical of the ideological superficies of life. The condemnation of aura easily becomes the dismissal of qualitatively modern art that distances itself from the logic of familiar things; the critique of aura thereby cloaks the products of mass culture in which profit is hidden and whose trace they bear even in supposedly socialist countries. Brecht did in fact value *Song*-style above atonality and twelve-tone technique, which was for him suspiciously romantic in its expressiveness. From these perspectives the so-called irrational currents of spirit are summarily chalked up to Fascism, ignoring their voice of protest against bourgeois reification by which they nevertheless continue to provoke. In conformity with East-bloc politics, a blind eye is turned toward the relation between enlightenment and mass deception.[8] Disenchanted technical procedures that dedicate themselves completely to appearances, as what they claim to be, function only too well for the transfiguration of these appearances. The failure of Benjamin's grandly conceived theory of reproduction remains that its bipolar categories make it impossible to distinguish between a conception of art that is free of ideology to its core and the misuse of aesthetic rationality for mass exploitation and mass domination, a possibility he hardly touches upon. The single technique dealt with by Benjamin that goes beyond camera rationalism is montage, which reached its acme in surrealism and was quickly weakened in film. But montage disposes over the elements that make up the reality of an unchallenged common sense, either to transform their intention or, at best, to awaken their latent language. It is powerless, however, insofar as it is unable to explode the individual elements. It is precisely montage that is to be criticized for possessing the remains of a complaisant irrationalism, for adaptation to material that is delivered ready-made from outside the work.

Following an internal logic whose stages will need to be described by an aesthetic historiography that does not yet exist, the principle of montage therefore became that of construction. There is no denying that even in the principle of construction, in the dissolution of materials and their subordination to an imposed unity, once again something smooth, harmonistic, a quality of pure logicality, is conjured up that seeks to establish itself as ideology. It is the fatality of all contemporary art that it is contaminated by the untruth of the ruling totality. Still, construction is currently the only possible form that the rational element in the artwork can take, just as at the outset, in the Renaissance, the emancipation of art from cultic heteronomy was part of the discovery of construction, then called "composition." In the artwork as monad, construction—its authority limited—is the plenipotentiary of logic and causality transferred to the artwork from the domain of objective knowledge. Construction is the synthesis of the diverse at the expense of the qualitative elements that it masters, and at the expense of the subject, which intends to extinguish itself as it carries out this synthesis. The affinity of construction with cognitive processes, or perhaps rather with their interpretation by the theory of knowledge, is no less evident than is their difference, which is that art does not make judgments and when it does, it shatters its own concept. What distinguishes construction from composition in the encompassing sense of pictorial composition, is the ruthless subordination not only of everything that originated from outside the artwork, but also of all partial elements immanent to the work. To this extent construction is the extension of subjective domination, which conceals itself all the more profoundly the further it is driven. Construction tears the elements of reality out of their primary context and transforms them to the point where they are once again capable of forming a unity, one that is no less imposed on them internally than was the heteronomous unity to which they were subjected externally. By means of construction, art desperately wants to escape from its nominalistic situation, to extricate itself by its own power from a sense of accidentalness and attain what is overarchingly binding or, if one will, universal. To this end art requires a reduction of its elements, which it threatens to enervate and degenerate into a victory over what is not present. The abstract transcendental and hidden subject of Kant's theory of schematism becomes the aesthetic subject. Yet construction at the same time critically reduces aesthetic subjectivity, just as constructivist approaches such as Mondrian's originally took a stand in opposition to those of expressionism. For if the synthesis of construction is to succeed, it must in spite of all aversion be read out of the elements themselves, and they never wholly accede in themselves to what is imposed on them; with complete justice construction countermands the organic as illusory. The subject in its quasi-logical universality is the functionary of this act, whereas the self-expression of the subject in the result becomes a matter of indifference. It counts among the most profound insights of Hegel's aesthetics that long before constructivism it recognized this truly dialectical relation and located the subjective success of the artwork in the disappearance of the subject in the artwork. Only by way of this disappearance, not by cozying up to reality, does the artwork break through merely subjective reason. This is the utopia of construction; its fallibility, on the other hand, is that it necessarily has a penchant to destroy what it integrates and to arrest the process in which it exclusively has its life. The loss of tension in constructive art today is not only the product of subjective weakness but a consequence of the idea of construction itself, specifically with regard to its semblance. Pursuing its virtually irreversible course, which tolerates nothing external to itself, construction wants to make itself into something real sui generis, even though it borrows the very purity of its principles from external technical functional forms. Functionless, however, construction remains trapped in art. The purely constructed, strictly objective artwork, which ever since Adolf Loos has been the sworn enemy of everything artisanal, reverses into the artisanal by virtue of its mimesis of functional forms: Purposelessness without purpose becomes irony. To date the only alternative to this has been the polemical intervention of the subject in subjective reason by a surplus of the subject's own manifestation beyond that in which it wants to negate itself. Only by carrying through this contradiction, and not by its false resolution, can art somehow still survive.

The need for objective art was not fulfilled in functional means and therefore encroached on autonomous means. It disavows art as the product of human labor, one that nevertheless does not want to be an object, a thing among other things. Art that is simply a thing is an oxymoron. Yet the development of this oxymoron is nevertheless the inner direction of contemporary art. Art is motivated by a conflict: Its enchantment, a vestige of its magical phase, is constantly repudiated as unmediated sensual immediacy by the progressive disenchantment of the world, yet without its ever being possible finally to obliterate this magical element. Only in it is art's mimetic character preserved, and its truth is the critique that, by its sheer existence, it levels at a rationality that has become absolute. Emancipated from its claim to reality, the enchantment is itself part of enlightenment: Its semblance disenchants the disenchanted world. This is the dialectical ether in which art today takes place. The renunciation of any claim to truth by the preserved magical element marks out the terrain of aesthetic semblance and aesthetic truth. Art inherits a comportment of spirit once directed toward essence, and with it the chance of perceiving mediately that which is essential yet otherwise tabooed by the progress of rational knowledge. Though it will not acknowledge it, for the disenchanted world the fact of art is an outrage, an afterimage of enchantment, which it does not tolerate. If, however, art unflinchingly acquiesces in this and posits itself blindly as sorcery, it degrades itself to an act of illusion in opposition to its own claim to truth and undermines itself with a vengeance. In the midst of the disenchanted world even the most austere idea of art, divested of every consolation, sounds romantic. Hegel's philosophical history of art, which construes romantic art as art's final phase, is confirmed even by antiromantic art, though indeed it is only through its darkness that this art can outmaneuver the demystified world and cancel the spell that this world casts by the overwhelming force of its appearance, the fetish character of the commodity. By their very existence artworks postulate the existence of what does not exist and thereby come into conflict with the latter's actual nonexistence. Yet this conflict is not to be conceived in the manner of jazz fans for whom what does not appeal to them is out of date because of its incongruity with the disenchanted world. For only what does not fit into this world is true. What is requisite of the artistic act no longer converges with the historical situation, which is not to say that they ever harmonized. This incongruity is not to be eliminated by adaptation: The truth, rather, is in carrying through their conflict. Conversely, the deaestheticization of art is immanent to art—whether it be art that unflinchingly pursues its autonomous order or art that sells itself off cheap—in accordance with the technological tendency of art, which is not to be halted by any appeal to a purportedly pure and unmediated inwardness. The concept of artistic technique emerged late: Even after the French Revolution, when the aesthetic domination of nature was becoming self-conscious, the concept was still lacking, though not its reality. Artistic technique is no cozy adaptation to an age that with foolish zeal labels itself technological, as if productive forces alone determined its structure, regardless of the relations of production that hold the former in check. As was not infrequently the case in modern movements after World War II, whenever aesthetic technology strove for the scientization of art rather than technical innovation, art was dazzled and went astray. Scientists, especially physicists, had no trouble pointing out many misunderstandings to artists who had become enraptured with the nomenclature, reminding them that the scientific terminology they used to name their technical procedures was being misattributed. The technologization of art is no less provoked by the subject—by the disillusioned consciousness and the mistrust of magic as a veil—than by the object: by the problem of how artworks may be bindingly organized. The possibility of the latter became problematic with the collapse of traditional procedures, however much their influence has extended into the current epoch. Only technology provided a solution; it promised to organize art completely in terms of that means-end relation that Kant had in general equated with the aesthetic. It is not that technique sprang out of the blue as a stopgap, although it is true that the history of art has known moments that are reminiscent of the technical revolution of material production. With the progressive sub-jectivization of artworks, free control over them ripened within the traditional procedures. Technologization established free control over the material as a principle. For its legitimation the development of technique can appeal to the fact that traditional masterworks since Palladio, though they relied only desultorily on knowledge of technical procedures, never-theless gained their authenticity from their level of technical integration, until finally technology exploded the traditional procedures. In retrospect, even as a constituent element of the art of the past, technique can be recognized with incomparable clarity compared with what is conceded by cultural ideology, which portrays what it calls the technical age of art as the decline of a previous age of human spontaneity. Certainly it is possible in the case of Bach to show the gaps between the structure of his music and the technical means that were available for its completely adequate performance; for the critique of aesthetic historicism this is relevant. Yet insights of this sort do not suffice for the entire complex of issues. Bach's experience led him to a highly developed compositional technique. On the other hand, in works that can be called archaic, expression is amalgamated with technique as well as with its absence or with what technique could not yet accomplish. It is in vain to try to decide what effects of pre-perspectival painting are due to expressive profundity or to some degree of technical insufficiency that itself becomes expression. Precisely for this reason archaic works, which are generally limited in their range of possibilities, always seem to have just enough available technique and no more than is required for the realization of the project. This imbues them with that deceptive authority that is misleading with regard to the technical aspect that is a condition of such authority. In the face of such works the effort to distinguish between what was wanted and what was still out of reach falls mute; in truth, this question is always misleading with regard to what is objectivated. Yet abandoning the question also has an element of obscurantism. Alois Riegl's concept of artistic volition [*Kunstwollen*], much as it helped to free aesthetic experience from abstract timeless norms, can scarcely be maintained; it is hardly ever the case that what is decisive in a work is what the artist intended. The fierce rigidity of the Etruscan Apollo at the Villa Giulia is a constituent of the content, regardless whether it was intended or not. And yet at critical points in the history of art the function of technique has been fundamentally trans-formed. When fully developed, technique establishes the primacy in art of making, in contradistinction to a receptivity of production, however that is conceived. Technique is able to become the opponent of art insofar as art represents—at changing levels—the repressed unmakable. However, the technologization of art is not synonymous with feasibility either, as the superficiality of cultural conservatism would prefer. Technologization, the extended arm of the nature-dominating subject, purges artworks of their immediate language. Technological requirements drive out the contingency of the individual who produces the work. The same process that traditionalists scorn as the loss of soul is what makes the artwork in its greatest achievements eloquent rather than merely the testimony of something psychological or human, as the contemporary prattle goes. Radicalized, what is called reification probes for the language of things. It narrows the distance to the idea of that nature that extirpates the primacy of human meaning. Emphatically modern art breaks out of the sphere of the portrayal of emotions and is transformed into the expression of what no significative language can achieve. Paul Klee's work is probably the best evidence of this from the recent past, and he was a member of the technologically minded Bauhaus.

If one teaches—as Adolf Loos did implicitly and technocrats since have happily reiterated—that real technical objects are beautiful, one predicates of them precisely that against which artistic *Sachlichkeit,* as an aesthetic innervation, is directed. Incidental beauty, measured in terms of opaque traditional categories such as formal harmony or even imposing grandeur, impinges on the real functionality in which functional works like bridges or industrial plants seek their law of form. It is apologetic to claim that functional works, by virtue of their fidelity to this law of form, are always beautiful; the aim is evidently to give consolation for what these works lack and assuage *Sachlichkeit's* bad conscience. By contrast, the autonomous work, functionally exclusive in itself, wants to achieve through its own immanent teleology what was once called beauty. If in spite of their division, purposeful and purposeless art nevertheless share the innervation of *Sachlichkeit,* the beauty of the autonomous technological artwork becomes problematic, a beauty that its model—the functional work —renounces. The beauty of the work suffers from functionless functioning. Because its external *terminus ad quem* atrophies, its internal telos wastes away; functioning—as a for-something-else—becomes superfluous, an ornamental end in itself. This sabotages an element of functionality, that necessity that arises from the partial elements of the artwork in accord with what these elements want and with regard to their own self-direction. The equalization of tension that the objective artwork borrowed from the functional arts is profoundly impeded. What becomes obvious is the disparity between the functionally thoroughly formed artwork and its actual functionlessness. Still, aesthetic mimesis of functionality cannot be revoked through recourse to the subjectively unmediated: This would only mask how much the individual and his psychology have become ideological with regard to the supremacy of social objectivity, a supremacy of which *Sachlichkeit* is correctly conscious. The crisis of *Sachlichkeit* is not a signal to replace it with something humane, which would immediately degenerate into consolation, the correlative of the actual rise of inhumanity. Thought through to the bitter end, *Sachlichkeit* itself regresses to a preartistic barbarism. Even the highly cultivated aesthetic allergy to kitsch, ornament, the superfluous, and everything reminiscent of luxury has an aspect of barbarism, an aspect—according to Freud—of the destructive discontent with culture. The antinomies of *Sachlichkeit* confirm the dialectic of enlightenment: That progress and regression are entwined. The literal is barbaric. Totally objectified, by virtue of its rigorous legality, the artwork becomes a mere fact and is annulled as art. The alternative that opens up in this crisis is: Either to leave art behind or to transform its very concept.

Notes

1 Karl Rosenkranz, *Ästhetik des Häßlichen* (Königsberg, 1853).

2 See Max Horkheimer and Adorno, *Dialectic of Enlightenment*, trans. John Cumming (New York, 1972).

3 See Arthur Rimbaud, "The Blacksmith," from *Poems 1870*, in *Complete Works*, trans. Wallace Fowlie (Chicago, 1966), p. 23.

4 [Gerhart Hauptmann, *Hannele's Ascension*, in *Three Plays*, trans. H. Frenz and M. Waggoner (New York, 1951), pp. 99–143.—trans.]

5 ["ein kleinster Übergang": The smallest transition, is a fundamental aesthetico-theological motif in both Walter Benjamin's and Adorno's writings. See Adorno, *Alban Berg: Master of the Smallest Link*, trans. Juliane Brand and Christopher Hailey (Cambridge, 1991).—trans.]

6 "Wolken ziehn wie schwere Träume," from Joseph von Eichendorff's "Zwielicht," in *Werke* ed. W. Rasch (Munich, 1955), p. 11.

7 See Walter Benjamin, "A Small History of Photography," in *One Way Street and Other Writings*, trans. Edmund Jephott and Kingley Shorter (London, 1979), pp. 240ff., and "The Work of Art in the Age of Mechanical Reproduction," in *Illuminations*, trans. Harry Zohn (New York, 1968), pp. 217ff.

8 See Horkheimer and Adorno, *Dialectic of Enlightenment*, pp. 120ff.

4
Natural beauty

Since Schelling, whose aesthetics is entitled the *Philosophy of Art*, aesthetic interest has centered on artworks. Natural beauty, which was still the occasion of the most penetrating insights in the *Critique of Judgment*, is now scarcely even a topic of theory. The reason for this is not that natural beauty was dialectically transcended, both negated and maintained on a higher plane, as Hegel's theory had propounded, but, rather, that it was repressed. The concept of natural beauty rubs on a wound, and little is needed to prompt one to associate this wound with the violence that the artwork—a pure artifact—inflicts on nature. Wholly artifactual, the artwork seems to be the opposite of what is not made, nature. As pure antitheses, however, each refers to the other: nature to the experience of a mediated and objectified world, the artwork to nature as the mediated plenipotentiary of immediacy. Therefore reflection on natural beauty is irrevocably requisite to the theory of art. Whereas thoughts on it, virtually the topic itself, have, paradoxically, a pedantic, dull, antiquarian quality, great art and the interpretation of it have, by incorporating what the older aesthetics attributed to nature, blocked out reflection on what is located beyond aesthetic immanence and yet is nevertheless its premise. The price of this repression was the transition to the ideological art religion (a name coined by Hegel) of the nineteenth century—the satisfaction in a reconciliation symbolically achieved in the artwork. Natural beauty vanished from aesthetics as a result of the burgeoning domination of the concept of freedom and human dignity, which was inaugurated by Kant and then rigorously transplanted into aesthetics by Schiller and Hegel; in accord with this concept nothing in the world is worthy of attention except that for which the autonomous subject has itself to thank. The truth of such freedom for the subject, however, is at the same time unfreedom: unfreedom for the other. For this reason the turn against natural beauty, in spite of the immeasurable progress it made possible in the comprehending of art as spiritual, does not lack an element of destructiveness, just as the concept of dignity does not lack it in its turn against nature. Schiller's variously interpreted treatise *On Grace and Dignity* marks the new development. The devastation that idealism sowed is glaringly evident in its victims—Johann Peter Hebel, for example—who were vanquished by the verdict passed by aesthetic dignity yet survived it by exposing through their own existence the finitude of the idealists who had judged their existence to be all too finite. Perhaps nowhere else is the desiccation of everything not totally ruled by the subject more apparent, nowhere else is the dark shadow of idealism more obvious, than in aesthetics. If the case of natural beauty were pending, dignity would be found culpable for having raised the human animal above the animal. In the experience of nature, dignity reveals itself as subjective usurpation that degrades what is not subordinate to the subject—the qualities—to mere material and expulses it from art as a totally indeterminate potential, even though art requires it according to its own concept. Human beings are not equipped positively with dignity; rather, dignity would be exclusively what they have yet to achieve. This is why Kant situated it in the intelligible character rather than consigning it to the empirical sphere. Under the sign of the dignity that was tacked on to human beings as they are—a dignity that was rapidly transformed into that official dignity that Schiller nevertheless mistrusted in the spirit of the eighteenth century—art became the tumbling mat of the true, the beautiful, and the good, which in aesthetic reflection forced valuable art out of the way of what the broad, polluted mainstream of spirit drew in its current.

The artwork, through and through θέσει, something human, is the plenipotentiary of φύσει, of what is not merely for the subject, of what, in Kantian terms, would be the thing itself. The identity of the artwork with the subject is as complete as the identity of nature with itself should some day be. The liberation of art from the heteronomy of the material, especially of natural objects, as well as the right to take every possible object as an object of art, first made art master of itself and expunged from it the rawness of what is unmediated by spirit. However, the course of this progress, which plowed under everything that did not accommodate to identity with spirit, was also a course of devastation. This has been well documented in the twentieth century by the effort to recover authentic artworks that succumbed to the terror of idealism's scorn. Karl Kraus sought to rescue linguistic objects as a part of his vindication of what capitalism has oppressed: animal, landscape, woman. The reorientation of aesthetic theory toward natural beauty is allied with Kraus's effort. Hegel obviously lacked the sensibility needed to recognize that genuine experience of art is not possible without the experience of that elusive dimension whose name—natural beauty—had faded. The substantiality of the experience of natural beauty, however, reaches deep into modern art: In Proust, whose *Recherche* is an artwork and a metaphysics of art, the experience of a hawthorne hedge figures as a fundamental phenomenon of aesthetic comportment. Authentic artworks, which hold fast to the idea of reconciliation with nature by making themselves completely a second nature, have consistently felt the urge, as if in need of a breath of fresh air, to step outside of themselves. Since identity is not to be their last word, they have sought consolation in first nature: Thus the last act of *Figaro* is played out of doors, and in *Freischütz* Agathe, standing on the balcony, suddenly becomes aware of the starry night. The extent to which this taking a breath depends on what is mediated, on the world of conventions, is unmistakable. Over long periods the feeling of natural beauty intensified with the suffering of the subject thrown back on himself in a mangled and administered world; the experience bears the mark of Weltschmerz. Even Kant had misgivings about art made by human beings and conventionally opposed to nature. "The superiority of natural beauty over that of art, namely, that—even if art were to excel nature in form—it is the only beauty that arouses a direct interest, agrees with the refined and solid way of thinking of all people who have cultivated their moral feeling."[1] Here it is Rousseau who speaks, and no less in the following sentence: "A man who has taste enough to judge the products of fine art with the greatest correctness and refinement may still be glad to leave a room in which he finds those beauties that minister to vanity and perhaps to social joys, and to turn instead to the beautiful in nature, in order to find there, as it were, a voluptuousness for the mind in a train of thought that he can never fully unravel. If that is how he chooses, we shall ourselves regard this choice of his with esteem and assume that he has a beautiful soul, such as no connoisseur and lover of art can claim to have because of the interest he takes in his objects."[2] The gesture of stepping out into the open is shared by these theoretical sentences with the artworks of their time. Kant lodged the sublime—and probably along with it all beauty that rises above the mere play of form—in nature. By contrast, Hegel and his generation achieved a concept of art that did not—as any child of the eighteenth century took for granted—"minister to vanity and social joys." But they thereby missed the experience that is still expressed unreservedly by Kant in the bourgeois revolutionary spirit that held the humanly made for fallible and that, because the humanly made was never thought fully to become second nature, guarded the image of first nature.

The degree to which the concept of natural beauty has been historically transformed is made most strikingly evident by the fact that it was probably only in the course of the nineteenth century that the concept was enlarged by a new domain: the cultural landscape, an artifactitious domain that must at first seem totally opposed to natural beauty. Historical works are often considered beautiful that have some relation to their geographical setting, as for instance hillside towns that are related to their setting by the use of its stone. A law of form does not, as in art, predominate in them; they are seldom planned, although sometimes the effect of a plan is produced by the arrangement of the town around a church or marketplace, just as economic-material conditions at times spawn artistic forms. Certainly these cultural landscapes do not bear the character of inviolability that the accepted view associates with natural beauty. Engraved as their expression is history, and engraved as their form is historical continuity, which integrates the landscapes dynamically as in artworks. The discovery of this aesthetic dimension and its appropriation through the collective sensorium dates back to romanticism, probably initially to the cult of the ruin. With the collapse of romanticism, that hybrid domain, cultural landscape, deteriorated into an advertising gimmick for organ festivals and phony security; the prevailing urbanism absorbs as its ideological complement whatever fulfills the desiderata of urban life without bearing the stigmata of market society on its forehead. But if a bad conscience is therefore admixed with the joy of each old wall and each group of medieval houses, the pleasure survives the insight that makes it suspicious. So long as progress, deformed by utilitarianism, does violence to the surface of the earth, it will be impossible—in spite of all proof to the contrary—completely to counter the perception that what antedates the trend is in its backwardness better and more humane. Rationalization is not yet rational; the universality of mediation has yet to be transformed into living life; and this endows the traces of immediacy, however dubious and antiquated, with an element of corrective justice. The longing that is assuaged and betrayed by them and made pernicious through spurious fulfillment is nevertheless legitimated by the denial of gratification continually imposed by the status quo. But perhaps the most profound force of resistance stored in the cultural landscape is the expression of history that is compelling, aesthetically, because it is etched by the real suffering of the past. The figure of the constrained gives happiness because the force of constraint must not be forgotten; its images are a memento. The cultural landscape, which resembles a ruin even when the houses still stand, embodies a wailful lament that has since fallen mute. If today the aesthetic relation to the past is poisoned by a reactionary tendency with which this relation is in league, an ahistorical aesthetic consciousness that sweeps aside the dimension of the past as rubbish is no better. Without historical remembrance there would be no beauty. The past, and with it the cultural landscape, would be accorded guiltlessly to a liberated humanity, free especially of nationalism. What appears untamed in nature and remote from history, belongs—polemically speaking—to a historical phase in which the social web is so densely woven that the living fear death by suffocation. Times in which nature confronts man over-poweringly allow no room for natural beauty; as is well known, agri-cultural occupations, in which nature as it appears is an immediate object of action, allow little appreciation for landscape. Natural beauty, purport-edly ahistorical, is at its core historical; this legitimates at the same time that it relativizes the concept. Wherever nature was not actually mastered, the image of its untamed condition terrified. This explains the strange predilection of earlier centuries for symmetrical arrangements of nature. In sympathy with the spirit of nominalism, the sentimental experience of nature delighted in the irregular and unschematic. The progress of civilization, however, easily deceives human beings as to how vulnerable they remain even now. Delight in nature was bound up with the conception of the subject as being-for-itself and virtually infinite in itself; as such the subject projected itself onto nature and in its isolation felt close to it; the subject's powerlessness in a society petrified into a second nature becomes the motor of the flight into a purportedly first nature. In Kant, as a result of the subject's consciousness of freedom, the fear of nature's force began to become anachronistic; this consciousness of freedom, however, gave way to the subject's anxiety in the face of perennial unfreedom. In the experience of natural beauty, consciousness of freedom and anxiety fuse. The less secure the experience of natural beauty, the more it is predicated on art. Verlaine's "la mer est plus belle que les cathédrales" is intoned from the vantage point of a high civilization and creates—as is the case whenever nature is invoked to throw light on the world human beings have made—a salutary fear.

Just how bound up natural beauty is with art beauty is confirmed by the experience of the former. For it, nature is exclusively appearance, never the stuff of labor and the reproduction of life, let alone the substratum of science. Like the experience of art, the aesthetic experience of nature is that of images. Nature, as appearing beauty, is not perceived as an object of action. The sloughing off of the aims of self-preservation—which is emphatic in art—is carried out to the same degree in aesthetic experience of nature. To this extent the difference between the two forms of beauty is hardly evident. Mediation is no less to be inferred from the relation of art to nature than from the inverse relation. Art is not nature, a belief that idealism hoped to inculcate, but art does want to keep nature's promise. It is capable of this only by breaking that promise; by taking it back into itself. This much is true in Hegel's theorem that art is inspired by negativity, specifically by the deficiency of natural beauty, in the sense that so long as nature is defined only through its antithesis to society, it is not yet what it appears to be. What nature strives for in vain, artworks fulfill: They open their eyes. Once it no longer serves as an object of action, appearing nature itself imparts expression, whether that of melancholy, peace, or something else. Art stands in for nature through its abolition in effigy; all naturalistic art is only deceptively close to nature because, analogous to industry, it relegates nature to raw material. The resistance to empirical reality that the subject marshals in the autonomous work is at the same time resistance to the immediate appearance of nature. For what becomes perceptible in nature no more coincides with empirical reality than does—according to Kant's grandly paradoxical conception—the thing itself with the world of "phenomena," the categorially constituted objects. Just as in early bourgeois times natural beauty originated from the historical progress of art, this progress has since gnawed away at natural beauty; something of this may have been distortedly anticipated in Hegel's depreciation of natural beauty. Rationality that has become aesthetic, a disposition over materials that fits them together according to their own immanent tendencies, is ultimately similar to the natural element in aesthetic comportment. Quasi-rational tendencies in art—the outcome of subjectivization—such as the critical rejection of topoi, the complete internal organization of individual works progressively approximate, though not by imitation, something natural that has been veiled by the mastery of the omnipotent subject; if anywhere, then it is in art that "origin is the goal."[3] That the experience of natural beauty, at least according to its subjective consciousness, is entirely distinct from the domination of nature, as if the experience were at one with the primordial origin, marks out both the strength and the weakness of the experience: its strength, because it recollects a world without domination, one that probably never existed; its weakness, because through this recollection it dissolves back into that amorphousness out of which genius once arose and for the first time became conscious of the idea of freedom that could be realized in a world free from domination. The anamnesis of freedom in natural beauty deceives because it seeks freedom in the old unfreedom. Natural beauty is myth transposed into the imagination and thus, perhaps, requited. The song of birds is found beautiful by everyone; no feeling person in whom something of the European tradition survives fails to be moved by the sound of a robin after a rain shower. Yet something frightening lurks in the song of birds precisely because it is not a song but obeys the spell in which it is enmeshed. The fright appears as well in the threat of migratory flocks, which bespeak ancient divinations, forever presaging ill fortune. With regard to its content, the ambiguity of natural beauty has its origin in mythical ambiguity. This is why genius, once it has become aware of itself, is no longer satisfied with natural beauty. As its prose character intensifies, art extricates itself completely from myth and thus from the spell of nature, which nevertheless continues in the subjective domination of nature. Only what had escaped nature as fate would help nature to its restitution. The more that art is thoroughly organized as an object by the subject and divested of the subject's intentions, the more articulately does it speak according to the model of a nonconceptual, nonrigidified significative language; this would perhaps be the same language that is inscribed in what the sentimental age gave the beautiful if threadbare name, "The Book of Nature." Along the trajectory of its rationality and through it, humanity becomes aware in art of what rationality has erased from memory and of what its second reflection serves to remind us. The vanishing point of this development—admittedly an aspect only of modern art—is the insight that nature, as something beautiful, cannot be copied. For natural beauty as something that appears is itself image. Its portrayal is a tautology that, by objectifying what appears, eliminates it. The hardly esoteric judgment that paintings of the Matterhorn and purple heather are kitsch has a scope reaching far beyond the displayed subject matter: What is innervated in the response is, unequivocally, that natural beauty cannot be copied. The uneasiness this causes flares up only in the face of extreme crudeness, leaving the tasteful zone of nature imitations all the more secure. The green forest of German impressionism is of no higher dignity than those views of the Königssee painted for hotel lobbies. French impressionists, by contrast, knew very well why they so seldom chose pure nature as a subject; why, when they did not turn to artificial subjects like ballerinas and racing jockeys or the dead nature of Sisley's winter scenes, they interspersed their landscapes with emblems of civilization that contributed to the constructive skeletonization of form, as Pissarro did, for example. It is hard to determine the extent to which the intensifying taboo on the replication of nature affects its image. Proust's insight that Renoir transformed the perception of nature not only offers the consolation that the writer imbibed from impressionism, it also implies horror: that the reification of relations between humans would contaminate all experience and literally become absolute. The face of the most beautiful girl becomes ugly by a striking resemblance to the face of a film star on whom it was carefully modeled: Even when nature is experienced as spontaneously individuated, as if it were protected from administration, the deception is predictable. Natural beauty, in the age of its total mediatedness, is transformed into a caricature of itself; not the least of the causes for this is the awe felt for natural beauty, which imposes asceticism on its contemplation for as long as it is overlaid with images of being a commodity. Even in the past the portrayal of nature was probably only authentic as *nature morte*: when painting knew to read nature as the cipher of the historical, if not as that of the transience of everything historical. The Old Testament prohibition on images has an aesthetic as well as a theological dimension. That one should make no image, which means no image *of* anything whatsoever, expresses at the same time that it is impossible to make such an image. Through its duplication in art, what appears in nature is robbed of its being-in-itself, in which the experience of nature is fulfilled. Art holds true to appearing nature only where it makes landscape present in the expression of its own negativity; Borchardt's "Verse bei Betrachtung von Landschaft-Zeichnungen geschrieben" [verses written while contemplating landscape drawings][4] expressed this inimitably and shockingly. Where painting and nature seem happily reconciled—as in Corot—this reconciliation is keyed to the momentary: An everlasting fragrance is a paradox.

Natural beauty, such as it is perceived unmediated in appearing nature, is compromised by the Rousseauian *retournons*. The mistakenness of the crude antithesis of technique and nature is obvious in the fact that precisely nature that has not been pacified by human cultivation, nature over which no human hand has passed—alpine moraines and taluses—resembles those industrial mountains of debris from which the socially lauded aesthetic need for nature flees. Just how industrial it looks in inorganic outer space will someday be clear. Even in its telluric expansion, as the imprint of total technique, the concept of idyllic nature would retain the provincialism of a minuscule island. In schema borrowed from bourgeois sexual morality, technique is said to have ravished nature, yet under transformed relations of production it would just as easily be able to assist nature and on this sad earth help it to attain what perhaps it wants. Consciousness does justice to the experience of nature only when, like impressionist art, it incorporates nature's wounds. The rigid concept of natural beauty thereby becomes dynamic. It is broadened by what is already no longer nature. Otherwise nature is degraded to a deceptive phantasm. The relation of appearing nature to what is inert and thing-like in its deadness is accessible to its aesthetic experience. For in every particular aesthetic experience of nature the social whole is lodged. Society not only provides the schemata of perception but peremptorily determines what nature means through contrast and similarity. Experience of nature is coconstituted by the capacity of determinate negation. With the expansion of technique and, even more important, the total expansion of the exchange principle, natural beauty increasingly fulfills a contrasting function and is thus integrated into the reified world it opposes. Coined in opposition to absolutism's wigs and formal gardens, the concept of natural beauty forfeited its power, because bourgeois emancipation under the sign of the alleged natural rights of human beings made the world of experience not less but more reified than it was in the eighteenth century. The unmediated experience of nature, its critical edge blunted and subsumed to the exchange relation such as is represented in the phrase "tourist industry," became insignificantly neutral and apologetic, and nature became a nature reserve and an alibi. Natural beauty is ideology where it serves to disguise mediatedness as immediacy. Even adequate experience of natural beauty obeys the complementary ideology of the unconscious. If in keeping with bourgeois standards it is chalked up as a special merit that someone has feeling for nature—which is for the most part a moralistic-narcissistic posturing as if to say: What a fine person I must be to enjoy myself with such gratitude—then the very next step is a ready response to such testimonies of impoverished experience as appear in ads in the personal column that claim "sensitivity to everything beautiful." Here the essence of the experience of nature is deformed. There is hardly anything left of it in organized tourism. To feel nature, and most of all its silence, has become a rare privilege and has in turn become commercially exploitable. This, however, does not amount to the condemnation of the category of natural beauty *tout court*. The disinclination to talk about it is strongest where love of it survives. The "How beautiful!" at the sight of a landscape insults its mute language and reduces its beauty; appearing nature wants silence at the same time that anyone capable of its experience feels compelled to speak in order to find a momentary liberation from monado-logical confinement. The image of nature survives because its complete negation in the artifact—negation that rescues this image—is necessarily blind to what exists beyond bourgeois society, its labor, and its commod-ities. Natural beauty remains the allegory of this beyond in spite of its mediation through social immanence. If, however, this allegory were substituted as the achieved state of reconciliation, it would be degraded as an aid for cloaking and legitimating the unreconciled world as one in which—as the claim goes—beauty is indeed possible.

The "Oh how beautiful," which according to a verse of Friedrich Hebbel disturbs the "celebration of nature,"[5] is appropriate to the tense concentra-tion vis-à-vis artworks, not nature. Its beauty is better known through unconscious apperception; in the continuity of such perception natural beauty unfolds, sometimes suddenly. The more intensively one observes nature, the less one is aware of its beauty, unless it was already involun-tarily recognized. Planned visits to famous views, to the landmarks of natural beauty, are mostly futile. Nature's eloquence is damaged by the objectivation that is the result of studied observation, and ultimately something of this holds true as well for artworks, which are only completely perceptible in *temps durée*, the conception of which Bergson probably derived from artistic experience. If nature can in a sense only be seen blindly, the aesthetic imperatives of unconscious apperception and remembrance are at the same time archaic vestiges incompatible with the increasing maturation of reason. Pure immediacy does not suffice for aesthetic experience. Along with the involuntary it requires volition, concentrating consciousness; the contradiction is ineluctable. All beauty reveals itself to persistent analysis, which in turn enriches the element of involuntariness; indeed, analysis would be in vain if the involuntary did not reside hidden within it. In the face of beauty, analytical reflection reconstitutes the *temps durée* through its antithesis. Analysis terminates in beauty just as it ought to appear to complete and self-forgetting unconscious perception. Thus analysis subjectively redescribes the course that the artwork objectively describes within itself: Adequate knowledge of the aesthetic is the spontaneous completion of the objective processes that, by virtue of the tensions of this completion, transpire within it. Genetically, aesthetic comportment may require familiarity with natural beauty in childhood and the later abandonment of its ideological aspect in order to transform it into a relation to artifacts.

As the antithesis of immediacy and convention became more acute and the horizon of aesthetic experience widened to include what Kant called the sublime, natural phenomena overwhelming in their grandeur began to be consciously perceived as beautiful. Historically this attitude of consciousness was ephemeral. Thus Karl Kraus's polemical genius—perhaps in concurrence with the *modern style* of a Peter Altenberg—spurned the cult of grandiose landscapes and certainly took no pleasure in high mountain ranges, which probably prompt undiminished joy only in tourists, whom the culture critic rightly scorned. This skepticism toward natural grandeur clearly originates in the artistic sensorium. As its powers of differentiation develop, it begins to react against the practice in idealist philosophy of equating grand designs and categories with the content of artworks. The confusion of the two has in the meantime become the index of art-alien comportment. Even the abstract magnitude of nature, which Kant still venerated and compared to moral law, is recognized as a reflex of bourgeois megalomania, a preoccupation with setting new records, quantification, and bourgeois hero worship. This critique, however, fails to perceive that natural grandeur reveals another aspect to its beholder: that aspect in which human domination has its limits and that calls to mind the powerlessness of human bustle. This is why Nietzsche in Sils Maria felt himself to be "two thousand meters above sea level, but even higher than that above all things human." These vicissitudes in the experience of natural beauty prohibit the establishment of any apriority of its theory as completely as art does. Whoever wishes to define the conceptual invariants of natural beauty would make himself as ridiculous as Husserl did when he reports that while ambulating he perceived the green freshness of the lawn. Whoever declaims on natural beauty verges on poetastery. Only the pedant presumes to distinguish the beautiful from the ugly in nature, but without such distinction the concept of natural beauty would be empty. Neither categories such as formal magnitude—which is contradicted by the micrological perception of the beautiful in nature, probably its most authentic form—nor the mathematical, symmetrical proportions favored by older aesthetics furnish criteria of natural beauty. According to the canon of universal concepts it is undefinable precisely because its own concept has its substance in what withdraws from universal conceptuality. Its essential indeterminateness is manifest in the fact that every part of nature, as well as everything made by man that has congealed into nature, is able to become beautiful, luminous from within. Such expression has little or nothing to do with formal proportions. At the same time, however, every individual object of nature that is experienced as beautiful presents itself as if it were the only beautiful thing on earth; this is passed on to every artwork. Although what is beautiful and what is not cannot be categorically distinguished in nature, the consciousness that immerses itself lovingly in something beautiful is compelled to make this distinction. A qualitative distinction in natural beauty can be sought, if at all, in the degree to which something not made by human beings is eloquent: in its expression. What is beautiful in nature is what appears to be more than what is literally there. Without receptivity there would be no such objective expression, but it is not reducible to the subject; natural beauty points to the primacy of the object in subjective experience. Natural beauty is perceived both as authoritatively binding and as something incomprehensible that questioningly awaits its solution. Above all else it is this double character of natural beauty that has been conferred on art. Under its optic, art is not the imitation of nature but the imitation of natural beauty. It develops in tandem with the allegorical intention that manifests it without deciphering it; in tandem with meanings that are not objectified as in significative language. The quality of these meanings may be thoroughly historical as in Hölderlin's "Winkel von Hardt" [the shelter at Hardt].[6] In this poem, a stand of trees becomes perceived as beautiful, as more beautiful than the others, because it bears, however vaguely, the mark of a past event; a rock appears for an instant as a primeval animal, while in the next instant the similarity slips away. This is the locus of one dimension of romantic experience that has outlasted romantic philosophy and its mentality. In natural beauty, natural and historical elements interact in a musical and kaleidoscopically changing fashion. Each can step in for the other, and it is in this constant fluctuation, not in any unequivocal order of relationships, that natural beauty lives. It is spectacle in the way that clouds present Shakespearian dramas, or the way the illuminated edges of clouds seem to give duration to lightning flashes. While art does not reproduce those clouds, dramas nonetheless attempt to enact the dramas staged by clouds; in Shakespeare this is touched on in the scene with Hamlet and the courtiers. Natural beauty is suspended history, a moment of becoming at a standstill. Artworks that resonate with this moment of suspension are those that are justly said to have a feeling for nature. Yet this feeling is—in spite of every affinity to allegorical inter-pretation—fleeting to the point of déjà vu and is no doubt all the more compelling for its ephemeralness.

Wilhelm von Humboldt occupies a position between Kant and Hegel in that he holds fast to natural beauty yet in contrast to Kantian formalism endeavors to concretize it. Thus in his writing on the Vasks, which was unfairly overshadowed by Goethe's *Italian Journey*, he presents a critique of nature that, contrary to what would be expected one hundred and fifty years later, has not become ridiculous in spite of its earnestness. Humboldt reproaches a magnificent craggy landscape for the lack of trees. His comment that "the city is well situated, yet it lacks a mountain" makes a mockery of such judgments: Fifty years later the same landscape would probably have seemed delightful. Yet this naïveté, which does not delimit the use of human taste at the boundary of extrahuman nature, attests to a relation to nature that is incomparably deeper than admiration that is content with whatever it beholds. The application of reason to landscape not only presupposes, as is obvious to anyone, the rationalistic-harmo-nistic taste of an epoch that assumes the attunement of even the extrahuman to the human. Beyond that, this attitude of reason to nature is animated throughout by a philosophy of nature that interprets nature as being meaningful in itself, a view Goethe shared with Schelling. This concept of nature, along with the experience of nature that inspired it, is irretrievable. But the critique of nature is not only the hubris of a spirit that has exalted itself as an absolute. It has some basis in the object. As true as the fact that every object in nature can be considered beautiful is the judgment that the landscape of Tuscany is more beautiful than the surroundings of Gelsenkirchen. Surely the waning of natural beauty accompanied the collapse of the philosophy of nature. The latter, however, perished not only as an ingredient of cultural history; the experience that was its substance, as well as the source of happiness in nature, was fundamentally transformed. Natural beauty suffers the same fate as does education: It is vitiated as the inevitable consequence of its expansion. Humboldt's descriptions of nature hold their own in any comparison; his depictions of the wildly turbulent Bay of Biscay occupy a position between Kant's most powerful passages on the sublime and Poe's portrayal of the maelstrom, but they are irretrievably bound up with their historical moment. Solger's and Hegel's judgment, which derived the inferiority of natural beauty from its emerging indeterminacy, missed the mark. Goethe still wanted to distinguish between objects that were worthy of being painted and those that were not; this lured him into glorifying the hunt for motifs as well as veduta painting, a predilection that discomfited even the pompous taste of the editor of the jubilee edition of Goethe's works. Yet because of its concreteness, the classifying narrowness of Goethe's judgments on nature is nevertheless superior to the sophisticated leveling maxim that everything is equally beautiful. Obviously, under the pressure of developments in painting the definition of natural beauty has been transformed. It has been too often remarked with facile cleverness that kitsch paintings have even infected sunsets. Guilt for the evil star that hangs over the theory of natural beauty is borne neither by the corrigible weakness of thought about it nor by the impoverished aim of such thought. It is determined, rather, by the indeterminateness of natural beauty, that of the object no less than that of the concept. As indeterminate, as antithetical to definitions, natural beauty is indefinable, and in this it is related to music, which drew the deepest effects in Schubert from such nonobjective similarity with nature. Just as in music what is beautiful flashes up in nature only to disappear in the instant one tries to grasp it. Art does not imitate nature, not even individual instances of natural beauty, but natural beauty as such. This denominates not only the aporia of natural beauty but the aporia of aesthetics as a whole. Its object is determined negatively, as indeterminable. It is for this reason that art requires philosophy, which interprets it in order to say what it is unable to say, whereas art is only able to say it by not saying it. The paradoxes of aesthetics are dictated to it by its object: "Beauty demands, perhaps, the slavish imitation of what is indeterminable in things."[7] If it is barbaric to say of something in nature that it is more beautiful than something else, the concept of beauty in nature as the concept of something that can be distinguished as such nevertheless bears that barbarism teleologically in itself, whereas the figure of the philistine remains prototypically that of a person who is blind to beauty. The origin of this paradox is the enigmatic character of nature's language. This insufficiency of natural beauty may in fact—in accord with Hegel's theory of aesthetic stages—have played a role in motivating emphatic art. For in art the evanescent is objectified and summoned to duration: To this extent art is concept, though not like a concept in discursive logic. The weakness of thought in the face of natural beauty, a weakness of the subject, together with the objective intensity of natural beauty demand that the enigmatic character of natural beauty be reflected in art and thereby be determined by the concept, although again not as something conceptual in itself. Goethe's "Wanderer's Night Song" is incomparable not because here the subject speaks—as in all authentic works, it is, rather, that the subject wants to fall silent by way of the work—but because through its language the poem imitates what is unutterable in the language of nature. No more should be meant by the ideal of form and content coinciding in a poem, if the ideal itself is to be more than a hollow phrase.

Natural beauty is the trace of the nonidentical in things under the spell of universal identity. As long as this spell prevails, the nonidentical has no positive existence. Therefore natural beauty remains as dispersed and uncertain as what it promises, that which surpasses all human immanence. The pain in the face of beauty, nowhere more visceral than in the experience of nature, is as much the longing for what beauty promises but never unveils as it is suffering at the inadequacy of the appearance, which fails beauty while wanting to make itself like it. This pain reappears in the relation to artworks. Involuntarily and unconsciously, the observer enters into a contract with the work, agreeing to submit to it on condition that it speak. In the pledged receptivity of the observer, pure self-abandonment —that moment of free exhalation in nature—survives. Natural beauty shares the weakness of every promise with that promise's inextinguishability. However words may glance off nature and betray its language to one that is qualitatively different from its own, still no critique of natural teleology can dismiss those cloudless days of southern lands that seem to be waiting to be noticed. As they draw to a close with the same radiance and peacefulness with which they began, they emanate that everything is not lost, that things may yet turn out: "Death, sit down on the bed, and you hearts, listen carefully: / An old man points into the glimmering light / Under the fringe of dawn's first blue: / In the name of God and the unborn, / I promise you: / World, never mind your woes, / All is still yours, for the day starts anew!"[8] The image of what is oldest in nature reverses dialectically into the cipher of the not-yet-existing, the possible: As its appearance this cipher is more than the existing; but already in reflecting on it this almost does it an injustice. Any claim that this is how nature speaks cannot be judged with assurance, for its language does not make judgments; but neither is nature's language merely the deceptive consolation that longing reflects back to itself. In its uncertainty, natural beauty inherits the ambiguity of myth, while at the same time its echo—consolation—distances itself from myth in appearing nature. Contrary to that philosopher of identity, Hegel, natural beauty is close to the truth but veils itself at the moment of greatest proximity. This, too, art learned from natural beauty. The boundary established against fetishism of nature—the pantheistic subterfuge that would amount to nothing but an affirmative mask appended to an endlessly repetitive fate—is drawn by the fact that nature, as it stirs mortally and tenderly in its beauty, does not yet exist. The shame felt in the face of natural beauty stems from the damage implicitly done to what does not yet exist by taking it for existent. The dignity of nature is that of the not-yet-existing; by its expression it repels intentional humanization. This dignity has been transformed into the hermetic character of art, into—as Hölderlin taught—art's renunciation of any usefulness whatever, even if it were sublimated by the addition of human meaning. For communication is the adaptation of spirit to utility, with the result that spirit is made one commodity among the rest; and what today is called meaning participates in this disaster. What in artworks is structured, gapless, resting in itself, is an after-image of the silence that is the single medium through which nature speaks. Vis-à-vis a ruling principle, vis-à-vis a merely diffuse juxtaposition, the beauty of nature is an other; what is reconciled would resemble it.

Hegel makes the transition to art beauty from natural beauty, whose necessity he initially concedes: "Now, as the physically objective idea, life that animates nature is *beautiful* in that as life the true, the idea, is immediately present in individual and adequate actuality in its first natural form."[9] This thesis, which begins by casting natural beauty as more impoverished than it is, presents a paradigm of discursive aesthetics: It is deduced from the identification of the real with the rational, or more specifically, from the definition of nature as the idea in its otherness. The idea is credited, condescendingly, to natural beauty's account. The beauty of nature unfolds from Hegel's theodicy of the real: Because the idea can take no other form than that in which it is realized, its first appearance or "first natural form" is "suitable" and therefore beautiful. This concept of natural beauty is immediately circumscribed dialectically; the concept of nature as spirit is taken no further because—probably with a polemical eye toward Schelling—nature is to be understood as spirit in its otherness, not directly reducible to that spirit. There is no mistaking the progress of critical consciousness here. The Hegelian movement of the concept seeks truth —which cannot be stated immediately—in the naming of the particular and the limited: of the dead and the false. This provides for the disappearance of natural beauty when it has scarcely been introduced: "Yet, because of this purely physical immediacy, the living beauty of nature is produced neither *for* nor *out* of *itself* as *beautiful*, nor for the sake of a beautiful appearance. The beauty of nature is beautiful only for another, i.e., for *us*, for the mind which apprehends beauty."[10] Thus the essence of natural beauty, the anamnesis of precisely what does not exist foran-other, is let slip. This critique of natural beauty follows an inner tendency of Hegel's aesthetics as a whole, follows its objectivistic turn against the contingence of subjective sentiment. Precisely the beautiful, which presents itself as independent from the subject, as absolutely something not made, falls under suspicion of being feebly subjective; Hegel equates this directly with the indeterminacy of natural beauty. Throughout, Hegel's aesthetics lacks receptivity for the speech of what is not significative; the same is true of his theory of language.[11] It can be argued immanently against Hegel that his own definition of nature as spirit in its otherness not only contrasts spirit with nature but also binds them together without, however, the binding element being investigated in his system's *Aesthetics* or *Philosophy of Nature*. Hegel's objective idealism becomes crass virtually unreflected partisanship for subjective spirit in the *Aesthetics*. What is true in this is that natural beauty, the unexpected promise of something that is highest, cannot remain locked in itself but is rescued only through that consciousness that is set in opposition to it. What Hegel validly opposes to natural beauty is of a part with his critique of aesthetic formalism and thus of a playful eighteenth-century hedonism that was anathema to the emancipated bourgeois spirit. "The form of natural beauty, as an abstract form, is on the one hand determinate and therefore restricted; on the other hand it contains a unity and an abstract relation to itself . . . This sort of form is what is called regularity and symmetry, also conformity to law, and finally harmony."[12] Hegel elsewhere speaks in sympathy with the advances of dissonance, though he is deaf to how much it has its locus in natural beauty. In pursuit of this intention of dissonance, aesthetic theory at its apex, in Hegel, took the lead over art; only as neutralized sanctimonious wisdom did it, after Hegel, fall behind art. In Hegel, the formal, "mathematical" relations that once supposedly grounded natural beauty are contrasted with living spirit and rejected as subaltern and pedestrian: The beauty of regularity is "a beauty of abstract understanding."[13] His disdain for rationalistic aesthetics, however, clouds his vision for what in nature slips through the conceptual net of this aesthetics. The concept of the subaltern occurs literally in the passage of natural beauty to art beauty: "Now this essential deficiency [of natural beauty] leads us to the necessity of the Ideal, which is not to be found in nature, and in comparison with it the beauty of nature appears subordinate."[14] Natural beauty, however, is subordinate not in itself but for those who prize it. To whatever degree the determinacy of art surpasses that of nature, the exemplar of art is provided by what nature expresses and not by the spirit with which men endow nature. The concept of a posited ideal, one that art should follow, and one that is "purified," is external to art. The idealist disdain for what is not spirit in nature takes vengeance on what in art is more than subjective spirit. The timeless ideal becomes hollow plaster; in the history of German literature the most obvious evidence for this is the fate of Hebbel's dramatic works, which share much with Hegel. Hegel deduces art rationalistically enough, strangely ignoring its historical genesis, from the insufficiency of nature: "Thus it is from the deficiencies of immediate reality that the necessity of the beauty of art is derived. The task of art must therefore be firmly established in art's having a calling to display the appearance of life, and especially of spiritual animation (in its freedom, externally too) and to make the external correspond with its concept. Only so is the truth lifted out of its temporal setting, out of its straying away into a series of finites. At the same time it has won an external appearance through which the poverty of nature and prose no longer peeps; it has won an existence worthy of truth."[15] The inner thread of Hegel's philosophy is revealed in this passage: Natural beauty gains legitimacy only by its decline, in such a way that its deficiency becomes the raison d'être of art beauty. At the same time natural beauty is subsumed on the basis of its "calling" to a purpose, and a transfiguring affirmative purpose at that, in obedience to a bourgeois topos dating back at least to d'Alembert and Saint-Simon. What Hegel chalks up as the deficiency of natural beauty—the characteristic of escaping from fixed concept—is however the substance of beauty itself. In Hegel's transition from nature to art, on the other hand, the much touted polysignificance of *Aufhebung* is nowhere to be found. Natural beauty flickers out without a trace of it being recognizable in art beauty. Because natural beauty is not thoroughly ruled and defined by spirit, Hegel considers it preaesthetic. But the imperious spirit is an instrument, not the content, of art. Hegel calls natural beauty prosaic. This phrase, which designates the asymmetry that Hegel overlooks in natural beauty, is at the same time unable to comprehend the development of more recent art, every aspect of which could be viewed as the infiltration of prose into formal principles. Prose is the ineradicable reflex of the disenchantment of the world in art, and not just its adaptation to narrow-minded usefulness. Whatever balks at prose becomes the prey of an arbitrarily decreed stylization. In Hegel's age the vector of this development could not yet be completely foreseen; it is in no way identical with realism, but rather is related to autonomous procedures that are free of any relation to representational realism and to topoi. In this regard Hegel's *Aesthetics* is reactionary in classicist fashion. In Kant the classicist conception of beauty was compatible with the conception of natural beauty; Hegel sacrifices natural beauty to subjective spirit, but subordinates that spirit to a classicism that is external to and incompatible with it, perhaps out of fear of a dialectic that even in the face of the idea of beauty would not come to a halt. Hegel's critique of Kant's formalism ought to have valorized nonformal concreteness. This critique was not, however, within Hegel's purview; it is perhaps for this reason that he confused the material elements of art with its representational content [*Inhalt*]. By rejecting the fleetingness of natural beauty, as well as virtually everything non-conceptual, Hegel obtusely makes himself indifferent to the central motif of art, which probes after truth in the evanescent and fragile. Hegel's philosophy fails vis-à-vis beauty: Because he equates reason and the real through the quintessence of their mediations, he hypostatizes the subjective preformation of the existing as the absolute; thus for him the nonidentical only figures as a restraint on subjectivity rather than that he determines the experience of the nonidentical as the telos and emancipation of the aesthetic subject. Progressive dialectical aesthetics becomes necessary to critique even Hegel's aesthetics.

The transition from natural beauty to art beauty is dialectical as a transition in the form of domination. Art beauty is what is objectively mastered in an image and which by virtue of its objectivity transcends domination. Artworks wrest themselves from domination by transforming the aesthetic attitude, shaped by the experience of natural beauty, into a type of productive labor modeled on material labor. As a human language that is both organizing as well as reconciled, art wants once again to attain what has become opaque to humans in the language of nature. Artworks have this much in common with idealist philosophy: They locate reconciliation in identity with the subject; in this respect idealist philosophy—as is explicit in Schelling—actually has art as its model, rather than the reverse. Artworks extend the realm of human domination to the extreme, not literally, though, but rather by the strength of the establishment of a sphere existing for itself, which just through its posited immanence divides itself from real domination and thus negates the heteronomy of domination. Only through their polar opposition, not through the pseudomorphosis of art into nature, are nature and art mediated in each other. The more strictly artworks abstain from rank natural growth and the replication of nature, the more the successful ones approach nature. Aesthetic objectivity, the reflection of the being-in-itself of nature, realizes the subjective teleological element of unity; exclusively thereby do artworks become comparable to nature. In contrast, all particular similarity of art to nature is accidental, inert, and for the most part foreign to art. The feeling of an artwork's necessity is synonymous with this objectivity. As Benjamin showed, the concept of necessity has generally been mishandled by historians of ideas. By dubbing it necessary, they try to understand or to legitimate historical material to which there is otherwise no relation, as for instance in the praise of a piece of dull music as a necessary preliminary stage to great music. The proof of such necessity can never be adduced; neither in the particular work nor in the historical relation of artworks and styles to each other is there any transparent lawfulness such as that established by the natural sciences, and as regards psychological necessity the situation is no better. The necessity of art cannot be propounded *more scientifico* but rather only insofar as a work, by the power of its internal unity, gives evidence of being thus-and-only-thus,[16] as if it absolutely must exist and cannot possibly be thought away. The being-in-itself to which artworks are devoted is not the imitation of something real but rather the anticipation of a being-in-itself that does not yet exist, of an unknown that—by way of the subject—is self-determining. Artworks say that something exists in itself, without predicating anything about it. In fact, the spiritualization that art has undergone during the past two hundred years and through which it has come to maturity has not alienated art from nature, as is the opinion of reified consciousness; rather, in terms of its own form, art has converged with natural beauty. A theory of art that, in conformity with subjective reason, simplistically identifies the tendency of art to subjectivization with the development of scientific reason, omits for the benefit of plausibility the content [*Gehalt*] and direction of artistic development. With human means art wants to realize the language of what is not human. The pure expression of artworks, freed from every thing-like interference, even from everything so-called natural, converges with nature just as in Webern's most authentic works the pure tone, to which they are reduced by the strength of subjective sensibility, reverses dialectically into a natural sound: that of an eloquent nature, certainly, its language, not the portrayal of a part of nature. The total subjective elaboration of art as a nonconceptual language is the only figure, at the contemporary stage of rationality, in which something like the language of divine creation is reflected, qualified by the paradox that what is reflected is blocked. Art attempts to imitate an expression that would not be interpolated human intention. The latter is exclusively art's vehicle. The more perfect the artwork, the more it forsakes intentions. Mediate nature, the truth content of art, takes shape, immediately, as the opposite of nature. If the language of nature is mute, art seeks to make this muteness eloquent; art thus exposes itself to failure through the insurmountable contradiction between the idea of making the mute eloquent, which demands a desperate effort, and the idea of what this effort would amount to, the idea of what cannot in any way be willed.

Notes

1 Immanuel Kant, *Critique of Judgment*, trans. Werner S. Pluhar (Indianapolis, 1987), p. 300.

2 Ibid., pp. 300–301.

3 [Karl Kraus's maxim, which became a motto both for Benjamin and Adorno.—trans.]

4 See Rudolf Borchardt, *Gedichte*, ed. M. L. Borchardt and H. Steiner (Stuttgart, 1957), pp. 113ff.

5 Friedrich Hebbel, "Herbstbild," in *Werke in zwei Bänden*, ed. G. Fricke (Munich, 1952), vol. 1, p. 12.

6 See Friedrich Hölderlin, "Winkel von Hardt," from *Gedichte nach 1800*, in *Sämtliche Werke*, vol. 2, ed. F. Beißner (Stuttgart, 1953), p. 120. [Adorno discusses this poem in detail in "Parataxis: On Hölderlin's Late Poetry," in *Notes to Literature*, trans. Shierry Weber Nicholsen (New York, 1992), pp. 111–112.—trans.]

7 Paul Valéry, *Windstriche: Aufzeichnungen und Aphorismen*, trans. B. Böschenstein et al. (Wiesbaden, 1959), p. 94. [Originally published in *OEuvres*, vol. 2 (Paris, 1957), p. 681.—trans.]

8 Rudolf Borchardt, "Tagelied," ["Tod, sitz aufs Bett, und Herzen, horcht hinaus: / Ein alter Mann zeigt in den schwachen Schein / Unterm Rand des ersten Blaus: / Für Gott, den Ungebornen, stehe / Ich euch ein: / Welt, und sei dir noch so wehe, / Es kehrt von Anfang, alles ist noch dein!"—trans.]

9 Georg Wilhelm Friedrich Hegel, *Aesthetics*, trans. T. M. Knox, vol. 1 (Oxford, 1975), p. 123. [Translation amended.—trans.]

10 Ibid.

11 See Adorno, *Hegel: Three Studies*, trans. Shierry Weber (Boston, 1993), pp. 89ff.

12 Hegel, *Aesthetics*, vol. 1, p. 134.
13 Ibid.
14 Ibid., p. 142.
15 Ibid., p. 152.
16 ["Sosein" is the German translation of the Latin "quiddity," the whatness, or essence of an object as opposed to its existence. In Adorno's work, however, "Sosein" becomes the equivalent of Beckett's "Comment c'est".—trans.]

5

Art beauty: Apparition, spiritualization, intuitability

Nature is beautiful in that it appears to say more than it is. To wrest this more from that more's contingency, to gain control of its semblance, to determine it as semblance as well as to negate it as unreal: This is the idea of art. This artifactual more does not in itself guarantee the metaphysical substance of art. That substance could be totally null, and still the artworks could posit a more as what appears. Artworks become artworks in the production of this more; they produce their own transcendence, rather than being its arena, and thereby they once again become separated from transcendence. The actual arena of transcendence in artworks is the nexus of their elements. By straining toward, as well as adapting to, this nexus, they go beyond the appearance that they are, though this transcendence may be unreal. Only in the achievement of this transcendence, not foremost and indeed probably never through meanings, are artworks spiritual. Their transcendence is their eloquence, their script, but it is a script without meaning or, more precisely, a script with broken or veiled meaning. Although this transcendence is subjectively mediated, it is manifested objectively, yet all the more desultorily. Art fails its concept when it does not achieve this transcendence; it loses the quality of being art. Equally, however, art betrays transcendence when it seeks to produce it as an effect. This implies an essential criterion of new art. Compositions fail as background music or as the mere presentation of material, just as those paintings fail in which the geometrical patterns to which they are reducible remain factually what they are; this is the reason for the relevance of divergences from mathematical forms in all those works that employ them. The striven-for shudder comes to nothing: It does not occur.

One of the paradoxes of artworks is that what they posit they are actually not permitted to posit; this is the measure of their substantiality.

The more cannot be adequately described by the psychological definition of a gestalt, according to which a whole is more than its parts. For the more is not simply the nexus of the elements, but an other, mediated through this nexus and yet divided from it. The artistic elements suggest through their nexus what escapes it. Here one comes up against an antinomy of the philosophy of history. In his treatment of the theme of aura—a concept closely related to the concept of the appearance that by virtue of its internal unity points beyond itself—Benjamin showed that, beginning with Baudelaire, aura in the sense of "atmosphere" is taboo;[1] already in Baudelaire the transcendence of the artistic appearance is at once effected and negated. From this perspective, the deaestheticization of art is not only a stage of art's liquidation but also the direction of its development. All the same, the socialized rebellion since Baudelaire against aura and atmosphere has not meant the simple disappearance of the crackling noise in which the more of the phenomenon announces itself in opposition to this phenomenon. One need only compare good poems by Brecht that are styled as protocol sentences with bad poems by authors whose rebellion against being poetic recoils into the preaesthetic. In Brecht's disenchanted poetry what is fundamentally distinct from what is simplistically stated constitutes the works' eminent rank. Erich Kahler may have been the first to recognize this; and it is best confirmed by the poem "Two Cranes."[2] Aesthetic transcendence and disenchantment converge in the moment of falling mute: in Beckett's oeuvre. A language remote from all meaning is not a speaking language and this is its affinity to muteness. Perhaps all expression, which is most akin to transcendence, is as close to falling mute as in great new music nothing is so full of expression as what flickers out—that tone that disengages itself starkly from the dense musical texture—where art by virtue of its own movement converges with its natural element.

The instant of expression in artworks is however not their reduction to the level of their materials as to something unmediated; rather, this instant is fully mediated. Artworks become appearances, in the pregnant sense of the term—that is, as the appearance of an other—when the accent falls on the unreality of their own reality. Artworks have the immanent character of being an act, even if they are carved in stone, and this endows them with the quality of being something momentary and sudden. This is registered by the feeling of being overwhelmed when faced with an important work. This immanent character of being an act establishes the similarity of all artworks, like that of natural beauty, to music, a similarity once evoked by the term muse. Under patient contemplation artworks begin to move. To this extent they are truly afterimages of the primordial shudder in the age of reification; the terror of that age is recapitulated vis-à-vis reified objects. The deeper the χωρισμός between the circumscribed, particular things and the paling essence, the more hollowly artworks gaze, the sole anamnesis of what could exist beyond the χωρισμός. Because the shudder is past and yet survives, artworks objectivate it as its afterimage. For if at one time human beings in their powerlessness against nature feared the shudder as something real, the fear is no less intense, no less justified, that the shudder will dissipate. All enlightenment is accompanied by the anxiety that what set enlightenment in motion in the first place and what enlightenment ever threatens to consume may disappear: truth. Thrown back on itself, enlightenment distances itself from that guileless objectivity that it would like to achieve; that is why, under the compulsion of its own ideal of truth, it is conjoined with the pressure to hold on to what it has condemned in the name of truth. Art is this mnemosyne. The instant of appearance in artworks is indeed the paradoxical unity or the balance between the vanishing and the preserved. Artworks are static as much as they are dynamic; art genres that fall below approved culture, such as circus tableaux and revues and probably mechanisms such as the water fountains of the seventeenth century, confess to what authentic[3] artworks conceal in themselves as their secret apriori. Artworks remain enlightened because they would like to make commensurable to human beings the remembered shudder, which was incommensurable in the magical primordial world. This is touched upon by Hegel's formulation of art as the effort to do away with foreignness.[4] In the artifact the shudder is freed from the mythical deception of its being-in-itself, without however the work's being reduced to subjective spirit. The increasing autonomy of artworks, their objectivation by human beings, presents the shudder as something unmollified and unprecedented. The act of alienation in this objectivation, which each artwork carries out, is corrective. Artworks are neutralized and thus qualitatively transformed epiphanies. If the deities of antiquity were said to appear fleetingly at their cult sites, or at least were to have appeared there in the primeval age, this act of appearing became the law of the permanence of artworks, but at the price of the living incarnation of what appears. The artwork as appearance is most closely resembled by the *apparition*,[5] the heavenly vision. Artworks stand tacitly in accord with it as it rises above human beings and is carried beyond their intentions and the world of things. Artworks from which the *apparition* has been driven out without a trace are nothing more than husks, worse than what merely exists, because they are not even useful. Artworks are nowhere more reminiscent of mana than in their extreme opposition to it, in the subjectively posited construction of ineluctability. That instant—which is what artworks are—crystallized, at least in traditional works, at the point where out of their particular elements they became a totality. The pregnant moment[6] of their objectivation is the moment that concentrates them as appearance, which is by no means just the expressive elements that are dispersed over the artworks. Artworks surpass the world of things by what is thing-like in them, their artificial objectivation. They become eloquent by the force of the kindling of thing and appearance. They are things whose power it is to appear. Their immanent process is externalized as their own act, not as what humans have done to them and not merely for humans.

The phenomenon of fireworks is prototypical for artworks, though because of its fleetingness and status as empty entertainment it has scarcely been acknowledged by theoretical consideration; only Valéry pursued ideas that are at least related. Fireworks are apparition κατ ἐξοχήν: They appear empirically yet are liberated from the burden of the empirical, which is the obligation of duration; they are a sign from heaven yet artifactual, an ominous warning, a script that flashes up, vanishes, and indeed cannot be read for its meaning. The segregation of the aesthetic sphere by means of the complete afunctionality of what is thoroughly ephemeral is no formal definition of aesthetics. It is not through a higher perfection that artworks separate from the fallibly existent but rather by becoming actual, like fireworks, incandescently in an expressive appearance. They are not only the other of the empirical world: Everything in them becomes other. It is this to which the preartistic consciousness of artworks responds most intensely. This consciousness submits to the temptation that first led to art and that mediates between art and the empirical. Although the preartistic dimension becomes poisoned by its exploitation, to the point that artworks must eliminate it, it survives sublimated in them. It is not so much that artworks possess ideality as that by virtue of their spiritualization they promise a blocked or denied sensuality. That quality can be comprehended in those phenomena from which artistic experience emancipated itself, in the relics of an art-alien art, as it were, the justly or unjustly so-called lower arts such as the circus, to which in France the cubist painters and their theoreticians turned, and to which in Germany Wedekind turned. What Wedekind called "corporeal art" has not only remained beneath spiritualized art, not only remained just its complement: In its intentionlessness, however, it is the archetype of spiritualized art. By its mere existence, every artwork, as alien artwork to what is alienated, conjures up the circus and yet is lost as soon as it emulates it. Art becomes an image not directly by becoming an *apparition* but only through the counter-tendency to it. The preartistic level of art is at the same time the memento of its anticultural character, its suspicion of its antithesis to the empirical world that leaves this world untouched. Important artworks nevertheless seek to incorporate this art-alien layer. When, suspected of being infantile, it is absent from art, when the last trace of the vagrant fiddler disappears from the spiritual chamber musician and the illusionless drama has lost the magic of the stage, art has capitulated. The curtain lifts expectantly even at the beginning of Beckett's *Endgame*; plays and stagings that eliminate the curtain fumble with a shallow trick. The instant the curtain goes up is the expectation of the *apparition*. If Beckett's plays, as crepuscularly grey as after sunset and the end of the world, want to exorcise circus colors, they yet remain true to them in that the plays are indeed performed on stage and it is well known how much their antiheros were inspired by clowns and slapstick cinema. Despite their *austerity* they in no way fully renounce costumes and sets: The servant Clov, who wishes in vain to break out, wears the laughably outmoded costume of a traveling Englishman; and the sandhill of *Happy Days* bears a similarity to geological formations of the American West; in general, the question remains whether in their material and visual organization even the most abstract paintings do not bear elements of a representationality that they hope to remove from circulation. Even artworks that incorruptibly refuse celebration and consolation do not wipe out radiance, and the greater their success, the more they gain it. Today this luster devolves precisely upon works that are inconsolable. Their distance from any purpose sympathizes, as from across the abyss of ages, with the superfluous vagrant who will not completely acquiesce to fixed property and settled civilization. Not least among the contemporary difficulties of art is that artworks are ashamed of *apparition*, though they are unable to shed it; no longer substantial in the Hegelian sense, having become self-transparent right into their constitutive semblance, which artworks find untrue in its transparentness, this transparentness gnaws away at their possibility.

An inane Wilhelmian army joke tells of an orderly who one fine Sunday morning is sent by his superior to the zoo. He returns very worked up and declares: "Lieutenant! Animals like that do not exist!" This form of reaction is as requisite of aesthetic experience as it is alien to art. Artworks are eliminated along with the youthful θαυμάζειν; Klee's *Angelus Novus* arouses this astonishment much as do the semihuman creatures of Indian mythology. In each genuine artwork something appears that does not exist. It is not dreamt up out of disparate elements of the existing. Out of these elements artworks arrange constellations that become ciphers, without, however, like fantasies, setting up the enciphered before the eyes as something immediately existing. The encipherment of the artwork, one facet of its *apparition*, is thus distinct from natural beauty in that while it too refuses the univocity of judgment, nevertheless in its own form, in the way in which it turns toward the hidden, the artwork achieves a greater determinacy. Artworks thus vie with the syntheses of significative thinking, their irreconcilable enemy.

The appearance of the nonexistent as if it existed motivates the question as to the truth of art. By its form alone art promises what is not; it registers objectively, however refractedly, the claim that because the nonexistent appears it must indeed be possible. The unstillable longing in the face of beauty, for which Plato found words fresh with its first experience, is the longing for the fulfillment of what was promised. Idealist aesthetics fails by its inability to do justice to art's *promesse du bonheur*. It reduces the artwork to what it in theoretical terms symbolizes and thus trespasses against the spirit in that artwork. What spirit promises, not the sensual pleasure of the observer, is the locus of the sensual element in art.——Romanticism wanted to equate what appears in the *apparition* with the artistic. In doing so, it grasped something essential about art, yet narrowed it to a particular, to the praise of a specific and putatively inwardly infinite comportment of art; in this, romanticism imagined that through reflection and thematic content it could grasp art's ether, whereas it is irresistible precisely because it refuses to let itself be nailed down either as an entity or as a universal concept. Its ether is bound up with particularization; it epitomizes the unsubsumable and as such challenges the prevailing principle of reality: that of exchangeability. What appears is not interchangeable because it does not remain a dull particular for which other particulars could be substituted, nor is it an empty universal that equates everything specific that it comprehends by abstracting the common characteristics. If in empirical reality everything has become fungible, art holds up to the world of everything-for-something-else images of what it itself would be if it were emancipated from the schemata of imposed identification. Yet art plays over into ideology in that, as the image of what is beyond exchange, it suggests that not everything in the world is exchangeable. On behalf of what cannot be exchanged, art must through its form bring the exchangeable to critical self-consciousness. The telos of artworks is a language whose words cannot be located on the spectrum; a language whose words are not imprisoned by a prestabilized universality. An important suspense novel by Leo Perutz concerns the color "drommet red";[7] subartistic genres such as *science fiction* credulously and therefore powerlessly make a fetish of such themes. Although the nonexisting emerges suddenly in artworks, they do not lay hold of it bodily as with the pass of a magic wand. The nonexisting is mediated to them through fragments of the existing, which they assemble into an *apparition*. It is not for art to decide by its existence if the nonexisting that appears indeed exists as something appearing or remains semblance. As figures of the existing, unable to summon into existence the nonexisting, artworks draw their authority from the reflection they compel on how they could be the overwhelming image of the nonexisting if it did not exist in itself. Precisely Plato's ontology, more congenial to positivism than dialectic is, took offense at art's semblance character, as if the promise made by art awakened doubt in the positive omnipresence of being and idea, for which Plato hoped to find surety in the concept. If the Platonic ideas were existence-in-itself, art would not be needed; the ontologists of antiquity mistrusted art and sought pragmatic control over it because in their innermost being they knew that the hypostatized universal concept is not what beauty promises. Plato's critique of art is indeed not compelling, because art negates the literal reality of its thematic content, which Plato had indicted as a lie. The exaltation of the concept as idea is allied with the philistine blindness for the central element of art, its form. In spite of all this, however, the blemish of mendacity obviously cannot be rubbed off art; nothing guarantees that it will keep its objective promise. Therefore every theory of art must at the same time be the critique of art. Even radical art is a lie insofar as it fails to create the possible to which it gives rise as semblance. Artworks draw credit from a praxis that has yet to begin and no one knows whether anything backs their letters of credit.

Artworks are images as *apparition*, as appearance, and not as a copy. If through the demythologization of the world consciousness freed itself from the ancient shudder, that shudder is permanently reproduced in the historical antagonism of subject and object. The object became as incommensurable to experience, as foreign and frightening, as mana once was. This permeates the image character. It manifests foreignness at the same time that it seeks to make experiential what is thing-like and foreign. For artworks it is incumbent to grasp the universal—which dictates the nexus of the existing and is hidden by the existing—in the particular; it is not for art, through particularization, to disguise the ruling universality of the administered world. Totality is the grotesque heir of mana. The image character of artworks passed over into totality, which appears more truly in the individual than in the syntheses of singularities. By its relation to what in the constitution of reality is not directly accessible to discursive conceptualization and none the less objective, art in the age of enlightenment holds true to enlightenment while provoking it. What appears in art is no longer the ideal, no longer harmony; the locus of its power of resolution is now exclusively in the contradictory and dissonant. Enlightenment was always also the consciousness of the vanishing of what it wanted to seize without any residue of mystery; by penetrating the vanishing—the shudder—enlightenment not only is its critique but salvages it according to the measure of what provokes the shudder in reality itself. This paradox is appropriated by artworks. If it holds true that the subjective rationality of means and ends—which is particular and thus in its innermost irrational—requires spurious irrational enclaves and treats art as such, art is nevertheless the truth of society insofar as in its most authentic products the irrationality of the rational world order is expressed. In art, denunciation and anticipation are syncopated. If *apparition* illuminates and touches, the image is the paradoxical effort to transfix this most evanescent instant. In art something momentary transcends; objectivation makes the artwork into an instant. Pertinent here is Benjamin's formulation of a dialectic at a standstill, which he developed in the context of his conception of a dialectical image. If, as images, artworks are the persistence of the transient, they are concentrated in appearance as something momentary. To experience art means to become conscious of its immanent process as an instant at a standstill; this may perhaps have nourished the central concept of Lessing's aesthetics, that of the "pregnant moment."

Artworks not only produce *imagines* as something that endures. They become artworks just as much through the destruction of their own *imagerie*; for this reason art is profoundly akin to explosion. When in Wedekind's *Spring Awakening* Moritz Stiefel shoots himself dead with a water pistol and the curtain falls as he says: "Now I won't ever be going home again,"[8] in this instant, as dusk settles over the city in the far distance, the unspeakable melancholy of the river landscape is expressed. Not only are artworks allegories, they are the catastrophic fulfillment of allegories. The shocks inflicted by the most recent artworks are the explosion of their appearance. In them appearance, previously a self-evident apriori of art, dissolves in a catastrophe in which the essence of appearance is for the first time fully revealed: and nowhere perhaps more unequivocally than in Wols's paintings.[9] Even this volatilization of aesthetic transcendence becomes aesthetic, a measure of the degree to which artworks are mythically bound up with their antithesis. In the incineration of appearance, artworks break away in a glare from the empirical world and become the counterfigure of what lives there; art today is scarcely conceivable except as a form of reaction that anticipates the apocalypse. Closely observed, even tranquil works discharge not so much the pent-up emotions of their makers as the works' own inwardly antagonistic forces. The result of these forces is bound up with the impossibility of bringing these forces to any equilibrium; their antinomies, like those of knowledge, are unsolvable in the unreconciled world. The instant in which these forces become image, the instant in which what is interior becomes exterior, the outer husk is exploded; their *apparition*, which makes them an image, always at the same time destroys them as image. In Benjamin's interpretation, Baudelaire's fable of the man who lost his aureole describes not just the demise of aura but aura itself; if artworks shine, the objectivation of aura is the path by which it perishes. As a result of its determination as appearance, art bears its own negation embedded in itself as its own telos; the sudden unfolding of appearance disclaims aesthetic semblance. Appearance, however, and its explosion in the artwork are essentially historical. The artwork in itself is not, as historicism would have it—as if its history accords simply with its position in real history—Being absolved from Becoming. Rather, as something that exists, the artwork has its own development. What appears in the artwork is its own inner time; the explosion of appearance blasts open the continuity of this inner temporality. The artwork is mediated to real history by its monadological nucleus. History is the content of artworks. To analyze artworks means no less than to become conscious of the history immanently sedimented in them.

The image character of works, at least in traditional art, is probably a function of the "pregnant moment." This could be illustrated by Beethoven's symphonies and above all in many of his sonata movements.

Movement at a standstill is eternalized in the instant, and what has been made eternal is annihilated by its reduction to the instant. This marks the sharp difference of the image character of art from how Klages and Jung conceived it: If, after the separation of knowledge into image and sign, thought simply equates the image with truth, the untruth of the schism is in no way corrected but made all the worse, for the image is no less affected by the schism than is the concept. Aesthetic images are no more translatable into concepts than they are "real"; there is no *imago* without the imaginary; their reality is their historical content, and the images themselves, including the historical images, are not to be hypostatized.—
—Aesthetic images are not fixed, archaic invariants: Artworks become images in that the processes that have congealed in them as objectivity become eloquent. Bourgeois art-religion of Diltheyian provenance confuses the *imagerie* of art with its opposite: with the artist's psychological repository of representations. But this repository is itself an element of the raw material forged into the artwork. The latent processes in artworks, which break through in the instant, are their inner historicity, sedimented external history. The binding character of their objectivation as well as the experiences from which they live are collective. The language of artworks is, like every language, constituted by a collective undercurrent, especially in the case of those works popularly stigmatized as lonely and walled up in the ivory tower; the eloquence of their collective substance originates in their image character and not in the "testimony"—as the cliché goes—that they supposedly wish to express directly to the collective. The specifically artistic achievement is an overarching binding character to be ensnared not thematically or by the manipulation of effects but rather by presenting what is beyond the monad through immersion in the experiences that are fundamental to this bindingness. The result of the work is as much the trajectory it traverses to its *imago* as it is the *imago* itself as the goal; it is at once static and dynamic. Subjective experience contributes images that are not images *of* something, and precisely they are essentially collective; thus and in no other way is art mediated to experience. By virtue of this experiential content,[10] and not primarily as a result of fixation or forming as they are usually conceived, artworks diverge from empirical reality: empiria through empirical deformation. This is the affinity of artworks to the dream, however far removed they are from dreams by their law of form. This means nothing less than that the subjective element of artworks is mediated by their being-in-themselves. The latent collectivity of this subjectivity frees the monadological artwork from the accidentalness of its

individuation. Society, the determinant of experience, constitutes artworks as their true subject; this is the needed response to the current reproach of subjectivism raised to art by both left and right. At every aesthetic level the antagonism between the unreality of the *imago* and the reality of the appearing historical content is renewed. The aesthetic images, however, emancipate themselves from mythical images by subordinating themselves to their own unreality; that is what the law of form means. This is the artworks' methexis in enlightenment. The view of art as politically engaged or didactic regresses back of this stage of enlightenment. Unconcerned with the reality of aesthetic images, this view shuffles away the antithesis of art to reality and integrates art into the reality it opposes. Only those artworks are enlightened that, vigilantly distant from the empirical, evince true consciousness.

That through which artworks, by becoming appearance, are more than they are: This is their spirit. The determination of artworks by spirit is akin to their determination as phenomenon,[11] as something that appears, and not as blind appearance. What appears in artworks and is neither to be separated from their appearance nor to be held simply identical with it—the nonfactual in their facticity—is their spirit. It makes artworks, things among things, something other than thing. Indeed, artworks are only able to become other than thing by becoming a thing, though not through their localization in space and time but only by an immanent process of reification that makes them self-same, self-identical. Otherwise one could not speak of their spirit, that is, of what is utterly unthinglike. Spirit is not simply *spiritus*, the breath that animates the work as a phenomenon; spirit is as much the force or the interior of works, the force of their objectivation; spirit participates in this force no less than in the phenomenality that is contrary to it. The spirit of artworks is their immanent mediation, which transforms their sensual moments and their objective arrangement; this is mediation in the strict sense that each and every element in the artwork becomes manifestly its own other. The aesthetic concept of spirit has been severely compromised not only by idealism but also by writings dating from the nascence of radical modernism, among them those of Kandinsky. In his justified revolt against sensualism, which even in *Jugendstil* accorded a preponderance to sensual satisfaction, Kandinsky abstractly isolated the contrary of this principle and reified it so that it became difficult to distinguish the "You should believe in spirit" from superstition and an arts-and-crafts enthusiasm for the exalted. The spirit in artworks transcends equally their status as a thing and the sensual phenomenon, and indeed only exists insofar as these are among its elements. Put negatively: In artworks nothing is literal, least of all their words; spirit is their ether, what speaks through them, or, more precisely, what makes artworks become script. Although nothing counts in artworks that does not originate in the configuration of their sensual elements—all other spirit in the artworks, particularly injected philosophical thematics and putatively expressed spirit, all discursive ingredients, are material like colors and tones—the sensual in artworks is artistic only if in itself mediated by spirit. Even the sensually most dazzling French works achieve their rank by the involuntary transformation of their sensual elements into bearers of a spirit whose experiential content is melancholic resignation to mortal, sensual existence; never do these works relish their suaveness to the full, for that suaveness is always curtailed by the sense of form. The spirit of artworks is objective, regardless of any philosophy of objective or subjective spirit; this spirit is their own content and it passes judgment over them: It is the spirit of the thing itself that appears through the appearance. Its objectivity has its measure in the power with which it infiltrates the appearance. Just how little the spirit of the work equals the spirit of the artist, which is at most one element of the former, is evident in the fact that spirit is evoked through the artifact, its problems, and its material. Not even the appearance of the artwork as a whole is its spirit, and least of all is it the appearance of the idea purportedly embodied or symbolized by the work; spirit cannot be fixated in immediate identity with its appearance. But neither does spirit constitute a level above or below appearance; such a supposition would be no less of a reification. The locus of spirit is the configuration of what appears. Spirit forms appearance just as appearance forms spirit; it is the luminous source through which the phenomenon radiates and becomes a phenomenon in the most pregnant sense of the word. The sensual exists in art only spiritualized and refracted. This can be elucidated by the category of "critical situation" in important artworks of the past, without the knowledge of which the analysis of works would be fruitless. Just before the beginning of the reprise of the first movement of Beethoven's *Kreutzer* sonata, which Tolstoy defamed as sensuous, the secondary subdominant produces an immense effect. Anywhere outside of the *Kreutzer* sonata the same chord would be more or less insignificant. The passage only gains significance through its place and function in the movement. It becomes crucially significant in that through its *hic et nunc* it points beyond itself and imparts the feeling of a critical situation over what precedes and follows it. This feeling cannot be grasped

115

as an isolated sensual quality, yet through the sensual constellation of two chords at a critical point it becomes as irrefutable as only something sensual can be. In its aesthetic manifestation, spirit is condemned to its locus in the phenomenon just as spirits were once thought to have been condemned to their haunts; if spirit does not appear, the artworks are as negligible as that spirit. Spirit is indifferent to the distinction drawn by the history of ideas between sensual and idealistic art. Insofar as there is sensual art, it is not simply sensual but embodies the spirit of sensuality; Wedekind's concept of carnal spirit registered this. Spirit, art's vital element, is bound up with art's truth content, though without coinciding with it. The spirit of works can be untruth. For truth content postulates something real as its substance, and no spirit is immediately real. With an ever increasing ruthlessness, spirit determines and pulls everything merely sensual and factual in artworks into its own sphere. Artworks thereby become more secular, more opposed to mythology, to the illusion of spirit—even its own spirit—as real. Thus artworks radically mediated by spirit are compelled to consume themselves. Through the determinate negation of the reality of spirit, however, these artworks continue to refer to spirit: They do not feign spirit, rather the force they mobilize against it is spirit's omnipresence. Spirit today is not imaginable in any other form; art offers its prototype. As tension between the elements of the artwork, and not as an existence sui generis, art's spirit is a process and thus it is the work itself. To know an artwork means to apprehend this process. The spirit of artworks is not a concept, yet through spirit artworks become commensurable to the concept. By reading the spirit of artworks out of their configurations and confronting the elements with each other and with the spirit that appears in them, critique passes over into the truth of the spirit, which is located beyond the aesthetic configuration. This is why critique is necessary to the works. In the spirit of the works critique recognizes their truth content or distinguishes truth content from spirit. Only in this act, and not through any philosophy of art that would dictate to art what its spirit must be, do art and philosophy converge.

The strict immanence of the spirit of artworks is contradicted on the other hand by a countertendency that is no less immanent: the tendency of artworks to wrest themselves free of the internal unity of their own construction, to introduce within themselves caesuras that no longer permit the totality of the appearance. Because the spirit of the works is not identical with them, spirit breaks up the objective form through which it is constituted; this rupture is the instant of *apparition*. If the spirit of artworks were literally identical with their sensual elements and their organization, spirit would be nothing but the quintessence of the appearance: The repudiation of this thesis amounts to the rejection of idealism. If the spirit of artworks flashes up in their sensual appearance, it does so only as their negation: Unitary with the phenomenon, spirit is at the same time its other. The spirit of artworks is bound up with their form, but spirit is such only insofar as it points beyond that form. The claim that there is no difference between articulation and the articulated, between immanent form and content, is seductive especially as an apology for modern art, but it is scarcely tenable. This becomes evident in the realization that techno- logical analysis does not grasp the spirit of a work even when this analysis is more than a crude reduction to elements and also emphasizes the artwork's context and its coherence as well as its real or putative initial constituents; it requires further reflection to grasp that spirit. Only as spirit is art the antithesis of empirical reality as the determinate negation of the existing order of the world. Art is to be construed dialectically insofar as spirit inheres in it, without however art's possessing spirit as an absolute or spirit's serving to guarantee an absolute to art. Artworks, however much they may seem to be an entity, crystallize between this spirit and its other. In Hegel's aesthetics the objectivity of the artwork was conceived as the truth of spirit that has gone over into its own otherness and become identical with this otherness. For Hegel, spirit is at one with totality, even with the aesthetic totality. Certainly spirit in artworks is not an intentional particular but an element like every particular constitutive of an artwork; true, spirit is that particular that makes an artifact art, though there is no spirit without its antithesis. In actual fact, history knows no artworks in which there is a pure identity of the spiritual and the nonspiritual. According to its own concept, spirit in artworks is not pure but rather a function of that out of which it arises. Those works that appear to embody such identity and are content with it are hardly ever the most important ones. Granted, that which in artworks is opposed to spirit is in no way the natural aspect of its materials and objects; rather, it is a limit. Materials and objects are as historically and socially preformed as are their methods; they are definitively transformed by what transpires in the works. What is heterogeneous in artworks is immanent to them: It is that in them that opposes unity and yet is needed by unity if it is to be more than a pyrrhic victory over the unresisting. That the spirit of artworks is not to be equated with their immanent nexus—the arrangement of their sensual elements —is evident in that they in no way constitute that gapless unity, that type of form to which aesthetic reflection has falsely reduced them. In terms of their own structure, they are not organisms; works of the highest rank are hostile to their organic aspect as illusory and affirmative. In all its genres, art is pervaded by intellective elements. It may suffice to note that without such elements, without listening ahead and thinking back, without expectation and memory, without the synthesis of the discrete and separate, great musical forms would never have existed. Whereas to a certain extent these functions may be attributed to sensual immediacy —that is, that particular complexes of elements incorporate qualities of what is antecedent and forthcoming—artworks nevertheless achieve a critical point where this immediacy ends; where they must be "thought," not in external reflection but on their own terms; the intellective mediation belongs to their own sensual arrangement and determines their perception. If there is something like a common characteristic of great late works, it is to be sought in the breaking through of form by spirit. This is no aberration of art but rather its fatal corrective. Its highest products are condemned to a fragmentariness that is their confession that even they do not possess what is claimed by the immanence of their form.

Objective idealism was the first to stress vigorously the spiritual as against the sensual element of art. It thus equated art's objectivity with spirit: In thoughtless accord with tradition, idealism identified the sensual with the accidental. Universality and necessity, which for Kant dictate the canon of aesthetic judgment even though they remain problematic, became construable for Hegel by means of the omnipotent category of spirit. The progress of this aesthetics beyond all previous thinking is evident; just as the conception of art was liberated from the last traces of feudal divertissement, its spiritual content, as its principal determination, was at least potentially wrested from the sphere of mere meaning, of intentions. Since Hegel conceives of spirit as what exists in and for itself, it is recognized in art as its substance and not as a thin, abstract layer hovering above it. This is implicit in the definition of beauty as the sensual semblance of the idea. Philosophical idealism, however, was in no way as kindly disposed toward aesthetic spiritualization as the theoretical construction would perhaps indicate. On the contrary, idealism set itself up as the defender of precisely that sensuality that in its opinion was being impoverished by spiritualization; that doctrine of the beautiful as the sensual semblance of the idea was an apology for immediacy as something meaningful and, in Hegel's own words, affirmative. Radical spiritualization is antithetical to this. This progress had a high price, however, for the spiritual element of art is not what idealist aesthetics calls spirit; rather, it is the mimetic impulse fixated as totality. The sacrifice made by art for this emancipation, whose postulate has been consciously formulated ever since Kant's dubious theorem that "nothing sensuous is sublime,"[12] is presumably already evident in modernity. With the elimination of the principle of representation in painting and sculpture, and of the exploitation of fragments in music, it became almost unavoidable that the elements set free—colors, sounds, absolute configurations of words—came to appear as if they already inherently expressed something. This is, however, illusory, for the elements become eloquent only through the context in which they occur. The superstitious belief in the elementary and unmediated, to which expressionism paid homage and which worked its way down into arts and crafts as well as into philosophy, corresponds to capriciousness and accidentalness in the relation of material and expression in construction. To begin with, the claim that in itself red possesses an expressive value was an illusion, and the putative expressive values of complex, multitonal sounds were in fact predicated on the insistent negation of traditional sounds. Reduced to "natural material" all of this is empty, and theories that mystify it have no more substance than the charlatanism of *Farbton* experiments. It is only the most recent physicalism that, in music for instance, carries out a reduction literally to elements: This is spiritualization that progressively exorcises spirit. Here the self-destructive aspect of spiritualization becomes obvious. While the metaphysics of spiritualization has become philosophically questionable, the concept is at the same time too universal to do justice to spirit in art. Nevertheless, the artwork continues to assert itself as essentially spiritual even when spirit is for all intents and purposes no longer to be presupposed as a substance. Hegel's aesthetics does not resolve the question of how it is possible to speak of spirit as a determination of the artwork without hypostatizing its objectivity as absolute identity. Thereby the controversy is in a sense referred back to the Kantian court of justice. In Hegel, the spirit of art was deducible from the system as one level of its manifestation and was, as it were, univocal in potentially each and every genre and artwork, but only by relinquishing the aesthetic attribute of ambiguity. Aesthetics is, however, not applied philosophy but rather in itself philosophical. Hegel's reflection that "the science of art has greater priority than does art itself"[13] is the admittedly problematical product of his hierarchical view of the relation of the domains of spirit to each other. On the other hand, in the face of growing theoretical interest in art, Hegel's theorem of the primacy of science has its prophetic truth in art's need of philosophy for the unfolding of its own content. Paradoxically, Hegel's metaphysics of spirit results in a certain reification of spirit in the artwork through the fixation of its idea. In Kant, however, the ambiguity between the feeling of necessity and the fact that this necessity is not a given but something unresolved is truer to aesthetic experience than is Hegel's much more modern ambition of knowing art from within rather than in terms of its subjective constitution from without. If this Hegelian philosophical turn is justified, it in no way follows from a systematic subordinating concept but rather from the sphere that is specific to art. Not everything that exists is spirit, yet art is an entity that through its configurations becomes something spiritual. If idealism was able to requisition art for its purposes by fiat, this was because through its own constitution art corresponds to the fundamental conception of idealism, which indeed without Schelling's model of art would never have developed into its objective form. Art cannot be conceived without this immanently idealistic element, that is, without the objective mediation of all art through spirit; this sets a limit to dull-minded doctrines of aesthetic realism just as those elements encompassed in the name of realism are a constant reminder that art is no twin of idealism.

In no artwork is the element of spirit something that exists; rather, it is something in a process of development and formation. Thus, as Hegel was the first to perceive, the spirit of artworks is integrated into an overarching process of spiritualization: that of the progress of consciousness. Precisely through its progressive spiritualization, through its division from nature, art wants to revoke this division from which it suffers and which inspires it. Spiritualization provided art anew with what had been excluded from it by artistic practice since Greek antiquity: the sensuously unpleasing, the repulsive; Baudelaire virtually made this development art's program. Hegel aimed at justifying the irresistibility of spiritualization in the theory of what he called the romantic artwork.[14] Since then, everything sensually pleasing in art, every charm of material, has been degraded to the level of the preartistic. Spiritualization, as the continuous expansion of the mimetic taboo on art, the indigenous domain of mimesis, works toward art's dissolution. But being also a mimetic force, spiritualization at the same time works toward the identity of the artwork with itself, thereby excluding the heterogeneous and strengthening its image character. Art is not infiltrated by spirit; rather, spirit follows artworks where they want to go, setting free their immanent language. Still, spiritualization cannot free itself of a shadow that demands its critique; the more substantial spiritual-ization became in art, the more energetically—in Benjamin's theory no less than in Beckett's literary praxis—did it renounce spirit, the idea. However, in that spiritualization is inextricable from the requirement that everything must become form, spiritualization becomes complicitous in the tendency that liquidates the tension between art and its other. Only radically spiritualized art is still possible, all other art is childish; inexorably, however, the childish seems to contaminate the whole existence of art.——The sensuously pleasing has come under a double attack. On the one hand, through the artwork's spiritualization the external must pass by way of spirit and has increasingly become the appearance of the inward. On the other hand, the absorption of resistant material and themes opposes the culinary consumption of art even if, given the general ideological tendency to integrate everything that resists integration, con-sumption undertakes to swallow everything up whole, however repulsive it might seem. In early impressionism, with Manet, the polemical edge of spiritualization was no less sharp than it was in Baudelaire. The further artworks distance themselves from the childish desire to please, the more what they are in themselves prevails over what they present to even the most ideal viewer, whose reflexes increasingly become a matter of indif-ference. In the sphere of natural beauty, Kant's theory of the sublime anticipates the spiritualization that art alone is able to achieve. For Kant, what is sublime in nature is nothing but the autonomy of the spirit in the face of the superior power of sensuous existence, and this autonomy is achieved only in the spiritualized artwork. Admittedly, the spiritualization of art is not a pristine process. Whenever spiritualization is not fully carried out in the concretion of the aesthetic structure, the emancipated spiritual element is degraded to the level of subaltern thematic material. Opposed to the sensuous aspect, spiritualization frequently turns blindly against that aspect's differentiation, itself something spiritual, and becomes abstract. In its early period, spiritualization is accompanied by a tendency to primitiv-ism and, contrary to sensuous culture, tends toward the barbaric: In their own name the fauvists made this their program. Regression shadows all opposition to affirmative culture. Spiritualization in art must prove its ability to rise above this threat of regression and to recover the suppressed differentiation; otherwise, art deteriorates into a violent act of spirit. All the same, spiritualization is legitimate as the critique of culture through art, which is part of culture and finds no satisfaction in its failure. The function of barbaric traits in modern art changes historically. The good souls who cross themselves in front of reproductions of the *Demoiselles d'Avignon* or while listening to Schoenberg's early piano pieces, are without exception more barbaric than the barbarism they fear. As soon as new dimensions emerge in art, they refuse older ones and initially prefer impoverishment and the renunciation of false richness, even of highly developed forms of reaction. The process of spiritualization in art is never linear progress. Its criterion of success is the ability of art to appropriate into its language of form what bourgeois society has ostracized, thereby revealing in what has been stigmatized that nature whose suppression is what is truly evil. The perennial indignation, unchanged by the culture industry, over the ugliness of modern art is, despite the pompous ideals sounded, hostile to spirit; it interprets the ugliness, and especially the unpleasing reproaches, literally rather than as a test of the power of spiritualization and as a cipher of the opposition in which this spiritualization proves itself. Rimbaud's postulate of the radically modern is that of an art that moves in the tension between *spleen et idéal*, between spiritualization and obsession with what is most distant from spirit. The primacy of spirit in art and the inroads made by what was previously taboo are two sides of the same coin. It is concerned with what has not yet been socially approved and preformed and thereby becomes a social condition of determinate negation. Spiritualization takes place not through ideas announced by art but by the force with which it penetrates layers that are intentionless and hostile to the conceptual. This is not the least of the reasons why the proscribed and forbidden tempt artistic sensibilities. Spiritualization in new art prohibits it from tarnishing itself any further with the topical preferences of philistine culture: the true, the beautiful, and the good. Into its innermost core what is usually called art's social critique or *engagement*, all that is critical or negative in art, has been fused with spirit, with art's law of form. That these elements are at present stubbornly played off against each other is a symptom of the regression of consciousness.

Theories that argue that art has the responsibility of bringing order —and, indeed, not a classificatory abstract order but one that is sensuously concrete—to the chaotic multiplicity of the appearing or of nature itself, suppress in idealistic fashion the telos of aesthetic spiritualization: to give the historical figures of the natural and repression of the natural their due. Accordingly, the relation of the process of spiritualization to the chaotic is historical. It has often been said, probably first by Karl Kraus, that in society as a whole it is art that should introduce chaos into order rather than the reverse. The chaotic aspects of qualitatively new art are opposed to order—the spirit of order—only at first glance. They are the ciphers of a critique of a spurious second nature: Order is in truth this chaotic. The element of chaos and radical spiritualization converge in the rejection of sleekly polished images of life; in this regard art that has been spiritualized to the extreme, such as that beginning with Mallarmé's, and the dream-chaos of surrealism are more closely related than their disciples realize; incidentally, there are cross-links between the young Breton and symbolism, as well as between the early German expressionists and George, whom they challenged. In its relation to the unmastered, spiritualization is antinomical. Because spiritualization always constrains the sensuous elements, its spirit fatefully becomes a being sui generis and thus according to its own immanent tendency spiritualization also works against art. Art's crisis is accelerated by spiritualization, which opposes selling artworks off as objects of sensuous gratification. Spiritualization becomes a counterforce to the gypsy wagon of wandering actors and musicians, the socially outcast. Yet however deep the compulsion may lie that art divest itself of every trace of being a show, of its ancient deceitfulness in society, art no longer exists when that element has been totally eradicated and yet it is unable to provide any protected arena for that element. No sublimation succeeds that does not guard in itself what it sublimates. Whether or not the spiritualization of art is capable of this will decide if art survives or if Hegel's prophecy of the end of art will indeed be fulfilled, a prophecy that, in the world such as it has become, amounts to the thoughtless and—in the detestable sense—realistic confirmation and reproduction of what is. In this regard, the rescue of art is eminently political, but it is also as uncertain in itself as it is threatened by the course of the world.

Insight into the growing spiritualization of art, by virtue of the development of its concept no less than by its relation to society, collides with a dogma that runs throughout bourgeois aesthetics: that of art's intuitability.[15] Already in Hegel spiritualization and intuitability could no longer be reconciled, and the first somber prophecies on the future of art were the result. Kant had already formulated the norm of intuitability in section 9 of the *Critique of Judgment*: "[T]he beautiful is that which pleases universally without a concept."[16] The "without a concept" may be said to converge with the quality of art's pleasingness as dispensation from the labor and exertion imposed—and not only since Hegel's philosophy—by the concept. Whereas art long ago relegated the ideal of pleasingness to musty antiquity, the theory of art has not been able to renounce the concept of intuitability, a monument to old-fashioned aesthetic hedonism, even though every modern artwork—by now even the older works —demands the labor of observation with which the doctrine of intuitability wanted to dispense. The advancement of intellective mediation into the structure of artworks, where this mediation must to a large extent perform what was once the role of pregiven forms, constrains the sensuously unmediated whose quintessence was the pure intuitability of artworks. Yet bourgeois consciousness entrenches itself in the sensuously unmediated because it senses that only its intuitability reflects a gaplessness and roundness of artworks that then, in whatever circuitous fashion, is attributed to the reality to which the artworks respond. If, however, art were totally without the element of intuition, it would be theory, whereas art is instead obviously impotent in itself when, emulating science, it ignores its own qualitative difference from the discursive concept; precisely art's spiritualization, as the primacy of its procedures, distances art from naïve conceptuality and the commonsense idea of comprehensibility. Whereas the norm of intuitability accentuates the opposition of art to discursive thinking, it suppresses nonconceptual mediation, suppresses the nonsensuous in the sensuous structure, which by constituting the structure already fractures it and puts it beyond the intuitability in which it appears. The norm of intuitability, which denies what is implicitly categorial in artworks, reifies intuitability itself as opaque and impenetrable, makes it in terms of its pure form into a copy of the petrified world, always alert for anything that might disturb the harmony the work purportedly reflects. In actuality, the concretion of artworks, in the *apparition* that ripples disconcertingly through them, goes far beyond the intuitability that is habitually held up against the universality of the concept and that stands in accord with the ever-same. The more inexorably the world is ruled throughout, ever-the-same, by the universal, the more easily the rudiments of the particular are mistaken for immediacy and confused with concretion, even though their contingency is in fact the stamp of abstract necessity. Artistic concretion is, however, neither pure existence, conceptless individualization, nor that form of mediation by the universal known as a type. In terms of its own determination, no authentic artwork is typical. Lukács's thinking is art-alien when he contrasts typical, "normal" works with atypical and therefore irrelevant ones. If he were right, artworks would be no more than a sort of anticipation of a science yet to be completed. The patently idealist assertion that the artwork of the present represents the unity of the universal and the particular is completely dogmatic. The assertion, a surreptitious borrowing of the theological doctrine of the symbol, is given the lie by the a priori fissure between the mediate and the immediate, from which no mature artwork has yet been able to escape; if this fissure is concealed rather than that the work immerses itself in it, the work is lost. It is precisely radical art that, while refusing the desideratum of realism, stands in a relation of tension to the symbol. It remains to be demonstrated that symbols or metaphors in modern art make themselves progressively independent of their symbolic function and thereby contribute to the constitution of a realm that is antithetical to the empirical world and its meanings. Art absorbs symbols in such a fashion that they are no longer symbolic; advanced artists have themselves carried out the critique of the character of the symbol. The ciphers and characters of modern art are signs that have forgotten themselves and become absolute. Their infiltration into the aesthetic medium and their refusal of intentionality are two aspects of the same process. The transformation of dissonance into compositional "material" is to be interpreted analogously. In literature, this transformation can be followed relatively early in the relationship between Strindberg and late Ibsen, where Strindberg is already anticipated. The increasing literalization of what was previously symbolic shockingly endows the spiritual element, which was emancipated through second reflection, with an independence that is mortally eloquent in the occult layer of Strindberg's work and becomes productive in the break from any form of replicability. That none of his works are a symbol points up that in none of them does the absolute reveal itself; otherwise art would be neither semblance nor play but rather something factually real. Given their constitutive refractedness, pure intuitability cannot be attributed to artworks. Art is preemptively mediated by its as-if character. If it were completely intuitable, it would become part of the empirical world that it resists. Its mediatedness, however, is not an abstract apriori but involves every concrete aesthetic element; even the most sensuous elements are always unintuitable by virtue of their relation to the spirit of the work. No analysis of important works could possibly prove their pure intuitability, for they are all pervaded by the conceptual. This is literally true in language and indirectly true even in the non-conceptual medium of music, where regardless of a work's psychological genesis the stupid and the intelligent can be explicitly distinguished. The desideratum of intuitability wants to conserve the mimetic element of art while remaining blind to the fact that this element survives only through its antithesis, the works' rational control over everything heterogeneous to them. Shorn of its antithesis, intuitability would become a fetish. In the aesthetic domain the mimetic impulse affects even the mediation, the concept, that which is not present. The concept is as indispensably intermixed in art as it is in language, though in art the concept becomes qualitatively other than collections of characteristics shared by empirical objects. The intermixture of concepts is not identical with asserting the conceptuality of art; art is no more concept than it is pure intuition, and it is precisely thereby that art protests against their separation. The intuitive element in art differs from sensuous perception because in art the intuitive element always refers to its spirit. Art is the intuition of what is not intuitable; it is akin to the conceptual without the concept. It is by way of concepts, however, that art sets free its mimetic, nonconceptual layer. Whether by reflection or unconsciously, modern art has undermined the dogma of intuitability. What remains true in the doctrine of intuitability is that it emphasizes the element of the incommensurable, that which in art is not exhausted by discursive logic, the sine qua non of all manifestations of art. Art militates against the concept as much as it does against domination, but for this opposition it, like philosophy, requires concepts. Art's so-called intuitability is an aporetic construction: With a pass of the magic wand it means to reduce to identity what is internally disparate and in process in artworks, and therefore this construction glances off art-works, none of which result in such identity. The word *Anschaulichkeit* [intuitability], itself borrowed from the theory of discursive knowledge, where it stipulates a formed content, testifies to the rational element in art as much as it conceals that element by dividing off the phenomenal element and hypostatizing it. Evidence of the aporia of the concept of aesthetic intuition is provided by the *Critique of Judgment*. The "Analytic of the Beautiful" concerns the "Elements of the Judgment of Taste." Of these Kant says in a footnote to section 1: "I have used the logical functions of judging to help me find the elements that judgment takes into considera-tion when it reflects (since even a judgment of taste still has reference to the understanding). I have examined the element of quality first, because an aesthetic judgment about the beautiful is concerned with it first."[17] This flagrantly contradicts the thesis that beauty pleases universally without a concept. It is admirable that Kant's aesthetics let this contradiction stand and expressly reflected on it without explaining it away. On the one hand, Kant treats the judgment of taste as a logical function and thus attributes this function to the aesthetic object to which the judgment would indeed need to be adequate; on the other hand, the artwork is said to present itself "without a concept," a mere intuition, as if it were simply extralogical. This contradiction, however, is in fact inherent in art itself, as the contradiction between its spiritual and mimetic constitution. The claim to truth, which involves something universal and which each artwork registers, is incompatible with pure intuitability. Just how fateful the insistence on the exclusively intuitable character of art has been is obvious from its consequences. In Hegel's terms, it serves the abstract separation of intuition and spirit. The more the work is said to be purely identical with its intuitability, the more its spirit is reified as an "idea," as an immutable content back of its appearance. The spiritual elements that are withdrawn from the structure of the phenomenon are hypostatized as its idea. The result usually is that intentions are exalted as the work's content, while correlatively intuition is allotted to sensuous satisfaction. The official assertion of artworks' common unity could, however, be refuted in each of those so-called classical works on which the assertion is founded: Precisely in these works the semblance of unity is what has been conceptually mediated. The dominant model is philistine: Appearance is to be purely intuitable and the content purely conceptual, corresponding to the rigid dichotomy between freedom and labor. No ambivalence is tolerated. This is the polemical point of attack for the break from the ideal of intuitability. Because aesthetic appearance cannot be reduced to its intuition, the content of artworks cannot be reduced to the concept either. The false synthesis of spirit and sensuousness in aesthetic intuition conceals their no less false, rigid polarity; the aesthetics of intuition is founded on the model of a thing: In the synthesis of the artifact the tension, its essence, gives way to a fundamental repose.

Intuitability is no *characteristica universalis* of art. It is intermittent. Aestheticians have hardly taken notice of this; one of the rare exceptions is Theodor Meyer, now virtually forgotten. He showed that there is no sensuous intuition, no set of images, that corresponds to what literature says; on the contrary, its concretion consists in its linguistic form rather than in the highly problematic optical representation that it supposedly provokes.[18] Literature does not require completion through sensuous representation; it is concrete in language and through it, it is suffused with the nonsensuous, in accordance with the oxymoron of nonsensuous intuition. Even in concept-alien art there is a nonsensuous element at work. Theories that deny this element for the sake of their *thema probandum* join forces with that philistinism that is always ready to dub the music it finds cozy a "feast for the ears." Precisely in its great and emphatic forms, music embodies complexes that can only be understood through what is sensuously not present, through memory or expectation, complexes that hold such categorical determinations embedded in their own structure. It is impossible, for instance, to interpret as a mere continuation the at times distant relations between the development of the first movement of the *Eroica* and the exposition, and the extreme contrast to this exposition established by the new theme: The work is intellective in itself, without in any way being embarrassed about it and without the integration of the work thereby impinging on its law of form. The arts seem to have moved so far in the direction of their unity in art that the situation is no different in the visual arts. The spiritual mediation of the artwork, by which it contrasts with the empirical world, cannot be realized without the inclusion of the discursive dimension. If the artwork were in a rigorous sense intuitable, it would be permanently relegated to the contingency of what exists sensuously and immediately, to which the artwork in fact opposes its own type of logicity. Its quality is determined by whether its concretion divests itself of its contingency by virtue of its integral elaboration. The puristic and to this extent rationalistic separation of intuition from the conceptual serves the dichotomy of rationality and sensuousness that society perpetrates and ideologically enjoins. Art would need rather to work in effigy against this dichotomy through the critique that it objectively embodies; through art's restriction to sensuousness this dichotomy is only confirmed. The untruth attacked by art is not rationality but rationality's rigid opposition to the particular; if art separates out intuitability and bestows it with the crown of the particular, then art endorses that rigidification, valorizing the detritus of societal rationality and thereby serving to distract from this rationality. The more gaplessly a work seeks to be intuitable and thus fulfill aesthetic precept, the more its spiritual element is reified, χωρίς from the appearance and isolated from the forming of *apparition*. Behind the cult of intuitability lurks the philistine convention of the body that lies stretched out on the sofa while the soul soars to the heights: Aesthetic appearance is to be effortless relaxation, the reproduction of labor power, and spirit is reduced handily to what is called the work's "message." Constitutively a protest against the claim of the discursive to totality, artworks therefore await answer and solution and inevitably summon forth concepts. No work has ever achieved the indifference of pure intuitability and binding universality that is presupposed a priori by traditional aesthetics. The doctrine of intuition is false because it phenomenologically attributes to art what it does not fulfill. The criterion of artworks is not the purity of intuition but rather the profundity with which they carry out the tension with the intellective elements that inhere in them. Nevertheless, the taboo on the nonintuitive elements of artworks is not without justification. What is conceptual in artworks involves judgment, and to judge is contrary to the artwork. Although judgments may occur in it, the work itself does not make judgments, perhaps because ever since Attic tragedy the work has been a hearing. If the discursive element takes primacy, the relation of the artwork to what is external to it becomes all too unmediated and the work accommodates itself even at those points where, as in Brecht, it takes pride in standing in opposition to reality: The work actually becomes positivistic. The artwork must absorb into its immanent nexus its discursive components in a movement that is contrary to the externally directed, apophantic movement that releases the discursive. The language of advanced lyrical poetry achieves this, and that is how it reveals its specific dialectic. It is evident that artworks can heal the wounds that abstraction inflicts on them only through the heightening of abstraction, which impedes the contamination of the conceptual ferment with empirical reality: The concept becomes a "parameter." Indeed, because art is essentially spiritual, it cannot be purely intuitive. It must also be thought: art itself thinks. The prevalence of the doctrine of intuition, which contradicts all experience of artworks, is a reflex to social reification. It amounts to the establishment of a special sphere of immediacy that is blind to the thing-like dimensions of artworks, which are constitutive of what in art goes beyond the thing as such. Not only do artworks, as Heidegger pointed out in opposition to idealism,[19] have things that function as their bearers—their own objectivation makes them into things of a second order. What they have become in themselves—their inner structure, which follows the work's immanent logic—cannot be reached by pure intuition; in the work what is available to intuition is mediated by the structure of the work, in contrast to which the intuitable is a matter of indifference. Every experience of artworks must go beyond what is intuitable in them. If they were nothing but intuitable they would be of subaltern importance, in Wagner's words: an effect without a cause. Reification is essential to artworks and contradicts their essence as that which appears; their quality of being a thing is no less dialectical than their intuitable element. But the objectivation of the artwork is not—as was thought by Friedrich Theodor Vischer, who no longer entirely understood Hegel—unitary with its material; rather, its objectivation is the result of the play of forces in the work and related to its thing-character as an act of synthesis. There is some analogy here to the double character of the Kantian thing as the transcendent thing-in-itself and as an object subjectively constituted through the law of its phenomena. For artworks are things in space and time; whether this holds for hybrid musical forms such as improvisation, once extinct and now resuscitated, is hard to decide; in artworks the element that precedes their fixation as things constantly breaks through the thing-character. Yet even in improvisation much speaks for their status as a thing: their appearance in empirical time and, even more important, the fact that they demonstrate objectivated, mostly conventional patterns. For insofar as artworks are works they are things in themselves, objectified by virtue of their particular law of form. That in drama not the text but the performance is taken to be what matters, just as in music not the score but the living sound is so regarded, testifies to the precariousness of the thing-character in art, which does not, however, thereby release the artwork from its participation in the world of things. For scores are not only almost always better than the performances, they are more than simply instructions for them; they are indeed the thing itself. Incidentally, both concepts of the artwork as thing are not necessarily distinct. The realization of music was, at least until recently, the interlinear version of the score. The fixation through print or scores is not external to the work; only through them does the work become autonomous from its genesis: That explains the primacy of the text over its performance. What is not fixated in art is—for the most part only illusorily—closer to the mimetic impulse but usually below—not above—the fixated, a vestige of an obsolete and usually regressive practice. The most recent rebellion against the fixation of artworks as reification, for instance the replacement of the mensural system with neumic-graphic imitations of musical gestures, is by comparison still significative and simply reification of an older level. Of course this rebellion would not be as extensive if the artwork did not suffer from its immanent condition as a thing. Only a philistine and stubborn faith in artists could overlook the complicity of the artwork's thing-character with social reification and thus with its untruth: the fetishization of what is in itself a process as a relation between elements. The artwork is at once process and instant. Its objectivation, a condition of aesthetic autonomy, is also rigidification. The more the social labor sedimented in the artwork is objectified and fully formed, the more the work echoes hollowly and becomes alien to itself.

Notes

1 Walter Benjamin, "On Some Motifs in Baudelaire," in *Illuminations*, trans. Harry Zohn (New York, 1968), pp. 155–200.

2 See Bertolt Brecht, "Die Liebenden," in *Gedichte II* (Frankfurt, 1960), p. 210.

3 ["authentische Kunstwerke": Whenever Adorno, the author of *Jargon der Eigentlichkeit* (*The Jargon of Authenticity*, trans. Knut Tarnowsky and Frederic Will, Evanston, 1976) and archcritic of Heideggerian "authenticity" (Eigentlichkeit), uses the concept of authenticity in a positive sense, he always employs the Greek/French loan word "Authentizität" rather than the German root word "Eigentlichkeit" or the adjective "echt."—trans.]

4 See Georg Wilhelm Friedrich Hegel, *Aesthetics*, trans. T. M. Knox (Oxford, 1975), vol. 1, p. 31: "Man does this [that is, he transposes the external world on which he impresses the seal of his inferiority—trans.] in order, as a free subject, to strip the external world of its inflexible foreignness and to enjoy in the shape of things only an external realization of himself."

5 [Although the word "apparition" exists in German as "Apparition," Adorno throughout uses the French concept and makes this obvious in the German by not capitalizing the first letter.—trans.]

6 ["der fruchtbare Moment": Gotthold Ephraim Lessing's concept of the highest moment of aesthetic tension, which he developed in his interpretation of the Laocoön sculpture. See his *Laocoön*, trans. Edward McCormick (Baltimore, 1962)—trans.]

7 See Leo Perutz, *Der Meister des jüngsten Tages* (Munich, 1924), p. 199.

8 [See Frank Wedekind, *Spring Awakening*, trans. Tom Osborne (London, 1969), p. 52.—trans.]

9 [Wols is the pseudonym of Wolfgang Schulze (1913–1951), a German expatriot and a key figure of French *art informelle*.—trans.]

10 ["Erfahrungsgehalt": This is a central concept of Adorno's philosophy, and it is easily lost track of in translation. See Adorno, "The Experiential Content of Hegel's Philosophy," in *Hegel: Three Studies*, trans. Shierry Weber (Boston, 1993), pp. 53ff.—trans.]

11 ["Phänomen"; "Phenomenon" is here implicitly contrasted with noumenon. —trans.]

12 Immanuel Kant, *Critique of Judgment*, trans. Werner S. Pluhar (Indianapolis, 1987), p. 97.

13 Hermann Lotze, *Geschichte der Aesthetik in Deutschland* (Munich, 1868), p. 190.

14 As in the whole of his philosophy, Hegel's doctrine of the artwork as spiritual, which he justly conceived historically, is the reflexive fulfillment of Kant's thought. Kant's "disinterested satisfaction" implies recognition of the aesthetic as spiritual through the negation of its own opposite.

15 ["Anschaulichkeit," the character of an object such that it is possible or necessary to enter into immediate, nonconceptual contact with it. Etymologically, this immediacy of relationship is modeled on vision. See M. Inwood, *A Hegel Dictionary* (London, 1992).—trans.]

16 Kant, *Critique of Judgment*, p. 61.

17 Ibid., p. 43.

18 See Theodor A. Meyer, *Das Stilgesetz der Poesie* (Leipzig, 1901).

19 Martin Heidegger, "The Origin of the Work of Art," in *Poetry, Language, and Thought* (New York, 1971), pp. 15–88.

6
Semblance and expression

The emancipation from the concept of harmony has revealed itself to be a revolt against semblance: Construction inheres tautologically in expression, which is its polar opposite. The rebellion against semblance did not, however, take place in favor of play, as Benjamin supposed, though there is no mistaking the playful quality of the permutations, for instance, that have replaced fictional developments. The crisis of semblance may engulf play as well, for the harmlessness of play deserves the same fate as does harmony, which originates in semblance. Art that seeks to redeem itself from semblance through play becomes sport. A measure of the intensity of the crisis of semblance is that it has befallen music, which *prima vista* is inimical to the illusory. In music, fictive elements wither away even in their sublimated form, which includes not only the expression of nonexistent feelings but even structural elements such as the fiction of a totality that is recognized as unrealizable. In great music such as Beethoven's—and probably this holds true far beyond the range of the temporal arts—the so-called primal elements turned up by analysis are usually eminently insubstantial. Only insofar as these elements asymptotically approximate nothingness do they meld—as a pure process of becoming—into a whole. As differentiated partial elements, however, time and again they want to be something previously existent: a motif or a theme. The immanent nothingness of its elementary determinations draws integral art down into the amorphous, whose gravitational pull increases the more thoroughly art is organized. It is exclusively the amorphous that makes the integration of the artwork possible. Through the completion of the work, by setting unformed nature at a distance, the natural element

133

returns as what has yet to be formed, as the nonarticulated. When artworks are viewed under the closest scrutiny, the most objectivated paintings metamorphose into a swarming mass and texts splinter into words. As soon as one imagines having a firm grasp on the details of an artwork, it dissolves into the indeterminate and undifferentiated, so mediated is it. This is the manifestation of aesthetic semblance in the structure of artworks. Under micrological study, the particular—the artwork's vital element—is volatilized; its concretion vanishes. The process, which in each work takes objective shape, is opposed to its fixation as something to point to, and dissolves back from whence it came. Artworks themselves destroy the claim to objectivation that they raise. This is a measure of the profundity with which illusion suffuses artworks, even the non-representational ones. The truth of artworks depends on whether they succeed at absorbing into their immanent necessity what is not identical with the concept, what is according to that concept accidental. The purposefulness of artworks requires the purposeless, with the result that their own consistency is predicated on the illusory; semblance is indeed their logic. To exist, their purposefulness must be suspended through its other. Nietzsche touched on this with the obviously problematic dictum that in an artwork everything can just as well be different from the way it is; presumably this holds true, only within the confines of an established idiom, within a "style" that guarantees some breadth of variation. If the immanent closure of artworks is not to be taken strictly, however, semblance overtakes them precisely at the point they imagine themselves best protected from it. They give the lie to the claim to closure by disavowing the objectivity they produce. They themselves, not just the illusion they evoke, are the aesthetic semblance. The illusory quality of artworks is condensed in their claim to wholeness. Aesthetic nominalism culminates in the crisis of semblance insofar as the artwork wants to be emphatically substantial. The irritation with semblance has its locus in the object itself. Today every element of aesthetic semblance includes aesthetic inconsistency in the form of contradictions between what the work appears to be and what it is. Through its appearance it lays claim to substantiality; it honors this claim negatively even though the positivity of its actual appearance asserts the gesture of something more, a pathos that even the radically pathos-alien work is unable to slough off. If the question as to the future of art were not fruitless and suspiciously technocratic, it would come down to whether art can outlive semblance. A typical instance of this crisis was the trivial revolt forty years ago against costumes in the theater: Hamlet in a suit, Lohengrin without a swan. This was perhaps not so much a revolt against the infringement of artworks on the prevailing realistic mentality as against their immanent *imagerie*, which they were no longer able to support. The beginning of Proust's *Recherche* is to be interpreted as the effort to outwit art's illusoriness: to steal imperceptibly into the monad of the artwork without forcibly positing its immanence of form and without feigning an omnipresent and omniscient narrator. The contemporary problem faced by all artworks, how to begin and how to close, indicates the possibility of a comprehensive and material theory of aesthetic form that would also need to treat the categories of continuity, contrast, transition, development, and the "knot," as well as, finally, whether today everything must be equally near the midpoint or can have different densities. During the nineteenth century aesthetic semblance was heightened to the point of phantasmagoria. Artworks effaced the traces of their production, probably because the victorious positivistic spirit penetrated art to the degree that art aspired to be a fact and was ashamed of whatever revealed its compact immediateness as mediated.[1] Artworks obeyed this tendency well into late modernism. Art's illusoriness progressively became absolute; this is concealed behind Hegel's term "art-religion," which was taken literally by the oeuvre of the Schopenhauerian Wagner. Modernism subsequently rebelled against the semblance of a semblance that denies it is such. Here the many efforts converge that are undisguisedly determined to pierce the artwork's hermetic immanent nexus, to release the production in the product, and, within limits, to put the process of production in the place of its results—an intention, incidentally, that was hardly foreign to the great representatives of the idealist epoch. The phantasmagorical side of artworks, which made them irresistible, became suspicious to them not only in the so-called neo-objective movements, that is, in functionalism, but also in traditional forms such as the novel. In the novel the illusion of peeping into a box and a world beyond, which is controlled by the fictive omnipresence of the narrator, joins forces with the claim to the reality of a factitious world that is at the same time, as fiction, unreal. Those antipodes, George and Karl Kraus, rejected the novel, but even the novelists Proust and Gide, who commented on the form's pure immanence by breaking through it, are testimony to the same malaise and not merely the often adduced anti-romantic mood of the time. The phantasmagorical dimension, which strengthens the illusion of the being-in-itself of works technologically, could be better understood as the rival of the romantic artwork, which from the beginning sabotaged the phantasmagorical dimension through irony. Phantasmagoria became an embarrassment because the gapless being-in-itself, after which the pure artwork strives, is incompatible with its determination as something humanly made and therefore as a thing in which the world of things is embedded a priori. The dialectic of modern art is largely that it wants to shake off its illusoriness like an animal trying to shake off its antlers. The aporias in the historical development of art cast their shadows over its possibility as a whole. Even antirealist movements such as expressionism took part in the rebellion against semblance. At the same time that it opposed the replication of the external world, however, it sought the undisguised manifestation of real psychical states and approximated the psychograph. In the aftermath of that rebellion, however, artworks are at the point of regressing to the status of a mere thing as if in punishment for the hubris of being more than art. The recent and for the most part childishly ignorant emulation of science is the most tangible symptom of this regression. Many works of contemporary music and painting, in spite of the absence of representational objectivity and expression, would rightly be subsumed by the concept of a second naturalism. Crudely physicalistic procedures in the material and calculable relations between parameters helplessly repress aesthetic semblance and thereby reveal the truth of their positedness. The disappearance of this positedness into their autonomous nexus left behind aura as a reflex of human self-objectivation. The allergy to aura, from which no art today is able to escape, is inseparable from the eruption of inhumanity. This renewed reification, the regression of artworks to the barbaric literalness of what is aesthetically the case,[2] and phantasmagorical guilt are inextricably intertwined. As soon as the artwork fears for its purity so fanatically that it loses faith in its possibility and begins to display outwardly what cannot become art—canvas and mere tones—it becomes its own enemy, the direct and false continuation of purposeful rationality. This tendency culminates in the *happening*. There is no separating what is legitimate in the rebellion against semblance as illusion from what is illusory—the hope that aesthetic semblance could rescue itself from the morass in which it is sunk by pulling itself up by the scruff of its own neck. Clearly the immanent semblance character of artworks cannot be freed from some degree of external imitation of reality, however latent, and therefore cannot be freed from illusion either. For everything that artworks contain with regard to form and materials, spirit and subject matter, has emigrated from reality into the artworks and in them has divested itself of its reality: Thus the artwork also becomes its afterimage. Even the purest aesthetic determination, appearance, is mediated to reality as its determinate negation. The difference of artworks from the empirical world, their semblance character, is constituted out of the empirical world and in opposition to it. If for the sake of their own concept artworks wanted absolutely to destroy this reference back to the empirical world, they would wipe out their own premise. Art is indeed infinitely difficult in that it must transcend its concept in order to fulfill it; yet in this process where it comes to resemble realia it assimilates itself to that reification against which it protests: Today *engagement* inescapably becomes aesthetic concession. The ineffability of illusion prevents the solution of the antinomy of aesthetic semblance by means of a concept of absolute appearance. Semblance, which heralds the ineffable, does not literally make artworks epiphanies, however difficult it may be for genuine aesthetic experience not to trust that the absolute is present in authentic artworks. It inheres in the grandeur of art to awaken this trust. That whereby art becomes an unfolding of truth is at the same time its cardinal sin, from which it cannot absolve itself. Art drags this sin along with it because it acts as if absolution had been bestowed on it.——That in spite of everything it remains an embarrassment for art to bear even the slightest trace of semblance cannot be separated from the fact that even those works that renounce semblance are cut off from real political effect, which was the original inspiration for the rejection of semblance by dadaism. Mimetic comportment—by which hermetic artworks criticize the bourgeois maxim that everything must be useful—itself becomes complicitous through the semblance of being purely in-itself, a semblance from which there is no escape even for art that destroys this semblance. If no idealist misunderstanding were to be feared, one could formulate the law of each and every work—and not miss by much naming art's inner lawfulness—as the obligation to resemble its own objective ideal and on no account that of the artist's. The mimesis of artworks is their resemblance to themselves. Whether univocally or ambiguously, this law is posited by the initial act of each artwork; by virtue of its constitution each work is bound by it. It divides aesthetic from cultic images. By the autonomy of their form, artworks forbid the incorporation of the absolute as if they were symbols. Aesthetic images stand under the prohibition on graven images. To this extent aesthetic semblance, even its ultimate form in the hermetic artwork, is truth. Hermetic works do not assert what transcends them as though they were Being occupying an ultimate realm; rather, through their powerlessness and superfluity in the empirical world they emphasize the element of powerlessness in their own content. The ivory tower—in disdain for which those who are led in democratic countries and the *Führer* of totalitarian countries are united—has in its unwavering mimetic impulse, which is an impulse toward self-likeness, an eminently enlightening aspect; its *spleen* is a truer consciousness than the doctrines of didactic or politically *engagé* art, whose regressive character is, almost without exception, blatantly obvious in the trivial wisdom those doctrines supposedly communicate. Therefore, in spite of the summary verdicts passed on it everywhere by those who are politically interested, radical modern art is progressive, and this is true not merely of the techniques it has developed but of its truth content. What makes existing artworks more than existence is not simply another existing thing, but their language. Authentic artworks are eloquent even when they refuse any form of semblance, from the phantasmagorical illusion to the faintest auratic breath. The effort to purge them of whatever contingent subjectivity may want to say through them involuntarily confers an ever more defined shape on their own language. In artworks the term expression refers to precisely this language. There is good reason that where this term has been technically employed longest and most emphatically, as the directive *espressivo* in musical scores, it demands nothing specifically expressed, no particular emotional content. Otherwise *espressivo* could be replaced by terms for whatever specific thing is to be expressed. The composer Artur Schnabel attempted to do just this, but without success.

No artwork is an undiminished unity; each must simulate it, and thus collides with itself. Confronted with an antagonistic reality, the aesthetic unity that is established in opposition to it immanently becomes a semblance. The integration of artworks culminates in the semblance that their life is precisely that of their elements. However, the elements import the heterogeneous into artworks and their semblance becomes apocryphal. In fact, every penetrating analysis of an artwork turns up fictions in its claim to aesthetic unity, whether on the grounds that its parts do not spontaneously cohere and that unity is simply imposed on them, or that the elements are prefabricated to fit this unity and are not truly elements. The plurality in artworks is not what it was empirically but rather what it becomes as soon as it enters their domain; this condemns aesthetic reconciliation as aesthetically specious. The artwork is semblance not only as the antithesis to existence but also in its own terms. It is beleaguered with inconsistencies. By virtue of their nexus of meaning, the organon of their semblance, artworks set themselves up as things that exist in themselves. By integrating them, meaning itself—that which creates unity—is asserted as being present in the work, even though it is not actual. Meaning, which effects semblance, predominates in the semblance character. Yet the semblance of meaning does not exhaustively define meaning. For the meaning of an artwork is at the same time the essence that conceals itself in the factual; meaning summons into appearance what appearance otherwise obstructs. This is the purpose of the organization of an artwork, of bringing its elements together into an eloquent relation. Yet it is difficult through critical examination to distinguish this aim from the affirmative semblance of the actuality of meaning in a fashion that would be definitive enough to satisfy the philosophical construction of concepts. Even while art indicts the concealed essence, which it summons into appearance, as monstrous, this negation at the same time posits as its own measure an essence that is not present, that of possibility; meaning inheres even in the disavowal of meaning. Because meaning, whenever it is manifest in an artwork, remains bound up with semblance, all art is endowed with sadness; art grieves all the more, the more completely its successful unification suggests meaning, and the sadness is heightened by the feeling of "Oh, were it only so." Melancholy is the shadow of what in all form is heterogenous, which form strives to banish: mere existence. In happy artworks, melancholy anticipates the negation of meaning in those that are undermined, the reverse image of longing. What radiates wordlessly from artworks is that *it is*, thrown into relief by *it*—the unlocatable grammatical subject—*is not*; it cannot be referred demonstratively to anything in the world that previously exists. In the utopia of its form, art bends under the burdensome weight of the empirical world from which, as art, it steps away. Otherwise, art's consummateness is hollow. The semblance of artworks is bound up with the progress of their integration, which they had to demand of themselves and through which their content seems immediately present. The theological heritage of art is the secularization of revelation, which defines the ideal and limit of every work. The contamination of art with revelation would amount to the unreflective repetition of its fetish character on the level of theory. The eradication of every trace of revelation from art would, however, degrade it to the undifferentiated repetition of the status quo. A coherence of meaning—unity—is contrived by art because it does not exist and because as artificial meaning it negates the being-in-itself for the sake of which the organization of meaning was undertaken, ultimately negating art itself. Every artifact works against itself. Those that are a tour de force, a balancing act, demonstrate something about art as a whole: They achieve the impossible. The impossibility of every artwork in truth defines even the simplest as a tour de force. The defamation of the virtuoso element by Hegel (who was nevertheless charmed by Rossini), which lives on in the rancor against Picasso, secretly makes common cause with an affirmative ideology that disguises the antinomical character of art and all its products: Works that satisfy this affirmative ideology are almost exclusively oriented to the topos challenged by the tour de force, that great works must be simple. It is hardly the worst criterion for the fruitfulness of aesthetic-technical analysis that it reveals why a work is a tour de force. The idea of art as a tour de force only appears fully in areas of artistic execution extrinsic to the culturally recognized concept of art; this may have founded the sympathy that once existed between avant-garde and music hall or variety shows, a convergence of extremes in opposition to a middling domain of art that satisfies audiences with inwardness and that by its culturedness betrays what art should do. Art is made painfully aware of aesthetic semblance by the fundamental insolubility of its technical problems; this is most blatant in questions of artistic presentation: in the performance of music or drama. Adequate performance requires the formulation of the work as a problem, the recognition of the irreconcilable demands, arising from the relation of the content [Gehalt] of the work to its appearance, that confront the performer. In uncovering the tour de force of an artwork, the performance must find the point of indifference where the possibility of the impossible is hidden. Since the work is antinomic, a fully adequate performance is actually not possible, for every performance necessarily represses a contrary element. The highest criterion of performance is if, without repression, it makes itself the arena of those conflicts that have been emphatic in the tour de force.——Works of art that are deliberately conceived as a tour de force are semblance because they must purport in essence to be what they in essence cannot be; they correct themselves by emphasizing their own impossibility: This is the legitimation of the virtuoso element in art that is disdained by a narrow-minded aesthetics of inwardness. The proof of the tour de force, the realization of the unrealizable, could be adduced from the most authentic works. Bach, whom a crude inwardness would like to claim, was a virtuoso in the unification of the irreconcilable. What he composed is the synthesis of harmonic thoroughbass and polyphonic thinking. This synthesis is seamlessly integrated into the logic of chordal progression divested, however, of its heterogeneous weight because it is the pure result of voice leading; this endows Bach's work with its singularly floating quality. With no less stringency the paradox of the tour de force in Beethoven's work could be presented: that out of nothing something develops, the aesthetically incarnate test of the first steps of Hegel's logic.

The semblance character of artworks is immanently mediated by their own objectivity. Once a text, a painting, a musical composition is fixed, the work is factually existent and merely feigns the becoming—the content—that it encompasses; even the most extreme developmental tensions in aesthetic time are fictive insofar as they are cast in the work in advance; actually, aesthetic time is to a degree indifferent to empirical time, which it neutralizes. Concealed in the paradox of the tour de force, of making the impossible possible, is the paradox of the aesthetic as a whole: How can making bring into appearance what is not the result of making; how can what according to its own concept is not true nevertheless be true? This is conceivable only if content is distinct from semblance; yet no artwork has content other than through semblance, through the form of that semblance. Central to aesthetics therefore is the redemption of semblance; and the emphatic right of art, the legitimation of its truth, depends on this redemption. Aesthetic semblance seeks to salvage what the active spirit —which produced the artifactual bearers of semblance—eliminated from what it reduced to its material, to what is for-an-other. In the process, however, what is to be salvaged itself becomes something dominated, if not actually produced, by it; redemption through semblance is itself illusory, and the artwork accepts this powerlessness in the form of its own illusoriness. Semblance is not the *characteristica formalis* of artworks but rather *materialis*, the trace of the damage artworks want to revoke. Only to the extent that its content is unmetaphorically true does art, the artifactual, discard the semblance produced by its artifactuality. However, if on the basis of its tendency toward replication, art acts as if it is what it appears to be, it becomes the fraud of *trompe l'oeil*, a sacrifice precisely to that element in it that it wants to conceal; what was formerly called *Sachlichkeit* is based on this. Its ideal was an artwork that, by refusing in any way to appear as other than it is, would become formed in such a way that what it appears to be and what it wants to be would potentially coincide. If the artwork were completely formed—and not by illusion or because the work was rattling hopelessly at the bars of its semblance character—that character would perhaps not have the last word. However, even *Sachlichkeit*'s objectification of the artwork did not succeed in casting off the cloak of semblance. To the extent that the artwork's form is not simply identical with its adequacy to practical purposes, it remains semblance vis-à-vis that reality from which it differs through its mere determination as an artwork even when it completely hides its facture. By canceling those elements of semblance that adhere to them, artworks actually strengthen the semblance that emanates from their existence, an existence that, by being integrated, takes on the density of something in-itself even though, as something posited, an artwork cannot be something in-itself. The work is no longer to be the result of any pregiven form; flourishes, ornament, and all residual elements of an overarching formal character are to be renounced: The artwork is to be organized from below. There is nothing, however, that guarantees in advance that the artwork, once its immanent movement has blasted away the overarching form, will in any way cohere, that its *membra disjecta* will somehow unify. This uncertainty has motivated artistic procedures to preforming all individual elements backstage—and the theatrical expression is pertinent—so that they will be capable of making the transition into a whole that the details, taken in their absolute contingency after the liquidation of all predetermined form, would otherwise refuse. Semblance thus prevails over its sworn enemies. The illusion is created that there is no illusion; that the diffuse and ego-alien harmonize with the posited totality, whereas the harmony itself is organized; that the process is presented from below to above, even though the traditional determination from above to below, without which the spiritual determination of the artwork cannot be conceived, persists. Usually the semblance character of artworks has been associated with their sensuous element, especially in Hegel's formulation of the sensuous semblance of the idea. This view of semblance stands in the Platonic-Aristotelian tradition, which distinguished between the semblance of the sensuous world on the one hand and essence or pure spirit as authentic being on the other. The semblance of artworks originates, however, in their spiritual essence. Spirit as something separated from its other, making itself independent in opposition to it and intangible in this being-for-itself, is necessarily illusory; all spirit, χωρίς from the corporeal, has in itself the aspect of raising what does not exist, what is abstract, to existence; this is the truth element of nominalism. Art carries out the test of the illusoriness of spirit as that of an essence sui generis by taking at its word spirit's claim to be an entity and placing it as such before the eyes. It is this, much more than the imitation of the sensual world by aesthetic sensuousness, that art has learned to renounce and that compels art to semblance. Spirit, however, is not only semblance but also truth; it is not only the imposture of something existing in-itself, but equally the negation of all false being-in-itself. Spirit's element of nonexistence and its negativity enter artworks, which do not sensualize spirit directly or make it a fixed thing but rather become spirit exclusively through the relation of their sensuous elements to each other. Therefore the semblance character of art is at the same time its methexis in truth. The flight of many contemporary manifestations of art into aleatory may be interpreted as a desperate answer to the ubiquity of semblance: The contingent is to pass into the whole without the *pseudos* of a prestabilized harmony. The result, however, is that on the one hand the artwork is subjected to a blind lawfulness, which can no longer be distinguished from total determination from above to below and, on the other hand, the whole is surrendered to accident and the dialectic of the particular and the whole is reduced to semblance in that no whole is actually achieved. The complete absence of illusion regresses to chaotic regularity, in which accident and necessity renew their fatal pact. Art gains no power over semblance by its abolition. The semblance character of artworks sets their form of knowledge in opposition to the concept of knowledge in Kant's first critique. Artworks are semblance in that they externalize their interior, spirit, and they are only known insofar as, contrary to the prohibition laid down by the chapter on amphiboles, their interior is known. In Kant's critique of aesthetic judgment, which is so subjectively conceived that an interior of the aesthetic object is not even mentioned, this interior is nevertheless implicitly presupposed by the concept of teleology. Kant subordinates artworks to the idea of something purposeful in and of itself, rather than consigning their unity exclusively to subjective synthesis through the knower. Artistic experience, immanently purposeful, does not amount to the categorial forming of the chaotic by the subject. Hegel's method, which was to give himself over to the complexion of aesthetic objects and to dismiss their subjective effects as accidental, puts Kant's thesis to the test: Objective teleology becomes the canon of aesthetic experience. The primacy of the object in art and the knowledge of its works from within are two sides of the same coin. In terms of the traditional distinction between thing and phenomenon, artworks—by virtue of their countertendency toward their status as a thing and ultimately toward reification altogether—have their locus on the side of appearances. But in artworks, appearance is that of essence, toward which it is not indifferent; in artworks, appearance itself belongs to the side of essence. They are truly characterized by that thesis in Hegel in which realism and nominalism are mediated: Art's essence must appear, and its appearance is that of essence and not an appearance for-another but rather art's immanent determination. Accordingly, no work of art, regardless what its maker thinks of it, is directed toward an observer, not even toward a transcendental subject of apperception; no artwork is to be described or explained in terms of the categories of communication. Artworks are semblance in that they help what they themselves cannot be to a type of second-order, modified existence; they are appearance because by virtue of aesthetic realization the nonexistent in them, for whose sake they exist, achieves an existence, however refracted. Yet the identity of essence and appearance can no more be achieved by art than it can be by knowledge of the real. The essence that makes the transition to appearance and defines it also explodes it; in being the appearance of what appears, what appears is always also a husk. This was denied by the aesthetic concept of harmony and all its related categories. They envisioned an equilibrium of essence and appearance, virtually by means of tact; in the candid idiom of yesteryear this was called the "artist's skillfulness." What is achieved is never aesthetic harmony but rather polish and balance; internal to everything in art that can justly be called harmonious there survives something desperate and mutually contradictory.[3] According to their internal constitution, artworks are to dissolve everything that is heterogeneous to their form even though they are form only in relation to what they would like to make vanish. They impede what seeks to appear in them according to their own apriori. They must conceal it, a concealment that their idea of truth opposes until they reject harmony. Without the memento of contradiction and nonidentity, harmony would be aesthetically irrelevant, just as according to the insight of Hegel's early work on the difference between Schelling's and Fichte's systems identity can only be conceived as identity with what is nonidentical. The more deeply artworks immerse themselves in the idea of harmony, of the appearing essence, the less they can be satisfied with that idea. From the perspective of the philosophy of history, it is hardly an improper generalization of what is all too divergent if one derives the antiharmonic gestures of Michelangelo, of the late Rembrandt, and of Beethoven's last works not from the subjective suffering of their development as artists but from the dynamic of the concept of harmony itself and ultimately from its insufficiency. Dissonance is the truth about harmony. If the ideal of harmony is taken strictly, it proves to be unreachable according to its own concept. Its desiderata are satisfied only when such unreachableness appears as essence, which is how it appears in the late style of important artists. Far beyond any individual oeuvre, this style has exemplary force: that of the historical suspension of aesthetic harmony altogether. The rejection of the ideal of classicism is not the result of the alternation of styles or, indeed, of an alleged historical temperament; it is, rather, the result of the coefficient of friction in harmony itself, which in corporeal form presents what is not reconciled as reconciled and thereby transgresses the very postulate of the appearing essence at which the ideal of harmony aims. The emancipation from this ideal is an aspect of the developing truth content of art.

The rebellion against semblance, art's dissatisfaction with itself, has been an intermittent element of its claim to truth from time immemorial. Art, whatever its material, has always desired dissonance, a desire suppressed by the affirmative power of society with which aesthetic semblance has been bound up. Dissonance is effectively expression; the consonant and harmonious want to soften and eliminate it. Expression and semblance are fundamentally antithetical. If expression is scarcely to be conceived except as the expression of suffering—joy has proven inimical to expression, perhaps because it has yet to exist, and bliss would be beyond expression —expression is the element immanent to art through which, as one of its constituents, art defends itself against the immanence that it develops by its law of form. Artistic expression comports itself mimetically, just as the expression of living creatures is that of pain. The lineaments of expression inscribed in artworks, if they are not to be mute, are demarcation lines against semblance. Yet, in that artworks as such remain semblance, the conflict between semblance—form in the broadest sense—and expression remains unresolved and fluctuates historically. Mimetic comportment—an attitude toward reality distinct from the fixated antithesis of subject and object—is seized in art—the organ of mimesis since the mimetic taboo—by semblance and, as the complement to the autonomy of form, becomes its bearer. The unfolding of art is that of a quid pro quo: Expression, through which nonaesthetic experience reaches most deeply into the work, becomes the archetype of everything fictive in art, as if at the juncture where art is most permeable to real experience culture most rigorously stood guard that the border not be violated. The expressive values of artworks cease to be immediately those of something alive. Refracted and transformed, they become the expression of the work itself: The term *musica ficta* is the earliest evidence of this. That quid pro quo not only neutralizes mimesis, it also derives from it. If mimetic comportment does not imitate something but rather makes itself like itself, this is precisely

145

what artworks take it upon themselves to fulfill. In their expression, artworks do not imitate the impulses of individuals, nor in any way those of their authors; in cases where this is their essential determination, they fall as copies precisely to the mercy of that reification that the mimetic impulse opposes. At the same time artistic expression enforces on itself history's judgment that mimesis is an archaic comportment, that as an immediate practice mimesis is not knowledge, that what makes itself like itself does not become truly alike, that mimetic intervention failed. Thus mimesis is banished to art that comports itself mimetically, just as art absorbs the critique of mimesis into itself by carrying out the objectivation of this impulse.

Although there has rarely been doubt that expression is an essential element of art—even the present hesitancy toward expression confirms its relevance and actually holds for art as a whole—its concept, like most key aesthetic concepts, is recalcitrant to the theory that wants to name it: What is qualitatively contrary to the concept per se can only with difficulty be brought within the bounds of its concept; the form in which something may be thought is not indifferent to what is thought. From the perspective of the philosophy of history, expression in art must be interpreted as a compromise. Expression approaches the transsubjective; it is the form of knowledge that—having preceded the polarity of subject and object—does not recognize this polarity as definitive. Art is secular, however, in that it attempts to achieve such knowledge within the bounds of the polarity of subject and object, as an act of autonomous spirit. Aesthetic expression is the objectification of the non-objective, and in fact in such a fashion that through its objectification it becomes a second-order nonobjectivity: It becomes what speaks out of the artifact not as an imitation of the subject. Yet precisely the objectivation of expression, which coincides with art, requires the subject who makes it and—in bourgeois terms—makes use of his own mimetic impulses. Art is expressive when what is objective, subjectively mediated, speaks, whether this be sadness, energy, or longing. Expression is the suffering countenance of artworks. They turn this countenance only toward those who return its gaze, even when they are composed in happy tones or glorify the *vie opportune* of rococo. If expression were merely the doubling of the subjectively felt, it would be null and void; the artist who condemns a work as being an impression rather than an invention knows this perfectly well. Rather than such feelings, the model of expression is that of extra-artistic things and situations. Historical processes and functions are already sedimented in them and speak out of them. Kafka is exemplary for the gesture of art when he carries out the retransformation of expression back into the actual occurrences enciphered in that expression—and from that he derives his irresistibility. Yet expression here becomes doubly puzzling because the sedimented, the expressed meaning, is once more meaningless; it is natural history that leads to nothing but what, impotently enough, it is able to express. Art is imitation exclusively as the imitation of an objective expression, remote from psychology, of which the sensorium was perhaps once conscious in the world and which now subsists only in artworks. Through expression art closes itself off to being-for-another, which always threatens to engulf it, and becomes eloquent in itself: This is art's mimetic consummation. Its expression is the antithesis of expressing something.

Such mimesis is the ideal of art, not its practical procedure, nor is it an attitude directed toward expressive values. The contribution made to expression by the artist is the power of mimicry, which in him releases the expressed; if what is expressed becomes the tangible content [*Inhalt*] of the artist's soul, and the artwork a copy of this content, the work degenerates into a blurred photograph. Schubert's resignation has its locus not in the purported mood of his music, nor in how he was feeling—as if the music could give a clue to this—but in the *It is thus*[4] that it announces with the gesture of letting oneself fall: This is its expression. Its quintessence is art's character of eloquence,[5] fundamentally distinct from language as its medium. It is worth speculating whether the former is incompatible with the latter; that would in part explain the effort of prose since Joyce to put discursive language out of action, or at least to subordinate it to formal categories to the point that construction becomes unrecognizable: The new art tries to bring about the transformation of communicative into mimetic language. By virtue of its double character, language is a constituent of art and its mortal enemy. Etruscan vases in the Villa Giulia are eloquent in the highest degree and incommensurable with all communicative language. The true language of art is mute, and its muteness takes priority over poetry's significative element, which in music too is not altogether lacking. That aspect of the Etruscan vases that most resembles speech depends most likely on their *Here I am* or *This is what I am*, a selfhood not first excised by identificatory thought from the interdependence of entities. Thus the rhinoceros, that mute animal, seems to say: "I am a rhinoceros." Rilke's line "for there is no place / without eyes to see you,"[6] which Benjamin held in high esteem, codified the nonsignificative language of artworks in an incomparable fashion: Expression is the gaze of artworks. Compared to significative language, the language of expression is older though unfulfilled: as if artworks, by molding themselves to the subject through their organization, recapitulated the way the subject originated, how it wrested itself free.[7] Artworks bear expression not where they communicate the subject, but rather where they reverberate with the protohistory of subjectivity, of ensoulment, for which tremolo of any sort is a miserable surrogate. This is the affinity of the artwork to the subject and it endures because this protohistory survives in the subject and recommences in every moment of history. Only the subject is an adequate instrument of expression however much, though it imagines itself unmediated, it is itself mediated. However much the expressed resembles the subject, however much the impulses are those of the subject, they are at the same time apersonal, participating in the integrative power of the ego without ever becoming identical with it. The expression of artworks is the nonsubjective in the subject; not so much that subject's expression as its copy; there is nothing so expressive as the eyes of animals—especially apes—which seem objectively to mourn that they are not human. By the transposition of impulses into artworks, which make them their own by virtue of their integration, these impulses remain the plenipotentiary in the aesthetic continuum of extra-aesthetic nature yet are no longer incarnate as its afterimage. This ambivalence is registered by every genuine aesthetic experience, and incomparably so in Kant's description of the feeling of the sublime as a trembling between nature and freedom. Such modification of mimesis is, without any reflection on the spiritual, the constitutive act of spiritualization in all art. Later art only develops this act, but it is already posited in the modification of mimesis through the work, provided that it does not occur through mimesis itself as, so to speak, the physiologically primordial form of spirit. The modification shares the guilt of the affirmative character of art because it mollifies the pain through imagination just as the spiritual totality in which this pain disappears makes it controllable and leaves it untransformed.

However much art is marked and potentiated by universal alienation, it is least alienated insofar as everything in it passes through spirit—is humanized—without force. Art oscillates between ideology and what Hegel confirmed as the native domain of spirit, the truth of spirit's self-certainty. No matter how much spirit may exert domination in art, its objectivation frees it from the aims of domination. In that aesthetic structures create a continuum that is totally spirit, they become the semblance of a blocked being-in-itself in whose reality the intentions of the subject would be fulfilled and extinguished. Art corrects conceptual knowledge because, in complete isolation, it carries out what conceptual knowledge in vain awaits from the nonpictorial subject-object relation: that through a subjective act what is objective would be unveiled. Art does not postpone this act ad infinitum but demands it of its own finitude at the price of its illusoriness. Through spiritualization, the radical domination of nature—its own—art corrects the domination of nature as the domination of an other. What establishes itself in the artwork as an alien and rudimentary fetish that endures in opposition to the subject is the plenipotentiary of the nonalienated; by contrast, however, what comports itself in the world as though it were unidentical nature is reduced all the more surely to the material of the domination of nature, to a vehicle of social domination, and is thus truly alienated. Expression, by which nature seeps most deeply into art, is at the same time what is not literally nature, a memento of what expression itself is not, of what could not have become concrete except through the *how* of that expression.

The mediation of expression in artworks through their spiritualization —which in expressionism's early period was evident to its most important exponents—implies the critique of that clumsy dualism of form and expression that orients traditional aesthetics as well as the consciousness of many genuine artists.[8] Not that this dichotomy is without any basis. The preponderance of expression at one point, and of the formal aspect at another, cannot be denied, especially in older art, which offered impulses a framework. Since then both elements have become inextricably mediated by each other. Where works are not fully integrated, not fully formed, they sacrifice precisely the expressivity for the sake of which they dispense with the labor and effort of form, and the supposedly pure form that disavows expression rattles mechanically. Expression is a phenomenon of interference, a function of technical procedures no less than it is mimetic. Mimesis is itself summoned up by the density of the technical procedure, whose immanent rationality indeed seems to work in opposition to expression. The compulsion exerted by integral works is equivalent to their eloquence, to what speaks in them, and no merely suggestive effect; suggestion is, furthermore, itself related to mimetic processes. This leads to a subjective paradox of art: to produce what is blind, expression, by way of reflection, that is, through form; not to rationalize the blind but to produce it aesthetically, "To make things of which we do not know what they are."[9] This situation, which has today been sharpened to an antithesis, has a long prehistory. In speaking of the precipitate of the absurd, the incommensurable, in every artwork, Goethe not only formulated the modern constellation of the conscious and unconscious but also envisioned the prospect that the sphere of art sheltered from consciousness as a preserve of the unconscious would become that *spleen* as which art understood itself to be in the second romanticism since Baudelaire: a virtually self-transcending preserve built into rationality. Pointing this out, however, does not dispatch art: Whoever argues against modernism in this fashion holds mechanically to the dualism of form and expression. What theorists take for a strictly logical contradiction is familiar to artists and unfolds in their work as that control over the mimetic element that summons up, destroys, and redeems its spontaneity. Spontaneity amid the involuntary is the vital element of art, and this ability is a dependable criterion of artistic capacity, though it does not gloss over the fatality of this capacity. Artists are familiar with this capacity as their sense of form. It provides the mediating category to the Kantian problematic of how art, which Kant considered blatantly nonconceptual, subjectively bears that element of the universal and the necessary that, according to the critique of reason, is reserved exclusively for discursive knowledge. The sense of form is the reflection, at once blind and binding, of the work in itself on which that reflection must depend; it is an objectivity closed to itself that devolves upon the subjective mimetic capacity, which for its part gains its force through its antithesis, rational construction. The blindness of the sense of form corresponds to the necessity in the object. The irrationality of the expressive element is for art the aim of all aesthetic rationality. Its task is to divest itself, in opposition to all imposed order, both of hopeless natural necessity and chaotic contingency. Aesthetic necessity becomes aware of its fictive element through the experience of contingency. But art does not seek to do justice to contingency by its intentional, fictive incorporation in order thus to depotentiate its subjective mediations. Rather, art does justice to the contingent by probing in the darkness of the trajectory of its own necessity. The more truly art follows this trajectory, the less self-transparent art is. It makes itself dark. Its immanent process has the quality of following a divining rod. To follow where the hand is drawn: This is mimesis as the fulfillment of objectivity; examples of automatic writing, including the Schoenberg who wrote *Erwartung*, were inspired by this utopia, only to be compelled to discover that the tension between expression and objectivation does not issue in their identity. There is no middle position between the self-censorship of the need for expression and the concessiveness of construction. Objectivation traverses the extremes. When untamed by taste or artistic understanding the need for expression converges with the bluntness of rational objectivity. On the other hand, art's "thinking of itself," its *noesis noeseos*, is not to be restrained by any preordained irrationality. Aesthetic rationality must plunge blindfolded into the making of the work rather than directing it externally as an act of reflection over the artwork. Artworks are smart or foolish according to their procedures, not according to the thoughts their author has about them. Such immanent understanding of the material assures that Beckett's work is at every point sealed tightly against superficial rationality. This is by no means the exclusive prerogative of modern art but equally evident in the abbreviations in late Beethoven, in the renunciation of superfluous and to this extent irrational ornamentation. Conversely, lesser artworks, facile music especially, are marked by an immanent stupidity, to which modernism's ideal of maturity was a polemical reaction. The aporia of mimesis and construction compels artworks to unite radicalism with deliberation, without the aid of any apocryphal, trumped-up hypotheses.

Deliberation, however, does not resolve the aporia. Historically, one of the roots of the rebellion against semblance is the allergy to expression; here, if anywhere in art, the relation between the generations plays a part. Expressionism became the father image. Empirically it has been confirmed that inhibited, conventional, and aggressive-reactionary individuals tend to reject "intraception"—self-awareness—in any form, and along with it expression as such, as being all too human.[10] They are the ones who, in a context of general estrangement from art, declare themselves with particular resentment against modernism. Psychologically they obey defense mechanisms with which a weakly developed ego repudiates whatever disturbs its restricted functional capacity and may, above all, damage its narcissism. This psychological posture is that of an *"intolerance to ambiguity,"* an impatience with what is ambivalent and not strictly definable; ultimately, it is the refusal of what is open, of what has not been predetermined by any jurisdiction, ultimately of experience itself. Immediately back of the mimetic taboo stands a sexual one: Nothing should be moist; art becomes hygienic. Many artistic directions identify with this taboo and with the witch hunt against expression. The antipsychologism of modernism has shifted its function. Once a prerogative of the avant-garde, which rebelled against *Jugendstil* as well as against a realism protracted by a turn toward inwardness, this antipsychologism was meanwhile socialized and made serviceable to the status quo. The category of inwardness, according to Max Weber's thesis, is to be dated back to Protestantism, which subordinated works to faith. Although inwardness, even in Kant, implied a protest against a social order heteronomously imposed on its subjects, it was from the beginning marked by an indifference toward this order, a readiness to leave things as they are and to obey. This accorded with the origin of inwardness in the labor process: Inwardness served to cultivate an anthropological type that would dutifully, quasi-voluntarily, perform the wage labor required by the new mode of production necessitated by the relations of production. With the growing powerlessness of the autonomous subject, inwardness consequently became completely ideological, the mirage of an inner kingdom where the silent majority are indemnified for what is denied them socially; inwardness thus becomes increasingly shadowy and empty, indeed contentless in itself. Art no longer wants to accommodate itself to this situation. Yet art is scarcely imaginable without the element of inwardness. Benjamin once said that in his opinion inwardness could go fly a kite. This was directed against Kierkegaard and the "philosophy of inwardness" that claimed him as their founder, even though that term would have been as antipathetic to the theologian as the word ontology. Benjamin had in mind abstract subjectivity that powerlessly sets itself up as substance. But his comment is no more the whole truth than abstract subjectivity is. Spirit—certainly Benjamin's own—must enter itself if it is to be able to negate what is opaque. This could be demonstrated by the antithesis of Beethoven and jazz, a contrast to which many musicians' ears are already beginning to be deaf. Beethoven is, in modified yet determinable fashion, the full experience of external life returning inwardly, just as time—the medium of music—is the inward sense; *popular music*, in all of its many varieties does not undergo this sublimation and is, as such, a somatic stimulant and therefore regressive vis-à-vis aesthetic autonomy. Even inwardness participates in dialectics, though not as Kierkegaard thought. The result of the liquidation of inwardness was by no means the surfacing of a type of person cured of ideology but rather one who never became an individual in the first place, the type David Riesmann termed "*outer-directed.*" This casts a reconciling light on the category of inwardness in art. In fact, the rabid denunciation of radically expressive works as being examples of hyperbolic late romanticism has become the predictable babble of all those who favor a return to the pristine. Aesthetic self-relinquishment in the artwork requires not a weak or conformist ego but a forceful one. Only the autonomous self is able to turn critically against itself and break through its illusory imprisonment. This is not conceivable as long as the mimetic element is repressed by a rigid aesthetic superego rather than that the mimetic element disappears into and is maintained in the objectivation of the tension between itself and its antithesis. All the same, semblance is most strikingly obvious in expression because it makes its appearance as if it were illusionless even while subsuming itself to aesthetic semblance; major criticism of expression has been sparked by its perception as theatrics. In the fully administered world, the mimetic taboo—a keystone of bourgeois ontology—encroached on the zone that had been tolerantly reserved for mimesis, whereby it beneficially revealed human immediacy to be a lie. Beyond this, however, the allergy to expression supports that hatred of the subject without which no critique of the commodity world would even be meaningful. The subject is abstractly negated. Indeed, the subject—which in compensation inflates itself the more powerless and functional it becomes—is false consciousness the moment it lays claim to expression by feigning a relevance that was withdrawn from it. Yet the emancipation of society from the supremacy of its relations of production has as its aim what these relations have to date impeded—the real establishment of the subject—and expression is not simply the hubris of the subject but the lament over its miscarriage as a cipher of its possibility. Certainly the allergy to expression may be most profoundly legitimated by the fact that something in expression tends toward mendacity, regardless of any aesthetic manipulation. Expression is a priori imitation. Latently implicit in expression is the trust that by being spoken or screamed all will be made better: This is a rudiment of magic, faith in what Freud polemically called the "omnipotence of thought." Yet expression is not altogether circumscribed by the magic spell. That it is spoken, that distance is thus won from the trapped immediacy of suffering, transforms suffering just as screaming diminishes unbearable pain. Expression that has been objectivated as language endures; what has once been said never fades away completely, neither the evil nor the good, neither the slogan of "the final solution" nor the hope of reconciliation. What accedes to language enters the movement of a humanness that does not yet exist; it is compelled toward language and alive only by virtue of its helplessness. Stumbling along behind its reification, the subject limits that reification by means of the mimetic vestige, the plenipotentiary of an undamaged life in the midst of mutilated life, which subverts the subject to ideology. The inextricability of reification and mimesis defines the aporia of artistic expression. There is no general test for deciding if an artist who wipes out expression altogether has become the mouthpiece of reified consciousness or of the speechless, expressionless expression that denounces it. Authentic art knows the expression of the expressionless, a kind of weeping without tears. By contrast, *Neue Sachlichkeit*'s polished extirpation of expression contributes to universal conformism and subordinates antifunctional art to a principle that originates entirely in functionality. This form of reaction fails to recognize in expression what is not metaphorical, not ornamental; the more unreservedly artworks open themselves to this, the more they become depositions of expression and effectively invert *Sachlichkeit*. At the very least it is evident that antiexpressive and, like Mondrian's, affirmatively mathematized artworks have by no means passed final judgment on expression. If the subject is no longer able to speak directly, then at least it should—in accord with a modernism that has not pledged itself to absolute construction—speak through things, through their alienated and mutilated form.

Notes

1 See Adorno, *In Search of Wagner*, trans. Rodney Livingstone (London, 1981), pp. 85ff.

2 ["was ästhetisch der Fall sei": This is a reference to Wittgenstein's *Tractatus Logico-Philosophicus*, see note 3 in "Situation."—trans.]

3 See Adorno, "On the Classicism of Goethe's *Iphigenie*," in *Notes to Literature*, trans. Shierry Weber Nicholsen, vol. 2 (New York, 1992), pp. 153ff.

4 ["So ist es": See note 16 on "Sosein" in "Natural Beauty."—trans.]

5 ["Sprachcharakter": There is no adequate translation for this concept as Adorno uses it. Its meaning, however, is partly elucidated by a group of related ideas in which Adorno conceives the artwork as something that is, or becomes "beredt" (fluent, expressive), where something comes to or finds "Sprache." This is a speech where language itself is not necessarily the medium. "Eloquence" has, as a potential, just this implication, and it has therefore been used, reluctantly, for all of the above concepts in one way or another. The problem is, of course, that the English concept tends to emphasize an unconflicted sort of fluency and persuasiveness. Adorno, however, is not at all concerned with persuasion but rather with expression as gesture, cipher, countenance, script and speech as it arises out of brokenness, fragmentariness or fissuredness. "Eloquence," furthermore, importantly forfeits the idea of script, which is a palpable aspect of "Sprachcharakter." But "script" would forfeit the quality of speaking and in any case, when Adorno wants to emphasize "script" he uses "Schrift" or, in other writings than *Aesthetic Theory*, "ecriture."—trans.]

6 Rainer Maria Rilke, "Archäischer Torso Apollos," in *Sämtliche Werke*, ed. E. Zinn, vol. 1 (Wiesbaden, 1955), p. 557. "Denn da ist keine Stelle, / die dich nicht sieht." [See also "Torso of an Archaic Apollo," in *Selected Poems*, trans. C.

F. MacIntyre (Berkeley, 1964), pp. 92–93.—trans.]

7 ["wie es entspringt, sich entringt": This passage is constructed out of the central concepts of Walter Benjamin's *The Origin of German Tragic Drama*, trans. John Osborne (London, 1977). In this line Adorno effectively explicates Benjamin's concept of origin—the *Ursprung*, the original leap—as both a leap out of and a wresting free. See Benjamin, *The Origin of German Tragic Drama*, p. 45.—trans.]

8 See Adorno, "Reminiscence," *Alban Berg: Master of the Smallest Link*, trans. Juliane Brand and Christopher Hailey (Cambridge, 1991), pp. 9ff.

9 [Here Adorno quotes the last line from his "Vers une musique informelle," in *Quasi una Fantasia*, trans. Rodney Livingstone (London, 1992), p. 322 (translation amended).—trans.]

10 [See Adorno et al., *The Authoritarian Personality* (New York, 1982), pp. 163ff.—trans.]

7
Enigmaticalness, truth content, metaphysics

The task of aesthetics is not to comprehend artworks as hermeneutical objects; in the contemporary situation, it is their incomprehensibility that needs to be comprehended. What is so resistlessly absorbed as a cliché by the watchword—the *absurd*—could only be recuperated by a theory that thinks its truth. It cannot simply be divided off from the spiritualization of artworks as counterpoint to that spiritualization, this counterpoint is, In Hegel's words, the ether of artworks; it is spirit itself in its omnipresence and not the intention of the enigma. For in that it negates the spirit that dominates nature, the spirit of artworks does not appear as spirit. It ignites on what is opposed to it, on materiality. In no way is spirit most present in the most spiritual artworks. Art is redemptive in the act by which the spirit in it throws itself away. Art holds true to the shudder, but not by regression to it. Rather, art is its legacy. The spirit of artworks produces the shudder by externalizing it in objects. Thus art participates in the actual movement of history in accord with the law of enlightenment: By virtue of the self-reflection of genius, what once seemed to be reality emigrates into imagination, where it survives by becoming conscious of its own unreality. The historical trajectory of art as spiritualization is that of the critique of myth as well as that toward its redemption: The imagination confirms the possibilities of what it recollects. This double movement of spirit in art describes its protohistory, which is inscribed in its concept, rather than its empirical history. The uncheckable movement of spirit toward what has eluded it becomes in art the voice that speaks for what was lost in the most distantly archaic.

Mimesis in art is the prespiritual; it is contrary to spirit and yet also that on which spirit ignites. In artworks, spirit has become their principle of construction, although it fulfills its telos only when it emerges from what is to be constructed, from the mimetic impulses, by shaping itself to them rather than allowing itself to be imposed on them by sovereign rule. Form objectivates the particular impulses only when it follows them where they want to go of their own accord. This alone is the methexis of artworks in reconciliation. The rationality of artworks becomes spirit only when it is immersed in its polar opposite. The divergence of the constructive and the mimetic, which no artwork can resolve and which is virtually the original sin of aesthetic spirit, has its correlative in that element of the ridiculous and clownish that even the most significant works bear and that, uncon-cealed, is inextricable from their significance. The inadequacy of classicism of any persuasion originates in its repression of this element; a repression that art must mistrust. The progressive spiritualization of art in the name of maturity only accentuates the ridiculous all the more glaringly; the more the artwork's own organization assimilates itself to a logical order by virtue of its inner exactitude, the more obviously the difference between the artwork's logicity and the logicity that governs empirically becomes the parody of the latter; the more reasonable the work becomes in terms of its formal constitution, the more ridiculous it becomes according to the standard of empirical reason. Its ridiculousness is, however, also part of a condemnation of empirical rationality; it accuses the rationality of social praxis of having become an end in itself and as such the irrational and mad reversal of means into ends. The ridiculous in art, which philistines recognize better than do those who are naïvely at home in art, and the folly of a rationality made absolute indict one other reciprocally; inciden-tally, when viewed from the perspective of the praxis of self-preservation, happiness—sex—is equally ridiculous, as can be spitefully pointed out by anyone who is not driven by it. Ridiculousness is the residue of the mimetic in art, the price of its self-enclosure. In his condemnation of this element, the philistine always has an ignominious measure of justification. The ridiculous, as a barbaric residuum of something alien to form, misfires in art if art fails to reflect and shape it. If it remains on the level of the childish and is taken for such, it merges with the calculated *fun* of the culture industry. By its very concept, art implies kitsch, just as by the obligation it imposes of sublimating the ridiculous it presupposes educa-tional privilege and class structure; *fun* is art's punishment for this. All the same, the ridiculous elements in artworks are most akin to their intention-less levels and therefore, in great works, also closest to their secret. Foolish subjects like those of *The Magic Flute* and *Der Freischütz* have more truth content through the medium of the music than does the *Ring*, which gravely aims at the ultimate. In its clownishness, art consolingly recollects prehistory in the primordial world of animals. Apes in the zoo together perform what resembles clown routines. The collusion of children with clowns is a collusion with art, which adults drive out of them just as they drive out their collusion with animals. Human beings have not succeeded in so thoroughly repressing their likeness to animals that they are unable in an instant to recapture it and be flooded with joy; the language of little children and animals seems to be the same. In the similarity of clowns to animals the likeness of humans to apes flashes up; the constellation animal/fool/clown is a fundamental layer of art.

As a thing that negates the world of things, every artwork is a priori helpless when it is called on to legitimate itself to this world; still, art cannot simply refuse the demand for legitimation by pointing to this apriority. It is hard to be astonished by art's enigmaticalness if it is taken neither as a source of pleasure, as it is for those alien to art, nor as an exceptional realm, as it is for the connoisseur, but as the substance of personal experience; yet this substance demands that the elements of art not be abandoned but secured when art is fundamentally challenged by its experience. An inkling of this is had when artworks are experienced in so-called cultural contexts that are alien or incommensurable to them. In these situations artworks are displayed naked to the test of their *cui bono*, a test from which they are protected only by the leaky roof of their own familiar context. In such situations the disrespectful question, which ignores the taboo surrounding the aesthetic zone, often becomes fateful to the quality of a work; observed completely externally the artworks' dubiousness is uncovered as relentlessly as when they are observed completely internally. The enigmaticalness of artworks remains bound up with history. It was through history that they became an enigma; it is history that ever and again makes them such, and, conversely, it is history alone—which gave them their authority—that holds at a distance the embarrassing question of their raison d'être. The enigmaticalness of artworks is less their irrationality than their rationality; the more methodi-cally they are ruled, the more sharply their enigmaticalness is thrown into relief. Through form, artworks gain their resemblance to language, seem-ing at every point to say just this and only this, and at the same time whatever it is slips away.

All artworks—and art altogether—are enigmas; since antiquity this has been an irritation to the theory of art. That artworks say something and in the same breath conceal it expresses this enigmaticalness from the perspective of language. This characteristic cavorts clownishly; if one is within the artwork, if one participates in its immanent completion, this enigmaticalness makes itself invisible; if one steps outside the work, breaking the contract with its immanent context, this enigmaticalness returns like a spirit. This gives further reason for the study of those who are alien to art: In their proximity the enigmaticalness of art becomes outrageous to the point that art is completely negated, unwittingly the ultimate criticism of art and, in that it is a defective attitude, a confirmation of art's truth. It is impossible to explain art to those who have no feeling for it; they are not able to bring an intellectual understanding of it into their living experience. For them the reality principle is such an obsession that it places a taboo on aesthetic comportment as a whole; incited by the cultural approbation of art, alienness to art often changes into aggression, not the least of the causes of the contemporary deaestheticization of art. Its enigmaticalness may in an elementary fashion confirm the so-called unmusical, who does not understand the "language of music," hears nothing but nonsense, and wonders what all the noise is about; the difference between what this person hears and what the initiated hear defines art's enigmaticalness. This is of course not restricted to music, whose aconceptuality makes it almost too obvious. Whoever refuses to reenact the work under the discipline it imposes falls under the empty gaze cast by a painting or poem, the same empty gaze that, in a sense, the art-alien encounter in music; and it is precisely the empty questioning gaze that the experience and interpretation of artworks must assimilate if they are not to go astray; failing to perceive the abyss is no protection from it; however consciousness seeks to safeguard itself from losing its way is fateful. There is no answer that would convince someone who would ask such questions as "Why imitate something?" or "Why tell a story as if it were true when obviously the facts are otherwise and it just distorts reality?" Artworks fall helplessly mute before the question "What's it for?" and before the reproach that they are actually pointless. If, for instance, one responded that fictive narration can touch more deeply on the essence of historical reality than can factual reportage, a possible reply would be that precisely this is a matter of theory, and that theory has no need of fiction. This manifestation of the enigmaticalness of art as incomprehension in the face of questions of putatively grand principle is familiar in the broader context of the bluff inherent in the question as to the meaning of life.[1] The awkwardness prompted by such questions can easily be confused with their irrefutability; their level of abstraction is so remote from what is effortlessly subsumed, that the actual question vanishes. Understanding art's enigmaticalness is not equivalent to understanding specific artworks, which requires an objective experiential reenactment from within in the same sense in which the interpretation of a musical work means its faithful performance. Understanding is itself a problematic category in the face of art's enigmaticalness. Whoever seeks to understand artworks exclusively through the immanence of consciousness within them by this very measure fails to understand them and as such understanding grows, so does the feeling of its insufficiency caught blindly in the spell of art, to which art's own truth content is opposed. If one who exits from this immanent context or was never in it registers the enigmaticalness with animosity, the enigmaticalness disappears deceptively into the artistic experience. The better an artwork is understood, the more it is unpuzzled on one level and the more obscure its constitutive enigmaticalness becomes. It only emerges demonstratively in the profoundest experience of art. If a work opens itself completely, it reveals itself as a question and demands reflection; then the work vanishes into the distance, only to return to those who thought they understood it, overwhelming them for a second time with the question "What is it?" Art's enigmaticalness can, however, be recognized as constitutive where it is absent: Artworks that unfold to contemplation and thought without any remainder are not artworks. Enigma here is not a glib synonym for "problem," a concept that is only aesthetically significant in the strict sense of a task posed by the immanent composition of works. In no less strict terms, artworks are enigmas. They contain the potential for the solution; the solution is not objectively given. Every artwork is a picture puzzle, a puzzle to be solved, but this puzzle is constituted in such a fashion that it remains a vexation, the preestablished routing of its observer. The newspaper picture puzzle recapitulates playfully what artworks carry out in earnest. Specifically, artworks are like picture puzzles in that what they hide—like Poe's letter—is visible and is, by being visible, hidden. The German language, in its protophilosophic description of aesthetic experience, rightly expresses that one understands something of art, not that one understands art. Connoisseurship of art is the combination of an adequate comprehension of the material and a narrow-minded incomprehension of the enigma; it is neutral to what is cloaked. Those who peruse art solely with comprehension make it into something straightforward, which is furthest from what it is. If one seeks to get a closer look at a rainbow, it disappears. Of all the arts, music is the prototypical example of this: It is at once completely enigmatic and totally evident. It cannot be solved, only its form can be deciphered, and precisely this is requisite for the philosophy of art. He alone would understand music who hears with all the alienness of the unmusical and with all of Siegfried's familiarity with the language of the birds. Understanding, however, does not extinguish the enigmaticalness of art. Even the felicitously interpreted work asks for further understanding, as if waiting for the redemptive word that would dissolve its constitutive darkening. Following artworks through in the imagination is the most complete, most deceptive surrogate for understanding, though obviously also a step toward it. Those who can adequately imagine music without hearing it possess that connection with it required for its understanding. Understanding in the highest sense—a solution of the enigma that at the same time maintains the enigma—depends on a spiritualization of art and artistic experience whose primary medium is the imagination. The spiritualization of art approaches its enigmaticalness not directly through conceptual elucidation, but rather by concretizing its enigmaticalness. The solution of the enigma amounts to giving the reason for its insolubility, which is the gaze artworks direct at the viewer. The demand of artworks that they be understood, that their content be grasped, is bound to their specific experience; but it can only be fulfilled by way of the theory that reflects this experience. What the enigmaticalness of artworks refers to can only be thought mediatedly. The objection to the phenomenology of art, as to any phenomenology that imagines it can lay its hands directly on the essence, is not that it is antiempirical but, on the contrary, that it brings thinking experience to a halt.

The much derided incomprehensibility of hermetic artworks amounts to the admission of the enigmaticalness of all art. Part of the rage against hermetic works is that they also shatter the comprehensibility of traditional works. It holds true in general that the works sanctioned by tradition and public opinion as being well understood withdraw behind their galvanized surface and become completely incomprehensible; those manifestly incomprehensible works that emphasize their enigmaticalness are potentially the most comprehensible. Art in the most emphatic sense lacks the concept even when it employs concepts and adapts its facade to comprehension. No concept that enters an artwork remains what it is; each and every concept is so transformed that its scope can be affected and its meaning refashioned. In Trakl's poems the word "sonata" acquires a unique importance by its sound and by the associations established by the poem; if one wanted to envision a particular sonata on the basis of the diffuse sounds that are suggested, the sense of the word in the poem could be missed just as the conjunct image would be incongruous with such a sonata and the sonata form itself. At the same time this would be legitimate, because the word coalesces out of fragments and scraps of sonatas and its very name is reminiscent of the sound that is meant and awakened in the work. The term sonata describes works that are highly articulated, motivically and thematically wrought, and internally dynamic; their unity is a clearly differentiated manifold, with development and reprise. The verse, "There are rooms filled with chords and sonatas"[2] retains little of this but has, rather, the feeling of the childish naming of names; it has more to do with the spurious title *Moonlight* sonata than with the composition itself and yet is no coincidence; without the sonatas that his sister played there would not have been the isolated sounds in which the melancholy of the poet sought shelter. Something of this marks even the poem's simplest words, which are drawn from communicative language; that is why Brecht's critique of autonomous art, that it simply reiterates what something is, misses the mark. Even Trakl's omnipresent "is" is alienated in the artwork from its conceptual sense: It expresses no existential judgment but rather its pale afterimage qualitatively transformed to the point of negation; the assertion that something is amounts to both more and less and includes the implication that something is not. When Brecht or William Carlos Williams sabotages the poetic and approximates an empirical report, the actual result is by no means such a report: By the polemical rejection of the exalted lyrical tone, the empirical sentences translated into the aesthetic monad acquire an altogether different quality. The antilyrical tone and the estrangement of the appropriated facts are two sides of the same coin. Judgment itself undergoes metamorphosis in the artwork. Artworks are, as synthesis, analogous to judgment; in artworks, however, synthesis does not result in judgment; of no artwork is it possible to determine its judgment or what its so-called message is. It is therefore questionable whether artworks can possibly be *engagé*, even when they emphasize their *engagement*. What works amount to, that in which they are unified, cannot be formulated as a judgment, not even as one that they state in words and sentences. Mörike has a little poem entitled "Mousetrap Rhyme." If one restricted interpretation to its discursive content, the poem would amount to no more than sadistic identification with what civilized custom has done to an animal disdained as a parasite:

Mousetrap Rhyme

The child circles the mousetrap three times and chants:

Little guest, little house.
Dearest tiny or grown-up mouse
boldly pay us a visit tonight
when the moon shines bright!
But close the door back of you tight,
you hear?
And careful for your little tail!
After dinner we will sing
After dinner we will spring
And make a little dance:
Swish, Swish!
My old cat will probably be dancing with.[3]

The child's taunt, "My old cat will probably be dancing with"—if it really is a taunt and not the involuntarily friendly image of child, cat, and mouse dancing, the two animals on their hind legs—once appropriated by the poem, no longer has the last word. To reduce the poem to a taunt is to ignore its social content [*Inhalt*] along with its poetic content. The poem is the nonjudgmental reflex of language on a miserable, socially conditioned ritual, and as such it transcends it by subordinating itself to it. The poem's gesture, which points to this ritual as if nothing else were possible, holds court over the gapless immanence of the ritual by turning the force of self-evidence into an indictment of that ritual. Art judges exclusively by abstaining from judgment; this is the defense of naturalism. Form, which shapes verse into the echo of a mythical epigram, negates its fatefulness. Echo reconciles. These processes, transpiring in the interior of artworks, make them truly infinite in themselves. It is not that artworks differ from significative language by the absence of meanings; rather, these meanings through their absorption become a matter of accident. The movements by which this absorption of meaning occurs are concretely prescribed by every aesthetically formed object.

Artworks share with enigmas the duality of being determinate and indeterminate. They are question marks, not univocal even through synthesis. Nevertheless their figure is so precise that it determines the point where the work breaks off. As in enigmas, the answer is both hidden and demanded by the structure. This is the function of the work's immanent logic, of the lawfulness that transpires in it, and that is the theodicy of the concept of purpose in art. The aim of artworks is the determination of the indeterminate. Works are purposeful in themselves, without having any positive purpose beyond their own arrangement; their purposefulness, however, is legitimated as the figure of the answer to the enigma. Through organization artworks become more than they are. In recent aesthetic debates, especially in the fine arts, the concept of *écriture* has become relevant, inspired probably by Klee's drawings, which approximate scrawled writing. Like a searchlight, this category of modern art illumines the art of the past; all artworks are writing, not just those that are obviously such; they are hieroglyphs for which the code has been lost, a loss that plays into their content. Artworks are language only as writing. If no artwork is ever a judgment, each artwork contains elements derived from judgment and bears an aspect of being correct and incorrect, true and false. Yet the silent and determinate answer of artworks does not reveal itself to interpretation with a single stroke, as a new immediacy, but only by way of all mediations, those of the works' discipline as well as those of thought and philosophy. The enigmaticalness outlives the interpretation that arrives at the answer. If the enigmaticalness of artworks is not localized in what is experienced in them, in aesthetic understanding—if the enigmaticalness only bursts open in the distance—the experience that immerses itself in the artworks and is rewarded with corroboration itself becomes enigmatic: the enigma that what is multivocally entwined can be univocally and compellingly understood as such. For the experience of artworks, whatever its starting point, is as Kant himself described it, necessarily immanent and transparent right into its most sublime nuance. The musician who understands the score follows its most minute impulses, and yet in a certain sense he does not know what he plays; the situation is no different for the actor, and precisely in this is the mimetic capacity made manifest most drastically in the praxis of artistic performance as the imitation of the dynamic curves of what is performed; it is the quintessence of understanding this side of the enigma. However, as soon as the experience of artworks flags, they present their enigma as a grimace.

Incessantly the experience of artworks is threatened by their enigmatical-ness. If enigmaticalness disappears completely from the experience, if experience supposes that it has become completely immanent to the object, the enigma's gaze suddenly appears again; thus is preserved the artworks' seriousness, which stares out of archaic images and is masked in traditional art by their familiar language until strengthened to the point of total alienation.

If the process immanent to artworks constitutes the enigma, that is, what surpasses the meaning of all its particular elements, this process at the same time attenuates the enigma as soon as the artwork is no longer perceived as fixed and thereupon vainly interpreted but instead once again produced in its objective constitution. In performances that do not do this, that do not interpret, the in-itself of the artworks, which such asceticism claims to serve, becomes the booty of its muteness; every noninterpretive performance is meaningless. If some types of art, drama, and to a certain extent music, demand that they be played and interpreted so that they can become what they are—a norm from which no one is exempt who is at home in the theater or on the podium and knows the qualitative difference between what is required there and the texts and scores—these types actually do no more than illuminate the comportment of an artwork, even those that do not want to be performed: This comportment is that each artwork is the recapitulation of itself. Artworks are self-likeness freed from the compulsion of identity. The Aristotelian dictum that only like can know like, which progressive rationality has reduced to a marginal value, divides the knowledge that is art from conceptual knowledge: What is essentially mimetic awaits mimetic comportment. If artworks do not make themselves like something else but only like themselves, then only those who imitate them understand them. Dramatic or musical texts should be regarded exclusively in this fashion and not as the quintessence of instructions for the performers: They are the congealed imitation of works, virtually of themselves, and to this extent constitutive although always permeated with significative elements. Whether or not they are performed is for them a matter of indifference; what is not, however, a matter of indifference is that their experience—which in terms of its ideal is inward and mute—imitates them. Such imitation reads the nexus of their mean-ing out of the *signa* of the artworks and follows this nexus just as imitation follows the curves in which the artwork appears. As laws of their imitation the divergent media find their unity, that of art. If in Kant discursive knowledge is to renounce the interior of things, then artworks are objects whose truth cannot be thought except as that of their interior. Imitation is the path that leads to this interior.

Artworks speak like elves in fairy tales: "If you want the absolute, you shall have it, but you will not recognize it when you see it." The truth of discursive knowledge is unshrouded, and thus discursive knowledge does not have it; the knowledge that is art, has truth, but as something incommensurable with art. Through the freedom of the subject in them, artworks are less subjective than is discursive knowledge. With unerring compass, Kant subordinated art to a concept of teleology whose positive application he did not concede to empirical understanding. However, the block that according to Kant's doctrine obstructs the in-itself to people, shapes that in-itself in artworks—the doctrine's proper domain, in which there is no longer to be any difference between what is in-itself and what is for-itself—as enigmatic figures: Precisely because they are blocked, artworks are images of being-in-itself. Ultimately, what lives on in art's enigmaticalness, through which art most abruptly opposes the unquestionable existence of objects of action, is the latter's own enigma. Art becomes an enigma because it appears to have solved what is enigmatical in existence, while the enigma in the merely existing is forgotten as a result of its own overwhelming ossification. The more densely people have spun a categorial web around what is other than subjective spirit, the more fundamentally have they disaccustomed themselves to the wonder of that other and deceived themselves with a growing familiarity with what is foreign. Art hopes to correct this, though feebly and with a quickly exhausted gesture. A priori, art causes people to wonder, just as Plato once demanded that philosophy do, which, however, decided for the opposite.

The enigma of artworks is their fracturedness. If transcendence were present in them, they would be mysteries, not enigmas; they are enigmas because, through their fracturedness, they deny what they would actually like to be. Only in the recent past—in Kafka's damaged parables—has the fracturedness of art become thematic. Retrospectively, all artworks are similar to those pitiful allegories in graveyards, the broken-off stelae. Whatever perfection they may lay claim to, artworks are lopped off; that what they mean is not their essence is evident in the fact that their meaning appears as if it were blocked. The analogy here to astrological superstition, which similarly depends on a purported relationship as much as it leaves this relationship obscure, is too insistently obvious to be dismissed lightly: Art's blemish is that it is bound up with superstition. Art all too happily, and irrationally, revalues this blemish as a merit. The much touted complexity of art is the falsely positive name for its enigmaticalness. This enigmaticalness, however, has an antiaesthetic aspect, which Kafka irrevocably unveiled. By their failure with regard to their own element of rationality, artworks threaten to relapse into myth, from which they have been precariously wrested. Art is mediated in spirit—the element of rationality—in that it produces its enigmas mimetically, just as spirit devises enigmas, but without being capable of providing the solution; it is in art's enigmaticalness, not in its meanings, that spirit is manifest. In fact, the praxis of important artists has an affinity with the making of puzzles, as is evident in the delight taken by composers over many centuries in enigmatic canons. Art's enigmatic image is the configuration of mimesis and rationality. This enigmaticalness emerged out of a historical process. Art is what remains after the loss of what was supposed to exercise a magical, and later a cultic, function. Art's why-and-wherefore—its archaic rationality, to put it paradoxically—was forfeited and transformed into an element of its being-in-itself. Art thus became an enigma; if it no longer exists for the purpose that it infused with meaning, then what is it? Its enigmaticalness goads it to articulate itself immanently in such a fashion that it achieves meaning by forming its emphatic absence of meaning. To this extent, the enigmaticalness of artworks is not all there is to them; rather, every authentic work also suggests the solution to its unsolvable enigma.

Ultimately, artworks are enigmatic in terms not of their composition but of their truth content. The indefatigably recurring question that every work incites in whoever traverses it—the "What is it all about?"—becomes "Is it true?"—the question of the absolute, to which every artwork responds by wresting itself free from the discursive form of answer. A taboo on any possible answer is all that discursive thought can offer. Art itself, which is the mimetic struggle against this taboo, seeks to impart the answer and yet, being nonjudging, does not impart it; thus art becomes as enigmatic as the terror born of the primordial world, which, though it metamorphoses, does not disappear; all art remains the seismogram of that terror. The key to art's enigma is missing, just as it has been lost for the writings of many peoples who have perished. The most extreme form in which the question posed by the enigmaticalness of art can be formulated is whether or not there is meaning. For no artwork is without its own coherence, however much this coherence may be transformed into its own opposite. Through the objectivity of the work, this coherence posits the claim to the objectivity of meaning in-itself. This claim is not only nonnegotiable, it is contravened by experience. Enigmaticalness peers out of every artwork with a different face but as if the answer that it requires—like that of the sphinx—were always the same, although only by way of the diversity, not the unity that the enigma, though perhaps deceptively, promises. Whether the promise is a deception—that is the enigma.

The truth content of artworks is the objective solution of the enigma posed by each and every one. By demanding its solution, the enigma points to its truth content. It can only be achieved by philosophical reflection. This alone is the justification of aesthetics. Although no artwork can be reduced to rationalistic determinations, as is the case with what art judges, each artwork through the neediness implicit in its enigmaticalness nevertheless turns toward interpretive reason. No message is to be squeezed out of *Hamlet*; this in no way impinges on its truth content. That great artists, the Goethe who wrote fairy tales no less than Beckett, want nothing to do with interpretations only underscores the difference of the truth content from the consciousness and the intention of the author and does so by the strength of the author's own self-consciousness. Artworks, especially those of the highest dignity, await their interpretation. The claim that there is nothing to interpret in them, that they simply exist, would erase the demarcation line between art and nonart. Ultimately, perhaps, even carpets, ornaments, all nonfigural things longingly await interpretation. Grasping truth content postulates critique. Nothing is grasped whose truth or untruth is not grasped, and this is the concern of critique. The historical development of works through critique and the philosophical development of their truth content have a reciprocal relation. The theory of art must not situate itself beyond art but must rather entrust itself to its laws of movement while recognizing that artworks hermetically seal themselves off against the consciousness of these laws of movement. Artworks are enigmatic in that they are the physiognomy of an objective spirit that is never transparent to itself in the moment in which it appears. The absurd, the category most refractory to interpretation, inheres in that spirit that is requisite to the interpretation of artworks. At the same time, the need of artworks for interpretation, their need for the production of their truth content, is the stigma of their constitutive insufficiency. Artworks do not achieve what is objectively sought in them. The zone of indeterminacy between the unreachable and what has been realized constitutes their enigma. They have truth content and they do not have it.

Positive science and the philosophy derived from it do not attain it. It is neither the work's factual content nor its fragile and self-suspendable logicality. Nor—despite traditional philosophy—is art's truth content its idea, even if that idea is so broad as to include the tragic or the conflict between the finite and the infinite. Indeed, in its philosophical construction such an idea rises above subjective intention. Yet, however applied, it remains external to the artwork and abstract. Even idealism's emphatic concept of the idea relegates artworks to examples of the idea as instances of what is ever-the-same. This passes sentence on the rule of the idea in art, just as this idea can no longer hold its ground to philosophical critique. The content [*Gehalt*] of art does not reduce without remainder into the idea, rather, this content is the extrapolation of what is irreducible; among academic aestheticians only Friedrich Theodor Vischer had an inkling of this. Just how little the truth content converges with the subjective idea, with the intention of the artist, is evident to the most rudimentary consideration. There are artworks in which the artist brought out clearly and simply what he wanted, and the result, nothing more than an indication of what the artist wanted to say, is thereby reduced to an enciphered allegory. The work dies as soon as philologists have pumped out of it what the artist pumped in, a tautological game whose schema is true also of many musical analyses. The difference between truth and intention in artworks becomes evident to critical consciousness when the object of the artist's intention is itself false, those usually eternal truths in which myth simply reiterates itself. Mythical inevitability usurps truth. Innumerable artworks suffer from the fact that they lay claim to being a process of constant self-transformation and development and yet subsist as an atemporal sequence of what is ever-the-same. It is at such points of fracture that technological critique becomes the critique of the untrue and thus allies itself with the truth content. There are good reasons to hold that in artworks technical failure is indicated by the metaphysically false. Artworks have no truth without determinate negation; developing this is the task of aesthetics today. The truth content of artworks cannot be immediately identified. Just as it is known only mediately, it is mediated in itself. What transcends the factual in the artwork, its spiritual content, cannot be pinned down to what is individually, sensually given but is, rather, constituted by way of this empirical givenness. This defines the mediatedness of the truth content. The spiritual content does not hover above the work's facture; rather, artworks transcend their factuality through their facture, through the consistency of their elaboration. The breath that surrounds them, that which is most akin to their truth content and is at once factual and not factual, is fundamentally distinct from mood in whatever way artworks once expressed mood; on the contrary, in the interest of the work's breath, mood is consumed by the forming process. In artworks, objectivity and truth are inseparable. Through the breath of objectivity and truth within themselves—composers are familiar with the idea of a composition's "breath"—artworks approach nature, but not by imitation, whose sphere encompasses mood. The more deeply works are formed, the more obstinate they become against any contrived semblance, and this obstinacy is the negative appearance of their truth. Truth is antithetical to the phantasmagorical element of artworks; thoroughly formed artworks that are criticized as formalistic are the most realistic works insofar as they are realized in themselves and solely by means of this realization achieve their truth content, what is spiritual in them, rather than merely signifying this content. However, it is no guarantee of their truth that artworks transcend themselves through their realization. Many works of the highest quality are true as the expression of a consciousness that is false in itself. This is recognized only by transcendent criticism, such as Nietzsche's critique of Wagner. The failing of that kind of critique, however, is not only that it judges the matter from on high rather than measuring itself by it. This criticism is also impeded by a narrow-minded notion of truth content, usually a cultural/philosophical notion that neglects the immanently historical element of aesthetic truth. The separation of what is true in itself from the merely adequate expression of false consciousness is not to be maintained, for correct consciousness has not existed to this day, and no consciousness has the lofty vantage point from which this separation would be self-evident. The complete presentation of false consciousness is what names it and is itself truth content. It is for this reason that works unfold not only through interpretation and critique but also through their rescue, which aims at the truth of false consciousness in the aesthetic appearance. Great artworks are unable to lie. Even when their content is semblance, insofar as this content is necessary semblance the content has truth, to which the artworks testify; only failed works are untrue. By reenacting the spell of reality, by sublimating it as an image, art at the same time liberates itself from it; sublimation and freedom mutually accord. The spell with which art through its unity encompasses the *membra disjecta* of reality is borrowed from reality and transforms art into the negative appearance of utopia. That by virtue of their organization artworks are more—not only as what is organized but also as the principle of organization—for as what is organized they obtain the semblance of being nonartifactual—determines them as spiritual. This determination, when recognized, becomes content. It is expressed by the artwork not only through its organization but equally through its disruption, which organization implies. This throws light on the contemporary predilection for the shabby and filthy as well as on the allergy to splendor and suaveness. Underlying this is the consciousness of the sordid aspects of culture hidden beneath its husk of self-contentment. Art that forswears the happy brilliance that reality withholds from men and women and thus refuses every sensual trace of meaning, is spiritualized art; it is, in its unrelenting renunciation of childish happiness, the allegory of the illusionless actuality of happiness while bearing the fatal proviso of the chimerical: that this happiness does not exist.

Philosophy and art converge in their truth content: The progressive self-unfolding truth of the artwork is none other than the truth of the philosophical concept. With good reason, idealism historically—in Schelling—derived its own concept of truth from art. The closed yet internally dynamic totality of idealist systems was read out of artworks. However, because philosophy bears upon reality and in its works is not autarchically organized to the same degree as are artworks, the cloaked aesthetic ideal of systems necessarily shattered. These systems are paid back in their own coin with the ignominious praise that they are philosophical artworks. The manifest untruth of idealism, however, has retrospectively compromised artworks. That in spite of their autarchy and by means of it they seek their other, what is external to their spell, drives the artwork beyond the identity with itself by which it is fundamentally determined. The disruption of its autonomy was not a fateful decline. Rather, it became art's obligation in the aftermath of the verdict over that in which philosophy was all too much like art. The truth content of artworks is not what they mean but rather what decides whether the work in itself is true or false, and only this truth of the work in-itself is commensurable to philosophical interpretation and coincides—with regard to the idea, in any case—with the idea of philosophical truth. For contemporary consciousness, fixated on the tangible and unmediated, the establishment of this relation to art obviously poses the greatest difficulties, yet without this relation art's truth content remains inaccessible: Aesthetic experience is not genuine experience unless it becomes philosophy.——The condition for the possibility that philosophy and art converge is to be sought in the element of universality that art possesses through its specification as language sui generis. This universality is collective just as philosophical universality, for which the transcendental subject was once the signum, points back to the collective subject. However, in aesthetic images precisely that is collective that withdraws from the I: Society inheres in the truth content. The appearing, whereby the artwork far surpasses the mere subject, is the eruption of the subject's collective essence. The trace of memory in mimesis, which every artwork seeks, is simultaneously always the anticipation of a condition beyond the diremption of the individual and the collective. This collective remembrance in artworks is, however, not χωρίς from the subject but rather takes place by way of the subject; in the subject's idiosyncratic impulse the collective form of reaction becomes manifest. For this reason, too, the philosophical interpretation of the truth content must unswervingly construe that truth content in the particular. By virtue of this content's subjectively mimetic expressive element, artworks gain their objectivity; they are neither pure impulse nor its form, but rather the congealed process that transpires between them, and this process is social.

Today the metaphysics of art revolves around the question of how something spiritual that is made, in philosophical terms something "merely posited," can be true. The issue is not the immediately existing artwork but its content [Gehalt]. The question of the truth of something made is indeed none other than the question of semblance and the rescue of semblance as the semblance of the true. Truth content cannot be something made. Every act of making in art is a singular effort to say what the artifact itself is not and what it does not know: precisely this is art's spirit. This is the locus of the idea of art as the idea of the restoration of nature that has been repressed and drawn into the dynamic of history. Nature, to whose imago art is devoted, does not yet in any way exist; what is true in art is something nonexistent. What does not exist becomes incumbent on art in that other for which identity-positing reason, which reduced it to material, uses the word nature. This other is not concept and unity, but rather a multiplicity. Thus truth content presents itself in art as a multiplicity, not as the concept that abstractly subordinates artworks. The bond of the truth content of art to its works and the multiplicity of what surpasses identification accord. Of all the paradoxes of art, no doubt the innermost one is that only through making, through the production of particular works specifically and completely formed in themselves, and never through any immediate vision, does art achieve what is not made, the truth. Artworks stand in the most extreme tension to their truth content. Although this truth content, conceptless, appears nowhere else than in what is made, it negates the made. Each artwork, as a structure, perishes in its truth content; through it the artwork sinks into irrelevance, something that is granted exclusively to the greatest artworks. The historical perspective that envisions the end of art is every work's idea. There is no artwork that does not promise that its truth content, to the extent that it appears in the artwork as something existing, realizes itself and leaves the artwork behind simply as a husk, as Mignon's prodigious verse prophesies. The seal of authentic artworks is that what they appear to be appears as if it could not be prevaricated, even though discursive judgment is unable to define it. If however it is indeed the truth, then along with the semblance truth abolishes the artwork. The definition of art is not fully encompassed by aesthetic semblance: Art has truth as the semblance of the illusionless. The experience of artworks has as its vanishing point the recognition that its truth content is not null; every artwork, and most of all works of absolute negativity, mutely say: *non confundar*. Artworks would be powerless if they were no more than longing, though there is no valid artwork without longing. That by which they transcend longing, however, is the neediness inscribed as a figure in the historically existing. By retracing this figure, they are not only more than what simply exists but participate in objective truth to the extent that what is in need summons its fulfillment and change. Not for-itself, with regard to consciousness, but in-itself, what is wants the other; the artwork is the language of this wanting, and the artwork's content [*Gehalt*] is as substantial as this wanting. The elements of this other are present in reality and they require only the most minute displacement into a new constellation to find their right position. Rather than imitating reality, artworks demonstrate this displacement to reality. Ultimately, the doctrine of imitation should be reversed; in a sublimated sense, reality should imitate the artworks. However, the fact that artworks exist signals the possibility of the nonexisting. The reality of artworks testifies to the possibility of the possible. The object of art's longing, the reality of what is not, is metamorphosed in art as remembrance. In remembrance what is qua what was combines with the nonexisting because what was no longer is. Ever since Plato's doctrine of anamnesis the not-yet-existing has been dreamed of in remembrance, which alone concretizes utopia without betraying it to existence. Remembrance remains bound up with semblance: for even in the past the dream was not reality. Yet art's imago is precisely what, according to Bergson's and

Proust's thesis, seeks to awaken involuntary remembrance in the empirical, a thesis that proves them to be genuine idealists. They attribute to reality what they want to save and what inheres in art only at the price of its reality. They seek to escape the curse of aesthetic semblance by displacing its quality to reality.—The *non confundar* of artworks marks the boundary of their negativity, comparable to the boundary marked out in the novels of the Marquis de Sade where he has no other recourse than to call the most beautiful *gitons du tableau "beaux comme des anges."* At this summit of art, where its truth transcends semblance, it is most mortally exposed. Unlike anything human, art lays claim to being unable to lie, and thus it is compelled to lie. Art does not have it in its power to decide over the possibility that everything may indeed not come to anything more than nothing; it has its fictiveness in the assertion implicit in its existence that it has gone beyond the limit. The truth content of artworks, as the negation of their existence, is mediated by them though they do not in any way communicate it. That by which truth content is more than what is posited by artworks is their methexis in history and the determinate critique that they exercise through their form. History in artworks is not something made, and history alone frees the work from being merely something posited or manufactured: Truth content is not external to history but rather its crystallization in the works. Their unposited truth content is their name.

In artworks the name is, however, strictly negative. Artworks say what is more than the existing, and they do this exclusively by making a constellation of how it is, "Comment c'est."[4] The metaphysics of art requires its complete separation from the religion in which art originated. Artworks are not the absolute, nor is the absolute immediately present in them. For their methexis in the absolute they are punished with a blindness that in the same instant obscures their language, which is a language of truth: Artworks have the absolute and they do not have it. In their movement toward truth artworks are in need of that concept that for the sake of their truth they keep at a distance. It is not up to art to decide whether its negativity is its limit or truth. Artworks are a priori negative by the law of their objectivation: They kill what they objectify by tearing it away from the immediacy of its life. Their own life preys on death. This defines the qualitative threshold to modern art. Modern works relinquish themselves mimetically to reification, their principle of death. The effort to escape this element is art's illusory element which, since Baudelaire, art has wanted to discard without resigning itself to the status of a thing among things. Those heralds of modernism Baudelaire and Poe were as artists the first technocrats of art. Without the admixture of poison, virtually the negation of life, the opposition of art to civilizatory repression would amount to nothing more than impotent comfort. If since early modernism art has absorbed art-alien objects that have been received without being fully transformed by its law of form, this has led mimesis in art to captitulate—as in montage—to its antagonist. Art was compelled to this by social reality. Whereas art opposes society, it is nevertheless unable to take up a position beyond it; it achieves opposition only through identification with that against which it remonstrates. This was already the content [*Gehalt*] of Baudelaire's satanism, much more than the punctual critique of bourgeois morality which, outdone by reality, became childishly silly. If art tried directly to register an objection to the gapless web, it would become completely entangled; thus, as occurs in such exemplary fashion in Beckett's *Endgame*, art must either eliminate from itself the nature with which it is concerned, or attack it. The only *parti pris* left to it, that of death, is at once critical and metaphysical. Artworks derive from the world of things in their performed material as in their techniques; there is nothing in them that did not also belong to this world and nothing that could be wrenched away from this world at less than the price of its death. Only by the strength of its deadliness do artworks participate in reconciliation. But in this they at the same time remain obedient to myth. This is what is Egyptian in each. By wanting to give permanence to the transitory—to life—by wanting to save it from death, the works kill it. With good reason the power of artworks to reconcile is sought in their unity, in the fact that, in accord with the ancient topos, they heal the wound with the spear that inflicted it. Reason, which in artworks effects unity even where it intends disintegration, achieves a certain guiltlessness by renouncing intervention in reality, real domination; yet even in the greatest works of aesthetic unity the echo of social violence is to be heard; indeed, through the renunciation of domination spirit also incurs guilt. The act that binds and fixates the mimetic and diffuse in the artwork not only does harm to amorphous nature. The aesthetic image is a protest against nature's fear that it will dissipate into the chaotic. The aesthetic unity of the multiplicitous appears as though it had done no violence but had been chosen by the multi-plicitous itself. It is thus that unity—today as real as was ever the diremption—crosses over into reconciliation. In artworks the destructive power of myth is mollified through the particularization of the repetition that myth exercises in empirical reality, repetition that the artwork summons into particularization at the closest proximity. In artworks, spirit is no longer the old enemy of nature. Assuaged, spirit reconciles. Art is not reconciliation in the classicistic sense: Reconciliation is the comportment of artworks by which they become conscious of the nonidentical. Spirit does not identify the nonidentical: It identifies with it. By pursuing its own identity with itself, art assimilates itself with the nonidentical: This is the contemporary stage of development of art's mimetic essence. Today, reconciliation as the comportment of the artwork is evinced precisely there where art countermands the idea of reconciliation in works whose form dictates intransigence. Yet even such irreconcilable reconciliation through form is predicated on the unreality of art. This unreality threatens art permanently with ideology. Art, however, does not sink to the level of ideology, nor is ideology the verdict that would ban each and every artwork from truth. On the basis of their truth, of the reconciliation that empirical reality spurns, art is complicitous with ideology in that it feigns the factual existence of reconciliation. By their own apriori, or, if one will, according to their idea, artworks become entangled in the nexus of guilt. Whereas each artwork that succeeds transcends this nexus, each must atone for this transcendence, and therefore its language seeks to withdraw into silence: An artwork is, as Beckett wrote, *a desecration of silence*

Art desires what has not yet been, though everything that art is has already been. It cannot escape the shadow of the past. But what has not yet been is the concrete. Nominalism is perhaps most deeply allied with ideology in that it takes concretion as a given that is incontestably available; it thus deceives itself and humanity by implying that the course of the world interferes with the peaceful determinacy of the existing, a determinacy that is simply usurped by the concept of the given and smitten with abstractness. Even by artworks the concrete is scarcely to be named other than negatively. It is only through the nonfungibility of its own existence and not through any special content [*Inhalt*] that the artwork suspends empirical reality as an abstract and universal functional nexus. Each artwork is utopia insofar as through its form it anticipates what would finally be itself, and this converges with the demand for the abrogation of the spell of self-identity cast by the subject. No artwork cedes to another. This justifies the indispensable sensual element of artworks: It bears their *hic et nunc* in which, in spite of all mediation, a certain independence is maintained; naïve consciousness, which always clings to this element, is not altogether false consciousness. The nonfungibility, of course, takes over the function of strengthening the belief that mediation is not universal. But the artwork must absorb even its most fatal enemy —fungibility; rather than fleeing into concretion, the artwork must present through its own concretion the total nexus of abstraction and thereby resist it. Repetition in authentic new artworks is not always an accommodation to the archaic compulsion toward repetition. Many artworks indite this compulsion and thereby take the part of what Karl Heinz Haag has called the unrepeatable; Beckett's *Play,* with the spurious infinity of its reprise, presents the most accomplished example. The black and grey of recent art, its asceticism against color, is the negative apotheosis of color. If in the extraordinary biographical chapters of Selma Lagerlöf's *Mårbacka,* a stuffed bird of paradise—something never before seen—cures a paralyzed child, the effect of this vision of utopia remains vibrant, but today nothing comparable would be possible: The tenebrous has become the plenipotentiary of that utopia. But because for art, utopia—the yet-to-exist—is draped in black, it remains in all its mediations recollection; recollection of the possible in opposition to the actual that suppresses it; it is the imaginary reparation of the catastrophe of world history; it is freedom, which under the spell of necessity did not—and may not ever—come to pass. Art's methexis in the tenebrous, its negativity, is implicit in its tense relation to permanent catastrophe. No existing, appearing artwork holds any positive control over the nonexisting. This distinguishes artworks from religious symbols, which in their appearance lay claim to the transcendence of the immediately present. The nonexisting in artworks is a constellation of the existing. By their negativity, even as total negation, artworks make a promise, just as the gesture with which narratives once began or the initial sound struck on a sitar promised what was yet to be heard, yet to be seen, even if it was the most fearsome; and the cover of every book between which the eye loses itself in the text is related to the promise of the camera obscura. The paradox of all modern art is that it seeks to achieve this by casting it away just as the opening of Proust's *Recherche* ingeniously slips into the book without the whirring of the camera obscura, the peep-show perspective of the omniscient narrator, renouncing the magic of the act and thereby realizing it in the only way possible. Aesthetic experience is that of something that spirit may find neither in the world nor in itself; it is possibility promised by its impossibility. Art is the ever broken promise of happiness.

Notes

1 See Adorno, "Meditations on Metaphysics," in *Negative Dialectics*, trans. E. B. Ashton, (New York, 1973), pp. 361ff.

2 Georg Trakl, "Psalm," trans. Dallas Wiebe, in *The Sixties* 8 (Spring, 1966), pp. 37–38.

3 Eduard Mörike, *Sämtliche Werke*, ed. J. Perfahl et al., vol. 1 (Munich, 1968), p. 855. [The original text is as follows.—trans.]

> Mausfallen-Sprüchlein
>
> Das Kind geht dreimal um die Falle und spricht:
>
> Kleine Gäste, kleines Haus.
> Liebe Mäusin, oder Maus,
> Stell dich nur kecklich ein
> Heut nacht beim Mondenschein!
> Mach aber die Tür fein hinter dir zu,
> Hörst du?
> Dabei hüte dein Schwänzchen!
> Nach Tische singen wir
> Nach Tische springen wir
> Und machen ein Tänzchen:
> Witt witt!
> Meine alte Katze tanzt wahrscheinlich mit.

4 [See note 16 on "Sosein" in "Natural Beauty."—trans.]

8
Coherence and meaning

Although artworks are neither conceptual nor judgmental, they are logical. In them nothing would be enigmatic if their immanent logicality did not accommodate discursive thought, whose criteria they nevertheless regularly disappoint. They most resemble the form of a syllogism and its prototype in empirical thought. That in the temporal arts one moment is said to follow from another is hardly metaphorical; that one event is said to be caused by another at the very least allows the empirical causal relation to shimmer through. It is not only in the temporal arts that one moment is to issue from another; the visual arts have no less a need of logical consistency. The obligation of artworks to become self-alike, the tension into which this obligation brings them with the substratum of their immanent contract, and ultimately the traditional desideratum of homeostasis require the principle of logical consistency: This is the rational aspect of artworks. Without its immanent necessity no work would gain objectivation; this necessity is art's antimimetic impulse, one borrowed externally, which unites the work as an interior. The logic of art, a paradox for extra-aesthetic logic, is a syllogism without concept or judgment. It draws consequences from phenomena that have already been spiritually mediated and to this extent made logical. Its logical process transpires in a sphere whose premises and givens are extralogical. The unity that artworks thereby achieve makes them analogous to the logic of experience, however much their technical procedures and their elements and the relation between them may distance them from those of practical empirical reality. The affiliation with mathematics that art established in the age of its dawning emancipation and that today, in the age of the dissolution of its idioms, once again emerges as predominant, marked art's emergent self-consciousness from its dimension of logical consistency. Indeed, on the basis of its formalism, mathematics is itself aconceptual; its signs are not signs of something, and it no more formulates existential judgments than does art; its aesthetic quality has often been noted. Of course, art deceives itself when, encouraged or intimidated by science, it hypostatizes its dimension of logical consistency and directly equates its own forms with those of mathematics, unconcerned that its forms are always opposed to those of the latter. Still, it is art's logicality that among its powers constitutes it most emphatically as second nature, as a being sui generis. It thwarts every effort to comprehend artworks on the basis of their effect: By way of their logical character, artworks are determined objectively in themselves without regard to their reception. Yet their logicality is not to be taken *à la lettre*. This is the point of Nietzsche's comment—though admittedly it amateurishly underestimates the logicality of art—that in artworks everything only appears as if it must be as it is and could not be otherwise. The logic of artworks demonstrates that it cannot be taken literally, in that it grants every particular event and resolution an incomparably greater degree of latitude than logic otherwise does; it is impossible to ignore the compelling hint of a relation with the logic of dreams in which comparably, a feeling of coercive logical consistency is bound up with an element of contingency. Through its retreat from empirical goals, logic in art acquires a shadowy quality of being at once binding and slack. Logic is all the less constrained the more obliquely preestablished styles provide the semblance of logicality and unburden the particular work of the need for its manufacture. Whereas logicality rules without the slightest misgiving in works commonly called classical, they nevertheless provide several, sometimes a plethora, of internal possibilities, just as thoroughbass music and commedia dell'arte and other preestablished forms permit improvisation more securely than do later fully organized and individualized works. Although superficially these individualized works are less logical and less transparently modeled according to quasi-conceptual schemata and formulas, internally they are far more severely concerned with logical consistency. However, while the logicality of artworks intensifies, while its claims become ever more literal—to the point of parody in totally determined works deduced from a minimum of basic material—the "as if" of this logicality is laid bare. What today seems absurd in art is the negative function of unbridled logical consistency. Art is thus made to pay for the fact that conclusions cannot be drawn without concept and judgment.

This figurative rather than real logic of art is difficult to distinguish from causality because in art there is no difference between purely logical forms and those that apply empirically; in art the archaic undifferentiatedness of logic and causality hibernates. Schopenhauer's *principia individuationis* —space, time, and causality—make a second, refracted appearance in art, in the sphere of what is most individuated. Their defraction, a necessary implication of art's illusoriness, endows art with its aspect of freedom. It is through this freedom, through the intervention of spirit, that the sequence and nexus of events is established. In the undifferentiatedness of spirit and blind necessity, art's logic is reminiscent of the strict lawfulness that governs the succession of real events in history. Schoenberg was known to speak of music as the history of themes. Crude unmediated space, time, and causality no more exist in art than, in keeping with the idealist philosophem, as a sphere totally apart, art exists beyond their determinations; they play into art as from a distance and in it are immediately transformed into something other. Thus, for example, there is no mistaking time as such in music, yet it is so remote from empirical time that, when listening is concentrated, temporal events external to the musical continuum remain external to it and indeed scarcely touch it; if a musician interrupts a passage to repeat it or to pick it up at an earlier point, musical time remains indifferent, unaffected; in a certain fashion it stands still and only proceeds when the course of the music is continued. Empirical time disturbs musical time, if at all, only by dint of its heterogeneity, not because they flow together. All the same, the formative categories of art are not simply qualitatively distinct from those external to them but, in spite of the latters' modification, incorporate their quality in a qualitatively other medium. If in external existence these forms are fundamental to the control of nature, in art they are themselves controlled and freely disposed over. Through the domination of the dominating, art revises the domination of nature to the core. In contrast to the semblance of inevitability that characterizes these forms in empirical reality, art's control over them and over their relation to materials makes their arbitrariness in the empirical world evident. As a musical composition compresses time, and as a painting folds spaces into one another, so the possibility is concretized that the world could be other than it is. Space, time, and causality are maintained, their power is not denied, but they are divested of their compulsiveness. Paradoxically, it is precisely to the extent that art is released from the empirical world by its formal constituents that it is less illusory, less deluded by subjectively dictated lawfulness, than is empirical knowledge. That the logic of artworks is a derivative of discursive logic and not identical with it, is evident in that art's logic—and here art converges with dialectical thought—suspends its own rigor and is ultimately able to make this suspension its idea; this is the aim of the many forms of disruption in modern art. Artworks that manifest a tendency toward integral construction disavow their logical rigor with what is heterogeneous to it: the indelible trace of mimesis, on which construction depends. The autonomous law of form of artworks protests against logicality even though logicality itself defines form as a principle. If art had absolutely nothing to do with logicality and causality, it would forfeit any relation to its other and would be an a priori empty activity; if art took them literally, it would succumb to the spell; only by its double character, which provokes permanent conflict, does art succeed at escaping the spell by even the slightest degree. Conclusions drawn without concept and judgment are from the outset divested of any apodicity and insist instead on a communication between objects that is easily masked by concept and judgment, whereas aesthetic consistency preserves this communication as the affinity of elements that remain unidentified. The oneness of aesthetic constituents with those of cognition is, however, the unity of spirit and thus the unity of reason; this Kant demonstrated in his theory of aesthetic purposefulness. If Schopenhauer's thesis of art as an image of the world once over bears a kernel of truth, then it does so only insofar as this second world is composed out of elements that have been transposed out of the empirical world in accord with Jewish descriptions of the messianic order as an order just like the habitual order but changed in the slightest degree. This second world, however, is directed negatively against the first; it is the destruction of what is simulated by familiar senses rather than the assemblage of the *membra disjecta* of existence. There is nothing in art, not even in the most sublime, that does not derive from the world; nothing that remains untransformed. All aesthetic categories must be defined both in terms of their relation to the world and in terms of art's repudiation of that world. In both, art is knowledge, not only as a result of the return of the mundane world and its categories, which is art's bond to what is normally called an object of knowledge, but perhaps even more importantly as a result of the implicit critique of the nature-dominating *ratio*, whose rigid determinations art sets in movement by modifying them. It is not through the abstract negation of the *ratio*, nor through a mysterious, immediate eidetic vision of essences, that art seeks justice for the repressed, but rather by revoking the violent act of rationality by emancipating rationality from what it holds to be its inalienable material in the empirical world. Art is not synthesis, as convention holds; rather, it shreds synthesis by the same force that affects synthesis. What is transcendent in art has the same tendency as the second reflection of nature-dominating spirit.

The comportment of artworks reflects the violence and domination of empirical reality by more than analogy. The closure of artworks, as the unity of their multiplicity, directly transfers the nature-dominating comportment to something remote from its reality; this is perhaps because the principle of self-preservation points beyond the possibility of its realization in the external world, there sees itself confuted by death, and is unable to reconcile itself to that; autonomous art is a work of contrived immortality, utopia and hubris in one; scrutinized from another planet they would all seem Egyptian. The purposiveness of artworks, through which they assert themselves, is only a shadow of the purposiveness external to them. This they resemble only in their form, through which, from their perspective at least, they are protected from decomposition. Kant's paradoxical formulation that the beautiful is what is purposive without a purpose, expresses—in the language of subjective transcendental philosophy—the heart of the matter with a fidelity that never ceases to distance the Kantian theorems from the methodological nexus in which they appear. For Kant artworks were purposive as dynamic totalities in which all particular elements exist for the sake of their purpose—the whole—just as the whole exists for the sake of its purpose, the fulfillment or redemption through the negation of its elements. At the same time, artworks were purposeless because they had stepped out of the means-ends relation of empirical reality. Remote from reality, the purposiveness of artworks has something chimerical about it. The relation of aesthetic to real purposiveness was historical: The immanent purposiveness of artworks was of external origin. In many instances, collectively fashioned aesthetic forms are once-purposive forms that have become purposeless. This is notably the case with ornaments, which drew heavily on mathematical-astronomical science. The course of this development was marked out by the origin of artworks in magic: They shared in a praxis meant to influence nature, separated from this praxis in the early history of rationality, and renounced the deception of any real influence. What is specific to artworks—their form—can never, as the sedimentation of content [*Inhalt*] fully disown its origin. Aesthetic success is essentially measured by whether the formed object is able to awaken the content [*Inhalt*] sedimented in the form. In general, then, the hermeneutics of artworks is the translation of their formal elements into content [*Inhalt*]. This content [*Inhalt*] does not, however, fall directly to art, as if this content only needed to be gleaned from reality. Rather, it is constituted by way of a countermovement. Content [*Inhalt*] makes its mark in those works that distance themselves from it. Artistic progress, to the degree that it can be cogently spoken of, is the epitome of this movement. Art gains its content [*Inhalt*] through the latter's determinate negation. The more energetic the negation, the more artworks organize themselves according to an immanent purposiveness, and precisely thereby do they mold themselves progressively to what they negate. The Kantian conception of a teleology of art modeled on that of organisms was rooted in the unity of reason, ultimately in the unity of divine reason as it is manifest in things-in-themselves. This idea had to go. All the same, the teleological determination of art guards its truth beyond that trivial notion rejected in the course of artistic development that the artist's fantasy and consciousness confer organic unity on his works. Art's purposiveness, free of any practical purpose, is its similarity to language; its being "without a purpose" is its nonconceptuality, that which distinguishes art from significative language. Artworks move toward the idea of a language of things only by way of their own language, through the organization of their disparate elements; the more they are syntactically articulated in themselves, the more eloquent they become in all their elements. The aesthetic concept of teleology has its objectivity in the language of art. Traditional aesthetics misses the mark because, in keeping with a general *parti pris*, it prejudges the relation of the whole and the part in favor of the whole. In contrast, dialectics does not give any instructions for the treatment of art, but inheres in it. The reflective power of judgment—which cannot take the subordinating concept as its starting point nor, consequently, the artwork as a whole, for it is never "given," and which follows the individual elements and goes beyond them by virtue of their own need—subjectively traces the movement of artworks in themselves. By the force of their dialectic, artworks escape myth, the blind and abstractly dominating nexus of nature.

Incontestably the quintessence of all elements of logicality, or, more broadly, coherence in artworks, is form. It is astonishing, however, how little aesthetics reflected on the category of form, how much it, the distinguishing aspect of art, has been assumed to be unproblematically given. The difficulty in getting a grasp on it is in part due to the entwinement of all aesthetic form with content [*Inhalt*]; form is not only to be conceived in opposition to content but through it if aesthetics is not to fall prey to an abstractness that habitually makes it the ally of reactionary art. Indeed, the concept of form has been the blind spot of aesthetics right up to Valéry, because everything about art is so inextricably tied up with it that the concept defies isolation. As little as art is to be defined by any other element, it is simply identical with form. Every other element can be negated in the concept of form, even aesthetic unity, the idea of form that first made the wholeness and autonomy of the artwork possible. In highly developed modern works, form tends to dissociate unity, either in the interest of expression or to criticize art's affirmative character. Long before the ubiquitous crisis, open forms existed. In Mozart the unity of the work was occasionally playfully tested by its relaxation. By juxtaposing relatively disjointed or contrasting elements, Mozart, the composer who is praised above all others for the rigor of his form, masterfully juggles the concept of form itself. He is so sure of its strength that he effectively lets go the reins and, on the basis of the security of the construction itself, gives the lead to centrifugal forces. For Mozart, the heir of an older tradition, the idea of unity as form is still so unshaken that it is able to bear the utmost pressure, whereas for Beethoven, in whom unity lost its substantiality under the nominalist assault, there is a need to assert unity far more strictly; unity preforms the multiplicitous contents a priori and thus tames them all the more triumphantly. Today artists would like to do away with unity altogether, though with the irony that those works that are supposedly open and incomplete necessarily regain something comparable to unity insofar as this openness is planned. For the most part, theory equates form with symmetry or repetition. There is no reason to deny that, if one wanted to reduce the concept of form to invariants, equality and repetition could be lined up in opposition to inequality, that is, to contrast and development. But little would be gained by setting up such categories. Musical analyses, for example, show that even in those works most diffuse and hostile to repetition, similarities are involved, that many parts correspond with others in terms of shared, distinguishing characteristics, and that it is only through the relation to these elements of identity that the sought-after nonidentity is achieved; without sameness of any sort, chaos itself would prevail as something ever-same. Indeed, the distinction between repetition that is superficial, heteronomously decreed, and incompletely mediated by specific details and, on the other hand, the ineluctable determination of the unlike by a degree of sameness, is a distinction that decisively outweighs all invariance. If this distinction is ignored by a concept of form sympathetic with invariance, the result is an affinity for that bestial phraseology that indulges in expressions like "consummate form." Because form is the central concept of aesthetics and is always presupposed by it in the givenness of art, aesthetics must gather all its forces to think the concept through. If aesthetics is not to be trapped in tautologies it must gain access to what is not simply immanent in the concept of form, yet the concept of form refuses to grant a voice to anything aesthetic that claims independence from it. An aesthetics of form is possible only if it breaks through aesthetics as the aesthetics of the totality of what stands under the spell of form. Whether art is in any way still possible depends precisely on this. The concept of form marks out art's sharp antithesis to an empirical world in which art's right to exist is uncertain. Art has precisely the same chance of survival as does form, no better. The participation of form in the crisis of art becomes evident in statements like those of Lukács, who said that in modern art the importance of form has been greatly overestimated.[1] Evident in this philistine call to arms is a discontent with art of which Lukács the cultural conservative is unconscious, as well as a concept of form that is inadequate to art. To hit upon the idea that form has been overestimated in art, one must fail to recognize that form is essential to art, that it mediates content [Inhalt]. Form is the artifacts' coherence, however self-antagonistic and refracted, through which each and every successful work separates itself from the merely existing. Lukács's unreflected concept of form, with its hue and cry over formalism, sets form in opposition to the content of poems, compositions, and paintings as an organization that can simply be lifted off the work. Form is thereby conceived as something superimposed, subjectively dictated, whereas it is substantial only when it does no violence to what is formed and emerges from it. Indeed, what is formed, the content [Inhalt] does not amount to objects external to form; rather, the content is mimetic impulses that are drawn into the world of images that is form. The innumerable and pernicious equivocations of the concept of form can be traced to its ubiquity, which produces the temptation to call everything and anything that is artistic in art form. In any case, the concept of form is fruitless if nothing more is meant than the trivial generality that the artwork's "material"—whether this means intentional objects or materials such as tones or colors—mediates instead of simply being present. It is just as inapt to define form as it is to define what is conferred by the subject and bears the stamp of that subject. What can rightly be called form in artworks fulfills the desiderata of that on which subjective activity takes place just as much as it is the product of subjective activity. In artworks,

187

form is aesthetic essentially insofar as it is an objective determination. Its locus is precisely there where the work frees itself from being simply a product of subjectivity. Form is thus not to be sought in the arrangement of pregiven elements, as the theory of pictorial composition held it to be prior to being debunked by impressionism; that nevertheless so many artworks, including precisely those that are applauded as classical, prove under careful scrutiny to be just such an arrangement is a fatal objection to traditional art. There is absolutely no reducing the concept of form to mathematical relations, as was envisioned by aesthetics of Zeising's era.[2] Such relations—whether explicitly invoked as principles during the Renaissance or latently coupled with mystical ideas, as perhaps occasionally in Bach—play a role as technical procedures, yet they are not form itself but rather its vehicle, the means by which the newly liberated subject, dependent strictly on its own resources, preforms otherwise chaotic and undifferentiated material. Just how little mathematical organization and everything related to it coincides with aesthetic form is audible in the recent history of twelve-tone technique, which in fact preforms the material by the establishment of numerical relations of permutated rows in which no tone may occur before the other tone has preceded it. Immediately it became evident that this preformation did not constitute form in the fashion expected by Erwin Stein's program, which not by accident carried the title *New Principles of Form*.[3] Schoenberg himself distinguished almost mechanically between the preparation of twelve-tone material and composition, and on account of this distinction he had reason to regret his ingenious technique. The heightened logical consistency of the following generation, however, which obliterated the distinction between the preparation of the material and actual composition, not only exchanged integration for music's self-alienation but incurred the loss of articulation, without which form is almost inconceivable. It is as if the immanent nexus of the work, when abandoned completely to itself without any interference, without the effort to hear the totality of form out of the heterogeneous, relapses into the raw and crude. In fact, the totally organized works of the serial phase have almost completely surrendered the means of differentiation in which they originated. Mathematization as a method for the immanent objectivation of form is chimerical. Its insufficiency can perhaps be clarified by the fact that artists resort to it during historical periods when the traditional self-evidence of forms dissolves and no objective canon is available. At these moments the artist has recourse to mathematics; it unifies the level of subjective reason attained by the artist with the semblance of an objectivity founded on categories such as universality and necessity; this is semblance because the organization, the relation of elements to each other that constitutes form, does not originate in the specific structure and fails when confronted with the particular. For this reason mathematization favors precisely those traditional forms that it at the same time denounces as irrational. Rather than embodying the abiding lawfulness of being, its own claim to legitimacy, the mathematical aspect of art despairingly strives to guarantee its possibility in a historical situation in which the objectivity of the conception of form is as requisite as it is inhibited by the level of consciousness.

Frequently the concept of form proves limited in that, depending on the circumstances, it locates form in one dimension regardless of others, as, for example, when musical form is located in temporal succession, as if simultaneity and polyphony do not contribute to form, or when in painting form is attributed to proportions of space and surface at the cost of the form-giving function of color. In contrast to this, aesthetic form is the objective organization within each artwork of what appears as bindingly eloquent. It is the nonviolent synthesis of the diffuse that nevertheless preserves it as what it is in its divergences and contradictions, and for this reason form is actually an unfolding of truth. A posited unity, it constantly suspends itself as such; essential to it is that it interrupts itself through its other just as the essence of its coherence is that it does not cohere. In its relation to its other—whose foreignness it mollifies and yet maintains—form is what is antibarbaric in art; through form art participates in the civilization that it criticizes by its very existence. Form is the law of the transfiguration of the existing, counter to which it represents freedom. Form secularizes the theological model of the world as an image made in God's likeness, though not as an act of creation but as the objectivation of the human comportment that imitates creation; not *creatio ex nihilo* but creation out of the created. The metaphorical expression is irresistible, that form in artworks is everything on which the hand has left its trace, everything over which it has passed. Form is the seal of social labor, fundamentally different from the empirical process of making. What artists directly perceive as form is best elucidated *e contrario* as an antipathy to the unfiltered in the artwork, to the grouping of color that is simply factual without being articulated or animated in itself; an antipathy to the rote musical sequence, the topos, the precritical. Form converges with critique. It is that through which artworks prove self-critical; what in the work rebels against any untransformed residue is really the bearer of form, and art is disavowed wherever support is given to the theodicy of the unformed, whether under the name of musicality or ham acting. By its critical implication, form annihilates practices and works of the past. Form repudiates the view that artworks are immediately given. If form is that in artworks by which they become artworks, it is equivalent with their mediatedness, their objective reflectedness into themselves. Form is mediation in that it is the relation of parts to each other and to the whole and as the elaboration of details. With regard to form, then, the much praised naïveté of artworks turns out to be hostile to art. What may appear intuitive and naïve in artworks, their constitution as something that presents itself as self-coherent, gapless, and therefore unmediated, derives from their mediatedness in themselves. It is only through this mediatedness that they become significative and their elements become signs. Everything in artworks that resembles language originates in form and is thus transformed into the antithesis of form, the mimetic impulse. Form seeks to bring the particular to speech through the whole. However, this is the melancholy of form, especially among artists in whose work form prevails. Form inevitably limits what is formed, for otherwise its concept would lose its specific difference to what is formed. This is confirmed by the artistic labor of forming, which is always a process of selecting, trimming, renouncing. Without rejection there is no form, and this prolongs guilty domination in artworks, of which they would like to be free; form is their amorality. They do injustice to what they form by following it. At least something of this was sensed by vitalism's endlessly rehearsed assurance, ever since Nietzsche, of the antithesis between form and life. Art becomes entangled in the guilt context of the living, not only because its distance allows the guilt context to prevail but even more importantly because it makes incisions in the living in order to help it to language and thus mutilates it. The myth of Procrustes recounts the philosophical protohistory of art. Yet the total condemnation of art does not follow from this any more than it does elsewhere from partial guilt in the context of total guilt. Whoever rails against art's putative formalism, against art being art, advocates the very inhumanity with which he charges formalism and does so in the name of cliques that, in order to retain better control of the oppressed, insist on adaptation to them. Whenever the inhumanity of spirit is indicted, it is a judgment passed against humanity; only that spirit does justice to humanity that, rather than serving it according to what it has become, immerses itself in that which unknown to humanity is its own. The campaign against formalism ignores the fact that form that befalls content [*Inhalt*] is itself sedimented content; this, and not regression to any pre-artistic emphasis on content, secures the primacy of the object in art. Aesthetic categories of form such as particularity, development and resolution of conflict, even the anticipation of reconciliation through homeostasis, are transparent with regard to their content even, and most of all, where they have separated themselves from the empirical objects. Precisely by distance from it art adopts its stance toward the empirical world in which conflicts appear immediate and as absolute cleavages; their mediation, implicitly contained in the empirical, becomes the for-itself of consciousness only by the act of stepping back from it, which is what art does. This stepping back is, as such, an act of knowledge. Those features of modern art on whose account it has been ostracized as formalistic derive without exception from the fact that in them content flickers incarnate, instead of having been peremptorily adjusted by an easily marketable harmony. Emancipated expression, in which all of modern art's forms originated, was a protest against romantic expression by a depositional character that is antagonistic to the forms. This was the source of their substantiality; Kandinsky coined the term "cerebral acts." The historicophilosophical significance of the emancipation of form is that it refuses to mollify alienation in the image, exclusively thereby incorporating the alienated; that it defines the alienated as such. The hermetic works bring more criticism to bear on the existing than do those that, in the interest of intelligible social criticism, devote themselves to conciliatory forms and silently acknowledge the flourishing culture industry. In the dialectic of form and content, the scale also tips toward form—against Hegel—because content, which his aesthetics wanted to salvage, degenerated to a positivistic given, a mold for the reification against which, according to Hegel's theory, art protests. Thus the more deeply the content [*Inhalt*] is experienced and transformed unrecognizably into formal categories, the less the unsublimated materials are commensurable with the content [*Gehalt*] of artworks. Everything appearing in the artwork is virtually content [*Inhalt*] as much as it is form, whereas form remains that by which the appearing determines itself and content remains what is self-determining. To the extent that aesthetics achieved an energetic concept of form, it legitimately opposed the preartistic view of art by seeking what is specifically aesthetic exclusively in form by seeking out form's transformations as such in the comportment of the aesthetic subject; this was axiomatic for the conception of art history as cultural history. But what promises to emancipate and thus strengthen the subject weakens it at the same time through its isolation. Hegel is right that all aesthetic processes are bound up with content [*Inhalt*], just as in the history of the plastic arts and literature new levels of the external world constantly become apparent and are discovered and assimilated, whereas others perish, lose their artistic potential, and no longer excite even the worst commercial painter to grant them a brief eternity on canvas. In this regard it is worth mentioning the studies of the Warburg Institute, many of which penetrated to the center of artistic content [*Gehalt*] through the analysis of motifs; in poetics Benjamin's study of the German baroque shows an analogous tendency, motivated by the rejection of the confusion of subjective intentions with aesthetic content [*Gehalt*] and, ultimately, of the alliance of aesthetics and idealist philosophy. The elements bound up with content [*Inhalt*] undergird the substance [*Gehalt*] in opposition to the pressure of subjective intention.

The articulation, by which the artwork achieves its form, also always coincides in a certain sense with the defeat of form. If a gapless and unforced unity of form and the formed succeeded, as is intended by the idea of form, this would amount to the achievement of the identity of the identical and nonidentical. But it is vis-à-vis the fact that this has not been achieved that the artwork is motivated to wall itself up in the imaginary confines of an identity that is merely for-itself. The arrangement of a whole in accordance with the sum of its complexes, which is the idea of articulation, is never completely adequate, whether as the division of a lava mass into a multitude of small garden plots or whether it is because of an external residue remaining after the divergent has been unified. A prototypical instance of this is the suitelike, unmastered randomness of the succession of movements in an integrated symphony. What may be called a work's level of form, a term employed in graphology ever since Ludwig Klages, depends on its degree of articulation. This concept calls a halt to the relativism of Riegl's "artistic will." There are types of art, as well as phases in its history, in which articulation was of little concern or was impeded by conventional procedures. Articulation's adequacy to artistic will, to the objective-historical sense of form that it bears, does not make it any less inferior: Under the constraint of an encompassing "It shall not be" such works fail to carry out what they are obliged to fulfill according to their own logicality. Like desk-bound white-collar workers whose ancestors were artists of an inferior level of form, their unconscious whispers in their ears that the utmost is not possible for the little men that they are; yet the utmost is nevertheless the law of form of what they undertook to do. It is rarely noted, even in art criticism, that neither individual nor collective art wills its own concept, which develops from within; rather like people who laugh even when there is nothing funny. Many artworks are undertaken with tacit resignation; for their diminished claim they are rewarded by making art historians and the public happy. It would be worthwhile to analyze to what degree such aesthetic resignation has since antiquity contributed to the division of high and low art, a division whose decisive reason is obviously that culture proved unsuccessful for precisely those who produced it. In any case, even so apparently formal a category as that of articulation has its material aspect: that of intervention in the *rudis indigestaque moles* of what is sedimented in the artwork this side of its autonomy; even aesthetic forms tend historically toward becoming material of a second order. The means, without which there would be no form, undermine form. This aporia is dodged, not solved, by works that renounce partial wholes of any significant dimension in order to protect their unity: This is the key objection to Webern's intensity without extension. Mediocre works, by contrast, leave the partial wholes unchallenged under the thin husk of their form, camouflaging them rather than melding them. It could almost be stated as a rule, one that testifies to the depth at which form and content [*Inhalt*] are mediated in each other, that the relation of the parts to the whole, an essential aspect of form, is constituted by way of detours. Artworks lose themselves in order to find themselves: The form category for this is the episode. In a collection of aphorisms from his expressionist phase published prior to World War I, Schoenberg noted that Ariadne provides no thread to follow through the interior of artworks.[4] This however does not imply aesthetic irrationalism. Their form, their whole, and their logicality are hidden from artworks to the same degree as the elements, the content [*Inhalt*], desire the whole. Art that makes the highest claim compels itself beyond form as totality and into the fragmentary. The plight of form is most emphatically manifest in the difficulty of bringing temporal art forms to a conclusion; in music composers often speak of the problem of a finale, and in literature the problem of a denouement, which came to a head in Brecht. Once having shaken itself free of convention, no artwork was able to end convincingly, and the continued use of traditional endings only simulate the temporal convergence of the particular elements with the concluding instant as a totality of form. In many modern works that have attracted a large audience, the form was artfully held open because they wanted to demonstrate that the unity of form was no longer bestowed on them. Spurious infinity, the inability to close, becomes a freely chosen principle of method and expression. Beckett's play, which, rather than stopping repeats itself word for word, is a reaction to this; almost fifty years ago, Schoenberg proceeded in similar fashion in the March of his Serenade: After the reprise had been abolished, it was resurrected out of desperation. What Lukács once called the "discharge of meaning" was the force that allowed the artwork, once it has confirmed its immanent determination, to end on the model of one who dies old, having led a full life. That this is denied artworks, that they can no more die than can the hunter Gracchus, is internalized by them directly as an expression of horror. The unity of artworks cannot be what it must be: the unity of the multiplicitous; in that unity synthesizes, it damages what is synthesized and thus the synthesis. Artworks suffer from their mediated totality no less than from their immediateness.

Against the philistine division of art into form and content it is necessary to insist on their unity; against the sentimental view of their indifference in the artwork it is necessary to insist that their difference endures even in their mediation. Not only is the perfect identity of the two chimerical, it would not redound to the success of the works: By analogy to Kant's maxim, they would become empty or blind, self-sufficient play or raw empiria. With regard to content [Inhalt], the concept of material best does justice to the mediated distinction. According to an almost universally accepted terminology in all the arts, material is what is formed. It is not the same as content [Inhalt], even if Hegel fatefully confounded the two. This can be explicated with regard to music. Its content [Inhalt] is in any case what occurs—partial events, motifs, themes, and their elaboration: changing situations. Content is not external to musical time but essential to it, as time is essential to content; content is everything that transpires in time. Material, by contrast, is what artists work with: It is the sum of all that is available to them, including words, colors, sounds, associations of every sort and every technique ever developed. To this extent, forms too can become material; it is everything that artists encounter about which they must make a decision. The idea, widespread among unreflective artists, of the open eligibility of any and all material is problematic in that it ignores the constraint inherent in technical procedures and the progress of material, which is imposed by various materials as well as by the necessity to employ specific materials. The choice of the material, its use, and the limitations of that use, are an essential element of production. Even innovative expansion of the material into the unknown, going beyond the material's given condition, is to a large extent a function of the material and its critique, which is defined by the material itself. The concept of material is presupposed by alternatives such as whether a composer works with sounds that are native to tonality and recognizable as its derivatives, or whether he radically eliminates them; analogous alternatives in painting are those between the representational and the nonrepresentational, the perspectival and the nonperspectival. The concept of material may first have taken conscious shape in the twenties, if one leaves aside the lingo of singers who, tortured by a sense of the dubiousness of their musicality, exult over their "material." Since Hegel's theory of the romantic artwork, the error has persisted that along with preestablished overarching forms even the bindingness of the materials with which the forms were concerned has disintegrated; the expansion of available materials, which scorns the old boundaries between the arts, is primarily the result of the historical emancipation of the concept of form in art. This expansion has been much overestimated by those external to it; it is offset by the renunciations demanded of the artist not only by taste but by the condition of the material. Of all the material that is abstractly employable, only the tiniest part does not collide with the condition of spirit and is as such concretely usable. Thus material is not natural material even if it appears so to artists; rather, it is thoroughly historical. Its supposedly sovereign position is the result of the collapse of every ontology of art, which has in turn affected the materials. They are no less dependent on the transformation of technique than is technique on the materials that it manipulates. It is obvious how much a composer who, for instance, works with tonal material receives this material from tradition. If, however, he turns critically against tradition through the use of an autonomous material, one completely purged of concepts such as consonance, dissonance, triad, and diatonicism, the negated is nevertheless retained in the negation. Such works speak by virtue of the taboos they radiate; the falseness or, at the least, the shock of every triad that they permit makes this obvious enough, and this is the objective cause of the comfortably prescribed monotonousness of radically modern art. The rigorousness of the most recent developments in music and painting, which right into the smallest detail of the emancipated material ruthlessly eliminates all traces of the traditional and the negated, obeys all the more recklessly—under the illusion of the pure givenness of a material without any intrinsic quality—the historical tendency. Stripping the material of any qualitative dimension, which superficially connotes its dehistoricization, is itself the material's historical propensity, the propensity of subjective reason. What defines its limits are that it leaves its historical determinations behind in the material.

What aesthetic terminology once called subject matter [*Stoff*] and Hegel the subject [*Sujet*] is not to be apodictically excluded from the concept of material. All the same, while the concept of subject matter remains a concern of art, in its immediacy, as a theme that can be lifted over from external reality and worked upon, it has, since Kandinsky, Proust, and Joyce, incontrovertibly declined. Parallel to the critique of the heterogeneously imposed, the aesthetically unassimilable, discontent has been growing with the so-called great themes to which Hegel as well as Kierkegaard, and more recently many Marxist theoreticians and playwrights attributed such eminence. The idea that works that occupy themselves with august events—whose sublimity is usually only the fruit of ideology and of respect for power and magnitude—are thereby augmented in their dignity was unmasked once van Gogh painted a stool or a few sunflowers in such a fashion that the images rage with the storm of all those emotions in the experience of which the individual of van Gogh's epoch for the first time registered the historical catastrophe. This having become evident, it could be shown in earlier art too how little its authenticity depends on the trumped-up or even actual relevance of its objects. What is the importance of Delft in Vermeer? Does it not hold that—as Kraus wrote, a gutter well painted is of greater value than a badly painted palace: "Out of a loose sequence of events . . . a world of perspectives, moods, and shocks takes shape for the more pellucid eye, and trashy poetry becomes the poetry of trash, damnable only to that official idiocy that holds a badly painted palace preferable to a well-painted gutter."[5] Hegel's aesthetics of content [*Inhalt*], an aesthetics of subject matter, in keeping with the spirit of many of his intentions, subscribes undialectically to the objectivation of art by way of a raw relation to objects. Essentially he excluded mimesis from his aesthetics. In German idealism the turn to the object was always coupled with philistinism, as is most crassly obvious in the comments on historical painting in the third book of the *World as Will and Representation*. In its relation to art, idealism's eternity is unmasked as kitsch, to which he who clings to idealism's inalienable categories is consigned. Brecht ignored this. In his essay "*Fünf Schwierigkeiten beim Schreiben der Wahrheit*" (five difficulties in writing the truth) he concludes: "Thus, it is for example not untrue to say that chairs provide a place to sit and that rain falls from above. Many poets write truths of this kind. They are like painters who cover the walls of sinking ships with still lifes. For them even what we have called our first difficulty in writing the truth does not exist and yet they have a clear conscience. They produce their daubs undisturbed by the mighty or by the screams of the ravaged. The absurdity of what they do produces in them a 'deep' pessimism that they sell at a good price and that would actually better suit those who watch these masters and their sales. At the same time it is anything but easy to recognize that their truths are truths about chairs or the rain, since they usually sound completely different, as if they were truths about important things. For the process of artistic production is precisely that of according importance to something. Only by taking a close look does one perceive that they are only saying: 'A chair is a chair' and 'Nobody can change the fact that rain falls from above.'"[6] This is a *blague*. It justly provokes the official culture mentality, which has even succeeded in integrating van Gogh's chair as a piece of furniture. Yet if one wanted to extract a norm out of this, it would be merely regressive. There is no point to making threats. A painted chair can actually be extremely significant, to the extent that one does not prefer to avoid this bloated word. Incomparably deeper and socially relevant experiences can be sedimented in the *how* of a painting than in faithful portraits of generals or revolutionary heros. All paintings of this sort retrospectively take their place in the *Galerie des Glaces de Versailles* of 1871, regardless whether the generals, eternalized in historical postures, were to have led red armies that occupy countries in which the revolution never took place. This problematic of thematic material whose relevance is directly borrowed from reality also befalls the intentions that are injected into the work. However spiritual these ideas may be in themselves, once introduced into the artwork they become no less subject matter than if they were Meier, the Basel mayor who promises to fetch the coal. As Hegel well knew, what artists can say they say only through the form [*Gestaltung*], not by letting that form deliver a message. Among the sources of error in the contemporary interpretation and critique of artworks the most disastrous is the confusion of the intention, what the artist supposedly wants to say, with the content [*Gehalt*] of the work. In reaction, the content of the artwork is increasingly lodged in what has not been cathected by the artist's subjective intentions, whereas content is blocked in works in which intention, whether as *fabula docet* or as philosophical thesis, demands primacy. The objection that an artwork is too reflected is not only ideology but has its element of truth in the work's being too little reflected: not reflected against the incursion of its own intention. The philological procedure, which imagines that it grasps securely the content of the work when it grasps its intention, passes judgment immanently on itself in that it tautologically extracts from artworks what was put into them earlier; the secondary literature on Thomas Mann is the most repellent example of this. Granted, this practice is fostered by a genuine tendency that has its source in literature; Naïve immediacy and its illusoriness has become threadbare for literature, which no longer disavows reflection and is thus compelled to strengthen the dimension of intention. This supplies an interpretive method alien to spirit with an easy surrogate for spirit. It is incumbent on artworks, just as occurred in modernism's greatest achievements, to incorporate the reflexive element by its further reflexivity into the work itself rather than tolerating it in the form of residual subject matter.

However little the intention of artworks is their content [*Gehalt*]—if only because no intention, however neatly presented, is assured of being realized by the work—still only a stubborn rigorism would disqualify intention as an element of the work. Intentions have their locus in the dialectic between the mimetic pole of artworks and their methexis in enlightenment; intentions have their locus not only in being the subjectively moving and organizing force that is thereupon extinguished in the work but also in the objectivity of the work itself. Because the artwork is not simply inert, intentions are endowed with an independence as specific as that of any other element of the artwork; one would need to ignore the complexion of important artworks for the sake of a *thema probandum* to deny that, however variable historically, their importance stands in relation to intention. If material in the artwork is truly resistant to the artwork's otherwise pure identity, the inner process of identity in artworks is essentially that between the material and intention. Without intention, without the immanent form of the principle of identity, form would not exist any more than it would without the mimetic impulse. The surplus of intentions reveals that the objectivity of artworks cannot be reduced simply to mimesis. The objective bearer of intentions, which synthesizes the individual intentions of artworks into a whole, is their meaning. It remains relevant in spite of everything problematic inherent to it and in spite of all the evidence that this is not all there is to artworks. The meaning of Goethe's *Iphigenie* is humanity. If this idea were merely intended abstractly by the poetic subject, if it were in Hegel's words simply a "maxim"—as indeed it is in Schiller—it would be irrelevant to the work.

In that, however, by means of language, humanity itself becomes mimetic—is itself expressed in the nonconceptual without sacrificing its conceptual element—meaning achieves a fruitful tension to the work's content [Gehalt], to what has been composed. The meaning of a poem such as Verlaine's "Clair de lune" cannot be univocally established, yet this is not to say that its meaning does not reach beyond the incomparable resonance of the verses. The poem's sensuality is itself an element of intention: Happiness and sadness, which accompany sexuality as soon as it descends into itself and negates spirit as ascetic, are the poem's content [Gehalt]; the flawlessly presented idea of sensuality divorced from sensuousness is the meaning. This trait, central to the whole of late nineteenth- and early twentieth-century French art, including Debussy, contains the potential of radical modernism, and there is no lack of actual historical ties. Conversely, it is the starting point, though not the telos of criticism, whether the intention is objectivated in what is composed; the fault lines between intention and result, rarely missing from recent art, are no less ciphers of the work's content than is the result. A higher level of critique, however, that of the truth or untruth of the content, often becomes immanent critique through the knowledge of the relation between intention and what has been written, painted, or composed. Intention does not always miscarry as the result of the inadequate form-giving powers of the subject. The untruth of intention interrupts the objective truth content. If what is supposed to be truth content is in itself untrue, that prohibits inner consistency. Such untruth tends to be mediated by the untruth of the intention, as is apparent at the highest level of form in Wagner's music. ——For traditional aesthetics, and to a large extent for traditional art as well, the determination of the totality of the artwork is its determination as a nexus of meaning. The reciprocal relation of whole and parts is supposed to shape the work as something meaningful to such an extent that the quintessence of this meaning coincides with the metaphysical content. Because the nexus of meaning is constituted by the relation of elements—and not in atomistic fashion in something given that is sensual —what can justly be called the spirit of artworks should be comprehensible in that nexus. That the spirit of an artwork is the configuration of its elements is more than a seductive idea; it attains its truth in the face of all crude reification or materialization of the spirit and content of artworks. Directly or indirectly everything that appears in the work contributes to such meaning, though not all that appears is necessarily of equal importance. The establishment of relative importance was one of the most effective means for aesthetic articulation, as is obvious enough in the differentiation between thetic main events and transitions, and between the essential and accidental yet requisite elements. These differentiations in traditional art were largely determined schematically. With the critique of schematic organization, the differentiations become dubious: Art tends toward processes in which everything that occurs is equidistant to the midpoint; where everything accidental arouses the suspicion of being superfluously ornamental. This is one of the most imposing difficulties in the articulation of recent art. Art's inexorable self-criticism, the requirement of drossless composition, underscores this difficulty and promotes chaos, the ever lurking precondition of all art. Even in works with the highest level of form, the crisis of differentiation has frequently resulted in a dimension of nondifferentiation. Efforts to defend against this have almost without exception, though often latently, had recourse to borrowings from the aesthetic resources that they oppose: Even here the total domination of the material and movement toward diffuseness converge.

That artworks, in accord with Kant's magnificently paradoxical formula, are "purposeless," that they are separated from empirical reality and serve no aim that is useful for self-preservation and life, precludes calling art's meaning its purpose, despite meaning's affinity to immanent teleology. Yet it becomes ever harder for artworks to cohere as a nexus of meaning. Ultimately they respond to this by rejecting the very concept of meaning. The more the emancipation of the subject demolished every idea of a preestablished order conferring meaning, the more dubious the concept of meaning became as the refuge of a fading theology. Even prior to Auschwitz it was an affirmative lie, given historical experience, to ascribe any positive meaning to existence. This has consequences that reach deep into aesthetic form. When artworks have nothing external to themselves to which they can cling without ideology, what they have lost cannot be restored by any subjective act. It was wiped out by their tendency toward subjectivization, which was no cultural-historical accident but conforms rather with the true state of things. Critical self-reflection, inherent in every artwork, sharpens the work's sensitivity not only toward every element that strengthens traditional meaning but also against the work's immanent meaning and those of its categories that provide meaning. For the meaning that is the synthesis of the artwork cannot merely be something that it has manufactured, its quintessence. At the same time the totality of the work presents meaning and produces it aesthetically, it reproduces it. Meaning is only legitimate in the artwork insofar as it is objectively more than the work's own meaning. In that artworks relentlessly chip away at the nexus in which meaning is founded, they turn against this nexus and against meaning altogether. The unconscious labor of the artistic *ingenium* on the meaning of the work as on something substantial and enduring transcends this meaning. The advanced production of recent decades has become self-conscious of this issue, has made it thematic and translated it into the structure of artworks. It is easy to convict neodadaism of a lack of political import and dismiss it as meaningless and purposeless in every sense of the word. But to do so is to forget that its products ruthlessly demonstrate the fate of meaning without any regard to themselves as artworks. Beckett's oeuvre already presupposes this experience of the destruction of meaning as self-evident, yet also pushes it beyond meaning's abstract negation in that his plays force the traditional categories of art to undergo this experience, concretely suspend them, and extrapolate others out of the nothingness. The dialectical reversal that occurs is obviously not a derivative of theology, which always heaves a sigh of relief whenever its concerns are treated in any way, no matter what the verdict, as if at the end of the tunnel of metaphysical meaninglessness—the presentation of the world as hell—a light glimmers; Günther Anders was right to defend Beckett against those who make his works out to be affirmative.[7] Beckett's plays are absurd not because of the absence of any meaning, for then they would be simply irrelevant, but because they put meaning on trial; they unfold its history. His work is ruled as much by an obsession with positive nothingness as by the obsession with a meaninglessness that has developed historically and is thus in a sense merited, though this meritedness in no way allows any positive meaning to be reclaimed. Nevertheless the emancipation of artworks from their meaning becomes aesthetically meaningful once this emancipation is realized in the aesthetic material precisely because the aesthetic meaning is not immediately one with theological meaning. Artworks that divest themselves of any semblance of meaning do not thereby forfeit their similitude to language. They enunciate their meaninglessness with the same determinacy as traditional artworks enunciate their positive meaning. Today this is the capacity of art: Through the consistent negation of meaning it does justice to the postulates that once constituted the meaning of artworks. Works of the highest level of form that are meaningless or alien to meaning are therefore more than simply meaningless because they gain their content [*Gehalt*] through the negation of meaning. Artwork that rigorously negates meaning is by this very rigor bound to the same density and unity that was once requisite to the presence of meaning. Artworks become nexuses of meaning, even against their will, to the extent that they negate meaning. Although the crisis of meaning is rooted in a problematic common to all art, the failure in the face of rationality, reflection is unable to repress the question whether art does not perhaps, through the demolition of meaning, throw itself into the arms of precisely that which strikes ordinary consciousness as absurd, the positivistically reified consciousness. The dividing line between authentic art that takes on itself the crisis of meaning and a resigned art consisting literally and figuratively of protocol sentences is that in significant works the negation of meaning itself takes shape as a negative, whereas in the others the negation of meaning is stubbornly and positively replicated. Everything depends on this: whether meaning inheres in the negation of meaning in the artwork or if the negation conforms to the status quo; whether the crisis of meaning is reflected in the works or whether it remains immediate and therefore alien to the subject. Key events may include certain musical works such as Cage's Piano Concerto, which impose on themselves a law of inexorable aleatoriness and thereby achieve a sort of meaning: the expression of horror. What governs Beckett's work, certainly, is a parodic unity of time, place, and action, combined with artfully fitted and balanced episodes and a catastrophe that consists solely in the fact that it never takes place. Truly, one of the enigmas of art, and evidence of the force of its logicality, is that all radical consistency, even that called absurd, culminates in similitude to meaning. This, however, is not confirmation of metaphysical substantiality, to which every thoroughly formed work would lay claim as confirmation of its illusoriness: Ultimately, art is semblance in that, in the midst of meaninglessness, it is unable to escape the suggestion of meaning. Artworks, however, that negate meaning must also necessarily be disrupted in their unity; this is the function of montage, which disavows unity through the emerging disparateness of the parts at the same time that, as a principle of form, it reaffirms unity. The relation between the technique of montage and photography is familiar. Montage has its appropriate place in film. The sudden, discontinuous juxtaposition of sequences, editing employed as an artistic means, wants to serve intentions without damaging the intentionlessness of life as it is, which is the actual interest of film. On no account is the principle of montage a trick to integrate photography and its derivatives into art despite the limitations defined by their dependence on empirical reality. Rather, montage goes beyond photography immanently without infiltrating it with a facile sorcery, but also without sanctioning as a norm its status as a thing: It is photography's self-correction. Montage originated in antithesis to mood-laden art, primarily impressionism. Impressionism dissolved objects —drawn primarily from the sphere of technical civilization or its amalgams with nature—into their smallest elements in order to synthesize them gaplessly into the dynamic continuum. It wanted aesthetically to redeem the alienated and heterogenous in the replica. The conception proved ever less adequate the more intense the superiority of the reified prosaic world over the living subject became: The subjectivization of objective reality relapsed into romanticism, as was soon blatantly obvious not only in *Jugendstil* but also in the later stages of authentic impressionism. It was against this that montage protested, which developed out of the pasted-in newspaper clippings and the like during the heroic years of cubism. The semblance provided by art, that through the fashioning of the heterogeneously empirical it was reconciled with it, was to be broken by the work admitting into itself literal, illusionless ruins of empirical reality, thereby acknowledging the fissure and transforming it for purposes of aesthetic effect. Art wants to admit its powerlessness vis-à-vis late-capitalist totality and to initiate its abrogation. Montage is the inner-aesthetic capitulation of art to what stands heterogeneously opposed to it. The negation of synthesis becomes a principle of form. In this, montage unconsciously takes its lead from a nominalistic utopia: one in which the pure facts are mediated by neither form nor concept and irremediably divest themselves of their facticity. The facts themselves are to be demonstrated in deictical fashion, as epistemology calls it. The artwork wants to make the facts eloquent by letting them speak for themselves. Art thereby begins the process of destroying the artwork as a nexus of meaning. For the first time in the development of art, affixed debris cleaves visible scars in the work's meaning. This brings montage into a much broader context. All modern art after impressionism, probably including even the radical manifestations of expressionism, has abjured the semblance of a continuum grounded in the unity of subjective experience, in the "stream of lived experience." The intertwinement, the organic commingling, is severed, the faith destroyed that one thing merges wholly with the other, unless the intertwinement becomes so dense and intricate as to obscure meaning completely. This is complemented by the aesthetic principle of construction, the blunt primacy of a planned whole over the details and their interconnection in the microstructure; in terms of this microstructure all modern art may be called montage. Whatever is unintegrated is compressed by the subordinating authority of the whole so that the totality compels the failing coherence of the parts and thus however once again asserts the semblance of meaning. This dictated unity corrects itself in accord with the tendencies of the details in modern art, the "instinctual life of sounds" or colors; in music, for example, in accord with the harmonic and melodic demand that complete use be made of the available tones of the chromatic scale. Certainly, this tendency in turn derives from the totality of the material, from the available spectrum, and is defined by the system rather than actually being spontaneous. The idea of montage and that of technological construction, which is inseparable from it, becomes irreconcilable with the idea of the radical, fully formed artwork with which it was once recognized as being identical. The principle of montage was conceived as an act against a surreptitiously achieved organic unity; it was meant to shock. Once this shock is neutralized, the assemblage once more becomes merely indifferent material; the technique no longer suffices to trigger communication between the aesthetic and the extra-aesthetic, and its interest dwindles to a cultural-historical curiosity. If, however, as in the commercial film, the intentions of montage are insisted upon, they are jarringly heavy-handed. Criticism of the principle of montage has implications for constructivism, in which montage has camouflaged itself, precisely because constructivist form succeeds only at the cost of the individual impulse, ultimately the mimetic element. As a result, constructivism is always in danger of rattling emptily. *Sachlichkeit* itself, as it is represented by constructivism within the bounds of nonfunctional art, is subject to the critique of semblance: What claims to be strictly adequate to its purpose fails because the work's formative process interferes with the impulses of what is to be formed; an immanent purposefulness is claimed that is in fact none at all, in that the work lets the teleology of the particular elements atrophy. *Sachlichkeit* turns out to be ideology: The drossless unity to which *Sachlichkeit* or the technical artwork pretends is never achieved. In those—admittedly minimal—hollows that exist between all particular elements in constructivist works, what has been standardized and bound together breaks apart in just the same way as do suppressed individual interests under total administration. After the default of any higher, subordinating jurisdiction, the process between the whole and the particular has been turned back to a lower court, to the impulse of the details themselves, in accord with the nominalistic situation. At this point, art is conceivable only on the condition that any pregiven subordinating standard be excluded. The blemishes that indelibly mark purely expressive, organic works offer an analogy to the antiorganic praxis of montage. This brings an antinomy into focus. Artworks that are commensurable to aesthetic experience are meaningful insofar as they fulfill an aesthetic imperative: the requirement that everything be required. This ideal, however, is directly opposed by the development that it itself set in motion. Absolute determination—which stipulates that everything is important to an equal degree and that nothing may remain external to the inner nexus of the work—converges, as György Ligeti perceived, with absolute arbitrariness. This gnaws away retrospectively at aesthetic lawfulness. It always has an element of positedness, of game rules and contingency. Since the beginning of the modern age, most notably in seventeenth-century Dutch painting and the early English novel, art has absorbed contingent elements of landscape and fate that were not as such construable out of any overarching *ordo* or idea of life in order to be able to grant them meaning freely within the aesthetic continuum. Ultimately, however, the impossibility of any subjectively established objectivity of meaning, which was hidden over the long epochs of the rise of the bourgeoisie, abandoned the nexus of meaning itself to that very contingency whose mastery once defined form. The development toward the negation of meaning is what meaning deserved. However, though this development is inevitable and has its own truth, it is accompanied by a hostility to art that is, although not to the same extent, narrow-mindedly mechanistic and, in terms of its propensity, reprivatizing; this development is allied with the eradication of aesthetic subjectivity by virtue of its own logic. Subjectivity is made to pay the price for the production of the untruth of aesthetic semblance. Even so-called absurd literature participates in this dialectic in the work of its most important representatives, in that as a nexus of meaning organized teleologically in itself it expresses the absence of meaning and thus through determinate negation maintains the category of meaning; this is what makes its interpretation possible, indeed, demands it.

Categories such as unity, or even harmony, have not tracelessly vanished as a result of the critique of meaning. The determinate antithesis of individual artworks toward empirical reality furthers the coherence of those artworks. Otherwise the gaps in the work's structure would be invaded, as occurs in montage, by the unwieldy material against which it protects itself. This is what is true in the traditional concept of harmony. What survives of this concept after the negation of the culinary has retracted to the category of the whole, even though the whole no longer takes precedence over the details. Although art revolts against its neutral-ization as an object of contemplation, insisting on the most extreme incoherence and dissonance, these elements are those of unity; without this unity they would not even be dissonant. Even when art unreservedly obeys the dictates of inspiration, the principle of harmony, metamor-phosed to the point of unrecognizability, is at work, because inspiration, if it is to count, must gel; that tacitly presupposes an element of organization and coherence, at least as a vanishing point. Aesthetic experience, no less in fact than theoretical experience, is constantly made aware that inspira-tions and ideas that do not gel impotently dissipate. Art's paratactical logicality consists in the equilibrium of what it coordinates, a homeostasis in which the concept of aesthetic harmony is sublimated as a last resort. With regard to its elements, such aesthetic harmony is negative and stands in a dissonant relation to them: They undergo something similar to what individual tones once underwent in the pure consonance of a triad. Thus aesthetic harmony qualifies in its own right as an element. The mistake of traditional aesthetics is that it exalts the relationship of the whole to the parts to one of entire wholeness, to totality, and hoists it in triumph over the heterogeneous as a banner of illusory positivity. The ideology of culture, in which unity, meaning, and positivity are synonyms, inevitably boils down to a *laudatio temporis acti*. As the sermon goes, society once enjoyed a blessed closure when every artwork had its place, function, and legitimation and therefore enjoyed its own closure, whereas today every-thing is constructed in emptiness and artworks are internally condemned to failure. However transparent the tenor of such ideas, which invariably maintain an all too secure distance from art and falsely imagine that they are superior to inner-aesthetic necessities, it is better to follow up what is insightful in them rather than to brush them aside on the basis of the role they play, since failure to investigate them might contribute to their preservation. On no account does an artwork require an a priori order in which it is received, protected, and accepted. If today nothing is harmoni-ous, this is because harmony was false from the beginning. The closure of the aesthetic, ultimately of the extra-aesthetic, system of reference does not necessarily correspond to the dignity of the artwork. The dubiousness of the ideal of a closed society applies equally to that of the closed artwork. It is incontestable that artworks have, as die-hard reactionaries never cease to repeat, lost their social embeddedness. The transition from this security into the open has become, for them, a *horror vacui*; that they address an anonymous and ultimately nonexistent audience has not been just a blessing, not even immanently: not for their authenticity and not for their relevance. What ranks as problematic in the aesthetic sphere has its origin here; the remainder became the plunder of boredom. Every new artwork, if it is to be one, is exposed to the danger of complete failure. If in his own time Hermann Grab praised the preformation of style in the keyboard music of the seventeenth and early eighteenth centuries because it precluded anything obviously bad, it could be rejoined that this style just as certainly excluded the possibility of what is emphatically good. Bach was so incomparably superior to the music that preceded him and that of his epoch because he broke through this preformation. Even the Lukács of *The Theory of the Novel* had to admit that the artworks that came after the end of the supposedly meaning-filled age had gained infinitely in richness and depth.[8] What speaks for the survival of the concept of harmony as an element is that artworks that remonstrate against the mathematical ideal of harmony and the requirement of symmetrical relations, striving rather for absolute asymmetry, fail to slough off all symmetry. In terms of its artistic value, asymmetry is only to be comprehended in its relation to symmetry; this has recently been confirmed by what Kahnweiler has called the phenomena of distortion in Picasso. Similarly, new music has shown reverence for the tonality that it abolished through the extreme sensitivity that it developed toward its rudiments. This is documented by Schoenberg's ironic comment from the early years of atonality that the "Mondfleck" of *Pierrot lunaire* was composed according to the strict rules of counterpoint, which only permitted prepared consonants and then only on unaccented beats. The further real domination of nature progresses, the more painful it becomes for art to admit the necessity of that progress within itself. In the ideal of harmony, art senses acquiescence to the administered world, even though art's opposition to this world continues, with steadily increasing autonomy, the domination of nature. Art concerns itself as much as it is contrary to itself. Just how much these innervations of art are bound up with its position in reality could be viscerally sensed in the bombed German cities of the postwar years. In the face of actual chaos the optical order that the aesthetic sensorium had long ago rejected once again became intensely alluring. However, rapidly advancing nature, the vegetation in the ruins, brought all vacation-minded romanticization of nature to a deserved end. For a brief historical moment what traditional aesthetics called "satisfying" harmonic and symmetrical relations returned. When traditional aesthetics, Hegel's included, praised harmony in natural beauty, it projected the self-satisfaction of domination onto the dominated.

What is qualitatively new in recent art may be that in an allergic reaction it wants to eliminate harmonizations even in their negated form, truly the negation of negation with its own fatality: the self-satisfied transition to a new positivity, to the absence of tension in so many paintings and compositions of the postwar decades. False positivity is the technological locus of the loss of meaning. What during the heroic years of modern art was perceived as its meaning maintained the ordering elements of traditional art as determinately negated; their liquidation results in a smoothly functioning but empty identity. Even artworks freed from harmonistic-symmetrical ideas are formally characterized by similarity and contrast, static and dynamic, exposition, transition, development, identity, and return. Works are unable to wipe out the difference between the first appearance of an element and its repetition, no matter how modified that may be. The capacity to sense and employ harmonic and symmetrical relations in their most abstract form has become progressively more subtle. Whereas in music a more or less tangible reprise was once required to establish symmetry, now a vague similarity of tone color at various points may suffice. Dynamic freed from every static reference and no longer discernible as such by its contrast to something fixed, is transformed into something that hovers and no longer has direction. In the manner of its appearance, Stockhausen's *Zeitmaße* evokes a through-composed cadence, a fully presented yet static dominant. Yet today such invariants become what they are only in the context of change; whoever tries to distill them from the dynamic complexion of history or from the individual work thereby misrepresents them.

Because the concept of spiritual order is itself worthless, it cannot be transposed from cultural cogitations to art. Opposites are intermixed in the ideal of the closure of the artwork: The irrevocable compulsion toward coherence, the ever fragile utopia of reconciliation in the image, and the longing of the objectively weakened subject for a heteronomous order, a constant of German ideology. Temporarily deprived of any direct satisfaction, authoritarian instincts revel in the imago of an absolutely closed culture where meaning is guaranteed. Closure for its own sake, independent of truth content and what this closure is predicated on, is a category that in fact deserves the ominous charge of formalism. Certainly this does not mean that positive and affirmative artworks, virtually the whole store of traditional art, are to be dismissed or defended on the basis of the all too abstract argument that, given their abrupt opposition to empirical life, they too are critical and negative. The philosophical critique of unreflective

nominalism prohibits any claim that the trajectory of progressive negativity, the negation of objectively binding meaning, is that of unqualified
progress in art. However much a song by Webern is more thoroughly
constructed, the universality of the language of Schubert's *Winterreise*
secures for it an element of superiority. Though it is nominalism that
helped art achieve its language in the first place, still there is no language
without the medium of a universality beyond pure particularization,
however requisite the latter. This overarching universality necessarily
bears a degree of affirmation: This can be sensed in the word understanding. Affirmation and authenticity are amalgamated to no small
degree. Yet this is no argument against any individual work; at most it is an
argument against the language of art as such. There is no art that is entirely
devoid of affirmation, since by its very existence every work rises above
the plight and degradation of daily existence. The more binding art is to
itself, the richer, denser, and more unified its works, the more it tends
toward affirmation—of whatever stamp—by suggesting that its own
qualities are those of a world existing in itself beyond art. This apriority of
the affirmative is art's ideological dark side. It projects the reflection of
possibility onto the existing even as the latter's determinate negation. This
element of affirmation withdraws from the immediacy of artworks and
what they say and becomes the fact that they continue to speak at all.[9]
That the world spirit never made good on its promise has the effect of
lending the affirmative works of the past a touching quality rather than
ensuring that they remain truly ideological; today, indeed, what appears
evil in consummate works is their own consummateness as a monument
to force rather than a transfiguration that is too transparent to spur any
opposition. According to cliché, great works are compelling. In being so,
they cultivate coercion to the same extent that they neutralize it; their guilt
is their guiltlessness. Modern art, with its vulnerability, blemishes, and
fallibility, is the critique of traditional works, which in so many ways are
stronger and more successful: It is the critique of success. It is predicated on
the recognition of the inadequacy of what appears to be adequate; this is
true not only with regard to its affirmative essence but also in that in its
own terms it is not what it wants to be. Instances are the jigsaw-puzzle
aspects of musical classicism—the mechanical moments in Bach's technique, the top-down construction in the paintings of the masters—which
reigned for centuries under the name composition before, as Valéry noted,
suddenly becoming a matter of indifference with the rise of impressionism.

Art's affirmative element and the affirmative element of the domination of nature are one in asserting that what was inflicted on nature was all for the good; by re-enacting it in the realm of imagination, art makes it its own and becomes a song of triumph. In this, no less than in its silliness, art sublimates the circus. In doing so, art finds itself in inextricable conflict with the idea of the redemption of suppressed nature. Even the most relaxed work is the result of a ruling tension that turns against the dominating spirit that is tamed in becoming the work. Prototypical of that is the concept of the classical. The experience of the model of all classicism—Greek sculpture—may retrospectively undermine confidence in it, as well as in later epochs. Classical art relinquished the distance to empirical existence that had been maintained by archaic images and carvings. According to traditional aesthetics, classical sculpture aimed at the identity of the universal and the particular—the idea and the individual—because already it could no longer depend on the sensual appearance of the idea. If the idea was to appear in sensual form, it would have to integrate the empirically individuated world of appearance with its principle of form. This sets a limit to full individuation, however, probably Greek classicism had not yet even experienced individuality; this occurred first, in concordance with the direction of social development, in Hellenic sculpture. The unity of the universal and the particular contrived by classicism was already beyond the reach of Attic art, let alone the art of later centuries. This is why classical sculptures stare with those empty eyes that alarm—archaically—instead of radiating that noble simplicity and quiet grandeur[10] projected onto them by eighteenth-century sentimentalism. Today what is compelling in antiquity is fundamentally distinct from the correspondence that developed with European classicism in the era of the French Revolution and Napoleon, even in that of Baudelaire. Whoever does not, in the guise of the archaeologist or philologist, sign a covenant with antiquity—which certainly since the rise of humanism has ever and again shown itself not to be disdained—will not find the normative claim of antiquity compelling. Without protracted study, scarcely any of it speaks, and the quality of the works themselves is certainly not beyond question. What is overwhelming is the level of form. Scarcely anything vulgar or barbaric seems to have been passed down, not even from the imperial age, even though there the beginnings of mass production are unmistakable. The floor mosaics of the villas in Ostia, which were presumably meant to be rented, are based on a single model. Ever since Attic classicism, the real barbarism of antiquity—the slavery, genocide, and contempt for human life—left few traces in art; just how chaste it kept itself, even in "barbaric cultures," does not redound to its credit. The formal immanence of antique art is probably to be explained by the fact that the sensual world had not yet been debased by sexual taboos, which would come to encompass a sphere reaching far beyond its own immediate area; Baudelaire's classicist longing is precisely for that. In capitalism, what forces art against art into an alliance with the vulgar is not only a function of commercialism, which exploits a mutilated sexuality, but equally the dark side of Christian inwardness. The concrete transience of the classical, however, which Hegel and Marx did not experience, exposes the transience of its concept and the norms deriving from it. The dilemma between superficial classicism and the demand that a work be coherent is apparently not one that arises from contrasting true classicism with plaster frauds. But this contrast is no more fruitful than that between modern and modernistic. What is excluded in the name of a putative authenticity as its degenerate form is usually contained in the former as its ferment, the excision of which leaves it sterile and harmless. The concept of classicism stands in need of differentiation: It is worthless so long as in peaceful juxtaposition it lays out in state Goethe's *Iphigenie* and Schiller's *Wallenstein*. In popular usage, the concept of classicism means social authority, achieved for the most part through economic control mechanisms; it is fitting that Brecht was no stranger to this usage. Classicism of this sort should rather be held against artworks, yet it is so external to them that by way of all sorts of mediations even authentic works may be bestowed with the accolade. The classical also refers to a standard of style, without its being thereby possible to distinguish between the model, its legitimate appropriation, and fruitless imitation as conclusively as would suit that *common sense* that assumes it can knowingly play off the classical against classicism. Mozart would be inconceivable apart from the classicism of the last years of the eighteenth century, with its stylistic imitation of the ancients, yet the trace of these quoted norms in his music provides no basis for any convincing objection to the specific quality of the classical Mozart. Ultimately, to call a work classical refers to its immanent success, the uncoerced yet ever fragile reconciliation of the one and the multiplicitous. It has nothing to do with style and mentality, and everything to do with accomplishment; here Valéry's comment applies that even a romantic artwork, successfully brought off, is by dint of its success classical.[11] This concept of the classical is strung taut to the highest degree; it alone is worthy of critique. The critique of the classical, however, is more than the critique of those formal principles by which the classical has, for the most part, been manifest. The ideal of form, which is identified with classicism, is to be translated back into content [*Inhalt*]. The purity of form is modeled on the purity of the subject, constituting itself, becoming conscious of itself, and divesting itself of the nonidentical: It is a negative relation to the nonidentical. Yet it implies the distinction of form from content, a distinction concealed by the classical ideal. Form is constituted only through dissimilarity, only in that it is different from the nonidentical; in form's own meaning, the dualism persists that form effaces. The counter-movement to myth—a countermovement that classicism shares with the acme of Greek philosophy—was turned directly against the mimetic impulse. Mimesis was displaced by objectifying imitation. This counter-movement thereby easily succeeded in subsuming art to Greek enlightenment and making taboo that by which art takes the side of the suppressed against the domination of the imposed concept or of what slips through domination's narrow mesh. Though in classicism the subject stands aesthetically upright, violence is done to it, to that eloquent particular that opposes the mute universal. In the much admired universality of the classical work the pernicious universality of myth—the inescapability of the spell—is perpetuated as the norm of the process of formation. In classicism, where the autonomy of art originated, art renounces itself for the first time. It is no accident that since that moment all classicisms have made ready alliance with science. To this day, the scientific mentality has harbored an antipathy toward art that refuses voluntary subservience to categorial thought and the desiderata of clear-cut divisions. Whatever proceeds as if there is no antinomy is antinomic and degenerates into what bourgeois phraseology is always ready to dub "formal perfection," about which nothing more need be said. It is not because of an irrational mentality that qualitatively modern movements frequently correspond, in Baudelaire's sense, with archaic, preclassical movements. They are, admittedly, no less exposed to the reactionary than is classicism by the delusion that the attitude to reality manifest in archaic works, from which the emancipated subject wrested itself, is to be reasserted, regardless of what has historically transpired. The sympathy of the modern with the archaic is not repressively ideological only when that sympathy turns toward what classicism discarded along the course of its development and refuses to endorse the pernicious pressure from which classicism freed itself. But the one is rarely to be found without the other. In place of the identity of the universal and the particular, classical works provide its abstract logical radius, effectively a hollow form hopelessly awaiting specification. The fragility of the classical paradigm gives the lie to its paradigmatical status and thus to the classical ideal itself.

Notes

1 See Georg Lukács, *The Meaning of Contemporary Realism* (London, 1962).

2 See Arnold Zeising, *Aesthetische Forschungen* (Frankfurt, 1885).

3 See Erwin Stein, "Neue Formprinzipien," in *Von neuer Musik* (Cologne, 1925), pp. 59ff.

4 See Arnold Schoenberg, "Aphorismen," in *Die Musik*, vol. 9 (1909–1910), pp. 159ff.

5 Karl Kraus, *Literatur und Lüge*, ed. H. Fischer (Munich, 1958), p. 14.

6 Bertolt Brecht, "Fünf Schwierigkeiten beim Schreiben der Wahrheit," in *Gesammelte Werke*, vol. 18 (Frankfurt, 1967), p. 225.

7 Günther Anders, *Die Antiquiertheit des Menschen* (Munich, 1956), pp. 213ff.

8 See Lukács, *The Theory of the Novel*, trans. A. Balarian (Cambridge, 1971).

9 Adorno, "Is Art Lighthearted?" in *Notes to Literature*, trans. Shierry Weber Nicholsen, vol. 2 (New York, 1992), pp. 247ff.

10 [Joachim Winckelmann's seminal characterization of Greek sculpture in "Thoughts on the Imitation of Greek Works in Painting and Sculpture" (1775).—trans.]

11 See Paul Valéry, *Œuvres*, ed. J. Hytier, vol. 2 (Paris, 1966), pp. 565ff.

9
Subject-object

Contemporary aesthetics is dominated by the controversy over whether it is subjective or objective. These terms, however, are equivocal. Variously the controversy may focus on the conclusion drawn from subjective reactions to artworks, in contrast to the *intentio recta* toward them, the *intentio recta* being considered precritical according to the current schema of epistemology. Or the two concepts could refer to the primacy of objective or subjective elements in the artworks themselves, in keeping, for instance, with the distinction made in the history of ideas between classical and romantic. Or, lastly, the issue may be the objectivity of the aesthetic judgment of taste. These various meanings need to be distinguished from each other. With regard to the first, the direction of Hegel's aesthetics was objective, whereas with regard to the second, his aesthetics probably emphasized subjectivity more decisively than did that of his predecessors, for whom the participation of the subject in the effect on an observer was limited even in the case of an ideal or transcendental observer. For Hegel, the subject-object dialectic transpires in the object itself. The relation of subject and object in the artwork too must not be forgotten, insofar as it is concerned with objects. This relation changes historically yet persists even in nonrepresentational works, for they take up an attitude to the object by placing it under a taboo. Still, the starting point of the *Critique of Judgment* was not simply inimical to an objective aesthetics. Its force was that, as throughout Kant's theories, it was not comfortably installed in any of the positions marked out by the system's strategies. Insofar as according to his theory aesthetics is constituted by the subjective judgment of taste, this judgment necessarily becomes not only a *constituens* of the objective work but rather bears in itself an objective necessity, however little this necessity can be reduced to universal concepts. Kant envisioned a subjectively mediated but objective aesthetics. The Kantian concept of the judgment of taste, by its subjectively directed query, concerns the core of objective aesthetics: the question of quality—good and bad, true and false—in the artwork. The subjective query is itself more aesthetic than is the epistemological *intentio obliqua* because the objectivity of the artwork is mediated in a manner that is qualitatively different from the objectivity of knowledge, being mediated more specifically through the subject. It is virtually tautological to claim that the determination whether an artwork is an artwork depends on the judgment whether it is, and that the mechanism of such judgments, far more than any investigation of the power of judgment as a psychic "ability," is the theme of the work. "The definition of taste on which I am basing this analysis is that it is the ability to judge the beautiful. But we have to analyze judgments of taste in order to discover what is required for calling an object beautiful."[1] The canon of the work is the objective validity of the judgment of taste that, while affording no guarantee, is nevertheless stringent. The situation of all nominalist art is thus prepared. Analogously with the critique of reason, Kant would like to ground aesthetic objectivity in the subject rather than to displace the former by the latter. Implicitly he holds that the element that unifies the objective and the subjective is reason, a subjective ability at the same time that, by virtue of its attributes of necessity and universality, it is the exemplar of all objectivity. For Kant, even the aesthetic is subordinated to the primacy of discursive logic: "I have used the logical functions of judging to help me find the elements that judgment takes into consideration when it reflects (since even a judgment of taste still has reference to the understanding). I have examined the element of quality first, because an aesthetic judgment about the beautiful is concerned first with it."[2] The strongest buttress of subjective aesthetics, the concept of aesthetic feeling, derives from objectivity, not the reverse. Aesthetic feeling says that something is thus, that something is beautiful; Kant would have attributed such aesthetic feeling, as "taste," exclusively to one who was capable of discriminating in the object. Taste is not defined in Aristotelian fashion by sympathy and fear, the affects provoked in the viewer. The contamination of aesthetic feeling with unmediated psychological emotions by the concept of arousal misinterprets the modification of real experience by artistic experience. It would otherwise be inexplicable why people expose themselves to aesthetic experience in the first place. Aesthetic feeling is not the feeling that is aroused: It is astonishment vis-à-vis what is beheld rather than vis-à-vis what it is about; it is a being overwhelmed by what is aconceptual and yet determinate, not the subjective affect released, that in the case of aesthetic experience may be called feeling. It goes to the heart of the matter, is the feeling for it and not a reflex of the observer. The observing subjectivity is to be strictly distinguished from the subjective element in the object, that is, from the object's expression as well as from its subjectively mediated form. The question, however, of what is and what is not an artwork cannot in any way be separated from the faculty of judging, that is, from the question of quality, of good and bad. The idea of a bad artwork has something nonsensical about it: If it miscarries, if it fails to achieve its immanent constitution, it fails its own concept and sinks beneath the apriori of art. In art, judgments of relative merit, appeals to fairness and toleration of the half-finished, all commonsense excuses and even that of humanity, are false; their indulgence damages the artwork by implicitly liquidating its claim to truth. As long as the boundary that art sets up against reality has not been washed away, tolerance for bad works—borrowed from reality—is a violation of art.

To be able to say with good reason why an artwork is beautiful, true, coherent, or legitimate does not mean reducing it to its universal concepts, even if this operation—which Kant both desired and contested—were possible. In every artwork, and not only in the aporia of the faculty of reflective judgment, the universal and the particular are densely intertwined. Kant touches on this when he defines the beautiful as "that which pleases universally without requiring a concept."[3] This universality, in spite of Kant's desperate effort, cannot be divorced from necessity; that something "pleases universally" is equivalent to the judgment that it must please each and every person, for otherwise it would be merely an empirical statement. Yet universality and implicit necessity remain ineluctable concepts, and their unity, as Kant conceived it, in the act of pleasing is external to the work. The requirement of the subsumption of particulars to the unifying concept transgresses against the idea of conceptualization from within that, by means of the concept of finality, was to correct in both parts of the *Critique of Judgment* the classificatory method of "theoretical," natural-scientific reason that emphatically rejects knowledge of the object from within. In this regard, Kant's aesthetics is a hybrid defenselessly exposed to Hegel's critique. His advance must be emancipated from absolute idealism; this is the task that today confronts aesthetics. The ambivalence of Kant's theory, however, is defined by his philosophy as a whole, in which the concept of purpose only extends the category into its regulative use and thus to this extent also circumscribes it. He knows what it is that art shares with discursive knowledge, but not that whereby art diverges qualitatively from it; the distinction becomes the quasi-mathematical one between the finite and the infinite. No single rule by which the judgment of taste must subsume its objects, not even the totality of these rules, has anything to say about the dignity of an artwork. So long as the concept of necessity, as constitutive of aesthetic judgment, is not reflected into itself, it simply reproduces the deterministic mechanism of empirical reality, that mechanism that itself only returns in artworks in a shadowy and modified form; yet the stipulation that beauty be universally pleasing presupposes a consent that is, though without admitting it, subordinate to social convention. If, however, these two elements are harnessed together in the intelligible realm then Kant's doctrine forfeits its content [*Inhalt*]. It is possible concretely to conceive of artworks that fulfill the Kantian judgment of taste and nevertheless miss the mark. Other works, indeed new art as a whole, contradict that judgment and are hardly universally pleasing, and yet they cannot thereby be objectively disqualified as art. Kant achieves his goal of the objectivity of aesthetics, just as he does that of the objectivity of ethics, by way of universally conceptual formalization. This formalization is, however, contrary to aesthetic phenomena as what is constitutively particular. What each artwork would need to be according to its pure concept is essential to none. Formalization, an act of subjective reason, forces art back into precisely that merely subjective sphere—ultimately that of contingency—from which Kant wanted to wrest it and which art itself resists. As contrary poles, subjective and objective aesthetics are equally exposed to the critique of a dialectical aesthetics: the former because it is either abstractly transcendental or arbitrary in its dependence on individual taste; the latter because it overlooks the objective mediatedness of art by the subject. In the artwork the subject is neither the observer nor the creator nor absolute spirit, but rather spirit bound up with, preformed and mediated by the object.

For the artwork and thus for its theory, subject and object are its own proper elements and they are dialectical in such a fashion that whatever the work is composed of—material, expression, and form—is always both. The materials are shaped by the hand from which the artwork received them; expression, objectivated in the work and objective in itself, enters as a subjective impulse; form, if it is not to have a mechanical relationship to what is formed, must be produced subjectively according to the demands of the object. What confronts artists with the kind of objective impenetrability with which their material so often confronts them, an impenetrability analogous to the construction of the given in epistemology, is at the same time sedimented subject; it is expression, that which appears most subjective, but which is also objective in that it is what the artwork exhausts itself on and what it incorporates; finally, it is a subjective comportment in which objectivity leaves its imprint. But the reciprocity of subject and object in the work, which cannot be that of identity, maintains a precarious balance. The subjective process of the work's production is, with regard to its private dimension, a matter of indifference. Yet the process also has an objective dimension that is a condition for the realization of its immanent lawfulness. It is as labor, and not as communication, that the subject in art comes into its own. It must be the artwork's ineluctable ambition to achieve balance without ever being quite able to do so: This is an aspect of aesthetic semblance. The individual artist also functions as the executor of this balance. It is hard to say whether, in the production process, he is faced with a self-imposed task; the marble block in which a sculpture waits, the piano keys in which a composition waits to be released, are probably more than metaphors for the task. The tasks bear their objective solution in themselves, at least within a certain variational range, though they do not have the univocity of equations. The act carried out by the artist is minimal, that of mediating between the problem that confronts him and is already determined, and the solution, which is itself similarly lodged in the material as a potential. If the tool has been called the extension of an arm, the artist could be called the extension of a tool, a tool for the transition from potentiality to actuality.

Art's linguistic quality gives rise to reflection over what speaks in art; this is its veritable subject, not the individual who makes it or the one who receives it. This is masked by the lyrical "I," which in confessing has over the centuries produced the semblance of the self-evidence of poetic subjectivity. But this subjectivity is on no account identical with the I that speaks in the poem. This is not only because of the poetic fictional character of poetry and of music, in which subjective expression scarcely ever coincides immediately with the condition of the composer. Far more important is that the grammatical I of the poem is only posited by the I that speaks latently through the work; the empirical I is a function of the spiritual I, not the reverse. The part played by the empirical I is not, as the topos of sincerity would have it, the locus of authenticity. It remains undecided whether the latent I, the speaking I, is the same in the different genres of art and whether or not it changes; it may vary qualitatively according to the materials of the arts; their sub-sumption under the dubious subordinating concept of art obscures this. In any case, this latent I is immanently constituted in the work through the action of the work's language; in relation to the work, the individual who produces it is an element of reality like others. The private person is not even decisive in the factual production of artworks. Implicitly the artwork demands the division of labor, and the individual functions accordingly. By entrusting itself fully to its material, production results in something universal born out of the utmost individuation. The force with which the private I is externalized in the work is the I's collective essence; it constitutes the linguistic quality of works. The labor in the artwork becomes social by way of the individual, though the individual need not be conscious of society; perhaps this is all the more true the less the individual is conscious of society. The intervening individual subject is scarcely more than a limiting value, something minimal required by the artwork for its crystallization. The emancipation of the artwork from the artist is no *l'art pour l'art* delusion of grandeur but the simplest expression of the work's constitution as the expression of a social relation that bears in itself the law of its own reification: Only as things do artworks become the antithesis of the reified monstrosity. Correspondingly, and this is key to art, even out of so-called individual works it is a We that speaks and not an I—indeed all the more so the less the artwork adapts externally to a We and its idiom. Here again music gives the most extreme expression to certain characteristics of the artistic, though this too by no means bestows any primacy on music. Music says We directly, regardless of its intentions. Even the depositional works of its expressionist phase register binding experiences, and the works' bindingness, their formative force, depends on whether these experiences actually speak through the works. In Western music it would be possible to demonstrate how much its most important discovery, the harmonic depth dimension, as well as all counterpoint and polyphony, is the We of the choric ritual that has penetrated into the material. The We introduces its literalness transformed as an immanently acting force and yet maintains the quality of speech. Literary forms, by their direct and ultimately inescapable participation in communicative language, are related to a We; for the sake of their own eloquence they must strive to free themselves of all external communicativeness. But this process is not—as it appears to be or seems to itself to be—one of pure subjectivization. Through this process the subject forms itself to collective experience all the more intimately the more it hardens itself against linguistically reified expression. The plastic arts speak through the How of apperception. Their We is simply the sensorium according to its historical condition pursued to the point that it breaks the relation to representational objectivity that was modified by virtue of the development of its language of form. Images say: "Behold!"; they have their collective subject in what they point to, which is outward, not inward as with music. In the potentiation of its linguistic quality the history of art—which is equivalent to that of progressive individualization—is at the same time its opposite. That this We is, however, not socially univocal, that it is hardly that of a determinate class or social positions, has its origin perhaps in the fact that to this day art in the emphatic sense has only existed as bourgeois art; according to Trotsky's thesis, no proletarian art is conceivable, only socialist art. The aesthetic We is a social whole on the horizon of a certain indeterminateness, though, granted, as determinate as the ruling productive forces and relations of an epoch. Although art is tempted to anticipate a nonexistent social whole, its non-existent subject, and is thereby more than ideology, it bears at the same time the mark of this subject's non-existence. The antagonisms of society are nevertheless preserved in it. Art is true insofar as what speaks out of it—indeed, it itself—is conflicting and unreconciled, but this truth only becomes art's own when it synthesizes what is fractured and thus makes its irreconcilability determinate. Paradoxically, art must testify to the unreconciled and at the same time envision its reconciliation; this is a possibility only for its nondiscursive language. Only in this process is its We concretized. What speaks out of it, however, is truly its subject insofar as it indeed speaks out of it rather than being something depicted by it. The title of the incomparable final piece of Schumann's *Scenes from Childhood*, "The Poet Speaks," one of the earliest models of expressionist music, takes cognizance of this. But the aesthetic subject is probably unrepresentable because, being socially mediated, it is no more empirical than the transcendental subject of philosophy. "The objectivation of the artwork takes place at the cost of the replication of the living. Artworks win life only when they renounce likeness to the human. 'The expression of an unadulterated feeling is always banal. The more unadulterated, the more banal. Not to be banal requires effort.'"[4]

The artwork becomes objective as something made through and through, that is, by virtue of the subjective mediation of all of its elements. The insight of the critique of knowledge that subjectivity and reification are correlative receives unparalleled confirmation in aesthetics. The semblance character of artworks, the illusion of their being-in-itself, refers back to the fact that in the totality of their subjective mediatedness they take part in the universal delusional context of reification, and, that, in Marxian terms, they need to reflect a relation of living labor as if it were a thing. The inner consistency through which artworks participate in truth also involves their untruth; in its most unguarded manifestations art has always revolted against this, and today this revolt has become art's own law of movement. The antinomy of the truth and untruth of art may have moved Hegel to foretell its end. Traditional aesthetics possessed the insight that the primacy of the whole over the parts has constitutive need of the diverse and that this primacy misfires when it is simply imposed from above. No less constitutive, however, is that no artwork has ever been fully adequate in this regard. Granted, the multiplicitous in the aesthetic continuum wants synthesis, yet at the same time, being determined extra-aesthetically, it withdraws from synthesis. The synthesis that is extrapolated out of multiplicity, which it has as a potential in itself, is unavoidably also the negation of this multiplicity. The equilibrium sought by form must misfire internally because externally, meta-aesthetically, it does not exist. Antagonisms that are unsolved in reality cannot be solved imaginatively either; they work their way into the imagination and are reproduced in imagination's own inconsistency; in fact, this happens in proportion to the intensity with which they pursue their coherence. Artworks must act as if the impossible were for them possible; the idea of the perfection of works, with which none can dispense except at the cost of its own triviality, was dubious. Artists have a hard fate not only because of their always uncertain fate in the world but because through their own efforts they necessarily work against the aesthetic truth to which they devote themselves. Inasmuch as subject and object have become disjoint in historical reality, art is possible only in that it passed through the subject. For mimesis of what is not administered by the subject has no other locus than in the living subject. The objectivation of art through its immanent execution requires the historical subject. If the artwork hopes through its objectivation to achieve that truth that is hidden from the subject, then this is so because the subject is itself not ultimate. The relation of the objectivity of the artwork to the primacy of the object is fractured. This objectivity bears witness to the primacy of the object in a condition of universal thralldom that only in the subject provides a place of refuge for what is in-itself, while at the same time the form of the objectivity of this in-itself, which is a semblance effected by the subject, is a critique of objectivity. This objectivity grants entry exclusively to the *membra disjecta* of the world of objects, which only in a state of decomposition becomes commensurable to the law of form.

Subjectivity, however, though a necessary condition of the artwork, is not the aesthetic quality as such but becomes it only through objectivation; to this extent subjectivity in the artwork is self-alienated and concealed. This is not comprehended by Riegl's concept of "artistic volition." Yet this concept discerns an element essential to immanent critique: that nothing external adjudicates over the niveau of artworks. They, not their authors, are their own measure; in Wagner's words, their self-posited law. The question of their own legitimation is not lodged beyond their fulfillment. No artwork is only what it aspires to be, but there is none that is more than this without aspiring to be something. This bears closely on spontaneity, although precisely it also involves the nonvolitional. Spontaneity manifests itself primarily in the conception of the work, through the design evident in it. But conception too is no ultimate category: It often transforms the self-realization of the artworks. It is virtually the seal of objectivation that under the pressure of its immanent logic the conception is displaced. This self-alien element that works contrary to the purported artistic volition is familiar, sometimes terrifyingly so, to artists as to critics; Nietzsche broached this issue at the end of *Beyond Good and Evil*. The element of self-alienness that occurs under the constraint of the material is indeed the seal of what was meant by "genius." If anything is to be salvaged of this concept it must be stripped away from its crude equation with the creative subject, who through vain exuberance bewitches the artwork into a document of its maker and thus diminishes it. The objectivity of artworks—a thorn in the side of the inhabitants of a society based on barter because they mistakenly expect that art will mollify the alienation—is translated back into the person who stands behind the work, even though he is usually only the character mask of those who want to promote the work as an article of consumption. If one does not simply want to abolish the concept of genius as a romantic residue, it must be understood in terms of its historicophilosophical objectivity. The divergence of subject and individual, adumbrated in Kant's antipsychologism and raised to the level of a principle in Fichte, takes its toll on art, too. Art's authenticity—what is binding in it—and the freedom of the emancipated individual become remote from each other. The concept of genius represents the attempt to unite the two with a wave of the wand; to bestow the

223

individual within the limited sphere of art with the immediate power of overarching authenticity. The experiential content of such mystification is that in art authenticity, the universal element, is no longer possible except by way of the *principium individuationis,* just as, conversely, universal bourgeois freedom is exclusively that of particularization and individuation. This relation, however, is treated blindly by the aesthetics of genius and displaced undialectically into an individual who is supposedly at the same time subject; the *intellectus archetypus,* which in the theory of knowledge is expressly the idea, is treated by the concept of genius as a fact of art. Genius is purported to be the individual whose spontaneity coincides with the action of the absolute subject. This is correct insofar as the individuation of artworks, mediated by spontaneity, is that in them by which they are objectivated. Yet the concept of genius is false because works are not creations and humans are not creators. This defines the untruth of any genius aesthetics that suppresses the element of finite making, the τέχνη in artworks, in favor of their absolute originality, virtually their *natura naturans;* it thus spawns the ideology of the organic and unconscious artwork, which flows into the murky current of irrationalism. From the start, the genius aesthetic shifted emphasis toward the individual—opposing a spurious universality—and away from society by absolutizing this individual. Yet whatever the misuse perpetrated by the concept of genius, it calls to mind that the subject in the artwork should not be reduced to its objectivation. In the *Critique of Judgment* the concept of genius became the refuge for everything of which hedonism had deprived Kant's aesthetics. However, with incalculable consequences, Kant restricted geniality exclusively to the subject, indifferent to its ego-alienness, which was later ideologically exploited by contrasting genius with scientific and philosophical rationality. The fetishization of the concept of genius that begins with Kant as the fetishization of dirempted, abstract subjectivity—to put it in Hegelian terms—already in Schiller's votive offerings took on a quality of crass elitism. The concept of genius becomes the potential enemy of artworks; with a sidelong glance at Goethe, the person back of the work is purported to be more essential than the artworks themselves. In the concept of genius the idea of creation is transferred with idealistic hubris from the transcendental to the empirical subject, to the productive artist. This suits crude bourgeois consciousness as much because it implies a work ethic that glorifies pure human creativity regardless of its aim as because the viewer is relieved of taking any trouble with the object itself: The viewer is supposed to be satisfied with the personality—essentially a kitsch biography—of the artist. Those who produce important artworks are not demigods but fallible, often neurotic and damaged, individuals. An aesthetic mentality, however, that wholly swept away the idea of genius would degenerate into a desolate, pedantic arts-and-crafts mentality devoted to tracing out stencils. The element of truth in the concept of genius is to be sought in the object, in what is open, not in the repetition of the imprisoned. Incidentally, the concept of genius as it came in vogue in the late eighteenth century was in no way charismatic; in that epoch, any individual could become a genius to the extent that he expressed himself unconventionally as nature. Genius was an attitude to reality, "ingenious doings," indeed almost a conviction or frame of mind; only later, perhaps given the insufficiency of mere conviction in artworks, did genius become a divine blessing. The experience of real unfreedom destroyed the exuberance of subjective freedom as freedom for all and reserved it as the exclusive domain of genius. It becomes ideology in inverse proportion to the world's becoming a less human one and the more consciousness of this—spirit—is neutralized. Privileged genius becomes the proxy to whom reality promises what it denies humanity as a whole. What deserves to be salvaged in genius is what is instrumental to the work. The category of geniality can best be documented when a passage is described as being ingenious. Fantasy alone does not suffice for its definition. The genial is a dialectical knot: It is what has not been copied or repeated, it is free, yet at the same time bears the feeling of necessity; it is art's paradoxical sleight of hand and one of its most dependable criteria. To be genial means to hit upon a constellation, subjectively to achieve the objective, it is the instant in which the methexis of the artwork in language allows convention to be discarded as accidental. The signature of the genial in art is that the new appears by virtue of its newness as if it had always been there; romanticism took note of this. The work of fantasy is less *creatio ex nihilo*, the belief of an art-alien religion of art, than the imagining of authentic solutions in the midst of the effectively preexisting nexus of works. Experienced artists may be overheard referring derisively to a passage: "Here he's a genius." They chastise the intrusion of fantasy into the logic of the work, an intrusion not subsequently integrated; instances of this are found not only in the work of self-promoting whiz kids but even at Schubert's niveau. The genial remains paradoxical and precarious because the freely discovered and the necessary cannot actually ever be completely fused. Without the ever present possibility of failure there is nothing genial in artworks.

Because of its element of something that had not existed before, the genial was bound up with the concept of originality: thus the concept *Originalgenie*. As is well known, prior to the age of genius the idea of originality bore no authority. That in their new works composers of the seventeenth and early eighteenth centuries made use of whole sections of their own earlier works and those of others, or that painters and architects entrusted their designs to students for completion, is easily misused to justify the stereotypical and routine and to denounce subjective freedom. Yet what this practice demonstrates is that originality had yet to become the object of critical reflection, by no means that there was no originality in artworks; one glance at the difference between Bach and his contemporaries suffices to make the point. Originality, the specificity of a determinate artwork, is not antithetical to the logicality of artworks, which implies a universal. Often originality emerges from a thoroughly consistent logical construction, of which mediocre talents are incapable. All the same, the question of the originality of older, archaic works is meaningless because the coercion exercised by collective consciousness, in which domination entrenches itself, was so extensive that originality, which presupposes something on the order of emancipated subjectivity, would be anachronistic. The concept of originality, as in Benjamin's sense of the "originary,"[5] does not so much summon up the primordial as the *yet to be* in works, their utopic trace. The original is the objective name of each work. If, however, originality arose historically, it is also enmeshed in historical injustice, in the predominance of bourgeois commodities that must touch up the ever-same as the ever-new in order to win customers. Yet with the growing autonomy of art, originality has turned against the market where it was never permitted to go beyond a certain limit. It withdrew into the artworks themselves, into the relentlessness of their integral organization. Originality remains touched by the historical fate of the category of individualness from which it was derived. Originality no longer obeys what it has been associated with ever since it began to be self-consciously reflected upon: a so-called individual style. Although the collapse of that style has meanwhile come to be decried by traditionalists, who are in fact defending conventional goods, in the most progressive works individual style, cunningly tricked out of the requirements of construction, takes on the quality of a blemish, a deficiency, or at the least a compromise. This is one of the most important reasons why advanced artistic production aims less at originality in a particular work than at the production of a new type. Originality is in the process of being transformed into the act of inventing types, a transformation in which originality is changed qualitatively without, however, disappearing in the process.

This transformation, which altogether severs originality from mere inspiration, the unique detail that once seemed to be the substance of originality, throws light on fantasy, its organon. Under the spell of the belief in the subject as the creator's successor, fantasy effectively meant the capacity to bring forth something determinately artistic out of nothing. Its crude concept, that of absolute invention, is the exact correlate of the modern scientific ideal of the strict reproduction of what already exists; here the bourgeois division of labor has furrowed a trench that divides art from any mediation with reality, just as it divides knowledge from everything that in any way transcends reality. This concept of fantasy was never essential to important artworks; the invention, for instance, of fantastic beings in contemporary plastic arts is of minor significance, just as the sudden intervention of a musical motif, though hardly to be discounted, remains powerless so long as it does not surpass its own factuality through what develops out of it. If everything in artworks, including what is most sublime, is bound up with what exists, which they oppose, fantasy cannot be the mere capacity to escape the existing by positing the nonexisting as if it existed. On the contrary, fantasy shifts whatever artworks absorb of the existing into constellations through which they become the other of the existing, if only through its determinate negation. If the effort is made to envision a strictly nonexisting object through what epistemologists dubbed fantasizing fiction, nothing is achieved that cannot be reduced—in its parts and even in the elements that constitute its coherence—to what already exists. Only under the spell of the totally empirical does what is qualitatively opposed to it appear, though it does so exclusively as something on a second order of existence modeled on the first. Art transcends the nonexisting only by way of the existing; otherwise it becomes the helpless projection of what in any case already exists. Accordingly, fantasy in artworks cannot be restricted to the sudden vision. Although there is no conceiving of fantasy devoid of spontaneity, fantasy, despite being closest to the *creatio ex nihilo*, is by no means art's one and all. Fantasy may be set in motion primarily by something concrete in the artwork, especially among those artists whose process of production works upward from below. Equally, however, fantasy is active in a dimension that a common prejudice holds to be abstract, namely in the dimension of the quasi-empty outline, which is then fleshed out and made good on through what prejudice considers the opposite of fantasy: "labor." Even specifically technological fantasy is not a recent development, as is evident in the compositional style of the Adagio of Schubert's string quintet as well as in the eddies of light in Turner's seascapes. Fantasy is also, and essentially so, the unrestricted availability of potential solutions that crystallize within the artwork. It is lodged not only in what strikes one both as existing and as the residue of something existing, but perhaps even more in the transformation of the existing. The harmonic variant of the main theme in the coda of the first movement of the *Appassionata*, with the catastrophic effect of the diminished seventh chord, is no less a product of fantasy than is the triadic theme of the brooding idea that opens the movement; with regard to genesis it cannot be excluded that the variant that is decisive for the whole might in fact have been Beethoven's initial idea, from which, retroactively as it were, the theme in its primary form was derived. It is no less of an achievement of fantasy that the later sections of the broadly cast development of the first movement of the *Eroica* give way to lapidary harmonic periods, as if suddenly there was no time for differentiation. The growing primacy of construction necessarily reduced the substantiality of the particular inspiration. Just how much labor and fantasy are implicated in each other—their divergence is invariably an index of failure—is supported by the experience of artists that fantasy is subject to command. They sense that the freedom to the involuntary is what distinguishes them from dilettantes. Even subjectively, the mediate and the immediate are in turn mediated in each other aesthetically and in knowledge. Not genetically, but in terms of its constitution, art is the most compelling argument against the epistemological division of sensuality and intellect. Reflection is fully capable of the act of fantasy in the form of the determinate consciousness of what an artwork at a certain point needs. The idea that consciousness kills, for which art supposedly provides unimpeachable testimony, is a foolish cliché in this context as anywhere else. Even its power to resolve objects into their components, its critical element, is fruitful for the self-reflection of the artwork: It excludes and modifies the inadequate, the unformed, and the incoherent. On the other hand, the category of aesthetic dumbness has its *fundamentum in re* as the lack of immanent reflection in works, which is evident, for instance, in the stupor of mechanical repetition. What is bad in artworks is a reflection that directs them externally, that forces them; where, however, they immanently want to go can only be followed by reflection, and the ability to do this is spontaneous. If each and every artwork involves a probably aporetic nexus of problems, this is the source of what is perhaps not the worst definition of fantasy. As the capacity to discover approaches and solutions in the artwork, fantasy may be defined as the differential of freedom in the midst of determination.

The objectivity of artworks is no more a residual determination than is any truth. Neoclassicism faltered because it deluded itself with the goal of achieving an ideal of objectivity, which appeared to it in apparently binding styles of the past, by way of a subjectively instituted procedure: It abstractly negated the subject in the work and formulated the imago of a subjectless in-itself, which the subject—itself no longer eliminable by any act of will—could throw into relief solely by means of injury to itself. A rigor that establishes restrictions by imitating long-past heteronomous forms obeys nothing other than that very subjective volition that is to be tamed. Valéry outlined the problem but did not solve it. Form that is merely chosen and posited, which Valéry himself sometimes defends, is as accidental as the chaotic "vitality" he despised. The aporia of art today is not to be cured through any willing subordination to authority. It remains an open question just how, without coercion, it would be possible, given an unmitigated nominalism, to achieve anything on the order of an objectivity of form; this is impeded by instituted closure. The tendency toward this instituted closure was synchronous with the rise of political fascism, whose ideology similarly feigned that a state freed from the desperation and insecurity of its subjects during the period of late liberalism could be hoped for only on the basis of the abdication of the subject. Of course, this abdication was prompted by more powerful subjects. Even in its fallibility and weakness, the subject who contemplates art is not expected simply to retreat from the claim to objectivity. Otherwise it would hold that those alien to art—the philistines devoid of any relation to art, who let it affect them as if they were a *tabula rasa*—would be the most qualified to understand and judge it, and the unmusical would be the best music critics. Like art itself, knowledge of it is consummated dialectically. The more the observer adds to the process, the greater the energy with which he penetrates the artwork, the more he then becomes aware of objectivity from within. He takes part in objectivity when his energy, even that of his misguided subjective "projection," extinguishes itself in the artwork. The subjective detour may totally miss the mark, but without the detour no objectivity becomes evident.——— Every step toward the perfection of artworks is a step toward their self-alienation, and this dialectically produces ever anew those revolts that are too superficially characterized as subjectivity's rebellion against formalism of whatever sort. The growing integration of artworks, their immanent exigency, is also their immanent contradiction. The artwork that carries through its immanent dialectic reflects it as resolved: This is what is aesthetically false in the aesthetic principle. The antinomy of aesthetic reification is also one between the ever fractured metaphysical claim of works to being exempted from time, and the transience of everything that establishes itself in time as enduring. Artworks become relative because they must assert themselves as absolute. Benjamin touched on this once in commenting that "there is no redemption for artworks." The perennial revolt of art against art has its *fundamentum in re*. If it is essential to artworks that they be things, it is no less essential that they negate their own status as things, and thus art turns against art. The totally objectivated artwork would congeal into a mere thing, whereas if it altogether evaded objectivation it would regress to an impotently powerless subjective impulse and flounder in the empirical world.

Notes

1 Immanuel Kant, *Critique of Judgment*, trans. Werner S. Pluhar (Indianapolis, 1987), p. 43.
2 Ibid.
3 Ibid., p. 64.
4 Adorno, *Notes to Literature*, trans. Shierry Weber Nicholsen, vol. 2 (New York, 1992), p. 163. [Translation amended.—trans.]
5 ["Der Begriff des Ursprünglichen": The reference to Benjamin has been interpolated here by the translator. See note 7 in "Semblance and Expression."—trans.]

10
Toward a theory of the artwork

That the experience of artworks is adequate only as living experience is more than a statement about the relation of the observer to the observed, more than a statement about psychological cathexis as a condition of aesthetic perception. Aesthetic experience becomes living experience only by way of its object, in that instant in which artworks themselves become animate under its gaze. This is George's symbolist teaching in the poem "The Tapestry,"[1] an *art poétique* that furnishes the title of a volume. Through contemplative immersion the immanent processual quality of the work is set free. By speaking, it becomes something that moves in itself. Whatever in the artifact may be called the unity of its meaning is not static but processual, the enactment of antagonisms that each work necessarily has in itself. Analysis is therefore adequate to the work only if it grasps the relation of its elements to each other processually rather than reducing them analytically to purported fundamental elements. That artworks are not being but a process of becoming can be grasped technologically. Their continuity is demanded teleologically by the particular elements. They are in need of continuity and capable of it by virtue of their incompleteness and, often, by their insignificance. It is as a result of their own constitution that they go over into their other, find continuance in it, want to be extinguished in it, and in their demise determine what follows them. This immanent dynamic is, in a sense, a higher-order element of what artworks are. If anywhere, then it is here that aesthetic experience resembles sexual experience, indeed its culmination. The way the beloved image is transformed in this experience, the way rigidification is unified with what is most intensely alive, effectively makes the experience the incarnate prototype of aesthetic experience. Yet it is not only the individual works that are immanently dynamic; so too is their relation to each other. Art is historical exclusively by way of individual works that have taken shape in themselves, not by their external association, not even through the influence that they purportedly exert over each other. This is why art mocks verbal definition. That whereby art's existence is constituted is itself dynamic as an attitude toward objectivity that both withdraws from and takes up a stance toward it and in this stance maintains objectivity transformed. Artworks synthesize ununifiable, nonidentical elements that grind away at each other; they truly seek the identity of the identical and the nonidentical processually because even their unity is only an element and not the magical formula of the whole. The processual quality of artworks is constituted in such a fashion that as artifacts, as something humanly made, they have their place a priori in the "native realm of spirit" but are, in order to become self-identical, in need of what is nonidentical, heterogeneous, and not already formed. The resistance to them of otherness, on which they are nevertheless dependent, compels them to articulate their own formal language, to leave not the smallest unformed particle as remnant. This reciprocity constitutes art's dynamic; it is an irresolvable antithesis that is never brought to rest in the state of being. Artworks are such only *in actu* because their tension does not terminate in pure identity with either extreme. On the other hand, it is only as finished, molded objects that they become force fields of their antagonisms; otherwise the encapsuled forces would simply run parallel to each other or dissipate. Artworks' paradoxical nature, stasis, negates itself. The movement of artworks must be at a standstill and thereby become visible. Their immanent processual character—the legal process that they undertake against the merely existing world that is external to them—is objective prior to their alliance with any party. All artworks, even the affirmative, are a priori polemical. The idea of a conservative artwork is inherently absurd. By emphatically separating themselves from the empirical world, their other, they bear witness that that world itself should be other than it is; they are the unconscious schemata of that world's transformation. Even for an artist like Mozart, who seems so unpolemical and who according to general agreement moves solely within the pure sphere of spirit, excepting the literary themes that he chose for his greatest operas, the polemical element is central in the power by which the music sets itself at a distance that mutely condemns the impoverishment and falsity of that from which it distances itself. In Mozart form acquires the power of that distancing as determinate negation; the reconciliation that it realizes is painfully sweet because reality to date has refused it. The resoluteness of distance—as presumably that of all classicism that is forceful rather than vacantly playing with itself—concretizes the critique of what has been repulsed. What crackles in artworks is the sound of the friction of the antagonistic elements that the artwork seeks to unify; it is script not least because, as in linguistic signs, its processual element is enciphered in its objectivation. The processual character of artworks is nothing other than their temporal nucleus. If duration becomes their intention in such a fashion that they expel what they deem ephemeral and by their own hand eternalize themselves in pure impregnable forms or, worse, by the ominous claim to the universally human, they cut short their lives and assimilate themselves into the concept that—as the fixed circumference of shifting contents—by its form pursues precisely that temporal stasis against which the drawn tension of the artwork defends itself. Artworks, mortal human objects, pass away all the more rapidly the more doggedly they stave it off. Although permanence cannot be excluded from the concept of their form, it is not their essence. Daringly exposed works that seem to be rushing toward their perdition have in general a better chance of survival than those that, subservient to the idol of security, hollow out their temporal nucleus and, inwardly vacuous, fall victim to time: the curse of neoclassicism. Speculating on survival by adding something perishable is hardly helpful. Today it is conceivable and perhaps requisite that artworks immolate themselves through their temporal nucleus, devote their own life to the instant of the appearance of truth, and tracelessly vanish without thereby diminishing themselves in the slightest. The nobility of such comportment would not be unworthy of art now that its loftiness has decayed to attitude and ideology. The idea of the permanence of works is modeled on the category of property and is thus ephemeral in the bourgeois sense; it was alien to many periods and important productions. It is said that when Beethoven finished the *Appassionata* he commented that it would still be played ten years later. Stockhausen's concept of electronic works—which, since they are not notated in the traditional sense but immediately "realized" in their material, could be extinguished along with this material—is a splendid one of an art that makes emphatic claim yet is prepared to throw itself away. Like other constituents through which art once became what it is, even its temporal nucleus has been exteriorized and explodes its concept. The common declarations against fashion that equate the transient with the nugatory are not only allied with the counterimage of an inwardness that has been compromised politically as well as aesthetically by its incapacity for exteriorization and a stubborn limitation to individual quiddity. In spite of its commercial manipulatability, fashion reaches deep into artworks; it does not simply exploit them. Such inventions as Picasso's rayonism are like transpositions from haute couture experiments, pinning dresses together around the body for an evening rather than tailoring them in a traditional manner. Fashion is one of the ways in which historical movement affects the sensorium and, through it, artworks, and this is so usually by way of minimal self-obtuse impulses.

The artwork is a process essentially in the relation of its whole and parts. Without being reducible to one side or the other, it is the relation itself that is a process of becoming. Whatever may in the artwork be called totality is not a structure that integrates the sum of its parts. Even objectified the work remains a developing process by virtue of the propensities active in it. Conversely, the parts are not something given, as which analysis almost inevitably mistakes them: Rather, they are centers of energy that strain toward the whole on the basis of a necessity that they equally preform. The vortex of this dialectic ultimately consumes the concept of meaning. When according to history's verdict the unity of process and result no longer succeeds; when, above all, the individual elements refuse to mold themselves to the ever latently preconceived totality, the gaping divergence tears meaning apart. If the artwork is nothing fixed and definitive in itself, but something in motion, then its immanent temporality is communicated to its parts and whole in such a fashion that their relation develops in time and that they are capable of canceling this relation. If artworks are alive in history by virtue of their own processual character, they are also able to perish in it. The indefeasibility of what is sketched on paper, painted on canvas, or carved in stone is no guarantee of the indefeasibility of what is essential to the artwork, its spirit, which is dynamic in itself. Artworks are on no account transformed exclusively by what reified consciousness takes to be the changing attitude of individuals toward works, which shifts according to the historical situation. Such change is external with regard to what transpires in the works themselves: the dissolution of their layers, one after the other, which was unforeseeable in the moment of the work's appearance; the determination of this transformation by their emerging and increasingly distinct law of form; the petrification of works that have become transparent, their decrepitude, and their falling silent. Ultimately their development is the same as their process of collapse.

The concept of an artifact, from which "artwork" is etymologically derived, does not fully comprise what an artwork is. Knowing that an artwork is something made does not amount to knowing that it is an artwork. The exaggerated accent on its fabrication, whether to lambast art as human deception or to denounce its artificiality or preciousness in opposition to the delusion of art as unmediated nature, stands in sympathetic accord with philistinism. The idea of providing a simple definition of art was dared only by those all-disposing philosophical systems that reserved a niche for every phenomenon. Hegel did indeed define beauty, but not art, presumably because he recognized its unity with, and difference from, nature. In art the difference between the thing made and its genesis—the making—is emphatic: Artworks are something made that has become more than something simply made. This was not contested until art began to experience itself as transient. The confounding of artworks with their genesis, as if genesis provided the universal code for what has become, is the source of the alienness of art scholarship to art: for artworks obey their law of form by consuming their genesis. Specifically aesthetic experience, self-abandonment to artworks, is indifferent to their genesis. Knowledge of the genesis is as external to aesthetic experience as is the history of the dedication of the *Eroica* to what musically transpires in that symphony. The attitude of authentic artworks toward extra-aesthetic objectivity is not so much to be sought in how this objectivity affects the process of production, for the artwork is in-itself a comportment that reacts to that objectivity even while turning away from it. Germane here is Kant's discussion of the real and the imitated nightingale in *Critique of Judgment*,[2] the theme of Andersen's famous fairy tale that has so often been turned into opera. Kant's reflection on it substitutes the knowledge of the origin of the phenomenon for the experience of that phenomenon. If the fictitious youth was indeed able to so perfectly imitate the nightingale that no difference could be discerned, this would cancel any interest in the question of the authenticity or nonauthenticity of the phenomenon, though it would be necessary to concede to Kant that such knowledge colors aesthetic experience: One sees a painting differently if one knows the name of the painter. No art is presuppositionless, and its presuppositions can no more be eliminated than art could be deduced from them. Rather than the Kantian artificer, Andersen with good instinct dealt with a toy; Stravinsky's opera characterizes the sound of that toy as a mechanical piping.[3] The difference from a natural song is perceptible in the phenomenon: As soon as the artifact wants to prompt the illusion of the natural, it founders.

The artwork is both the result of the process and the process itself at a standstill. It is what at its apogee rationalist metaphysics proclaimed as the principle of the universe, a monad: at once a force field and a thing. Artworks are closed to one another, blind, and yet in their hermeticism they represent what is external. Thus it is, in any case, that they present themselves to tradition as that living autarchy that Goethe was fond of calling entelechy, the synonym for monad. It is possible that the more problematic the concept of teleology becomes in organic nature the more intensively it condensed itself in artworks. As an element of an over-arching context of the spirit of an epoch, entwined with history and society, artworks go beyond their monadic limit even though they lack windows. The interpretation of an artwork as an immanent, crystallized process at a standstill approximates the concept of the monad. The thesis of the monadological character of artworks is as true as it is problematic. Their stringency and internal structuration are borrowed from their intellectual domination of reality. To this extent what is transcendent to them is imported into them as that by which they in the first place become an immanent nexus. These categories are, however, so completely mod ified that only the shadow of bindingness remains. Irrevocably, aesthetics presupposes immersion in the particular work. There is no denying the progress made even in academic art scholarship through the demand for immanent analysis and the renunciation of methods concerned with everything but the artwork. At the same time, however, immanent analysis bears an aspect of self-deception. There is no determination of the particularity of an artwork that does not, as a universal, according to its form, go beyond the monad. It is delusive to claim the concept, which must be introduced externally to the monad in order to open it up from within and thus to shatter it, has its source exclusively in the object. The monadological constitution of artworks in themselves points beyond itself. If it is made absolute, immanent analysis falls prey to ideology, against which it struggled when it wanted to devote itself to the artworks internally rather than deducing their worldviews. Today it is already evident that immanent analysis, which was once a weapon of artistic experience against philistinism, is being misused as a slogan to hold social reflection at a distance from an absolutized art. Without social reflection, however, the artwork is not to be understood in relation to that of which it constitutes one element, nor is it to be deciphered in terms of its own content. The blindness of the artwork is not only a corrective of the nature-dominating universal, it is also its correlative; as always the blind and the empty belong together in their abstractness. No particular in the artwork is legitimate without also becoming universal through its particularization. True, as an investigative procedure subsumption never reveals aesthetic content, but if subsumption is rejected altogether, no content would be thinkable; aesthetics would have to capitulate in front of the artwork as before a *factum brutum*. The aesthetically determined particular is to be referred to the element of its universality exclusively by way of its monadological closure. With a regularity that is indicative of something structural, immanent analyses—if their contact with what has been formed is close enough—lead to universal determinations that emerge directly from the most extreme specification. Certainly this is also due to the analytical method: Explanation amounts to the reduction to what is already known, whose synthesis with what is to be explained inescapably involves a universal. But the reversal of the particular into the universal is no less determined by the individual object. Where it is concentrated in itself to an extreme, it executes tensions that originate in the genre. Exemplary here are Anton Webern's works, in which sonata movements shrink to aphorisms. Aesthetics is not obliged, as under the spell of its object, to exorcise concepts. Rather, its responsibility is to free concepts from their externality to the particular object and to bring them within the work. If anywhere, then it is in aesthetics that Hegel's formulation of the movement of the concept has its locus. The reciprocal relation of the universal and the particular, which takes place unconsciously in artworks and which aesthetics must bring to consciousness, is what truly necessitates a dialectical approach. It could be objected that a residual dogmatic trust is operative here; external to the Hegelian system, it could be claimed, the movement of the concept has no sphere of legitimacy; the object can only be grasped as the life of the concept if the totality of what is objective coincides with spirit. To that the reply is that the monads, which artworks are, lead by way of their own principle of particularization to the universal. The universal determinations of art are not simply an exigency of their conceptual reflection. They testify to the boundaries of the principle of individuation, which is no more to be ontologized than is its opposite. Artworks get ever closer to these boundaries the more uncompromisingly they pursue the *principium individuationis*; the artwork that appears as something universal bears the accidental quality of being an example of its genre: It is spuriously individual. Even dada, the purely deictic gesture, was as universal as the demonstrative pronoun; that expressionism was more powerful as an idea than in its works perhaps has its origins in the fact that its utopia of the pure τόδε τι is itself a fragment of false consciousness. Yet the universal becomes substantial in artworks only by its self-transformation. Thus in Webern the universal musical form of the development becomes a "knot" and renounces its developmental function. Its place is taken by a succession of segments of differing levels of intensity. As a result the knot, like passages, become something wholly other, something more present and less relational than any development section ever was. Not only does the dialectic of the universal and particular descend into the depths of the universal in the midst of the particular. At the same time it destroys the invariance of the universal categories.

Just how little a universal concept of art suffices for artworks is demonstrated by the artworks themselves in that, as Valéry noted, few fulfill the strict concept. Guilt for this is borne not only by the weakness of artists in the face of the formidable concept of their object, but also by the concept itself. The more single-mindedly artworks devote themselves to the emerging idea of art, the more precarious becomes the relation of artworks to their other, a relation that is itself demanded by the concept. But this relation can be conserved only at the price of precritical consciousness, desperate naïveté: Today this is one of art's aporia. It is evident that supreme works are not the most pure, but tend to contain an extra-artistic surplus, especially an untransformed material element that burdens their immanent composition; however, it is no less evident that once the complete immanent elaboration of artworks, unsupported by anything unreflected that is other than art, has taken shape as an aesthetic norm, it is not possible willfully to reintroduce impure elements. The crisis of the pure artwork in the wake of the European catastrophes cannot be solved by breaking out of the pure work into an extra-aesthetic materiality whose moralistic pathos is pitched to obscure the fact that it is the easy way out; the line of least resistance is hardly suited to being established as the norm. The antinomy of pure versus impure art is subordinate to the more general antinomy that art is not the subordinating concept of its genres. These differ as much specifically as they diverge from one another.[4] The question beloved of traditionalist apologists of every stripe—"But is that still music?"—is fruitless; it is concrete, however, to analyze the deaesthetization of art as a praxis that, devoid of reflection and this side of art's own dialectic, progressively delivers art over to the extra-aesthetic dialectic. By contrast, that stereotypical question wants to use art's abstract subordinating concept to constrain the movement of those discrete, mutually distinguishing elements in which art consists. Currently, however, art stirs most energetically where it decomposes its subordinating concept. In this decomposition, art is true to itself: It breaks the mimetic taboo on the impure as a hybrid.—The inadequacy of the concept of art is registered by the linguistic sensorium in the expression a *Sprachkunstwerk*, a literary artwork. Not without a certain legitimacy, a literary historian coined it as a synonym for poetry in the largest sense. But the concept also does damage to poetic works that are artworks and yet, because of their relatively autonomous discursive element, not only artworks or not artworks throughout. Art likewise is in no way simply equivalent with artworks, for artists are always also at work on art and not only on artworks. Art as such is independent even of the artworks' consciousness. Functional forms and cult objects may develop historically into artworks; to deny this implies making oneself dependent on art's self-understanding, whose dynamic development is lodged in its own concept. The distinction urged by Benjamin between the artwork and the document[5] holds good insofar as it rejects works that are not in themselves determined by the law of form; many works, however, are objectively artworks even when they do not present themselves as art. The name of exhibitions entitled "Documenta," which provide an enormous service, glosses over this problem and thus abets a historicist aesthetic consciousness that they, being museums of the contemporary, want to oppose. Concepts of this sort, and especially those of the so-called classics of modernism, contribute all too well to the loss of tension in post-World War II art, much of which goes slack the moment it appears. They comfortably adapt to the model of an epoch that likes to call itself the atomic age.

The historical moment is constitutive of artworks; authentic works are those that surrender themselves to the historical substance of their age without reservation and without the presumption of being superior to it. They are the self-unconscious historiography of their epoch; this, not least of all, establishes their relation to knowledge. Precisely this makes them incommensurable with historicism, which, instead of following their own historical content, reduces them to their external history. Artworks may be all the more truly experienced the more their historical substance is that of the one who experiences it. The bourgeois world of art is ideologically blind even in the supposition that artworks that lie far enough in the past can be better understood than those of their own time. The layers of experience borne by important contemporary artworks, that which wants to speak in them, are—as objective spirit—incomparably more commensurable to contemporaries than are works whose historico-philosophical presuppositions are alienated from actual consciousness. The more intensively one seeks to comprehend Bach, the more puzzling is the gaze he returns, charged as it is with all the power that is his. Unless corrupted by willful stylization, a living composer would hardly be able to write a fugue that is better than a conservatory exercise or a parody or a feeble imitation of the *Well-Tempered Clavier*. The most extreme shocks and gestures of alienation of contemporary art—seismograms of a universal and inescapable form of reaction—are nearer than they appear to be by virtue of historical reification. What is considered to be intelligible to all is what has become unintelligible; what the manipulated repel as all too strange is what is secretly all too comprehensible, confirming Freud's dictum that the uncanny is repulsed only because it is all too familiar. What is blessed on the other side of the Iron Curtain as cultural heritage and accepted on this side as western tradition is exclusively manipulable experiences that can be turned on and off at will. They are more than familiar to convention, whereas the familiar can scarcely be actualized any longer. These experiences die off in the same instant that they become immediately accessible; their tensionless accessibility seals their fate. This is to be demonstrated equally by the fact that obscure and doubtlessly uncomprehended works are laid out in state in the pantheon of the classics and stubbornly repeated,[6] as by the fact that—except for a vanishing few that are reserved as exceptions for the most extreme avant-garde—the performances of traditional works turn out false and nonsensical: objectively incomprehensible. To make this evident, opposition is needed to the semblance of comprehensibility that has grown like a patina over each of these works and their performances. The aesthetic consumer is allergic to having this demonstrated: With some justification he feels that he is being robbed of what he protects as his possession, though he does not know that he is already robbed of it as soon as he claims it as his own. Foreignness to the world is an element of art: Whoever perceives it other than as foreign fails to perceive it at all.

Spirit in artworks is posited by their structure, it is not something added from outside. This is responsible in no small way for the fetish character of artworks: Because their spirit emerges from their constitution, spirit necessarily appears as something-in-itself, and they are artworks only insofar as spirit appears to be such. Nevertheless artworks are, along with the objectivity of their spirit, something made. Reflection must equally comprehend the fetish character, effectively sanction it as an expression of its objectivity, and critically dissolve it. To this extent an art-alien element, which art senses, is admixed to aesthetics. Artworks organize what is not organized. They speak on its behalf and violate it; they collide with it by following their constitution as an artifact. The dynamic that each artwork encapsulates is what is eloquent in it. One of the paradoxes of artworks is that, though they are dynamic in themselves, they are fixated, whereas it is only by being fixated that they are objectivated. Thus it is that the more insistently they are observed the more paradoxical they become: Each artwork is a system of irreconcilables. Their process itself could not be presented without fixation; improvisations are usually no more than juxtapositions, so to speak, marching in place. The written word and musical notation, if glimpsed for once strictly externally, are a disconcerting paradox of something existent that is in its own terms a process of becoming. The mimetic impulses that motivate the artwork, that integrate themselves in it and once again disintegrate it, are fragile, speechless expression. They only become language through their objectivation as art. Art, the rescue of nature, revolts against nature's transitoriness. Artworks become like language in the development of the bindingness of their elements, a wordless syntax even in linguistic works. What these works say is not what their words say. In art's intentionless language the mimetic impulses are bequeathed to the whole, which synthesizes them. In music an event or situation is able retroactively to shape a preceding development into something awesome even when it was not that in the first place. Such retroactive metamorphosis is exemplary as a metamorphosis by way of the spirit of the works. Artworks are distinguished from the gestalts on which psychological theory is based in that in artworks the elements are not merely maintained in a sort of independence, as is indeed possible in gestalts. Insofar as artworks appear, they are not—as psychical gestalts are purported to be—immediately given. By their spiritual mediation they enter into a contradictory relation with each other that appears in them at the same time that they strive to solve it. The elements are not arranged in juxtaposition but rather grind away at each other or draw each other in; the one seeks or repulses the other. This alone constitutes the nexus of the most demanding works. The dynamic of artworks is what speaks in them; through spiritualization the works attain the mimetic impulses that primarily their spirit subjugates. Romantic art hopes to conserve the mimetic element by refraining from mediating it through form; the whole is to say what the particular scarcely still has the capacity to say. Nevertheless, romantic art cannot simply ignore the compulsion toward objectivation. It degrades what objectively refuses synthesis to something that is disconnected. If it dissociates itself in details, it inclines nonetheless, contrary to its superficial qualities, to the abstractly formal. In one of the greatest composers, Robert Schumann, this quality is bound up essentially with the tendency toward disintegration. The purity with which his work shapes an unreconciled antagonism is what gives it its power and rank. Precisely because of the abstract being-for-itself of form, the romantic artwork regresses back of the classicist ideal, which it rejects as formalistic. In classicism the mediation of the whole and part was far more emphatically sought, though admittedly not without traces of resignation in the whole, which oriented itself to types, but in the particular as well, which was tailored to the whole. At every point the declining forms of romanticism tend toward the academic. Under this aspect, a sturdy typology of artworks emerges unavoidably. One type moves from above, from the whole down; the other moves in the opposite direction. That both types have endured fairly distinctly is demonstrated by the antinomy that produces them and that is not to be resolved by any type: the irreconcilability of the universal and the particular. Rather than schematically extinguishing the particular, as was the predominant praxis of the age preceding him, Beethoven, showing an elective affinity for the spirit of the mature bourgeois spirit of the natural sciences, faced the antinomy of the universal and the particular by qualitatively neutralizing the particular. He thus did more than merely integrate music as a continuum of what is in the process of becoming, more than merely shield the form from the emerging threat of empty abstraction. In foundering, the particular elements dissolve into each other and determine the form through the process of their foundering. In Beethoven the particular is and is not an impulse toward the whole, something that only in the whole becomes what it is, yet in itself tends toward the relative indeterminateness of basic tonal relations and toward amorphousness. If one hears or reads his extremely articulated music closely enough, it resembles a continuum of nothing. The tour de force of each of his great works is literally Hegelian, in that the totality of nothing determines itself as a totality of being, though it does so only as semblance and not with the claim of absolute truth. Yet this claim to absolute truth is at the very least suggested as the works' ultimate content by the composition's immanent stringency. The element of nature is represented by a polar opposition between the latently diffuse and ungraspable on the one hand, and the compelling force that constrains and shapes it on the other. The demon, the compositional subject that forges and hurls whole blocks, faces the undifferentiated smallest unities into which each and every movement is dissociated; ultimately there is no material at all but only the unadorned system of basic tonal relations.——Artworks are, however, again paradoxical in that not even their dialectic is literal; it does not transpire as does history, their secret model. In accord with the concept of the artifact, their dialectic is reproduced in existing works, which is the opposite of the process that they at the same time are: This is paradigmatic of art's illusory element. It remains to be shown, extrapolating from Beethoven, that in terms of their technical praxis all authentic works are tours de force: Many artists of the late bourgeois era—Ravel, Valéry—recognized this as their own task. Thus the once disdained concept of the "artiste" recovers its dignity. That trick is no primitive form of art and no aberration or degeneration but art's secret, a secret that it keeps only to give it away at the end. Thomas Mann alludes to this with his provocative comment that art is a higher form of prank. Technological as well as aesthetic analyses become fruitful when they comprehend the tour de force in works. At the highest level of form the detested circus act is reenacted: the defeat of gravity, the manifest absurdity of the circus—Why all the effort?—is *in nuce* the aesthetic enigma. This comes to bear on questions of artistic performance. To perform a play or a composition correctly means to formulate it correctly as a problem in such a fashion that the incompatible demands it makes on the performer are recognized. The task of a rendering that will do justice to a work is in principle infinite.

By its opposition to the empirical world each artwork programmatically, as it were, establishes its unity. What has passed by way of spirit determines itself in its oneness against the accidental and chaotic that are embedded in nature. Unity is more than merely formal: By its force artworks wrest themselves free from fatal disintegration. The unity of artworks is their caesura from myth. In themselves, and in accord with their immanent determination, they achieve a unity that is impressed upon the empirical objects of rational knowledge: Unity emerges from their own elements, from the multiplicity; thus they do not extirpate myth but mollify it. Turns of phrase such as that a certain painter well understood how to compose figures in a harmonious scene, or that the timing and placing of a pedal point in a Bach prelude have an especially felicitous effect—Goethe himself was on occasion not averse to formulations of this type—now have an archaic and provincial quality because they lag behind the concept of immanent unity and, admittedly, at the same time avow the surplus of arbitrary will in every work. Such comments praise what is defective in innumerable works, even if it is a defect that is constitutive of art. The material unity of artworks is all the more illusory the more its forms and elements are topoi and do not emerge immediately from the complexion of the individual work. One aspect of the opposition of modern art to immanent semblance, its insistence on the real unity of the unreal, is that it no longer tolerates anything universal in the form of an unreflected immediacy in itself. That the unity of the work does not, however, completely originate in the work's individual impulses is not due simply to how these impulses are manipulated. Semblance is defined by these impulses as well. While gazing longingly and needingly toward the unity they could fulfill and reconcile, they always at the same time flee from it. The prejudice of the idealist tradition in favor of unity and synthesis has neglected this. Unity is motivated not least of all by the fact that according to their own propensity the individual elements seek to escape it. Dispersed multiplicity does not offer itself neutrally to aesthetic synthesis as does epistemology's chaotic material, which, devoid of quality, neither anticipates nor eludes its forming. If the unity of artworks is also inescapably the violence done to multiplicity—symptomatic of which is the use in aesthetic criticism of expressions such as "mastery over the material"—multiplicity must, like the ephemeral and alluring images of nature in antiquity's myths, fear unity. The unity of logos, because it mutilates, is enmeshed in the nexus of its guilt. Homer's tale of Penelope, who in the evening unraveled what she had accomplished during the day, is a self-unconscious allegory of art: What cunning Penelope inflicts on her artifacts, she actually inflicts on herself. Ever since Homer's verses this episode is not the addition or rudiment for which it is easily mistaken, but a constitutive category of art: Through this story, art takes into itself the impossibility of the identity of the one and the many as an element of its unity. Artworks, no less than reason, have their cunning. If the diffuseness and individual impulses of artworks were left to their own immediacy, to themselves, they would blow away without a trace. Artworks register what would otherwise vanish. Through unity the impulses forfeit their independence; it is only metaphorically that they are any longer spontaneous. This compels criticism even of very great artworks. The idea of greatness as a rule is bound up with the element of unity, sometimes at the cost of its relation to the nonidentical; for this reason the concept of greatness itself is dubious in art. The authoritarian effect of great artworks, especially in architecture, both legitimates and indicts them. Integral form is inseparable from domination, though it sublimates it; the instinct against it is specifically French. Greatness is the guilt that works bear, but without this guilt they would remain insufficient. This is perhaps the reason for the superiority of major fragments, and the fragmentary character of others that are more finished, over fully complete works. This has always been registered by various types of form that are not among the most highly regarded. The quodlibet and medley in music, and in literature the apparently comfortable epic suspension of the ideal of dynamic unity, testify to this need. In every instance the renunciation of unity as a principle of form itself remains unity sui generis, however mediocre the quality. Yet this unity is not binding, and an element of this absence of bindingness is probably binding in all artworks. As soon as unity becomes stable, it is already lost.

The degree to which unity and multiplicity are internal to each other in artworks can be grasped in terms of the question of their intensity. Intensity is the mimesis achieved through unity and ceded by the multiplicity to the totality, although this totality is not immediately present in such a fashion that it could be perceived as an intensive force; the power accumulated in the totality is, so to speak, restored to the detail. That in many of its elements the artwork becomes more intense, thickens, and explodes, gives the impression of being an end in itself; the great unities of composition and construction seem to exist only for the purpose of such intensity. Accordingly, contrary to current aesthetic views, the whole in truth exists only for the sake of its parts—that is, its καιρός the instant —and not the reverse; what works in opposition to mimesis ultimately seeks to serve it. One who reacts preartistically, who loves various passages of a composition or painting without considering the form, perhaps without noticing it, perceives something that is rightfully driven out by aesthetic cultivation yet remains essential to it. Whoever lacks an appreciation for beautiful passages—in painting, too, as with Proust's Bergotte, who, seconds before his death, is captivated by a small section of a yellow wall in a Vermeer painting—is as alien to the artwork as one who is incapable of experiencing its unity. All the same, such details gain their luminosity only by virtue of the whole. Many measures in Beethoven sound like the sentence in *Elective Affinities*: "Like a star hope fell from the heavens below"; this is true of the Adagio of the Sonata in D Minor, op. 31, no. 2. It only requires playing the passage first in context and then alone to be able to recognize how much its incommensurableness, radiating over the passage, owes to the work as a whole. The passage becomes extraordinary because its expression is raised above what precedes it by the concentration of a lyrical, humanized melody. It is individuated in relation to, and by way of, the totality; it is its product as well as its suspension. Even totality, the gapless fittedness of artworks, is no ultimate category. Although it is intransigent in the face of regressive-atomistic perception, it is relativized because its force is proved exclusively in the particular into which it radiates.

The concept of an artwork implies that of its success. Failed artworks are not art: Relative success is alien to art; the average is already the bad. The average is incompatible with the medium of particularization. Middling artworks, the healthy soil of minor masters so appreciated by historians of a similar stamp, presuppose an ideal similar to what Lukács had the audacity to defend as a "normal artwork." However, being the negation of the spurious universal of the norm, art tolerates neither normal works nor middling ones that correspond to a norm or establish their meaning in terms of their distance to it. There is no scale for the ranking of artworks; their self-identity mocks the dimension of "more or less." For success, inner consistency is an essential element, but in no way the only one. That the artwork touch on something, the richness of the detail in the whole, the gesture of generosity even in the most brittle works: These are models of the demands that are present to art without their being reducible to the coordinates of inner consistency; their plenitude would probably elude general theoretical reflection. Yet they suffice for casting doubt not only on the concept of consistency but on that of success, which is in any case distorted by its association with the image of the straining model student. Yet the idea of success is all the same requisite if art is not to be abandoned to crude relativism; and the idea of success is active in the self-criticism that resides in each artwork and makes it one in the first place. Immanent to consistency is that it is not all there is to art; this distinguishes its emphatic concept from its academic correlative. What is only and thoroughly consistent, is not consistent. What is nothing but consistent, regardless of what is to be formed, ceases to be something in-itself and degenerates into something completely for-an-other: This defines academic polish. Academic works are bad because the elements their logicality should synthesize engender no counter-impulses and in fact do not exist. The work undertaken by their unity is superfluous, tautological, and, insofar as it appears as the unity of something, inconsistent. These works are dry, which is in general what results when mimesis withers; according to the doctrine of temperament, Schubert—the mimic par excellence—would be sanguine, moist. The mimetically diffuse can be art because art is in sympathy with diffuseness; this is not the case for unity, which strangles the diffuse element of art to honor art. An artwork whose form springs from its truth content, however, is emphatically successful. It is not obliged to erase the traces of the process by which it has come to be what it is, its artificiality; the phantasmagorical is its opposite in that through its appearance it portrays itself as achieved instead of carrying through the process whereby it might actually succeed; this is the only moral of artworks. By pursuing it, artworks approximate themselves to a natural-ness that is not unjustly demanded of art; they distance themselves from it as soon as they take the image of naturalness under their own charge. The idea of success is intolerant of administration, for it postulates objective aesthetic truth. Admittedly there is no aesthetic truth without the logi-cality of the work. But to become aware of it requires consciousness of the whole process, which is sharpened as the critical problem posed by the work. The objective quality of the work is mediated through this process. Artworks have mistakes and can be vitiated by them, but there is no single mistake that the true consciousness of the process would not be able to legitimate as correct, thereby annulling the judgment. One is not neces-sarily a pedant to raise objections on the basis of compositional experience to the first movement of Schoenberg's String Quartet in F-sharp Minor. The immediate continuation of the first main theme in the viola anticipates precisely the motive of the second theme and as a result damages the economy that demands the binding contrast of a prolonged thematic dualism. If, however, one thinks through the movement as a whole, as a single instant, then the similarity is meaningful as an anticipation. Or: On the grounds of orchestrational logic it could be objected that in the last movement of Mahler's Ninth Symphony, at the reintroduction of the main strophe, its melody twice appears in the same characteristic color—that of the solo horn—rather than being subjected to the principle of coloristic variation. On the first occasion, however, this sound is so penetrating, indeed exemplary, that the music does not disengage itself from it and yields to it: Thus the repetition turns out to be correct. The answer to the concrete aesthetic question of why a work can justly be said to be beautiful, consists in the casuistic pursuit of just such self-reflecting logic. The empirical interminability of these reflections changes nothing in the objectivity of what they grasp. The objection lodged by healthy common sense—that the monadological rigor of immanent critique and the categorical claim of aesthetic judgment are incompatible because every norm trespasses on the immanence of the work, whereas without any norm the work is no more than accidental—perpetuates that abstract division of the universal and particular that makes artworks null and void. That whereby it is possible to distinguish what is correct and what is false in an artwork according to its own measure is the elements in which universality imposes itself concretely in the monad. In what is formed in itself or incompatible with itself a universal is lodged, even though it is impossible to pull it away from the specific form and hypostatize it.

The ideological, affirmative aspect of the concept of the successful artwork has its corrective in the fact that there are no perfect works. If they did exist, reconciliation would be possible in the midst of the unreconciled, to which realm art belongs. In perfect works art would transcend its own concept; the turn to the friable and the fragmentary is in truth an effort to save art by dismantling the claim that artworks are what they cannot be and what they nevertheless must want to be; the fragment contains both those elements. The rank of an artwork is defined essentially by whether it exposes itself to, or withdraws from, the irreconcilable. Even in so-called formal elements there is by virtue of their relation to the unreconcilable a return of content [*Inhalt*] that is refracted by their law. This dialectic in the form constitutes its depth; without it form would be what philistines take it to be: empty play. Yet depth is not to be equated with the abyss of subjective inwardness, which is said to yawn wide in artworks; rather, it is an objective category of works; the clever chatter about the superficiality of depth is as sophistic as is its solemn praise. In superficial works, synthesis does not intervene in the heterogeneous elements to which it refers but runs parallel with them. Those works are deep that neither mask the divergent or antagonistic nor leave it unreconciled. By forcing it into appearance that issues from the unreconciled, they incorporate the possibility of conciliation. Giving form to antagonisms does not reconcile or eliminate them. By appearing and determining all labor in the artwork, they become something essential; by becoming thematic in the aesthetic image, their substantiality emerges with all the more plasticity. Certainly many historical phases provided greater possibilities of reconciliation than does the contemporary historical situation, which radically refuses it. As the nonviolent integration of what diverges, however, the artwork at the same time transcends the antagonisms of existence without perpetrating the deception that they no longer exist. The deepest antinomy of artworks, the most threatening and fruitful, is that they are irreconcilable by way of reconciliation, whereas actually their constitutive irreconcilability at the same time deprives them too of reconciliation. Yet they converge with knowledge through their synthetic function, the joining of the disjoint.

It is not possible to conceive the rank or quality of an artwork apart from its degree of articulation. In general, artworks are more valuable in direct relation to how articulated they are, when nothing dead, nothing unformed, remains; when there is no part that has not been passed through in the forming process. The more deeply this process has penetrated, the more successful the work. Articulation is the redemption of the many in the one. For artistic praxis the demand for articulation means that every specific form idea must be driven to its extreme. For its realization in the artwork, even the form idea that is the opposite of distinctness—the vague—requires the utmost distinctness of form, as in Debussy. Distinctness is not to be confused with bombastic, exalted gesturing, even though irritation with the latter originates more in anxiety than in critical consciousness. That *style flamboyant*, which still stands in poor repute, may be perfectly appropriate and "objective" according to the requirements of something that is to be presented. Even when the temperate, expressionless, disciplined, and middling is sought, it must be carried out with the utmost energy; the indecisive and mediocre is as bad as the harlequinade and the excitement that, through the choice of inappropriate means, becomes exaggerated. The more articulated the work, the more its idea becomes eloquent; mimesis receives succor from its counterpole. Although the category of articulation, correlative with the principle of individuation, was not reflected until the modern age, it has objectively retroactive force even over works of the past: Their rank cannot be isolated from the later course of history. Many older works must fall because, built on stereotypes, they dispensed with articulation. Prima facie the principle of articulation, as a principle of artistic procedure, bears analogy to the progress of subjective reason, taking it in strictly formal terms that the dialectical treatment of art relegates to being one element among others. This idea of articulation, however, would be too cheap. For articulation does not consist of differentiation that serves exclusively as a means for unification; rather, it consists in the realization of that differentiated something that is—as Hölderlin wrote—good.[7] Aesthetic unity gains its dignity through the multiplicitous itself. It does justice to the heterogeneous. The generosity of artworks, the antithesis of their immanent discipline, is an aspect of their richness, however ascetically hidden that richness may be; abundance protects them from ignominious rehashing. It promises what reality denies, but as an element subordinate to the law of form, not as a treasure that the work holds in its hands ready for the taking. The degree to which aesthetic unity is itself a function of multiplicity is evident in works that out of abstract enmity to unity seek to dissolve themselves into the multiplicitous, to renounce that whereby the differentiated becomes something differentiated in the first place. Works that are absolutely in flux, whose plurality is without reference to unity, thereby become undifferentiated, monotonous, and indifferent.

The truth content of artworks, on which their rank ultimately depends, is historical right into its innermost cell. It is, however, not related to history in such a fashion that it, and thus the rank of artworks, simply varies with time. Of course such variation takes place, and artworks of quality, for example, are able to strip themselves of their outer layers in the course of history. In the process, however, truth content—quality—does not fall prey to historicism. History is immanent to artworks, not an external fate or fluctuating estimation. Truth content becomes historical by the objectivation of correct consciousness in the work. This consciousness is no vague timeliness, no καιρός that would justify the course of a world history, that is not the development of truth. Rather, ever since freedom emerged as a potential, correct consciousness has meant the most progressive consciousness of antagonisms on the horizon of their possible reconciliation. The criterion of the most progressive consciousness is the level of productive forces in the work, part of which, in the age of art's constitutive reflectedness, is the position that consciousness takes socially. As the materialization of the most progressive consciousness, which includes the productive critique of the given aesthetic and extra-aesthetic situation, the truth content of artworks is the unconscious writing of history bound up with what has until now been repeatedly vanquished. Admittedly, just what is progressive is never so obvious as the innervation of fashion would like to dictate; it too has need of reflection. The determination of what is progressive involves the state of theory as a whole, for the decision cannot be resolved on the basis of isolated elements. By virtue of its artisanal dimension, all art has a quality of blind making. This element of the spirit of the times is permanently suspect of being reactionary. Even in art the operational dulls the critical edge; it is here that the self-confidence of the technical forces of production is compelled to recognize the limit of its identity with the utmost progressive consciousness. No modern work of rank, however stylistically and sub-jectively oriented to the past, is able to avoid this. Regardless of how much Anton Bruckner sought for theological restoration through his works, they are more than this ostensible intention. They participate in truth content precisely because, in spite of everything, they appropriated the harmonic and instrumental discoveries of their period; what they desire as eternal becomes substantial exclusively as modern and in opposition to the modern. Rimbaud's *il faut être absolument moderne,* itself modern, remains normative. However, because art's temporal nucleus is not its thematic actuality but its immanent organization, Rimbaud's norm—whatever it owes to reflection—finds its resonance in what is in a certain sense an unconscious impulse of disgust for the musty and stagnant. The capacity for sensing this is bound up with what is anathema to cultural con-servatism: fashion. It has its truth as the unconscious consciousness of the temporal nucleus of art and is normatively legitimate insofar as it is not manipulated by the culture industry and torn away from objective spirit. Great artists since Baudelaire have conspired with fashion; if they denounced it, these denunciations were given the lie by the impulses of their own work. Although art resists fashion when it seeks to level art heteronomously, it is allied with it in its instinct for the historical moment and in its aversion to provincialism and the subaltern, the refusal of which delineates the only humanly worthy concept of artistic niveau. Even such artists as Richard Strauss, perhaps even Monet, diminished in quality when, seemingly happy with themselves and with what they had achieved, they forfeited the power for historical innervation and the appropriation of the most progressive materials.

The subjective impulse that registers what is to be done is the appear-ance of something objective transpiring back of this impulse, the develop-ment of productive forces, which art in its innermost has in common with society and at the same time opposes through its own development. In art, development has multiple meanings. It is one of the means that crystallize in art's autarchy; further, it is the absorption of techniques that originate socially, external to art, and that, because they are alien and antagonistic, do not always result in progress; and, lastly, human productive forces also develop in art, in the form of subjective differentiation, for example, although such progress is often accompanied by the shadow of regression in other dimensions. Progressive consciousness ascertains the condition of the material in which history is sedimented right up to the moment in

which the work answers to it; precisely by doing so, progressive consciousness is also the transforming critique of technique; in this moment,
consciousness reaches out into the open, beyond the status quo. It is not
possible to eliminate from this consciousness the element of spontaneity, it
is in that element that the spirit of the age indicates its determinacy and
surpasses its mere reproduction. What does not simply reiterate given
procedures is itself historically produced in accord with Marx's comment
that each epoch solves the tasks that are posed to it;[8] in each epoch the
aesthetic forces of production, the talents, emerge that—as if by second
nature—correspond to the level of technique and by a sort of secondary
mimesis drive it further; the categories that are held to be extratemporal
natural endowments are just so temporally mediated: Thus even the
cinematographic gaze may appear innate. Aesthetic spontaneity is vouch-
safed by its relation to extra-aesthetic reality: It is the determinate
opposition to reality by way of adaptation to it. Just as spontaneity, which
traditional aesthetics wanted to exempt from time as the creative principle,
is temporal in itself, it participates in time that is individualized in the
particular; by doing so, it gains the possibility of becoming objective in
artworks. The concept of artistic volition is right in that it conceives the
intrusion of the temporal into what is artistic, however impossible it is to
reduce the artistic to the subjective denominator that is implicit in the idea
of volition. In *Parsifal*, just as in all artworks, even in those of the so-called
temporal arts, time becomes space.

By virtue of what it stores within itself no less than by its own rationality,
which it transposes to the logicality of artworks, the spontaneous subject is
something universal; as that which brings forth a work in the here and
now, it is a temporal particular. This was registered by the ancient doctrine
of genius, but it was falsely attributed to charisma. This coincidence of the
universal and the particular goes over into artworks, whereby the subject
becomes aesthetically objective. Artworks are therefore transformed objectively, on no account simply in terms of their reception: The force bound
up in them lives on. And yet reception should not be schematically
neglected; Benjamin once spoke of the traces that the innumerable eyes of
beholders have left behind on many paintings,[9] and Goethe's dictum that
it is hard to judge what once made a great impression indicates more than
merely respect for established opinion. The transformation of works is not
prevented by their fixation in stone or on canvas, in literary texts or
musical scores, even if the will, mythically trapped as ever, does its part in
this fixation to seal the works away from time. The fixated is a sign, a

function, not something in-itself; the process between what has been fixated and the spirit is the history of works. If each work is in a condition of equilibrium, each may yet once again enter into motion. The elements of equilibrium are irreconcilable with each other. The development of artworks is the afterlife of their immanent dynamic. What works say through the configuration of their elements in different epochs means something objectively different, and this ultimately affects their truth content. Works may become uninterpretable and fall mute; often their quality suffers; in general, the inner transformation of works most often involves a decline, a collapse into ideology. The past offers up ever fewer works of value. The so-called cultural reserve shrinks: The neutralization of culture as a "reserve" is the external aspect of the internal collapse of works. The historical transformation of artworks extends to their level of form. Although today no emphatic art can be imagined that does not lay claim to the highest level of form, this is no guarantee of survival. Conversely, works that may have held no great ambition for themselves sometimes display qualities they hardly had initially. Mathias Claudius and Johann Peter Hebel show greater powers of enduring than do more ambitious authors like Friedrich Hebbel or the Flaubert of *Salammbô*; parody, which thrives better at the lower than at the higher level of form, codifies the relationship. Levels of form should be maintained and relativized.

However, if finished works only become what they are because their being is a process of becoming, they are in turn dependent on forms in which their process crystallizes: interpretation, commentary, and critique. These are not simply brought to bear on works by those who concern themselves with them; rather they are the arena of the historical development of artworks in themselves, and thus they are forms in their own right. They serve the truth content of works as something that goes beyond them, which separates this truth content—the task of critique—from elements of its untruth. If the unfolding of the work in these forms is not to miscarry, they must be honed to the point where they become philosophical. It is from within, in the movement of the immanent form of artworks and the dynamic of their relation to the concept of art, that it ultimately becomes manifest how much art—in spite of, and because of, its monadological essence—is an element in the movement of spirit and of social reality. The relation to the art of the past, as well as the barriers to its apperception, have their locus in the contemporary condition of consciousness as positively or negatively transcended; the rest is nothing more than empty erudition. All inventorying consciousness of the artistic past is false. Only a liberated, reconciled humanity will someday perhaps be able to devote itself to the art of the past without ignominy, without that infamous rancor at contemporary art, and thus make amends to the dead. The opposite of a genuine relation to the historical substance of artworks —their essential content—is their rash subsumption to history, their assignment to a historical moment. In Zermatt the Matterhorn, the child's image of the absolute mountain, gives the appearance of being the only mountain on earth; from the Gorn Ridge it appears as one link in a colossal chain. But Gorn Ridge can only be approached from Zermatt. The situation is no different with regard to perspectives on artworks.

The interdependence of quality and history should not be conceived according to the stubborn cliché of a crude history of ideas that insists that history is the court that determines quality. This wisdom is a historicophilosophical rationalization of its own inadequacy, as if no judgment were possible in the here and now. Such humility is in no way superior to a pontificating judge of art. Cautious, postured neutrality is always ready to bow to ruling opinions. Its conformism extends even into the future. For this neutrality puts its trust in the course of world spirit, in an afterworld in which the authentic would be ever secure, whereas under its unceasing spell the world spirit confirms and bequeaths the old untruth. Occasional great discoveries or exhumations, such as those of El Greco, Büchner, and Lautréamont, have been powerful just because they make evident that the course of history as such in no way makes common cause with what is good. Even with regard to important artworks the course of history must—as Benjamin put it—be brushed against the grain,[10] and no one is able to say what important works have been destroyed in the history of art, so deeply forgotten are they that they are not to be retrieved, or so slandered that they are beyond call: Rarely has the violence of historical reality tolerated even intellectual revisions. All the same, the idea of the judgment of history is not simply nugatory. For centuries, examples of the incomprehension of contemporaries have abounded; ever since the end of feudal traditionalism the demand for the new and original has necessarily collided with whatever views are prevailing; simultaneous reception becomes ever more difficult. It is nevertheless striking how few artworks of the highest rank were brought to light even in the epoch of historicism, which ransacked everything it could lay hands on. It must be reluctantly admitted, moreover, that the most famous works of the most famous masters—themselves fetishes in commodity culture—are indeed often, though not always, superior in quality to those that have been neglected. In the judgment of history, domination in the form of prevailing opinion entwines with the unfolding truth of artworks. As the antithesis to existing society, truth is not exhausted according to society's laws. Rather, truth has its own laws, which are contrary to those of society; and in real history it is not only repression that grows but also the potential for freedom, which is unanimous with the truth content of art. The merits of a work, its level of form, its internal construction, tend to become recognizable only as the material ages or when the sensorium becomes dulled to the most striking features of the work. Beethoven could probably be heard as a composer only after the gesture of the titanic—his primary effect—was outstripped by the crasser effects of younger composers like Berlioz. The superiority of the great impressionists over Gauguin became evident only after his innovations had paled in the face of later developments. For quality to unfold historically, however, depends not just on it but on what came afterward, and it sets in relief what preceded it; perhaps some relation rules between quality and the process of perishing. Inherent in many artworks is the force to break through the social barrier that they establish. Whereas Kafka's writings violate the collusion of the novel reader by the explosive empirical impossibility of what is narrated, it is precisely by virtue of this violation that they become understandable to all. The view trumpeted in unison by Westerners and Stalinists of the incomprehensibility of modern art for the most part holds true descriptively; what is false in this view, however, is that they treat this reception as a fixed entity and ignore the interventions in consciousness of which incompatible works are capable. In the administered world, artworks are only adequately assimilated in the form of the communication of the uncommunicable, the breaking through of reified consciousness. Works in which the aesthetic form, under pressure of the truth content, transcends itself occupy the position that was once held by the concept of the sublime. In them, spirit and material polarize in the effort to unite. Their spirit experiences itself as sensually unrepresentable, while on the other hand their material, that to which they are bound external to their boundary, experiences itself as irreconcilable with the unity of the work. Kafka's writings are no more artworks than they could ever have been religious documents. The material —according to Benjamin, the language in particular—becomes desolate, starkly conspicuous; spirit is imbued with the quality of a second-order abstractness. Kant's doctrine of the feeling of the sublime all the more describes an art that shudders inwardly by suspending itself in the name of an illusionless truth content, though without, as art, divesting itself of its semblance character. The enlightenment concept of nature contributed to the invasion of the sublime into art. Along with the critique of the absolutist world of forms that made nature taboo as monstrous, boorish, and plebeian—a critique that was itself part of the general cultural-historical movement of the late eighteenth century—artistic practice was penetrated by that which Kant had reserved for nature as sublime and which came increasingly into conflict with taste. The unleashing of the elemental was one with the emancipation of the subject and thus with the self-consciousness of spirit. This self-consciousness spiritualized art as nature. Art's spirit is the self-recognition of spirit itself as natural. The more art integrates into itself what is nonidentical, what is immediately opposed to spirit, the more it must spiritualize itself. Conversely, spiritualization for its part introduced into art what is sensually displeasing and repugnant and what had previously been taboo for art; the sensually unpleasant has an affinity with spirit. The emancipation of the subject in art is the emancipation of art's own autonomy; if art is freed from consideration of its recipient, its sensual facade becomes increasingly a matter of indifference. The facade is transformed into a function of the content, which derives its force from what is not socially approved and prearranged. Art is spiritualized not by the ideas it affirms but through the elemental—the intentionless—that is able to receive the spirit in itself; the dialectic of the elemental and spirit is the truth content. Aesthetic spirituality has always been more compatible with the *fauve*, the savage, than with what has already been appropriated by culture. Spiritualized, the artwork becomes in itself what was previously attributed to it as its cathartic effect on another spirit: the sublimation of nature. The sublime, which Kant reserved exclusively for nature, later became the historical constituent of art itself. The sublime draws the demarcation line between art and what was later called arts and crafts. Kant covertly considered art to be a servant. Art becomes human in the instant in which it terminates this service. Its humanity is incompatible with any ideology of service to humankind. It is loyal to humanity only through inhumanity toward it.

By its transplantation into art the Kantian definition of the sublime is driven beyond its boundaries. According to this definition, spirit, in its empirical powerlessness vis-à-vis nature, experiences its intelligible essence as one that is superior to nature. However, given that the sublime is supposed to be felt in the face of nature, the theory of subjective constitution implies that nature itself is sublime; self-reflection in the face of its sublimity anticipates something of a reconciliation with nature. Nature, no longer oppressed by spirit, frees itself from the miserable nexus of rank second nature and subjective sovereignty. Such emancipation would be the return of nature, and it—the counterimage of mere existence—is the sublime. Though the traits of domination evident in its dimensions of power and magnitude, the sublime speaks against domination. This is touched on by Schiller's dictum that the human being is only fully human when at play; with the consummation of his sovereignty he leaves behind the spell of sovereignty's aim. The more empirical reality hermetically excludes this event, the more art contracts into the element of the sublime; in a subtle way, after the fall of formal beauty, the sublime was the only aesthetic idea left to modernism. Even the hubris of art as a religion, the self-exaltation of art as the absolute, has its truth content in the allergy against what is not sublime in art, against that play that is satisfied with the sovereignty of spirit. What Kierkegaard subjectivistically terms "aesthetic seriousness," the heritage of the sublime, is the reversal of works into what is true by virtue of their content. The ascendancy of the sublime is one with art's compulsion that fundamental contradictions not be covered up but fought through in themselves; reconciliation for them is not the result of the conflict but exclusively that the conflict becomes eloquent. Thus, however, the sublime becomes latent. Art that is compelled toward a truth content that is the locus of unarbitrated contradictions is not capable of the positivity of negation that animated the traditional concept of the sublime as the presence of the infinite. This corresponds to the decline of the categories of play. Even in the nineteenth century a famous classicist theory defined music, in opposition to Wagner, as the play of sounding, moving forms; the similarity of the process of musical events with the optical patterns of the kaleidoscope, a brooding Biedermeier invention, was frequently underscored. This similarity need not be denied out of the desire to hold culture pure: The collapsing constellations of symphonic music, as in Mahler's works, have their true analogue in the kaleidoscopic patterns in which a series of slightly varying images collapses and a qualitatively transformed constellation emerges. It is just that in music what is conceptually indeterminate, its flux and articulation, is exceedingly determinate, and in the totality of these determinations that it itself establishes it achieves a content ignored by the concept of the play of forms. What parades as sublimity rings hollow, whereas what plays imperturbably regresses to the triviality from which it was born. Admittedly, as art became dynamic, as its immanent determination became that of being an action, its play character also secretly intensified; thus, a half century before Beckett, Debussy entitled his most important orchestral work *Jeux*. The critique of profundity and seriousness, which once took aim at the overbearing presumptions of provincial inwardness—in that it justifies an industrious and mindless participation, activity for its own sake—is no less ideological than what it criticizes. Indeed, the sublime ultimately reverses into its opposite. To speak of the sublime with regard to specific artworks is at this point impossible without the twaddle of culture religion, and this results from the dynamic of the category of the sublime itself. The dictum that the sublime is only a step removed from the ridiculous pronounced by Napoleon at the moment when his luck turned has been overtaken by history and fulfilled in all its horror. At the time the dictum referred to a grandiose style, a pathos-laden discourse that, as a result of a disproportion between its high claims and its pedestrian reality, had a comic effect. But the targeted faux pas actually transpires within the concept of the sublime itself. The sublime was supposedly the grandeur of human beings who are spiritual and dominate nature. If, however, the experience of the sublime reveals itself as the self-consciousness of human beings' naturalness, then the composition of the concept changes. Even in Kant's formulation it was tinged with the nothingness of man; in this nothingness, the fragility of the empirical individual, the eternity of his universal destiny—his spirit—was to unfold. If, however, spirit itself is reduced to its natural dimension, then the annihilation of the individual taking place within it is no longer transcended positively. Through the triumph of the intelligible essence in the individual who stands firm spiritually against death, man puffs himself up as if in spite of everything, as the bearer of spirit, he were absolute. He thus becomes comical. Advanced art writes the comedy of the tragic: Here the sublime and play converge. The sublime marks the immediate occupation of the artwork by theology, an occupation that vindicates the meaning of existence one last time by virtue of its collapse. Against this verdict art is powerless. Something in Kant's construction of the sublime resists the objection that he reserved it exclusively for a feeling for nature because he had not yet experienced great subjective art. Unwittingly his doctrine expresses that the sublime is incompatible with the semblance character of art, in a way reminiscent perhaps of what Haydn implied in his reaction to Beethoven when he called him the Great Mogul. As bourgeois art stretched out its hand toward the sublime and thereby came into its own, the movement of the sublime toward its own negation was already implied. Theology for its part resists aesthetic integration. The sublime as semblance has its own absurdity and contributes to the neutralization of truth; this is the accusation of art in Tolstoy's *Kreutzer Sonata*. In any case, what is presented as evidence against the aesthetics of subjective feeling is that the feelings are illusory. Yet the feelings are real; the semblance is a quality of the aesthetic objects. Kant's asceticism toward the aesthetically sublime objectively anticipates the critique of heroic classicism and the emphatic art derived from it. However, by situating the sublime in overpowering grandeur and setting up the antithesis of power and powerlessness, Kant directly affirmed his unquestioning complicity with domination. Art must find domination a source of shame and seek to overturn the perdurable, the desideratum of the concept of the sublime. Even Kant was by no means unaware that the sublime is not quantitative grandeur as such: With profound justification he defined the concept of the sublime by the resistance of spirit to the overpowering. The feeling of the sublime does not correspond immediately with what appears; towering mountains are eloquent not as what crushes overwhelmingly but as images of a space liberated from fetters and strictures, a liberation in which it is possible to participate. The legacy of the sublime is unassuaged negativity, as stark and illusionless as was once promised by the semblance of the sublime. This is however at the same time the legacy of the comic, which was always nourished by a feeling for the diminutive, the ludicrously pompous and insignificant, and which, for the most part, shored up established domination. The nonentity is comic by the claim to relevance that it registers by its mere existence and by which it takes the side of its opponent; once seen through, however, the opponent—power, grandeur—has itself become a nonentity. Tragedy and comedy perish in modern art and preserve themselves in it as perishing.

Notes

1 See Stefan George, "The Tapestry," from *The Tapestry of Life*, in *The Works of Stefan George*, trans. Marx and Merwitz (Chapel Hill, 1974), p. 185. [The tapestry is merely "barren lines," its parts "at strife . . . until one night the fabric leaps to life."—trans.]

2 See Immanuel Kant, *Critique of Judgment*, trans. Werner S. Pluhar (Indianapolis, 1987), p. 169.

3 [See Hans Christian Andersen, "The Nightingale," in *The Complete Fairy Tales and Stories*, trans. E. C. Haugaard (New York, 1974), pp. 203–212; see also Igor Stravinsky, *The Nightingale.*—trans.]

4 See Adorno, "Die Kunst und die Künste," in *Ohne Leitbild, Gesammelte Schriften*, vol. 10.1 (Frankfurt, 1977), pp. 168ff.

5 See Walter Benjamin, *One Way Street and Other Writings*, trans. Edmund Jephott and Kingley Shorter (London, 1979), p. 66.

6 See Adorno, *Moments musicaux* (Frankfurt, 1964), pp. 167ff.

7 See Friedrich Hölderlin, *Gedichte nach 1800*, in *Sämtliche Werke*, ed. F. Beißner, vol. 2 (Stuttgart, 1953), p. 328.

8 Karl Marx, Preface to *A Contribution to the Critique of Political Economy*, trans. N. Stone (Chicago, 1904), p. 12. ["Mankind always takes up only such problems as it can solve.—trans.]

9 See Benjamin, "Some Motifs in Baudelaire," in *Illuminations*, trans. Harry Zohn (New York, 1968), p. 188.

10 Benjamin, "Theses on the Philosophy of History," in *Illuminations*, p. 257.

11
Universal and particular

What befell the categories of the tragic and the comic testifies to the decline of aesthetic genres as such. Art has been caught up in the total process of nominalism's advance ever since the medieval *ordo* was broken up. The universal is no longer granted art through types, and older types are being drawn into the whirlpool. Croce's art-critical reflection that every work be judged, as the English say, *on its own merits* raised this historical tendency to the level of theoretical aesthetics. Probably no important artwork ever corresponded completely to its genre. Bach, from whom the academic rules of the fugue were derived, wrote no transition section modeled on sequencing in double counterpoint, and the requirement to deviate from mechanical models was ultimately incorporated even in conservatory rules. Aesthetic nominalism was the consequence, which Hegel himself overlooked, of his doctrine of the primacy of dialectical stages over the abstract totality. But Croce, who tardily drew the implied consequences, dilutes the dialectic by simply dismissing, along with the genres, the element of universality rather than seriously undertaking to transcend it. This is in keeping with the general tendency of Croce's work to adapt the rediscovered Hegel to the reigning spirit of his age by means of a more or less positivistic doctrine of development. Just as the arts as such do not disappear tracelessly in the general concept of art, the genres and forms do not merge perfectly into the individual art forms. Unquestionably, Attic tragedy was also the crystallization of no less a universal than the reconciliation of myth. Great autonomous art originated in agreement with the emancipation of spirit; it could no more be conceived without an element of universality than could the latter. The *principium individuationis*, however, which implies the need for the aesthetically particular, is not only universal as a principle in its own right, it is inherent to the self-liberating subject. Its universal—spirit—is in terms of its own meaning not lodged beyond the particular individuals who bear it. The χωρισμός between subject and individual belongs to a late stage of philosophical reflection that was conceived for the sake of exalting the subject as the absolute. The substantial element of genres and forms has its locus in the historical needs of their materials. Thus the fugue is bound up with tonal relations; and it was virtually demanded by tonality as its telos once it had displaced modality and reigned supreme in imitative praxis. Specific procedures, such as the real or tonal answer of a fugue theme, became musically meaningful only when traditional polyphony found itself confronted with the new task of transcending the homophonic gravitational pull of tonality, of integrating tonality into polyphonic space and at the same time introducing contrapuntal and harmonic concepts. All the peculiarities of fugal form could be derived from these necessities, of which the composers themselves were in no way conscious. Fugue is the form in which polyphony that has become tonal and fully rationalized is organized; to this extent the fugue as form reaches beyond its individual realizations and yet does not exist apart from them. For this reason, too, the emancipation from the model is universally prefigured by the model. If tonality is no longer binding, then fundamental categories of the fugue such as the distinction between *dux* and *comes*—the standardized structure of response—and, in particular, the element of reprise in the fugue, which serves the return of the principal key, become functionless and technically false. If the differentiated and dynamic need for expression of individual composers no longer seeks objectivation in the fugue—which, incidentally, was far more differentiated than it now seems from the perspective of the consciousness of freedom—the form has at the same time become objectively impossible. Whoever persists in employing this form, which so quickly became archaizing, must "construct" it to the point that what emerges is its bare idea rather than its concreteness; the same holds for other forms. The construction of a predeterminant form acquires an "as if" quality that contributes to its destruction. The historical tendency itself has a universal element. Fugues became fetters historically. Forms can be inspiring. Thorough motivic work, and hence the concrete structuration of music, is predicated on the universal element in the fugal form. Even *Figaro* would never have become what it is if its music had not sought after what opera demands, and that implicitly poses the question of what opera is. The fact that Schoenberg, whether voluntarily or not, continued Beethoven's reflections on how quartets should be written, brought about that expansion of counterpoint that proceeded to revolutionize musical material as a whole. The glorification of the artist as creator does him an injustice because it attributes to conscious invention something that is anything but that. Whoever creates authentic forms fulfills them.——Croce's insight, which swept aside the residue of scholasticism and old-fashioned rationalism, preceded the artworks themselves, a development that neither Croce, who was at heart a classicist, nor his mentor Hegel would have approved. Yet the drive toward nominalism does not originate in reflection but in the artwork's own impulse, and to this extent it originates in a universal of art. From time immemorial, art has sought to rescue the special; progressive particularization was immanent to it. Successful works have always been those in which specification has flourished most extensively. The universal aesthetic genre concepts, which ever and again established themselves as norms, were always marked by a didactic reflection that sought to dispose over the quality, which was mediated by particularization, by measuring them according to common characteristics even though these common characteristics were not necessarily what was essential to the works. The authenticity of individual works is stored away in the genre. Still, the propensity toward nominalism is not simply identical with the development of art into its concept-alien concept. The dialectic of the universal and the particular does not, as does the murky concept of the symbol, eliminate their difference. The *principium individuationis* in art, its immanent nominalism, is not a given but a directive. This directive not only encourages particularization and thus the radical elaboration of individual works. Bringing together the universals by which artworks are oriented, it at the same time obscures the boundary against unformed, raw empiria and thus threatens the structuration of works no less than it sets it in motion. Prototypical of this is the rise of the novel in the bourgeois age, the rise of the nominalistic and thus paradoxical form par excellence; every loss of authenticity suffered by modern art derives from this dialectic. The relation of the universal and the particular is not so simple as the nominalistic tendency suggests, nor as trivial as the doctrine of traditional aesthetics, which states that the universal must be particularized. The simple disjunction of nominalism and universalism does not hold. As August Halm,[1] now disgracefully forgotten, once pointed out when writing of music: The existence and teleology of objective genres and types is as true as the fact that they must be attacked in order to maintain their substantial element. In the history of forms, subjectivity, which produces them, is qualitatively transformed and disappears into them. To the extent that Bach produced the form of the fugue on the basis of the initial efforts of his predecessors, and to the extent that it was his subjective product and in a sense fell mute after him, the process in which he produced it was objectively determined: the jettisoning of what was rudimentary and insufficiently perfected. What he achieved drew the consequences from what awaited and was needed yet still incoherent in the older *canzona* and *ricercare*. The genres are no less dialectical than the particular. Although they originated historically and are transient, they do all the same have something in common with Platonic ideas. The more authentic the works, the more they follow what is objectively required, the object's consistency, and this is always universal. The power of the subject resides in its methexis in the universal, not in the subject's simple self-announcement. The forms hold sway over the subject up to that moment when the coherence of the works no longer coincides with the forms. They are exploded by the subject for the sake of coherence, which is a matter of objectivity. The individual work does not do justice to the genres by subsuming itself to them but rather through the conflict in which it long legitimated them, then engendered them, and ultimately canceled them. The more specific the work, the more truly it fulfills its type: The dialectical postulate that the particular is the universal has its model in art. This was first recognized and already defused in Kant. From the perspective of teleology, reason functions in aesthetics as total, identity-positing reason. Itself purely a product, in Kant's terms the artwork ultimately knows nothing of the nonidentical. Its purposefulness, which transcendental philosophy renders taboo in discursive knowledge by making it inaccessible to the subject, becomes manipulable in art. The universality in the particular is described virtually as preestablished; the concept of genius must function to guarantee it, though this is never made explicit. In the simplest sense of the word, individuation distances art from the universal. That art must *à fond perdu* become individuated makes its universality problematic; Kant was aware of this. If art is supposed whole and unfragmented, it is bound from the outset to fail; if it is jettisoned in order to be won, there is no guarantee that it will return; it is lost insofar as the individuated does not on its own, without any deus ex machina, go over into the universal. The sole path of success that remains open to artworks is also that of their progressive impossibility. If recourse to the pregiven universality of genres has long been of no avail, the radically particular work verges on contingency and absolute indifference, and no intermediary provides for compromise.

In antiquity, the ontological view of art, on which genre aesthetics is based, was part of aesthetic pragmatism in a fashion that is now scarcely imaginable. As is well known, Plato's assessment of art shifted according to his estimation of its presumptive political usefulness. Aristotle's aesthetics remained an aesthetics of effect, though certainly more enlightened in the bourgeois sense and humanized insofar as it sought the effect of art in the affects of individuals, in accord with Hellenistic tendencies toward privatization. The effects postulated by both philosophers may already in their own time have become fictive. Still, the alliance of genre aesthetics and pragmatism is not so absurd as it may at first seem. Early on, the conventionalism latent in all ontology accommodated itself to pragmatism as the universal determination of ends; the *principium individuationis* is opposed not only to genres but to any subsumption by the prevailing praxis. Immersion in the individual work, which is contrary to genres, leads to an awareness of that work's immanent lawfulness. The works become monads and are thus withdrawn from any disciplinary effect they could exercise externally. If the discipline exerted or buttressed by artworks becomes their own lawfulness, they forfeit their crudely authoritarian character vis-à-vis human beings. Authoritarian attitudes and insistence on optimally pure and unadultered genres are compatible; to authoritarian thinking, unregimented concretion appears defiled and impure; the theory of The *Authoritarian Personality* noted this as *intolerance of ambiguity,* and it is unmistakable in all hierarchical art and society.[2] To be sure, whether the concept of pragmatism can without distortion be applied to antiquity is an open question. As a doctrine of the measurability of intellectual works in terms of their real effect, pragmatism presupposes a break between inner and outer, between the individual and collectivity, that was only beginning to take shape in antiquity, where it never attained the completeness it achieved in the bourgeois world; collective norms did not have anything approaching the same status they have in modern society. Yet today the temptation to overemphasize the divergences between chronologically remote theorems, without being concerned with the invariance of their repressive traits, seems again to have increased. The complicity of Plato's judgments on art with these repressive elements is so obvious that ontological *entêtement* is needed to explain it away with the protestation that back then it all meant something completely different.

Advancing philosophical nominalism liquidated the universals long before the genres and the claims they made revealed themselves to art as posited and fragile conventions, as dead and formulaic. Genre aesthetics asserted itself even in the age of nominalism, right through German idealism, and this was probably not only thanks to Aristotle's authority. The idea of art as an irrational reserve, to which everything is relegated that does not fit into scientism, may also have had a part in this anachronism; there is even better reason to suppose that it was only with the help of genre concepts that theoretical reflection believed it could avoid aesthetic relativism, which to undialectical opinion is bound up with radical individuation. The conventions themselves become enticing—*prix du progrès*—to the extent that they were rendered powerless. They appear as afterimages of an authenticity of which art despairs without making them obligatory; that they cannot be taken seriously becomes a surrogate for an unachievable merriment; in that merriment, so willingly cited, the vanishing element of aesthetic play seeks refuge. Having become function-less, the conventions serve as masks. Yet these count among art's ancestors; in the rigidification that makes it a work in the first place, all art is reminiscent of masks. Quoted and distorted conventions are part of enlightenment in that they absolve the magic masks by recapitulating them in play, though they are almost always inclined to establish them-selves positively and to become integrated into art as a force of repression. In any case, conventions and genres did not just stand in the service of society; many, however, such as the topos of the maid-turned-master, were already a blunted form of rebellion. As a whole, the distance of art from the crudely empirical in which its autonomy developed would never have been achieved had it not been for conventions; probably no one ever mistook the commedia dell'arte naturalistically. If this form of theater was only able to thrive in what was still a closed society, this society provided the preconditions for art to come into existence through an opposition in which its social opposition was cloaked. Nietzsche's defense of conven-tions, which originated in unrelenting opposition to the development of nominalism as well as in resentment toward progress in the aesthetic domination of material, rings false because he misinterpreted conventions literally, as agreements arbitrarily established and existing at the mercy of volition. Because he overlooked the sedimented social compulsion in conventions and attributed them to pure play, he was equally able to trivialize or defend them with the gesture of "Precisely!" This is what brought his genius, which was superior in its differentiation to that of all his contemporaries, under the influence of aesthetic reaction; ultimately he was no longer able to distinguish levels of form. The postulate of the particular has the negative aspect of serving the reduction of aesthetic distance and thereby joining forces with the status quo; what is repulsive in its vulgarity does not simply damage the social hierarchy but serves to compromise art with art-alien barbarism. By becoming the formal laws of artworks, conventions inwardly shored up works and made them resistant to the imitation of external life. Conventions contain an element that is external and heterogenous to the subject, reminding it of its own boundaries and the ineffability of its own accidentalness. The stronger the subject becomes and, complementarily, the more the social categories of order and the spiritual categories derived from these social categories weaken, the less it is possible to reconcile the subject and conventions. The increasing fissure between inner and outer leads to the collapse of conventions. If the fragmented subject then freely posits conventions, the contradiction degrades them to being mere administered events: As the result of choice or decree they fail to provide what the subject expected from them. What later appeared in artworks as the specific, unique, and nonsubstitutable quality of each individual work and became important as such was a deviation from the genre that had reached a point where it turned into a new quality, one mediated by the genre. That universal elements are irrevocably part of art at the same time that art opposes them, is to be understood in terms of art's likeness to language. For language is hostile to the particular and nevertheless seeks its rescue. Language mediates the particular through universality and in the constellation of the universal, but it does justice to its own universals only when they are not used rigidly in accord with the semblance of their autonomy but are rather concentrated to the extreme on what is specifically to be expressed. The universals of language receive their truth content by way of a process that countervails them. "Every salutary effect of language, indeed each that is not essentially destructive, depends on its (the word's, language's) secret. In however many forms language may prove to be effective, it is not through the mediation of contents [*Inhalten*] but through the purest disclosure of its dignity and essence. And if I prescind from other forms of efficacy—such as poetry and prophecy—it appears to me that the crystal-pure elimination of the unutterable from language is the given and most accessible form for us to act within, and to this extent through, language. This elimination of the unutterable seems to me to converge precisely with a properly objective, functional style and to indicate the relation between knowledge and action within the linguistic magic. My concept of objective and at the same time highly political style and writing is this: to focus on what is denied to the word; only where this sphere of the wordless discloses itself with unutterably pure force can a magical spark spring between word and dynamic act, unifying them. Only the intensive aiming of words toward the nucleus of the innermost muteness can be effective. I do not believe that the word at any point stands at a greater remove from the divine than does 'genuine' action, that is, if it is otherwise unable to lead to the divine except by its own self and its own purity. Taken as a means it becomes a rank natural growth."[3] What Benjamin calls the elimination of the unutterable is no more than the concentration of language on the particular, the refusal to establish its universals as metaphysical truth. The dialectical tension between Benjamin's extremely objectivistic and accordingly universalistic metaphysics of language and a formulation that agrees almost literally with Wittgenstein's famous maxim—which was, incidentally, published five years after Benjamin's letter and thus unknown to him—may be transposed to art, with the admittedly decisive proviso that the ontological asceticism of language is the only way to say the unutterable. In art, universals are strongest where art most closely approaches language; that is, when something speaks, that, by speaking, goes beyond the here and now. Art succeeds at such transcendence, however, only by virtue of its tendency toward radical particularization; that is, only in that it says nothing but what it says by virtue of its own elaboration, through its immanent process. The element that in art resembles language is its mimetic element; it only becomes universally eloquent in the specific impulse, by its opposition to the universal. The paradox that art says it and at the same time does not say it, is because the mimetic element by which it says it, the opaque and particular, at the same time resists speaking.

When conventions are in an ever unstable equilibrium with the subject they are called styles. The concept of style refers as much to the inclusive element through which art becomes language—for style is the quintessence of all language in art—as to a constraining element that was somehow compatible with particularization. The styles deserved their much bemoaned collapse as soon as this peace became recognized as an illusion. What is to be lamented is not that art renounced styles but rather that art, under the spell of its authority, feigned styles; this is the origin of all lack of style in the nineteenth century. Objectively, mourning over the loss of style, which is usually nothing but an incapacity for individuation, stems from the fact that after the collapse of the collective bindingness of art, or the semblance of such bindingness—for the universality of art always bore a class character and was to this extent particular—artworks were no longer radically elaborated, any more so than the early automobile succeeded at freeing itself from the model of the buggy, or early photographs from the model of portraiture. The inherited canon has been dismantled; artworks produced in freedom cannot thrive under an enduring societal unfreedom whose marks they bear even when they are daring. Indeed, in the copy of style—one of the primal aesthetic phenomena of the nineteenth century—that specifically bourgeois trait of promising freedom while prohibiting it can be sought. Everything is to be at the service of the hand that grasps it, but the grasping hand regresses to the repetition of what is available, which is not actually that at all. In truth, bourgeois art, because it is radically autonomous, cannot to be conflated with the prebourgeois idea of style; by stubbornly ignoring this consequence, bourgeois art expresses the antinomy of bourgeois freedom itself. This antinomy results in the absence of style: There is nothing left—as Brecht said—to hold on to under the compulsion of the market and the necessity of adaptation, not even the possibility of freely producing authentic art; for this reason what has already been condemned to oblivion is resurrected. The Victorian terrace houses that deface Baden parody villas all the way into the *slums*. However, the devastations that are chalked up to an age without style and criticized on aesthetic grounds are in no way the expression of the spirit of an age of kitsch but, rather, products of something extra-aesthetic, that is, of the false rationality of an industry oriented to profit. Because capital mobilizes for its own purposes what strikes it as being the irrational elements of art, it destroys these elements. Aesthetic rationality and irrationality are equally mutilated by the curse of society. The critique of style is repressed by its polemical-romantic ideal; carried to its extreme, this critique would encompass the whole of traditional art. Authentic artists like Schoenberg protested fiercely against the concept of style; it is a criterion of radical modernism that modernism reject the concept. The concept of style never fully did justice to the quality of works; those works that seem most exactly to represent their style have always fought through the conflict with it; style itself was the unity of style and its suspension. Every work is a force field, even in its relation to style, and this continues to be the case in modernism, where, unbeknownst to modernism and precisely there where it renounced all will to style, something resembling style formed under the pressure of the immanent elaboration of works. The higher the ambition of artworks, the more energetically they carry out the conflict with style, even when this requires renouncing that success in which they already sense affirmation. Retrospectively, style may be exalted only because in spite of its repressive aspects it was not simply stamped externally on artworks but was rather—as Hegel liked to say in regard to antiquity—to a certain degree substantial. Style permeated the artwork with something like objective spirit; indeed, it even teased out elements of specification, which it required for its own realization. During periods in which objective spirit was not completely commandeered and spontaneity had yet to be totally administered, there was also still felicity in style. Constitutive in Beethoven's subjective art was the totally dynamic form of the sonata, in other words, the late-absolutist style of Viennese classicism that only came into its own once Beethoven carried out its implications. Nothing of the sort is possible any longer, for style has been liquidated. Instead, the concept of the chaotic is uniformly conjured up. It merely projects the inability to follow the specific logic of a particular work back onto this work; with astonishing regularity the invectives against new art are enunciated in tandem with a demonstrable lack of comprehension, often even of any basic knowledge. There is no avoiding the recognition that the bindingness of styles is a reflex of society's repressive character, which humanity intermittently and ever under the threat of regression seeks to shake off; without the objective structure of a closed and thus repressive society, it would be impossible to conceive an obligatory style. With regard to individual artworks the concept of style is at best applicable as the quintessence of the elements that are eloquent in it: The work that does not subsume itself to any style must have its own style or, as Berg called it, its own "tone." It is undeniable that with regard to the most recent developments, those works that are elaborated in themselves converge. What the academic study of history calls a "personal style" is vanishing. If it protestingly seeks to survive, it almost inevitably collides with the immanent lawfulness of the individual work. The complete negation of style seems to reverse dialectically into style. The discovery of conformist traits in nonconformism[4] has, however, become no more than a truism, good only to help the bad conscience of conformists secure an alibi from what wants change. This in no way diminishes the dialectic through which the particular becomes universal. That in nominalistically advanced artworks the universal, and sometimes the conventional, reappears results not from a sinful error but from the character of artworks as language, which progressively produces a vocabulary within the windowless monad.

Thus expressionist poetry—as Mautz has shown—employs certain color conventions that can also be found in Kandinsky's book.[5] Expression, the fiercest antithesis to abstract universality, requires such conventions in order to be able to speak as its concept promises. If expression restricts itself to the locus of the absolute impulse, it would be unable to determine it adequately enough for this impulse to speak out of the artwork. Even though in all its aesthetic media expressionism, contrary to its idea, drew on style-like elements, only among its lesser representatives was this in the interest of accommodation to the market: In all other cases this phenomenon followed directly from its idea. For its own realization, expressionism must accept aspects that reach beyond the τόδε τι, and this in turn compromises its realization.

Naïve faith in style goes hand in hand with rancor against the concept of progress in art. Conservative cultural philosophy, stubbornly insensible to the immanent tendency that motivates artistic radicalism, has the habit of sagely explaining that the concept of progress is itself outmoded and endures only as a bad relic of the nineteenth century. This provides a semblance of intellectual superiority over the supposed technological dependency of avant-garde artists, as well as a certain demagogical effect; an intellectual benediction is bestowed on a widespread anti-intellectualism that has degenerated into the cultivated terrain of the culture industry. The ideological character of such efforts, however, is no dispensation from reflection on the relation of art to progress. As Hegel and Marx knew, in art the concept of progress is more refracted than in the history of the technical forces of production. To its very core, art is enmeshed in the historical movement of growing antagonisms. In art there is as much and as little progress as in society. Hegel's aesthetics suffers not least of all because—like his system as a whole—it oscillates between thinking in invariants and unrestrained dialectical thinking, and although it grasped, as no previous system had, the historical element of art as the "development of truth," it nevertheless conserved the canon of antiquity. Instead of drawing dialectics into aesthetic progress, Hegel brought this progress to a halt; for him it was art and not its prototypical forms that was transient. The consequences in Communist countries one hundred years later could not have been foreseen: Their reactionary art theory is nourished, not without Marx's approval, on Hegel's classicism. That according to Hegel art was once the adequate stage of spirit and now no longer is, demonstrates a trust in the real progress of consciousness of freedom that has since been bitterly disappointed. Hegel's theorem of art as the consciousness of needs is compelling, and it is not outdated. In fact, the end of art that he prognosticated did not occur in the one hundred fifty years that have since lapsed. It is in no way the case that what was destined to perish has simply been forced along, emptily; the quality of the most important works of the epoch and particularly those that were disparaged as decadent is not open to discussion with those who would simply like to annul that quality externally and thus from below. Even given the most extreme reductionism in art's consciousness of needs, the gesture of self-imposed muteness and vanishing, art persists, as in a sort of differential. Because there has not yet been any progress in the world, there is progress in art; "*il faut continuer.*" Admittedly, art remains caught up in what Hegel called world spirit and is thus an accomplice, but it could escape this guilt only by destroying itself and thus directly abetting speechless domination and deferring to barbarism. Artworks that want to free themselves of their guilt weaken themselves as artworks. One would only succeed in holding true to the monodimensionality of the world spirit if one were to insist on reducing it exclusively to the concept of domination. Artworks that, in epochs of liberation that go beyond the historical instant, are fraternally allied with the world spirit, owe it their breath, vigor, and indeed everything by which they go beyond the ever-sameness of the administered world. In these works, the subject opens its eyes, nature awakens to itself, and the historical spirit itself participates in this awakening. As much as progress in art is not to be fetishized but to be confronted with its truth content, it would be pitiful to distinguish between good progress as temperate and bad progress as what has run wild. Oppressed nature expresses itself more purely in works criticized as artificial, which with regard to the level of the technical forces of production, go to the extreme, than it does in circumspect works whose *parti pris* for nature is as allied with the real domination of nature as is the nature lover with the hunt. Progress in art is neither to be proclaimed nor denied. No later work, even were it the work of the greatest talent, could match the truth content of Beethoven's last quartets without reoccupying their position point by point with regard to material, spirit, and procedures.

The difficulty of coming to a general judgment about the progress of art has to do with a difficulty presented by the structure of its history. It is inhomogeneous. At most, series are to be discerned that have a successive continuity that then breaks off, often under social pressure that can indeed be that of conformity; to this day, continuity in artistic developments has required relatively stable social conditions. Continuities in genres parallel social continuity and homogeneity; it can be supposed that there was little change in the Italian public's attitude to opera from the time of the Neapolitans to Verdi, perhaps even to Puccini; and a similar continuity of genre, marked by a relatively consistent development of means and prohibitions, can be seen in late medieval polyphony. The correspondence between closed historical developments in art and, possibly, static social structures indicates the limits of the history of genres; any abrupt change of social structure, such as occurred with the emergence of a bourgeois public, brings about an equally abrupt change in genres and stylistic types. Thoroughbass music, which in its beginnings was primitive to the point of regression, repressed the highly developed Dutch and Italian polyphony; its powerful revival in Bach was marginalized tracelessly for decades after his death. Only desultorily is it possible to speak of a transition from one work to another. Spontaneity, the compulsion toward the yet ungrasped, without which art is unthinkable, would otherwise have no place and its history would be mechanically determined. This holds true for the production of individually significant artists; the continuity of their work is often fragmented, not only in the case of the work of purportedly protean natures who seek security by switching models but even in the case of the most discriminating. They sometimes produce works that are starkly antithetical to what they have already completed, either because they consider the possibilities of one type of work to be exhausted or as a preventative to the danger of rigidification and repetition. In the works of many artists, production develops as if the new works wanted to recover what the earlier work, in becoming concretized and therefore, as ever, limiting itself, had had to renounce. No individual work is ever what traditional idealist aesthetics praises as a totality. Each is inadequate as well as incomplete, an extract from its own potential, and this runs contrary to its direct continuation if one leaves out of consideration various series of works in which painters, in particular, try out a conception with an eye to its possibilities for development. This discontinuous structure is, however, no more causally necessary than it is accidental and disparate. Even if there is no transition from one work to another, their succession nevertheless stands under the unity of the problem posed. Progress, the negation of what exists through new beginnings, takes place within this unity. Problems that previous work either did not solve or spawned in the course of their own solutions await attention, and that sometimes necessitates a break. Yet not even the unity of the problem provides an uninterrupted structure for the history of art. Problems can be forgotten; historical antitheses can develop in which the thesis is no longer preserved. Just how little progress in art has been a phylogenetically unbroken course can be learned ontogenetically. Innovators rarely have more power over what is old than did their predecessors. No aesthetic progress without forgetting; hence, all progress involves regression. Brecht made forgetting his program on cultural-critical grounds that are justly suspicious of cultural tradition as a golden chain of ideologies. Phases of forgetting and, complementarily, those of the reemergence of what has long been taboo—for example, the reprise of the didactic poem in Brecht—usually involve genres rather than individual works; this is also true of taboos such as that which has today fallen on subjective—and especially erotic—poetry, which was once an expression of emancipation. In fact, the continuity of art can be construed only from a very great distance. Rather, the history of art has nodal points. Although partial histories of genre have their legitimacy—such as those of landscape painting, portraiture, the opera—they should not be overtaxed. This is strikingly corroborated by the history of parody and contrafactum in older music. In Bach's oeuvre it is his technique, the complexion and density of the composition, that is truly progressive and more to the point than whether he wrote secular or religious, vocal or instrumental music; to this extent nominalism retrospectively affects the knowledge of older music. The impossibility of a univocal construction of the history of art and the fatality of all disquisitions on its progress—which exists and then again does not exist—originate in art's double character as being socially determined in its autonomy and at the same time social. When the social character of art overwhelms its autonomy, when its immanent structure explosively contradicts its social relations, autonomy is sacrificed and with it art's continuity; it is one of the weaknesses of the history of ideas that it idealistically ignores this. For the most part, when continuity shatters it is the relations of production that win out over the forces of production; there is no cause to chime in with such social triumph. Art develops by way of the social whole; that is to say, it is mediated by society's ruling structure. Art's history is not a string of individual causalities; no univocal necessities lead from one phenomenon to the next. Its history may be called necessary only with regard to the total social tendency, not in reference to its individual manifestations. Its pat construction from above is as false as faith in the incommensurable genius of individual works that transports them out of the realm of necessity. A noncontradictory theory of the history of art is not to be conceived: The essence of its history is contradictory in itself.

Undoubtedly, the historical materials and their domination—technique—advance; discoveries such as those of perspective in painting and polyphony in music are the most obvious examples. Beyond this, progress is also undeniable in the logical development of established methodology, as is evident in the differentiation of harmonic consciousness between the age of thoroughbass composition and the threshold of new music, or in the transition from impressionism to pointillism. Such unmistakable progress is, however, not necessarily that of quality. Only blindness could deny the aesthetic means gained in painting from Giotto and Cimabue to Piero della Francesca; however, to conclude that Piero's paintings are therefore better than the frescos of Assisi would be schoolmarmish. Whereas with regard to a particular work the question of quality can be posed and decided, and whereas relations are thereby indeed implicit in the judgment of various works, such judgments become art-alien pedantry as soon as comparison is made under the heading of "better than": Such controversies are in no way immune from cultural nonsense. However much works are distinguished from each other by their quality, they are at the same time incommensurable. They communicate with each other exclusively by way of antitheses: "Every work is the mortal enemy of the other."[6] They become comparable only by annihilating themselves, by realizing their life through their mortality. It is difficult to distinguish—and if at all then only *in concreto*—which archaic and primitive traits result from technique and which from the objective idea of the work; the two can be separated only arbitrarily. Even flaws may become eloquent, whereas what is excellent may in the course of history narrow the truth content. The history of art is just that antinomical. The subcutaneous structure of Bach's most important instrumental works can only be brought out in performance by means of an orchestral palette that he did not have at his disposal; yet it would be ridiculous to wish for perspective in medieval paintings, which would rob them of their specific expression.——Progress can be surpassed by progress. The reduction, and ultimately the canceling, of perspective in modern painting produces correspondences with preperspectival works that raises in estimation the distant past above the more recent past; these correspondences become philistine, however, if primitive and superseded methods are employed for modern works and progress in the mastery over the material is disparaged and revoked. Even progressive mastery over the material is sometimes paid for with a loss in the mastery over the material. The greater familiarity with exotic musics that had previously been dismissed as primitive suggests that Western music's polyphony and rationalization—which are inseparable and which opened up all its richness and depths—dulled the power of differentiation that is alive in the minimal rhythmic and melodic variations of monadic music; the rigidity —and, for European ears, the monotony—of exotic music was obviously the condition for this differentiation. Ritual pressure strengthened the capacity to differentiate in a narrow sphere, where it was tolerated, whereas European music, under less pressure, was less in need of such correctives. As a result, only Western music achieved full autonomy—the status of art—and the consciousness that is immanent to it cannot arbitrarily leave it in order to broaden itself in some fashion. Undeniably, a finer capacity to differentiate, which is always an aspect of the aesthetic mastery over material, is bound up with spiritualization; it is the subjective correlative of objective control, the capacity to sense what has become possible, as a result of which art becomes freer to its own task: the protest against the mastery over material itself. Volition within the involuntary is the paradoxical formula for the possible dissolution of the antinomy of aesthetic domination. The mastery over the material implies spiritualization, though this spiritualization, as the autonomy of spirit vis-à-vis its other, immediately endangers itself again. The sovereign aesthetic spirit has a tendency to communicate itself rather than to give voice to what is at stake, which alone would fulfill the idea of spiritualization. The *prix du progrès* is inherent in progress itself, and this is most apparent in the declining authenticity and bindingness of art and in the growing sense of accidentalness; this is directly identical with progress of the domination of the material, as seen in the intensification of the elaboration of the individual work. It is uncertain whether this loss is factual or merely semblance. For naïve consciousness, as for that of the musician, a song from *Die Winterreise* may seem more authentic than one by Webern, as if the former had hit upon something objective whereas in the latter the content is narrowed to merely individual experience. Yet this distinction is dubious. In works with the dignity of Webern's music, differentiation —which to untutored ears damages the objectivity of the content—is of a piece with the developing capacity to shape the work more precisely, to purge it of all residue of the schematic, and precisely this is what is called objectivation. Intimate experience of authentic modern art loses the feeling of contingency that arises as long as a language is perceived to be necessary that has not been demolished simply by the subjective need for expression but rather by this need in the process of objectivation. Clearly artworks themselves are not indifferent to the transformation of their binding element into monad. That they appear to become more indifferent is not simply the result of their diminishing social effect. There is reason to think that works, through the shift to pure immanence, forfeit their coefficient of friction, an element of their essence; that they also become more indifferent in themselves. However, that radically abstract images can be displayed in public spaces without irritating anyone does not justify any restoration of representational art, which is a priori comforting even when Che Guevara is chosen for the goal of reconciliation with the object. Finally, progress is not only that of the domination of material and spiritualization but also the progress of spirit in Hegel's sense of the consciousness of freedom. Whether the domination of the material in Beethoven goes beyond that in Bach can be disputed endlessly; with regard to various dimensions, each had superior mastery of the material. Although the question of whom to rank higher is idle, the same cannot be said of the insight that the voice of the maturity of the subject, the emancipation from and reconciliation with myth—that is, the truth content—reached a higher development in Beethoven than in Bach. This criterion surpasses all others.

The aesthetic name for mastery over material—technique, a borrowing from antiquity, which ranked the arts among artisanal activities—is of recent date in its present acceptation. It bears the traces of a phase in which, analogous to science, methods were considered to be independent of their object. In retrospect, all artistic procedures that form the material and allow themselves to be guided by it coalesce under the technological aspect, including those procedures that originated in the artisanal praxis of the medieval production of goods, a praxis from which art, resisting integration into capitalism, never completely diverged. In art the threshold between craft and technique is not, as in material production, a strict quantification of processes, which is incompatible with art's qualitative telos; nor is it the introduction of machines; rather, it is the predominance of conscious free control over the aesthetic means, in contrast to tradition-alism, under the cover of which this control matured. Vis-à-vis content [Gehalt], the technical aspect is only one aspect among many others; no artwork is nothing but the quintessence of its technical elements. That any view of artworks that perceives nothing but how they are made falls short of aesthetic experience is admittedly a standard apologetic topos preferred by cultural ideology, yet it nevertheless remains true in opposition to the functionalist view of art at the point where functionalism is forsaken.

Technique is, however, constitutive of art, because in it is condensed the fact that each artwork is a human artifact and that what is artistic in it becomes a human product. Technique and content must be distinguished; what is ideological is the abstraction that extracts the supratechnical from what is purportedly merely technique, as if in important works technique and content did not produce each other reciprocally. Shakespeare's nominalistic breakthrough into mortal and infinitely rich individuality—as content—is as much a function of an antitectonic, quasi-epic succession of short scenes as this episodic technique is under the control of the content: a metaphysical experience that explodes the meaning-giving order of the old unities. In the priestly word "message" the dialectical relation of content and technique is reified as a simple dichotomy. Technique has key significance for the knowledge of art; it alone leads reflection to the interior of works, though of course only on condition that one speak their language. Because the content is not something made, technique does not circumscribe art as a whole, yet it is exclusively from its concretion that the content can be extrapolated. Technique is the definable figure of the enigma in artworks, at once rational and conceptless. It authorizes judgment in a region that does not make judgments. Certainly the technical questions of artworks become infinitely complex and cannot be solved on the basis of a single maxim. Yet in principle they can be immanently decided. Technique, as the measure of the "logic" of works, is also the measure of the suspension of logic. The surgical excision of technique would suit a vulgar mentality, but it would be false. For the technique of a work is constituted by its problems, by the aporetic task that it objectively poses to itself. It is only with regard to this problem that the technique of a work can be discerned and the question answered as to whether or not it suffices, just as inversely the objective problem of the work must be inferred from its technical complexion. If no work can be understood without an understanding of its technique, technique conversely cannot be understood without an understanding of the work. The degree to which, beyond the specification of a particular work, a technique is universal or monadological varies historically, yet even in idolized eras, when style was binding, technique had the responsibility of assuring that style did not abstractly rule the work but entered into the dialectic of the work's individuation. How much more significant technique is than art-alien irrationalism would like to admit is obvious in that, presupposing the capacity for the experience of art, experience unfolds all the more richly the more deeply consciousness penetrates the artwork's technical complexion. Understanding grows along with an understanding of the technical treatment of the work. That consciousness kills is a nursery tale; only false consciousness is fatal. *Métier* initially makes art commensurable to consciousness because for the most part it can be learned. What a teacher finds fault with in a student's work is the first model of a lack of *métier*; corrections are the model of *métier* itself. These models are preartistic insofar as they recapitulate preestablished patterns and rules; they take a step beyond this when they become the comparison of technical means with the sought-after goal. At a primitive level of education, beyond which, admittedly, the usual study of composition rarely goes, the teacher finds fault with parallel fifths and in their place suggests better voiceleading; but if he is not a pedant, he will demonstrate to the student that parallel fifths are legitimate artistic means for intended effects, as in Debussy, and that external to tonality the prohibition loses its meaning altogether. *Métier* ultimately sloughs off its provisional, limited shape. The experienced eye that surveys a score or a drawing ascertains, almost mimetically, before any analysis, whether the objet d'art has *métier* and innervates its level of form. Yet this does not suffice. An account is necessary of the work's *métier*, which appears as a breath—the aura of artworks—in strange contrast to the dilettante's image of artistic skill. The auratic element, paradoxically apparent and bound up with *métier*, is the memory of the hand that, tenderly, almost caressingly, passed over the contours of the work and, by articulating them, also mollified them. This relation of aura and *métier* can be brought out by analysis, which is itself lodged in *métier*. In contrast to the synthesizing function of artworks, which is familiar to all, the analytical element is strangely ignored. Its locus is the counterpole to synthesis, that is, it focuses on the economy of the elements out of which the work is composed; yet, no less than synthesis, it inheres objectively in the artwork. The conductor, who analyzes a work in order to perform it adequately rather than mimicking it, recapitulates a precondition of the possibility of the work itself. Analysis provides clues to a higher concept of *métier*: In music, for instance, the "flow" of a piece is concerned with whether it is thought in individual measures or in phrases that reach over and above them; or whether impulses are followed through and pursued rather than being left to peter out in patchwork. This movement in the concept of technique provides the true *gradus ad Parnassum*. Only in the course of an aesthetic casuistry, however, does this become completely evident. When Alban Berg answered in the negative the naïve question whether Strauss was not to be admired at least for his technique, he pointed up the arbitrariness of Strauss's method, which carefully calculates a series of effects without seeing to it that, in purely musical terms, one event emerges from, or is made requisite by, another. This technical critique of highly technical works obviously disregards a conception of composition that asserts the principle of shock as fundamental and actually transfers the unity of the composition into the irrational suspension of what traditional style called logicality, unity. It could be argued that this concept of technique ignores the immanence of the work and has external origins, specifically in the ideal of a school that, like Schoenberg's, anachronistically maintains the idea of developing variation, a vestige of traditional musical logic, in order to mobilize it against tradition. But this argument avoids the actual artistic issue. Berg's critique of Strauss's *métier* hits the mark because whoever refuses logic is incapable of the elaboration of the work that serves that *métier* to which Strauss himself was committed. True, already in Berlioz the breaks and leaps of the *imprévu* were sought after; they at the same time disrupt the thrust of the music's course, which is replaced by the thrusting gesture. Music organized in such temporal-dynamic fashion as that of Strauss is incompatible with a compositional method that does not coherently organize temporal succession. Ends and means are contradictory. The contradiction cannot be assuaged simply within the realm of means, but instead extends to the goal itself, the glorification of contingency, which celebrates as an unencumbered life something that is no more than the anarchy of commodity production and the brutality of those who control it. There is a false concept of continuity implicit in the view of artistic technique as a straight line of progress independent from content; movements espousing the liberation of technique are capable of being affected by the untruth of the content. Just how inwardly technique and content—contrary to accepted opinion—are mutually defining was expressed by Beethoven when he said that many of the effects that are commonly attributed to the natural genius of the composer are in truth due to the adroit use of the diminished seventh chord; the dignity of such sober assessment condemns all the chatter about creativity; Beethoven's objectivity was the first time justice was done equally to aesthetic illusion and the illusionless. The recognition of inconsistencies between technique—an artwork's intention, especially its expressive-mimetic dimension—and its truth content sometimes provokes revolts against technique. Self-emancipation at the price of its goal is endogenous to the concept of technique. It has a propensity to become an end-in-itself as a sort of contentless proficiency. Fauvism was a reaction against this in painting; the analogous reaction in music was the rise of Schoenberg's free atonality in opposition to the orchestral brilliance of the *neu-deutsch* school. In his essay "Problems in Teaching Art,"[7] Schoenberg —who, more than any other musician of his epoch, insisted on consistent craftsmanship—expressly attacked blind faith in technique. Reified technique sometimes provokes correctives that border on the "wild," the barbaric, the technically primitive and art-alien. What can truly be called modern art was hurled out by this primitive impulse, which, because it could not domesticate itself, transformed itself at every point once again into technique. Yet this impulse was in no way regressive. Technique is not an abundance of means but rather the accumulated capacity to be suited to what the object itself demands. This idea of technique is sometimes better served by the reduction of means than by piling it up and exhausting the work. Schoenberg's economical Piano Pieces, op. 11, with all the wonderful ungainliness of their innovativeness, are technically superior to the orchestration of Strauss's *Heldenleben,* of which only a part of the score is acoustically perceptible; here the means are no longer adequate even to their most immediate end, the sounding appearance of what is imagined. It is possible that the mature Schoenberg's second technique, the twelve-tone system, fell short of what was achieved by the earlier act of suspension involved in his first technique, atonality. But even the emancipation of technique, which draws technique into its particular dialectic, is not simply the original sin of routine, which is how it appears to the unalloyed need for expression. Because of its close bond with content, technique has a legitimate life of its own. In the process of change, art habitually finds itself in need of those elements that it was previously obliged to renounce. This neither explains nor excuses the fact that to date, artistic revolutions have been reactionary, but it is certainly bound up with it. Prohibitions, including the prohibition on luxuriating plentitude and complexity, have a regressive aspect; this is one of the reasons why prohibition, however saturated it may be with refusal, ultimately collapses. This constitutes one of the dimensions in the process of objectivation. When, some ten years after World War II, composers had had enough of post-Webernian pointillism—a striking example of which is Boulez's *Marteau sans maître*—the process repeated itself, this time as the critique of the ideology of any absolute new beginning, of starting out with a clean slate. Four decades earlier the transition from Picasso's *Demoiselles d'Avignon* to synthetic cubism may have had a related meaning. The same historical experiences are expressed in the rise and fall of technical allergies as are expressed in the content; in this, content communicates with technique.——Kant's idea of purposefulness, which as he conceived it established the connection between art and the interior of nature, is most closely related to technique. Technique is that whereby artworks are organized as purposeful in a way that is denied to empirical existence; only through technique do they become purposeful. Because of its sobriety the emphasis on technique in art alienates philistines: It makes art's provenance in prosaic praxis—of which art stands in horror—all too obvious. Nowhere does art make itself so guilty of illusoriness as in the irrevocable technical aspect of its sorcery, for only through technique, the medium of art's crystallization, does art distance itself from the prosaic. Technique insures that the artwork is more than an agglomeration of what is factually available, and this more is art's content.

In the language of art, expressions like technique, *métier*, and craft are synonyms. This points up that anachronistic aspect of craft that Valéry's melancholy did not overlook. It admixes something idyllic with art's existence in an age in which nothing true is any longer permitted to be harmless. On the other hand, however, whenever autonomous art has seriously set out to absorb industrial processes, they have remained external to it. Mass reproduction has in no way become its immanent law of form to the extent that identification with the aggressor would like to suggest. Even in film, industrial and aesthetic-craftsmanlike elements diverge under socioeconomic pressure. The radical industrialization of art, its undiminished adaptation to the achieved technical standards, collides with what in art resists integration. If technique strives for industrialization as its vanishing point, it does so at the cost of the immanent elaboration of the work and thus at the cost of technique itself. This instills into art an archaic element that compromises it. The fanatic predilection that generations of youth have had for jazz unconsciously protests against this and at the same time manifests the implicit contradiction, for production that adapts to industry or, at the least, acts as if it had done so, falls helplessly behind the artistic-compositional forces of production in terms of its own aesthetic complexion. The current tendency, evident in media of all kinds, to manipulate accident is probably an effort to avoid old-fashioned and effectively superfluous craftsmanlike methods in art without delivering art over to the instrumental rationality of mass production. The suspicious question as to art in the age of technology, as unavoidable as it is a socially naïve slogan of the epoch, can be approached only by reflection on the relation of artworks to purposefulness. Certainly artworks are defined by technique as something that is purposeful in itself. The work's *terminus ad quem*, however, has its locus exclusively in itself, not externally. Therefore the technique of its immanent purposefulness also remains "without a purpose," whereas technique itself constantly has extra-aesthetic technique as its model. Kant's paradoxical formulation expresses an antinomical relation, though the antinomist did not make it explicit: In the process of becoming increasingly technical, which irrevocably binds them to functional forms, artworks come into contradiction with their purposelessness. In applied arts, products are, for example, adapted to the streamlined form that serves to reduce air resistance, even though the chairs will not be meeting with this resistance. Applied arts are, however, a prophetic warning for art. Art's irrevocably rational element, which is concentrated as its technique, works against art. It is not that rationality kills the unconscious, the substance of art, or whatever; technique alone made art capable of admitting the unconscious into itself. But precisely by virtue of its absolute autonomy the rational, purely elaborated artwork would annul its difference from empirical existence; without imitating it, the artwork would assimilate itself to its opposite, the commodity. It would be indistinguishable from completely functional works except that it would have no purpose, and this, admittedly, would speak against it. The totality of inner-aesthetic purposefulness develops into the problem of art's purposefulness beyond its own sphere, a problem for which it has no answer. The judgment holds that the strictly technical artwork comes to ruin, and those works that restrict their own technique are inconsequential. If technique is the quintessence of art's language, it at the same time inescapably liquidates its language. In art no less than in other domains the concept of the technical force of production cannot be fetishized. Otherwise it would become a reflex of that technocracy that is a form of domination socially disguised under the semblance of rationality. Technical forces of production have no value in themselves. They receive their importance exclusively in relation to their purpose in the work, and ultimately in relation to the truth content of what has been written, composed, or painted. Of course, such purposefulness of technical means in art is not transparent. Purpose often hides in technology without the latter's adequacy to the purpose being immediately ascertainable. Thus the discovery and rapid development of instrumental technique in the early nineteenth century bore the technocratic traces of Saint-Simonian technocracy. How this instrumental integration of works in all their dimensions was related to purpose only became evident at a later stage, and at that point once again qualitatively transformed orchestral technique. In art the entwinement of purpose and technical means is an admonition for the circumspect invocation of categorial judgments on their quid pro quo. Likewise, it is uncertain whether adaptation to extra-aesthetic technique necessarily amounts, inner-aesthetically, to progress. This could hardly be claimed in the case of the *Symphonie fantastique*, a pendant to early world fairs, in comparison with the contemporaneous late work of Beethoven. Beginning in those years, the erosion of subjective mediation, which almost always accompanies technologization, took its toll on music, as is evident in the lack of real compositional elaboration in Berlioz's work; the technological artwork is by no means a priori more consistent than that which, in response to industrialization, turns inward, intent on producing the effect of an "effect without a cause." What hits the mark in the various reflections on art in what journalists call the technological age, which is just as much marked by the social relations of production as by the level of productive forces, is not so much the adequacy of art to technical development as the transformation of the experiential forms sedimented in artworks. The question is that of the aesthetic world of imagery: Preindustrial imagery irretrievably had to collapse. The sentence with which Benjamin's reflections on surrealism began—"It no longer feels right to dream about the blue flower"[8]—gets to the heart of the matter. Art is mimesis of the world of imagery and at the same time its enlightenment through forms of control. The world of imagery, itself thoroughly historical, is done an injustice by the fiction of a world of images that effaces the relations in which people live. The utilization of available technical means in accord with the critical consciousness of art does not offer a solution to the problem whether and how art is possible that, as an uneducable innocence thinks of it, would be relevant in today's world; on the contrary, any solution demands the authenticity of a form of experience that does not lay claim to an immediacy it has lost. Today immediacy of aesthetic comportment is exclusively an immediate relationship to the universally mediated. That today any walk in the woods, unless elaborate plans have been made to seek out the most remote forests, is accompanied by the sound of jet engines overhead not only destroys the actuality of nature as, for instance, an object of poetic celebration. It affects the mimetic impulse. Nature poetry is anachronistic not only as a subject: Its truth content has vanished. This may help clarify the anorganic aspect of Beckett's as well as of Celan's poetry. It yearns neither for nature nor for industry; it is precisely the integration of the latter that leads to poetization, which was already a dimension of impressionism, and contributes its part to making peace with an unpeaceful world. Art, as an anticipatory form of reaction, is no longer able—if it ever was—to embody pristine nature or the industry that has scorched it; the impossibility of both is probably the hidden law of aesthetic nonrepresentationalism. The images of the postindustrial world are those of a corpse; they want to avert atomic war by banning it, just as forty years ago surrealism sought to save Paris through the image of cows grazing in the streets, the same cows after which the people of bombed-out Berlin rebaptized *Kurfürstendamm* as *Kudamm*.[9] In relation to its telos, all aesthetic technique falls under the shadow of irrationality, which is the opposite of that for which aesthetic irrationalism criticizes technique; and this shadow is anathema to technique. Of course, an element of universality cannot be eliminated from technique any more than from the movement of nominalism as a whole. Cubism and composition with twelve tones related only to one another[10] are, in terms of their idea, universal procedures in the age of the negation of aesthetic universality. The tension between objectivating technique and the mimetic essence of artworks is fought out in the effort to save the fleeting, the ephemeral, the transitory in a form that is immune to reification and yet akin to it in being permanent. It is probably only in this Sisyphean struggle that the concept of artistic technique took shape; it is akin to the tour de force. This is the focal point of Valéry's theory, a rational theory of aesthetic irrationality. Incidentally, art's impulse to objectivate the fleeting, not the permanent, may well run through the whole of its history. Hegel failed to recognize this and for this reason, in the midst of dialectics, failed to recognize the temporal core of art's truth content. The subjectivization of art throughout the nineteenth century, which at the same time unbound its technical forces of production, did not sacrifice the objective idea of art but rather, by bringing it fully into time, set it in sharper, purer relief than any classicist purity ever achieved. Thus the greatest justice that was done to the mimetic impulse becomes the greatest injustice, because permanence, objectivation, ultimately negates the mimetic impulse. Yet the guilt for this is borne not by art's putative decline but by the idea of art itself.

Aesthetic nominalism is a process that transpires in the form and that ultimately becomes form; even here the universal and the particular are mediated. The nominalistic prohibitions on predefined forms are, as prescriptions, canonical. The critique of forms is entwined with the critique of their formal adequacy. Prototypical in this regard is the distinction between closed and open forms, which is relevant to all theory of form. Open forms are those universal genre categories that seek an equilibrium with the nominalistic critique of universality that is founded on the experience that the unity of the universal and the particular, which is claimed by artworks, fundamentally fails. No pregiven universal unprotestingly receives a particular that does not derive from a genre. The perpetuated universality of forms becomes incompatible with form's own meaning; the promise of something rounded, overarching, and balanced is not fulfilled. For this is a promise made to what is heterogeneous to the forms, which probably never tolerated identity with them. Forms that rattle on after their moment is past do the form itself injustice. Form that has become reified with regard to its other is no longer form. The sense of form in Bach, who in many regards opposed bourgeois nominalism, did not consist in showing respect for traditional forms but rather in keeping them in motion, or better: in not letting them harden in the first place; Bach was nominalistic on the basis of his sense of form. A not unrancorous cliché praises the novel for its gift of form, yet the cliché has its justification not in the novel's happy manipulation of forms but in its capacity for maintaining the lability of forms to what is formed, of yielding to it out of sensual sympathy rather than simply taming it. The sense for forms instructs on their problematic: that the beginning and end of a musical phrase, the balanced composition of a painting, stage rituals such as death or marriage of heroes are vain because they are arbitrary: What is shaped does not honor the form that shapes. If, however, the renunciation of ritual in the idea of an open genre—which is itself often conventional enough, like the rondo—is free of the lie of necessity, the idea of the genre becomes all the more exposed to contingency. The nominalistic artwork should become an artwork by being organized from below to above, not by having principles of organization foisted on it. But no artwork left blindly to itself possesses the power of organization that would set up binding boundaries for itself: Investing the work with such a power would in fact be fetishistic. Unchecked aesthetic nominalism liquidates—just as philosophical critique does with regard to Aristotle—all forms as a remnant of a spiritual being-in-itself. It terminates in a literal facticity, and this is irreconcilable with art. In an artist with the incomparable level of form of Mozart it would be possible to show how closely that artist's most daring and thus most authentic formal structures verge on nominalistic collapse. The artifactual character of the artwork is incompatible with the postulate of pure relinquishment to the material. By being something made, artworks acquire that element of organization, of being something directed, in the dramaturgical sense, that is anathema to the nominalistic sensibility. The historical aporia of aesthetic nominalism culminates in the insufficiency of open forms, a striking example of which is Brecht's difficulty in writing convincing conclusions to his plays. A qualitative leap in the general tendency to open form is, moreover, not to be overlooked. The older open forms were based on traditional forms that they modified but from which they maintained more than just the external trappings. The classical Viennese sonata was a dynamic yet closed form, and this closure was precarious; the rondo, with the intentional freedom in the alternation of refrain and couplets, was a decidedly open form. All the same, in the fiber of what was composed, the difference was not so substantial. From Beethoven to Mahler, the sonata rondo was much employed, which transplanted the development section of the sonata to the rondo, thus balancing off the playfulness of the open form with the bindingness of the closed form. This was possible because the rondo form was itself never literally pledged to contingency but rather, in the spirit of a nominalistic age and in recollection of the much older spirit of the rounded canon, the alternation between choir and soloist adapted to the demand for an absence of constraint in an established form. The rondo lent itself better to cheap standardization than did the dynamically developing sonata, whose dynamic, in spite of its closure, did not permit typification. The sense of form, which in the rondo at the very least gave the impression of contingency, required guarantees in order not to explode the genre. Antecedent forms in Bach, such as the Presto of his *Italian* concerto, were more flexible, less rigid, more complexly elaborated than were Mozart's rondos, which belonged to a later stage of nominalism. The qualitative reversal occurred when in place of the oxymoron of the open form a new procedure appeared that, indifferent to the genres, completely followed the nominalistic commandment; paradoxically, the results had greater closure than their conciliatory predecessors; the nominalistic urge for authenticity resists the playful forms as descendants of feudal divertissement. The seriousness in Beethoven is bourgeois. Contingency impinged on form. Ultimately, contingency is a function of growing structuration. This explains apparently marginal events such as the temporally contracting scope of musical compositions, as well as the miniature format of Klee's best works. Resignation vis-à-vis time and space gave ground to the crisis of nominalistic form until it was reduced to a mere point, effectively inert. *Action painting, l'art informelle,* and aleatorical works may have carried the element of resignation to its extreme: The aesthetic subject exempts itself of the burden of giving form to the contingent material it encounters, despairing of the possibility of undergirding it, and instead shifts the responsibility for its organization back to the contingent material itself. The gain here is, however, dubious. Form purportedly distilled from the contingent and the heterogeneous itself remains heterogeneous and, for the artwork, arbitrary; in its literalness it is alien to art. Statistics are used to console for the absence of traditional forms. This situation holds embedded in itself the figure of its own critique. Nominalistic artworks constantly require the intervention of the guiding hand they conceal in the service of their principle. The extremely objective critique of semblance incorporates an illusory element that is perhaps as irrevocable as the aesthetic semblance of all artworks. Often in artistic products of chance a necessity is sensed to subordinate these works to, effectively, a stylizing procedure of selection. *Corriger la fortune*: This is the fateful writing on the wall of the nominalistic artwork. Its *fortune* is nothing of the kind but rather that fateful spell from which artworks have tried to extricate themselves ever since art lodged its claim against myth in antiquity. Beethoven's music, which was no less affected by nominalism than was Hegel's philosophy, is incomparable in that the intervention enjoined by the problematic of form is permeated with autonomy, that is, with the freedom of the subject that is coming to self-consciousness. He legitimated what, from the standpoint of the artwork that was to be developed entirely on its own terms, must have seemed like an act of coercion on the basis of its own content. No artwork is worthy of its name that would hold at bay what is accidental in terms of its own law of form. For form is, according to its own concept, the form of something, and this something must not be permitted to become merely the tautology of form. But the necessity of this relation of form to its other undermines form; form cannot set itself up vis-à-vis the heterogeneous as that purity that as form it wants to be just as much as it requires the heterogeneous. The immanence of form in the heterogeneous has its limits. Nevertheless the history of the whole of bourgeois art was not possible except as the effort if not to solve the antinomy of nominalism then at least to give it shape, to win form from its negation. In this the history of modern art is not merely analogous to the history of philosophy: It is the same history. What Hegel called the unfolding of truth occurred as the same process of unfolding both in art and philosophy.

The necessity of bringing about the objectivation of the nominalistic element, which this element at the same time resists, engenders the principle of construction. Construction is the form of works that is no longer imposed on them ready-made yet does not arise directly out of them either, but rather originates in its reflection through subjective reason. Historically, the concept of construction originated in mathematics; it was applied to substantive concerns for the first time in Schelling's speculative philosophy, where it was to serve as the common denominator of the diffusely contingent and the need for form. The concept of construction in art comes close to this. Because art can no longer rely on any objectivity of universals and yet by its own concept is none the less the objectivation of impulses, objectivation becomes functionalized. By demolishing the security of forms, nominalism made all art *plein air* long before this became an unmetaphoric slogan. Thinking and art both became dynamic. It is hardly an unfair overgeneralization to say that nominalistic art has a chance of objectivation only through immanent development, through the processual character of every particular artwork. Dynamic objectivation, however, the determination of the work as existing in itself, involves a static element. In construction the dynamic reverses completely into the static: The constructed work stands still. Nominalism's progress thus reaches its own limit. In literature the prototype of dynamization was intrigue, in music the prototype was the development section. In Haydn's developments a self-preoccupied busyness, opaque to itself in terms of its own purpose, became an objective determining basis of what is perceived as an expression of subjective humor. The individual activity of the motifs as they pursue their separate interests, all the while assured by a sort of residual ontology that through this activity they serve the harmony of the whole, is unmistakably reminiscent of the zealous, shrewd, and narrow-minded demeanor of intrigants, the descendants of the dumb devil; his dumbness infiltrates even the emphatic works of dynamic classicism, just as it lingers on in capitalism. The aesthetic function of such means was dynamically, through development, to confirm the process ignited by a unique element: The premises immediately posited by the work are fulfilled as its result. There is a kind of cunning of unreason that strips the intrigant of his narrow-mindedness; the tyrannical individual becomes the affirmation of the process. The reprise, peculiarly long-lived in the history of music, embodies to an equal degree affirmation and—as the repetition of what is essentially unrepeatable—limitation. Intrigue and development are not only subjective activity, temporal development for itself. They also represent unleashed, blind, and self-consuming life in the works. Against it, artworks are no longer a bulwark. Every intrigue, literally and figuratively, says: This is how things are, this is what it's like out there. In the portrayal of this "Comment c'est" the unwitting artwork is permeated by its other, its own essence, the movement toward objectivation, and is motivated by that heterogeneous other. This is possible because intrigue and development, which are subjective aesthetic means, when transplanted into the work acquire that quality of subjective objectivation that they have in the external world, where they reproach social labor and its narrow-mindedness with its potential superfluity. This superfluity is truly the point at which art coincides with the real world's business. To the extent to which a drama—itself a sonatalike product of the bourgeois era—is in musical terms "worked," that is, dissected into the smallest motifs and objectivated in their dynamic synthesis, to this extent, and right into the most sublime moments, the echo of commodity production can be heard. The common nexus of these art-technical procedures and material processes, which has developed in the course of industrialization, has yet to be clarified but is nevertheless strikingly evident. With the emergence of intrigue and development, however, commodity production not only migrates into artworks in the form of a heterogeneous life but indeed also as their own law: nominalistic artworks were unwitting *tableaux économiques*. This is the historicophilosophical origin of modern humor. Certainly it is through external industry that life is reproduced. It is a means to an end. But it subordinates all ends until it itself becomes an end in itself and truly absurd. This is recapitulated in art in that the intrigues, plots, and developments, as well as the depravity and crime of detective novels, absorb all interest. By contrast, the conclusions to which they lead sink to the level of the stereotypical. Thus real industry, which by its own definition is only a for-something, contradicts its own definition and becomes silly in itself and ridiculous for the artist. Through the form of his finales, Haydn, one of the greatest composers, showed the futility of the dynamics by which they are objectivated, and did so in a way that became paradigmatical for art; this is the locus of whatever may justly be called humor in Beethoven. However, the more intrigue and dynamics become ends in themselves—intrigue already reached the level of thematic frenzy in *Les liaisons dangereuses*—the more comic do they become in art as well; and the more does the affect associated subjectively with this dynamic effectively become rage over the lost penny: It becomes the element of indifference in individuation. The dynamic principle, by means of which art was long and insistently justified in hoping for homeostasis between the universal and the particular, is rejected. Even its magic is shorn away by the sense for form; it begins to seem inept. This experience can be traced back to the middle of the nineteenth century. Baudelaire, the apologist of form no less than the poet of the *vie moderne*, expressed this in the dedication of *Le spleen de Paris* when he wrote that he can break off where he pleases, and so may the reader, "for I have not strung his wayward will to the endless thread of some unnecessary plot."[11] What was organized by nominalistic art by means of development is stigmatized as superfluous once the intention of its function is recognized, and this becomes an irritant. With this comment, the chief figure of the whole of *l'art pour l'art* effectively capitulates: His *dégoût* extends to the dynamic principle that engenders the work as autonomous in itself. Since that moment the law of all art has been its antilaw. Just as for the bourgeois nominalistic artwork the necessity of a static form decayed, here it is the aesthetic dynamic that decays in accord with the experience first formulated by Kürnberger but flashing up in each line and stanza of Baudelaire, that life no longer exists. This has not changed in the situation in which contemporary art finds itself. Art's processual character has been overtaken by the critique of semblance, and not merely as the critique of aesthetic universality but rather as that of progress in the midst of what is ever-the-same. Process has been unmasked as repetition and has thus become an embarrassment to art. Enciphered in modern art is the postulate of an art that no longer conforms to the disjunction of the static and dynamic. Beckett, indifferent to the ruling cliché of development, views his task as that of moving in an infinitely small space toward what is effectively a dimensionless point. This aesthetic principle of construction, as the principle of *Il faut continuer*, goes beyond stasis; and it goes beyond the dynamic in that it is at the same time a principle of treading water and, as such, a confession of the uselessness of the dynamic. In keeping with this, all constructivistic techniques tend toward stasis. The telos of the dynamic of the ever-same is disaster; Beckett's writings look this in the eye. Consciousness recognizes the limitedness of limitless self-sufficient progress as an illusion of the absolute subject, and social labor aesthetically mocks bourgeois pathos once the superfluity of real labor came into reach. The dynamic in artworks is brought to a halt by the hope of the abolition of labor and the threat of a glacial death; both are registered in the dynamic, which is unable to choose on its own. The potential of freedom manifest in it is at the same time denied by the social order, and therefore it is not substantial in art either.

That explains the ambivalence of aesthetic construction. Construction is equally able to codify the resignation of the weakened subject and to make absolute alienation the sole concern of art—which once wanted the opposite—as it is able to anticipate a reconciled condition that would itself be situated beyond static and dynamic. The many interrelations with technocracy give reason to suspect that the principle of construction remains aesthetically obedient to the administered world; but it may terminate in a yet unknown aesthetic form, whose rational organization might point to the abolition of all categories of administration along with their reflexes in art.

Notes

1 [August Halm (1869–1929), the musicologist and author of *Harmonielehre* (1905) and essays collected in *Von Form und Sinn der Musik* (1978).—trans.]

2 [See Adorno et al., *The Authoritarian Personality* (New York, 1982), pp. 275ff.—trans.]

3 See Walter Benjamin, *The Correspondence of Walter Benjamin 1910–1940*, ed. Gershom Scholem and T. W. Adorno, trans. Manfred Jacobson and Evelyn Jacobson (Chicago, 1994), p. 80.

4 See Adorno, *Minima Moralia*, trans. E. F. N. Jephcott (London, 1974), pp. 206ff.

5 See Kurt Mautz, "Die Farbensprache der expressionistischen Lyrik," in *Deutsche Vierteljahrsschrift für Literaturwissenschaft und Geistesgeschichte*, vol. 31 (1957), pp. 198ff. [See also Wassily Kandinsky, *Concerning the Spiritual in Art*, trans. M. T. H. Sadler (New York, 1946).—trans.]

6 [Adorno is quoting from his "Die Kunst und die Künste," in *Ohne Leitbild, Gesammelte Schriften*, vol. 10.1 (Frankfurt, 1977).—trans.]

7 See Arnold Schoenberg, "Problems in Teaching Art," in *Style and Idea*, ed. Leonard Stein, trans. Leo Black (Berkeley, 1975), pp. 365–368.

8 See Walter Benjamin, *Schriften*, ed. T. W. Adorno and G. Adorno, vol. 1 (Frankfurt, 1955), p. 421. [The "blue flower" is the "blaue Blume" of Novalis's *Heinrich von Ofterdingen*, which became a symbol of romantic longing.—trans.]

9 [A punning abbreviation of "Avenue of the Elector" to "Avenue of the Cows".—trans.]

10 [Schoenberg's own description of his technique in "Composition with Twelve Tones," in *Style and Idea*, pp. 214–245.—trans.]

11 Charles Baudelaire, "To Arsène Houssaye," in *The Poems in Prose*, trans. F. Scarfe (London, 1989), p. 25.

12
Society

Prior to the emancipation of the subject, art was undoubtedly in a certain sense more immediately social than it was afterward. Its autonomy, its growing independence from society, was a function of the bourgeois consciousness of freedom that was itself bound up with the social structure. Prior to the emergence of this consciousness, art certainly stood in opposition to social domination and its *mores*, but not with an awareness of its own independence. There had been conflicts between art and society desultorily ever since art was condemned in Plato's state, but the idea of a fundamentally oppositional art was inconceivable, and social controls worked much more immediately than in the bourgeois era until the rise of totalitarian states. On the other hand, the bourgeoisie integrated art much more completely than any previous society had. Under the pressure of an intensifying nominalism, the ever present yet latent social character of art was made increasingly manifest; this social character is incomparably more evident in the novel than it was in the highly stylized and remote epics of chivalry. The influx of experiences that are no longer forced into a priori genres, the requirement of constituting form out of these experiences, that is, from below: This is "realistic" in purely aesthetic terms, regardless of content [*Inhalt*]. No longer sublimated by the principle of stylization, the relation of content to the society from which it derives at first becomes much less refracted, and this is not only the case in literature. The so-called lower genres too held their distance from society, even when, like Attic comedy, they made bourgeois relations and the events of daily life thematic; the flight into no-man's-land is not just one of Aristophanes' antics but rather an essential element of his form. If, in one regard, as a product of the social labor of spirit, art is always implicitly a *fait social*, in becoming bourgeois art its social aspect was made explicit. The object of bourgeois art is the relation of itself as artifact to empirical society; Don Quixote stands at the beginning of this development. Art, however, is social not only because of its mode of production, in which the dialectic of the forces and relations of production is concentrated, nor simply because of the social derivation of its thematic material. Much more importantly, art becomes social by its opposition to society, and it occupies this position only as autonomous art. By crystallizing in itself as something unique to itself, rather than complying with existing social norms and qualifying as "socially useful," it criticizes society by merely existing, for which puritans of all stripes condemn it. There is nothing pure, nothing structured strictly according to its own immanent law, that does not implicitly criticize the debasement of a situation evolving in the direction of a total exchange society in which everything is heteronomously defined. Art's asociality is the determinate negation of a determinate society. Certainly through its refusal of society, which is equivalent to sublimation through the law of form, autonomous art makes itself a vehicle of ideology: The society at which it shudders is left in the distance, undisturbed. Yet this is more than ideology: Society is not only the negativity that the aesthetic law of form condemns but also, even in its most objectionable shape, the quintessence of self-producing and self-reproducing human life. Art was no more able to dispense with this element than with critique until that moment when the social process revealed itself as one of self-annihilation; and it is not in the power of art, which does not make judgments, to separate these two elements intentionally. A pure productive force such as that of the aesthetic, once freed from heteronomous control, is objectively the counterimage of enchained forces, but it is also the paradigm of fateful, self-interested doings. Art keeps itself alive through its social force of resistance; unless it reifies itself, it becomes a commodity. Its contribution to society is not communication with it but rather something extremely mediated: It is resistance in which, by virtue of inner-aesthetic development, social development is reproduced without being imitated. At the risk of its self-alienation, radical modernity preserves art's immanence by admitting society only in an obscured form, as in the dreams with which artworks have always been compared. Nothing social in art is immediately social, not even when this is its aim. Not long ago even the socially committed Brecht found that to give his political position artistic expression it was necessary to distance himself precisely from that social reality at which his works took aim. Jesuitical machinations were needed sufficiently to camouflage what he wrote as socialist realism to escape the inquisition. Music betrays all art. Just as in music society, its movement, and its contradictions appear only in shadowy fashion—speaking out of it, indeed, yet in need of identification—so it is with all other arts. Whenever art seems to copy society, it becomes all the more an "as-if." For opposite reasons, Brecht's China in the *Good Woman of Setzuan* is no less stylized than Schiller's Messina in *The Bride of Messina*. All moral judgments on the characters in novels or plays have been senseless even when these judgments have justly taken the empirical figures back of the work as their targets; discussions about whether a positive hero can have negative traits are as foolish as they sound to anyone who overhears them from so much as the slightest remove. Form works like a magnet that orders elements of the empirical world in such a fashion that they are estranged from their extra-aesthetic existence, and it is only as a result of this estrangement that they master the extra-aesthetic essence. Conversely, by exploiting these elements the culture industry all the more successfully joins slavish respect for empirical detail, the gapless semblance of photographic fidelity, with ideological manipulation. What is social in art is its immanent movement against society, not its manifest opinions. Its historical gesture repels empirical reality, of which artworks are nevertheless part in that they are things. Insofar as a social function can be predicated for artworks, it is their functionlessness. Through their difference from a bewitched reality, they embody negatively a position in which what is would find its rightful place, its own. Their enchantment is disenchantment. Their social essence requires a double reflection on their being-for-themselves and on their relations to society. Their double character is manifest at every point; they change and contradict themselves. It was plausible that socially progressive critics should have accused the program of *l'art pour l'art*, which has often been in league with political reaction, of promoting a fetish with the concept of a pure, exclusively self-sufficient artwork. What is true in this accusation is that artworks, products of social labor that are subject to or produce their own law of form, seal themselves off from what they themselves are. To this extent, each artwork could be charged with false consciousness and chalked up to ideology. In formal terms, independent of what they say, they are ideology in that a priori they posit something spiritual as being independent from the conditions of its material production and therefore as being intrinsically superior and beyond the primordial guilt of the separation of physical and spiritual labor. What is exalted on the basis of this guilt is at the same time debased by it. This is why artworks with truth content do not blend seamlessly with the concept of art; *l'art pour l'art* theorists, like Valéry, have pointed this out. But the guilt they bear of fetishism does not disqualify art, any more so than it disqualifies anything culpable; for in the universally, socially mediated world nothing stands external to its nexus of guilt. The truth content of artworks, which is indeed their social truth, is predicated on their fetish character. The principle of heteronomy, apparently the counterpart of fetishism, is the principle of exchange, and in it domination is masked. Only what does not submit to that principle acts as the plenipotentiary of what is free from domination; only what is useless can stand in for the stunted use value. Artworks are plenipotentiaries of things that are no longer distorted by exchange, profit, and the false needs of a degraded humanity. In the context of total semblance, art's semblance of being-in-itself is the mask of truth. Marx's scorn of the pittance Milton received for *Paradise Lost*, a work that did not appear to the market as socially useful labor,[1] is, as a denunciation of useful labor, the strongest defense of art against its bourgeois functionalization, which is perpetuated in art's undialectical social condemnation. A liberated society would be beyond the irrationality of its *faux frais* and beyond the ends-means-rationality of utility. This is enciphered in art and is the source of art's social explosiveness. Although the magic fetishes are one of the historical roots of art, a fetishistic element remains admixed in artworks, an element that goes beyond commodity fetishism. Artworks can neither exclude nor deny this; even socially the emphatic element of semblance in artworks is, as a corrective, the organon of truth. Artworks that do not insist fetishistically on their coherence, as if they were the absolute that they are unable to be, are worthless from the start; but the survival of art becomes precarious as soon as it becomes conscious of its fetishism and, as has been the case since the middle of the nineteenth century, insists obstinately on it. Art cannot advocate delusion by insisting that otherwise art would not exist. This forces art into an aporia. All that succeeds in going even minutely beyond it is insight into the rationality of its irrationality. Artworks that want to divest themselves of fetishism by real and extremely dubious political commitment regularly enmesh themselves in false consciousness as the result of inevitable and vainly praised simplification. In the shortsighted praxis to which they blindly subscribe, their own blindness is prolonged.

The objectivation of art, which is what society from its external perspective takes to be art's fetishism, is itself social in that it is the product of the division of labor. That is why the relation of art to society is not to be sought primarily in the sphere of reception. This relation is anterior to reception, in production. Interest in the social decipherment of art must orient itself to production rather than being content with the study and classification of effects that for social reasons often totally diverge from the artworks and their objective social content. Since time immemorial, human reactions to artworks have been mediated to their utmost and do not refer immediately to the object; indeed, they are now mediated by society as a whole. The study of social effect neither comes close to understanding what is social in art nor is it in any position to dictate norms for art, as it is inclined to do by positivist spirit. The heteronomy, which reception theory's normative interpretation of phenomena foists on art, is an ideological fetter that exceeds everything ideological that may be inherent in art's fetishization. Art and society converge in the artwork's content [*Gehalt*], not in anything external to it. This applies also to the history of art. Collectivization of the individual takes place at the cost of the social force of production. In the history of art, real history returns by virtue of the life of the productive force that originates in real history and is then separated from it. This is the basis of art's recollection of transience. Art preserves it and makes it present by transforming it: This is the social explanation of its temporal nucleus. Abstaining from praxis, art becomes the schema of social praxis: Every authentic artwork is internally revolutionary. However, whereas society reaches into art and disappears there by means of the identity of forces and relations, even the most advanced art has, conversely, the tendency toward social integration. Yet contrary to the cliché that touts the virtues of progress, this integration does not bring the blessings of justice in the form of retrospective confirmation. More often, reception wears away what constitutes the work's determinate negation of society. Works are usually critical in the era in which they appear; later they are neutralized, not least because of changed social relations. Neutralization is the social price of aesthetic autonomy. However, once artworks are entombed in the pantheon of cultural commodities, they themselves —their truth content—are also damaged. In the administered world neutralization is universal. Surrealism began as a protest against the fetishization of art as an isolated realm, yet as art, which after all surrealism also was, it was forced beyond the pure form of protest. Painters for whom the quality of *peinture* was not an issue, as it was for André Masson, struck a balance between scandal and social reception. Ultimately, Salvador Dalí became an exalted society painter, the Laszlo or Van Dongen of a generation that liked to think of itself as being *sophisticated* on the basis of a vague sense of a crisis that had in any case been stabilized for decades. Thus the false afterlife of surrealism was established. Modern tendencies, in which irrupting shock-laden contents [*Inhalte*] demolish the law of form, are predestined to make peace with the world, which gives a cozy reception to unsublimated material as soon as the thorn is removed. In the age of total neutralization, false reconciliation has of course also paved the way in the sphere of radically abstract art: Nonrepresentational art is suitable for decorating the walls of the newly prosperous. It is uncertain whether that also diminishes the immanent quality of artworks; the excitement with which reactionaries emphasize this danger speaks against its reality. It would be truly idealistic to locate the relation of art and society exclusively as mediated in problems of social structure. Art's double character—its autonomy and *fait social*—is expressed ever and again in the palpable dependencies and conflicts between the two spheres. Frequently there are direct socioeconomic interventions in artistic production, a contemporary instance of which is the long-term contracts between painters and art merchants who favor what is called work with a "personal touch," or more bluntly, a gimmick. That German expressionism vanished so quickly may have its artistic reasons in the conflict between the idea of an artwork, which remained its goal, and the specific idea of the absolute scream. Expressionist works could not totally succeed without betraying themselves. Also important was that the genre became politically obsolete as its revolutionary impetus went unrealized and the Soviet Union began to prosecute radical art. Nor should it be concealed that the authors of that movement, which went unreceived until forty or fifty years later, had to make a living and were compelled, as Americans say, *to go commercial*; this could be demonstrated in the case of most German expressionist writers who survived World War I. What is sociologically to be learned from the fate of the expressionists is the primacy of the bourgeois profession over the need for expression that inspired the expressionists in however naïve and diluted a fashion. In bourgeois society artists, like all who are intellectually productive, are compelled to keep at it once they have taken on the trade name of artist. Superannuated expressionists not unwillingly chose marketably promising themes. The lack of any immanent necessity for production, coupled with the concurrent economic compulsion to continue, is apparent in the product as its objective insignificance.

Among the mediations of art and society the thematic, the open or covert treatment of social matters, is the most superficial and deceptive.

The claim that the sculpture of a coal miner a priori says more, socially, than a sculpture without proletarian hero, is by now echoed only where art is used for the purpose of "forming opinion," in the wooden language of the peoples' democracies of the Eastern bloc, and is subordinated to empirical aims, mostly as a means for improving production. Emile Meuniers' idealized coal miner and his realism dovetail with a bourgeois ideology that dealt with the then still visible proletariat by certifying that it too was beautiful humanity and noble nature. Even unvarnished naturalism is often of a part with a deformed bourgeois character structure, a suppressed—in psychoanalytic terms, anal—pleasure. It feeds on the suffering and decay it scourges; like *Blut-und-Boden* authors, Zola glorified fertility and employed anti-Semitic clichés. On the thematic level, in the language of indictment, no boundary can be drawn between aggressiveness and conformism. An agitprop chorus of the unemployed with the performance directive that it be performed in an "ugly" fashion, may have functioned around 1930 as a certificate of correct political opinion, though it hardly ever testified to progressive consciousness; but it was always uncertain if the artistic stance of growling and raw technique really denounced such things or identified with them. Real denunciation is probably only a capacity of form, which is overlooked by a social aesthetic that believes in themes. What is socially decisive in artworks is the content [*Inhalt*] that becomes eloquent through the work's formal structures. Kafka, in whose work monopoly capitalism appears only distantly, codifies in the dregs of the administered world what becomes of people under the total social spell more faithfully and powerfully than do any novels about corrupt industrial trusts. The thesis that form is the locus of social content [*Gehalt*] can be concretely shown in Kafka's language. Its objectivity, its Kleistian quality has often been remarked upon, and readers who measure up to Kafka have recognized the contradiction between that objectivity and events that become remote through the imaginary character of so sober a presentation. However, this contrast becomes productive not only because the quasi-realistic description brings the impossible menacingly close. At the same time this critique of the realistic lineaments of Kafka's form, a critique that to socially committed ears seems all too artistic, has its social aspect. Kafka is made acceptable by many of these realistic lineaments as an ideal of order, possibly of a simple life and modest activity in one's assigned station, an ideal that is itself a mask of social repression. The linguistic habitus of "the world is as it is" is the medium through which the social spell becomes aesthetic appearance. Kafka wisely guards against naming it, as if otherwise the spell would be broken whose insurmountable omnipresence defines the arena of Kafka's work and which, as its apriori, cannot become thematic. His language is the instrument of that configuration of positivism and myth that has only now become obvious socially. Reified consciousness, which presupposes and confirms the inevitability and immutableness of what exists, is—as the heritage of the ancient spell—the new form of the myth of the ever-same. Kafka's epic style is, in its archaism, mimesis of reification. Whereas his work must renounce any claim to transcending myth, it makes the social web of delusion knowable in myth through the *how*, through language. In his writing, absurdity is as self-evident as it has actually become in society. Those products are socially mute that do their duty by regurgitating *tel quel* whatever social material they treat and count this metabolic exchange with second nature as the glory of art as social reflection. The artistic subject is inherently social, not private. In no case does it become social through forced collectivization or the choice of subject matter. In the age of repressive collectivization, art has the power to resist the compact majority—a resistance that has become a criterion of the work and its social truth—in the lonely and exposed producer of art, while at the same time this does not exclude collective forms of production such as the composers' workshop that Schoenberg envisioned. By constantly admitting into the production of his work an element of negativity toward his own immediacy, the artist unconsciously obeys a social universal: In every successfully realized correction, watching over the artist's shoulder is a collective subject that has yet to be realized. The categories of artistic objectivity are unitary with social emancipation when the object, on the basis of its own impulse, liberates itself from social convention and controls. Yet artworks cannot be satisfied with vague and abstract universality such as that of classicism. Rather, they are predicated on fissuredness and thus on the concrete historical situation. Their social truth depends on their opening themselves to this content. The content becomes their subject, to which they mold themselves, to the same extent that their law of form does not obscure the fissure but rather, in demanding that it be shaped, makes it its own concern.——However profound and still largely obscure the part of science has been in the development of artistic forces of production, and however deeply, precisely through methods learned from science, society reaches into art, just so little is artistic production scientific, even when it is a work of integral constructivism. In art, all scientific discoveries lose their literal character: This is evident in the modification of optical-perspectival laws in painting and in the natural overtone relations in music. When art, intimidated by technique, tries to conserve its miniature terrain by proclaiming its transformation into science, it misconceives the status of the sciences in empirical reality. On the other hand, the aesthetic principle is not to be played out as sacrosanct—as would suit irrationalism—in opposition to the sciences. Art is not an arbitrary cultural complement to science but, rather, stands in critical tension to it. When, for instance, the cultural and human sciences are rightly accused of a lack of spirit, this is almost always at the same time a lack of aesthetic discernment. It is not without reason that the certified sciences demand furiously to be left in peace whenever art, whatever they attribute to it, intervenes in their sphere; that someone can write is cause for suspicion on scientific grounds. Crudeness of thinking is the incapacity to differentiate within a topic, and differentiation is an aesthetic category as much as one of understanding. Science and art are not to be fused, but the categories that are valid in each are not absolutely different. Conformist consciousness prefers the opposite, partly because it is incapable of distinguishing the two and partly because it refuses the insight that identical forces are active in nonidentical spheres. The same holds true with regard to morality. Brutality toward things is potentially brutality toward people. The raw —the subjective nucleus of evil—is a priori negated by art, from which the ideal of being fully formed is indispensable: This, and not the pronouncement of moral theses or the striving after moral effects, is art's participation in the moral and makes it part of a more humanly worthy society.

Social struggles and the relations of classes are imprinted in the structure of artworks; by contrast, the political positions deliberately adopted by artworks are epiphenomena and usually impinge on the elaboration of works and thus, ultimately, on their social truth content. Political opinions count for little. It is possible to argue over how much Attic tragedy, including those by Euripides, took part in the violent social conflicts of the epoch; however, the basic tendency of tragic form, in contrast to its mythical subjects, the dissolution of the spell of fate and the birth of subjectivity, bears witness as much to social emancipation from feudal-familial ties as, in the collision between mythical law and subjectivity, to the antagonism between fateful domination and a humanity awakening to maturity. That this antagonism, as well as the historicophilosophical tendency, became an apriori of form rather than being treated simply as thematic material, endowed tragedy with its social substantiality: Society appears in it all the more authentically the less it is the intended object.

Real partisanship, which is the virtue of artworks no less than of men and women, resides in the depths, where the social antinomies become the dialectic of forms: By leading them to language through the synthesis of the work, artists do their part socially; even Lukács in his last years found himself compelled toward such considerations. Figuration, which articulates the wordless and mute contradictions, thereby has the lineaments of a praxis that is not simply flight from real praxis; figuration fulfills the concept of art itself as a comportment. It is a form of praxis and need not apologize that it does not act directly, which it could not do even if it wanted to; the political effect even of so-called committed art is highly uncertain. The social standpoint of artists may serve to interfere with conformist consciousness, but in the actual development of works they become insignificant. That he expressed abominable views when Voltaire died says nothing about the truth content of Mozart's works. At the actual time when artworks appear there is certainly no abstracting from their intention; whoever would attempt an assessment of Brecht exclusively on the basis of the artistic merit of his works would fail him no less than one who judges his meaning according to his theses. The immanence of society in the artwork is the essential social relation of art, not the immanence of art in society. Because the social content of art is not located externally to its *principium individuationis* but rather inheres in individuation, which is itself a social reality, art's social character is concealed and can only be grasped by its interpretation.

Yet even in artworks that are to their very core ideological, truth content can assert itself. Ideology, socially necessary semblance, is by this same necessity also the distorted image of the true. A threshold that divides the social consciousness of aesthetics from the philistine is that aesthetics reflects the social critique of the ideological in artworks, rather than mechanically reiterating it. Stifter provides a model of the truth content of an oeuvre that is undoubtedly ideological in its intentions. Not only the conservative-restorative choice of thematic material and the *fabula docet* are ideological, but so is the objectivistic deportment of the form, which suggests a micrologically tender world, a meaningfully correct life that lends itself to narration. This is why Stifter became the idol of a retrospectively noble bourgeoisie. Yet the layers of his work that once provided him with his half-esoteric popularity have with time peeled away and vanished. This, however, is not the last word on Stifter, for the reconciling, conciliatory aspects, especially in his last works, are exaggerated. Here objectivity hardens into a mask and the life evoked becomes a defensive ritual. Shimmering through the eccentricity of the average is the secret and denied suffering of the alienated subject and an unreconciled life. The light that falls over his mature prose is drained and bleak, as if it were allergic to the happiness of color; it is, as it were, reduced to a pencil sketch by the exclusion of everything unruly and disturbing to a social reality that was as incompatible with the mentality of the poet as with the epic apriori that he took from Goethe and clung to. What transpires, in opposition to the will of his prose, through the discrepancy between its form and the already capitalist society devolves upon its expression; ideological exaggeration endows his work mediately with its nonideological truth content, with its superiority over all consoling, assiduously pastoral literature, and it won for it that authentic quality that Nietzsche admired. Stifter is the paradigm of how little poetic intention, even that meaning that is directly embodied or represented in an artwork, approximates its objective content; in his work the content is truly the negation of the meaning, yet this content would not exist if the meaning were not intended by the work and then canceled and transformed by the work's own complexion. Affirmation becomes the cipher of despair and the purest negativity of content contains, as in Stifter, a grain of affirmation. The iridescence that emanates from artworks, which today taboo all affirmation, is the appearance of the affirmative *ineffabile*, the emergence of the nonexisting as if it did exist. Its claim to existence flickers out in aesthetic semblance; yet what does not exist, by appearing, is promised. The constellation of the existing and nonexisting is the utopic figure of art. Although it is compelled toward absolute negativity, it is precisely by virtue of this negativity that it is not absolutely negative. By no means do artworks primarily develop this inwardly antinomial affirmative element as a result of their external attitude to what exists, that is, to society; rather, it develops immanently in them and immerses them in twilight. No beauty today can evade the question whether it is actually beautiful and not instead surreptitiously acquired by static affirmation. The antipathy toward applied arts is, indirectly, the bad conscience of art as a whole, which makes itself felt at the sound of every musical chord and at the sight of every color. There is no need for social criticism of art to investigate this externally: It emerges from the inner-aesthetic formations themselves. The heightened sensitivity of the aesthetic sensorium converges asymptotically with the socially motivated irritability toward art.——In art, ideology and truth cannot be neatly distinguished from each other. Art cannot have one without the other, and this reciprocity in turn is an enticement toward the ideological

305

misuse of art as much as it is an enticement toward summarily finishing it off. It is only a step from the utopia of the self-likeness of artworks to the stink of the heavenly roses that art scatters here below as do the women in Schiller's tirade. The more brazenly society is transformed into a totality in which it assigns everything, including art, to its place, the more completely does art polarize into ideology and protest; and this polarization is hardly to art's advantage. Absolute protest constrains it and carries over to its own raison d'être; ideology thins out to an impoverished and authoritarian copy of reality.

In the culture resurrected after the catastrophe, art—regardless of its content and substance [*Inhalt* and *Gehalt*]—has even taken on an ideo-logical aspect by its mere existence. In its disproportion to the horror that has transpired and threatens, it is condemned to cynicism; even where it directly faces the horror, it diverts attention from it. Its objectivation implies insensitivity to reality. This degrades art to an accomplice of the barbarism to which it succumbs no less when it renounces objectivation and directly plays along, even when this takes the form of polemical commitment. Every artwork today, the radical ones included, has its conservative aspect; its existence helps to secure the spheres of spirit and culture, whose real powerlessness and complicity with the principle of disaster becomes plainly evident. But this conservative element—which, contrary to the trend toward social integration, is stronger in advanced works than in the more moderate ones—does not simply deserve oblivion. Only insofar as spirit, in its most advanced form, survives and perseveres is any opposition to the total domination of the social totality possible. A humanity to which progressive spirit fails to bequeath what humanity is poised to liquidate would disappear in a barbarism that a reasonable social order should prevent. Art, even as something tolerated in the administered world, embodies what does not allow itself to be managed and what total management suppresses. Greece's new tyrants knew why they banned Beckett's plays, in which there is not a single political word. Asociality becomes the social legitimation of art. For the sake of reconciliation, authentic works must blot out every trace of reconciliation in memory. All the same, the unity that even dissociative works do not escape is not without a trace of the old reconciliation. Artworks are, a priori, socially culpable, and each one that deserves its name seeks to expiate this guilt. Their possibility of surviving requires that their straining toward synthesis develop in the form of their irreconcilability. Without the synthesis, which confronts reality as the autonomous artwork, there would be nothing external to reality's spell; the principle of the isolation of spirit, which casts a spell around itself, is also the principle that breaks through the spell by making it determinate.

That the nominalistic tendency of art toward the destruction of all preestablished categories of order has social implications is evident in the enemies of modern art, right up to Emil Staiger. Their sympathy for what they call a *Leitbild*, a guiding principle, is precisely their sympathy for social, particularly sexual, repression. The bond between a socially reactionary posture and hatred for the artistically modern, which the analysis of the obedient character makes apparent, is documented by new and old fascist propaganda, and it is also confirmed by empirical social research.[2] The rage against the purported destruction of sacrosanct cultural goods, which for that reason alone can no longer be experienced as such, serves to mask the real destructive wishes of the indignant. For the ruling consciousness, any consciousness that would have the world other than it is always seems chaotic because it deviates from a petrified reality. Inevitably those who rail loudest against the anarchy of modern art, which for the most part hardly exists, convince themselves of what they presume to be the nature of their enemy on the basis of crude errors at the simplest level of information; indeed, there is no responding to them, because what they have decided in advance to reject they are not willing to experience in the first place. In this the division of labor incontestably bears part of the blame. The non-specialist will no more understand the most recent developments in nuclear physics than the lay person will straightaway grasp extremely complex new music or painting. Whereas, however, the incomprehensibility of physics is accepted on the assumption that in principle its rationality can be followed and its theorems understood by anyone, modern art's incomprehensibility is branded as schizoid arbitrariness, even though the aesthetically incomprehensible gives way to experience no less than does the scientifically obscure. If art is capable of realizing its humane universality at all, then it is exclusively by means of the rigorous division of labor: Anything else is false consciousness. Works of quality, those that are fully formed in themselves, are objectively less chaotic than innumerable works that have orderly facades somehow slapped on while underneath their own structure crumbles. Few are disturbed by this. Deep down and contrary to its better judgment, the bourgeois character tends to cling to what is inferior; it is fundamental to ideology that it is never fully believed and that it advances from self-disdain to self-destruction. The semi-educated consciousness insists on the

"I like that," laughing with cynical embarrassment at the fact that cultural trash is expressly made to dupe the consumer: As a leisure-time occupation, art should be cozy and discretionary; people put up with the deception because they sense secretly that the principle of their own sane realism is the fraud of equal exchange. It is within this false and at the same time art-alien consciousness that the fictional element of art, its illusoriness, develops in bourgeois society: *Mundus vult decipi* is the categorical imperative of artistic consumption. This taints all supposedly naïve artistic experience, and to this extent it is not naïve. The dominant consciousness is objectively led to this dank attitude because the administered must renounce the possibility of maturity, including aesthetic maturity, that is postulated by the order that they cling to as their own and at any price. The critical concept of society, which inheres in authentic artworks without needing to be added to them, is incompatible with what society must think of itself if it is to continue as it is; the ruling consciousness cannot free itself from its own ideology without endangering society's self-preservation. This confers social relevance on apparently derivative aesthetic controversies.

That society "appears" in artworks with polemical truth as well as ideologically, is conducive to historicophilosophical mystification. Speculation all too easily falls prey to the idea of a harmony between society and artworks that has been preestablished by the world spirit. But theory must not capitulate to that relationship. The process that transpires in artworks and is brought to a standstill in them, is to be conceived as the same social process in which the artworks are embedded; according to Leibniz's formulation, they represent this process windowlessly. The elements of an artwork acquire their configuration as a whole in obedience to immanent laws that are related to those of the society external to it. Social forces of production, as well as relations of production, return in artworks as mere forms divested of their facticity because artistic labor is social labor; moreover, they are always the product of this labor. In artworks, the forces of production are not in-themselves different from social productive forces except by their constitutive absenting from real society. Scarcely anything is done or produced in artworks that does not have its model, however latently, in social production. The binding force of artworks, beyond the jurisdiction of their immanence, originates in this affinity. If artworks are in fact absolute commodities in that they are a social product that has rejected every semblance of existing for society, a semblance to which

commodities otherwise urgently cling, the determining relation of production, the commodity form, enters the artwork equally with the social force
of production and the antagonism between the two. The absolute commodity would be free of the ideology inherent in the commodity form,
which pretends to exist for-another, whereas ironically it is something
merely for-itself: It exists for those who hold power. This reversal of
ideology into truth is a reversal of aesthetic content, and not immediately
a reversal of the attitude of art to society. Even the absolute commodity
remains salable and has become a "natural monopoly." That artworks are
offered for sale at the market—just as pots and statuettes once were—is not
their misuse but rather the simple consequence of their participation in the
relations of production. Thoroughly nonideological art is indeed probably
completely impossible. Its mere antithesis to empirical reality does not
suffice to make it so; Sartre[3] rightly accented that the principle of *l'art pour
l'art*, which has prevailed in France since Baudelaire, just as in Germany
the aesthetic ideal of art prevailed as an institution of moral reform, was
taken up by the bourgeoisie as a means for the neutralization of art with
the same willingness with which in Germany art was appropriated as a
costumed ally of social control and order. What is ideological in the
principle of *l'art pour l'art* does not have its locus in the energetic antithesis
of art to the empirical world but rather in the abstractness and facile
character of this antithesis. The idea of beauty advocated by *l'art pour l'art*,
at least as it has developed since Baudelaire, was not to be classical
formalism, yet it did indeed exclude all content [*Inhalt*] as disruptive that
did not, before undergoing the law of form and thus precisely anti-
artistically, submit to a dogmatic canon of beauty: It is in this spirit that
George in a letter excoriates Hofmannsthal for having allowed the painter
in the *Death of Titian* to die of the plague.[4] *L'art pour l'art*'s concept of beauty
becomes at once strangely empty and imprisoned by thematic material, a
sort of *Jugendstil* arrangement as revealed in Ibsen's formulaic descriptions
of vine leaves entwined in locks of hair and of dying in beauty. Beauty,
powerless to define itself and only able to gain its definition by way of its
other, a sort of aerial root, becomes entangled in the fate of artificial
ornamentation. This idea of beauty is limited because it sets itself up as
directly antithetical to a society rejected as ugly rather than, as Baudelaire
and Rimbaud did, extracting this antithesis from the content [*Inhalt*]
—from the imagery of Paris, in Baudelaire's instance—and putting it to the
test: Only in this fashion could sheer distance become the intervention of
determinate negation. It is precisely the autarchy of neoromantic and

symbolist beauty, its timidity vis-à-vis those social elements in which form exclusively becomes form, that accounts for its rapid transformation into something so easily consumable. This beauty deceives about the commodity world by setting it aside; this qualifies it as a commodity. Their latent commodity form has inner-artistically condemned the works of *l'art pour l'art* to kitsch, as which they are today ridiculed. In Rimbaud it would be possible to show that bitterly sarcastic opposition to society cohabits uncritically with a submissiveness comparable to Rilke's rapture over cabaret songs and the fragrance of an old chest; ultimately it was affirmation that triumphed, and the principle of *l'art pour l'art* was not to be saved. It is for this reason that socially the situation of art is today aporetic. If art cedes its autonomy, it delivers itself over to the machinations of the status quo; if art remains strictly for-itself, it nonetheless submits to integration as one harmless domain among others. The social totality appears in this aporia, swallowing whole whatever occurs. That works renounce communication is a necessary yet by no means sufficient condition of their unideological essence. The central criterion is the force of expression, through the tension of which artworks become eloquent with wordless gesture. In expression they reveal themselves as the wounds of society; expression is the social ferment of their autonomous form. The principal witness for this is Picasso's *Guernica* that, strictly incompatible with prescribed realism, precisely by means of inhumane construction, achieves a level of expression that sharpens it to social protest beyond all contemplative misunderstanding. The socially critical zones of artworks are those where it hurts; where in their expression, historically determined, the untruth of the social situation comes to light. It is actually this against which the rage at art reacts.

Artworks are able to appropriate their heterogeneous element, their entwinement with society, because they are themselves always at the same time something social. Nevertheless, art's autonomy, wrested painfully from society as well as socially derived in itself, has the potential of reversing into heteronomy; everything new is weaker than the accumulated ever-same, and it is ready to regress back into it. The *We* encapsuled in the objectivation of works is not radically other than the external *We*, however frequently it is the residue of a real *We* that is past. That is why collective appeal is not simply the original sin of artworks; rather, something in their law of form implies it. It is not out of obsession with politics that great Greek philosophy accorded aesthetic effect so much more weight than its objective tenor would imply. Ever since art has come within the purview of theoretical reflection, the latter has been tempted—by raising itself above art—to sink beneath art and surrender it to power relations. What is today called situating a work involves exiting from the aesthetic sphere; the cheap sovereignty that assigns art its social position, after dismissing its immanence of form as a vain and naïve self-delusion, tends to treat the work as if it were nothing but what its social function condemns it to. The good and bad marks Plato distributed to art according to whether or not it conformed to the military virtues of the community he confused with utopia, his totalitarian rancor against real or spitefully invented decadence, even his aversion to the lies of poets, which are after all nothing but art's semblance character, which Plato hoped to summon to the support of the status quo—all this taints the concept of art in the same moment in which it was first consciously reflected upon. The purging of the affects in Aristotle's *Poetics* no longer makes equally frank admission of its devotion to ruling interests, yet it supports them all the same in that his ideal of sublimation entrusts art with the task of providing aesthetic semblance as a substitute satisfaction for the bodily satisfaction of the targeted public's instincts and needs: Catharsis is a purging action directed against the affects and an ally of repression. Aristotelian catharsis is part of a superannuated mythology of art and inadequate to the actual effects of art. In return, artworks have realized in themselves, by spiritualization, what the Greeks projected on their external effect: They are, in the process they carry out between the law of form and their material content, their own catharsis. Sublimation, even aesthetic sublimation, incontestably participates in civilatory progress and even in inner-artistic progress itself, but it also has its ideological side: Art, as a surrogate satisfaction, by virtue of the fact that it is spurious, robs sublimation of the dignity for which the whole of classicism made propaganda, a classicism that survived for more than two thousand years under the protection of Aristotle's authority. The doctrine of catharsis imputes to art the principle that ultimately the culture industry appropriates and administers. The index of its untruth is the well-founded doubt whether the salutary Aristotelian effect ever occurred; substitute satisfaction may well have spawned repressed instincts.——Even the category of the new, which in the artwork represents what has yet to exist and that whereby the work transcends the given, bears the scar of the ever-same underneath the constantly new. Consciousness, fettered to this day, has not gained mastery over the new, not even in the image: Consciousness dreams *of* the new but is not able to dream the new itself. If the emancipation of art was possible only through the appropriation of the commodity character, through which art gained the semblance of its being-in-itself, then in the course of that development the commodity character was dropped from the artworks; *Jugendstil* played no small role in this, with its ideology of the reintroduction of art into life as well as with the sensations of Wilde, d'Annunzio, and Maeterlinck, who served as preludes to the culture industry. Progressive subjective differentiation, the heightening and expansion of the sphere of aesthetic stimuli, made these stimuli manipulable; they were able to be produced for the cultural marketplace. The attunement of art to the most fleeting individual reactions was bound up with the reification of these reactions; art's growing similarity to subjective physical existence distanced it—as far as the majority of artistic production was concerned—from its objectivity and at the same time commended it to the public; to this extent the watchword *l'art pour l'art* was the mask of its opposite. What is true in the uproar over decadence is that subjective differentiation has an aspect of ego-weakness, an aspect shared with the mentality of the culture industry's customers and something the culture industry knew how to exploit. Kitsch is not, as those believers in erudite culture would like to imagine, the mere refuse of art, originating in disloyal accommodation to the enemy; rather, it lurks in art, awaiting ever recurring opportunities to spring forth. Although kitsch escapes, implike, from even a historical definition, one of its most tenacious characteristics is the prevarication of feelings, fictional feelings in which no one is actually participating, and thus the neutralization of these feelings. Kitsch parodies catharsis. Ambitious art, however, produces the same fiction of feelings; indeed, this was essential to it: The documentation of actually existing feelings, the recapitulation of psychical raw material, is foreign to it. It is in vain to try to draw the boundaries abstractly between aesthetic fiction and kitsch's emotional plunder. It is a poison admixed to all art; excising it is today one of art's despairing efforts. The vulgar is related in a complementary fashion to the manufactured and bartered-off feeling, and indeed vulgarity is an aspect of every salable feeling. It is as hard to say what is vulgar in artworks as to answer Erwin Ratz's question[5] how it is that art, whose a priori gesture protests against vulgarity, is yet capable of being integrated with the vulgar. Only in a mutilated fashion does the vulgar represent the plebeian that is held at a distance by the so-called high arts. When art has allowed itself, without condescension, to be inspired by a plebeian element, art has gained in an authentic weightiness that is the opposite of the vulgar. Art becomes vulgar through condescension: when, especially by means of humor, it appeals to deformed consciousness and confirms it. It suits domination if what it has made out of the masses and what it drills into them can be chalked up to their own guilty desires. Art respects the masses by presenting itself to them as what they could be rather than by adapting itself to them in their degraded condition. Socially, the vulgar in art is the subjective identification with objectively reproduced humiliation. In place of what is withheld from them, the masses reactively, resentfully, enjoy what is produced by renunciation and usurps the place of what has been renounced. It is ideology that low art, entertainment, is socially legitimate and self-evident; it is solely that condition that expresses the omnipresence of repression. The model of aesthetic vulgarity is the child in the advertisement, taking a bite of chocolate with eyes half-closed, as if it were a sin. The repressed returns in the vulgar, bearing the marks of repression; it is the subjective expression of the failure of that sublimation that art praises so overzealously as catharsis and for which it gives itself credit because it senses how little sublimation, like all culture, has actually turned out to date. In the age of total administration, culture no longer needs to humiliate the barbarians it has created; it suffices that by its rituals it strengthens the barbarism that has subjectively been sedimenting over centuries. That art stands as a reminder of what does not exist, prompts rage; this rage is transferred to the image of that otherness and befouls it. The archetypes of the vulgar that the art of the emancipatory bourgeoisie held in check, sometimes ingeniously—in its clowns, servants, and Papagenos—are the grinning advertisement beauties whose praise of toothpaste brands unites the billboards of all lands; those who know they are being cheated by so much feminine splendor blacken out the all too brilliant teeth of these archetypes and in total innocence make the truth visible above the gleam of culture. This, at least, is perceived by the vulgar. Because aesthetic vulgarity undialectically imitates the invariants of social degradation, it has no history; its eternal return is celebrated by graffiti. No subject matter is ever to be taboo and excluded from art as vulgar; vulgarity is a relation to the material and to those to whom the appeal is made. The expansion of the vulgar to the totality has meanwhile swallowed up what once laid claim to the noble and sublime: This is one of the reasons for the liquidation of the tragic. It succumbed in the denouement of the second act of Budapest operettas. Today, everything that goes under the name of "light" art is to be rejected; that also applies, however, to what is noble, the abstract antithesis to reification and at the same time its booty. Ever since Baudelaire, the noble has been associated with political reaction, as if democracy as such, the quantitative category of masses, and not the perpetuation of oppression were the source of the vulgar. Fidelity to the noble in art should be maintained, just as the noble should reflect its own culpability, its complicity with privilege. Its refuge remains exclusively the unflinching power of resistance in the act of forming. The noble becomes spurious and itself vulgar when it extols itself, for to this day there has not been anything noble. Contradiction gnaws at the noble ever since Hölderlin's verse that nothing sacred is any longer fit for use,[6] the same contradiction that an adolescent might have sensed who read a socialist journal with political sympathy and at the same time was put off by the language and mentality and the ideological undercurrent of a culture for all. What that paper in fact promoted, of course, was not the potential of a freed people but rather people as the complement of class society, the statically conceived universal of voters who must be reckoned with.

The counterconcept to aesthetic comportment is, quite simply, the concept of the philistine, which often overlaps with the vulgar yet remains distinct from it by its indifference or hatred, whereas vulgarity greedily smacks its lips. Socially implicated in the guilt of those who lay claim to aesthetic nobility, the philistine's disdain grants intellectual labor an immediately higher rank than manual labor. That art benefits from certain advantages becomes, for art's self-consciousness and for those who react aesthetically, something better in-itself. This ideological element in art stands in need of permanent self-correction. Art is capable of this because, as the negation of practical life, it is itself praxis, and indeed not simply on the basis of its genesis and the fact that, like every artifact, it is the result of activity. Just as its content is dynamic in itself and does not remain self-identical, in the course of their history the objectivated artworks themselves once again become practical comportments and turn toward reality. In this, art and theory are allied. Art recapitulates praxis in itself, modified and in a sense neutralized, and by doing so it takes up positions toward reality. Beethoven's symphonic language, which in its most secret chemistry is the bourgeois process of production as well as the expression of capitalism's perennial disaster, at the same time becomes a *fait social* by its gesture of tragic affirmation: Things are as they must and should be and are therefore good. At the same time, this music belongs to the revolutionary process of bourgeois emancipation, just as it anticipates its apologetics. The more deeply artworks are deciphered, the less their antithesis to praxis remains absolute; they themselves are something other than their origin, their fundament, that is, this very antithesis to praxis, and they unfold the mediation of this antithesis. They are less than praxis and more: less, because, as was codified once and for all in Tolstoy's *Kreutzer Sonata*, they recoil before what must be done, perhaps even thwart it, although they are less capable of this than is suggested by Tolstoy's renegade asceticism. Their truth content cannot be separated from the concept of humanity. Through every mediation, through all negativity, they are images of a transformed humanity and are unable to come to rest in themselves by any abstraction from this transformation. Art, however, is more than praxis because by its aversion to praxis it simultaneously denounces the narrow untruth of the practical world. Immediate praxis wants to know nothing of this as long as the practical organization of the world has yet to succeed. The critique exercised a priori by art is that of action as a cryptogram of domination. According to its sheer form, praxis tends toward that which, in terms of its own logic, it should abolish; violence is immanent to it and is maintained in its sublimations, whereas artworks, even the most aggressive, stand for nonviolence. They are a constant indictment of the workaday bustle and the practical individual, back of which is concealed the barbaric appetite of the species, which is not human as long as it permits itself to be ruled by this appetite and is fused with domination. The dialectical relation of art to praxis is that of its social effect. That artworks intervene politically is doubtful; when it does happen, most often it is peripheral to the work; if they strive for it, they usually succumb to their own terms. Their true social effect is an extremely indirect participation in spirit that by way of subterranean processes contributes to social transformation and is concentrated in artworks; they only achieve such participation through their objectivation. The effect of artworks is not that they present a latent praxis that corresponds to a manifest one, for their autonomy has moved far beyond such immediacy; rather, their effect is that of recollection, which they evoke by their existence. If the historical genesis of artworks refers back to causal contexts, these do not disappear tracelessly in them; the process enacted internally by each and every artwork works back on society as the model of a possible praxis in which something on the order of a collective subject is constituted. However little the external effect matters in art, and however important its form is, its intrinsic form nevertheless has an effect. Therefore the critical analysis of the effect of artworks has a great deal to say about what artworks, in their character as things, have sealed up in themselves; this could be demonstrated in the ideological effect of Wagner's music. It is not social reflection on artworks and their inner chemistry that is false but rather the subordination of artworks to abstract social correlations determined from above that are indifferent to the tension between the historical causal nexus and the content of the work. Just how far artworks intervene on a practical level is incidentally determined not only by them but far more importantly by the social moment. Beaumarchais's comedies were certainly not politically committed in the style of Brecht or Sartre, yet they in fact had a certain political effect because their tangible content [*Inhalt*] harmonized with a social movement that relished finding itself flattered in them. Because it is second-hand, the social effect of art is obviously paradoxical; what is attributed to its spontaneity in fact depends on the general social tendency. Conversely, Brecht's work, which, beginning with *Saint Joan of the Stock-yards*, wanted to provoke social change, was probably socially powerless, and the astute Brecht by no means deceived himself on this score. Its effect is captured by the English expression of *preaching to the saved*. His theater of alienation intended to motivate the viewer to think. Brecht's postulate of a thinking comportment converges, strangely enough, with the objective discernment that autonomous artworks presuppose in the viewer, listener, or reader as being adequate to them. His didactic style, however, is intolerant of the ambiguity in which thought originates: It is authoritarian. This may have been Brecht's response to the ineffectuality of his didactic plays: As a virtuoso of manipulative technique, he wanted to coerce the desired effect just as he once planned to organize his rise to fame. Nevertheless, it is not least of all due to Brecht that the artwork gained self-consciousness of itself as an element of political praxis and thus acquired a force opposed to its ideological blindness. Brecht's cult of practicality became an aesthetic constituent of his works and it is not to be eliminated from what in his work stands at a remove from the realm of causal contexts, namely their truth content. The acute reason today for the social inefficacy of artworks—those that do not surrender to crude propa-ganda—is that in order to resist the all-powerful system of communication they must rid themselves of any communicative means that would perhaps make them accessible to the public. Artworks exercise a practical effect, if they do so at all, not by haranguing but by the scarcely apprehensible transformation of consciousness; in any case, agitative effects dissipate rapidly, presumably because even artworks of that type are perceived under the general category of irrationality: Their principle, of which they cannot rid themselves, stalls the immediate practical impulse. Aesthetic cultivation leads away from the preaesthetic contamination of art and reality. The distance acquired, which is its result, not only reveals the objective character of the artwork. It also affects the subjective comportment, in that it severs primitive identifications and puts the recipient qua empirical psychological person out of action, which benefits his relation to the work. Subjectively, art requires self-exteriorization; this is what was meant by Brecht's critique of empathic aesthetics. This exteriorization is, however, practical insofar as it determines the person who experiences art and steps out of himself as a ζῷον πολιτικόν, just as art itself is objectively praxis as the cultivation of consciousness; but it only becomes this by renouncing persuasion. Whoever takes up an objective stance vis-à-vis the artwork will hardly allow himself to become enthused by it in the fashion prescribed by the idea of a direct appeal. This would be incompatible with the comprehending attitude appropriate to the cognitive character of artworks. By the affront to reigning needs, by the inherent tendency of art to cast different lights on the familiar, artworks correspond to the objective need for a transformation of consciousness that could become a transformation of reality. The moment they hope to achieve the effect under whose absence they suffer by adapting to existing needs they deprive people of precisely that which—to take the jargon of needs seriously and turn it against itself—they could "offer" them. Aesthetic needs are fairly vague and unarticulated: the practices of the culture industry have not changed this as much as they would like the world to believe and, indeed, as much as many like to claim. That culture failed implies that there actually are no subjective cultural needs independent of supply and the mechanisms of distribution. The need for art is itself largely ideological: Life would be possible without art, too, not only objectively but also with regard to the psychological economy of consumers who in modified circumstances are easily moved to changing their taste, in that their taste follows the line of least resistance. In a society that has disaccustomed men and women from thinking beyond themselves, whatever surpasses the mere reproduction of their life and those things they have been drilled to believe they cannot get along without, is superfluous. What is true in the most recent rebellion against art is that—in the face of the absurdly incessant scarcity, the expanding and self-reproducing barbarism, the ever present threat of total catastrophe—phenomena that are not preoccupied with the maintenance of life take on a ridiculous aspect. Whereas artists can afford to be indifferent to a cultural mechanism that in any case swallows up everything and excludes nothing, not even what is relatively good, this mechanism nevertheless tinges everything that thrives within it with something of its objective indifference. What Marx was still able to presuppose, to some degree innocently, as cultural needs in the concept of a society's general level of achievement, has its dialectic in the fact that in the meantime one does culture a greater honor by forgoing it and not taking part in its festivals than by agreeing to be force-fed. Aesthetic motifs are no less critical of cultural needs than are empirically real ones. Artworks want to break up the eternal exchange of need and satisfaction, instead of doing injustice to unfulfilled needs by supplying them with substitute satisfactions. Every aesthetic and sociological theory of need makes use of what bears the characteristically old-fashioned name of lived aesthetic experience.[7] Its insufficiency is evident in the constitution of lived artistic experiences themselves, if such exist. The supposition of lived artistic experiences is based on the assumption of an equivalence between the content of experience—put crudely, the emotional expression of works—and the subjective experience of the recipient. A listener is, in other words, to become excited when the music seems to do so, whereas to the extent that one understands anything, one should become emotionally all the more disinterested the pushier the work's gesticulations become. Science could hardly think up anything more alien to art than those experiments that presume to measure aesthetic effect and aesthetic experience by recording the heartbeat. The fount of any such equivalence remains murky. What purportedly is to be lived or relived in the work —according to popular assumption, the feelings of the author—is itself only a partial element in works and certainly not the decisive one. Works are not depositions of impulses—in any case such depositions are always much disliked by listeners and least likely to be empathically "reexperienced"; they are, rather, radically modified by the autonomous nexus of the artwork. The interplay of the constructive and the mimetically expressive elements in art is simply suppressed or distorted by the theory of lived experience: The equivalence it posits is not an equivalence at all; rather, one particular aspect is abstracted. This aspect, again removed from the aesthetic nexus of the work and translated back into the empirical world, for a second time becomes an other of what in any case it is in the work. The shock aroused by important works is not employed to trigger personal, otherwise repressed emotions. Rather, this shock is the moment in which recipients forget themselves and disappear into the work; it is the moment of being shaken. The recipients lose their footing; the possibility of truth, embodied in the aesthetic image, becomes tangible. This immediacy, in the fullest sense, of relation to artworks is a function of mediation, of penetrating and encompassing experience [*Erfahrung*]; it takes shape in the fraction of an instant, and for this the whole of consciousness is required, not isolated stimuli and responses. The experience of art as that of its truth or untruth is more than subjective experience: It is the irruption of objectivity into subjective consciousness. The experience is mediated through subjectivity precisely at the point where the subjective reaction is most intense. In Beethoven many situations are *scènes à faire*, perhaps even with the flaw of being staged. The entrance of the reprise in the Ninth Symphony, which is the result of the symphonic process, celebrates its original introduction. It resonates like an overwhelming "Thus it is." The shudder is a response, colored by fear of the overwhelming; by its affirmation the music at the same time speaks the truth about untruth. Non-judging, artworks point—as with their finger—to their content without its thereby becoming discursive. The spontaneous reaction of the recipient is mimesis of the immediacy of this gesture. In it, however, artworks are not exhausted. The position that this musical passage, once integrated, achieves by its gesture is subject to critique: It poses the question whether the power of being thus-and-not-otherwise—at the epiphany of which such moments in art are aimed—is the index of its truth. Full comprehending experience [*Erfahrung*], which terminates in judgment on the nonjudging work, demands a decision and, by extension, the concept. The lived experience [*Erlebnis*] is exclusively an element of such comprehending experience and faulty because it is subject to persuasion. Works such as the Ninth Symphony exercise a mesmerizing effect: The force they achieve through their structure becomes the force of their effect. In the development of music after Beethoven the suggestive force of works, initially borrowed from society, has been shunted back to society and become agitative and ideological. Shudder, radically opposed to the conventional idea of experience [*Erlebnis*], provides no particular satisfaction for the I; it bears no similarity to desire. Rather, it is a memento of the liquidation of the I, which, shaken, perceives its own limitedness and finitude. This experience [*Erfahrung*] is contrary to the weakening of the I that the culture industry manipulates. For the culture industry the idea of the shudder is idle nonsense; this is probably the innermost motivation for the deaestheticization of art. To catch even the slightest glimpse beyond the prison that it itself is, the I requires not distraction but rather the utmost tension; that preserves the shudder, an involuntary comportment, incidentally, from becoming regression. In his *Aesthetic of the Sublime* Kant faithfully presented the power of the subject as the precondition of the sublime. True, the annihilation of the I in the face of art is to be taken no more literally than is art. Because, however, what are called aesthetic experiences [*Erlebnisse*] are as such psychologically real, it would be impossible to understand them if they were simply part and parcel of the illusoriness of art. Experiences are not "as if." The disappearance of the I in the moment of the shudder is not real; but delirium, which has a similar aspect, is nevertheless incompatible with artistic experience. For a few moments the I becomes aware, in real terms, of the possibility of letting self-preservation fall away, though it does not actually succeed in realizing this possibility. It is not the aesthetic shudder that is semblance but rather its attitude to objectivity: In its immediacy the shudder feels the potential as if it were actual. The I is seized by the unmetaphorical, semblance-shattering consciousness: that it itself is not ultimate, but semblance. For the subject, this transforms art into what it is in-itself, the historical voice of repressed nature, ultimately critical of the principle of the I, that internal agent of repression. This subjective experience [*Erfahrung*] directed against the I is an element of the objective truth of art. Whoever experiences [*erlebt*] artworks by referring them to himself, does not experience them; what passes for experience [*Erlebnis*] is a palmed-off cultural surrogate. Even of this surrogate one's conceptions are simplifications. The products of the culture industry, more shallow and standardized than any of its fans can ever be, may simultaneously impede the identification that is their goal. The question as to what the culture industry inflicts on men and women is probably all too naïve: Its effect is much more diffuse than the form of the question suggests. The empty time filled with emptiness does not even produce false consciousness but is an exertion that leaves things just as they are.

The element of objective praxis inherent in art is transformed into subjective intention when, as a result of society's objective tendency and of the critical reflection of art, art's antithesis to society becomes irreconcilable. The accepted term for this subjective intention is commitment. Commitment is a higher level of reflection than tendency; it is not simply out to correct unpleasant situations, although the committed all too easily sympathize with the idea of solving problems by means of "appropriate measures."[8] Commitment aims at the transformation of the preconditions of situations, not at merely making recommendations; to this extent it inclines toward the aesthetic category of essence. The polemical self-consciousness of art presupposes its spiritualization; the more sensitized art becomes toward that sensual immediacy with which it was formerly equated, the more critical its posture becomes toward raw reality, which—an extension of the rank growth of first nature—reproduces itself socially in ever expanded form. It is not only formally that the critically reflexive tendency toward spiritualization sharpens the relation of art to its subject matter. Hegel's break from sensualist aesthetics was of a part both with the spiritualization of the artwork and with the accentuation of its subject matter. Through spiritualization the artwork is transformed, in itself, into what was once blindly attested to be its effect on other spirits.——The concept of commitment is not to be taken too literally. If it is made the yardstick of censorship, it recapitulates in its attitude toward artworks that element of dominating supervision to which they stood opposed prior to all supervisable commitment. This does not amount, however, to jettisoning categories such as that of a program or its crude progeny according to the whim of an aesthetics of taste. What they register becomes their legitimate subject matter in a phase in which they are motivated by the longing and the will that the world be other than it is. But this gives them no dispensation from the law of form; even spiritual content [*Inhalt*] remains material and is consumed by the artworks, even when their self-consciousness insists that this subject matter is essence. Brecht taught nothing that could not have been understood apart from his didactic plays, indeed, that could not have been understood more concisely through theory, or that was not already well known to his audience: That the rich are better off than the poor; that the way of the world is unjust; that repression persists within formal equality; that objective evil transforms private goodness into its own opposite; that—admittedly a dubious wisdom—goodness requires the masks of evil. But the sententious vehemence with which he translates these hardly dew-fresh insights into scenic gestures lends his works their tone; the didacticism led him to his dramaturgical innovations, which overthrew the moribund theater of philosophy and intrigue. In his plays, theses took on an entirely different function from the one their content [*Inhalt*] intended. They became constitutive; they made the drama anti-illusory and contributed to the collapse of the unitary nexus of meaning. It is this, not commitment, that defines their quality, yet their quality is inseparable from the commitment in that it becomes their mimetic element. Brecht's commitment does for the work what it gravitates toward on its own: It undermines it. As often occurs, in commitment, something that is sealed up in art becomes external by means of growing control and practicability. Artworks became for-themselves what they previously were in-themselves. The immanence of artworks, their apparently a priori distance from the empirical, would not exist without the prospect of a world transformed by self-conscious praxis. In *Romeo and Juliet* Shakespeare was not promoting love without familial guardianship; but without the longing for a situation in which love would no longer be mutilated and condemned by patriarchal or any other powers, the presence of the two lost in one another would not have the sweetness—the wordless, imageless utopia—over which, to this day, the centuries have been powerless; the taboo that prohibits knowledge of any positive utopia also reigns over artworks. Praxis is not the effect of works; rather, it is encapsuled in their truth content. This is why commitment is able to become an aesthetic force of production. In general, the bleating against tendentious art and against commitment is equally subaltern. The ideological concern to keep culture pure obeys the wish that in the fetishized culture, and thus actually, everything remains as it was. Such indignation has much in common with the opposing position's indignation that has been standardized in the phrase about the obsolete ivory tower from which, in an age zealously proclaimed an age of mass communication, art must issue. The common denominator is the message; although Brecht's good taste steered him away from the word, the idea was not foreign to the positivist in him. The two positions are intensely self-contradictory. *Don Quixote* may have served a particular and irrelevant program, that of abolishing the chivalric romance, which had been dragged along from feudal times into the bourgeois age. This modest program served as the vehicle by which the novel became an exemplary artwork. The antagonism of literary genres in which Cervantes's work originated was transformed, in his hands, into an antagonism of historical eras of, ultimately, metaphysical dimension: the authentic expression of the crisis of immanent meaning in the demystified world. Works such as *Werther*, which have no programmatic aspect, contributed significantly to the emancipation of bourgeois consciousness in Germany. Goethe, by giving shape to the collision of society with the feelings of an individual who, finding himself alone and unloved, is driven to suicide, protested powerfully against a hardened petty bourgeoisie without even naming it. However, what the two basic censorial positions of bourgeois consciousness hold in common—that the artwork must not want to change the world and that it must be there for all—is a *plaidoyer* for the status quo; the former defends the domestic peace of artworks with the world and the latter remains vigilant that the sanctioned forms of public consciousness be maintained. Today, hermetic and committed art converge in the refusal of the status quo. Interference is prohibited by reified consciousness because it reifies the already reified artwork; for reified consciousness the work's objectivation in opposition to society appears as its social neutralization. That side of artworks that faces outward is falsified as their essence without any regard to the process of their formation or, ultimately, their truth content. No artwork, however, can be socially true that is not also true in-itself; conversely, social false consciousness is equally incapable of becoming aesthetically authentic. Social and immanent aspects of artworks do not coincide, but neither do they diverge so completely as the fetishism of culture and praxis would like to believe. That whereby the truth content of artworks points beyond their aesthetic complexion, which it does only by virtue of that aesthetic complexion, assures it its social significance. This duality is not a stipulation that rules abstractly over the sphere of art. It is art's vital element and lodged within each and every work. Art becomes something social through its in-itself, and it becomes in-itself by means of the social force of production effective in it. The dialectic of the social and of the in-itself of the artwork is the dialectic of its own constitution to the extent that it tolerates nothing interior that does not externalize itself, nothing external that is not the bearer of the inward, the truth content.

The dual nature of artworks as autonomous structures and social phenomena results in oscillating criteria: Autonomous works provoke the verdict of social indifference and ultimately of being criminally reactionary; conversely, works that make socially univocal discursive judgments thereby negate art as well as themselves. Immanent critique can possibly break through this rigid alternative. Stefan George certainly merited the reproach of being socially reactionary long before he propounded the maxims of his secret Germany, just as the poor-peoples' poetry of the late 1880s and 1890s, Arno Holz's, for instance, deserves to be criticized as being crudely unaesthetic.[9] Both types, however, should be confronted with their own concept. George's self-staged aristocratic posturings contradict the self-evident superiority that they postulate and thereby fail artistically; the verse "And—that we lack not a bouquet of myrrh"[10] is laughable, as is the verse on the Roman emperor who, after having his brother murdered, gently gathers up the purple train of his toga.[11] The brutality of George's social attitude, the result of failed identification, appears in his poetry in the violent acts of language that mar the purity of the self-sufficient work after which George aspired. In programmatic aestheticism, false social consciousness becomes the shrill tone that gives it the lie. Without ignoring the difference in quality between George, who was a great poet in spite of everything, and the mediocre naturalists, they have in common the fact that the social and critical content of their plays and poems is almost always superficial. It lags far behind what was already fully elaborated by social theory, in which they were scarcely interested. Arno Holz's parody of political hypocrisy, *Social Aristocrats*, suffices to prove this. Because artistically they overwhelmed society with verbiage, they felt duty bound to a vulgar idealism, as for instance in the image of the worker who dreams of something higher, whatever it may be, and who through the fate of his class origin is prevented from achieving it. The question of the provenance of his solidly bourgeois ideal of upward mobility is ignored. Naturalism's innovations—the renunciation of traditional categories of form, the distilling of the self-contained plots and even, as at points in Zola, the abandonment of the continuity of empirical time—are more advanced than its concept. The ruthless, effectively aconceptual presentation of empirical detail in *Savage Paris* destroyed the familiar surface coherence of the novel in a fashion not unlike that of its later monadic-associative form. As a result, naturalism regressed except when it took the most extreme risks. Carrying out intentions contradicts its principle. Yet naturalist plays abound in passages whose intention is plain: People are to speak plainly, yet in following the author's stage directions they speak as no one would ever speak. In the realist theater it is already inconsistent that even before they open their mouths people know so precisely what it is they are going to say. Perhaps it would be impossible to organize a realistic play according to its conception without its becoming, *à contre coeur*, dadaistic; through its unavoidable minimum of stylization, however, realism admits its impossibility and virtually abolishes itself. Taken in hand by the culture industry, it has become mass deception. The spiritedly unanimous rejection of Sudermann[12] may be because his box office successes let out of the bag what the most talented naturalists hid: the manipulated, fictive aspect of every gesture that lays claim to being beyond fiction when, instead, fiction envelops every word spoken on stage, however it resists and defends itself. These products, a priori cultural goods, are easily coaxed to become a naïve and affirmative image of culture. Even aesthetically there are not two types of truth. How the contradictory desiderata can reciprocally interpenetrate without being averaged out as a mediocre compromise between a purportedly good form and an appropriate social content [*Inhalt*] can be learned from Beckett's dramatic art. Its associative logic, in which one sentence draws after it the next sentence or the reply, just as in music a theme motivates its continuation or its contrast, scorns all imitation of its empirical appearance. The result is that, hooded, the empirically essential is incorporated according to its exact historical importance and integrated into the play character of the work. The latter expresses the objective condition both of consciousness and of the reality that shapes it. The negativity of the subject as the true form of objectivity can only be presented in radically subjective form, not by recourse to a purportedly higher reality. The grimacing clowns, childish and bloody, into which Beckett's subject is decomposed, are that subject's historical truth; socialist realism is, by comparison, simply childish. In *Godot* the relation of domination and servitude, along with its senile lunatic form, is thematic in a phase in which control over others' labor continues, even though humanity no longer needs it for its self-preservation. This motif, truly one of the essential laws of contemporary society, is taken further in *Endgame*. In both works Beckett's technique hurls it to the periphery: Hegel's chapter is transformed into anecdotes with sociocritical no less than dramaturgical function. In *Endgame* the tellurian partial catastrophe, the bloodiest of Beckett's clown jokes, is presupposed both thematically and formally in that it has obliterated art's constituent, its genesis. Art emigrates to a standpoint that is no longer a standpoint at all because there are no longer standpoints from which the catastrophe could be named or formed, a word that seems ridiculous in this context. *Endgame* is neither a play about the atom bomb nor is it contentless; the determinate negation of its content [*Inhalt*] becomes its formal principle and the negation of content altogether. Beckett's oeuvre gives the frightful answer to art that, by its starting point, by its distance from any praxis, art in the face of mortal threat becomes ideology through the harmlessness of its mere form, regardless of its content. This explains the influx of the comic into emphatic works. It has a social aspect. In that their effectively blindfolded movement originates exclusively in themselves, their movement becomes a walking in place and declares itself as such, just as the unrelenting seriousness of the work declares itself as frivolous, as play. Art can only be reconciled with its existence by exposing its own semblance, its internal emptiness. Its most binding criterion today is that in terms of its own complexion, unreconciled with all realistic deception, it no longer tolerates anything harmless. In all art that is still possible, social critique must be raised to the level of form, to the point that it wipes out all manifestly social content [*Inhalt*].

With the continuing organization of all cultural spheres the desire grows to assign art its place in society theoretically and indeed practically; this is the aim of innumerable *round table* conferences and symposia. Once art has been recognized as a social fact, the sociological definition of its context considers itself superior to it and disposes over it. Often the assumption is that the objectivity of value-free positivistic knowledge is superior to supposedly subjective aesthetic standpoints. Such endeavors themselves call for social criticism. They tacitly seek the primacy of administration, of the administered world even over what refuses to be grasped by total socialization or at any rate struggles against it. The sovereignty of the topographical eye that localizes phenomena in order to scrutinize their function and right to exist is sheer usurpation. It ignores the dialectic of aesthetic quality and functional society. A priori, in conformist fashion, the accent falls, if not on art's ideological effect, then at least on the consumability of art, while dismissing all that in which today social reflection would have its object: This is decided in advance, in conformist fashion. Because the expansion of technical administrative procedures is fused with the scientific apparatus of investigation, it appeals to those sorts of intellectuals who indeed sense something of the new social necessities but nothing of the necessities of art. Their mentality is that of an imaginary sociological lecture on culture whose title should be: "The Function of Television for the Adaptation of Europe to the Developing Countries." Social reflection on art has nothing to contribute in this spirit other than to make it thematic and thereby resist it. Then, as now, Steuermann's[13] comment holds good that the more that is done for culture, the worse it turns out.

For contemporary consciousness, and especially for student activists, the immanent difficulties of art, no less than its social isolation, amount to its condemnation. This is a sign of the historical situation, and those who want to abolish art would be the last to admit it. The avant-gardist disruptions of aesthetically avant-garde performances are as chimerical as the belief that they are revolutionary and that revolution is a form of beauty: Obtuseness to art is below, not above, culture, and commitment itself is often nothing but a lack of talent or concentration, a slackening of energy. Their most recent trick, which was admittedly already practiced by Fascism, revalorizes ego-weakness, the incapacity for sublimation, as a superior quality and sets a moral premium on the line of least resistance. It is claimed that the age of art is over; now it is a matter of realizing its truth content, which is facilely equated with art's social content: The verdict is totalitarian. What today lays claim to having been read solely out of the material, and what in its dullness indeed offers the most compelling reason for the verdict on art, in fact does the greatest violence to the material. The moment art is prohibited and it is decreed that it must no longer be, art—in the midst of the administrative world—wins back the right to exist, the denial of which itself resembles an administrative act. Whoever wants to abolish art cherishes the illusion that decisive change is not blocked. Exaggerated realism is unrealistic. The making of every authentic work contradicts the *pronunciamento* that no more can be made. The abolition of art in a half-barbaric society that is tending toward total barbarism makes itself barbarism's social partner. Although their constant refrain is concreteness, they judge abstractly and summarily, blind to the precise and unsolved tasks and possibilities that have been repressed by the most recent aesthetic actionism, such as the tasks and possibilities of a truly freed music that traverses the freedom of the subject rather than being abandoned to thing-like alienated contingency. Yet there is no arguing over the question whether art is necessary. The question itself is falsely posed because the necessity of art—if the idea must be maintained when the issue is the realm of freedom—is its nonnecessity. To evaluate art according to the standard of necessity covertly prolongs the principle of exchange, the philistine's concern for what can be gotten for it. The verdict that it is no longer possible to put up with it, the obedient contemplation of a purportedly given state, is itself a shop-worn bourgeois gesture, the wrinkled brow that worries, "Where is this all going to end?" Yet precisely this type of teleology is inimical to art insofar as art stands as plenipotentiary for the in-itself that does not yet exist. In terms of their historicophilosophical significance, works are all the more important the less they coincide with their stage of development. The question is a surreptitious form of social control. Many contemporary works can be characterized as an anarchy that effectively implies a wish to be quit of it all. The summary judgment passed on art, which is itself inscribed on those works that would like to substitute themselves for art, resembles the verdict pronounced by Lewis Carroll's Queen of Hearts: "Off with their heads." After these beheadings to the sound of a pop, in which the sound of *Popular Music* resonates, the head grows back. Art has everything to fear but the nihilism of impotence. By its social proscription, art is degraded to precisely that role of *fait social* that it refuses to resume. The Marxist theory of ideology, which is ambiguous in itself, is falsified as a total theory of ideology in Mannheimian fashion and blindly applied to art. If ideology is socially false consciousness, it does not follow that all consciousness is ideological. Beethoven's last quartets are consigned to the underworld of obsolete semblance only on the basis of ignorance and incomprehension. Whether art is still possible today cannot be decided from above, from the perspective of the relations of production. The question depends, rather, on the state of the forces of production. It encompasses what is possible but not yet realized: an art that refuses to let itself be terrorized by positivist ideology. As legitimate as Herbert Marcuse's critique of the affirmative character of culture was,[14] its thesis requires the investigation of the individual artwork: Otherwise it would become an anticulture league, itself no better than any cultural asset. Rabid criticism of culture is not radical. If affirmation is indeed an aspect of art, this affirmation is no more totally false than culture—because it failed—is totally false. Culture checks barbarism, which is worse; it not only represses nature but conserves it through its repression; this resonates in the concept of culture, which originates in agriculture. Life has been perpetuated through culture, along with the idea of a decent life; its echo resounds in authentic artworks. Affirmation does not bestow a halo on the status quo; in sympathy with what exists, it defends itself against death, the telos of all domination. Doubting this comes only at the price of believing that death itself is hope.

The double character of art—something that severs itself from empirical reality and thereby from society's functional context and yet is at the same time part of empirical reality and society's functional context—is directly apparent in the aesthetic phenomena, which are both aesthetic and *faits sociaux*. They require a double observation that is no more to be posited as an unalloyed whole than aesthetic autonomy and art can be conflated as something strictly social. This double character becomes physiognomically decipherable, whether intentionally so or not, when one views or listens to art from an external vantage point, and, certainly, art always stands in need of this external perspective for protection from the fetishization of its autonomy. Music, whether it is played in a café or, as is often the case in America, piped into restaurants, can be transformed into something completely different, of which the hum of conversation and the rattle of dishes and whatever else becomes a part. To fulfill its function, this music presupposes distracted listeners no less than in its autonomous state it expects attentiveness. A medley is sometimes made up of parts of artworks, but through this montage the parts are fundamentally transformed. Functions such as warming people up and drowning out silence recasts music as something defined as mood, the commodified negation of the boredom produced by the grey-on-grey commodity world. The sphere of entertainment, which has long been integrated into production, amounts to the domination of this element of art over all the rest of its phenomena. These elements are antagonistic. The subordination of autonomous artworks to the element of social function buried within each work and from which art originated in the course of a protracted struggle, wounds art at its most vulnerable point. Yet someone sitting in a café who is suddenly struck by the music and listens intensely may feel odd to himself and seem foolish to others. In this antagonism the fundamental relation of art and society appears. The continuity of art is destroyed when it is experienced externally, just as medleys willfully destroy it in the material. Heard in the corridors of the concert hall, little remains of one of Beethoven's orchestral works than the imperial kettle drum; even in the score the drums represent an authoritarian gesture, which the work borrowed from society in order to sublimate it in the elaboration of the composition. For art's two characters are not completely indifferent to each other. If a work of authentic music strays into the social sphere of background music, it may unexpectedly transcend that sphere by the purity that is stained by social function. On the other hand, the derivation of authentic works from social functions, as in the case of Beethoven's kettle drums, cannot be washed away; Wagner's irritation with those vestiges of divertissement in Mozart has since been sharpened into a *soupçon* even against those works that voluntarily bid farewell to entertainment. After the age of aesthetic autonomy, the position of artists in society, to the extent that it is significant with regard to mass reception, tends to revert into heterogeneity. If prior to the French Revolution artists were lackeys, they have since become entertainers. The culture industry calls its *crack* performers by their first name, just as head waiters and hair dressers chummily refer to the *jet set*. The demolition of the difference between the artist as aesthetic subject and the artist as empirical person also attests to the abolition of the distance of the artwork from the empirical world, without however art's thereby returning to a realm of freedom, which in any case does not exist. This deceptively manufactured proximity of art serves profit. From the vantage point of art, its double character clings to each of its works as a flaw of its dishonest origin, just as socially artists were once treated as dishonest persons. This same origin, however, is also the locus of its mimetic essence. Its dishonesty, which contradicts the dignity laid claim to by its autonomy, which puffs itself up out of guilt over its participation in society, redounds to its honor as mockery of the honesty of socially useful labor.

The relation of social praxis and art, always variable, may well have changed radically once again over the last forty or fifty years. During World War I and prior to Stalin, artistic and politically advanced thought went in tandem; whoever came of age in those years took art to be what it in no way historically had been: a priori politically on the left. Since then the Zhdanovs and Ulbrichts have not only enchained the force of artistic production with the dictate of socialist realism but actually broken it; socially the aesthetic regression for which they are responsible is transparent as a petty bourgeois fixation. By comparison, during the decades after the Second War, with the world divided into two political blocs, the ruling interests in the West have signed a revocable peace with radical art; abstract painting is subsidized by heavy German industry, and in France de Gaulle's minister of culture is André Malraux. Avant-garde doctrines, if their opposition to *communis opinio* is grasped with sufficient abstractness and if they remain to some degree moderate, are sometimes susceptible to elitist reinterpretation, as has been the case with Pound and Eliot. Benjamin already noted the fascist penchant in futurism, which can be traced back to peripheral aspects of Baudelaire's modernism.[15] All the same, when Benjamin in his later work distanced himself from the aesthetic avant-garde at those points where it failed to toe the Communist Party line, Brecht's hatred of Tui intellectuals may well have played a part. The elitist isolation of advanced art is less its doing than society's; the unconscious standards of the masses are the same as those necessary to the preservation of the relations in which the masses are integrated, and the pressure of heteronomous life makes distraction compulsory, thus prohibiting the concentration of a strong ego that is requisite to the experience of the nonstereotypical. This breeds resentment: the resentment of the masses toward what is denied them by the education that is reserved for the privileged; and—ever since Strindberg and Schoenberg—resentment of the aesthetically progressive toward the masses. The yawning schism between their aesthetic *trouvailles* and a political posture that is manifest in the content [*Inhalt*] and intention of works, significantly damages artistic consistency. The social interpretation of older literature in terms of its political content [*Inhalt*] is of uncertain value. The interpretation of Greek myths, such as Vico's interpretation of that of Cadmus, was ingenious. Yet the reduction of Shakespeare's plays to the idea of class struggle, as Brecht meant to do, goes too far and misses what is essential, except in those dramas where class struggle is clearly a theme. This is not to claim that what is essential is indifferent to society and, in human terms, timeless:

That is drivel. Rather, the social element is mediated by the objective formal posture of the plays, what Lukács called their "perspective." What is social in Shakespeare is categories such as those of the individual and passion: traits such as Caliban's bourgeois concreteness and the corrupt Venetian merchants, the conception of a semimatriarchal world in *Macbeth* and *King Lear*; the complete disgust for power in *Antony and Cleopatra* as well as Prospero's gesture of resignation. By contrast, the conflicts of patricians and plebeians drawn from Roman history are merely cultural goods. In Shakespeare, the more literally the Marxist thesis is held that all history is that of class struggle, the more dubious it appears. Class struggle objectively presupposes a high level of social integration and differentiation, and subjectively it requires class consciousness, which first developed rudimentarily in bourgeois society. It is nothing new to note that class itself, the social subsumption of atoms to a general concept that expresses their constitutive as well as heterogeneous relations, is structurally a bourgeois reality. Social antagonisms are as old as the hills; only desultorily did they become class struggles: where market economies related to bourgeois society began to take shape. For this reason the interpretation of everything historical as class struggle has a slightly anachronistic *air* just as the model of all of Marx's constructions and extrapolations was that of liberal entrepreneurial capitalism. True, social antagonisms shimmer through Shakespeare's plays at every point, yet they are manifest in individuals and are collective only in crowd scenes that follow topoi such as that of the suggestibility of mobs. From a social perspective it is at least evident that Shakespeare could not have been Bacon. That early bourgeois dialectical dramatist beheld the *theatrum mundi* not from the perspective of progress but from that of the victims of progress. Severing this ensnarement through social as well as aesthetic maturation is made prohibitively difficult by the social structure. If in art formal characteristics are not facilely interpretable in political terms, everything formal in art nevertheless has substantive implications and they extend into politics. The liberation of form, which genuinely new art desires, holds enciphered within it above all the liberation of society, for form—the social nexus of everything particular—represents the social relation in the artwork; this is why liberated form is anathema to the status quo. This is confirmed by psychoanalysis. It holds that all art, the negation of the reality principle, protests against the image of the father and is to this extent revolutionary. This objectively implies the political participation of the unpolitical. So long as social imbrication was not yet so agglomerated that form itself became subversive protest, the relation of artworks to existing social reality was less contentious. Without altogether surrendering to this reality, art was able to appropriate social elements without any great to-do, to continue clearly to resemble society, and to communicate with it. Today the socially critical aspect of artworks has become opposition to empirical reality as such because the latter has become its own self-duplicating ideology, the quintessence of domination. Whether art in turn becomes socially irrelevant—empty play and decoration of social bustle—depends on the extent to which its constructions and montages are simultaneously de-montages, destroying while receiving the elements of reality and shaping them freely as something other. The unity of art's aesthetic and social criteria is constituted by whether, in transcending empirical reality, it succeeds at concretizing its relation to what it has transcended; in doing so it gains a sort of prerogative. Without letting itself be put upon by political activists to provide the messages that suit them, art would then harbor no doubt as to what it is after. Fearless of any contradiction, Picasso and Sartre opted for a politics that disdained what they stood for aesthetically and only put up with them to the extent that their names had propaganda value. Their attitude is impressive because they do not subjectively dissolve the contradiction, which has an objective justification, by the univocal commitment to one thesis or its opposite. The critique of their attitude is pertinent only as one of the politics for which they vote; the smug assertion that they only hurt themselves misses the point. Hardly last among the aporia of the age is that no thought holds true that does not do damage to the interests, even the objective interests, of those who foster it.

Today the nomenclature of formalism and socialist realism is used, with great consequence, to distinguish between the autonomous and the social essence of art. This nomenclature is employed by the administered world to exploit for its own purposes the objective dialectic that inheres in the double character of each and every artwork: These two aspects are severed from each other and used to divide the sheep from the goats. This dichotomization is false because it presents the two dynamically related elements as simple alternatives. The individual artist is supposed to choose. Thanks to an ever present social master plan, inclination is always encouraged in the antiformalistic directions; the others are pronounced narrow specializations restricted to the division of labor and possibly even susceptible to naïve bourgeois illusions. The loving care with which apparatchiks lead refractory artists out of their isolation tallies with the assassination of Meyerhold.[16] In truth the abstract antithesis of formalistic and antiformalistic art cannot be maintained once art wants to be more than an open or covert *pep talk*. Around the time of World War I, or somewhat later modern painting polarized into cubism and surrealism. But cubism itself revolted, in terms of its actual content [*Inhalt*], against the bourgeois idea of a gaplessly pure immanence of artworks. Conversely, important surrealists such as Max Ernst and André Masson, who refused to collude with the market and initially protested against the sphere of art itself, gradually turned toward formal principles, and Masson largely abandoned representation, as the idea of shock, which dissipates quickly in the thematic material, was transformed into a technique of painting. With the intention to unmask the habitual world in a flash of light as semblance and illusion, the step toward nonrepresentational art has teleologically already been taken. Constructivism, officially the antagonist of realism, has by virtue of its anti-illusory language deeper relations with the historical transformation of reality than does a realism long overlaid with a romantic varnish because its principle—the sham reconciliation with the object —has gradually become romantic. With regard to content, the impulses of constructivism were those of the ever problematic adequacy of art to the disenchanted world, which could no longer be achieved by traditional realism without becoming academic. Today whatever proclaims itself *informelle*[17] becomes aesthetic only by articulating itself as form; otherwise it would amount to no more than a document. In the case of such exemplary artists of the epoch as Schoenberg, Klee, and Picasso, the expressive mimetic element and the constructive element are of equal intensity, not by seeking a happy mean between them but rather by way of the extremes: Yet each is simultaneously content-laden, expression is the negativity of suffering, and construction is the effort to bear up under the suffering of alienation by exceeding it on the horizon of undiminished and thus no longer violent rationality. Just as in thought, form and content are as distinct as they are mediated in one another, so too in art. The concepts of progress and reaction are hardly applicable to art as long as the abstract dichotomy of form and content is acceded to. This dichotomy is recapitulated in assertion and counterassertion. Some call artists reactionary because they purportedly champion socially reactionary theses or because through the form of their works they supposedly aid political reason in some admittedly discreet and not quite graspable fashion; others dub artists reactionary for falling behind the level of artistic forces of production. But the content [*Gehalt*] of important artworks can deviate from the opinion of their authors. It is obvious that Strindberg repressively inverted Ibsen's bourgeois-emancipatory intentions. On the other hand, his formal innovations, the dissolution of dramatic realism and the reconstruction of dreamlike experience, are objectively critical. They attest to the transition of society toward horror more authentically than do Gorki's bravest accusations. To this extent they are also socially progressive, the dawning self-consciousness of that catastrophe for which the bourgeois individualistic society is preparing: In it the absolutely individual becomes a ghost as in *Ghost Sonata*. In counterpoint to this are the greatest works of naturalism: the unmitigated horror of the first act of Hauptmann's *Hannele's Ascension* causes the reversal of faithful reproduction into the wildest expression. Social criticism of a politically decreed resuscitation of realism is important, however, only if it does not capitulate vis-à-vis *l'art pour l'art*. What is socially untrue in that protest against society has become socially evident. The carefully chosen words, for instance, of a Barbey d'Aurevilly have since dulled to an old-fashioned naïveté hardly befitting any artificial paradise; Aldous Huxley was already struck by the emerging comicalness of Satanism. The evil that both Baudelaire and Nietzsche found to be lacking in the liberalistic nineteenth century, was for them nothing more than the mask of drives no longer subject to Victorian repression. As a product of the repressed drives of the twentieth century, evil broke through the civilizatory hurdles with a bestiality compared to which Baudelaire's outrageous blasphemies took on a harmlessness that contrasts grotesquely with their pathos. Despite his preeminence, Baudelaire presaged *Jugendstil*. Its lie was the beautification of life without its transformation; beauty itself thereby became vacuous and, like all abstract negation, allowed itself to be integrated into what it negated. The phantasmagoria of an aesthetic world undisturbed by purposes of any kind became an alibi for the subaesthetic world.

It can be said that philosophy, and theoretical thought as a whole, suffers from an idealist prejudice insofar as it disposes solely over concepts; only through them does it treat what they are concerned with, which it itself never has. Its labor of Sisyphus is that it must reflect the untruth and guilt that it takes on itself, thereby correcting it when possible. It cannot paste its ontic substratum into the text; by speaking of it, philosophy already makes it into what it wants to free itself from. Modern art has registered dissatisfaction with this ever since Picasso disrupted his pictures with scraps of newspaper, an act from which all montage derives. The social element is aesthetically done justice in that it is not imitated, which would effectively make it fit for art, but is, rather, injected into art by an act of sabotage. Art itself explodes the deception of its pure immanence, just as the empirical ruins divested of their own context accommodate themselves to the immanent principles of construction. By conspicuously and willfully ceding to crude material, art wants to undo the damage that spirit —thought as well as art—has done to its other, to which it refers and which it wants to make eloquent. This is the determinable meaning of the meaningless intention-alien element of modern art, which extends from the hybridization of the arts to the *happenings*.[18] It is not so much that traditional art is thereby sanctimoniously condemned by an arriviste judgment but that, rather, the effort is made to absorb even the negation of art by its own force. What is no longer socially possible in traditional art does not on that account surrender all truth. Instead it sinks to a historical, geological stratum that is no longer accessible to living consciousness except through negation but without which no art would exist: a stratum of mute reference to what is beautiful, without all that strict a distinction between nature and work. This element is contrary to the disintegrative element into which the truth of art has changed; yet it survives because as the forming force it recognizes the violence of that by which it measures itself. It is through this idea that art is related to peace. Without perspective on peace, art would be as untrue as when it anticipates reconciliation. Beauty in art is the semblance of the truly peaceful. It is this toward which even the repressive violence of form tends in its unification of hostile and divergent elements.

It is false to arrive at aesthetic realism from the premise of philosophical materialism. Certainly, art, as a form of knowledge, implies knowledge of reality, and there is no reality that is not social. Thus truth content and social content are mediated, although art's truth content transcends the knowledge of reality as what exists. Art becomes social knowledge by grasping the essence, not by endlessly talking about it, illustrating it, or somehow imitating it. Through its own figuration, art brings the essence into appearance in opposition to its own semblance. The epistemological critique of idealism, which secures for the object an element of primacy, cannot simply be transposed to art. Object in art and object in empirical reality are entirely distinct. In art the object is the work produced by art, as much containing elements of empirical reality as displacing, dissolving, and reconstructing them according to the work's own law. Only through such transformation, and not through an ever falsifying photography, does art give empirical reality its due, the epiphany of its shrouded essence and the merited shudder in the face of it as in the face of a monstrosity. The primacy of the object is affirmed aesthetically only in the character of art as the unconscious writing of history, as anamnesis of the vanquished, of the repressed, and perhaps of what is possible. The primacy of the object, as the potential freedom from domination of what is, manifests itself in art as its freedom from objects. If art must grasp its content [*Gehalt*] in its other, this other is not to be imputed to it but falls to it solely in its own immanent nexus. Art negates the negativity in the primacy of the object, negates what is heteronomous and unreconciled in it, which art allows to emerge even through the semblance of the reconciliation of its works.

At first glance one argument of dialectical materialism bears persuasive force. The standpoint of radical modernism, it is claimed, is that of solipsism, that of a monad that obstinately barricades itself against inter-subjectivity; the reified division of labor has run amok. This derides the humanity that awaits realization. However, this solipsism—the argument continues—is illusory, as materialistic criticism and long before that great philosophy have demonstrated; it is the delusion of the immediacy of the for-itself that ideologically refuses to admit its own mediations. It is true that theory, through insight into universal social mediation, has con-ceptually surpassed solipsism. But art, mimesis driven to the point of self-consciousness, is nevertheless bound up with feeling, with the immediacy of experience; otherwise it would be indistinguishable from science, at best an installment plan on its results and usually no more than social reporting. Collective modes of production by small groups are already conceivable, and in some media even requisite; monads are the locus of experience in all existing societies. Because individuation, along with the suffering that it involves, is a social law, society can only be experienced individually. The substruction of an immediately collective subject would be duplicitous and would condemn the artwork to untruth because it would withdraw the single possibility of experience that is open to it today. If on the basis of theoretical insight art orients itself correctively, according to its own mediatedness, and seeks to escape from the monadic character that it has recognized as social semblance, historical truth remains external to it and becomes untruth: The artwork heteronomously sacrifices its immanent determination. According to critical theory, mere consciousness of society does not in any real sense lead beyond the socially imposed objective structure, any more than the artwork does, which in terms of its own determinations is itself a part of social reality. The capacity that dialectical materialism antimaterialistically ascribes to and demands of the artwork is achieved by that artwork, if at all, when in its objectively imposed monadologically closed structure it pushes its situation so far that it becomes the critique of this situation. The true threshold between art and other knowledge may be that the latter is able to think beyond itself without abdicating, whereas art produces nothing valid that it does not fill out on the basis of the historical standpoint at which it finds itself. The innervation of what is historically possible for it is essential to the artistic form of reaction. In art, substantiality means just this. If for the sake of a higher social truth art wants more than the experience that is accessible to it and that it can form, that experience becomes less, and the objective truth that it posits as its measure collapses as a fiction that patches over the fissure between subject and object. They are so falsely reconciled by a trumped-up realism that the most utopian phantasies of a future art would be unable to conceive of one that would once again be realistic without falling back into unfreedom. Art possesses its other immanently because, like the subject, immanence is socially mediated in itself. It must make its latent social content eloquent: It must go within in order to go beyond itself. It carries out the critique of solipsism through the force of externalization in its own technique as the technique of objectivation. By virtue of its form, art transcends the impoverished, entrapped subject; what wants willfully to drown out its entrapment becomes infantile and makes out of its heteronomy a social-ethical accomplishment. It may be objected here that the various peoples' democracies are still antagonistic and that they therefore preclude any but an alienated standpoint, yet it is to be hoped that an actualized humanism would be blessedly free of the need for modern art and would once again be content with traditional art. This concessional argument, however, is actually not all that distinct from the doctrine of overcoming individualism. To put it bluntly, it is based on the philistine cliché that modern art is as ugly as the world in which it originates, that the world deserves it and nothing else would be possible, yet surely it cannot go on like this forever. In truth, there is nothing to overcome; the word itself is *index falsi*. There is no denying that the antagonistic situation, what the young Marx called alienation and self-alienation, was not the weakest agency in the constitution of modern art. But modern art was certainly no copy, not the reproduction of that situation. In denouncing it, transposing it into the image, this situation became its other and as free as the situation denies the living to be. If today art has become the ideological complement of a world not at peace, it is possible that the art of the past will someday devolve upon society at peace; it would, however, amount to the sacrifice of its freedom were new art to return to peace and order, to affirmative replication and harmony. Nor is it possible to sketch the form of art in a changed society. In comparison with past art and the art of the present it will probably again be something else; but it would be preferable that some fine day art vanish altogether than that it forget the suffering that is its expression and in which form has its substance. This suffering is the humane content that unfreedom counterfeits as positivity. If in fulfillment of the wish a future art were once again to become positive, then the suspicion that negativity were in actuality persisting would become acute; this suspicion is ever present, regression threatens unremittingly, and freedom—surely freedom from the principle of possession—cannot be possessed. But then what would art be, as the writing of history, if it shook off the memory of accumulated suffering.

Notes

1 See Karl Marx and Friedrich Engels, *Theories of Surplus Value*, vol. 1 (Moscow, 1968), p. 389.

2 [See Adorno et al., *The Authoritarian Personality* (New York, 1982).—trans.]

3 Jean-Paul Sartre, *What Is Literature* (New York, 1965), p. 21.

4 See *Briefwechsel zwischen George und Hofmannsthal*, ed. R. Boehringer (Munich and Düsseldorf, 1953), p. 42.

5 [Erwin Ratz (1893–1973), the Austrian musicologist, a student of Schoenberg and later of Webern, best known for his *Einführung in die musikalische Formenlehre* (1968).—trans.]

6 See Friedrich Hölderlin, "At One Time I Questioned the Muse," in *Friedrich Hölderlin: Poems and Fragments*, trans. Michael Hamburger (Cambridge, 1966), pp. 537–539.

7 [This discussion is based on the distinction between "Erlebnis," or lived experience, and "Erfahrung," or comprehended experience, a distinction for which there is no comparable pair of succinct English concepts.—trans.]

8 [See Brecht's play *The Measures Taken*, in *Collected Plays*, ed. R. Mannheim and John Willett (New York, 1971), in which spontaneous human sympathy is sacrificed to the ostensibly higher good of party discipline.—trans.]

9 [Arno Holz (1863–1929), a leading German naturalist writer who in poems, plays, and essays ironically and satirically criticized contemporary politics and religion.—trans.]

10 See Stefan George, "Neuländische Liebesmahle II," in *Werke*, ed. R. Boehringer, vol. 1 (Munich and Düsseldorf, 1958), p. 14.

11 "O mutter meiner mutter und Erlauchte," ibid., p. 50.

12 [Hermann Sudermann (1857–1928), a leading naturalist writer best known for plays that are often melodramatic and remote from the political reality they

claim to treat.—trans.]

13 [Edward Steuermann (1892–1964), the pianist, composer, and longtime friend and teacher of Adorno.—trans.]

14 [See Marcuse, "Über den affirmativen Charakter der Kultur," in *Schriften*, vol. 3 (Frankfurt, 1979), pp. 186–226.—trans.]

15 See Walter Benjamin, "The Work of Art in the Age of Mechanical Reproduction," in *Illuminations*, trans. Harry Zohn (New York, 1968).

16 [Karl Theodor Kasimer Meyerhold (1874–1940), the Russian actor and director whose theater, charged with formalism, was closed in 1938, after which he was arrested and probably executed.—trans.]

17 ["Art informelle," the European art movement that paralleled American abstract expressionism. See Adorno's "Vers une musique informelle," in *Quasi una Fantasia*, trans. Rodney Livingstone (London, 1992), pp. 269–322.—trans.]

18 [Here Adorno to some extent presupposes familiarity with his description of the hybridization or fragmentation of the arts, the "Verfransung" of art, which is the topic of his essay "Die Kunst und die Künste," in *Ohne Leitbild, Gesammelte Schriften*, vol. 10.1 (Frankfurt, 1977), pp. 432–453.—trans.]

13
Paralipomena

Aesthetics presents philosophy with the bill for the fact that the academic system degraded it to being a mere specialization. It demands of philosophy precisely what philosophy has neglected to do: that it extract phenomena from their existence and bring them to self-reflection; this would be the reflection of what is petrified in the sciences, not a specialized science located beyond them. Aesthetics thereby yields to what its object, like any object, immediately seeks. Every artwork, if it is to be fully experienced, requires thought and therefore stands in need of philosophy, which is nothing but the thought that refuses all restrictions. Understanding [*Verstehen*] and criticism are one; the capacity of understanding, that of comprehending what is understood as something spiritual, is none other than that of distinguishing in the object what is true and false, however much this distinction must deviate from the procedure of ordinary logic. Emphatically, art is knowledge, though not the knowledge of objects. Only he understands an artwork who grasps it as a complex nexus of truth, which inevitably involves its relation to untruth, its own as well as that external to it; any other judgment of artworks would remain arbitrary. Artworks thus demand an adequate relation to themselves. They postulate what was once the aim of the philosophy of art, which, in its present form, it no longer accomplishes, neither vis-à-vis contemporary consciousness nor vis-à-vis current artworks.

The idea of a value-free aesthetics is nonsense. To understand artworks, as Brecht, incidentally, well knew, means to become aware of their logicality and its opposite, and of their fissures and their significance. No one can understand Wagner's *Meistersinger* who fails to perceive that element denounced by Nietzsche of a narcissistically self-staging positivity, that is, its element of untruth. The diremption of understanding and value is a scientific institution; without values nothing is understood aesthetically, and vice versa. In art, more than in any other sphere, it is right to speak of value. Like a mime, every work says: "I'm good, no?"; to which what responds is a comportment that knows to value.

While the effort of aesthetics today presupposes the critique of its universal principles and norms as binding, this effort is itself necessarily restricted to the medium of universal thought. It is not within the purview of aesthetics to abolish this contradiction. Aesthetics must acknowledge the contradiction and reflect it, obedient to the theoretical need that art categorically registers in the age of its reflection. The necessity, however, of such universality in no way legitimates a positive doctrine of aesthetic invariants. In the obligatorily universal determinations, historical processes have sedimented what—to vary an Aristotelian formula—art was. The universal determinations of art are what art developed into. The historical situation of art, which has lost any sense of art's very raison d'être, turns to the past in the hope of finding the concept of art, which retrospectively acquires a sort of unity. This unity is not abstract but is, rather, the unfolding of art according to its own concept. At every point, therefore, the theory of art presupposes concrete analyses, not as proofs and examples but as its own condition. Benjamin, who philosophically potentiated to the extreme the immersion in concrete artworks, was himself motivated toward a turn to universal reflection in his theory of reproduction.[1]

The requirement that aesthetics be the reflection of artistic experience without relinquishing its resolutely theoretical character can best be fulfilled by incorporating the movement of the concept into the traditional categories and confronting them with artistic experience. At the same time, no continuum between the poles is to be construed. The medium of theory is abstract and this is not to be masked by the use of illustrative examples. And yet, a spark may occasionally flash up—as it did in Hegel's *Phenomenology of Spirit*—between the concretion of spiritual experience and the medium of the universal concept. This can occur in such a fashion that the concrete is not merely an illustration but rather the thing itself, around which abstract reasoning turns, yet without which the name is not to be found. To this end, aesthetics must take its orientation from the process of production, which encompasses the objective problems and desiderata presented by the products themselves. The primacy of the sphere of production in artworks is the primacy of their nature as products of social labor, by contrast with the contingency of their subjective origins. The relation to the traditional categories, however, is unavoidable because only the reflection of these categories makes it possible to open theory to artistic experience. In the transformation of the categories, which such reflection expresses and effects, historical experience penetrates theory. Through the historical dialectic, which thought liberates in the traditional categories, these categories lose their spurious abstractness without sacrificing the universal that inheres in thought: Aesthetics aims at concrete universality. The most ingenious analyses of individual works are not necessarily aesthetics; this is their inadequacy as well as their superiority over what is called the science of art. Recourse to the traditional categories is legitimated by actual artistic experience, for these categories do not simply vanish from contemporary works but return in their negation. Experience culminates in aesthetics: It makes coherent and conscious what transpires in artworks obscurely and unelucidated, and what insufficiently transpires in the particular artwork. In this regard, even a nonidealistic aesthetics is concerned with "ideas."

The qualitative difference between art and science does not simply consist in using the latter as an instrument for knowing the former. The categories employed by science stand in so obtuse a relation to the inner-artistic categories that their direct projection onto the extra-aesthetic categories inevitably wipes out what the investigation was supposed to explain. The growing relevance of technology in artworks must not become a motive for subordinating them to that type of reason that produced technology and finds its continuation in it.

What survives of the classical is the idea of artworks as something objective, mediated by subjectivity. Otherwise art would in fact be an arbitrary, insignificant, and perhaps historically outdated amusement. It would be reduced to the level of an ersatz produced by a society whose energy is no longer consumed by the acquisition of means of subsistence and in which, nevertheless, direct instinctual satisfaction is limited. Art opposes this as the tenacious protest against a positivism that would prefer to subordinate it to a universal heteronomy. Not that art, drawn into the social web of delusion, could not actually be what it opposes. Yet its existence is incompatible with the forces that want to humble and subsume it. What speaks out of important artworks is opposed to subjective reason's claim to totality. Its untruth becomes manifest in the objectivity of artworks. Cut loose from its immanent claim to objectivity, art would be nothing but a more or less organized system of stimuli-conditioning reflexes that art would autistically and dogmatically attribute to that system rather than to those on which it has an effect. The result would be the negation of the difference between artworks and merely sensual qualities; it would be an empirical entity, nothing more than—in American argot—a *battery of tests*, and the adequate means for giving an account of art would be program analysis or surveys of average group reactions to artworks or genres—except that, perhaps out of respect for recognized branches of culture, positivism seems seldom to go to the extremes logically implied by its own method. If, as a theory of knowledge, it contests all objective meaning and classes as art every thought that is irreducible to protocol sentences, it *a limine*—though without admitting it—negates art, which it takes no more seriously than does the tired businessman who uses it as a massage; if art corresponded with positivistic criteria, positivism would be art's transcendental subject. The concept of art toward which positivism tends converges with that of the culture industry, which indeed formulates its products as those of a system of stimuli, which is what the subjective theory of projection considers art to be. Hegel's argument against a subjective aesthetics based on the sensibility of recipients took issue with its arbitrariness. But this was not the end of it. The culture industry, using statistical averages, calculates the subjective element of reaction and establishes it as universal law. It has become objective spirit. This however in no way weakens Hegel's critique. For the universality of contemporary style is the negative immediacy, the liquidation of every claim to truth raised by the work as well as the permanent deception of the recipients by the implicit assurance that it is for their own good that the money with which they are furnished by concentrated economic power is once again taken away from them. This all the more directs aesthetics—and sociology as well, insofar as it performs a subsidiary function for subjective aesthetics as a sociology of putative communication—to the objectivity of the artwork. In their actual research, positivistically minded scientists working, for instance, with the *Murray Test*, oppose any analysis of the objective expressive content of the test images, which they consider excessively dependent on the observer and thus scientifically unacceptable; ultimately they would need to proceed in this manner with artworks that are not, as in that test, aimed at their recipients but rather confront those recipients with their—the artworks'—objectivity. As with any apologetic for art, positivism would have an easy time with the bare asseveration that artworks are no sum of stimuli, dismissing artworks as rationalization and projection, good for winning social status, modeled on the relation that millions of cultural philistines have to art. Or, more radically, positivism could disqualify the objectivity of art as a vestige of animism that, like any other vestige, is obliged to give way to enlightenment. Whoever refuses to be swindled out of the experience of objectivity or refuses to cede authority over art to the art-alien must proceed immanently, must join with subjective forms of reaction, of which art and its content are—in positivist human under-standing—mere reflections. What is true in positivism is the platitude that without the experience of art nothing can be known about it and there can be no discussion of it. But precisely this experience contains the distinction that positivism ignores: To put it drastically, this is whether one uses a hit song, in which there is nothing to understand, as a backdrop for all kinds of psychological projections, or whether one understands a work by submitting to the work's own discipline. What philosophical aesthetics held to be liberating in art—in philosophical argot, what transcended time and space—was the self-negation of the contemplator who is virtually extinguished in the work. This extinguishing is exacted by the artworks and is the *index veri et falsi*; only he who submits to its objective criterion understands it; he who is unconcerned about it is a consumer. The subjective element is nevertheless maintained in an adequate relation to art: The greater the effort to participate in the realization of the work and its structural dynamic, the more contemplation the subject invests in the work, the more successfully does the subject, forgetting itself, become aware of the work's objectivity; even in the work's reception, subjectivity mediates objectivity. Not just in the sublime, as Kant thought, but in all beauty the subject becomes conscious of its own nullity and attains beyond it to what is other. Kant's doctrine of the sublime falls short only in that it established the counterpart to this nullity as a positive infinity and situates it in the intelligible subject. Pain in the face of beauty is the longing for what the subjective block closes off to the subject, of which the subject nevertheless knows that it is truer than itself. Experience, which would without violence be free of the block, results from the surrender of the subject to the aesthetic law of form. The viewer enters into a contract with the artwork so that it will speak. Those who brag of having "got" something from an artwork transfer in philistine fashion the relation of possession to what is strictly foreign to it; they extend the comportment of unbroken self-preservation, subordinating beauty to that interest that beauty, according to Kant's ever valid insight, transcends. That there would nevertheless be no beauty without the subject, that beauty becomes what is in-itself only by way of its for-other, is the fault of the self-positing of the subject. Because this self-positing disrupted beauty, it has need of its recollection by the subject in the image. The melancholy of evening is not the mood of he who feels it, yet it grips only him who has himself been so differentiated, has so much become subject, that he is not blind to it. Only the strong and developed subject, the product of all control over nature and its injustice, has the power both to step back from the object and to revoke its self-positing. The subject of aesthetic subjectivism, however, is weak, "*outer directed.*"[2] The overestimation of the subjective element in the artwork and the lack of a relation to the artwork are equivalent. The subject only becomes the essence of the artwork when it confronts it foreignly, externally, and compensates for the foreignness by substituting itself for the work. Of course the objectivity of the artwork is not completely and adequately open to knowledge, and in the works it is never beyond question; the difference between what is demanded by the problem posed by the works and the solution to this demand gnaws away at their objectivity. This objectivity is not a positive fact but rather an ideal toward which the work and knowledge of it tend. Aesthetic objectivity is not unmediated; he who thinks he holds it in the palm of his hand is led astray by it. If it were unmediated it would coincide with the sensuous phenomena of art and would suppress its spiritual element, which is, however, fallible both for itself and for others. Aesthetics effectively means the study of the conditions and mediations of the objectivity of art. Hegel's argumentation against Kant's subjectivistic grounding of aesthetics is too facile: In that the object is a priori spirit, the Hegelian immersion in the object or in its categories—which in Hegel still coincide with the genres —transpires without meeting any resistance. The collapse of the absolute- ness of spirit brings down with it the absoluteness of artworks. This is why it is so difficult for aesthetics not to capitulate to positivism and perish in it. Yet the dismemberment of the metaphysics of spirit does not expel spirit: Its spiritual element is strengthened and concretized once it is recognized that not everything in it must be spirit, which, incidentally, Hegel himself did not hold. If the metaphysics of spirit was patterned on art, after the collapse of metaphysics the spirit of art is, so to speak, restituted. The inadequate subjective-positivistic theorems of art must be demonstrated in art itself, not deduced from a philosophy of spirit. Aesthetic norms that are said to correspond to the perceiving subject's invariant forms of reaction are empirically invalid; thus the academic psychology is false that, in opposing new music, propounds that the ear is unable to perceive highly complex tonal phenomena that deviate too far from the natural overtone relations: There is no disputing that there are individuals who have this capacity and there is no reason why everyone should not be able to have it; the limitations are not transcendental but social, those of second nature. If an empirically oriented aesthetics uses quantitative averages as norms, it unconsciously sides with social conformity. What such an aesthetics classifies as pleasing or painful is never a sensual given of nature but something preformed by society as a whole, by what it sanctions and censors, and this has always been challenged by artistic production. Subjective reactions such as disgust for the suave, a motive force in new art, are elements of resistance to the heteronomous social order that have migrated into the sensorium. In general, the supposed basis of art is predicated on subjective forms of reaction and comportments; even the apparent accidents of taste are governed by a latent compulsion, albeit not always that of the material itself; any subjective form of reaction that is indifferent to the work is extra-aesthetic. At the very least, however, every subjective element in artworks is also motivated by the material itself. The sensibility of the artist is essentially the capacity to hear what is transpiring within the material, to see with the work's own eyes. The more strictly aesthetics, in accord with Hegel's postulate, is constructed on the movement of the material itself, the more objective it becomes and the less it confuses subjectively founded, dubious invariants with objectivity. It was Croce's achievement to have dialectically done away with every standard external to the work; Hegel's classicism prevented him from doing the same. In his *Aesthetics* he broke off the dialectic just as he did in the political thought of the *Philosophy of Right*. Only on the basis of the experience of radically nominalistic new art is Hegel's aesthetics to be fully realized; here even Croce hesitated.

Aesthetic positivism, which replaced the theoretical decipherment of artworks by taking inventories of their effects, can claim to be true only insofar as it denounces that fetishization of artworks that is itself part and parcel of the culture industry and aesthetic decline. Positivism draws attention to the dialectical element that no artwork is ever pure. For many aesthetic forms, such as opera, the effect was constitutive; if the internal movement of the genre compels it to renounce the primacy of effect, then the genre essentially becomes impossible. Whoever naïvely takes the artwork for the pure in-itself, as which all the same it must be taken, becomes the naïve victim of the work as self-posited and takes semblance for a higher reality, blind to the constitutive element in art. Positivism is the bad consciousness of art: It reminds art that it is not unmediatedly true.

Whereas the thesis of the projective character of art ignores its objectivity—its quality and truth content—and is unable to conceive an emphatic concept of art, it is important as the expression of a historical tendency. What in philistine fashion it inflicts on artworks corresponds to the positivistic caricature of enlightenment, of unfettered subjective reason. Reason's social superiority penetrates the works. This tendency, which would like to render artworks impossible through their deaestheticization, cannot be arrested by insisting that art must exist: Nowhere is that chiseled in stone. The theory of art as a subjective projection ultimately terminates in the negation of art, and this must be kept in mind if the theory of projection itself is not to be ignominiously neutralized according to the model of the culture industry. But positivistic consciousness has, as false consciousness, its own difficulties: It needs art as an arena in which it may dispose of what does not have any place in its own suffocatingly narrow space. Moreover, positivism, ever credulously devoted to the factually given, is obliged somehow to come to terms with art, simply because it exists. The positivists try to rescue themselves from this dilemma by taking art no more seriously than does a *tired businessman*. This allows them to be tolerant toward artworks, which, according to the positivist's own thought, no longer exist.

Just how little artworks are subsumed in their genesis, and how much, for this reason, philological methods do them an injustice, can be graphically demonstrated. Schikaneder had no need to dream up Bachofen.[3] The libretto of *The Magic Flute* amalgamates the most disparate sources without unifying them. Objectively, however, the work reveals the conflict between matriarchy and patriarchy, between lunar and solar principles. This explains the resilience of the text, long defamed as worse than mediocre by pedants. The libretto occupies a boundary line between banality and profundity, but is protected from the former because the coloratura role of the Queen of the Night is not presented as an "evil force."

Aesthetic experience crystallizes in the individual work. Still, no particular aesthetic experience occurs in isolation, independently of the continuity of experiencing consciousness. The temporally sequestered and atomistic is as contrary to aesthetic experience as it is to all experience: In the relation to artworks as monads, the pent-up force of aesthetic consciousness constituted beyond the individual work must participate. It is in this sense that "understanding art" is meaningful. The continuity of aesthetic experience is colored by all other experience and by all knowledge, though, of course, it is only confirmed and corrected in the actual confrontation with the phenomenon.

To intellectual reflection, to taste that considers itself able to judge the matter from above, Stravinsky's *Renard* may well seem a more suitable treatment of Wedekind's *Lulu* than does Berg's music. The musician knows, however, how far superior Berg's work is to Stravinsky's and in its favor it willingly sacrifices the sovereignty of the aesthetic standpoint; artistic experience is born out of just such conflicts.

The feelings provoked by artworks are real and to this extent extra-aesthetic. By contrast to these feelings, a cognitive posture that runs counter to the observing subject is more applicable, more just to the aesthetic phenomenon, without confusing it with the empirical existence of the observing subject. In that, however, the artwork is not only aesthetic but sub- and supra-aesthetic; in that it originates in empirical layers of life, has the quality of being a thing, a *fait social*, and ultimately converges with the meta-aesthetic in the idea of truth, it implies a critique of any chemically pure attitude to art. The experiencing subject, from which aesthetic experience distances itself, returns in aesthetic experience as a transaesthetic subject. The aesthetic shudder once again cancels the distance held by the subject. Although artworks offer themselves to observation, they at the same time disorient the observer who is held at the distance of a mere spectator; to him is revealed the truth of the work as if it must also be his own. The instant of this transition is art's highest. It rescues subjectivity, even subjective aesthetics, by the negation of subjectivity. The subject, convulsed by art, has real experiences; by the strength of insight into the artwork as artwork, these experiences are those in which the subject's petrification in his own subjectivity dissolves and the narrowness of his self-positedness is revealed. If in artworks the subject finds his true happiness in the moment of being convulsed, this is a happiness that is counterposed to the subject and thus its instrument is tears, which also express the grief over one's own mortality. Kant sensed something of this in his aesthetic of the sublime, which he excluded from art.

An absence of naïveté—a reflective posture—toward art clearly also requires naïveté, insofar as aesthetic consciousness does not allow its experiences to be regulated by what is culturally approved but rather preserves the force of spontaneous reaction toward even the most avant-garde movements. However much individual and even artistic consciousness is mediated by society, by the prevailing objective spirit, it remains the geometric site of that spirit's self-reflection and broadens it. Naïveté toward art is a source of blindness; but whoever lacks it totally is truly narrowminded and trapped in what is foisted upon him.

The "isms" must be defended as watchwords, as witnesses to the universal state of reflection, and, insofar as they function in the formation of movements, as the successors of what tradition once performed. This arouses the rage of the dichotomous bourgeois mind. Although it insists on planning and willing everything, under its control art is supposed to be, like love, spontaneous, involuntary; and unconscious. Historicophilosophically this is denied it. The taboo on watchwords is reactionary.

The concept of the new has inherited what once the individualistic concept of originality wanted to express and which in the meantime is opposed by those who do not want the new, who denounce it as unoriginal and all advanced forms as indistinguishable.

If recent art movements have made montage their principle, subcutaneously all artworks have always shared something of this principle; this could be demonstrated in detail in the puzzle technique of the great music of Viennese classicism, which nevertheless corresponds perfectly with the idea of organic development in that era's philosophy.

The distortion of the structure of history by the *parti pris* for real or putatively great events also affects the history of art. Indeed, history always crystallizes in the qualitatively new, but the antithesis must also be held in mind: that the sudden appearance of a new quality, the dialectical reversal, is virtually a non-entity. This enervates the myth of artistic creativity. The artist carries out a minimal transition, not the maximal *creatio ex nihilo*. The differential of the new is the locus of productivity. It is the infinitesimally small that is decisive and shows the individual artist to be the executor of a collective objectivity of spirit in contrast to which his own part vanishes. This was implicitly recognized in the idea of genius as receptive and passive, which opens a view to that in artworks that makes them more than their primary definition, more than artifacts. Their desire to be thus and not otherwise functions in opposition to the character of an artifact by driving it to its extreme; the sovereign artist would like to annul the hubris of creativity. Herein lies the morsel of truth to be found in the belief that everything is always possible. The keys of each and every piano hold the whole *Appassionata*; the composer need only draw it out, but this, obviously, required Beethoven.

In spite of the aversion to what in modernism is regarded as antiquated, the situation of art vis-à-vis *Jugendstil* has in no way changed as radically as that aversion would like to suppose. This could explain both the aversion to *Jugendstil* and the undiminished actuality of Schoenberg's *Pierrot*, as well as of many works by Maeterlinck and Strindberg, which, though they are not identical with *Jugendstil*, can nevertheless be attributed to it. *Jugendstil* was the first collective effort to extract from art an otherwise absent meaning; the collapse of this effort paradigmatically circumscribes the contemporary aporia of art. This effort exploded in expressionism; functionalism and its counterparts in nonapplied arts were its abstract negation. The key to contemporary anti-art, with Beckett at its pinnacle, is perhaps the idea of concretizing this negation, of culling aesthetic meaning from the radical negation of metaphysical meaning. The aesthetic principle of form is in itself, through the synthesis of what is formed, the positing of meaning even when meaning is substantively rejected. To this extent, whatever it wills or states, art remains theology; its claim to truth and its affinity to untruth are one and the same. This emerged specifically in *Jugendstil*. The situation culminates in the question of whether, after the fall of theology and in its total absence, art is still possible. But if, as in Hegel—who was the first to express historicophilosophical doubts as to this possibility—this necessity subsists, art retains an oracular quality; it is ambiguous whether the possibility of art is a genuine witness to what endures of theology or if it is the reflection of an enduring spell.

As is evident in its name, *Jugendstil* is a declaration of permanent puberty: It is a utopia that barters off its own unrealizability.

Hatred of the new originates in a concealed tenet of bourgeois ontology: that the transient should be transient, that death should have the last word.

The idea of making a sensation was always bound up with the effort to *épater le bourgeois* and was adapted to the bourgeois interest of turning everything to a profit.

However certain it is that the concept of the new is shot through with pernicious social characteristics—especially with that of *nouveauté*—on the market it is equally impossible, ever since Baudelaire, Manet, and *Tristan*, to dispense with it; efforts to do away with it, faced with its putative contingency and arbitrariness, have only heightened both.

351

Ever and again the menacing category of the new radiates the allure of freedom, more compellingly than it radiates its inhibiting, leveling, sometimes sterile aspects.

The category of the new, as the abstract negation of the category of the permanent, converges with permanence: The invariance of the new is its weakness.

Modernism emerged as something qualitatively new, in opposition to exhausted given forms; for this reason it is not purely temporal; this helps to explain why on the one hand it acquired those invariable features for which its critics gladly indict it and why, on the other hand, the new cannot simply be dismissed as being obsolete. In it the inner-aesthetic and the social interlock. The more art is compelled to oppose the standardized life stamped out by the structure of domination, the more it evokes chaos: Chaos forgotten becomes disaster. This explains the mendacity of the clamor about the putative spiritual terror of modern art, clamor that surpasses that terror of the world to which art stands opposed. The terror of a form of reaction that puts up with nothing but the new is salutary for the shame it casts on the banality of official culture. Those who embarrass themselves by blathering that art must not forget humanity, or when—in the face of bewildering works—they ask where the message is, will be reluctantly compelled, perhaps even without genuine conviction, to sacrifice cherished habits; shame can, however, inaugurate a process in which the external pervades the inner, a process that makes it impossible for the terrorized to go on bleating with the others.

It is impossible to consider the emphatic aesthetic idea of the new apart from the industrial procedures that increasingly dominate the material production of society; whether they are mediated by the exhibition of works, as Benjamin seems to have assumed, remains to be decided.[4] Industrial techniques, however, the repetition of identical rhythms and the repetitive manufacture of an identical object based on a pattern, at the same time contain a principle antithetical to the new. This exerts itself as a force in the antinomy of the aesthetically new.

Just as there is nothing that is simply ugly, per se, and just as anything ugly can become beautiful through its function, so there is nothing that is simply beautiful: It is trivial to note that the most beautiful sunset, the most beautiful girl, faithfully painted, can become repellent. And yet the element of immediacy in the beautiful, as in the ugly, is not to be suppressed: No lover capable of perceiving distinctions—and this capacity is the precondition of love—will allow the beauty of the beloved to perish.

Beauty and ugliness are neither to be hypostatized nor relativized; their relation is revealed in stages where one frequently becomes the opposite of the other. Beauty is historical in itself as what wrests itself free.[5]

Just how little empirical productive subjectivity and its unity converge with the constitutive aesthetic subject or, indeed, with objective aesthetic quality is attested by the beauty of many cities. Perugia and Assisi show the highest degree of form and coherence, probably without its ever having been intended or envisioned, although it is important not to underestimate the degree of planning even in a second nature that seems organic. This impression is favored by the gentle swell of a mountain, the reddish hue of stones, that is, by the extra-aesthetic that, as material of human labor, is itself one of the determinants of form. Here historical continuity acts as subject, truly an objective spirit that permits itself to be directed by the extra-aesthetic without requiring the individual architect to be conscious of it. This historical subject of beauty also largely directs the work of the individual artist. Although the beauty of these cities seems to be the result of strictly external factors, its source is internal. Immanent historicity becomes manifest, and with this manifestation aesthetic truth unfolds.

The identification of art with beauty is inadequate, and not just because it is too formal. In what art became, the category of the beautiful is only one element, one that has moreover undergone fundamental change: By absorbing the ugly, the concept of beauty has been transformed in itself, without, however, aesthetics being able to dispense with it. In the absorption of the ugly, beauty is strong enough to expand itself by its own opposite.

Hegel was the first to oppose aesthetic sentimentalism that seeks to discern the inherent content of the artwork not in the work itself but rather in its effect. This sentimentalism later became a concern with mood, a concept that has its own historical importance. For better or worse, nothing better defines Hegel's aesthetics than its incompatibility with the element of an artwork's mood. He insists, as he does throughout his philosophy, on the sturdiness of the concept. This redounds to the objectivity of the artwork rather than to its effects or to its merely sensuous facade. The progress that Hegel thus achieved was, however, bought at the price of a certain art-alienness; the objectivity was bought at the cost of reification, an excess of materiality. This progress threatens to set aesthetics back to the pre-artistic, to the concrete comportment of the bourgeois, who wants to be able to find a fixed content [Inhalt] in a painting or a play that he can grasp as well as depend on. In Hegel the dialectic of art is limited to the genres and their history, and it is not sufficiently introduced into the theory of the individual work. That natural beauty rebuffs definition by spirit leads Hegel, in a short circuit, to disparage what in art is not spirit qua intention. The correlative of intention is reification. The correlative of absolute making is always the made as a fixed object. Hegel mistakes what is not thing-like in art, which is inseparable from the concept of art as being opposed to the empirical world of things. Polemically he attributes what is not thing-like in art to natural beauty as its encumbering indeterminacy. But it is precisely in this element that natural beauty possesses something without which the artwork would revert back into a nonaesthetic facticity. Those who in experiencing nature are unable to distinguish it from objects to be acted upon—the distinction that constitutes the aesthetic—are incapable of artistic experience. Hegel's thesis, that art beauty originates in the negation of natural beauty, and thus in natural beauty, needs to be turned around: The act that initially gives rise to the consciousness of something beautiful must be carried out in the immediate experience if it is not already to postulate what it constitutes. The conception of natural beauty communicates with natural beauty: Both want to restore nature by renouncing its mere immediacy. In this context Benjamin's concept of aura is important: "The concept of aura proposed above with reference to historical objects may usefully be illustrated with reference to the aura of natural ones. We define the aura of the latter as the unique phenomenon of a distance, however close it may be. While resting on a summer afternoon to let one's gaze follow a mountain range on the horizon or a branch that casts its shadow over one—that is to breathe the aura of those mountains, or of that branch."[6] Here what is called aura is known to artistic experience as the atmosphere of the artwork, that whereby the nexus of the artwork's elements points beyond this nexus and allows each individual element to point beyond itself. Precisely this constituent of art, for which the existential-ontological term "being attuned" provides only a distorted equivalent, is what in the artwork escapes its factual reality, what, fleeting and elusive—and this could hardly have been conceived in Hegel's time—can nevertheless be objectivated in the form of artistic technique. The reason why the auratic element does not deserve Hegel's ban is that a more insistent analysis can show that it is an objective determination of the artwork. That aspect of an artwork that points beyond itself is not just a part of its concept but can be recognized in the specific configuration of every artwork. Even when artworks divest themselves of every atmospheric element—a development inaugurated by Baudelaire—it is conserved in them as a negated and shunned element. Precisely this auratic element has its model in nature, and the artwork is more deeply related to nature in this element than in any other factual similarity to nature. To perceive the aura in nature in the way Benjamin demands in his illustration of the concept requires recognizing in nature what it is that essentially makes an artwork an artwork. This, however, is that objective meaning that surpasses subjective intention. An artwork opens its eyes under the gaze of the spectator when it emphatically articulates something objective, and this possibility of an objectivity that is not simply projected by the spectator is modeled on the expression of melancholy, or serenity, that can be found in nature when it is not seen as an object of action. The distancing that Benjamin stresses in the concept of aura is a rudimentary model of the distancing of natural objects—as potential means—from practical aims. The threshold between artistic and preartistic experience is precisely that between the domination of the mechanism of identification and the innervations of the objective language of objects. Just as the exemplary instance of the philistine is a reader who judges his relation to artworks on the basis of whether he can identify with the protagonists, so false identification with the immediately empirical person is the index of complete obtuseness toward art. This false identification abolishes the distance at the same time that it isolates the consumption of aura as "something higher." True, even an authentic relation to the artwork demands an act of identification: The object must be entered and participated in—as Benjamin says, it is necessary "to breathe its aura." But the medium of this relationship is what Hegel called freedom toward the object: The spectator must not project what transpires in himself on to the artwork in order to find himself confirmed, uplifted, and satisfied in it, but must, on the contrary, relinquish himself to the artwork, assimilate himself to it, and fulfill the work in its own terms. In other words, he must submit to the discipline of the work rather than demand that the artwork give him something. The aesthetic comportment, however, that avoids this, thereby remaining blind to what in the artwork is more than factually the case, is unitary with the projective attitude, that of *terre à terre*, which characterizes the contemporary epoch as a whole and deaestheticizes artworks. Correlatively, artworks become on the one hand things among things and, on the other, containers for the psychology of the spectator. As mere things they no longer speak, which makes them adequate as receptacles for the spectator. The concept of mood, so opposed by Hegel's objective aesthetics, is therefore insufficient, because it is precisely mood that reverses what

Hegel calls the truth in the artwork into its own opposite by translating it into what is merely subjective—a spectator's mode of reaction—and represents it in the work itself according to the model of this subjectivity.

Mood in artworks once meant that in which the effect and the internal constitution of works formed a murky amalgam that went beyond their individual elements. As the semblance of sublimity, mood delivered the artwork over to the empirical. Although one of the limits of Hegel's aesthetics is its blindness to this element of mood, it is at the same time its dignity that caused it to avoid the twilight between the aesthetic and the empirical subject.

Rather than that, as Kant thought, spirit in the face of nature becomes aware of its own superiority, it becomes aware of its own natural essence. This is the moment when the subject, vis-à-vis the sublime, is moved to tears. Recollection of nature breaks the arrogance of his self-positing: "My tears well up; earth, I am returning to you."[7] With that, the self exits, spiritually, from its imprisonment in itself. Something of freedom flashes up that philosophy, culpably mistaken, reserves for its opposite, the glorification of the subject. The spell that the subject casts over nature imprisons the subject as well: Freedom awakens in the consciousness of its affinity with nature. Because beauty is not subordinate to natural causality imposed by the subject on phenomena, its realm is that of a possible freedom.

No more than in any other social realm is the division of labor in art a plain evil. When art reflects the social coercion in which it is harnessed and by doing so opens up a perspective on reconciliation, it is spiritualization; this spiritualization, however, presupposes the division of manual and intellectual labor. Only through spiritualization, and not through stubborn rank natural growth, do artworks break through the net of the domination of nature and mold themselves to nature; only from within does one issue forth. Otherwise art becomes infantile. Even in spirit something of the mimetic impulse survives, that secularized mana, what moves and touches us.

In many works of the Victorian era, not only in England, the force of sexuality and the sensuality related to it becomes even more palpable through its concealment; this could be shown in many of Theodor Storm's novellas. In early Brahms, whose genius has not been sufficiently appreciated to this day, there are passages of an overwhelming tenderness, such as could be expressed only by one who was deprived of it. Once again, it is a gross simplification to equate expression and subjectivity. What is subjectively expressed does not need to resemble the expressing subject. In many instances what is expressed will be precisely what the expressing subject is not; subjectively, all expression is mediated by longing.

Sensual satisfaction, punished at various times by an ascetic authoritarianism, has historically become directly antagonistic to art; mellifluous sounds, harmonious colors, and suaveness have become kitsch and trademarks of the culture industry. The sensual appeal of art continues to be legitimate only when, as in Berg's *Lulu* or in the work of André Masson, it is the bearer or a function of the content rather than an end in itself. One of the difficulties of new art is how to combine the desideratum of internal coherence, which always imports a certain degree of evident polish into the work, with opposition to the culinary element. Sometimes the work requires the culinary, while paradoxically the sensorium balks at it.

By defining art as something spiritual, however, the sensual element is not simply negated. Even the insight, hardly anathema to traditional aesthetics, that aesthetically only what is realized in sensual material counts, is superficial. What has been attributed to the highest artworks as metaphysical power has, over millennia, been fused with an element of sensuous happiness that autonomous formation has always opposed. It is only by grace of that element that art is intermittently able to become an image of bliss. The comforting motherly hand that strokes one's hair gives sensuous pleasure. Extreme spirituality reverses into the physical. In its *parti pris* for sensual appearance, traditional aesthetics sensed something that has since been lost, but took it too immediately. Without the harmonious sonority of a string quartet, the D-flat-major passage of the slow movement of Beethoven's op. 59, no. 1, would not have the power of consolation: The promise that the content is real—which makes it truth content—is bound up with the sensual. Here art is as materialistic as is all metaphysical truth. That today this element is proscribed probably involves the true crisis of art. Without recollection of this element, however, there would no longer be art, any more than if art abandoned itself entirely to the sensual.

Artworks are things that tend to slough off their reity. However, in artworks the aesthetic is not superimposed on the thing in such a fashion that, given a solid foundation, their spirit could emerge. Essential to artworks is that their thingly structure, by virtue of its constitution, makes them into what is not a thing; their reity is the medium of their own transcendence. The two are mediated in each other: The spirit of artworks is constituted in their reity, and their reity, the existence of works, originates in their spirit.

As regards form, artworks are things insofar as the objectivation that they give themselves resembles what is in-itself, what rests within itself and determines itself; and this has its model in the empirical world of things, indeed by virtue of their unity through the synthesizing spirit; they become spiritualized only through their reification, just as their spiritual element and their reity are melded together; their spirit, by which they transcend themselves, is at the same time their lethality. This they have implicitly always borne in themselves, and ineluctable reflection has exposed it.

Narrow limits are set to the thing character of art. In the temporal arts especially, in spite of the objectivation of their texts, their non-thingly quality survives in the momentariness of their appearance. That a piece of music or a play is written down bears a contradiction that the sensorium recognizes in the frequency with which the speeches of actors on stage ring false because they are obliged to enunciate something as if it were spontaneous even though it is imposed by the text. But the objectivation of musical scores and dramatic texts cannot be summoned back to improvisation.

The crisis of art, which has today reached the point of endangering its very possibility, affects both of its poles equally: On the one hand its meaning and thereby essentially its spiritual content; and on the other its expression and thereby its mimetic element. One depends on the other: There is no expression without meaning, without the medium of spiritualization; no meaning without the mimetic element: without art's eloquence,[8] which is now in the process of perishing.

Aesthetic distance from nature is a movement toward nature; in this, idealism did not deceive itself. The telos of nature, the focal point toward which the force fields of art are organized, compels art toward semblance, to the concealment of what in it belongs to the external world of things.

Benjamin's dictum—that the paradox of an artwork is that it appears[9]—is by no means as enigmatic as it may sound. Every artwork is in fact an oxymoron. Its own reality is for it unreal, it is indifferent to what it essentially is, and at the same time it is its own precondition; in the context of reality it is all the more unreal and chimerical. The enemies of art have always understood this better than those of its apologists who have fruitlessly sought to deny its constitutive paradox. Aesthetics is powerless that seeks to dissolve the constitutive contradiction rather than conceiving of art by way of it. The reality and unreality of artworks are not layers superimposed on each other; rather, they interpenetrate everything in art to an equal degree. An artwork is real only to the extent that, as an artwork, it is unreal, self-sufficient, and differentiated from the empirical world, of which it nevertheless remains a part. But its unreality—its determination as spirit—only exists to the extent that it has become real; nothing in an artwork counts that is not there in an individuated form. In aesthetic semblance the artwork takes up a stance toward reality, which it negates by becoming a reality sui generis. Art protests against reality by its own objectivation.

No matter where an interpreter enters his text, he always encounters a boundless profusion of desiderata that he must fulfill, although it is impossible to fulfill any one of them without causing another to suffer; he runs up against the incompatibility of what the works themselves want in their own terms, and what they want of him; the compromises that result, however, are detrimental because of the indifference inherent in indecision. Fully adequate interpretation is a chimera. This is not the least of what grants primacy to the ideal reading over performing: for reading—and in this it is comparable to Locke's infamous universal triangle—tolerates the coexistence of opposites because it is at once sensuous and nonsensuous intuition. This paradox of an artwork becomes apparent in a gathering of devotees around an artist to whom a particular problem or difficulty has been naïvely pointed out in a work in progress, whereupon he turns to his interlocutor with a condescending, desperate smile and replies: "But that's just the trick!" He rebukes one who knows nothing of the constitutive impossibility under which he works, and mourns over the a priori futility of his effort. The fact that he tries it nevertheless is the dignity of all virtuosos despite all the exhibitionism and the straining after effect. Virtuosity should not confine itself to the reproduction of a work but should, rather, fully enter the facture, which it is compelled to do by its sublimation. Virtuosity makes the paradoxical essence of art, the possibility of the impossible, appear. Virtuosos are the martyrs of artworks; in many of their achievements, whether those of ballerinas or coloratura sopranos, something sadistic has become sedimented, some traces of the torture required to carry it out. It is no coincidence that the name "artist" is borne both by the circus performer and one who has most turned away from effect, who champions the audacious idea of art, to fulfill its pure concept. If the logicality of artworks is also always their enemy, the absurd constitutes the countertendency to logicality even in traditional art, long before it became a philosophical program; this is proof that in art absolute logicality is empty. There is no net under authentic artworks that could protect them in their fall.

If in an artwork a process of development is objectivated and brought to an equilibrium, this objectivation thereby negates the process and reduces it to a mere as-if; this is probably why in the wake of the contemporary rebellion of art against semblance the forms of aesthetic objectivation have been rejected and the attempt was made to replace a merely simulated process of development with an immediate, improvisational process of becoming, even though the power of art, its dynamic element, could not exist without such fixation and thus without its semblance.

Duration of the transient, an element of art that at the same time perpetuates the mimetic heritage, is one of the categories that dates back to primeval times. In the judgment of many authors, the image itself, regardless of the level of differentiation of its content, is a phenomenon of regeneration. Frobenius reports of pygmies who "at the moment of sunrise drew the animal that they would later kill in order to resurrect it in a higher sense the following morning after the ritual smearing of the image with blood and hair . . . Thus the pictures of the animals represent their immortalization and apotheosis, effectively raising them into the firmament as eternal stars."[10] Yet it is apparent that precisely in early history the achievement of duration was accompanied by consciousness of its futility, perhaps even that such duration—in the spirit of the prohibition on graven images—was tied up with a sense of guilt toward the living. According to Walther Resch, the most archaic period was dominated by "a marked fear of portraying human beings."[11] One could well suppose that early on the nonreplicatory aesthetic images were already filtered through a prohibition on images, a taboo: Even the antimagical element of art has a magical origin. This is indicated by the no less ancient "ritual destruction of the image": At the very least "the image should bear marks of destruction so that the animal would no longer 'roam about.'"[12] This taboo originates in a fear of the dead, which was a motivation for embalming them in order—so to speak—to keep them alive. There is much to favor the speculation that the idea of aesthetic duration developed out of the process of mummification. This is substantiated by Felix Speiser's research on wood figurines of the New Hebrides,[13] to which Fritz Krause refers: "The line of development led from mummified figures to exact bodily replications in figure and skull statues, and from skulls mounted on poles to wooden and tree-fern statues."[14] Speiser interprets this shift as a "transition from the preservation and simulation of the bodily presence of the dead to the symbolic indication of their presence, and this constitutes the transition to the statue in the proper sense of the term."[15] This transition may well be that of the neolithic separation of material and form, the origin of "signification." One of the models of art may be the corpse in its transfixed and imperishable form. In that case, the reification of the formerly living would date back to primordial times, as did the revolt against death as a magical nature-bound practice.

As semblance perishes in art, the culture industry has developed an insatiable illusionism, the ultimate form of which Huxley constructed in the *"feelies"* of his *Brave New World*; the allergy to semblance runs in counterpoint to its commercial omnipotence. The elimination of semblance is the opposite of vulgar conceptions of realism, which in the culture industry is the exact complement of semblance.

Ever since the beginning of the modern age and the emergence of the self-reflecting diremption of subject and object, bourgeois reality—in spite of the limitations set by its incomprehensibility—has had a trace of unreality, of the illusory, just as in philosophy reality became a web of subjective determinations. The more irritating this illusoriness, the more obstinately did consciousness veil the reality of the real. Art, on the other hand, posited itself as semblance, far more emphatically than in previous periods, when it was not sharply distinguished from description and reporting. To this extent it sabotages the false claim to reality of a world dominated by the subject, the world of the commodity. This is the crystallization of art's truth content; it sets reality into relief by the self-positing of semblance. Thus semblance serves truth.

Nietzsche called for "an antimetaphysical but artistic" philosophy.[16] This would be a mix of Baudelaire's *spleen* with *Jugendstil*, with a subtle absurdity: as if art would obey the emphatic claim of this dictum if it were not the Hegelian unfolding of truth and itself a bit of the metaphysics Nietzsche condemned. There is nothing more anti-artistic than rigorous positivism. Nietzsche knew that well. That he allowed the contradiction to stand without developing it fits well with Baudelaire's cult of the lie and the chimerical, aerial concept of the beautiful in Ibsen. Nietzsche, that most consistent figure of enlightenment, did not deceive himself that sheer consistency destroys the motivation and meaning of enlightenment. Rather than carrying out the self-reflection of enlightenment, he perpetrated one conceptual *coup de main* after the other. They express that truth itself, the idea of which kindles enlightenment, does not exist without semblance, which it nevertheless wants to extirpate for the sake of truth; with this element of truth art stands in solidarity.

Art is directed toward truth, it is not itself immediate truth; to this extent truth is its content. By its relation to truth, art is knowledge; art itself knows truth in that truth emerges through it. As knowledge, however, art is neither discursive nor is its truth the reflection of an object.

Shoulder-shrugging aesthetic relativism is itself reified consciousness; it is not so much a melancholy skepticism conscious of its own incapacity as resentment of art's claim to truth, a claim that yet alone legitimated that greatness of artworks without the fetishization of which the relativists would have nothing to discuss. Their comportment is reified in that it is passively external and modeled on consumption rather than that it enters into the movement of those artworks in which the question of their truth becomes conclusive. Relativism is the split-off self-reflection of the isolated subject and as such indifferent to the work. Even aesthetically it is hardly ever meant in earnest; earnestness is just what it finds unbearable. Whoever says of an experimental new work that it is impossible to judge such a thing imagines that his incomprehension has effectively annihilated the work. That there are those who perpetually engage in aesthetic arguments, all the while indifferent as to the position they have taken, vis-à-vis aesthetics, is a more compelling refutation of relativism than any philosophical rebuttal: The idea of aesthetic truth finds justice for itself in spite of and in its problematic. However, the strongest support for the critique of aesthetic relativism is the definitiveness of technical questions. The automatically triggered response that technique may indeed permit categorical judgments, but that neither art nor its content do, dogmatically divides the latter from technique. However certain it is that artworks are more than the quintessence of their procedures, which is to say their "technique," it is just as certain that they have objective content only insofar as it appears in them, and this occurs solely by the strength of the quintessence of their technique. Its logic leads the way to aesthetic truth. Certainly no continuum stretches from aesthetic precepts learned in school to aesthetic judgment, yet even the discontinuity of this trajectory obeys a necessity: The highest questions of the truth of a work can be translated into categories of its coherence.[17] When this is not possible, thought reaches one of the boundaries of human restrictedness beyond the limitation of the judgment of taste.

The immanent coherence of artworks and their meta-aesthetic truth converge in their truth content. This truth would be simply dropped from heaven in the same way as was Leibniz's preestablished harmony, which presupposes a transcendent creator, if it were not that the development of the immanent coherence of artworks serves truth, the image of an in-itself that they themselves cannot be. If artworks strive after an objective truth, it is mediated to them through the fulfillment of their own lawfulness. That artworks fulfill their truth better the more they fulfill themselves: This is the Ariadnian thread by which they feel their way through their inner darkness. But this is no self-deception. For their autarchy originated in what they themselves are not. The protohistory of artworks is the introduction of the categories of the real into their semblance. However, the movement of the categories in the autonomy of the work is not defined solely by the laws of this semblance; rather, they preserve the directional constants that they received from the external world. The question posed by artworks is how the truth of reality can become their own truth. The canon of this transformation is untruth. Their pure existence criticizes the existence of a spirit that exclusively manipulates its other. What is socially untrue, flawed, and ideological is communicated to the structure of artworks as flawed, indeterminate, and inadequate. For the manner in which artworks react, their objective "attitude toward objectivity," remains an attitude toward reality.[18]

An artwork is always itself and simultaneously the other of itself. Such otherness can lead astray, because the constitutive meta-aesthetic element volatilizes the instant one pulls it away from the aesthetic and imagines that one holds it isolated in one's hands.

The recent historical tendency to emphasize the work itself, in opposition to the subject—at least to the subject's manifestation in the work —further undermines the distinction of artworks from reality, in spite of the subjective origin of this tendency. Increasingly, works acquire a second-order existence that obscures what is human in them. Subjectivity disappears into artworks as the instrument of their objectivation. The subjective imagination, of which artworks as ever stand in need, becomes recognizable as the turning back of the objective onto the subject and of the necessity of guarding the line of demarcation around the artwork. Imagination is the capacity to do this. It shapes what reposes in itself rather than arbitrarily concocting forms, details, fables, or whatever. Indeed, the truth of artworks cannot be otherwise conceived than in that what is transsubjective becomes readable in the subjectively imagined in-itself. The mediation of the transsubjective is the artwork.

The mediation between the content of artworks and their composition is subjective mediation. It consists not only in the labor and struggle of objectivation. What goes beyond subjective intention and its arbitrariness has a correlative objectivity within the subject: in the form of that subject's experiences, insofar as their locus is situated beyond the conscious will. As their sedimentation, artworks are imageless images, and these experiences mock representational depiction. Their innervation and registration is the subjective path to truth content. The only adequate concept of realism, which no art today dare shun, would be an unflinching fidelity to these experiences. Provided they go deeply enough, they touch on historical constellations back of the facades of reality and psychology. Just as the interpretation of traditional philosophy must excavate the experiences that motivated the categorial apparatus and deductive sequences in the first place, the interpretation of artworks penetrates to this subjectively experienced kernel of experience, which goes beyond the subject; interpretation thereby obeys the convergence of philosophy and art in truth content. Whereas it is this truth content that artworks speak in themselves, beyond their meaning, it takes shape in that artworks sediment historical experiences in their configuration, and this is not possible except by way of the subject: The truth content is no abstract in-itself. The truth of important works of false consciousness is situated in the gesture with which they indicate the strength of this false consciousness as inescapable, not in immediately possessing as their content the theoretical truth, although indeed the unalloyed portrayal of false consciousness irresistibly makes the transition to true consciousness.

The claim that the metaphysical content of the slow movement of Beethoven's Quartet op. 59, no. 1, must be true provokes the objection that what is true in it is the longing, but that that fades powerlessly into nothingness. If, in response, it were insisted that there is no yearning expressed in that D-flat passage, the assertion would have an obviously apologetic ring that could well be met by the objection that precisely because it appears as if it were true it must be a work of longing, and art as a whole must be nothing but this. The rejoinder would be to reject the argument as drawn from the arsenal of vulgar subjective reason. The automatic *reductio ad hominem* is too pat, too easy, to be an adequate explanation of what objectively appears. It is cheap to present these too facile measures, simply because they have rigorous negativity on their side, as illusionless depth, whereas capitulation vis–à–vis evil implies identification with it. The power of the passage in Beethoven is precisely its distance from the subject; it is this that bestows on those measures the stamp of truth. What was once called the "authentic" [*echt*][19] in art—a word still used by Nietzsche though now unsalvageable—sought to indicate this distance.

The spirit of artworks is not their meaning and not their intention, but rather their truth content, or, in other words, the truth that is revealed through them. The second theme of the Adagio of Beethoven's D-minor Sonata, op. 31, no. 2, is not simply a beautiful melody—there are certainly more buoyant, better formed, and even more original melodies than this one—nor is it distinguished by exceptional expressivity. Nevertheless, the introduction of this theme belongs to what is overwhelming in Beethoven's music and that could be called the spirit of his music: hope, with an authenticity [*authentizität*] that—as something that appears aesthetically—it bears even beyond aesthetic semblance. What is beyond the semblance of what appears is the aesthetic truth content: that aspect of semblance that is not semblance. The truth content is no more the factual reality of an artwork, no more one fact among others in an artwork, than it is independent from its appearance. The first thematic complex of that movement, which is of extraordinary, eloquent beauty, is a masterfully wrought mosaic of contrasting shapes that are motivically coherent even when they are registrally distant. The atmosphere of this thematic complex, which earlier would have been called mood, awaits—as indeed all mood probably does—an event that only becomes an event against the foil of this mood. The F-major theme follows with a rising thirty-second-note gesture. Against the dark, diffuse backdrop of what preceded, the accompanied upper voice that characterizes the second theme acquires its dual character of reconciliation and promise. Nothing transcends without that which it transcends. The truth content is mediated by way of, not outside of, the configuration, but it is not immanent to the configuration and its elements. This is probably what crystallized as the idea of all aesthetic mediation. It is that in artworks by which they participate in their truth content. The pathway of mediation is construable in the structure of artworks, that is, in their technique. Knowledge of this leads to the objectivity of the work itself, which is so to speak vouched for by the coherence of the work's configuration. This objectivity, however, can ultimately be nothing other than the truth content. It is the task of aesthetics to trace the topography of these elements. In the authentic artwork, what is dominated—which finds expression by way of the dominating principle—is the counterpoint to the domination of what is natural or material. This dialectical relationship results in the truth content of artworks.

The spirit of artworks is their objectivated mimetic comportment: It is opposed to mimesis and at the same time the form that mimesis takes in art.

As an aesthetic category, imitation cannot simply be accepted any more than it can simply be rejected. Art objectivates the mimetic impulse, holding it fast at the same time that it disposes of its immediacy and negates it. From this dialectic the imitation of reality draws the fatal consequence. Objectivated reality is the correlative of objectivated mimesis. The reaction to what is not-I becomes the imitation of the not-I. Mimesis itself conforms to objectivation, vainly hoping to close the rupture between objectivated consciousness and the object. By wanting to make itself like the objectivated other, the artwork becomes unlike that other. But it is only by way of its self-alienation through imitation that the subject so strengthens itself that it is able to shake off the spell of imitation. That in which artworks over millennia knew themselves to be images of something reveals itself in the course of history, their critic, as being inessential to them. There would have been no Joyce without Proust, nor Proust without Flaubert, on whom Proust looked down. It was by way of imitation, not by avoiding it, that art achieved its autonomy; in it art acquired the means to its freedom.

Art is not a replica any more than it is knowledge of an object; if it were it would be dragged down to the level of being a mere duplication, of which Husserl delivered such a stringent critique in the sphere of discursive knowledge. On the contrary, art reaches toward reality, only to recoil at the actual touch of it. The characters of its script are monuments to this movement. Their constellation in the artwork is a cryptogram of the historical essence of reality, not its copy. Such comportment is related to mimetic comportment. Even artworks that announce themselves as replicas are such only peripherally; by reacting to reality they become a second-order reality, subjective reflection, regardless whether the artists have reflected or not. Only artwork that makes itself imageless as something existing in itself [achieves the essence, and this requires a developed aesthetic domination of nature].[20]

If the precept held that artists are unknowing to the point of not knowing what an artwork is, this would collide with the ineluctable necessity today of reflection in art; it can hardly be conceived other than by way of the artists' consciousness. Such unknowingness in fact often becomes a blemish in the work of important artists, especially within cultural spheres where art still to some extent has a place; unknowingness, for instance in the form of a lack of taste, becomes an immanent deficiency. The point of indifference between unknowingness and necessary reflection, however, is technique. It not only permits reflection but requires it, yet it does so without destroying the fruitful tenebrosity of works by taking recourse to the subordinating concept.

The artwork's enigmaticalness is the shudder, not however in its living presence but as recollection.

The artwork of the past neither coincided with its cultic element nor stood in simple opposition to it. Rather, art tore itself free from cult objects by a leap in which the cultic element was both transformed and preserved, and this structure is reproduced on an expanding scale at every level of its history. All art contains elements by virtue of which it threatens to fail its laboriously won and precarious concept: The epic threatens to fail as rudimentary historiography, tragedy as the afterimage of a judicial proceeding, the most abstract work as an ornamental pattern, and the realistic novel as protosociology or reportage.

The enigmaticalness of artworks is intimately bound up with history. It was history that once changed them into enigmas and continues to do so; conversely, it is history alone, which invested them with authority, that keeps from them the embarrassing question of their raison d'être.

Artworks are archaic in the age in which they are falling silent. But when they no longer speak, their muteness itself speaks.

Not all advanced art bears the marks of the frightening; these marks are most evident where not every relation of the *peinture* to the object has been severed, where not every relation of dissonance to the fulfilled and negated consonance has been broken off: Picasso's shocks were ignited by the principle of deformation. Many abstract and constructive works lack these shocks; it is an open question whether the force of still-unrealized reality free of fear is active in these works or if—and this may well be the case—the harmony of abstract works is deceptive just as was the social euphoria of the first decades after the European catastrophe; even aesthetically, however, such harmony is apparently in decline.

Problems of perspective, which were once the decisive agent in the development of painting, may reemerge, this time emancipated from all functions of replication. It is worth considering if it is possible to conceive of absolutely nonrepresentational art in the visual domain; if everything that appears, even when reduced to its utmost, does not bear traces of the world of objects; all such speculations become untrue as soon as they are exploited for the purposes of any sort of restoration. Knowledge has its subjective limits in the inability of the knower to resist the temptation of extrapolating the future from his own situation. The taboo on invariants is, however, also an interdiction on such extrapolation. The future indeed is no more to be positively depicted than invariants are to be posited; aesthetics is concentrated in the postulates of the instant.

To the same extent that it cannot be defined what an artwork is, aesthetics is unable to renounce the desire for such a definition if it is not to be guilty of making false promises. Artworks are images that do not contain replicas of anything, therefore they are imageless; they are essence as appearance. They do not fulfill the requirements of Platonic archetypes or reflections, especially in that they are not eternal but historical through and through. The pre-artistic comportment that approaches art most closely and ultimately leads to it is a comportment that transforms experience into the experience of images; as Kierkegaard expressed it: "My booty is images." Artworks are the objectivations of images, objectivations of mimesis, schemata of experience that assimilate to themselves the subject that is experiencing.

Forms of the so-called lowbrow arts, such as the circus tableau, in which at the finale all the elephants kneel on their hind legs, while on each trunk stands a gracefully posed, impassive ballerina, are unintentional archetypal images of what the philosophy of history deciphers in art; from its disdained forms much can be gleaned of art's secret which is so well hidden back of its current level of development, as if art had never been otherwise.

Beauty is the exodus of what has objectivated itself in the realm of means and ends from this realm.

The idea of an objectivity that is nonobjectivated—and therefore an objectivity that cannot adequately be given in intentions—appears in aesthetic purposefulness as well as in the purposelessness of art. But art comes into possession of this idea only by way of the subject, only through that rationality from which purposefulness derives. Art is a polarization: Its spark connects a self-alienated subjectivity turned in on itself with what is not organized by rationality; it connects the block that separates the subject with what philosophy once called the in-itself. Art is incommensurable with the realm between these poles, that of *constituta*.

Kant's purposefulness without a purpose is a principle that emigrated out of empirical reality and the realm of the purposes of self-preservation and found its way into a remote realm, formerly that of the sacred. The purposefulness of artworks is dialectical as the critique of the practical positing of purposes. It takes sides with repressed nature, to which it owes the idea of a purposefulness that is other than that posited by humanity; an idea, obviously, that was undermined by the rise of natural science. Art is the rescue of nature—or of immediacy—through its negation, that is, total mediation. It makes itself like what is free of domination by the limitless domination over its material; this is what is hidden back of Kant's oxymoron.

Art, the afterimage of human repression of nature, simultaneously negates this repression through reflection and draws close to nature. The subjectively instituted totality of artworks does not remain the totality imposed on the other, but rather, by its distance from this other, becomes the imaginative restitution of the other. Neutralized aesthetically, the domination of nature renounces its violence. In the semblance of the restoration of the mutilated other to its own form, art becomes the model of the nonmutilated. Aesthetic totality is the antithesis of the untrue whole. If art, as Valéry once said, wants to be indebted only to itself, this is because art wants to make itself the likeness of an in-itself, of what is free of domination and disfigurement. Art is the spirit that negates itself by virtue of the constitution of its own proper realm.

Evidence that the domination of nature is no accident of art, no original sin resulting from some subsequent amalgamation with the civilizing process, is given at the very least by the fact that the magical practices of aboriginal peoples bear in themselves undifferentiatedly the element of the domination of nature: "The profound effect produced by the image of animals is simply explained by the fact that the image, by its characteristic features, psychologically exercises the same effect as does the object itself, and so as a result of his psychological alteration the person believes that he has been touched by magic. On the other hand, from the fact that the motionless image is entirely subject to his own powers, he comes to believe that the represented animal can be tracked and subdued; therefore the image appears to him as a means of power over the animal."[21] Magic is a rudimentary form of that causal thinking that ultimately liquidates magic.

Art is mimetic comportment that for the purpose of its objectivation disposes over the most advanced rationality for the control of its material and procedures. This contradiction is art's answer to the contradiction of the *ratio* itself. If the telos of reason is a fulfillment that is in-itself necessarily not rational—happiness is the enemy of rationality and purpose, of which it nevertheless stands in need—art makes this irrational telos its own concern. In this, art draws on an unrestrained rationality in its technical procedures, which are, in the supposedly "technical world," constrained by the relations of production and thus remain irrational.——In the age of technology, art is spurious when it masks universal mediation as a social relation.

The rationality of artworks has as its aim opposition to empirical existence: The rational shaping of artworks effectively means their rigorous elaboration in-themselves. As a result they come into contrast with the world of the nature-dominating *ratio*, in which the aesthetic *ratio* originates, and become a work for-themselves. The opposition of artworks to domination is mimesis of domination. They must assimilate themselves to the comportment of domination in order to produce something qualitatively distinct from the world of domination. Even the immanently polemical attitude of artworks against the status quo internalizes the principle that underlies the status quo, and that reduces it to the status of what merely exists; aesthetic rationality wants to make good on the damage done by nature-dominating rationality.

The proscription of the element of willful domination in art is not aimed at domination but at the expiation of domination, in that the subject places the control of itself and its other in the service of the nonidentical.

The category of formation [*Gestaltung*], which is embarrassing when it is cited as an autonomous ideal, must be supplemented by the concept of the work's structure. Yet the quality of the work is all the higher, the work all the more formed, the less it is disposed over. Formation means nonformation.

It is precisely the integrally constructed artworks of modernism that starkly illuminate the fallibility of logicality and formal immanence; to fulfill their concept they must outfox it; this is documented in Klee's diary entries. One of the tasks of an artist who insistently seeks the extreme is both to realize the logic of "coming to the end"—Richard Strauss was in this regard strangely insensitive—and to interrupt this logic, to suspend it, so as to cancel its mechanical aspect, its flawed predictability. The requirement of becoming assimilated to the work is precisely that of intervening in it so that it does not become an infernal machine. Perhaps the gestures of intervention, with which Beethoven, as if by an act of will, provided the later parts of his development sections, are early evidence of this experience. The fertile instant of the artwork otherwise becomes lethal to itself.

The difference between aesthetic and discursive logicality can be demonstrated in George Trakl's poetry. The succession of images—"so beautiful how image follows image"[22]—certainly does not constitute a nexus of meaning according to logical procedures and causality such as those that govern the apophantic realm, especially the realm of existential judgments. This is not contravened by Trakl's "it is," which the poet chose for its paradoxical force: In this context "it is" means that "what is not, is." In spite of the initial impression of a web of associations, his poetic textures are not those of a freely shifting order. Indirectly and obscurely logical categories play a part, as, for instance, in the musically rising or falling curves of the individual elements, the distribution of light and dark, the relations between beginning, continuation, and conclusion. The pictorial elements participate in formal categories, but they are legitimated only by virtue of these relations, which organize the poems and raise them above the contingency of mere conceits. Aesthetic form has its rationality even in poetic association. In it, as one moment calls up the next, there is something of the force of stringency demanded by the conclusions in logic and music. In fact, in a letter in which he criticized an irksome imitator, Trakl spoke of the aesthetic means he had acquired; none of them lacks an element of logicality.

Aesthetics of Form and Aesthetics of Content [*Inhalt*].——Ironically, in the contest between the two, the aesthetics of content holds the upper hand by the fact that the content [*Gehalt*] of works and of art as a whole—its ultimate end—is not formal but concrete. Yet this content [*Gehalt*] becomes concrete only by virtue of aesthetic form. If form must be at the center of aesthetics, aesthetics develops its content by rendering forms eloquent.

The results of formal aesthetics cannot simply be rejected. However little they do justice to undiminished aesthetic experience, this experience is unthinkable without formal elements such as mathematical proportions and symmetry and dynamic formal categories such as tension and release. Without the functions these categories fulfill, the great works of the past would be as incomprehensible as it would be impossible to hypostatize these elements as aesthetic criteria. They were always only elements and as such inseparable from the manifold elements of content; they never had immediate value except in relation to what they formed. They are paradigms of the dialectic. It is according to what is formed that they are modified; with the emergence of radical modern art they were thoroughly transformed by negation: Their effect is indirect as a result of being avoided and annulled; prototypical here—as Valéry noted—is, since Manet, the relation of artists to the traditional rules of pictorial composition. Their authority makes itself felt in the opposition of specific works to them. A category such as that of an artwork's proportions is only meaningful to the extent that it also encompasses the overthrow of proportions, in other words, their own dynamic. By way of such a dialectic, throughout modernism, the formal categories have been reestablished at ever higher levels: The quintessence of the dissonant was harmony; the quintessence of dynamic tensions was equilibrium. This would be inconceivable if the formal categories had not themselves been suffused with content. The formal principle according to which artworks should be both tension and equilibrium registers the antagonistic content of aesthetic experience, that of an unreconciled reality that nevertheless wants reconciliation. Even static formal categories, such as that of the golden mean, are congealed content, that of reconciliation itself. In artworks it is only as a result that harmony has ever amounted to anything; when it was simply posited and asserted it was already ideology, which is what the newly won homeostasis also ultimately became. Conversely, and this is effectively an apriori of art, all material in art developed by way of a process of formation that was then abstracted as the categories of form. These categories were in turn transformed through their relation to the material. Forming means the adequate completion of this transformation. This may explicate immanently the concept of the dialectic in art.

The formal analysis of an artwork, and what can properly be called form in an artwork, only has meaning in relation to the work's concrete material. The construction of the most impeccable diagonals, axes, and vanishing lines in a picture, the most stringent motivic economy in a musical composition, remains a matter of indifference so long as the construction is not developed specifically out of that particular picture or composition. No other use of the concept of construction in art is legitimate; otherwise the concept inevitably becomes a fetish. Many analyses contain everything except the reason why a painting or a piece of music is held to be beautiful or from what they derive their right to exist. Such analytical methods are in fact vulnerable to the critique of aesthetic formalism. But although it is not defensible simply to insist on the reciprocity of form and content—rather, this reciprocity needs to be demonstrated in detail—the formal elements, at every point referring back to content, preserve their tendency to become content. Crude materialism and a no less crude classicism agree in the mistaken belief that there is some sort of pure form. The official doctrine of materialism overlooks the dialectic even of the fetish character in art. Precisely when form appears emancipated from any preestablished content [*Inhalt*], the forms themselves acquire their own expression and content [*Inhalt*]. Surrealism operated in this fashion in many of its works, and Klee did throughout: The contents [*Inhalte*] sedimented in the forms awake as they age. This is what befell *Jugendstil* at the hands of surrealism, which polemically severed ties with it. Aesthetically, the *solus ipse* becomes aware of the world, which is his own, and that isolates him as *solus ipse* in the same instant that he jettisons the conventions of the world.

The concept of tension frees itself from the suspicion of being formalistic in that, by pointing up dissonant experiences or antinomical relations in the work, it names the element of "form" in which form gains its substance by virtue of its relation to its other. Through its inner tension, the work is defined as a force field even in the arrested moment of its objectivation. The work is at once the quintessence of relations of tension and the attempt to dissolve them.

In opposition to mathematical theories of harmony, it must be asserted that aesthetic phenomena cannot be mathematically conceived. In art, equal is not equal. This has become obvious in music. The return of analogous passages of the same length does not fulfill what the abstract concept of harmony promises: The repetition is irksome rather than satisfying, or, in less subjective terms, it is too long for the form; Mendelssohn was probably one of the first composers to have acted upon this experience, which made itself felt right up until the serial school's self-critique of mechanical correspondences. This self-critique became more intense with the emerging dynamization of art and the *soupçon* felt for all identity that does not become a nonidentity. The hypothesis may be risked that the well-known differences that distinguish the "artistic volition" of the visual arts of the baroque from those of the Renaissance were inspired by the same experience. All relations that appear natural, and are to this extent abstract invariables, undergo necessary modifications before they can function as aesthetic means; the modification of the natural overtone series by tempered tuning is the most striking example of this. Most often these modifications are ascribed to the subjective element, which supposedly finds the rigidity of a heteronomously imposed material order insupportable. But this plausible interpretation remains all too remote from history. It is only late that art takes recourse to so-called natural materials and relations in revolt against incoherent and unbelievable traditionalism: This revolt, in a word, is bourgeois. The mathematization of strictly quantifiable artistic materials and of the technical procedures spun out of them is in fact itself an achievement of the emancipated subject, of "reflection" that then rebels against its emancipation. Primitive procedures have nothing of this. What passes for natural facts and natural law in art is not primordially given but rather an inner-aesthetic development; it is mediated. Such nature in art is not the nature for which it longs; rather it has been projected upon art by the natural sciences, to compensate it for the loss of preestablished structures. What is striking in pictorial impressionism is the modernity of the physiologically perceivable, quasi-natural elements. Second reflection therefore demands the critique of all reified natural elements; just as they once emerged, they will pass away. After World War II consciousness—in the illusion of being able to begin anew without the transformation of society—clung to allegedly primordial phenomena; these are as ideological as the forty German marks of new currency per person with which the economy was supposed to be rebuilt from the ground up. Clearcutting is a character mask of the status quo; what is different does not hide its historical dimension. This is not to say that in art there are no mathematical relations. But they can only be grasped in relation to a historically concrete configuration, they cannot be hypostatized.

The concept of homeostasis, an equilibrium of tension that asserts itself only in the totality of an artwork, is probably bound up with that instant in which the artwork visibly makes itself independent: It is the instant when the homeostasis, if not immediately established, can be envisioned. The resulting shadow over the concept of homeostasis corresponds to the crisis of this idea in contemporary art. At precisely that point when the work comes into its own self-possession, becomes sure of itself, when it suddenly "fits" together, it no longer fits because the fortunately achieved autonomy seals its reification and deprives it of the openness that is an aspect of its own idea. During the heroic age of expressionism, these reflections were not far from painters like Kandinsky who, for instance, observed that an artist who believes he has found his style has thereby already lost it. Yet the problem is not as subjectively psychological as that epoch held; rather it is grounded in the antinomy of art itself. The openness toward which it tends and the closure—the "perfection"—by which it approximates the idea of its being-in-itself, of being completely uncompromised, a being-in-itself that is the agent of openness, are incompatible.

That the artwork is a result means that, as one of its elements, it should bear no residue of the dead, unworked, unformed, and sensitivity to this is an equally definitive element of all art criticism; the quality of each and every work depends on this element just as much as this element atrophies everywhere that cultural-philosophical cogitation hovers freely above the works. The first look that glides over a musical score, the instinct that—in front of a painting—judges its dignity, is guided by a consciousness of the degree to which it is fully formed, its integral structuration, and by a sensitivity to what is crude, which often enough coincides with what convention imposes on artworks and what the philistine wherever possible chalks up to its transsubjectivity. Even when artworks suspend the principle of their integral structuration and open themselves to the crude, they reflect the postulate of this principle. Those works are fully elaborated over which the forming hand has most delicately felt its way; this idea is exemplarily embodied in the French tradition. In good music not a measure is superfluous or rings hollow, not a measure is isolated from the phrase, just as no instrumental sound is introduced that—as musicians put it—has not truly been "heard," drawn by subjective sensibility from the specific character of the instrument before the passage is entrusted to it. The instrumental combination of a musical complex must be fully heard; it is the objective weakness of early music that only by exception did it achieve this mediation. The feudal dialectic of master and servant takes refuge in these artworks, whose very existence has a feudal quality.

That old and silly cabaret phrase, "Love, it's so erotic" provokes the variation: "Art, it's so aesthetic"; this is to be taken with deep seriousness as a memento of what has been repressed by its consumption. The quality that is at stake here reveals itself primarily in acts of reading, including the reading of musical scores: It is the quality of the trace that aesthetic forming leaves behind in what it forms without doing violence to it: It is the conciliatory element of culture in art that characterizes even its most violent protestation. It is implicit in the word *métier*, and it cannot simply be translated as craft [*Handwerk*]. The relevance of this element seems to have intensified in the history of modernism; in spite of Bach's optimal level of form, it would be rather anachronistic to discuss his work in terms of *metier*; even for Mozart and Schubert, and certainly for Bruckner, it is not quite right; but it applies to Brahms, Wagner, and even Chopin. Today this quality is the *differentia specifica* of art in opposition to the deluge of philistinism, and at the same time it is a criterion of mastery. Nothing crude may remain, even the simplest must bear that civilizatory trace. That trace is what is redolent of art in the artwork.

Even the concept of ornament against which *Sachlichkeit* revolts has its dialectic. To point out that the baroque is decorative does not say everything about it. It is *decorazione assoluta*, as if it had emancipated itself from every purpose, even the theatrical, and developed its own law of form. It ceases to decorate anything and is, on the contrary, nothing but decoration; thus it eludes the critique of the decorative. With regard to baroque works of exalted dignity the objections to "plaster art" are misdirected: The pliant material perfectly fulfills the formal apriori of absolute decoration. In these works, through progressive sublimation, the great world theater, the *theatrum mundi*, became the *theatrum dei*, the sensual world became a spectacle for the gods.

If the artisanal bourgeois mind expected from the solidity of things that they, holding out against time, can be bequeathed, this idea of solidity has gone over to the rigorous working out of objets d'art. Nothing in the circumference of art should be left in its rawness; this intensifies the closure of artworks vis-à-vis empirical reality and is associated with the idea of protecting artworks from their transience. Paradoxically, aesthetic bourgeois virtues such as that of solidity have emigrated into antibourgeois avant-garde art.

In so plausible and apparently universally valid a demand as that of clarity—the articulation of every element in the artwork—it is possible to show how every invariant of aesthetics motivates its own dialectic. A second specifically artistic logic is able to surpass the first, that of the distinct. Artworks of high quality are able, for the sake of the densest possible relations, to neglect clarity and bring into proximity with one another complexes that, with regard to the requirement of clarity, would need to be strictly distinguished. The idea of many artworks that want to realize the experience of vagueness actually demands that the boundaries of their constitutive elements be effaced. But in such artworks the vague must be made distinct. Authentic works that defy the exigency of clarity all the same posit it implicitly in order to negate it; essential to these works is not an absence of clarity but rather negated clarity. Otherwise they would be simply amateurish.

Hegel's dictum that the owl of Minerva begins its flight at dusk is confirmed in art. So long as the existence and function of artworks in society was self-evident and a sort of consensus ruled between the self-certainty of society and the place of artworks in it, no question of aesthetic meaningfulness arose: Its meaningfulness was a foregone conclusion. Aesthetic categories are first subjected to philosophical reflection when art, in Hegel's language, is no longer substantial, no longer immediately present and obvious.

The crisis of meaning in art, immanently provoked by the unstoppable dynamism of nominalism, is linked with extra-aesthetic experience, for the inner-aesthetic nexus that constitutes meaning reflects the meaningfulness of the world and its course as the tacit and therefore all the more powerful apriori of artworks.

The artwork's nexus, as its immanent life, is the afterimage of empirical life on which the reflection of the artwork falls and bestows a reflection of meaning. However, the concept of a nexus of meaning thereby becomes dialectical. The process that immanently reduces the artwork to its own concept, without casting an eye on the universal, reveals itself in the history of art on a theoretical level only after the nexus of meaning itself, and thus its traditional concept, becomes uncertain.

In aesthetics, as in all other domains, rationalization of means necessarily implies their fetishization. The more directly they are disposed over, the more they tend objectively to become ends in themselves. It is this that is truly fatal in the most recent developments in art, not the rejection of any sort of anthropological invariants or the sentimentally bemoaned loss of naïveté. The ends, that is, the works, are replaced by their possibilities; vacuous schemata of works take the place of the works themselves; thus the works themselves become a matter of indifference. With the intensification of subjective reason in art, these schemata become subjective in the sense of being arbitrarily elaborated independently of the works. As is frequently indicated by the titles of these works, the means employed become ends in themselves, as do the materials employed. This is what is false in the loss of meaning. Just as true and false must be distinguished in the concept of meaning, there is also a false collapse of meaning. Its index is affirmation, the glorification of the status quo in a cult of pure materials and pure mastery; both are thereby falsely severed.

That today positivity is blocked amounts to a verdict over the positivity of the past, but not over the longing that first stirred within it.

Aesthetic splendor is not just affirmative ideology; it is also the reflected glimmer of life free of oppression: In its defiance of ruin it takes the side of hope. Splendor is not only the cheap tricks of the culture industry. The higher the quality of a work, the greater its brilliance, and this is most strikingly the case in the instance of those grey-on-grey works of modernism that eclipse Hollywood's technicolor.

Mörike's poem of the abandoned girl is profoundly sad in a way that goes far beyond the theme itself. Verses such as "Suddenly I realized / unfaithful boy / that all night / I dreamt of you"[23] express without any reserve dreadful experiences: here that of awakening from the sensed fragility of sleep's comfort directly into despair. Nevertheless, even this poem has its affirmative element. Despite the authenticity of feeling, this element is lodged in the form, even though that form defends itself against the consolation of secure symmetry through strophic meter. In the tender fiction of a folksong the girl speaks as one among many: Traditional aesthetics would praise the poem for its prototypical qualities. What has been lost since that time is the latent community in which all loneliness was embedded, a situation in which society whispers consolation to one who is as alone as in the earliest dawn. As the tears have run dry, this consolation has become inaudible.

As component parts of the encompassing whole, artworks are not simply things. They participate specifically in reification because their objectivation is modeled on the objectivation of things external to them; it is in this sense, if at all, and not as imitations of any particular reality, that artworks are to be understood as copies. The concept of classicality, which cannot be reduced exclusively to ideology, applies to those artworks that have largely succeeded in such objectivation and thus to those that are most reified. By disowning its own dynamic the objectivated artwork opposes its own concept. Therefore aesthetic objectivation is always also fetishism and provokes permanent rebellion. As Valéry recognized, just as no artwork can escape the idea of its classicality, every authentic work must struggle against it; and in this antinomy, not least of all, art has its life. Under the compulsion to objectivation, artworks tend toward petrification: It is immanent to the principle of their perfection. In that artworks seek to rest in themselves as what exists in-itself, they seal themselves in; yet it is only insofar as they are open that they go beyond the status of being mere entities. Because the process, which all artworks are, dies off in the course of their objectivation, all classicism progressively approximates mathematical relations. The rebellion against classicality is raised not only by the subject, who feels repressed, but by the truth claim of artworks, with which the ideal of classicality collides. Conventionalization is not external to the objectivation of artworks, nor a result of their decline. Rather, it lurks within them; the overarching bindingness that artworks achieve through their objectivation assimilates them to an ever dominating universality. The classicistic ideal of drossless perfection is no less illusory than the longing for a pure uncoerced immediacy. Classicistic works lack validity and not just because the ancient models are too remote for imitation; the all-powerful principle of stylization is incompatible with the impulses with which it lays claim to unity, a claim on which its prerogative is founded: The achieved incontestability of any and all classicism has something underhanded about it. Beethoven's late works mark the revolt of one of the most powerful classicistic artists against the deception implicit in the principle of his own work. The rhythm of the periodic return of romantic and classicist currents in art, to the extent that such movements can truly be discerned in the history of art, bears witness to the antinomical character of art itself as it is most palpably manifest in the relation of its metaphysical claim of being situated above and beyond time to its actual transience as a merely human work. Indeed, artworks become relative because they must assert themselves as absolute. The perfectly objectivated artwork would be a thing existing absolutely in-itself and no longer an artwork. If the work became nature, as idealism expects, it would be annulled. Ever since Plato, bourgeois consciousness has deceived itself that objective antinomies could be mastered by steering a middle course between them, whereas the sought-out mean always conceals the antinomy and is torn apart by it. The precariousness of classicism is that of the artwork in terms of its own concept. The qualitative leap—the leap by which art approaches the boundary that marks its ultimate muteness—is the consummation of its antinomy.

Valéry so honed the concept of classicality that, elaborating on Baudelaire, he dubbed the successful romantic artwork classical.[24] This strains the idea of classicality to the breaking point. Modern art already registered this more than forty years ago. It is only in its relation to this, as to a disaster, that neoclassicism can be adequately understood. It is directly evident in surrealism. It toppled the images of antiquity from their Platonic heaven. In the paintings of Max Ernst they roam about as phantoms among the burghers of the late nineteenth century, for whom they have been neutralized as mere cultural goods and truly transformed into specters. Wherever the art movements that converged temporarily in Picasso and others external to the *groupe* took up the theme of antiquity, it led aesthetically directly to hell, just as it did theologically for Christianity. Antiquity's embodied epiphany in prosaic everyday life, which has a long prehistory, disenchants it. Formerly presented as an atemporal norm, antiquity now acquires a historical status, that of the bourgeois idea reduced to its bare contours and rendered powerless. Its form is deformation. Inflated interpretations of neoclassicism such as Cocteau's *ordre après le désordre*, as well as the surrealist interpretation decades later of a romantic liberation of fantasy and association, falsify the phenomena to the point of harmlessness: Following Poe's lead, they summon up the shudder of the instant of disenchantment as enchantment. That this instant was not to be fixed for eternity damned the followers of these movements either to restoration or to a powerless ritual of revolutionary gesturing. Baudelaire proved to be correct: Emphatic modern art does not thrive in Elysian fields beyond the commodity but is, rather, strengthened by way of the experience of the commodity, whereas classicality itself becomes a commodity, an exemplary daub. Brecht's mockery of the cultural treasure secured by its guardians in the form of plaster statues originates in the same context; that a positive concept of classicality worked its way into his thought later on, as it also did in the aesthetics of Stravinsky, whom Brecht scorned as a *Tui* intellectual, was as inevitable as it was revelatory of the rigidification of the Soviet Union into an authoritarian state. Hegel's attitude toward classicality was as ambivalent as the attitude of his philosophy toward the alternative between ontology and dynamics. He glorified the art of the Greeks as eternal and unsurpassable and recognized that the classical artwork had been surpassed by what he called the romantic artwork. History, whose verdict he sanctioned, had itself decided against invariance. His sense of the obsolescence of art may well have been colored by a presentiment of such progress. In strictly Hegelian terms, classicism, along with its modern sublimated form, is responsible for its own fate. Immanent critique—its most magnificent model, on the most magnificent object, is Benjamin's study of the *Elective Affinities*—pursues the fragility of canonical works into the depths of their truth content; the full potential of such critique still remains to be developed and discovered. Art indeed never embraced the ideal of classicality all that rigorously; to do so, it would have needed to be harder on itself than it in general has been, and when it was, then it really damaged itself and did itself injustice. The freedom of art vis-à-vis the *Dira necessitas* of the factual is incompatible with classicality in the sense of perfect univocity, which is as much borrowed from the compulsion of inevitability as it is opposed to it by virtue of its transparent purity. *Summum ius summa iniuria* is an aesthetic maxim. The more art pursues the logic of classicism and seeks to become an incorruptible reality sui generis, the more indurately it prevaricates an impenetrable threshold between itself and empirical reality. There is some justice to the speculation that, in its relation between what it lays claim to and what it is, art becomes all the more problematic the more rigorously, the more objectively, indeed—if one will—the more classically it proceeds, though with the caveat that the situation of art is not in the least improved when it makes things easier for itself.

When Benjamin criticized the application to art of the category of necessity,[25] he was concerned with the cultural historian's subterfuge of claiming that one artwork or another was necessary for the course of art's development. In fact, this concept of necessity does fulfill the subaltern apologetic function of attesting that without some stale old works, of which there is nothing other to praise, there would have been no getting any further.

The other in art inheres in art's own concept and in every instant threatens to crush it just as neo-Gothic New York churches and Regensburg's medieval city center were destroyed when they became traffic impediments. Art is no fixed set of boundaries but rather a momentary and fragile balance, comparable to the dynamic balance between the ego and the id in the psychological sphere. Bad artworks become bad only because they objectively raise the claim to being art, a claim they disavow subjectively, as Hedwig Courths-Mahler[26] did in a notable letter. The critique that demonstrates how bad they are nevertheless honors them as artworks. They are artworks and then again they are not.

In the course of history, works that were not produced as art or were produced prior to the age of its autonomy are able to become art, and the same is possible in the case of contemporary works that challenge their own status as art. This obviously does not happen, however, in the sense of constituting a putatively valuable preliminary step toward something worthwhile. On the contrary, as occurred in the instance of surrealism, specific aesthetic qualities may emerge that were rejected by an anti-art deportment that never achieved its goal of becoming a political force; this is the shape of the careers of important surrealists such as Masson. Equally, what once was art may cease to be art. The availability of traditional art for its own depravation has retroactive power. Innumerable paintings and sculptures have been transformed in their own essence to mere decoration as a result of their own offspring. Anyone who would decide to paint cubistically in 1970 would be providing posters useful for advertisements, and the originals, too, are not safe from being sold off cheap.

Tradition could be salvaged only by its separation from the spell of inwardness. Great artworks of the past were never identical with inwardness; most exploded it through externalization. Strictly speaking, every artwork is a critique of inwardness in that it externalizes appearance and thus is contrary to the ideology of inwardness, which tradition equates with the hoarded-up treasure of subjective recollection.

The interpretation of art based on its origin is dubious across the board: from biographical research on the study of cultural-historical influences to ontological sublimations of the concept of origin. All the same, origin is not radically external to the work. It is an implicit part of artworks that they are artifacts. The configurations sedimented in each address the context from which it issued. In each its likeness to its origins is thrown into relief by what it became. This antithetic is essential to its content. Its immanent dynamic crystallizes the dynamic external to it and indeed does so by virtue of its aporetic character. Regardless of their individual endowments and contrary to them, if artworks are unable to achieve their monadological unity, they succumb to real historical pressure; it becomes the force that inwardly dislocates them. This is not the least of the reasons why an artwork is adequately perceived only as a process. If however the individual work is a force field, a dynamic configuration of its elements, this holds no less for art itself as a whole. Therefore art cannot be understood all at once, but only in terms of its elements, in a mediated fashion. One of these elements is that by which artworks contrast with what is not art; their attitude to objectivity changes.

The historical tendency reaches profoundly into the aesthetic criteria. It decides, for instance, whether someone is a mannerist. That is what Saint-Saëns accused Debussy of being. Frequently the new appears as a sort of mannerism; whether the new is more than that can be discerned only by knowledge of the historical tendency. Yet the tendency is no arbiter either. In it true and false consciousness commingle; it too is open to criticism. For this reason the process that transpires between tendency and mannerism is never finished and requires tireless revision; mannerism is as much a protest against the historical tendency as that historical tendency unmasks what is merely contingent and arbitrary in a mannerism as the trademarks of the work.

Proust, and after him Kahnweiler, argued that painting had transformed vision and thus the objects. However authentic this experience may be, it may have been formulated too idealistically. The reverse might also be supposed: that the objects themselves were historically transformed, that the sensorium conformed to this, and that painting then found the ciphers for this transformation. Cubism could be interpreted as a form of reaction to a stage of the rationalization of the social world that undertook its geometrical organization; in these terms cubism was an attempt to bring within the bounds of experience what is otherwise contrary to it, just as impressionism had sought to do at an earlier and not yet fully planned stage of industrialization. By contrast, what is qualitatively new in cubism is that, whereas impressionism undertook to awaken and salvage a life that was becoming numb in the commodity world by the strength of its own dynamic, cubism despaired of any such possibility and accepted the heteronomous geometrization of the world as its new law, as its own order, and thus made itself the guarantor of the objectivity of aesthetic experience. Historically, cubism anticipated something real, the aerial photographs of bombed-out cities during World War II. It was through cubism that art for the first time documented that life no longer lives. This recognition was not free of ideology: Cubism substituted the rationalized order for what had become unexperienceable and thereby confirmed it. This probably drove Picasso and Braque beyond cubism, though their later works were not necessarily superior to it.

The attitude of artworks to history in turn varies historically. Lukács declared in an interview about recent literature, especially Beckett: Just wait ten, fifteen years and you'll see what people will say then. He thus adopted the standpoint of a paternalistic, far-seeing businessman who wants to dampen the enthusiasm of his son; implicitly he invokes for art durability and ultimately the category of possession. Still, artworks are not indifferent to the dubious judgment of history. At times quality has historically asserted itself against precisely those works that were simply content to swim with the tides of the Zeitgeist. It is rare that works that have won great renown have not in some way deserved it. The development of legitimate renown, however, necessarily coincided with the unfolding of the inner law of those artworks through interpretation, commentary, and critique. This quality is not directly produced by the *communis opinio*, least of all by that manipulated by the culture industry, a public judgment whose relation to the work is questionable. It is a disgraceful superstition that fifteen years after the fact the judgment of an anti-intellectual journalist or a musicologist of the good old school should be held to be more significant than what is perceived in the instant of the work's appearance.

The afterlife of artworks, their reception as an aspect of their own history, transpires between a do-not-let-yourself-be-understood and a wanting-to-be-understood; this tension is the atmosphere inhabited by art.

Many early works of new music, beginning with the those of Schoenberg's middle period and with Webern's works, have a character of untouchability, a refractoriness that rebuffs the listener by the strength of their objectivation, which becomes a life of its own; it is as if recognizing the priority of such works already does them an injustice.

The philosophical construction of the unequivocal primacy of the whole over the part is as alien to art as it is epistemologically untenable. In important works, details never merge tracelessly into the totality. Certainly the autonomization of the details, when they become indifferent to the nexus of the work and reduce it to a subordinating schema, is accompanied by the regression of the work to the preartistic. Yet artworks distinguish themselves productively from the merely schematic exclusively by the element of the autonomy of their details; every authentic work is the result of centripetal and centrifugal forces. Anyone who listens to music seeking out the beautiful passages is a dilettante; but whoever is unable to perceive beautiful passages, the varying density of invention and texture in a work, is deaf. Until the most recent developments in art, differentiation between the intensive and the secondary within a whole was an accepted artistic means; the negation of the whole through partial wholes is itself demanded by the whole. If today this possibility is disappearing, this is not only the triumph of a structuration that at every instant wants to be equally near the midpoint without falling slack; it is also the result of the lethal potential inherent in the contraction of the means of articulation. Art cannot be radically separated from the instant of being touched, of enchantment, that instant of elevation, without being confounded in the indifferent. This instant, however much it is also a function of the whole, is nevertheless essentially particular: The whole never offers itself to aesthetic experience in that immediacy without which aesthetic experience cannot be constituted. Aesthetic asceticism toward the detail and the atomistic comportment of the recipient indeed has an aspect of renunciation and threatens to deprive art of its very ferment.

That autonomous details are essential to the whole is confirmed by the repulsive quality of aesthetically concrete details that bear the trace of being prescribed from above, of in truth being heteronomous. When Schiller in *Wallenstein's Camp*[27] rhymes the words "Potz Blitz" with "Gustel von Blasewitz" he outstrips in abstractness the most pallid classicism; this aspect renders plays like *Wallenstein* insupportable.

At present, the details of artworks tend to be submerged in the whole through integration: not, however, under the pressure of planning but rather because they are themselves drawn to their own annihilation. What gives details meaning, *cachet*, and distinguishes them from the indifferent is that by which they seek to go beyond themselves, the precondition immanent to them of their synthesis. It is their death drive that permits the integration of the details. Their tendency to dissociation and their tendency to unification are not radically opposed to each other: In that it is posited and therefore insufficient, the detail is inevitably relativized. Disintegration inheres in the depth of integration and shimmers through it. Indeed the whole, the more detail it absorbs, itself effectively becomes a detail, one element among others, a singularity. The craving of the detail for its own annihilation becomes the demand of the whole. And indeed precisely because it—the whole—extinguishes the detail. If they have truly disappeared into the whole, if the whole becomes an aesthetic particular, its rationality loses its rationality, which was nothing other than the relation of the particulars to the whole, to the aim that defined them as means. If the synthesis is no longer a synthesis of something, it becomes null. The vacuity of the technically integrated structure is a symptom of its disintegration through tautological indifference. In the opacity of the perfectly unspontaneous work, a work that has totally rejected subjective inspiration, functionless functioning transforms the element of opacity into the fatality that art always bore in itself as its mimetic inheritance. This can be explicated in the musical category of inspiration. Schoenberg, Berg, and even Webern refused to give it up; they criticized Krenek and Steuermann. Actually, constructivism no longer grants any role to inspiration, which is unplanned arbitrariness. Schoenberg's inspirations, which—as he confirmed—also underlay his twelve-tone compositions, are simply indebted to the limits set by his constructive procedures, limits that others chalked up to a lack of consequentiality. But if the element of inspiration were fully liquidated, if composers were not permitted to be inspired by forms as a whole, which would instead be predetermined exclusively by the material, the result would lose its objective interest and fall mute. By contrast, the plausible demand for the restitution of inspiration suffers from powerlessness: In art one can hardly postulate a countervailing force to the programmatic programmatically. Compositions that, out of disgust with their own abstractness, strive for moments of inspiration, protean subsidiary forms and their endowment with character, expose themselves to the objection of being retrospective; as if in these works second aesthetic reflection—out of fear of the fatality inherent to rationalization—simply ignored the constraints of rationalization on the basis of a subjective decision. Kafka's obsessively varied situation—whatever one does, it is done wrong—has become the situation of art itself. Art that rigorously bans inspiration is condemned to indifference; but if inspiration is fetched back, it pales to a shadow, almost to a fiction. Already in Schoenberg's authentic works, such as his *Pierrot lunaire*, inspirations were ingeniously unauthentic, fractured, and shrunken to a sort of minimum existence. The question of the weight of details in new artworks is indeed so relevant because no less than in the totality of new artworks—the sublimation of organized society—society is also embodied in the details: Society is the fertile soil that sublimates aesthetic form. The details of artworks behave just as do individuals in society who, by their own interests largely opposed to society, are not only *faits sociaux* but society itself, reproduced by and reproducing it and therefore asserting themselves against it. Art is the appearance of the social dialectic of the universal and the individual mediated by the subjective spirit. It goes beyond this dialectic insofar as it does not simply carry out this dialectic but reflects it through form. Figuratively, its particularization makes good on the perpetuated injustice of society to the individuals. What hinders it in this restitution is that it is unable to perform anything that it cannot extract as a concrete possibility from the society in which it has its locus. Contemporary society is altogether remote from any structural transformation that would give individuals their due and thus dissipate the spell of individuation.

On the Dialectic of Construction and Expression—That each element dialectically reverses into the other is a maxim of contemporary art: Its structures must no longer endeavor to find some compromise between construction and expression but seek, rather, the extremes, so that in them, through them, an equivalent can be found for what an older aesthetics called synthesis. This is fundamental to the qualitative definition of modern art. The plurality of possibilities that was available up to the threshold of modern art, and which had grown extraordinarily during the nineteenth century, has been displaced by polarization. The polarization socially requisite is manifest in artistic polarization.[28] Where organization is necessary, in structuring material life and in the human relations that depend on it, there is too little organization, too much is ceded to an anarchistic private sphere. Art has a latitude of play in which models of planning can be developed that would not be tolerated by the social relations of production. On the other hand, the irrational administration of the world has been heightened to the virtual liquidation of the ever precarious existence of the particular. Where it survives it is made to serve a complementary ideology of the omnipotence of the universal. Individual interest that refuses this universal converges with the interest of universal, realized rationality. Rationality would become rational only once it no longer repressed the individuated in whose unfolding rationality has its right to exist. Yet the emancipation of the individual could succeed only to the extent that the individual grasps the universal on which individuals depend. Even socially, a reasonable order of the public world could be achieved only if, at the other extreme, opposition to the overly complex as well as inadequate organization were to suffuse individual consciousness. If the individual sphere in a certain sense lags behind the organized world, organization should nevertheless exist for the sake of the individual. The irrationality of organization still provides a measure of freedom to individuals. Their vestigiality becomes the last resort of what would go beyond progressive domination. This dynamic of what is out-of-date endows taboo expression aesthetically with the right of a resistance that lays its finger directly on the untruth of the whole. In spite of its ideological distortedness, the division of public and private in art is a given in such a fashion that art is unable to carry out any sort of transformation without establishing some relation to the givenness of this division. What in social reality would amount to powerless consolation has far more concrete chances as a plenipotentiary within the sphere of aesthetics.

In themselves, artworks ineluctably pursue nature-dominating reason by virtue of their element of unity, which organizes the whole. But through the disavowal of real domination this principle returns transformed, truncated, in a shadowy fashion, to put it metaphorically, which is perhaps the only way to describe it. Reason in artworks is reason as gesture: They synthesize like reason, but not with concepts, propositions, and syllogisms—where these forms occur in art they do so only as subordinated means—rather, they do so by way of what transpires in the artworks. Their synthetic function is immanent; it is the unity of their self, without immediate relation to anything external given or determined in some way or other; it is directed to the dispersed, the aconceptual, quasi-fragmentary material with which in their interior space artworks are occupied. Through this reception, as well as through the modification of synthesizing reason, artworks participate in the dialectic of enlightenment. Even in its aesthetically neutralized form, however, nature-dominating reason has something of the dynamic that once inhered in its external form. However much it is separated from this dynamic, the identity of the principle of reason effects a development internally and externally that is similar to the external dialectic: Windowless, artworks participate in civilization. That by which artworks distinguish themselves from the diffuse coincides with the achievements of reason qua reality principle. In artworks this reality principle is as active as its counterpart. Art carries out the correction of self-preserving reason, but not by simply setting itself in opposition to it; rather, the correction of reason is carried out by the reason immanent to artworks themselves. Whereas the unity of artworks derives from the violence that reason does to things, this unity is at the same time the source of the reconciliation of the elements of artworks.

It can hardly be contested that Mozart provided the prototype for the balance between form and the formed, that which is fleeting and centrifugal. This balance, however, is only as authentic as it is in his music because its thematic and motivic cells, the monads out of which it is composed—however much they are conceived with an eye to contrast and precise difference—seek to pull apart even while the tactful hand binds them together. The absence of violence in Mozart's music has its source in the fact that within an overarching balance the qualitative thusness of the details is not allowed to atrophy, and what can rightfully be called his genius of form is not his mastery of forms—which was for him in any case a given—but his capacity to employ them without an element of domination, using them to bind the diffuse without restraint. Form in Mozart is the equilibrium found in centrifugal forces, not their subjugation. This is most evident in the large operatic forms, as in the finale of the second act of *Figaro*, a form that is neither composed nor a synthesis—unlike instrumental music it is not obliged to refer to schemas that are legitimated by the synthesis of what they subsume—but rather a pure configuration of adjoined parts whose character is won from the shifting dramaturgical situation. Such works, no less than many of his most audacious instrumental movements, such as several of his violin concertos, tend as profoundly, if not as obviously, toward disintegration as do Beethoven's last quartets. Mozart's classicality is immune to the charge of classicism only because it is situated on the boundary of a disintegration that in Beethoven's late work—which is so much more the work of subjective synthesis—was surpassed in the critique of this synthesis. Disintegration is the truth of integral art.

Mozart, whom a harmonistic aesthetics to all appearances plausibly claims as its foundation, towers over its norms by virtue of what is itself, in the contemporary idiom, a formal dimension: his capacity to unify the ununifiable by doing justice to what the divergent musical characters require without dissolving it into an obligatory continuum. In this regard, Mozart is the composer of Viennese classicism who is most remote from the established classical ideal and thereby achieves a higher ideal, what might be called authenticity [*Authentizität*]. It is this element by which, even in music, in spite of its nonrepresentationality, the distinction can be made between formalism as an empty game and that for which there is no other term than the disreputable one of profundity.

The formal law of an artwork is that all its elements and its unity must be organized in conformity with their own specific character.

Because artworks are not the unity of a multiplicity but rather the unity of the one and the many, they do not coincide with phenomenality.

Unity is semblance, just as the semblance of artworks is constituted by their unity.

The monadological character of artworks would not have formed without the guilt of the monstrous monadological character of society, but only by its means do artworks achieve that objectivity that transcends solipsism.

Art has no universal laws, though in each of its phases there certainly are objectively binding taboos. They radiate from canonical works. Their very existence defines what forthwith is no longer possible.

So long as forms were available with a certain immediacy, works could be concretized within them; their concretion could, in Hegel's language, be termed the substantiality of the forms. In the course of the total nominalistic movement, the more this substantiality was vitiated—from a critical perspective, justly so—the more its nevertheless continuing existence became a fetter for concrete works. What was once objectivated productive force was transformed into aesthetic relations of production and collided with the forces of production. Forms, that by which artworks seek to become artworks, themselves require autonomous production. This at the same time threatens them: The concentration on forms as a means of aesthetic objectivity distances them from what is to be objectivated. It is for this reason that currently models, the ideas of the possibility of artworks, so often overshadow the works themselves. In the substitution of means for ends it is possible to recognize the expression of a total social movement as well as the crisis of the artwork. Relentless reflection gravitates toward the annihilation of what is reflected. There is complicity between reflection, to the extent that it does not reflect on itself, and the merely posited form that is indifferent to what it forms. On their own, even the most exacting formal principles are worthless if the authentic works, for the sake of which the principles were sought, fail to materialize; aesthetic nominalism has today culminated in this simple antinomy.

So long as genres were givens, the new flourished within them. Increasingly, however, newness has shifted to the genres, because they are scarce. Important artists have responded to the nominalistic situation less through new works than through models of their possibility, through types; this contributes further to the undermining of the traditional category of artwork.

The problematic of style is strikingly apparent in works of the highly stylized domain of early modernism such as Debussy's *Pelléas*. Without making the slightest concession, with exemplary purity, this lyrical drama pursues its *principium stilisationis*. The inconsistencies that result are in no way the fault of that supposed thin-bloodedness that is criticized by those who are no longer able to follow the work's principle of stylization. The monotony of the piece is striking and well known. The rigor of the work's refusals prohibits the formation of contrasts as cheap and banal or reduces them to mere intimations. This damages the articulation, the organization of form by subsidiary structures, that is so indispensable to a work whose ultimate criterion is unity of form; here stylization ignores the recognition that a unity of style must be the unity of a multiplicity. The uninterrupted psalmody, particularly of the vocal line, lacks what older musical terminology called *Abgesang*, a concluding phrase or section: redemption, fulfillment, pouring forth. Its sacrifice in the interest of a feeling for a past that is eons distant causes a rupture in the work, as if what had been promised had not been redeemed. Taste, raised to the level of totality, rebels against the dramatic gesture of the music, and at the same time the work cannot do without its staging. The work's consummateness also leads to the impoverishment of the technical means, the persevering homophony becomes meager, and the orchestration, though devoted to the exploitation of tone color, becomes grey on grey. These problems of stylization point to problems in the relation of art and culture. Any classificatory schema that subsumes art as a branch of culture is inadequate. Incontestably *Pelléas* is culture without any desire to denounce it. This is of a part with the speechlessly mythical hermeticism of the subject matter, which precisely thereby neglects what the subject seeks. Artworks require transcendence of culture if they are to satisfy culture; this is a powerful motivation of radical modernism.

Light is thrown on the dialectic of the universal and particular by a remark of Arnold Gehlen. Picking up on Konrad Lorenz, he interprets the specifically aesthetic forms, those of natural beauty as well as that of the ornament, as "releasing devices" [*Auslöserqualitäten*] that serve to relieve overstimulated human beings. According to Lorenz all means of release share improbability paired with simplicity. Gehlen transposes this idea to art on the assumption that "our pleasure in pure sounds ('spectral sounds') and their integral harmonies . . . is an exact analogy, on the acoustic level, to the releasing effect of 'improbability.'"[29] "Artistic imagination is inexhaustible in the 'stylization' of natural forms, that is, in their symmetrical and simplified rendering, in the interest of the optimal extraction of releasing effects."[30] If such simplification indeed constitutes what may specifically be called form, then through its link to improbability the abstractive element simultaneously becomes the opposite of universality and thus the element of particularization. In the idea of the particular, on which art depends—as is most obviously the case in narration, which intends to be the report of a particular, rather than a quotidian, event—the same improbability is contained that is evident in the apparently universal, in the geometrically pure forms of ornament and stylization. The improbable, as the secularization of mana, would be at once universal and particular, aesthetic regularity as an improbable regularity turned against the status quo; spirit is not simply the contrary of particularization, it is also, by virtue of the improbable, its precondition. In all art, spirit was always what dialectical reflection only later showed it to be: concretion, and not abstract.

Art's social fate is not simply imposed on it externally, but is equally the unfolding of art's own concept.

Art is not indifferent to its double character. Its pure immanence becomes for it an immanent burden. Art seeks autarchy, which at the same time threatens it with sterility. Wedekind recognized this in Maeterlinck and mocked him and his kind as "artistic artists"; Wagner made the same controversy thematic in the *Meistersinger*; and the same motif, with anti-intellectual overtones, is unmistakable in Brecht. Escape from art's domain of immanence easily turns demagogical in the name of the people; what the "artistic artist" mocks, ogles the barbaric. Yet art, for the sake of its own self-preservation, desperately seeks to escape its sphere. For art is not only social by virtue of its own movement, as a priori opposition to a heteronomous society. Society itself, in its concrete form, always reaches into art. The question of what is possible, of productive formal approaches, is immediately determined by the situation of society. Insofar as art is constituted by subjective experience, social content penetrates to its core, though not literally, but rather in a modified, fragmentary, and shadowy fashion. This, not psychology, is the true affinity of artworks to dreams.

Culture is refuse, yet art—one of its sectors—is nevertheless serious as the appearance of truth. This is implicit in the double character of fetishism.

Art is bewitched in that the ruling criterion of its being-for-other is semblance—the exchange relation that has been established as the measure of all things—whereas, however, the other, the in-itself of the work, becomes ideology as soon as it posits itself as such. The alternative, that between: *"What do I get out of it?"* and "To be German means doing something for its own sake,"[31] is detestable. The untruth of the for-other has become obvious in that what is supposedly done for the self only compounds self-betrayal; the thesis of being-in-itself is fused with elitist narcissism and thus also serves what is base.

Because artworks register and objectivate levels of experience that are fundamental to the relation to reality yet are almost always concealed by reification, aesthetic experience is socially as well as metaphysically compelling.

The distance of the aesthetic realm from that of practical aims appears inner-aesthetically as the distance of aesthetic objects from the observing subject; just as artworks cannot intervene, the subject cannot intervene in them; distance is the primary condition for any closeness to the content of works. This is implicit in Kant's concept of absence of interest, which demands of aesthetic comportment that it not grasp at the object, not devour it. Benjamin's definition of aura[32] touched on this inner-aesthetic element, though it relegated it to a past stage and declared it invalid for the contemporary age of technical reproducibility. Identifying with the aggressor, he all too promptly allied himself with the historical tendency that remands art to the empirical domain of practical ends. As a phenomenon, distance is what in artworks transcends their mere existence; their absolute nearness would be their absolute integration.

Compared with authentic art, degraded, dishonored, and administered art is by no means without aura: The opposition between these antagonistic spheres must always be conceived as the mediation of one through the other. In the contemporary situation, those works honor the auratic element that abstain from it; its destructive conservation—its mobilization for the production of effects in the interest of creating mood—has its locus in amusement. Entertainment art adulterates on the one hand the real layer of the aesthetic, which is divested of its mediation and reduced to mere facticity, to information and reportage; on the other hand, it rips the auratic element out of the nexus of the work, cultivates it as such, and makes it consumable. Every close-up in commercial film mocks aura by contriving to exploit the contrived nearness of the distant, cut off from the work as a whole. Aura is gulped down along with the sensual stimuli; it is the uniform sauce that the culture industry pours over the whole of its manufacture.

Stendhal's dictum of art as the *promesse du bonheur* implies that art does its part for existence by accentuating what in it prefigures utopia. But this utopic element is constantly decreasing, while existence increasingly becomes merely self-equivalent. For this reason art is ever less able to make itself like existence. Because all happiness found in the status quo is an ersatz and false, art must break its promise in order to stay true to it. But the consciousness of people, especially that of the masses who in an antagonistic society are separated by cultural privilege from consciousness of such a dialectic, hold fast to the promise of happiness; rightfully so, but in its immediate, material form. This provides the opening for the culture industry, which plans for and exploits the need for happiness. The culture industry has its element of truth in its fulfillment of a need that originates in the ever increasing renunciation demanded by society; but the sort of concessions it provides renders it absolutely false.

In the midst of a world dominated by utility, art indeed has a utopic aspect as the other of this world, as exempt from the mechanism of the social process of production and reproduction: It always has something of the feeling of the moment when the Thespian cart rolls into town in Smetana's *The Bartered Bride*. But even to see the tight-rope walkers costs something. What is other is swallowed up by the ever-same and yet survives in it as semblance: semblance even in the materialist sense. Art must distill all its elements, spirit included, from an unvarying uniformity and must transform them all. By its bare difference from the uniform, art is a priori the critic of the uniform, even when it accommodates itself to what it criticizes and effectively moves within its presuppositions. Unconsciously every artwork must ask itself if and how it can exist as utopia: always only through the constellation of its elements. The artwork transcends not by the bare and abstract difference from the unvarying but rather by taking the unvarying into itself, taking it apart, and putting it back together again; such composition is what is usually called aesthetic creativity. Accordingly, the truth content of artworks is to be judged in terms of the extent to which they are able to reconfigure the other out of the unvarying.

The spirit in the artwork and in the reflection on it becomes suspect because it can affect the commodity character of the work and its commercial value; to this the collective unconscious is exceedingly sensitive. Granted, this widespread suspiciousness is fueled by a deep mistrust of official culture, its goods, and the diligently advertised assurance that people are participating in all this through pleasure. The greater the precision with which the ambivalent inner self realizes that it is being cheated by official culture of what is promised—the promise of which in any case constitutes the debasement of culture—the more stubbornly it fixes its teeth ideologically in what in no way exists even in the mass experience of art. This is colored by the detritus of vitalism's wisdom: that consciousness kills.

When it is a matter of art, the bourgeois habit of attaching itself fiercely and with cowardly cynicism to something once it has seen through it as false and untrue becomes an insistence that: "What I like may be bad, a fraud, and fabricated to dupe people, but I don't want to be reminded of that and in my free time I don't want to exert myself or get upset." The element of semblance in art develops historically into this subjective obstinacy, which, in the age of the culture industry, integrates art into empirical reality as a synthetic dream and excludes reflection on art as well as the reflection immanent to art. Ultimately what underlies this is the fact that the perpetuation of existing society is incompatible with consciousness of itself, and art is punished for every trace of such consciousness. From this perspective as well, ideology—false consciousness—is socially necessary. Nevertheless, in the reflection of the observer, the authentic artwork gains rather than being diminished. If one were to take the art consumer at his word, it would be necessary to demonstrate to him that it is through full knowledge of the work and not from the first sensual impression that he would, to use a phrase he uses so lightly, get more out of the work. The experience of art becomes incomparably richer through undistracted knowledge of it. The intellectual study of a work reflects back on its sensual perception. Such subjective reflection is legitimate in that it, so to speak, recapitulates the immanent process of reflection that objectively transpires in the aesthetic object, a process of which the artist need by no means necessarily be conscious.

For art, "good enough" is never good enough. The idea of minor and middling masters is one of the treasured notions of the history of art and especially of music; it is the projection of a consciousness that is obtuse to the life of the work in itself. No continuum leads from bad by way of the middling to the good; what does not succeed is a priori bad because the idea of success and coherence is inherent to the idea of art; this is what motivates the incessant disputes over the quality of artworks, however sterile these disputes generally are. Art, according to Hegel the appearance of truth, is objectively intolerant, even of the socially dictated pluralism of peacefully coexisting spheres, which ever and again provides ideologues with excuses. Especially intolerable is the term "satisfying entertainment," which is glibly used by committees that would like to vindicate the commodity character of art in the eyes of their infirm consciences. A daily newspaper explained why Colette is treated as entertainment in Germany whereas in France she enjoys the highest regard: It is because there people do not distinguish between entertainment and serious art but only between good and bad. In fact, on the other side of the Rhine Colette plays the role of a sacred cow. In Germany, on the other hand, the rigid dichotomy of high and low art serves as fortifications for a petit bourgeois faith in the merits of cultural erudition. Artists who by official criteria belong to the lower sphere, but who show more talent than many of those who fulfill long-decayed standards, are robbed of their due. In the well-turned phrase of the social critic Willy Haas, there is good bad literature and bad good literature; the case in music is no different. All the same, the distinction between entertainment and autonomous art, to the extent that it does not close its eyes to the untenability of the concept of standards or ignore the unregimented stirrings below, has its substance in the qualities of the works. Certainly the distinction requires the most extreme differentiation; moreover, even in the nineteenth century these spheres were not so unreconcilably split as they are today in the age of cultural monopoly. There is no dearth of works that, on account of gratuitous formulations that range from the sketchy to the stereotypical—works that have subordinated their own coherence to the calculation of their effect and have their locus in the subaltern sphere of aesthetic circulation—yet nevertheless go beyond it by virtue of subtle qualities. When and if their value as amusement evaporates, they may be able to become more than they were to start with. Even the relation of lower to higher art has its historical dynamic. What was once tailored to consumer taste may later, in the face of totally rationalized and administered consumption, appear as an afterimage of humanity. Even works that are not fully worked through, not fully executed, cannot invariably be rejected by these criteria but are legitimate where works correct themselves by the expedient of establishing their own level of form and not setting themselves up to be more than they are. Thus Puccini's extraordinary talent was expressed far more convincingly in unpretentious early works like *Manon Lescaut* and *La Bohème* than in the later, more ambitious works that degenerate into kitsch because of the disproportion between substance and presentation. None of the categories of theoretical aesthetics can be employed rigidly, as unshakable criteria. Whereas aesthetic objectivity can only be grasped in the immanent critique of individual works, the necessary abstractness of categories becomes a source of error. It is up to aesthetic theory, which is unable to progress to immanent critique, at least to delineate models of its self-correction through the second reflection of its categories. In this context, Offenbach and Johann Strauss are relevant; antipathy toward official culture and its taste for classical knock-offs motivated Karl Kraus to a particular insistence on such phenomena, as well as on such literary phenomena as Nestroy.[33] Obviously it is necessary to be wary of the ideology of those who, because they are incapable of the discipline of authentic works, provide salable excuses. Yet the division of the spheres, objective in that it is a historical sedimentation, is not absolute. Lodged even in the highest work is an element that is for-other, a mortal remnant of seeking applause. Perfection, beauty itself, asks: "Am I not beautiful?" and thus sins against itself. Conversely, the most lamentable kitsch, which yet necessarily appears as art, cannot help raising a claim to what it disdains, the element of being in-itself, which it betrays. Colette was talented. She succeeded in making something as graceful as the small novel *Mitsou* and something as enigmatic as the heroine's attempted escape in *The Innocent Libertine*. Altogether she was a refined and linguistically cultivated version of Vicky Baum.[34] She provided unbearably heartwarming pseudonature and did not balk in the face of intolerable scenes such as the end of the novel in which to general approbation the frigid heroine finally finds pleasure in the arms of her legitimate spouse. Colette delighted her audience with family novels set in a milieu of high-class prostitution. The most significant objection to French art, which nourished the whole of modernism, is that the French have no word for kitsch, precisely that which is a source of pride in Germany. The truce between the domains of entertainment and serious art bears witness to the neutralization of culture: Because no spirit is binding for culture's spirit, culture offers its wares in a selection for *highbrows, middlebrows*, and *lowbrows*. The social need for amusement and what is called relaxation is exploited by a society whose involuntary members would otherwise hardly put up with the burden and monotony of their life and who in their allotted and administered leisure time are hardly capable of taking in anything but what is forced on them by the culture industry, and that in truth includes the pseudo-individualization of novels à la Colette. But the need for entertainment does not improve it; it barters off and dulls the dregs of serious art and comes up with meager, abstractly standardized, and incoherent results. Entertainment, including its more exalted products and especially those that seek a touch of nobility, has become vulgar ever since the exchange society caught hold of artistic production and made it too a commodity. Art is vulgar when it degrades people by cancelling its distance from an already degraded humanity; it confirms what the world has made of them rather than that its gesture revolts against it. Insofar as they embody the identification of people with their own debasement, the grinning cultural commodities are vulgar. No direct relation exists between social need and aesthetic quality, not even in the sphere of so-called functional art. The need to construct buildings in Germany in the decades after World War II was probably more pressing than it had been for centuries. Yet postwar German architecture is pitiful. Voltaire's equation of *vrai besoin* and *vrai plaisir* does not hold aesthetically; the quality of artworks can be meaningfully brought into relation with social need only when mediated by a theory of society as a whole, not on the basis of what a people need at any given time, which can for that reason be all the more easily imposed on them.

One of the defining elements of kitsch may well be the simulation of nonexisting feelings and thus their neutralization along with the neutralization of the aesthetic phenomenon. Kitsch is art that cannot be or does not want to be taken seriously and yet through its appearance postulates aesthetic seriousness. But, however illuminating this may be, it is not adequate, and this applies not only to that broad range of base and unsentimental kitsch. Emotion is simulated; but whose emotion? The author's? But the author's emotion cannot be reconstructed, nor is any correlation to it a criterion of art. All aesthetic objectivation diverges from the immediate impulse. Or is it the emotion of those to whom the author ascribes it? Then these emotions would be as fictional as the dramatis personae themselves. If the definition of kitsch is to be meaningful, the expression of the artwork must be considered in itself an *index veri et falsi;* but to judge the expressive authenticity of a work leads to such endless complications—one of which is the historical transformation of the truth content of the means of expression—that they could only be solved casuistically and even then not definitively. Kitsch is qualitatively distinct both from art and from its proliferation, as is predetermined by the contradiction that autonomous art must dispose over the mimetic impulses that are themselves opposed to such control. Through the artwork the mimetic impulses already undergo the injustice that culminates in the abolition of art and its substitution by the schemata of fiction. The critique of kitsch must be vigilant, though it takes its toll on art as well. The revolt of art against its a priori affinity with kitsch was one of the essential laws of development in its recent history, and it participates in the destruction of works. What once was art can later become kitsch. Perhaps this history of collapse is the history of the correction of art, its true progress.

In the face of the obvious dependency of fashion on the profit motive and its embeddedness in capitalist industry—which, for instance in the art market, which finances painters but overtly or covertly demands in exchange that they furnish whatever style of work the market expects of them, extends into so-called artistic fashions and directly undermines autonomy—fashion in art is no less corruptible than the zeal of ideological art agents who transform every apology into advertisement. What makes it worth salvaging, however, is that though it hardly denies its complicity with the profit system, it is itself disdained by that system. By suspending aesthetic values such as those of inwardness, timelessness, and profundity, fashion makes it possible to recognize the degree to which the relation of art to these qualities, which are by no means above suspicion, has become a pretext. Fashion is art's permanent confession that it is not what it claims to be. For its indiscreet betrayals fashion is as hated as it is a powerful force in the system; its double character is a blatant symptom of its antinomy. Fashion cannot be separated from art as neatly as would suit bourgeois art religion. Ever since the aesthetic subject polemically distanced itself from society and its prevailing spirit, art communicates with this objective spirit, however untrue it is, through fashion. Fashion is certainly no longer characterized by that spontaneity and simple originality that was earlier, and probably wrongly, attributed to it: It is entirely manipulated and in no way a direct adaptation to the demands of the marketplace, even if these demands are sedimented in it and the consensus of the marketplace is still requisite for fashion to succeed. Because, however, manipulation in the age of monopoly capitalism is itself the prototype of ruling social relations of production, fashion's *octroi* itself represents a socially objective power. If, in one of the most remarkable passages of his *Aesthetics*, Hegel defined the task of art as the appropriation of the alien,[35] fashion—doubtful of any possibility of such spiritual reconciliation—appropriates alienation itself. For fashion, alienation becomes the living model of a social being-thus-and-not-otherwise [*So-und-nicht-anders-Sein*], to which it surrenders as if in ecstasy. If it is not to betray itself, art must resist fashion, but it must also innervate fashion in order not to make itself blind to the world, to its own substance. In his poetic work and in his essays, Baudelaire was the first to practice this double relation toward fashion. Of this his eulogy for Constantin Guys[36] is the most compelling evidence. For Baudelaire, the artist *de la vie moderne* is he who remains in self-control while abandoning himself to what is completely ephemeral. Even the first artist of the highest importance who rejected communication did not shut out fashion: Much of Rimbaud's poetry resonates with the tone of Parisian literary cabarets. Radically oppositional art, which ruthlessly renounced everything heterogeneous to it, in its ruthlessness also attacked the fiction of a subject existing purely for-itself, the disastrous illusion of a strictly self-engaging integrity that usually functions to hide a provincial pharisaism. In the age of the growing powerlessness of subjective spirit vis-à-vis social objectivity, fashion registers the alien excess of objectivity in subjective spirit, which is painful yet all the same a corrective of the illusion that subjective spirit exists purely within itself. Against its detractors, fashion's most powerful response is that it participates in the individual impulse, which is saturated with history; it did so paradigmatically in *Jugendstil*, in the paradoxical universality of loneliness as a style. The disdain of fashion, however, is provoked by its erotic element, in which fashion reminds art of what it never fully succeeded in sublimating. Through fashion, art sleeps with what it must renounce and from this draws the strength that otherwise must atrophy under the renunciation on which art is predicated. If art, as semblance, is the clothing of an invisible body, fashion is clothing as the absolute. As such, they stand in accord with each other. The concept of the "latest mode" is a wretched one—linguistically, mode is allied with modernism—for it serves to defame in art what usually contains more truth than what claims to be unaffected by all the excitement and thus manifests a lack of sensitivity that disqualifies it artistically.

In the concept of art, play is the element by which art immediately raises itself above the immediacy of praxis and its purposes. Yet it is at the same time oriented toward the past, toward childhood, if not animality. In play, art—through its renunciation of functional rationality—at the same time regresses back of rationality. The historical compulsion for art to mature functions in opposition to its playfulness, though it does not cast it off altogether; any straightforward recourse to playful forms, on the other hand, inevitably stands in the service of restorative or archaizing social tendencies. Playful forms are without exception forms of repetition. When they are employed affirmatively they are joined with the repetition compulsion, to which they adapt and which they sanction as normative. In blunt opposition to Schillerian ideology, art allies itself with unfreedom in the specific character of play. Thereby art incorporates an element alien to it; the most recent deaestheticization of art covertly exploits the element of play at the cost of all others. When Schiller celebrates the play drive as quintessentially human because it is free of purpose, he, being the loyal bourgeois he was, interpreted the opposite of freedom as freedom, in accord with the philosophy of his age. The relationship of play to praxis is more complex than Schiller's *Aesthetic Education* makes it appear. Whereas all art sublimates practical elements, play in art—by its neutralization of praxis—becomes bound up specifically with its spell, the compulsion toward the ever-same, and, in psychological dependence on the death instinct, interprets obedience as happiness. In art, play is from the outset disciplinary; it fulfills the taboo on expression that inheres in the ritual of imitation; when art exclusively plays, nothing remains of expression. Secretly, play is in complicity with fate, a plenipotentiary of the weight of the mythical, which art would like to throw off; the repressive aspect is obvious in such phrases as that of the rhythm of the blood, with which the formal playfulness of dance is so readily invoked. If games of chance are the opposite of art, as forms of play they nevertheless extend into art. The putative play drive has ever been fused with the primacy of blind collectivity. Only when play becomes aware of its own terror, as in Beckett, does it in any way share in art's power of reconciliation. Art that is totally without play is no more thinkable than if it were totally without repetition, yet art is nevertheless able to define the remainder of horror within itself as being negative.

Huizinga's much celebrated *Homo Ludens* has reintroduced the category of play as central to aesthetics, and not only there: Culture, he argues, originates as play. "To speak of the 'play element in culture' . . . is not to imply that among the various activities of civilized life an important place is reserved for play, nor that civilization has arisen out of play by some evolutionary process, in the sense that something that was originally play passed into something that was no longer play and could henceforth be called culture. Rather, I wish to show that . . . culture is initially played."[37] Huizinga's thesis succumbs to the critique of the definition of art by its origin. All the same, his thesis has its truth and its untruth. If one grasps the concept of play as abstractly as he does, it is clear that he is defining not something specific but merely forms of comportment, which somehow distance themselves from the praxis of self-preservation. He fails to realize how much the element of play is itself an afterimage of praxis rather than of semblance. In all play, action has fundamentally divested itself of any relation to purpose, but in terms of its form and execution the relation to praxis is maintained. The element of repetition in play is the afterimage of unfree labor, just as sports—the dominant extraaesthetic form of play—is reminiscent of practical activities and continually fulfills the function of habituating people to the demands of praxis, above all by the reactive transformation of physical displeasure into secondary pleasure, without their noticing that the contraband of praxis has slipped into it. Huizinga's thesis not only that human beings play with language but that language itself originates in play, sovereignly ignores the practical necessities contained in language, of which language frees itself only eventually, if ever. There is, furthermore, an apparent convergence of Huizinga's theory of language with Wittgenstein's; he, too, fails to grasp the constitutive relation of language to the extralinguistic. Nevertheless, Huizinga's theory of play leads him to insights that are closed to the magical and religious-metaphysical reductions of art. He recognized that from the perspective of the subject, aesthetic comportments that he comprehends under the name of play are at once true and untrue. This helps him to reach a remarkably compelling idea of humor: "One would like . . . to ask whether the primitive's belief in his holiest myths is not, even from the beginning, tinged with a certain element of humor."[38] "A half-joking element verging on make-believe is inseparable from true myth."[39] The religious festivals of primitive peoples are not those "of a complete ecstasy and illusion. . . . There is no lack of an underlying consciousness of things 'not being authentic.'"[40] "Whether one is sorcerer or sorcerized, one is always knower and dupe at once. But one chooses to be the dupe."[41] It is in this consciousness of the untruth of the true that all art participates in humor, as do above all the dark works of modernism; Thomas Mann emphasized this quality in Kafka,[42] and in Beckett it is obvious. In Huizinga's formulation, "The unity and indivisibility of belief and disbelief, the indissoluble connection between sacred seriousness and pretense and 'fun,' are best understood in the concept of play."[43] What is here predicated of play holds true for all art as well. Less tenable, however, is Huizinga's interpretation of the "hermetic character of play," which collides with his own dialectical definition of play as a unity of "belief and disbelief." His insistence on a unity in which ultimately the play of animals, children, primitives, and artists is not qualitatively but only gradually distinguished, anesthetizes consciousness of the contradictoriness of the theory and fails to make good on Huizinga's own insight into the aesthetically constitutive nature of the contradiction.

On Surrealist Shock and Montage.——The paradox that what occurs in the rationalized world nevertheless has history is shocking not least because by virtue of its historicity the capitalist *ratio* itself is revealed as irrational. Alarmed, the sensorium becomes aware of the irrationality of the rational.

Praxis would be the ensemble of means for minimizing material necessity, and as such it would be identical with pleasure, happiness, and that autonomy in which these means are sublimated. This however is impeded by practicality, which denies pleasure in the spirit of a society in which the ideal of full employment is substituted for that of the abolition of labor. The rationalism of a mentality that refuses to allow itself to look beyond the means-ends relation and confront it with its own ends is irrational. Praxis itself is fetishized. This contradicts its own concept, necessarily that of a for-other, which the concept loses the moment it is established as an absolute. This other is art's—and theory's—moving force. The irrationality of which practicality accuses art is the corrective of its own irrationality.

The relation of art and society has its locus in art itself and its development, not in immediate partisanship, in what today is called *commitment*. It is equally fruitless to seek to grasp this relation theoretically by constructing as an invariant the nonconformist attitudes of art throughout history and opposing it to affirmative attitudes. There is no dearth of artworks that could only with difficulty be forced into a nonconformist tradition—which is in any case thoroughly fissured—whose objectivity nevertheless maintains a profoundly critical stance toward society.

The demise of art, which is today being proclaimed with as much glibness as resentment, would be false, a gesture of conformism. The desublimation, the immediate and momentary gain of pleasure that is demanded of art, is inner-aesthetically beneath art; in real terms, however, that momentary pleasure is unable to grant what is expected of it. The recently adopted insistence on culturing uncultivation, the enthusiasm for the beauty of street battles, is a reprise of futurist and dadaist actions. The cheap aestheticism of short-winded politics is reciprocal with the faltering of aesthetic power. Recommending jazz and rock-and-roll instead of Beethoven does not demolish the affirmative lie of culture but rather furnishes barbarism and the profit interest of the culture industry with a subterfuge. The allegedly vital and uncorrupted nature of such products is synthetically processed by precisely those powers that are supposedly the target of the Great Refusal:[44] These products are the truly corrupt.

The thesis that the end of art is imminent or has already occurred recurs throughout history, and especially since the beginning of the modern age; Hegel reflects this thesis philosophically, he did not invent it. Though today it poses as being anti-ideological, it was until recently the ideology of historically decadent groups who took their own end to be the end of all things. The shift is probably marked by the Communist ban on modern art, which suspended the immanent aesthetic movement in the name of social progress; the mentality of the apparatchiks, however, who thought this up, was the old petit bourgeois consciousness. Inevitably the thesis of the end of art can be heard at dialectical nodal points where a new form suddenly emerges that is directed polemically against the established form. Since Hegel the prophecy of the imminent end of art has more often been a component of a cultural philosophy that pronounces its judgment from on high than an element of actual artistic experience; in decrees totalitarian measures were prepared. The situation has, however, always looked different from within art. The Beckettian zero point—the last straw for a howling philosophy of culture—is, like the atom, infinitely full. It is not inconceivable that humanity would no longer need a closed, immanent culture once it actually had been realized; today, however, the threat is a false destruction of culture, a vehicle of barbarism. The "*Il faut continuer*," the conclusion of Beckett's *The Unnamable*, condenses this antinomy to its essence: that externally art appears impossible while immanently it must be pursued. What is new is that art must incorporate its own decline; as the critique of the spirit of domination it is the spirit that is able to turn against itself. The self-reflection of art penetrates to its own foundation and concretizes itself in it. The political significance, however, which the thesis of the end of art had thirty years ago, as for instance indirectly in Benjamin's theory of reproduction, is gone; incidentally, despite his desperate advocacy of mechanical reproduction,[45] in conversation Benjamin refused to reject contemporary painting: Its tradition, he argued, must be preserved for times less somber than our own. Nevertheless, in the face of the threatened transformation into barbarism it is better for art to come to a silent halt rather than to desert to the enemy and aid a development that is tantamount to integration into the status quo for the sake of its superior power. The lie in the intellectuals' proclamation of the end of art resides in their question as to what the point is of art, what its legitimation is vis-à-vis contemporary praxis. But the function of art in the totally functional world is its functionlessness; it is pure superstition to believe that art could intervene directly or lead to an intervention. The instrumentalization of art sabotages its opposition to instrumentalization; only where art respects its own immanence does it convict practical reason of its lack of reason. Art opposes the hopelessly antiquated principle of *l'art pour l'art* not by ceding to external purposes but by renouncing the illusion of a pure realm of beauty that quickly reveals itself as kitsch. By determinate negation artworks absorb the *membra disjecta* of the empirical world and through their transformation organize them into a reality that is a counterreality, a monstrosity; this was Baudelaire's interpretation of the watchword of *l'art pour l'art* when he used it. Just how little this is the time for the abolition of art is apparent in its concretely open yet untried possibilities, which languish as if under a spell. Even when art in protest works itself free it remains unfree, for even the protest is constrained. Clearly it would be miserable apologetics to claim that the end of art cannot be envisioned. In response, art can do no better than close its eyes and grit its teeth.

Sealing art off from empirical reality became an explicit program in hermetic poetry. In the face of all of its important works—those of Celan, for instance—it is justified to ask to what extent they are indeed hermetic; as Peter Szondi points out, that they are self-contained does not mean that they are unintelligible. On the contrary, hermetic poetry and social elements have a common nexus that must be acknowledged. Reified consciousness, which through the integration of highly industrialized society becomes integral to its members, fails to perceive what is essential to the poems, emphasizing instead their thematic content and putative informational value. Artistically people can only be reached any longer by the shock that imparts a blow to what pseudo-scientific ideology calls communication; for its part art is integral only when it refuses to play along with communication. Hermetic procedures are, however, motivated by the growing pressure to separate the poetry from the thematic material and from the intentions. This pressure has extended from reflection to poetry, which seeks to take under its own auspices its raison d'être, and this effort is at the same time its immanent law of movement. Hermetic poetry—the idea of which originated in the period of *Jugendstil* and has something in common with the then prevalent concept of the "will to style"—can be seen as poetry that sets out to produce, from itself, what otherwise only emerges historically: its essential content; this effort has a chimerical aspect in that it requires the transformation of emphatic content into intention. Hermetic poetry makes thematic and treats explicitly what earlier in art occurred without its having been aimed at: To this extent Valéry's idea of a reciprocal relation between artistic production and self-reflection in the course of poetic production is already formulated in Mallarmé. Out of his desire for a utopian art free of everything art-alien, Mallarmé was apolitical and therefore extremely conservative. But by his rejection of the sort of unctuous message as preached by every conservative voice today, he converges with his political counterpole, dadaism; in literary history there is never a scarcity of intermediaries. In the more than eighty years since Mallarmé, hermetic poetry has been transformed, partly in response to the social tendency: The cliché about the ivory tower no longer applies to the windowless monadic works. The beginnings were not free of the small-mindedness and desperate rapture of an art religion that convinced itself that the world was created for the sake of a beautiful verse or a well-turned phrase. In the work of the most important contemporary representative of German hermetic poetry, Paul Celan, the experiential content of the hermetic was inverted. His poetry is permeated by the shame of art in the face of suffering that escapes both experience and sublimation. Celan's poems want to speak of the most extreme horror through silence. Their truth content itself becomes negative. They imitate a language beneath the helpless language of human beings, indeed beneath all organic language: It is that of the dead speaking of stones and stars. The last rudiments of the organic are liquidated; what Benjamin noted in Baudelaire, that his poetry is without aura, comes into its own in Celan's work. The infinite discretion with which his radicalism proceeds compounds his force. The language of the lifeless becomes the last possible comfort for a death that is deprived of all meaning. The passage into the inorganic is to be followed not only in thematic motifs; rather, the trajectory from horror to silence is to be reconstructed in the hermetic works. Distantly analogous to Kafka's treatment of expressionist painting, Celan transposes into linguistic processes the increasing abstraction of landscape, progressively approximating it to the inorganic.

By appearing as art, that which insists that it is realistic injects meaning into reality, which such art is pledged to copy without illusion. In the face of reality this is a priori ideological. Today the impossibility of realism is not to be concluded on inner-aesthetic grounds but equally on the basis of the historical constellation of art and reality.

Today the primacy of the object and aesthetic realism are almost absolutely opposed to each other, and indeed when measured by the standard of realism: Beckett is more realistic than the socialist realists who counterfeit reality by their very principle. If they took reality seriously enough they would eventually realize what Lukács condemned when during the days of his imprisonment in Romania he is reported to have said that he had finally realized that Kafka was a realist writer.

The primacy of the object is not to be confused with the various attempts to extract art from its subjective mediation and to siphon objectivity into it from the outer world. Art puts the prohibition on positive negation to the test, showing that indeed negation of the negative is not the positive, that it does not accomplish the reconciliation with an object that is unreconciled with itself.

The thesis that the sum of taboos implies a canon of what is correct appears incompatible with the philosophical critique of the concept that the negation of the negation is a positive,[46] a concept that both in theory and in the social practice it implies signifies the sabotage of the negative labor of understanding [*Verstand*]. In the idealist model of dialectics, this negative labor of understanding is transformed into an antithesis that is constrained by the fact that its critique is to serve the legitimation of the thesis at a higher level. Granted, in this regard art and theory are not absolutely different. The moment idiosyncrasies, the aesthetic plenipotentiaries of negation, are raised to the level of positive rules, they freeze into anonymous abstractions vis-à-vis the particular artwork and artistic experience, and they mechanically subsume the interrelatedness of the artwork's elements at the expense of that interrelatedness. Through canonization, advanced artistic means easily acquire a restorative cast and become allied with structural elements against which the very same idiosyncrasies, themselves transformed into rules, once struggled. If in art everything is a question of nuance, this is no less true of the nuance between proscription and prescription. Speculative idealism, which culminated in Hegel's doctrine of positive negation, may have been borrowed from the idea of the absolute identity of artworks. Given their immanent economic principle and their artifactuality, artworks can in fact in themselves be much more consistent—and in the logical sense of the term more positive—than is theory, which is directly concerned with empirical reality. It is only through the progress of reflection that the principle of identity proves to be illusory even in the artwork, because its other is constitutive of its autonomy; to this extent artworks too are alien to positive negation.

With regard to the aesthetic object, the thesis of the primacy of the object means the primacy of the object itself, the artwork, over its maker as well as over its recipients. As Schoenberg said, "After all, I paint a picture, not a chair." Through this immanent primacy, the primacy of the external world is aesthetically mediated; unmediatedly, as the primacy of whatever the artwork presents, the primacy of the object would amount to the circumvention of the double character of the artwork. In the artwork, the concept of positive negation gains a new meaning: Aesthetically it is possible to speak of such positivity to the extent that the canon of historically necessary prohibitions serves the primacy of the object, that is, its immanent coherence.

Artworks present the contradictions as a whole, the antagonistic situation as a totality. Only by mediation, not by taking sides, are artworks capable of transcending the antagonistic situation through expression. The objective contradictions fissure the subject; they are not posited by the subject or the manufacture of his consciousness. This is the true primacy of the object in the inner composition of artworks. The subject can be fruitfully extinguished in the aesthetic object only because the subject itself is mediated through the object and is simultaneously the suffering subject of expression. The antagonisms are articulated technically; that is, they are articulated in the immanent composition of the work, and it is this process of composition that makes interpretation permeable to the tensions external to it. The tensions are not copied but rather form the work; this alone constitutes the aesthetic concept of form.

Even in a legendary better future, art could not disavow remembrance of accumulated horror; otherwise its form would be trivial.

Notes

1 See Walter Benjamin, "The Work of Art in the Age of Mechanical Reproduction," in *Illuminations,* trans. Harry Zohn (New York, 1968), pp. 217ff.

2 [See David Riesmann, *The Lonely Crowd* (New Haven, 1958).—trans.]

3 [Emanuel Johann Jakob Schikaneder (1751–1812), the German actor, singer, and playwright who made his career in Austria and is now known primarily as the author of the libretto for Mozart's *The Magic Flute.* Johann Jakob Bachofen (1815–1887), the mythologist and author of the romantic, diffuse, and seminal *Das Mutterrecht.*—trans.]

4 Benjamin, "The Work of Art in the Age of Mechanical Reproduction," in *Illuminations,* pp. 222–223.

5 ["das sich Entringende": See note 7 in "Semblance and Expression." —trans.]

6 Benjamin, "The Work of Art in the Age of Mechanical Reproduction," in *Illuminations,* pp. 222–223.

7 [From Johann Wolfgang von Goethe, *Faust,* conclusion of scene 1, "Night." —trans.]

8 [See note 5 on "Sprachcharakter" in "Semblance and Expression."—trans.]

9 "The paradox of everything that can rightly be called beautiful is that it appears." See Benjamin, *Schriften,* ed. Th. W. Adorno and G. Adorno, vol. 1 (Frankfurt, 1955), p. 549.

10 Quoted in Erik Holm, "Felskunst im südlichen Afrika," in *Kunst der Welt: Die Steinzeit* (Baden-Baden, 1960), pp. 197ff.

11 Walther F. E. Resch, "Gedanken zur stilistischen Gliederung der Tierdarstellungen in der nordafrikanishen Felsbildkunst," in *Paideuma, Mitteilungen zur Kulturkunde,* vol. 11 (1965).

12 Holm, *Felskunst im südlichen Afrika,* in *Kunst der Welt: Die Steinzeit,* p. 198.

13 See Felix Speiser, *Ethnographische Materialien aus den Neuen Hebriden und den Banks-Inseln* (Berlin, 1923).

14 Fritz Krause, "Maske und Ahnenfigur: Das Motiv der Hülle und das Prinzip der Form," in *Kulturanthropologie*, ed. W. E. Mühlmann and E. W. Müller (Cologne and Berlin, 1966), p. 228.

15 Speiser, *Ethnographische Materialien*, p. 390.

16 Friedrich Nietzsche, *Werke in drei Bänden*, ed. Karl Schlechta, vol. 3 (Munich and Vienna, 1956), p. 481.

17 The whole *In Search of Wagner* [trans. Rodney Livingstone (London, 1981)—trans.] had no other purpose than to mediate the critique of the truth content of Wagner's compositions with their technological structure and its fragility.

18 *In Search of Wagner* sought to demonstrate the mediation of the meta-aesthetic and the artistic in the work of an important artist. If in various sections the study is still oriented too psychologically to the artist, nevertheless the intent was a material aesthetics that would give a social and substantive voice to the autonomous and particularly the formal categories of art. The book is concerned with the objective meditations that constitute the truth content of the work, not with the genesis of the oeuvre or with analogies. Its intention was a contribution to philosophical aesthetics, not to the sociology of knowledge. What irritated Nietzsche about Wagner, the showiness, the bombast, and the affirmativeness and foisting pushiness that are evident right into the deepest molecule of the compositional technique, is one with the social ideology that the texts overtly espouse. Sartre's dictum that a good novel cannot be written from the perspective of anti-Semitism (see Jean-Paul Sartre, *What Is Literature?* New York, 1965, p. 58) puts the matter succinctly.

19 [See note 3 on "authenticity" in "Art Beauty: Apparition, Spiritualization, Intuitability."—trans.]

20 [The phrase in square brackets was crossed out in the manuscript, but the sentence was not otherwise revised.—ed. note in the original German edition.]

21 Katesa Schlosser, *Der Signalismus in der Kunst der Naturvölker: Biologisch-psychologische Gesetzlichkeiten in den Abweichungen von der Norm des Vorbildes* (Kiel, 1952), p. 14.

22 ["Wie schön sich Bild an Bildchen reiht," from "Verklärter Herbst" (transfigured autumn), one of Georg Trakl's best-known short poems, in *Georg Trakl: Dichtungen und Briefe* (Salzburg, 1969), p. 37.—trans.]

23 Eduard Mörike, *Sämtliche Werke*, ed. J. Perfahl et al., vol. 1 (Munich, 1968), p. 703.

24 Paul Valéry, *Œuvres*, ed. T. Hytier, vol. 2 (Paris, 1966), pp. 565ff.

25 Walter Benjamin, *The Origin of German Tragic Drama*, trans. John Osborne (London, 1977), p. 60.

26 [Hedwig Courths-Mahler (1867–1950) was the author of more than two hundred pulp novels.—trans.]

27 [*Wallenstein's Camp* is the prelude to the *Wallenstein* trilogy (1797–1799).—trans.]

28 See Adorno, "Individuum und Organisation," in *Individuum und Organisation*, ed. F. Neumark (Darmstadt, 1954), pp. 21ff.

29 Arnold Gehlen, "Über einige Kategorien des entlasteten, zumal des ästhetischen Verhaltens," in *Studien zur Anthropologie und Soziologie* (Neuwied and Berlin, 1963), p. 70.

30 Ibid., p. 69.

31 [A German nationalist maxim attributed to Richard Wagner.—trans.]

32 Benjamin, "The Work of Art in the Age of Mechanical Reproduction," in *Illuminations*, pp. 222ff.

33 [Johann Nepomuk Nestroy (1801–1862), the Austrian singer, actor, playwright, inveterate improvisor, and caustic literary and social critic whose modern reputation was the result of his advocacy by Karl Kraus.—trans.]

34 [Vicki Baum (1888–1960), the first German novelist whose career, techniques, and promotion were deliberately modeled by her publishing house, Ullstein, on the American formula of the best-seller. Baum is known as one of Ullstein's most successful ventures.—trans.]

35 [See note 4 in "Art Beauty: Apparition. Spiritualization, Intuitability."]

36 Charles Baudelaire, *The Painter of the Modern Life*, trans. and ed. Jonathan Mayne (New York, 1964), pp. 5ff.

37 Johann Huizinga, *Homo Ludens* (Boston, 1950), p. 46.

38 Ibid., p. 127.

39 Ibid., p. 140.

40 Ibid., p. 29.

41 Ibid., p. 30.

42 See Thomas Mann, *Altes und Neues. Kleine Prosa aus fünf Jahrzehnten* (Frankfurt, 1953), pp. 556ff.

43 Huizinga, *Homo Ludens*, p. 31.

44 ["The Great Refusal" was a central idea of Herbert Marcuse's *One Dimensional Man* (Boston, 1964), and it became a rallying cry of the American and German New Left.—trans.]

45 See Benjamin, "The Work of Art in the Age of Mechanical Reproduction," in *Illuminations*, pp. 222ff.

46 Cf. Adorno *Negative Dialectics* (New York, 1973), pp. 158–161.

14

Theories on the Origin of Art Excursus

The attempts to derive aesthetics from the origins of art as its essence are inevitably disappointing.[1] If the concept of origin is situated beyond history, the question takes on an ontological cast far removed from that solid ground that the prestigious concept of origin evokes; moreover, any invocation of the concept of origin that is divested of its temporal element transgresses against the simple meaning of the word, to which the philosophers of origin claim to be privy. Yet to reduce art historically to its prehistorical or early origins is prohibited by its character, which is the result of historical development. The earliest surviving manifestations of art are not the most authentic, nor do they in any way circumscribe art's range; and rather than best exemplifying what art is, they make it more obscure. It needs to be taken into account that the oldest surviving art, the cave paintings, belongs as a whole to the visual domain. Next to nothing is known of the music or poetry of the epoch; there are no indications of anything prehistoric that may have differed qualitatively from the optical works. Among aestheticians Croce was probably the first to condemn, in Hegelian spirit, the question of the historical origin of art as aesthetically irrelevant: "Since this 'spiritual' activity is its [history's] object, the absurdity of propounding the historical problem of the origin of art becomes evident . . . If expression is a form of consciousness, how can one look for the historical origin of what is not a product of nature and is presupposed by human history? How can one assign a historical genesis to a thing that is a category by means of which all historical processes and facts are understood?"[2] However correct the intention may be not to confound what is oldest with the concept of the thing-itself, which only

411

becomes what it is in the first place through its development, Croce's argumentation is dubious. By simply identifying art with expression, which is "presupposed by human history," he once again defines art as what it should never be for the philosophy of history: a "category," an invariant form of consciousness, something that is static in form, even if Croce conceives it as pure activity or spontaneity. His idealism, no less than the Bergsonian streak in his aesthetics, keeps him from being able to perceive the constitutive relation of art to what it itself is not, to what is not the pure spontaneity of the subject; this fundamentally limits his critique of the question of origin. Still, the legion of empirical studies that have since been dedicated to the question hardly give cause to revise Croce's verdict. It would be too easy to blame this on the advancing positivism that, out of fear of being contradicted by any next fact, no longer dares to undertake the construction of univocal theory and mobilizes the accumulation of facts in order to prove that genuine science can no longer put up with theory on a grand style. Ethnology, in particular, which according to the current division of labor has the responsibility of interpreting prehistoric findings, has let itself be intimidated by the tendency stretching back to Frobenius to explicate everything archaically puzzling in terms of religion, even when the findings themselves contradict such summary treatment. Nevertheless the scientific exclusion of the question of origin, which corresponds to the philosophical critique of origin, testifies to something more than the powerlessness of science and the terror of positivistic taboos. Melville J. Herskovits's study *Man and His Work*[3] is characteristic of the interpretive pluralism that even a disillusioned science is unable to renounce. If contemporary science renounces any monistic answer to the question of the origin of art, the question of what art originally was and has remained ever since, it thereby discloses an element of truth. Art did not become a unified whole until a very late stage. There is reason to doubt whether such integration is not more that of the concept than that of what it claims to comprehend. The forced quality of the term *Sprachkunstwerk*—the linguistic artwork—now popular among Germanists, awakens suspicion by its unceremonial subsumption of poetry to art through the mediation of language, even though art unquestionably became unified in the course of the process of enlightenment. The most archaic artistic manifestations are so diffuse that it is as difficult as it is vain to try to decide what once did and did not count as art. In later ages as well, art consistently resisted the process of unification in which it was simultaneously caught up. Its own concept is not indifferent to this. What seems to grow hazy in the half-light of prehistory is vague not only because of its distance but because it guards something of the indeterminate, of what is inadequate to the concept, which progressive integration tirelessly menaces. It is perhaps not irrelevant that the oldest cave paintings, whose naturalism is always so readily affirmed, demonstrated the greatest fidelity to the portrayal of movement, as if they already aspired to what Valéry ultimately demanded: the painstaking imitation of the indeterminate, of what has not been nailed down.[4] If so, the impulse of these paintings was not naturalistic imitation but, rather, from the beginning a protest against reification. Blame for ambiguity is not, or not only, to be ascribed to the limitedness of knowledge but is characteristic of prehistory itself. Univocity exists only since the emergence of subjectivity.

The so-called problem of origin echoes in the controversy over whether naturalistic depiction or symbolic-geometrical forms came first. Implicit in this question is the hope that it will provide what is needed to discern the primordial essence of art. This hope is deceptive. Arnold Hauser opens his *Social History of Art* with the thesis that during the Paleolithic age naturalism was older: "The monuments of primitive art . . . clearly suggest . . . that naturalism has the prior claim, so that it is becoming more and more difficult to maintain the theory of the primacy of an art remote from life and nature."[5] The polemical overtone against the neoromantic doctrine of the religious origin of art is unmistakable. Yet this important historian straight away restricts the thesis of the priority of naturalism. Hauser, while still employing the two habitually contrasting theses, criticizes them as anachronistic: "The dualism of the visible and the invisible, of the seen and the merely known, remains absolutely foreign to Paleolithic art."[6] He recognizes the element of undifferentiatedness from reality in the earliest art, as well as the undifferentiatedness from reality of the sphere of semblance.[7] Hauser maintains something akin to the priority of naturalism on the basis of a theory of magic that asserts the "reciprocal dependence of the similar."[8] For him, similarity is effectively replicability, and it exercises practical magic. Accordingly, Hauser divides magic sharply from religion, the former exclusively serving to procure means of sustenance. This sharp division is obviously hard to reconcile with the theorem of a primordial undifferentiatedness. On the other hand, it helps to establish replication as fundamental, even though other scholars, such as Erik Holm, contest the hypothesis of the utilitarian-magical function of the replica.[9] Hauser, by contrast, contends that "the Paleolithic hunter and painter thought he was in possession of the thing itself in the picture, thought he had won power over the portrayed by the portrayal."[10] With certain reservations, Resch also tends toward this position.[11] On the other hand, Katesa Schlosser finds that the most striking characteristic of Paleolithic portrayal is the deviation from the natural image; this deviation, however, is not attributed to any "archaic irrationalism" but rather, following Lorenz and Gehlen,[12] is interpreted as an expressive form of a biological *ratio*. Clearly, the thesis of magical utilitarianism and naturalism stands up in the face of the evidence no more than does Holm's thesis of the religious origin of art. His explicit use of the concept of symbolization already postulates for the earliest period a dualism that Hauser first attributes to the Neolithic period. This dualism, according to Holm, serves a unitary organization of art just as within this dualism there appears the structure of an articulated and therefore necessarily hierarchical and institutionalized society—one in which production already plays a role. He argues that cult and a unitary canon of forms were established during the same period, and that art was thus divided into a sacred and a profane sphere, that is, into idol sculpture and decorative ceramics. This construction of the animistic phase is paralleled by the construction of preanimism or, as science today prefers to call it, the "nonempirical world view," which is marked by the "essential unity of all life." But the objective impenetrability of the oldest phenomena rebuffs this construction: A concept like the "essential unity of all life" already presupposes a division between form and material in the earliest phase or, at the least, oscillates between the idea of such a division and the idea of unity. The stumbling block here is the concept of unity. Its current use obscures everything, including the relation between the one and the many. In truth, unity should be conceived as it was reflected upon for the first time in Plato's *Parmenides*: as the unity of the many. The undifferentiated character of prehistory is not a unity of this sort but falls rather on the other side of the dichotomy in which unity has meaning only as a polarity. As a result, such investigations as Fritz Krause's "Masks and Ancestral Figures" also encounters difficulties. According to Krause, in the oldest nonanimistic representations "form is bound up with the material rather than being separable from it. Any change of the essence is possible only through a change of material *and* form, that is, through the complete transformation of the body. This explains the metamorphosis of essences into one another."[13] Krause rightly argues against the conventional concept of the symbol that the transformation that takes place in mask ceremonies is not symbolic but rather "formative magic," a term borrowed from the developmental psychologist Heinz Werner.[14] For the Indians, he claims, the mask is not simply the demon whose force is transferred to its bearer: Rather, the bearer himself becomes the incarnation of the demon and is extinguished as a self.[15] There are grounds for doubting this: Every member of a tribe, the masked included, clearly recognizes the difference between his own face and the mask, a difference that according to the neoromantic construction should be imperceptible. Face and mask are no more one and the same than the bearer of the mask can be taken for the incarnation of the demon. Contrary to Krause's claim, the element of dissimulation inheres in the phenomenon: Neither the often totally stylized form nor the fact that the bearer of the mask is only partially covered affects the interpretation of the "essential transformation of the bearer by the mask."[16] Something on the order of belief in real transformation is of course equally part of the phenomenon in just the same way that children playing do not distinguish sharply between themselves and the role played yet can at any moment be called back to reality. Even expression is hardly primordial; it too developed historically, perhaps from animism. When a clan member imitatively makes himself into a totemic animal or a fearful divinity, something other than the self-contained individual is expressed. Although expression is seemingly an aspect of subjectivity, in it—externalization—there dwells just as much that is not the self, that probably is the collective. In that the subject, awakening to expression, seeks collective sanction, expression is already evidence of a fissure. It is only with the stabilization of the subject in self-consciousness that expression becomes autonomous as the expression of the subject, while maintaining the gesture of making itself into something. Replication could be interpreted as the reification of this comportment, and it is thus the enemy of precisely that impulse that is rudimentarily objectivated as expression. At the same time such reification by means of replication is also emancipatory: It helps to free expression by placing it at the disposal of the subject. Once people were perhaps as expressionless as animals, who neither laugh nor cry, though their shapes are objectively expressive, something the animals probably do not sense. This is recalled first by gorillalike masks, later by artworks. Expression, art's quasi-natural element, is as such already something other than pure nature.—The extremely heterogeneous interpretations are made possible by an objective ambiguity. Even the claim that heterogeneous elements are intermeshed in prehistoric artistic phenomena is anachronistic. It is more likely that division and unity arose under the pressure to be freed from the spell of the diffuse, accompanied by the emergence of a more secure social organization. In his conspectus Herskovits coherently argues that developmental theories that deduce art from a primarily symbolical or realistic "principle of validity" are untenable given the contradictory diversity of prehistoric and primitive art. The sharp contrast drawn between primitive conventionalism—in the sense of stylization—and Paleolithic realism isolates a single aspect. It is not possible to discern the general preponderance of one principle over another in earliest times any more than this could be done today among surviving primitive peoples. Paleolithic sculpture is said to be for the most part highly stylized, contrary to the contemporary "realistic" portrayals of the cave paintings; this realism, however, as Herskovits points out, is marked by heterogeneous elements, foreshortenings, for example, that cannot be interpreted as being either perspectival or symbolic. The art of primitive people today is just as complex; realistic elements have in no way suppressed fully stylized forms, least of all in sculpture. Immersion in art's origins tantalizes aesthetic theory with various apparently typical procedures, but just as quickly they escape the firm grip that modern interpretational consciousness imagines it possesses.

Art anterior to the Paleolithic period is not known. But it is doubtless that art did not begin with works, whether they were primarily magical or already aesthetic. The cave drawings are stages of a process and in no way an early one. The first images must have been preceded by a mimetic comportment—the assimilation of the self to its other—that does not fully coincide with the superstition of direct magical influence; if in fact no differentiation between magic and mimesis had been prepared over a long period of time, the striking traces of autonomous elaboration in the cave paintings would be inexplicable. But once aesthetic comportment, prior to all objectivation, set itself off from magical practices, however rudimentarily, this distinction has since been carried along as a residue; it is as if the now functionless mimesis, which reaches back into the biological dimension, was vestigially maintained, foreshadowing the maxim that the superstructure is transformed more slowly than the infrastructure. In the traces of what has been overtaken by the general course of things, all art bears the suspicious burden of what did not make the grade, the regressive. But aesthetic comportment is not altogether rudimentary. An irrevocable necessity of art and preserved by it, aesthetic comportment contains what has been belligerently excised from civilization and repressed, as well as the human suffering under the loss, a suffering already expressed in the earliest forms of mimesis. This element should not be dismissed as irrational. Art is in its most ancient relics too deeply permeated with rationality. The obstinacy of aesthetic comportment, which was later ideologically glorified as the eternal natural power of the play drive, testifies rather that to this day no rationality has been fully rational, none has unrestrictedly benefited humanity, its potential, or even a "humanized nature." What marks aesthetic comportment as irrational according to the criteria of dominant rationality is that art denounces the particular essence of a *ratio* that pursues means rather than ends. Art reminds us of the latter and of an objectivity freed from the categorial structure. This is the source of art's rationality, its character as knowledge. Aesthetic comportment is the capacity to perceive more in things than they are; it is the gaze under which the given is transformed into an image. Whereas this comportment can be effortlessly impugned as inadequate by the status quo, the latter can indeed only be experienced through this comportment. A final intimation of the rationality in mimesis is imparted by Plato's doctrine of enthusiasm as the precondition of philosophy and emphatic knowledge, which he not only demanded on a theoretical level but demonstrated at the decisive point in the *Phaedrus*. This Platonic doctrine has degenerated into a cultural commodity, yet without forfeiting its truth content. Aesthetic comport ment is the unimpaired corrective of reified consciousness that has in the meantime burgeoned as totality. That which in aesthetic comportment propels itself toward the light and seeks to escape the spell manifests itself *e contrario* in those who do without it, the aesthetically insensible. To study them would be of inestimable value for the analysis of aesthetic comport-ment. Even in terms of the standards of the dominant rationality they are in no way the most progressive or developed; nor are they simply those who lack a particular expendable quality. On the contrary, their entire constitution is deformed to a pathological degree: They concretize. Those whose thought is no more than projection are fools, which artists must not be on any account; those, however, who do not project at all fail to grasp reality and instead repeat and falsify it by crushing out what glimmered however distantly to preanimistic consciousness: the communication of all dispersed particulars with each other. This consciousness is no more true than one that confused fantasy and reality. Comprehension occurs only when the concept transcends what it wants to grasp. Art puts this to the test; thinking that proscribes such comprehension becomes outright stu-pidity and misses the object because it subjugates it. Art legitimates itself within the confines of the spell in that rationality becomes powerless when aesthetic comportment is repressed or, under the pressure of socialization, no longer even constituted. As was already pointed out in the *Dialectic of Enlightenment*, strict positivism crosses over into the feeble-mindedness of the artistically insensible, the successfully castrated. The narrowminded wisdom that sorts out feeling from knowing and rubs its hands together when it finds the two balanced is—as trivialities sometimes are—the caricature of a situation that over the centuries of the division of labor has inscribed this division in subjectivity. Yet feeling and understanding are not absolutely different in the human disposition and remain dependent even in their dividedness. The forms of reaction that are subsumed under the concept of feeling become futile enclaves of sentimentality as soon as they seal themselves off from their relation to thought and turn a blind eye toward truth; thought, however, approaches tautology when it shrinks from the sublimation of the mimetic comportment. The fatal separation of the two came about historically and is revocable. *Ratio* without mimesis is self-negating. Ends, the raison d'être of *raison*, are qualitative, and mimetic power is effectively the power of qualitative distinction. The self-negation of reason clearly has its historical necessity: The world, which is objectively losing its openness, no longer has need of a spirit that is defined by its openness; indeed, it can scarcely put up with the traces of that spirit. With regard to its subjective side, the contemporary loss of experience may largely coincide with the bitter repression of mimesis that takes the place of its metamorphosis. What in various sectors of German ideology is still called an artistic sensibility is just this repression of mimesis raised to a principle, as which it is transformed into artistic insensibility. Aesthetic comportment, however, is neither immediately mimesis nor its repression but rather the process that mimesis sets in motion and in which, modified, mimesis is preserved. This process transpires equally in the relation of the individual to art as in the historical macrocosm; it congeals in the immanent movement of each and every artwork, in its tensions and in their possible resolution. Ultimately, aesthetic comportment is to be defined as the capacity to shudder, as if goose bumps were the first aesthetic image. What later came to be called subjectivity, freeing itself from the blind anxiety of the shudder, is at the same time the shudder's own development; life in the subject is nothing but what shudders, the reaction to the total spell that transcends the spell. Consciousness without shudder is reified consciousness. That shudder in which subjectivity stirs without yet being subjectivity is the act of being touched by the other.

Aesthetic comportment assimilates itself to that other rather than sub-ordinating it. Such a constitutive relation of the subject to objectivity in aesthetic comportment joins eros and knowledge.

Notes

1 The author is grateful to Miss Renate Wieland, a graduate student in the Department of Philosophy at the University of Frankfurt, for her critical synopsis of the themes of this excursus.

2 Benedetto Croce, *Aesthetic*, trans. Douglas Ainslie (New York, 1956), p. 132.

3 See Melville J. Herskovits, *Man and His Work* (New York, 1948).

4 See Paul Valéry, *Œuvres*, vol. 2 (Paris, 1957), p. 681.

5 Arnold Hauser, *The Social History of Art*, vol. 1 (London, 1962), p. 1.

6 Ibid., p. 3.

7 Ibid., p. 5.

8 Ibid., p. 7. [Translation amended—trans.]

9 Erik Holm, "Felskunst im südlichen Afrika," in *Kunst der Welt: Die Steinzeit* (Baden-Baden, 1960), p. 196.

10 Hauser, *The Social History of Art*, vol. 1, p. 4.

11 See Walther F. E. Resch, "Gedanken zur stilistischen Gliederung der Tierdarstellungen in der nordafrikanischen Felsbildkunst," in *Paideuma, Mitteilungen zur Kulturkunde*, vol. 11 (1965), pp. 108ff.

12 See Konrad Lorenz, "Die angeborenen Formen möglicher Erfahrung," in *Zeitschrift für Tierpsychologie*, vol. 5, p. 258; Arnold Gehlen, "Über einige Kategorien des entlasteten, zumal des ästhetischen Verhaltens," in *Studien zur Anthropologie und Soziologie* (Neuwied and Berlin, 1963), pp. 69ff.

13 See Fritz Krause, "Maske und Ahnenfigur: Das Motiv der Hülle und das Prinzip der Form," in *Kulturanthropologie*, ed. W. E. Mühlmann and E. W. Müller (Cologne and Berlin, 1966), p. 231.

14 Heinz Werner, *Einführung in die Entwicklungspsychologie* (Leipzig, 1926), p. 269.

15 Krause, "Maske und Ahnenfigur," pp. 223ff.
16 Ibid., p. 224.

15
Draft Introduction

The concept of philosophical aesthetics has an antiquated quality, as does the concept of a system or that of morals. This feeling is in no way restricted to artistic praxis and the public indifference to aesthetic theory. Even in academic circles, essays relevant to aesthetics have for decades now noticeably diminished. This point is made in a recent dictionary of philosophy: "There is scarcely another philosophical discipline that rests on such flimsy presuppositions as does aesthetics. Like a weather vane it is 'blown about by every philosophical, cultural, and scientific gust; at one moment it is metaphysical and in the next empirical; now normative, then descriptive; now defined by artists, then by connoisseurs; one day art is supposedly the center of aesthetics and natural beauty merely preliminary, the next day art beauty is merely second-hand natural beauty.' Moritz Geiger's description of the dilemma of aesthetics has been true since the middle of the nineteenth century. There is a double reason for this pluralism of aesthetic theories, which are often even left unfinished: It resides on the one hand in the fundamental difficulty, indeed impossibility, of gaining general access to art by means of a system of philosophical categories, and on the other, in the fact that aesthetic statements have traditionally presupposed theories of knowledge. The problematic of theories of knowledge returns directly in aesthetics, because how aesthetics interprets its objects depends on the concept of the object held by the theory of knowledge. This traditional dependency, however, is defined by the subject matter itself and is already contained in the terminology."[1] Although this well describes the situation, it does not sufficiently explain it; the other philosophical disciplines, including the theory of knowledge

and logic, are no less controversial and yet interest in them has not flagged
to a similar extent. The unusual situation of aesthetics is discouraging.
Croce introduced radical nominalism into aesthetic theory. Almost simultaneously, important thinking left behind the so-called fundamental
problems of aesthetics and became immersed in specific formal and
material problems, as is the case with Lukács's *Theory of the Novel*,
Benjamin's critique of *Elective Affinities*, which developed into an emphatic
treatise, and his *Origin of German Tragic Drama*.² If the last-named work
cunningly defends Croce's nominalism, it at the same time takes into
account a situation where consciousness no longer hopes that fundamental principles will lead to insight into the traditionally great questions
of aesthetics, especially those of a metaphysical dimension, but instead
seeks insight in spheres that formerly held the status of exempla. Philosophical aesthetics found itself confronted with the fatal alternative
between dumb and trivial universality on the one hand and, on the other,
arbitrary judgments usually derived from conventional opinions. Hegel's
program, that thought should not proceed from above but rather relinquish itself to the phenomena, was first brought within reach in aesthetics
by a nominalism in opposition to which Hegel's own aesthetics, given its
classicist components, preserved far more abstract invariants than was
coherent with dialectical method. This at the same time threw into
question the possibility of aesthetic theory as a traditional theory. For the
idea of the concrete, on which each and every artwork, indeed any
experience of beauty, is fixed, prohibits—similarly as in the study of
art—distancing itself from determinate phenomena in the way that
philosophical consensus had so long and falsely supposed possible in the
spheres of the theory of knowledge or ethics. A general theory of the
aesthetically concrete would necessarily let slip what interested it in the
object in the first place. The reason for the obsolescence of aesthetics is that
it scarcely ever confronted itself with its object. By its very form, aesthetics
seems sworn to a universality that culminates in inadequacy to the
artworks and, complementarily, in transitory eternal values. The academic
mistrust of aesthetics is founded in the academicism immanent to it. The
motive for the lack of interest in aesthetic questions is primarily the
institutionalized scientific, scholarly anxiety vis-à-vis what is uncertain
and contested, not fear of provincialism and of how backward the
formulation of issues is with respect to the nature of those issues. The
synoptical, contemplative perspective that science expects of aesthetics has

meanwhile become incompatible with progressive art, which—as in Kafka—has lost patience with any contemplative attitude.[3] Aesthetics today therefore begins by diverging from what it treats, having become suspicious of the passive, possibly even culinary, pleasures of spectators. As its standard, contemplative aesthetics presupposes that taste by which the observer disposes over the works from a distance. Taste, on account of its subjectivistic prejudice, itself stands in need of theoretical reflection not only as to why it fails in the face of the most recent modernism but why it may long have been inadequate to advanced art. This critique was anticipated by Hegel's demand that the work itself take the place of the judgment of taste;[4] yet in his own aesthetics the object did not extricate itself from the perspective—still matted together with taste—of the detached spectator. It was the system that enabled his thought to be fruitful even where it remained at all too great a distance from its objects. Hegel and Kant were the last who, to put it bluntly, were able to write major aesthetics without understanding anything about art. That was possible so long as art itself was oriented to encompassing norms that were not questioned in individual works and were liquified only in the work's immanent problematic. True, there has probably scarcely ever been a work that was important in any regard that did not, by virtue of its own form, mediate these norms and thus virtually transform them. Yet these norms were not simply liquidated; something of them towered over and above the individual works. The great philosophical aesthetics stood in concordance with art to the extent that they conceptualized what was evidently universal in it; this was in accordance with a stage in which philosophy and other forms of spirit, such as art, had not yet been torn apart. Because the same spirit ruled in philosophy and art, philosophy was able to treat art in a substantial fashion without surrendering itself to the works. Certainly artworks regularly succumbed to the effort—motivated by the nonidentity of art with its universal determinations—to conceive them in their specificity: This resulted in speculative idealism's most painfully mistaken judgments. Kant, who was not pledged to prove that a posteriori was the apriori, was precisely for this reason less fallible. Imprisoned by eighteenth-century art,[5] which he would not have hesitated to call precritical—that is, preceding the full emancipation of the subject—he did not compromise himself to the same extent as Hegel by art-alien assertions. He even accorded more space to later radical modern possibilities than did Hegel,[6] who confronted art so much more courageously. After them came the sensitive connoisseurs, who occupied the mediocre middle ground between the thing-itself as postulated by Hegel and the concept. They combined a culinary relation to art with an incapacity for philosophical construction. Georg Simmel was typical of such sensitivity, despite his decisive predilection for the aesthetically individual. The right medium for understanding art is either the unwavering asceticism of conceptualization, doggedly refusing to allow itself to be irritated by facts, or the unconscious consciousness in the midst of the work itself; art is never understood by the appreciative, snugly empathetic spectator; the capriciousness of such an attitude is from the beginning indifferent to what is essential to works, their binding force. Aesthetics was productive only so long as it undiminishedly respected the distance from the empirical and with windowless thoughts penetrated into the content of its other; or when, with a closeness bordering on embodiment, it judged the work from within, as sometimes occurs in the scattered remarks of individual artists, which are important not as the expression of a personality that is hardly authoritative with regard to the work, but because often, without recurring to the subject, they document something of the experiential force of the work. These reports are often constrained by the naïveté that society insists on finding in art. Artists either stubbornly resist aesthetics with artisanal rancor, or the antidilettantes devise dilettantic theories that make do. If their comments are to convey anything to aesthetics, they require interpretation. Artisanal instruction that wants polemically to usurp the position of aesthetics ultimately develops into positivism, even when it includes sympathy with metaphysics. Advice on how best to compose a rondo is useless as soon as there are reasons—of which artisanal instruction is ignorant—why rondos can no longer be written. Its general rules are in need of philosophical development if they are to be more than a decoction of conventions. When they balk at this transition, they almost inevitably seek succor in a murky Weltanschauung. After the demise of idealistic systems, the difficulty of an aesthetics that would be more than a desperately reanimated branch of philosophy is that of bringing the artist's closeness to the phenomena into conjunction with a conceptual capacity free of any subordinating concept, free of all decreed judgments; committed to the medium of concepts, such an aesthetics would go beyond a mere phenomenology of artworks. On the other hand, the effort, under the pressure of the nominalistic situation, to make a transition to what has been called an empirical aesthetics, is in vain. If, for example, in compliance with the prescript of such scientization, one wanted to reach general aesthetic norms by abstracting from empirical descriptions and classifying them, the results would be incomparably meager when compared with the substantive and incisive categories of the speculative systems. Applied to current artistic practice, such distillates would be no more appropriate than artistic ideals ever were. All aesthetic questions terminate in those of the truth content of artworks: Is the spirit that a work objectively bears in its specific form true? For empiricism this is, as superstition, anathema. For it, artworks are bundles of indeterminate stimuli. What they are in themselves is beyond judgment; any claim to know is a projection. Only subjective reactions to artworks can be observed, measured, and generalized. As a result, the actual object of aesthetics escapes study. It is replaced by what is at bottom a preaesthetic sphere that has proved to be socially that of the culture industry. Hegel's achievement is not criticized in the name of a purportedly greater scientific acumen but is instead forgotten in favor of vulgar adaptation. That empiricism recoils from art—of which in general it has hardly ever taken notice (with the exception of the unique and truly free John Dewey) other than insofar as it attributes all knowledge that does not agree with its rules of the game to be poetry—can be explained by the fact that art constitutively dismisses these rules of the game, because art is an entity that is not identical with its empiria. What is essential to art is that which in it is not the case,[7] that which is incommensurable with the empirical measure of all things. The compulsion to aesthetics is the need to think this empirical incommensurability.

The objective difficulties in this are compounded subjectively by broad resistance. For most people, aesthetics is superfluous. It disturbs the weekend pleasures to which art has been consigned as the complement to bourgeois routine. In spite of far-reaching alienness to art, this subjective resistance helps give expression to something closely allied to art. For art allies itself with repressed and dominated nature in the progressively rationalized and integrated society. Yet industry makes even this resistance an institution and changes it into coin. It cultivates art as a natural reserve for irrationalism, from which thought is to be excluded. It thereby allies itself with the platitude—a bowdlerized theorem of aesthetics—that art must be a direct object of pleasure, whereas instead art at every point participates in concepts. This fundamentally confuses the ever problematic primacy of intuition in art with the enjoinder that art not be thought about because successful artists themselves supposedly never did so. The result of this mentality is a bloated concept of naïveté. In the domain of pure feeling—the phrase appears in the title of the aesthetics of a preeminent neo-Kantian[8]—a taboo is placed on anything akin to logicality, in spite of the elements of stringency in the artwork, whose relation to extra-aesthetic logic and causality could be elucidated only by philosophical aesthetics.[9] Feeling thus becomes its own opposite: It is reified. Art is actually the world once over, as like it as it is unlike it. In the managed world of the culture industry, aesthetic naïveté has changed its function. What once was praised of artworks, when they were poised on the pedestal of their classicality, as their abiding quality—that of noble simplicity—has become an exploitable means for attracting customers. The consumers, whose naïveté is confirmed and drilled into them, are to be dissuaded from entertaining stupid ideas about what has been packed into the pills they are obliged to swallow down. The simplicity of times past is translated into the stupidity of the culture consumer who, gratefully and with a metaphysically clear conscience, buys up the industry's trash, which is in any case inescapable. As soon as naïveté is taken up as a point of view, it no longer exists. A genuine relation between art and consciousness's experience of it would consist in education, which schools opposition to art as a consumer product as much as it allows the recipient a substantial idea of what an artwork is. Art today, even among those who produce it, is largely cut off from such education. The price art pays for this is the permanent temptation of the subartistic, even in the range of the most refined techniques. The naïveté of artists has degenerated into naïve pliancy vis-à-vis the culture industry. Naïveté was never the natural essence of the artist but rather the self-evidence with which he conducted himself in an imposed social situation, that is, it was an aspect of conformism. The unqualified acceptance of social forms was the real criterion of artistic naïveté. The justification of naïveté is bound up with the extent to which the subject assents to or resists these forms, the extent to which these forms can still lay claim to self-evidence. Ever since the surface of life, the immediacy it makes available to people, has become ideology, naïveté has reversed into its own opposite; it has become the reflex of reified consciousness to a reified world. Artistic production that refuses to relinquish the impulse against the ossification of life and is thus truly naïve, becomes what according to the game rules of conventional society is the opposite of naïveté; admittedly, it has stored up in it as much naïveté as the comportment of art has of noncompliance with the reality principle, something of the childish and—according to social norms—the infantile. It is the opposite of established naïveté, and it is condemned. Hegel, and even more perspicaciously, Karl Gustav Jochmann,[10] knew this.

AESTHETIC THEORY

Yet they were compelled to understand it in the context of their classicism and so attributed the end of art to it. Art's naïve and reflexive elements have, in truth, always been much more internal to each other than the longing that arose during the rise of industrial capitalism wanted to recognize. The history of art since Hegel has shown up what was mistaken in his premature eschatology of art. Its mistake was that it perpetuated the conventional ideal of naïveté. Even Mozart, who played the role of the divinely gifted, capering prodigy in the bourgeois household, was—as every page of his correspondence with his father documents—incomparably more reflexive than the popular profile of him lets on; reflexive, however, not in the sense of a freely hovering abstract intelligence but in the compositional material itself. Just how much the work of another household divinity of pure intuition—Raphael—has reflection as its objective condition is evident in the geometrical organization of his paintings. Art without reflection is the retrospective fantasy of a reflexive age. Theoretical considerations and scientific findings have at all times been amalgamated with art, often as its bellwether, and the most important artists were not those who hesitated. Well-known instances of this are Piero della Francesca's discovery of aerial perspective and the aesthetic speculations of the Florentine Camerata, in which opera originated. The latter is paradigmatic of a form that, once it had become the darling of the public, was cloaked after the fact with the aura of naïveté, whereas it originated in theory, literally in an invention.[11] Similarly, it was only the introduction of equal temperament in the seventeenth century that permitted modulation through the circle of fifths and, with it, Bach, who gratefully acknowledged this in the title of his great keyboard composition. Even in the nineteenth century, impressionist technique in painting was based on the rightly or wrongly interpreted scientific analysis of retinal processes. Of course the theoretical and reflexive elements in art seldom went untransformed. At times, art misunderstood the sciences to which it appealed, as is perhaps the case most recently with electronic music. Yet the productive impulse was little harmed by the rationality that was brought to bear on it. The physiological theorems of the impressionists were probably foils for the in part fascinated, in part socially critical experiences of the metropolis and the dynamic of their paintings. By means of the discovery of a dynamic immanent to the reified world, they wanted to resist reification, which was most palpable in metropolitan life. In the nineteenth century, natural scientific explanations functioned as the self-unconscious agent of art. The basis of this affinity between art and science was that the *ratio* to which the most progressive art of the epoch reacted was none other than the *ratio* of the natural sciences. Whereas in the history of art, scientific theories tend to wither away, without them artistic practices would no more have developed than, inversely, these theorems can adequately explain such practices. This has consequences for reception: It is inadequate if it is less reflexive than the object it receives. Not knowing what one sees or hears bestows no privileged direct relation to works but instead makes their perception impossible. Consciousness is not a layer in a hierarchy built over perception; rather, all elements of aesthetic experience are reciprocal. No artwork consists in the super-imposition of layers; that is exclusively the result of the calculation of the culture industry, that is, a result of reified consciousness. It can, for instance, be noted in extended, complex music that there is a constantly varying threshold between what is primarily perceived and what is determined by the reflexive perception of consciousness. The under-standing of the meaning of a fleeting musical passage often depends on the intellective comprehension of its function in a whole that is not present; the purportedly immediate experience itself depends on what goes beyond pure immediacy. The ideal perception of artworks would be that in which what is mediated becomes immediate; naïveté is the goal, not the origin.

Yet the flagging interest in aesthetics is not only predicated on aesthetics as a discipline but equally, and indeed more so, on its object. Insofar as aesthetics concerns itself primarily with the how rather than with the fact of art, it seems silently to imply the possibility of art. This position has become uncertain. Aesthetics can no longer take the fact of art for granted in the way that Kant's theory of knowledge presupposed the mathematical natural sciences. Although traditional theory was in no way encumbered by such concerns, aesthetic theory cannot escape the reality that art that holds fast to its concept and refuses consumption becomes antiart, and that art's distress with itself following the real catastrophes and faced with the coming ones stands in moral disproportion to its continued existence. At its Hegelian zenith, philosophical aesthetics prognosticated the end of art. Although aesthetics later forgot this, art senses it all the more deeply. Even if art remained what it once was and can no longer remain, it would become something wholly different in the society that is emerging and by virtue of its changed function in that society. Artistic consciousness rightly mistrusts reflection that by its very topic and by the style expected of it disports itself as if a firm foundation existed, whereas it is retrospectively dubious that any such solid foundation ever existed; it was and was not already that ideology into which the contemporary cultural bustle, along with its art department, is clearly being transformed. The question of the possibility of art is so relevant that it has taken a form that mocks its putatively more radical formulation of whether and how art is even possible at all. The question has instead become that of the concrete possibility of art today. The uneasiness with art is not only that of a stagnating social consciousness vis-à-vis the modern. At every point this uneasiness extends to what is essential to art, to its most advanced works. Art, for its part, seeks refuge in its own negation, hoping to survive through its death. Thus contemporary theater turns against the status of being a plaything, a peepshow with glitter; against imitating the world even with sets strung with barbed wire. The pure mimetic impulse—the happiness of producing the world once over—which animates art and has stood in age-old tension with its antimythological, enlightening component, has become unbearable under the system of total functional rationality. Art and happiness both arouse the suspicion of infantilism, although the anxiety that such infantilism inspires is itself regression, the misconstrual of the raison d'être of all rationality; for the movement of the principle of self-preservation, to the extent that it is not fetishized, leads by its own force to the desideratum of happiness; nothing stronger speaks for art. In the contemporary novel the impulses against the fiction of the constant presence of the narrator participate in art's self-disgust. This has in large measure defined the history of narration since Proust, though the genre has been unable to shake off completely the rubric "fiction," which stands at the head of the best-seller lists, however much aesthetic semblance has become social anathema. Music struggles to free itself of the element by which Benjamin, somewhat overgenerously, defined all art prior to the age of its technical reproducibility: aura, the sorcery that emanates from music, even if it were antimusic, whenever it commences to sound. Yet art does not labor on traits of this sort as it does on correctable residues of its past, for these traits seem inextricably grown together with art's own concept. The more, however, art itself—in order not to barter away semblance for lies—is driven to reflect on its own presuppositions and when possible to absorb into its own form such reflection as if it were a counterpoison, the more skeptical it becomes toward the presumption of having self-consciousness imposed on it externally. Aesthetics is compelled to drag its concepts helplessly behind a situation of art in which art, indifferent to what becomes of it, seeks to undermine those concepts without which it can hardly be conceived. No theory, aesthetic theory included, can dispense with the element of universality. This tempts aesthetics to take the side of invariants of precisely the sort that emphatic modern art must attack. The mania of cultural studies for reducing the new to the ever-same, as for example the claim that surrealism is a form of mannerism, the lack of any sense for the historical situation of artistic phenomena as the index of their truth, corresponds to the tendency of philosophical aesthetics toward those abstract rules in which nothing is invariant other than that they are ever and again given the lie by spirit as it takes shape. What sets itself up as an eternal aesthetic norm is something that developed and is transient; the claim to imperishability has become obsolete. Even a university-certified schoolmaster would hesitate to apply to prose such as Kafka's *Metamorphosis* or *The Penal Colony*, in which the secure aesthetic distance to the object is shockingly undermined, a sanctioned criterion such as that of disinterested satisfaction; anyone who has experienced the greatness of Kafka's writing must sense how awkwardly inapplicable to it any talk of art is. The situation is no different in the case of a priori genres such as the tragic or comic in contemporary drama, however much contemporary works may be marbled by them in the way that the enormous apartment building in Kafka's parable is marbled with medieval ruins. Although Beckett's plays can no longer be taken for tragic or comic, they are not therefore, as would suit academic aesthetics, hybrids on the order of tragicomedy. On the contrary, Beckett's plays pass historical judgment over these categories as such, faithful to the historical innervation that there is no more laughing over the classics of comic theater except in a state of renewed barbarism. In accord with the tendency of modern art to make its own categories thematic through self-reflection, plays like *Godot* and *Endgame*—in the scene in which the protagonists decide to laugh—are more the tragic presentation of comedy's fate than they are comic; in the actors' forced laughter, the spectator's mirth vanishes. Early in the century already, Wedekind named a *pièce à clef*, whose target was the publisher of *Simplicissimus*,[12] a "satire on satire." Academic philosophers adopt a false superiority when they survey the history of art to procure for themselves the satisfaction of *nil admirari* and, living in the domestic company of eternal values, derive from the ever-sameness of things the profit of separating out what is truly different and endangers the status quo, in order to dismiss it as a rehashing of the classics. This attitude is in league with a sociopsychologically and institutionally reactionary attitude. It is only in the process of critical self-consciousness that aesthetics is able once again to reach art, if it was ever capable of this in the first place.

Although art, frightened by the traces left by aesthetics, mistrusts it as something that had fallen far behind its own development, it must at the same time secretly fear that an aesthetics that was no longer anachronistic would sever the threads of life, which are already stretched to the limit. Such an aesthetics, it is feared, would lay claim to deciding if and how art should survive after the fall of metaphysics, to which art owes its existence and content. The metaphysics of art has become the court of judgment that rules over art's continued existence. The absence of theological meaning, however modified, culminates in art as the crisis of its own meaning. The more ruthlessly artworks draw the consequences from the contemporary condition of consciousness, the more closely they themselves approximate meaninglessness. They thereby achieve a historically requisite truth, which, if art disowned it, would condemn art to doling out powerless consolation and to complicity with the status quo. At the same time, however, meaningless art has begun to forfeit its right to exist; in any case, there is no longer any art that has remained inviolable. To the question as to why it exists, art has no other response than what Goethe called the dregs of absurdity, which all art contains. This residue rises to the surface and denounces art. Just as it is rooted at least in part in fetishes, art, through its relentless progress, relapses back into fetishism and becomes a blind end in itself, revealing itself as untruth, a sort of collective delusion, as soon as its objective truth content, its meaning, begins to waver. If psychoanalysis followed its own principle to its culmination, it would—like all positivism—necessarily demand the end of art, just as it tends to analyze it away in the treatment of patients. If art is sanctioned exclusively as sublimation, as a means for the maintenance of psychic economy, its truth content is contravened and art lingers on only as a pious deception. The truth of all artworks would, on the other hand, not exist without the fetishism that now verges on becoming art's untruth. The quality of artworks depends essentially on the degree of their fetishism, on the veneration that the process of production pays to what lays claim to being self-produced, to the seriousness that forgets the pleasure taken in it. Only through fetishism, the blinding of the artwork vis-à-vis the reality of which it is part, does the work transcend the spell of the reality principle as something spiritual.

From these perspectives, aesthetics proves to be not so much obsolete as necessary. Art does not stand in need of an aesthetics that will prescribe norms where it finds itself in difficulty, but rather of an aesthetics that will provide the capacity for reflection, which art on its own is hardly able to achieve. Words such as material, form, and formation, which flow all too easily from the pens of contemporary artists, ring trite; to cure contemporary language of this is one of the art-practical functions of aesthetics. Above all, however, aesthetics is demanded by the development of artworks. If they are not timelessly self-same, but rather become what they are because their own meaning is a process of becoming, they summon forth forms of spirit—commentary and critique, for example—through which this process is fulfilled. These forms remain weak, however, so long as they do not reach the truth content of the works. They only become capable of this by being honed to aesthetics. The truth content of an artwork requires philosophy. It is only in this truth content that philosophy converges with art or extinguishes itself in it. The way toward this is defined by the reflected immanence of works, not by the external application of philosophemes. The truth content of works must be rigorously distinguished from all philosophy that is pumped into them by authors or theorists; the difference between the two, it must be suspected, has for close to two hundred years been unbridgeable.[13] On the other hand, aesthetics brusquely repudiates the claim of philology however useful it may be in other contexts—that it assures the truth content of artworks. In the age of the irreconcilability of traditional aesthetics and contemporary art, the philosophical theory of art has no choice but, varying a maxim of Nietzsche's, by determinate negation to think the categories that are in decline as categories of transition. The elucidated and concrete dissolution of conventional aesthetic categories is the only remaining form that aesthetics can take; it at the same time sets free the transformed truth of these categories. If artists are compelled to permanent reflection, that reflection needs to be wrested free of its accidentalness so that it does not degenerate into arbitrary, amateurish auxiliary hypotheses, homemade rationalizations, or into arbitrary declarations of intentions framed by a Weltanschauung, without any justification from what is actually achieved. No one should any longer entrust himself naïvely to the technological *parti pris* of contemporary art; otherwise this art would consign itself totally to the substitution of the goal—that is, the work—by the means, the procedures by which it was produced. The propensity toward this harmonizes all too fundamentally with the general direction of society toward the apotheosis of means, production for the sake of production, total employment and all that is part of it, because the goals themselves—the rational organization of humanity—are blocked. Whereas in philosophy, aesthetics fell out of fashion, the most advanced artists have sensed the need for it all the more strongly. It is clear that even Boulez is far from envisioning a normative aesthetics of the traditional sort but sees, rather, the necessity of a historicophilosophical theory of art. What he means by "orientation esthétique" could best be translated as the critical self awareness of the artist.[14] If, as Hegel thought, the hour of naïve art is past, art must embody reflection and take it to the point where it no longer remains external and foreign to it; this would be the role of aesthetics today. Boulez's central point is that he had been puzzled by the current opinion of avant-garde artists, who believe that annotated instructions for the employment of technical procedures already amount to an artwork; on the contrary, the only criterion—according to Boulez—is what the artist does, not how and with whatever advanced means he intended to make it. Boulez, too, realizes, with regard to the contemporary artistic process, that insight into the historical situation—through which the antithetical relation to tradition is mediated—converges with binding implications for production. The dogmatic separation of craft and aesthetics, which Schoenberg decreed out of a then justified critique of a praxis-alien aesthetics, a separation that was self-evident to the artists of his generation as well as to those of the Bauhaus, is disavowed by Boulez in the name of craft and *métier*. Even Schoenberg's *Theory of Harmony* was only able to maintain this separation because he limited himself in this book to means that had long not been his own; had he discussed those he would have been irresistibly compelled to undertake aesthetic reflection, given that he lacked didactically communicable rules for the new craft. Such reflection responds to the fatal aging of the modern as a result of the tensionlessness of the totally technical artwork. This tensionlessness can hardly be dealt with in an exclusively inner-technical fashion, even though in technical criticism something of the supratechnical constantly registers. That significant contemporary art is a matter of indifference in a society that tolerates it, marks art itself as something indifferent that in spite of all its effort might equally well be something else or nothing at all. What currently passes for technical criteria in no way facilitates judgment on the level of artistic achievement and most often relegates it to the obsolete category of taste. As Boulez points out, many works, of which the question as to their value no longer makes sense, are beholden solely to their abstract opposition to the culture industry, not to their content or the capacity to realize it. The critical decision they elude could only be the responsibility of an aesthetics that proves itself equal to the most advanced developments to the same extent that it matches and supersedes the latter with its power of reflection. This aesthetics is obliged to renounce the concept of taste, in which the claim of art to truth is in danger of coming to a miserable end. The guilt lies with previous aesthetics that, by virtue of taking its starting point in the subjective judgment of taste, peremptorily deprived art of its claim to truth. Hegel, who took this claim seriously and emphasized art's opposition to pleasurable or useful play, was for this reason the enemy of taste, without however being able to break through its contingency in the concrete analyses of his *Aesthetics*. It is to Kant's credit that he recognized the aporia of aesthetic objectivity and the judgment of taste. He did indeed carry out an aesthetic analysis of the judgment of taste in terms of its elements, but he conceived them at the same time as latent, aconceptually objective elements. In so doing he pointed up the nominalistic threat to every emphatic theory—a threat that cannot be dismissed by any act of will—and at the same time perceived the elements in which theory goes beyond itself. By virtue of the intellective movement of his object, a movement that effectively closed its eyes to the object, Kant brought into thought the deepest impulses of an art that only developed in the one hundred fifty years after his death: an art that probed after its objectivity openly, without protection of any kind. What needs to be carried through is what in the theories of Kant and Hegel awaits redemption through second reflection. Terminating the tradition of philosophical aesthetics must amount to giving it its due.

The dilemma of aesthetics appears immanently in the fact that it can be constituted neither from above nor from below, neither from concepts nor from aconceptual experience. The only possibility for aesthetics beyond this miserable alternative is the philosophical insight that fact and concept are not polar opposites but mediated reciprocally in one another. This must be appropriated by aesthetics, for art again stands in need of aesthetics now that criticism has shown itself to be so disoriented by false and arbitrary judgments that it fails vis-à-vis art. Yet if aesthetics is to amount neither to art-alien prescriptions nor to the inconsequential classification of what it happens upon, then it is only conceivable as dialectical aesthetics; dialectical method is not unsuitably defined as the refusal to rest content with the diremption of the deductive and inductive that dominates rigid, indurative thought, and this is expressly rejected by the earliest formulations of dialectics in German idealism, those of Fichte.[15] Aesthetics must no more lag behind art than behind philosophy. Although it abounds in the most important insights, Hegel's aesthetics no more satisfied the concept of dialectics in his main works than did other material parts of the system. This is not easy to correct. Aesthetic dialectics is not to presuppose a metaphysics of spirit, which in Hegel as in Fichte was to guarantee that the individual, with which induction begins, and the universal, which provides the basis for deduction, are one. What was volatilized in emphatic philosophy cannot be revived by aesthetics, itself a philosophical discipline. Kant's theory is more apposite to the contemporary situation, for his aesthetics attempts to bind together consciousness of what is necessary with consciousness that what is necessary is itself blocked from consciousness. It follows its course, in effect, blindly. His aesthetics feels its way in the dark and yet is led by a compulsion toward what it seeks. This is the puzzle in which all aesthetic efforts today are bound up: Aesthetics, not entirely helpless, seeks to untangle the knot. For art is, or at any rate was until the most recent developments, under the impress of its semblance, what metaphysics, which is without semblance, always wanted to be. When Schelling declared art the organon of philosophy he involuntarily admitted what great idealistic speculation either passed over in silence or denied in the interest of its self-preservation. Correspondingly, Schelling did not, as is well known, carry through the thesis of identity as relentlessly as did Hegel. The aesthetic contours of Hegel's philosophy, that of a gigantic "as if," were then recognized by Kierkegaard and could be demonstrated in detail in his *Logic*.[16] Art is that—for the most part material—existent that is determined as spirit in precisely the fashion that idealism simply asserted extra-aesthetic reality to be. Experience is obscured by the naïve cliché that depicts the artist as an idealist or, depending on taste, as a fool in the service of the purportedly absolute reason of his work. Artworks are, in terms of their own constitution, objective as well as—and not only because they have their genesis in spiritual processes—spiritual; otherwise they would be in principle indistinguishable from eating and drinking. The contemporary debates originating in Soviet aesthetics, which insist that the claim to the primacy of the law of form as the primacy of the spiritual is an idealistic view of social reality, are groundless. Only as spirit is art the opposite of empirical reality, which becomes the determinate negation of the existing world order. Art is to be dialectically construed insofar as spirit inheres in it, without art's possessing it or giving surety of it as something absolute. However much they seem to be entities, artworks are crystallizations of the process between spirit and its other. This implies the difference from Hegel's aesthetics. There the objectivity of the artwork is the truth of spirit: It is spirit that has gone over into its own otherness and become identical with itself. For Hegel, spirit is one with totality, also with the totality in art. After the collapse of the general thesis of Idealism, however, spirit is strictly one aspect of artworks; granted, it is that aspect that makes the artifact art, yet it is not in any way present without what is opposed to it. Spirit no more devours its opposite than history has known pure artworks that have achieved the identity of spirit and nonspirit. Constitutively, the spirit of artworks is not pure. Those works that seem to embody such identity are not the most important. What in artworks opposes spirit is, however, on no account what is natural in their materials and objects; they constitute merely a limiting value in artworks. They bear what is opposed to them in themselves; their materials are historically and socially preformed as are their procedures, and their heterogeneous element is that in them that resists their unity and is needed by its unity for it to be more than a Pyrrhic victory over the unresisting. In this, aesthetic reflection is unanimous with the history of art, which irresistibly moved the dissonant into the center of the work until finally its difference from consonance was destroyed. Art thereby participates in the suffering that, by virtue of the unity of its process, finds its way to language rather than disappearing. It is because it recognizes this and allies art with the consciousness of need that Hegel's aesthetics, in spite of its harmonistic elements and its faith in the sensual appearance of the idea, is distinguished from merely formal aesthetics. He who was first to envision the end of art named the most compelling reason for its continuation: the continuation of needs, mute in themselves, that await the expression that artworks fulfill by proxy. However, if the element of spirit is immanent to artworks, this implies that this element is not identical with the spirit that produces them, not even with the collective spirit of the epoch. The determination of the spirit in artworks is the highest task of aesthetics; for this reason it is all the more pressing that aesthetics not let philosophy prescribe to it that category of spirit. *Common sense*, inclined to equate the spirit of artworks with what their makers infuse into them, must rapidly enough discover that artworks are so coconstructed by the opposition of the artistic material, by their own postulates, by historically contemporary models and procedures that are elemental to a spirit that may be called—in a condensed fashion that deviates from Hegel—objective, that their reduction to subjective spirit becomes absurd. This sets the question of the spirit of artworks at a distance from their genesis. The dynamic relation of material and labor, as Hegel developed it in the dialectic of the master and the slave, is pregnantly reproduced in art. If that chapter of the *Phenomenology* historically conjures up feudalism, art itself, its mere existence, bears an archaic quality. The reflection on this is inseparable from reflection on art's right to continue to exist. Today the neotroglodytes are more aware of this than is the naïveté of an unperturbed cultural consciousness.

Aesthetic theory, wary of a priori construction and cautious of an increasing abstractness, has as its arena the experience of the aesthetic object. The artwork is not to be known simply externally but demands of theory that, at whatever level of abstraction, it be understood. Philosophically the concept of understanding and categories such as empathy have been compromised by Dilthey and his followers. If one sets aside such theorems and insists on an understanding of artworks that would be knowledge determined strictly through their objectivity, difficulties amass. In advance it must be admitted that, if knowledge is anywhere achieved in layers, this is so in aesthetics. Any fixation of the starting point of this layering in experience would be arbitrary. It reaches back far behind aesthetic sublimation, where it is indivisible from lived perception. Experience remains related to such perception, while at the same time it only becomes what it is by distancing itself from immediacy, into which it stands permanently in danger of sinking back, as happens to those excluded from education who use the present rather than the past tense when narrating the events of a film or play; yet, without any trace of such immediacy, artistic experience is no less in vain than when it capitulates to immediacy. In Alexandrian fashion it circumvents the claim to an immediacy of existence that is registered by every artwork, whether it wants to or not. Pre-artistic experience of the aesthetic is indeed false, in that it identifies and counteridentifies with artworks as in empirical life and, if possible, even to a heightened degree, and thus precisely by way of a comportment that subjectivism holds to be the instrument of aesthetic experience. By approaching the artwork aconceptually, this comportment remains trapped within the radius of taste, and its relation to the work is no less oblique than if it misused art to illustrate philosophical positions. The malleable, readily identifying sensibility collapses when faced with the severity of the artwork; yet obdurate thought cheats itself of the element of receptivity, without which it is no longer thought. Preartistic experience requires projection,[17] yet aesthetic experience—precisely by virtue of the a priori primacy of subjectivity in it—is a countermovement to the subject. It demands something on the order of the self-denial of the observer, his capacity to address or recognize what aesthetic objects themselves enunciate and what they conceal. Aesthetic experience first of all places the observer at a distance from the object. This resonates in the idea of disinterested observation. Philistines are those whose relation to artworks is ruled by whether and to what degree they can, for example, put themselves in the place of the actors as they come forth; this is what all parts of the culture industry are based on and they foster it insistently in their customers. The more artistic experience possesses its objects and the closer it approaches them in a certain sense, the farther it is at the same time shifted away from them; artistic enthusiasm is art-alien. It is thus that aesthetic experience, as Schopenhauer knew, breaks through the spell of obstinate self-preservation; it is the model of a stage of consciousness in which the I no longer has its happiness in its interests, or, ultimately, in its reproduction.——That, however, to follow the course of action in a novel or a drama and note the various motivations, or adequately to recognize the thematic content of a painting, does not amount to understanding the works is as obvious as that they cannot be understood apart from such aspects. There are exact scholarly descriptions of artworks, even analyses—thematic analyses of music, for example—that miss everything essential. A second layer of understanding is that of the intention of the work, that which the work itself states and what traditional aesthetics calls its idea, an example of which would be the guiltiness of subjective morality in Ibsen's *Wild Duck*. The intention of the work is, however, not equivalent with its content, and thus its understanding remains provisional. The question remains at this level of understanding whether the intention is realized in the structure of the work; whether the form carries out the play of forces, the antagonisms, that objectively govern the work over and beyond its intention. Moreover, the understanding of the intention does not yet grasp the truth content of the work. For this reason the understanding of works is essentially a process, one apart from all biographical accidentalness and in no way comparable to that ominous lived experience [*Erlebnis*] that is supposed to deliver up all secrets with a wave of the magic wand and indeed provide a doorway into the object. Understanding has as its idea that one become conscious of the artwork's content by way of the full experience [*Erfahrung*] of it. This concerns the work's relation to its material, to its appearance and intention, as much as it concerns its own truth or falseness in terms of the artworks' specific logic, which instructs as to the differentiation between what is true and false in them. Artworks are understood only when their experience is brought to the level of distinguishing between true and not true or, as a preliminary stage, between correct and incorrect. Critique is not externally added into aesthetic experience but, rather, is immanent to it. The comprehension of an artwork as a complexion of truth brings the work into relation with its untruth, for there is no artwork that does not participate in the untruth external to it, that of the historical moment. Aesthetics that does not move within the perspective of truth fails its task; usually it is culinary. Because the element of truth is essential to artworks, they participate in knowledge, and this defines the only legitimate relation to them. Consigning them to irrationality profanes what is important in them under the pretext of what is putatively ultimate. The knowledge of artworks is guided by their own cognitive constitution: They are the form of knowledge that is not knowledge of an object. This paradox is also the paradox of artistic experience. Its medium is the obviousness of the incomprehensible. This is the comportment of artists; it is the objective reason back of their often apocryphal and helpless theories. The task of a philosophy of art is not so much to explain away the element of incomprehensibility, which speculative philosophy has almost invariably sought to do, but rather to understand the incomprehensibility itself. This incomprehensibility persists as the character of art, and it alone protects the philosophy of art from doing violence to art. The question of comprehensibility becomes urgent to the extreme in the face of the contemporary production of art. For the category of comprehensibility, if it is not to be situated in the subject and thus condemned to relativity, postulates something objectively comprehensible in the artwork. If the artwork assumes the expression of incomprehensibility and in its name destroys its own internal comprehensibility, the traditional hierarchy of comprehension collapses. Its place is taken by reflection on art's enigmatic character. Yet, it is precisely the so-called literature of the absurd—a pastiche concept tacked onto such heterogeneous material that it now serves only the misunderstanding of facile agreement—that proves that understanding, meaning, and content are not equivalents. The absence of meaning becomes intention, though not always with the same consequence. A play like Ionesco's *Rhinoceros*, for instance, though it insists that common sense accede in the metamorphosis of people into rhinos, permits the clear inference of what used to be called the idea of an artwork in its internal opposition to sheepish, standardized consciousness, to which the well-functioning I is more successfully adapted than one who has not completely kept up with dominant instrumental rationality. The intention of radical absurdity may have originated in art's need to translate the condition of metaphysical meaninglessness into a language of art that would cast meaning aside; thus it was, perhaps, a polemical act against Sartre, whose works firmly and subjectively posit this metaphysical experience. In Beckett the negative metaphysical content affects the content along with the form. The work does not, however, thereby become something simply incomprehensible; the well-founded refusal of its author to offer explanations for so-called symbols is faithful to an aesthetic tradition that has elsewhere been dismissed. A relation, not identity, operates between the negativity of the metaphysical content and the eclipsing of the aesthetic content. The metaphysical negation no longer permits an aesthetic form that would itself produce metaphysical affirmation; and yet this negation is nevertheless able to become aesthetic content and determine the form.

The concept of artistic experience, a concept into which aesthetics is transformed and which by its desideratum of understanding is incompatible with positivism, nevertheless in no way coincides with the currently popular concept of work-immanent analysis. Yet work-immanent analysis, which is self-evident to artistic experience and its hostility to philology, unquestionably marks decisive progress in scholarship. Various branches of art scholarship, such as the academic study of music, only awoke from their pharisaical lethargy when they caught up with this method rather than busying themselves with everything except what concerns the structure of artworks. But in its adaptation by scholarship work-immanent analysis, by virtue of which scholarship hoped to cure itself of its alienness to art, has in turn taken on a positivist character that it wants to go beyond. The strictness with which it concentrates on its object facilitates the disowning of everything in the artwork that—a fact to the second power—is not present, not simply the given facts of the matter. Even motivic-thematic musical analyses, though an improvement on glib commentaries, often suffer from the superstition that analyzing the work into basic materials and their transformations leads to the understanding of what, uncomprehended and correlative to the asceticism of the method, is gladly chalked up to a faulty irrationality. The work-immanent approach is indeed not all that removed from mindless craft, although its diagnoses are for the most part immanently correctable because they suffer from insufficient technical insight. Philosophical aesthetics, closely allied with the idea of work-immanent analysis, has its focal point where work-immanent analysis never arrives. Second reflection must push the complex of facts that work-immanent analysis establishes, and in which it has its limit, beyond itself and penetrate to the truth content by means of emphatic critique. Work-immanent analysis is in itself narrow-minded, and this is surely because it wants to knock the wind out of social reflection on art. That art on the one hand confronts society autonomously, and, on the other hand, is itself social, defines the law of its experience. Whoever experiences only the material aspect of art and puffs this up into an aesthetics is philistine, yet whoever perceives art exclusively as art and ensconces this as its prerogative deprives himself of its content. For the content of art cannot simply be art, unless it is to be reduced to an indifferent tautology. Contemplation that limits itself to the artwork fails it. Its inner construction requires, in however mediated a fashion, what is itself not art.

Experience alone is in no position to legislate aesthetically because a boundary is prescribed to it by the philosophy of history. If experience crosses this limit it degenerates into empathic appreciation. Many artworks of the past, and among them the most renowned, are no longer to be experienced in any immediate fashion and are failed by the fiction of such immediacy. If it is true that the rhythm of history is accelerating geometrically, then even artworks that do not reside in the distant past are being pulled into this process. They bear a stubborn semblance of spontaneous accessibility, which must be destroyed to permit their comprehension. Artworks are archaic when they can no longer be experienced. This boundary is not fixed, nor is it simply continuous; rather, it is fragmentary and dynamic and can be liquefied by *correspondance*. The archaic is appropriated as the experience of what is not experiential. The boundary of experientiality, however, requires that the starting point of any such appropriation be the modern. It alone throws light on the past, whereas academic custom for the most part limits itself to the past, rebounds from it, and at the same time, by violating the distance, transgresses the irretrievable. Ultimately, however, even in the most extreme refusal of society, art is essentially social and not understood when this essence is misunderstood.[18] Artistic experience thereby forfeits its prerogatives. Guilt for this is borne by a delusory process that takes place between the categories. Artistic experience is brought of its own accord into movement by the contradiction that the constitutive immanence of the aesthetic sphere is at the same time the ideology that undermines it. Aesthetic experience must overstep itself. It traverses its antithetical extremes rather than settling peacefully into a spurious median between them. It neither renounces philosophical motifs, which it transforms rather than drawing conclusions from them, nor does it exorcise from itself the social element. One is no more equal to a Beethoven symphony without comprehending its so-called purely musical course than if one is unable to perceive in it the echo of the French Revolution;[19] how these two aspects are mediated in the phenomenon belongs to the obstinate and equally unavoidable themes of philosophical aesthetics. Not experience alone but only thought that is fully saturated with experience is equal to the phenomenon. It is not for aesthetics to adapt itself aconceptually to aesthetic phenomena. Consciousness of the antagonism between interior and exterior is requisite to the experience of art. The description of aesthetic experiences, theory and judgment, is insufficient. What is required is experience of works rather than thoughts simply applied to the matter, yet no artwork adequately presents itself as immediately given; none is to be understood strictly on its own terms. All works are formed in themselves according to their own logic and consistency as much as they are elements in the context of spirit and society. The two aspects are not to be neatly separated, as is the scientific habit. True consciousness of the external world participates in the work's immanent coherence; the spiritual and social standpoint of an artwork can only be discerned on the basis of its internal crystallization. There is nothing artistically true whose truth is not legitimated in an overarching context; and there is no artwork whose consciousness is true that does not prove itself in terms of aesthetic quality. The kitsch of the Soviet bloc says something about the untruth of the political claim that social truth has been achieved there. If the model of aesthetic understanding is a comportment that moves immanently within the artwork, and if understanding is damaged as soon as consciousness exits this sphere, then consciousness must in return remain constantly mobile both internally and externally to the work, in spite of the opposition to which this mobility of thought exposes itself. To whoever remains strictly internal, art will not open its eyes, and whoever remains strictly external distorts artworks by a lack of affinity. Yet aesthetics becomes more than a rhapsodic back and forth between the two standpoints by developing their reciprocal mediation in the artwork itself.

As soon as the artwork is considered from an external vantage, bourgeois consciousness tends to become suspicious of alienness to art, even though in its own relation to artworks bourgeois consciousness tends to disport itself externally to them. The suspicion must be kept in mind that artistic experience as a whole is in no way as immediate as the official art religion would have it. Every experience of an artwork depends on its ambience, its function, and, literally and figuratively, its locus. Overzealous naïveté that refuses to admit this distorts what it considers so holy. In fact, every artwork, even the hermetic work, reaches beyond its monadological boundaries by its formal language. Each work, if it is to be experienced, requires thought, however rudimentary it may be, and because this thought does not permit itself to be checked, each work ultimately requires philosophy as the thinking comportment that does not stop short in obedience to the prescriptions stipulated by the division of labor. By virtue of the universality of thought, every reflection demanded by the artwork is also an external reflection; its fruitfulness is determined according to what it illuminates interior to the work. Inherent to the idea of aesthetics is the intention of freeing art, through theory, from its induration, which it suffers as a result of the inescapable division of labor. Understanding artworks is not χωρίς from their explanation; not from their genetic explanation but from that of their complexion and content, though this is not to say that explanation and understanding are identical. Understanding has as much need of the nonexplanatory level of the spontaneous fulfillment of the work as it does of the explanatory level; understanding goes beyond the art understanding of connoisseurs. Explanation ineluctably involves the tracing back of the new and the unknown to the known, even if what is best in the work struggles against it. Without such reduction, which violates the works, they could not survive. Their essence, what is uncomprehended in them, requires acts of identification and comprehension; it is thereby falsified as something familiar and old. To this extent the life of artworks is ultimately contradictory. Aesthetics must become conscious of this paradox and it must not act as if its opposition to tradition could dispense with rational means. Aesthetics moves within the medium of universal concepts even in the face of the radically nominalist situation of art and in spite of the utopia of the particular that aesthetics prizes along with art. This is not only the difficulty of aesthetics but also its *fundamentum in re*. If, in the experience of the real, it is the universal that is mediated, in art it is the particular that is mediated; just as nonaesthetic knowledge, in its Kantian formulation, poses the question of the possibility of universal judgment, the question posed by every artwork is how, under the domination of the universal, a particular is in any way possible. This binds aesthetics—however little its method can amount to subsumption by the abstract concept—to concepts, though admittedly to those whose telos is the particular. If anywhere, Hegel's theory of the movement of the concept has its legitimacy in aesthetics; it is concerned with the dynamic relation of the universal and the particular, which does not impute the universal to the particular externally but seeks it rather in the force fields of the particular itself. The universal is the stumbling block of art: By becoming what it is, art cannot be what it wants to become. Individuation, which is art's own law, has its boundaries set by the universal. Art leads beyond, and yet not beyond; the world it reflects remains what it is because it is merely reflected by art. Even dada, as the deictic gesture into which the word is transformed in the effort to shake off its conceptuality, was as universal as the childishly reiterated demonstrative word that dadaism took as its motto. Whereas art dreams the absolutely monado-logical, it is both happily and unhappily suffused with the universal. Art must contract to the geometrical point of the absolute τόδε τι and go beyond it. This imposed the objective limit to expressionism; art would have been compelled to go beyond it even if the artists had been less accommodating: They regressed behind expressionism. Whenever art-works on their way toward concretion polemically eliminate the universal, whether as a genre, a type, an idiom, or a formula, the excluded is maintained in them through its negation; this state of affairs is constitutive of the modern.

Insight into the life of the universal in the midst of aesthetic particular-ization, however, drives universality beyond the semblance of that static being-in-itself that bears the primary responsibility for the sterility of aesthetic theory. The critique of invariants does not aim at their exclusion but, rather, conceives them in their own variability. Aesthetics is not involved with its object as with a primordial phenomenon. Because phenomenology and its successors oppose conceptual procedures that move from the top down as well as those that move up from below, they are important to aesthetics, which shares in this opposition. As a phenom-enology of art, phenomenology would like to develop art neither by deducing it from its philosophical concept nor by rising to it through comparative abstraction; rather, phenomenology wants to say what art is. The essence it discerns is, for phenomenology, art's origin and at the same time the criterion of art's truth and falsehood. But what phenomenology has conjured up in art as with a wave of the magic wand, remains extremely superficial and relatively fruitless when confronted with actual artworks. Whoever wants something more must engage a level of content that is incompatible with the phenomenological commandment of pure essentiality. The phenomenology of art comes to grief on the presupposition of the possibility of being without presupposition. Art mocks efforts to reduce it to pure essentiality. It is not what it was fated to have been from time immemorial but rather what it has become. It is no more fruitful to pursue the question of the individual origin of artworks in the face of their objectivity, which subsumes the work's subjective elements, than it is to search out art's own origin. It is not an accident but rather its law that art wrested itself free. Art never completely fulfilled the determinations of its pure concept as it acquired them and indeed struggled against them; according to Valéry, the purest artworks are on no account the highest. If art were reduced to fundamental elements of artistic comportment, such as the instinct for imitation, the need for expression, or magical imagery, the results would be arbitrary and derivative. These elements play their part; they merge with art and survive in it; but not one of them is the whole of it. Aesthetics is not obliged to set off on the hopeless quest for the primal archetype of art, rather it must think such phenomena in historical constellations. No isolated particular category fully conceives the idea of art. It is a syndrome that is dynamic in itself. Highly mediated in itself, art stands in need of thinking mediation; this alone, and not the phenomenologist's purportedly originary intuition, leads to art's concrete concept.[20]

Hegel's central aesthetic principle, that beauty is the sensuous semblance of the idea, presupposes the concept of the idea as the concept of absolute spirit. Only if the all-encompassing claim of absolute spirit is honored, only if philosophy is able to reduce the idea of the absolute to the concept, would Hegel's aesthetic principle be compelling. In a historical phase in which the view of reality as the fulfillment of reason amounts to bloody farce, Hegel's theory—in spite of the wealth of genuine insight that it unlocked—is reduced to a meager form of consolation. If his conception of philosophy carried out a fortunate mediation of history with truth, the truth of the philosophy itself is not to be isolated from the misfortune of history. Certainly Hegel's critique of Kant holds good. Beauty that is to be more than symmetrically trimmed shrubbery is no mere formula reducible to subjective functions of intuition; rather, beauty's fundament is to be sought in the object. But Hegel's effort to do this was vitiated because it unjustly postulated the meta-aesthetical identity of subject and object in the whole. It is no accidental failing on the part of individual thinkers but rather predicated on an objective aporia that today philosophical interpretations of literary works—especially when, as in Heidegger, poetic language is mythologically exalted—fail to penetrate the construction of the works to be interpreted and instead prefer to work them up as the arena for philosophical theses: Applied philosophy, a priori fatal, reads out of works that it has invested with an *air* of concretion nothing but its own theses. If aesthetic objectivity, in which the category of the beautiful is itself only one element, remains canonical for all convincing reflection, it no longer devolves upon a preestablished conceptual structure anterior to aesthetics and begins to hover, as incontestable as it is precarious. The locus of aesthetics has become exclusively the analysis of contexts, in the experience of which the force of philosophical speculation is drawn in without depending on any fixed starting positions. The aesthetic theories of philosophical speculation are not to be conserved as cultural monuments, but neither are they to be discarded, and least of all in favor of the putative immediacy of artistic experience: Implicitly lodged in artistic experience is the consciousness of art, that is, philosophy, with which the naïve consideration of works imagines it has disposed. Art does not exist as the putative lived experience of the subject who encounters it as a tabula rasa but only within an already developed language of art. Lived experiences are indispensable, but they are no final court of aesthetic knowledge. Precisely those elements of art that cannot be taken immediately in possession and are not reducible to the subject require consciousness and therefore philosophy. It inheres in all aesthetic experience to the extent that it is not barbarically alien to art. Art awaits its own explanation. It is achieved methodically through the confrontation of historical categories and elements of aesthetic theory with artistic experience, which correct one another reciprocally.

Hegel's aesthetics gives a true account of what needs to be accomplished. The deductive system, however, prevents that dedication to objects that is systematically postulated. Hegel's work places thought under an obligation, even though his own answers are no longer binding. If the most powerful aesthetics—Kant's and Hegel's—were the fruits of systematic thinking, the collapse of these systems has thrown them into confusion without, however, destroying them. Aesthetics does not proceed with the continuity of scientific thinking. The particular aesthetics of the various philosophies cannot be reduced to a common formulation as their truth; rather their truth is to be sought in their conflict. To do so, it is necessary to renounce the erudite illusion that an aesthetician inherits problems from others and is now supposed to go calmly to work on them. If the idea of objectivity remains the canon of all convincing aesthetic reflection, then its locus is the contradiction of each and every aesthetic object in itself, as well as that of philosophical ideas in their mutual relation. That aesthetics, in its desire to be more than chatter, wants to find its way out into the open, entirely exposed, imposes on it the sacrifice of each and every security that it has borrowed from the sciences; no one expressed this necessity with greater candor than the pragmatist John Dewey. Because aesthetics is not supposed to judge art from an external and superior vantage point, but rather to help its internal propensities to theoretical consciousness, it cannot settle into a zone of security to which every artwork that has in any way succeeded gives the lie. Artworks, right up to those of the highest level, know the lesson taught to the bungler whose fingers stumble on the piano keys or who sketches carelessly: The openness of artworks—their critical relation to the previously established, on which their quality depends—implies the possibility of complete failure, and aesthetics alienates itself from its object the moment that by its own form it deceives on this score. That no artist knows with certainty whether anything will come of what he does, his happiness and his anxiety, which are totally foreign to the contemporary self-understanding of science, subjectively registers something objective: the vulnerability of all art. The insight that perfect artworks scarcely exist brings into view the vanishing point of this vulnerability. Aesthetics must unite this open vulnerability of its object with that object's claim to objectivity as well as with aesthetics' own claim to objectivity. If aesthetics is terrorized by the scientific ideal it recoils from this paradox; yet this paradox is aesthetics' vital element. The relation between determinacy and openness in aesthetics is perhaps clarified by the fact that the ways available to experience and thought that lead into artworks are infinitely many, yet they converge in truth content. This is obvious to artistic praxis, and theory should follow it much more closely than it has. Thus at a rehearsal the first violinist of a string quartet told a musician who was helping out, though himself not actively playing, to contribute whatever critique and suggestions occurred to him; each of these remarks, to the extent that they were just, directed the progress of the work ultimately to the same point, to the correct performance. Even contradictory approaches are legitimate, such as those that concern the form and those that concern the relatively tangible thematic levels. Right up to the present, all transformations of aesthetic comportment, as transformations of the comportment of the subject, involved changes in the representational dimension; in every instance new layers emerged, were discovered by art and adapted to it, while others perished. Until that period when representational painting declined, even in cubism still, the work could be approached from the representational side as well as from that of pure form. Aby Warburg's studies and those of his school are evidence of this. Motif studies, such as Benjamin's on Baudelaire, are able under certain conditions to be more productive aesthetically, that is, with regard to specifically formal questions, than the official formal analysis that seems to have a closer relation to art. Formal analysis had, and indeed still has, much to recommend it over dogmatic historicism. However, by extracting and thus isolating the concept of form from its dialectic with its other, it in turn tends toward petrification. At the opposite extreme, Hegel too did not escape the danger of such ossification. What even his sworn enemy Kierkegaard so admired him for, the accent he put on content [*Inhalt*] vis-à-vis form, did not merely announce opposition to empty and indifferent play, that is, the relation of art to truth, which was his preeminent concern. Rather, at the same time it revealed an over-estimation of the thematic content of artworks regardless of their dialectic with form. As a result, an art-alien and philistine element entered Hegel's aesthetics, which manifests its fatal character in the aesthetics of dialectical materialism, which in this regard had no more misgivings about Hegel than did Marx. Granted, pre-Hegelian and even Kant's aesthetics had no emphatic concept of the artwork and relegated it to the level of a sublimated means of pleasure. Still, Kant's emphasis on the work's formal constituents, through which the work becomes art in the first place, does more honor to the truth content of art than Hegel does, who directly intended this but never developed it out of art itself. The elements of form, which are those of sublimation, are—compared to Hegel—still bound by the eighteenth century at the same time that they are more progressive and modern; formalism, which is justly attributed to Kant, two hundred years later became the virulent password of anti-intellectual reaction. All the same, a weakness is unmistakable in the fundamental approach of Kant's aesthetics, apart from the controversy between formal and so-called content aesthetics. This weakness concerns the relation of his approach to the specific contents of the critique of aesthetic judgment. Parallel to his theory of knowledge, Kant seeks to establish—as if it were obvious—the subjective-transcendental foundation for what he called, in eighteenth-century fashion, the "feeling of the beautiful." According to the *Critique of Pure Reason*, however, the artifacts would be *constituta* and thus fall within the sphere of objects, a sphere situated external to the transcendental problematic. In this sphere, according to Kant, the theory of art was already potentially a theory of objects and at the same time a historical theory. The relation of subjectivity to art is not, as Kant has it, that of a form of reaction to artworks; rather, that relation is in the first place the element of art's own objectivity, through which art objects are distinguished from other things. The subject inheres in their form and content [*Gehalt*] and only secondarily, and in a radically contingent fashion, insofar as people respond to them. Admittedly, art points back to a condition in which there was no fixed dichotomy between the object and reaction to it; this was responsible for mistaking forms of reaction that are themselves the correlative of reified objectification as a priori. If it is maintained that, just as in the life process of society, production rather than reception is primary in art and in aesthetics, this implies the critique of traditional, naïve aesthetic subjectivism. Recourse is not to be had to lived experience, creative individuality, and the like; rather, art is to be conceived in accord with the objectively developing lawfulness of production. This is all the more to be insisted upon because the problematic—defined by Hegel—of the affects released by the artwork has been hugely magnified by their manipulation. The subjective contexts of reception are frequently turned, according to the will of the culture industry, against the object that is being reacted to. Yet artworks respond to this by withdrawing even more into their own structure and thus contribute to the contingency of the work's effects, whereas in other historical periods there existed, if not harmony, then at least a certain proportion between the work and the response it received. Artistic experience accordingly demands a comprehending rather than an emotional relation to the works; the subject inheres in them and in their movement as one of their elements; when the subject encounters them from an external perspective and refuses to obey their discipline, it is alien to art and becomes the legitimate object of sociology.

Aesthetics today should go beyond the controversy between Kant and Hegel and not simply level it. Kant's concept of what is pleasing according to its form is retrograde with regard to aesthetic experience and cannot be restored. Hegel's theory of content [*Inhalt*] is too crude. Music certainly has a determinate content—what transpires in it—and yet it nevertheless mocks the idea of content endorsed by Hegel. His subjectivism is so total, his idea of spirit so all-pervasive, that the differentiation of spirit from its other, and thus the determination of that other, does not come into play in his aesthetics. Because for him everything proves to be subject, what is specific to the subject—the spirit as an element of artworks—atrophies and capitulates to the thematic element, exempt from the dialectic. He is not to be spared the reproach that in his *Aesthetics*, in spite of magnificent insights, he became caught up in the philosophy of reflection against which he struggled. Contrary to his own thinking, he followed the primitive notion that content or material is formed or "worked over" by the aesthetic subject; in any case he liked to play off primitive notions against reflection by way of reflection. It is precisely in the artwork that, in Hegel's terms, content and material must always already be subject. It is only by way of this subjectivity that the work becomes something objective, that is, other. For the subject is in itself objectively mediated; by virtue of its artistic figuration its own—latent—objective content [*Gehalt*] emerges. No other idea of the content [*Inhalt*] of art holds good; official Marxist aesthetics no more understood the dialectic than it understood aesthetics. Form is mediated in-itself through content—not however in such a fashion that form confronts what is simply heterogeneous to it—and content is mediated by form; while mediated the two must be distinguished, but the immanent content [*Inhalt*] of artworks, their material and its movement, is fundamentally distinct from content [*Inhalt*] as something detachable, such as a plot in a play or the subject of a painting, which Hegel in all innocence equated with content [*Inhalt*]. Hegel, like Kant, lagged behind the aesthetic phenomena: Hegel missed what is specifically aesthetic, and Kant missed its depth and richness. The content [*Inhalt*] of a picture is not simply what it portrays but rather all the elements of color, structures, and relations it contains; the content of music is, for instance, as Schoenberg put it, the history of a theme. The object portrayed may also count as an element of content; in literature, the action or the narrated story may also count; content, however, is no less what all of this undergoes in the work, that whereby it is organized and whereby it is transformed. Form and content are not to be confused, but they should be freed from their rigid antithesis, which is insufficient to both extremes. Bruno Liebruck's insight that Hegel's politics and philosophy of right inhere more in the *Logic* than in the lectures and writings devoted to these material disciplines holds true also for Hegel's aesthetics: It has yet to be raised to an undiminished dialectic. At the beginning of the second part, Hegel's *Logic* shows that the categories of reflection had their own origin and development and yet were all the same valid as such; in the same spirit Nietzsche in the *Twilight of the Idols* dismantled the myth that nothing that develops is able to be true. Aesthetics must make this insight its own. What sets itself up in aesthetics as an eternal norm is, in that it became what it is, transitory and obsolete by virtue of its own claim to immortality. By contrast, however, the contemporary exigencies and norms that issue from the dynamic of history are not accidental and arbitrary but, by virtue of their historical content [*Gehalt*], objective; what is ephemeral in aesthetics is what is fixed, its skeleton. Aesthetics is under no obligation to deduce the objectivity of its historical content [*Gehalt*] in historicizing fashion, as being the inevitable result of the course of history; rather, this objectivity is to be grasped according to the form of that historical content. It is not, as the trivial paradigm would have it, that aesthetics moves and is transformed in history: History is immanent to the truth content of aesthetics. For this reason it is the task of the historicophilosophical analysis of the situation to bring to light in a rigorous fashion what was formerly held to be the apriori of aesthetics. The slogans that were distilled out of the situation are more objective than the general norms according to which, as is philosophical custom, they are to justify themselves; certainly it needs to be shown that the truth content of great aesthetic manifestos and similar documents has taken the place once held by philosophical aesthetics. The aesthetics that is needed today would be the self-consciousness of the truth content of what is radically temporal. This clearly demands, as the counterpoint to the analysis of the situation, that traditional aesthetic categories be confronted with this analysis; it is exclusively this confrontation that brings the artistic movement and the movement of the concept into relation.

That today a general methodology cannot, as is customary, preface the effort of reconceiving aesthetics, is itself of a part with methodology. The guilt for this is borne by the relation between the aesthetic object and aesthetic thought. The insistence on method cannot be stringently met by opposing another method to the one already approved. So long as the work is not entered—in keeping with Goethe's maxim—as a chapel would be entered, all the talk about objectivity in matters of aesthetics, whether it be the objectivity of artistic content or that of its knowledge, remains pure assertion. The chattering, automated objection that insists that claims to objectivity are only subjective opinions, or that the aesthetic content in which aesthetics that aims at objectivity terminates is nothing but projection, can be met fully only by the proof of objective artistic content in artworks themselves. The fulfillment of this proof legitimates method at the same time that it precludes its supposition. If aesthetic objectivity were presupposed as the abstract universal principle of the fulfillment of the method, without support from any system, it would be at a disadvantage; the truth of this objectivity is constituted by what comes later, in the process of its development, not by what is simply posited. The process has nothing but the development of truth to oppose as a principle to the insufficiency of the principle. Certainly the fulfillment of aesthetic objectivity requires critical reflection on principles. This protects it from irresponsible conjecture. Spirit that understands artworks, however, wards off its hubris through the strength of objectivated spirit, which artworks actually already are in themselves. What spirit requires of subjective spirit is that spirit's own spontaneity. The knowledge of art means to render objectified spirit once again fluid through the medium of reflection. Aesthetics must, however, take care not to believe that it achieves its affinity to art by—as if with a pass of a magic wand and excluding conceptual detours—enunciating what art is. The mediatedness of thought is qualitatively different from that of artworks. What is mediated in art, that through which the artwork becomes something other than its mere factuality, must be mediated a second time by reflection: through the medium of the concept. This succeeds, however, not through the distancing of the concept from the artistic detail, but by thought's turn toward it. When, just before the close of the first movement of Beethoven's sonata *Les Adieux*, an evanescently fleeting association summons up in the course of three measures the sound of trotting horses, the swiftly vanishing passage, the sound of disappearance, which confounds any effort to pin it down anywhere in the context of the phrase, says more of the hope of return than would any general reflection on the essence of the fleetingly enduring sound. Only a philosophy that could grasp such micrological figures in its innermost construction of the aesthetic whole would make good on what it promises. For this, however, aesthetics must itself be internally developed, mediated thought. If aesthetics, nevertheless, wanted to conjure up the secret of art with primal words, it would receive for its trouble nullities, tautologies, or at best formal characteristics from which that very essence evaporates that is usurped by linguistic style and the "care" for origins. Philosophy is not as lucky as Oedipus, who irrevocably answered the puzzle posed to him, even if the hero's luck proved delusional. Because the enigmaticalness of art is articulated only in the constellation of each particular work, by virtue of its technical procedures, concepts are not only the difficulty inherent in their decipherment but also their chance for decipherment. According to its own essence, in its particularization, art is more than simply its particularity; it is mediated even in its immediacy, and to this extent it bears an elective affinity with concepts. Common sense justly demands that aesthetics not envelop itself in a self-enclosing nominalism devoted strictly to the particular analyses of artworks, however indispensable the latter may be.

Whereas it must not let its freedom to singularity atrophy, second reflection—whose hour, in aesthetics, has indeed come—moves in a medium removed from artworks. Without some trace of resignation in the face of its undiminished ideal, aesthetics would become the victim of the chimera of concreteness that is the concreteness of art—and even there is not beyond suspicion—but is in no way the concreteness of theory. As a protest against abstracting and classifying procedures, aesthetics all the same requires abstractions and indeed has as its object the classificatory genres. Art's genres, however repressive they became, are not simply *flatus vocis*, even though the opposition to universal conceptuality is fundamental to art. Every artwork, even if it presents itself as a work of perfect harmony, is in itself the nexus of a problem. As such it participates in history and thus oversteps its own uniqueness. In the problem nexus of each and every artwork, what is external to the monad, and that whereby it is constituted, is sedimented in it. It is in the dimension of history that the individual aesthetic object and its concept communicate. History is inherent to aesthetic theory. Its categories are radically historical; this endows its development with an element of coercion that, given its illusory aspect, stands in need of criticism yet nevertheless has enough force to break the hold of an aesthetic relativism that inevitably portrays art as an arbitrary juxtaposition of artworks. However dubious it is from the perspective of the theory of knowledge to say of an artwork, or indeed of art as a whole, that it is "necessary"—no artwork must unconditionally exist—their relation to each other is nevertheless mutually conditioning, and this is evident in their internal composition. The construction of such problem nexuses leads to what art has yet to become and that in which aesthetics would ultimately have its object. The concrete historical situation of art registers concrete demands. Aesthetics begins with reflection on them; only through them does a perspective open on what art is. For art and artworks are exclusively what they are able to become. In that no artwork is capable of resolving its immanent tension fully, and in that history ultimately attacks even the idea of such resolution, aesthetic theory cannot rest content with the interpretation of given artworks and their concept. By turning toward their truth content, aesthetics is compelled—as philosophy—beyond the works. The consciousness of the truth of artworks is, precisely as philosophical truth, in accord with the apparently most ephemeral form of aesthetic reflection, the manifesto. The principle of method here is that light should be cast on all art from the vantage point of the most recent artworks, rather than the reverse, following the custom of historicism and philology, which, bourgeois at heart, prefers that nothing ever change. If Valéry's thesis is true that the best in the new corresponds to an old need, then the most authentic works are critiques of past works. Aesthetics becomes normative by articulating such criticism. This, however, has retroactive force, and from it alone is it possible to expect what general aesthetics offered merely as a hope and a sham.

Notes

1 Ivo Frenzel, "Ästhetik," in *Philosophie*, ed. A. Diemer and I. Frenzel, vol. 11 (Frankfurt, 1958), p. 35.

2 See Benjamin, *The Origin of German Tragic Drama*, trans. John Osborne (London, 1977), pp. 43ff.

3 See Adorno, "Notes on Kafka," in *Prisms*, trans. Samuel Weber and Shierry Weber (Cambridge, 1981), pp. 243ff.

4 See Georg Wilhelm Friedrich Hegel, *Aesthetics*, trans. T. M. Knox, vol. 1 (Oxford, 1975), p. 34.

5 Apart from the doctrine of disinterested satisfaction, which originates directly from the formal subjectivism of Kant's aesthetics, the historical boundaries of Kant's aesthetics are most apparent in his doctrine that the sublime belongs exclusively to nature, not to art. The art of his epoch, of which he philosophically gave a summary description, is characterized by the fact that without concerning itself with Kant and probably without being informed of his verdict, it immersed itself in the ideal of the sublime; this is above all true of Beethoven, whom incidently even Hegel never mentions. This historical limit was simultaneously a limit set up against the past, in the spirit of an age that disdained the baroque and whatever tended toward the baroque in Renaissance works as too much bound up with the recent past. It is deeply paradoxical that nowhere does Kant come closer to the young Goethe and bourgeois revolutionary art than in his description of the sublime; the young poets, the contemporaries of his old age, shared his sense of nature and by giving it expression vindicated the feeling of the sublime as an artistic rather than a moral reality. "Consider bold, overhanging, and, as it were, threatening rocks, thunderclouds piling up in the sky and moving about accompanied by lightning and thunderclaps, volcanos with all their destructive power, hurri-

canes with all the devastation they leave behind, the boundless ocean heaved up, the high waterfall of a mighty river, and so on. Compared to the might of any of these, our ability to resist becomes an insignificant trifle. Yet the sight of them becomes all the more attractive the more fearful it is, provided we are in a safe place. And we like to call these objects sublime because they raise the soul's fortitude above its usual middle range and allow us to discover in ourselves an ability to resist that is of a quite different kind, and that gives us the courage to believe that we could be a match for nature's seeming omnipotence." Kant, *Critique of Judgment*, trans. Werner S. Pluhar (Indianapolis, 1987), p. 120.

6 "The sublime, however, can also be found in a formless object, insofar as we present unboundedness, either [as] in the object or because the object prompts us to present it, while yet we add to this unboundedness the thought of its totality." Ibid., p. 98.

7 See Donald Brinkmann, *Natur und Kunst: Zur Phänomenologie des ästhetischen Gegenstandes* (Zurich and Leipzig, 1938).

8 [Adorno is referring to Hermann Cohen, *Ästhetik des reinen Gefühls* (Leipzig, 1912).—trans.]

9 See Arthur Schopenhauer, *The World as Will and Representation* (New York, 1963), pp. 521ff.

10 [Karl Gustav Jochmann (1789–1830), the German scholar and political author known for his *Studies on Protestantism* and, most important, *On Language*, a sociopolitical study of language. See Walter Benjamin, "Carl Gustav Jochmann: Die Rückschritte der Poesie," in *Schriften*, ed. T. W. Adorno and G. Adorno, vol. 2.2 (Frankfurt, 1955), pp. 572ff.—trans.]

11 See Hanns Gutman, "Literaten haben die Oper erfunden," in *Anbruch*, vol. 11 (1929), pp. 256ff.

12 [A satirical Munich weekly that appeared 1896–1944, published initially by A. Langer and Th. Heine.—trans.]

13 See Adorno, "Parataxis: On Hölderlin's Late Poetry," in *Notes to Literature*, trans. Shierry Weber Nicholsen, vol. 2 (New York, 1992), pp. 109ff.

14 See Pierre Boulez, "Nécessité d'une orientation esthétique," in *Zeugnisse: Theodor W. Adorno zum Sechzigsten Geburtstag*, ed. M. Horkheimer (Frankfurt, 1963), p. 334ff.

15 See Johann Gottlieb Fichte, "First Introduction to the Science of Knowledge," in *J. G. Fichte: Science of Knowledge*, ed. and trans. Peter Heath and John Lachs (Cambridge, 1982), pp. 3–28.

16 See Adorno, *Hegel: Three Studies*, trans. Shierry Weber (Boston, 1993).

17 See Max Horkheimer and Adorno, *Dialectic of Enlightenment*, trans. John Cumming (New York, 1972), pp. 187–200.

18 See Adorno, "On Lyric Poetry and Society," in *Notes to Literature*, vol. 1, pp. 34ff.

19 See Adorno, *Introduction to the Sociology of Music*, trans. Ashton (New York, 1976), chapter 12.
20 See Adorno, "Über das gegenwärtige Verhältnis von Philosophie und Musik," in *Filosofia dell'arte* (Rome and Milan, 1953), pp. 5ff.

16
Editors' Afterword

Gretel Adorno and Rolf Tiedemann

Adorno's metaphor for works of art applies literally to the last philosophical text on which he worked: "The fragment is the intrusion of death into the work. While destroying it, it removes the stain of semblance." The text of *Aesthetic Theory*, as it was in August 1969, which the editors present here as faithfully as possible, is the text of a *work in progress*, this is not the form in which Adorno would have published this book. Several days before his death he wrote in a letter that the final version "still needed a desperate effort" but that "basically it is now a matter of organization and hardly that of the substance of the book." Of this substance, according to Adorno, "essentially everything is, as one says, all there." The remaining final revision, which Adorno hoped to finish by the middle of 1970, would have involved much shifting of passages within the text as well as abbreviations of it; the insertion of the fragments collected here as the "Paralipomena" had been reserved for this final revision; and the "Draft Introduction" would have been replaced by another. Finally, Adorno would have improved many stylistic details. Thus the work as a whole remained a torso that, along with *Negative Dialectics*[1] and a volume planned on moral philosophy, "will show what I have to throw into the scale."[2] If the comment does injustice to Adorno's other books, from *Kierkegaard: Construction of the Aesthetic*[3] to *Alban Berg*[4]—an injustice that only the author could possibly possess the slightest right to inflict—it all the same gives a sense of *what* work was intruded upon, *what* work broken off. For even if the "fragmentary accrues as expression to the work"—the expression of

459

the critique of what is systematically fixed and closed in itself, the critique that most fundamentally motivates Adorno's philosophy—and removes the stain of semblance in which, according to Adorno's insight, all spirit necessarily becomes ensnared, still this hardly counterbalances the destruction to which the text of *Aesthetic Theory* testifies. Adorno employs the concept of the fragment in a double sense. He means on the one hand, something productive: that theories that bear a systematic intention must collapse in fragments in order to release their truth content. Nothing of the sort holds for the *Aesthetic Theory*. Its fragmentariness is the intrusion of death into a work before it had entirely realized its law of form. Essential to Adorno's philosophy as a whole is that no meaning be extracted from the ravages of death that would permit collusion with them. Two biographical fragments of comparable rank held eminent importance for Adorno: Right up to the end of his life he refused to acquiesce that Benjamin's *Arcades Project* was beyond saving or that the instrumentation of Berg's *Lulu* had to remain incomplete. As little as an edition of *Aesthetic Theory* can disguise the fragmentary character of the work, or should even attempt to do so, it is just as impossible to be reconciled with it. There is no acquiescing in something that is incomplete merely because of contingency, and yet true fidelity, which Adorno himself practiced incomparably, prohibits that hands be laid on the fragmentary to complete it.

Adorno resumed his teaching at the University of Frankfurt in the winter semester of 1949–1950, and already in the summer term 1950 he held a seminar on aesthetics. In the following years he lectured four more times on the same topic, the final course extending over the summer and winter terms of 1967–1968, when large parts of the *Aesthetic Theory* were already written. Precisely when he conceived the plan for a book on aesthetics is not known; occasionally Adorno spoke of it as one of the projects that "I've been putting off my whole life." He began making notes for the planned aesthetics in June 1956 at the latest. The wish of his friend Peter Suhrkamp, who died in 1959, to have an aesthetics from Adorno for his press, may have contributed to the concretization of the project. More important, obviously, was Adorno's intention of integrating his ideas on aesthetics and to develop as a theory what until then he had notated in his many writings on music and literature. These ideas had often been taken to be, if not downright rhapsodic, then mere flashes of insight. The primacy of substantive thought in Adorno's philosophy may have blocked any view of the unity of his philosophical consciousness. For Adorno the material studies on art comprise not "applications but rather integral elements of aesthetic theory itself."—On May 4, 1961, Adorno began to dictate the first version of *Aesthetic Theory*, which consisted of relatively short paragraphs. The work was soon broken off in favor of *Negative Dialectics*. After this was finished in the summer of 1966, Adorno undertook a new version of the aesthetics on October 25, 1966. The division into paragraphs gave way to one by chapters. He devoted great effort to the "schematization," a detailed disposition of the book. Already by the end of January 1967, approximately one fourth of the text had been completed in dictation. Dictation continued throughout 1967. More or less as an aside Adorno wrote studies such as the introduction to Durkheim[5] and the preface to the selection of Rudolf Borchardt's poems.[6] According to a diary note, "The rough dictation of *Aesthetic Theory* was finished" on December 25, 1967; the entry appears to have been premature, however, for on January 8, 1968, he wrote in a letter, "The rough draft is almost complete," and on January 24 finally, "Meanwhile I have finished the first draft of my big book on aesthetics."—The dictated version comprises, along with the introduction, seven chapters entitled: "Situation," "What Art Was, or On Primal History," "Materialism," "Nominalism," "Society," "Watchwords," and "Metaphysics." With the exception of several paragraphs, the 1961 text was wholly subsumed in the new version. But even this new version is scarcely recognizable in the final draft that is published here. Adorno commented in a letter on the preparation of the final version in relation to the first draft: "Only then does the real task begin, that is, the final revision; for me the second drafts are always the decisive effort, the first only assembles the raw material . . .: They are an organized self-deception by which I maneuver myself into the position of the critic of my own work, the position that is for me always the most productive." In the critical revision of *Aesthetic Theory*, however, it turned out that this time the second draft was itself only a provisional version.

After completion of the draft the work came to a halt. Adorno turned his attention to sociological essays such as the keynote address for the 16th Congress of German Sociologists and the introduction to the *Positivism Dispute in German Sociology*;[7] at the same time he wrote the book on Berg. Adorno always took these distractions from his "main task" as salutary correctives. In addition, however, there were the discussions with the student protest movement and a growing involvement in university politics; from the former much originated that went into the "Marginalia to Theory and Practice,"[8] but the latter fruitlessly consumed time and energy. It was not until the beginning of September 1968 that he was able to continue work on *Aesthetic Theory*. First he critically annotated the entire text as a preliminary to the actual revision. This consisted in a detailed, handwritten reformulation of the typescript of the dictated material, a reformulation in which no sentence remained unchanged and scarcely one remained where it stood; innumerable passages were added and not a few, some of them lengthy, were rigorously deleted. In the course of this revision, which Adorno began on October 9, 1968, the division into chapters was relinquished. It was superseded by a continuous text that was to be articulated only spatially; the text was finished on March 5, 1969. Three chapters of the old version were left out of the main text; two of them—"Watchwords" and "Situation"—were both corrected in March; the revision of the final chapter, "Metaphysics," was completed on May 14. In the following weeks many additions were written that in the course of the third revision would have been incorporated in the main text and would to some extent have replaced passages with which Adorno was still not satisfied. The last dated text was inscribed July 16, 1969.

The presentation of the book, which may appreciably burden its reception, is the result not only of the fragmentary character of *Aesthetic Theory*. During work on the second draft Adorno found himself confronted with problems he had not anticipated. These concerned the organization of the text and above all the problem of the relation of the presentation to what is presented. Adorno gives an account of these issues in his correspondence: "It is interesting that in working there obtrudes from the *content* [*Inhalt*] various implications for the form that I long expected but that now indeed astonish me. It is simply that from my theorem that there is no philosophical first principle, it now also results that one cannot build an argumentative structure that follows the usual progressive succession of steps, but rather that one must assemble the whole out of a series of partial complexes that are, so to speak, of equal weight and concentrically arranged all on the same level; their constellation, not their succession, must yield the idea." In another letter Adorno speaks of the difficulties in the presentation of *Aesthetic Theory*: "These difficulties consist . . . in this, that a book's almost ineluctable movement from antecedent to consequence proved so incompatible with the content that for this reason any organization in the traditional sense—which up until now I have continued to follow (even in *Negative Dialectics*)—proved impracticable. The book must, so to speak, be written in equally weighted, paratactical parts that are arranged around a midpoint that they express through their constellation." The problems of a paratactical form of presentation, such as they appear in the last version of *Aesthetic Theory*, with which Adorno would not have said he was content, are objectively determined: They are the expression of the attitude of thought to objectivity. Philosophical parataxis seeks to fulfill the promise of Hegel's program of a pure contemplation by not distorting things through the violence of preforming them subjectively, but rather by bringing their muteness, their nonidentity, to speech. Using Hölderlin's work, Adorno presented the implications of a serializing procedure, and he noted of his own method that it had the closest affinities with the aesthetic texts of the late Hölderlin. A theory, however, that is sparked by the *individuum ineffabile*, that wants to make amends to the unrepeatable, the non-conceptual, for what identifying thought inflicts on it, necessarily comes into conflict with the abstractness to which, as theory, it is compelled. By its philosophical content [*Gehalt*], Adorno's aesthetic is driven to paratactical presentation, yet this form is aporetic; it demands the solution of a problem of whose ultimate insolubility, in the medium of theory, Adorno had no doubt. At the same time, however, the bindingness of theory is bound to the obligation that labor and the effort of thought not renounce the effort to solve the insoluble. This paradoxy could also provide a model for the reception of this work. The difficulties that confront the πόρος the direct access to the text of *Aesthetic Theory*, could not have been cleared away by further revision of the text, yet doubtlessly in such a fully articulated text these difficulties would have been articulated and thus minimized.——Adorno planned to work through *Aesthetic Theory* a third time, a revision in which the text would have taken its definitive form, as soon as he returned from his vacation, which turned out to be his last.

This volume, which makes no claim to being a critical-historical edition, contains the complete text of the final version. Only those passages of the initial dictated version that were not incorporated in the second revision were omitted; even when Adorno did not explicitly strike them out, they must be regarded as having been rejected by him. On the other hand, because of their pertinence a number of shorter, uncorrected fragments are collected in the "Paralipomena." The corrected draft introduction, though it was discarded by Adorno, is appended to the text; its substantive importance prohibited its exclusion.——Idiosyncrasies of spelling have been maintained. The punctuation remains unchanged as well, although it still largely follows an oral rhythm; for publication Adorno would undoubtedly have adjusted it to standard practice. Because the hand-written corrections made the manuscript difficult for Adorno himself to read, occasional anacoluthic and elliptical formulations remain; these were discreetly corrected. Beyond such grammatical intrusions the editors felt under obligation to refrain wherever possible from conjecture, however frequently this was suggested by the repetitions, occasionally also by contradictions. Innumerable formulations and passages, which the editors were convinced Adorno would have changed, were incorporated unchanged. Conjectures were made only in instances where they were required to exclude misunderstandings of meaning.

The ordering of the book posed substantial difficulties. The corrected main text was the basic manuscript, into which the earlier mentioned, reworked but unintegrated three chapters were inserted. The chapter entitled "Situation"—a philosophy of history of modernité, which was the first chapter of the original version—had to be placed relatively early: Central to *Aesthetic Theory* is the insight that only from the most advanced contemporary art is light cast on the work of the past. According to a note, Adorno intended to combine the chapters "Situation" and "Watchwords," and the editors proceeded accordingly. The insertion of the chapter "Metaphysics" at the end of the section on "Enigmatic Character" followed compellingly from that section's course of thought.——With regard to particular passages, it was necessary to reorganize a number of them. In marginalia in the text Adorno himself had considered most of these shifts. In many instances, the shifts undertaken by the editors intended to accentuate the book's paratactical principle of presentation; they were not intended to sacrifice the book to a deductive hierarchical structure of presentation.——Those fragments treated by the editors as "Paralipomena" were in part later additions and in part "extracts": passages excised from the original text that Adorno intended to place elsewhere. The integration of these fragments into the main text proved to be impracticable. Only seldom did Adorno mark the exact place where he wanted them, and almost always there were a number of possible places for their insertion. Furthermore, the insertion of these texts would have required the formulation of transitional phrases, which the editors did not feel authorized to undertake. The organization of the "Paralipomena" is the work of the editors.——The passage headings are also additions made by the editors, who were often enough able to draw on *"headings,"* the descriptive keywords with which Adorno notated the majority of the manuscript pages.

A quotation from Friedrich Schlegel was to have served as a motto for *Aesthetic Theory*: "What is called the philosophy of art usually lacks one of two things: either the philosophy or the art." Adorno had intended to dedicate the book to Samuel Beckett.

The editors want to thank Elfriede Olbrich, Adorno's secretary of many years, who undertook the decipherment and copying of the text.

July 1970

Notes

1 [Translated by E. B. Ashton (New York, 1963).—trans.]
2 [Although Adorno did not write the book on moral philosophy, his lectures on the topic will be published as *Probleme der Moralphilosophie* in volume 10 of his posthumous writings.—trans.]
3 [Translated, edited, and with an introduction by Robert Hullot-Kentor (Minneapolis, 1989).—trans.]
4 [Translated with introduction and annotation by Juliane Brand and Christopher Hailey (Cambridge, 1991).—trans.]
5 ["Einleitung zu Emile Durkheim *Soziologie und Philosophie*," in *Gesammelte Schriften*, vol. 8, p. 245.—trans.]
6 ["Charmed Language: On the Poetry of Rudolf Borchardt," in *Notes to Literature*, trans. Shierry Weber Nicholsen, vol. 2 (New York, 1992), p. 193.—trans.]
7 [Translated by Glyn Adley and David Frisby (London, 1976).—trans.]
8 [Adorno, "Marginalia zu Theorie und Praxis," in *Stichworte, Gesammelte Schriften*, vol. 10.1 (Frankfurt, 1977), p. 759.—trans.]

Index

Compiled by Hassan Melehy

Theodor W. Adorno (1903–69), philosopher, sociologist, composer, and musicologist, is one of the last century's major figures in cultural criticism. Along with Max Horkheimer, he was a founder of the Institut für Sozialforschung at the Johann Wolfgang Goethe University in Frankfurt. Fleeing the Nazis in 1933, he spent the war years in the United States and returned to Germany in 1949 to teach and reestablish the Institut. Adorno's books include *The Dialectic of Enlightenment* (1944), *Philosophy of Modern Music* (1948), *Negative Dialectics* (1966), and *Aesthetic Theory* (1970).

Robert Hullot-Kentor is a writer and lives in Palo Alto, California. He has taught comparative literature at Stanford University and has been a Mellon Faculty Fellow at Harvard University. He was a fellow at the Getty Institute and in the University Professors Program at Boston University. He has written widely on Theodor W. Adorno and translated many of his works including *Kierkegaard: Construction of the Aesthetic* (Minnesota, 1989).